The Spectacle of Flight

Flight is the essence of the spirit.
It nurtures the soul.
It is awesome. Often ethereal. Glorious.
Emotionally wondrous and all-pervading. Intangible.
Louise Thaden

THE SPECTACLE OF FLIGHT

Aviation and the Western Imagination

1920–1950

ROBERT WOHL

YALE UNIVERSITY PRESS

NEW HAVEN AND LONDON

2005

Set in Bembo by SNP Best-set Typesetter Ltd, Hong Kong
Printed in China through Worldprint

Library of Congress Cataloging-in-Publication Data
Wohl, Robert.
The spectacle of flight : aviation and the Western imagination, 1920-1950 / Robert Wohl.
p. cm.
Includes bibliographical references and index.
ISBN 0-300-10692-0 (cl : alk. paper)
1. Aeronautics--History. 2. Aeronautics and civilization. I. Title.
TL515.W64 2005
629.13'009--dc22
2004022234

A catalogue record for this book is available from the British Library.

Frontispiece: Alan Cobham piloted this Singapore flying boat throughout Africa in 1927–1928.
He, his wife, and his crew celebrated their crossing of the equator "by a ceremony involving
champagne and a fine lunch that ended with brandy and cigars, all enjoyed while airborne."

FOR ROBERT AND ALEX

High flyers

Contents

Acknowledgements

Historians sometimes think of themselves as solitary workers, toiling away in the depths of dusty libraries and archives. They could not be more wrong. They are constantly accompanied by the personalities on whom they work and, among historians, by their predecessors and their contemporaries, a contrapuntal chorus of harmonious and sometimes dissonant voices that appear in their notes. Beyond the invisible yet omnipresent company that historians keep, one of the keenest pleasures their books afford is the opportunities they create to make new friendships and to consolidate old ones; and this was certainly true in the case of *The Spectacle of Flight*.

In Paris Patrick Fridenson has been a consistent supporter of my work and an endless source of information. Many of the ideas presented here were first introduced in lectures that he organized and sponsored at the Ecole des Hautes Pratiques en Sciences Sociales. I also wish to thank Christophe Prochasson and Marc Ferro for giving me the opportunity to address their seminars at that time. The late Emmanuel Chadeau, whose knowledge of French aviation in the interwar period was unparalleled, never ceased to instruct and amuse me. I shall miss his exuberance and his wit. In Rome the Contessa Maria Fede Caproni opened access to her archive in a splendid and convivial setting that made it easy to forget that I was supposed to be working. Though he had never before met me, Gregory Alegi generously organized a brief Roman sojourn that turned out to be remarkably fruitful for my work. Thanks to him, I was able to enjoy the stimulating company of Franco Briganti, Baldassare Catalonotto, and Paolo Balbo and visit the Ministero dell'Aeronautica where Colonel Salva Gagliano was a gracious host. Since then Gregory has provided me with rare books, photographs, films, and unexpected documents and has never failed to answer my endless stream of questions about Italian aviation during the interwar years. In 1994–1995 Tom Crouch, Von Hardesty, and Dominick Pisano were instrumental in obtaining for me an appointment as the Lindbergh Professor at the National Air and Space Museum in Washington, D.C. It was in those idyllic circumstances that I was able to begin the writing of this book. Through their writings and their conversation, Tom, Von, and Dom have taught me much about my topic.

More recently, Wayne and Yvone Rowe have chased down books and films in France that would otherwise have been beyond my reach. Yvone has patiently produced translations for French passages whose subtleties would otherwise have escaped me. I might add that many decades ago she inspired my fascination with French civilization and the French language, which I would like to think is reflected in these pages. Huston Paschal, co-curator of the North Carolina Museum of Art's exhibition 2003 exhibit *Defying Gravity*, bestowed on me the gift that every author needs – a reader impatient to have access to his next work – and created opportunities for me to broaden my horizons when thinking about the impact of aviation on the visual arts. Nor can I forget the contribution of my dear and very old friend Françoise Dubost, who responded to a plea for help on short notice and produced for me unsuspected material that substantially enriched the book. To all these persons – and to others I have not named – I am immensely grateful for their assistance and their friendship.

Authors are more dependent on their editors than they would often like to admit. I have been extremely fortunate in having two of exceptional ability and commitment. John Nicoll had the inspired idea of breaking what had started as a single book into volumes and created the format that has been used in both *A Passion for Wings* and *The Spectacle of Flight*. No author could have a better tutor in the art of producing illustrated books; nor could one ask for a more enthusiastic and supportive editor. In the wake of John's departure from Yale University Press, Robert Baldock came to my rescue in what appeared to be a dire situation and steered the manuscript sure-handedly through the process of production. Communicating by e-mail from Yale's London office, Robert's associate Sandy Chapman went to extraordinary lengths to accommodate my ambitions for the book's design. I also wish to thank the manuscript's reader, Peter Fritzsche, who produced a thoughtful critique on short notice that helped me to understand more clearly what I was trying (and not trying) to do in this book.

In a time when people complain about the failings of public institutions, the UCLA libraries – and especially UCLA's Interlibrary Loan Service – provided indispensable support. Rare publications were often produced on the shortest of notice and then retrieved after having been returned. It is no exaggeration to say that this book would have been very different – and much poorer – had it not been for the conscientiousness and efficiency of the persons in charge of these services who, laboring in the shadows, sustain scholarly enterprises such as mine.

As in the case of *A Passion for Wings*, my main debt is to my wife, Marisol. There is no aspect of the book in which she has not been deeply involved. She helped to shape the chapters as they were being written; she took responsibility for the collection of illustrations and discovered rare pictures that had escaped my research; and when we entered the final states of the layout, she miraculously found solutions to what seemed like insoluble problems in the process of design. Whenever I was in doubt, I relied on her judgment. The reward I can offer her is meager: never again to be forced to watch another aviation movie with Pat O'Brien and James Cagney.

X

Introduction: The Spectacle of Flight

And if I live to be one hundred, I shall never forget the splendor of flying back across [Long Island] Sound into the gorgeous sunsets of late summer with brilliant flashes of purple, red and yellow streaking the sky and reflecting from the water. It is such moments that keep pilots in the air.

Ruth Nichols, 1957[1]

THIS is not the book that I originally set out to write. I had intended to do a one-volume cultural history of aviation. My starting point was the discovery I made that in the early twentieth century some had perceived the achievement of powered flight primarily as an *aesthetic* event. When I began my research, cultural histories of aviation were few and far between.[2] I therefore had the exhilarating sensation of entering an intellectual territory that, if not unexplored, was imperfectly known. The material I found was so rich that what I had originally conceived as an introduction to the present book became a volume in its own right, *A Passion for Wings: Aviation and the Western Imagination, 1908–1918*.[3]

The Spectacle of Flight pursues some of the themes first developed in the earlier book into the decades following the Great War, and in that sense it can be regarded as a sequel to *A Passion for Wings*. Like its predecessor, it deals with the aesthetic dimension of flight and aviation as a source of cultural inspiration. But I have embedded this central motif within contexts that, though sometimes anticipated in the earlier volume, emerge with much greater force and clarity here. The chronological sweep is larger than in the previous book – three decades rather than one – and whereas *A Passion for Wings* focused on early responses to the new technology of flight there is more of an emphasis in this volume on the way in which aeronautical events were initially represented and then selectively remembered within national communities. The political uses of aviation figure more prominently here; and the airplane appears even more clearly than it did in the earlier volume as one of the exemplars of the modernist aesthetic, especially in the 1930s when avant-garde designers and architects praised it for its embodiment of purity of line and clearness of function.[4] No other machine seemed to represent as fully humankind's deter-

Pl. 1. The Russian illustrator Rojan (Feodor Rojankovsky) imagines the world down below as it is perceived by elegantly attired air travelers in this colorful 1929 lithograph that associates flight with fashionable images of modernity, such as steamships, trains, automobiles, modernist buildings, and cocktails.

Pl. 2. John MacGilchrist evokes the excitement inspired by seeing a sleek Lockheed Sirius *Zooming Over Manhattan* in this 1930 etching. Charles Lindbergh and his wife Anne flew a modified version of this plane during their 1931 flight to the Orient.

Pl. 3. Four views of the Savoia Marchetti S.55 X, used by Italo Balbo and his squadron of twenty-four planes to fly from Rome to Chicago in 1933. The modernist architect and city planner Le Corbusier chose these photographs to illustrate a book he published in 1935 entitled *Aircraft*. He ended his introduction to that book with the following words: "The airplane, in the sky, carries our hearts above mediocre things. The airplane has given us the bird's-eye view. When the eye sees clearly, the mind makes a clear decision."

mination to escape from age-old limitations, to defy the power of gravity, and to obliterate the tyranny of time and space.

The main focus of my interest in the cultural history of aviation was always the 1920s and 1930s. From the beginning, I sensed something different about this period, though I would have been hard put to find the words with which to define that elusive quality that hovered tantalizingly before my eyes. I now understand that it had to do with the meanings that people then attached to flight. It is difficult for us to appreciate this today because the airplane has been reduced to a faster way of getting from one place to another. This was not always so. How strange to think that men and women once believed that flying was a sacred and transcendent calling that more than justified its cost in lives. Remembering his decision to become an airmail pilot, Antoine de Saint-Exupéry could think of no better comparison than entering a monastery.[5]

I owe it to my readers to warn them that this is a very personal book. It is not conceived as a survey, and there are many important aspects of the cultural history of aviation that I do not treat. I have written about people who caught my fancy and held my interest over a period of years. The story of Lindbergh's triumphal flight and what he made of it seemed a natural place to begin. My emphasis is not so much on what Lindbergh did, or how he did it, but instead on the response to his exploit – in Europe as well as the United States – and on Lindbergh's ongoing effort to construct what he perceived as an authentic narrative of his life and its meaning. Barnstormer, military aviator, airmail pilot, record-maker, prophet and trailblazer of civil aviation, Lindbergh epitomized the history of flight during the interwar years, just as he was later in the vanguard of those who expressed disillusionment with the destruction it had wrought during the Second World War and anxieties regarding its future. He remains a problematic and, in my view, misunderstood figure. I do not underestimate the degree to which Lindbergh himself contributed to this situation. In his virtues and his defects, he reflects the country that first deified him, then demonized him. Yet there is no doubt that in 1927 he embodied the traits that Americans longed to have. I confess to being surprised by the prominence that Lindbergh has in this book; I did not anticipate it. He casts a shadow over every chapter.[6]

Italy stands out in the interwar period for the systematic attempt by Mussolini's Fascist government to encourage the development of an aviation culture. At the center of this story lies Italy's air minister, Italo Balbo. Even today Balbo remains a controversial personality in Italy; it has been easier to ignore him than to grapple with his contradictions, which reflect the contradictions of many others of his time.[7] But whatever one thinks about Balbo's politics, his seven years at the helm of the Italian Air Ministry were an important aspect of the aviation story during the interwar years and they have to be put in a deeper context that looks back to Mussolini's realization that the modernist cachet of fascism could be enhanced by its identification with flying and Gabriele D'Annunzio's earlier contribution to the rhetoric and imagery of flight.

Born at the same time, the technologies of aviation and cinema developed step by step along parallel lines. I devote a chapter to the encounter between Hollywood and flight and trace the emergence of the aviation picture, a genre with which the studios became enamored during the years between 1927 and 1939. Film determined, as no other cultural form did, the way people saw and understood flight and aviators in this period. Hence the importance of seeing which aspects of the aviation story the Hollywood studios chose to emphasize. I dwell on the paradox that whereas Hollywood proved remarkably adept at transforming aviation into thrilling spectacle, it was markedly less successful at portraying the changes that were taking place in the aviation world. The last film I discuss in Chapter 3, *Only Angels Have Wings*, is set in a remote corner of Latin America, far away from the concerns of America's aviators in 1939. I do not believe that this was mere chance; it was easier for Hollywood to deal with aviation's past than with its present.

No one disputes the primacy of Antoine de Saint-Exupéry among aviation writers; no one before or since wrote so eloquently or poetically about flight. But Saint-Exupéry's writings have to be set in the larger context of French aviation literature and the French people's longstanding love affair with the airline known as Aéropostale. It was not Saint-Exupéry but another writer, Joseph Kessel, who laid the groundwork for the myth of Aéropostale; and it was he who wrote the foundational biography of Aéropostale's most famous pilot, Jean Mermoz. How the myth of Aéropostale developed and how it was later nurtured is the theme of Chapter 4.

I thought originally that this volume would end in 1939; but as appealing as this date might appear as a point of closure, it turned out to be unfeasible in terms of the story that I tell. Many of my themes come to full fruition either during or immediately after the Second World War. Thus, Chapter 5 takes up the fear of bombing that developed during the interwar years and then goes on to show the range of cultural responses that bombing inspired, as it moved from a threat to a destructive reality during the years between 1936 and 1945. The predictions of an obscure Italian military theorist, Giulio Douhet, that many regarded as far-fetched (or demented) when he first published them in the early 1920s, had become accepted practice by the end of the Second World War. By then, the mass slaughter of civilians from the air was regarded as a necessary and legitimate means of bringing the enemy to its knees.

I end with some reflections on the meanings that aviation assumed for those who engaged in it between 1920 and 1950, and I assess the extent to which the airplane created the new civilization that Gabriele D'Annunzio and others had predicted during the years before 1914. The theme of this last chapter is the paradox that aviation's relentless progress, won at the cost of so many lives, meant the end of a romantic dream that flourished like a delicate but doomed flower in the conditions of the 1920s and early 1930s. Its withering and death were only a matter of time.

I call the book *The Spectacle of Flight*. Though it may seem improbable to the jaded and now uneasy air traveler of today, the airplane remained during its first four decades of existence a magical contrivance that had little to do with most people's everyday lives. To the extent that the general public had contact with flight during the years covered by this book, it was largely through the form of spectacle. Hence they experienced flight vicariously through the public celebration of the exploits of aviation heroes and images diffused by various forms of mass culture: bestselling books, newspapers, popular magazines, comic strips, radio, and, above all, motion pictures. Aviators, like sports figures and actors, became celebrities, and subsequently the early history of aviation has to be understood within the framework of the rise of a certain type of mass culture. Though few famous aviators acknowledged it as openly as Sir Alan Cobham was willing to do, flyers were showmen. At a banquet in New York, when Cobham was on a lecture tour, he was not at all surprised (or offended) to be taken for an entertainer.[8] Lindbergh's refusal to embrace this role began the breach between himself and his earlier admirers.

Aviators themselves were taken by the spectacular aspect of flight, and it was a theme to which they often returned when describing their experiences in the air. Indeed, I shall argue that one of the great attractions of flight for the men and women who engaged in it during the 1920s and 1930s was the visual excitement that it offered, an excitement that was often combined with a sense of awe that merged on mysticism and a feeling of contact with the divine. Lindbergh was not alone in feeling like a god when he climbed over mountains and looked down on "the cloud strewn sky, the white-capped peaks, the rain filled valleys, mine. I owned the world that hour I rode over it, cutting through my sky, laughing proudly down on my mountains, so small, so beautiful, so formidable, I could dive at a peak; I could touch a cloud; I could climb far above them all."[9]

Yet the supreme spectacle, even if a gruesome one, took place in the skies over Europe and Japan during the Second World War when they were illuminated by batteries of searchlights, antiaircraft fire, and tracer bullets as bombers delivered their deadly cargo and cities were consumed in raging storms of flame. Both the airmen who dropped the bombs and the earthlings who suffered their attacks have confessed to watching the raids with morbid fascination. Albert Speer later confessed that he had constantly to remind himself of the "cruel reality" of the bombing raids in Berlin "in order not to be completely entranced by the scene: the illumination of the parachute flares, which the Berliners called 'Christmas trees,' followed by flashes of explosions which were caught by the clouds of smoke, the innumerable probing searchlights, the excitement when a plane was caught and tried to escape the cone of light, the brief flaming torch when it was hit. No doubt about it, this apocalypse provided a magnificent spectacle."[10]

There is a strong emphasis throughout this book on personalities; I have not strayed far from individual lives. I have been primarily interested in what my protagonists felt, said, and later remembered – and in what their contemporaries thought and said about them. My ambition is to bring the reader as close as possible to an era that is now irremediably past, but not beyond the reach of the historical imagination.

Aviation attracted people who sought strong emotions and valued intense experience above long life. The ones I chose to write about were, almost without exception, keenly sensitive to the aesthetic dimension of flight. Naturally, they belong to a minority of flyers who are no doubt unrepresentative; but they are the ones we remember, and rightly so. It is surprising in retrospect how many aviators in this period were driven to share their experiences with others in written form, and how successful they were in doing so.

Because this book is to a considerable extent about the meanings aviation had for people during the period between 1920 and 1950, I have tried to convey those meanings

Pl. 4.   Sir Alan Cobham later recalled: "It was not going to be an easy landing. The tide was low at Westminister [in London on 1 October 1926], and the wind was blowing across the [Thames] river: the great bulk of the Houses of Parliament would slow it down a little, but might also create turbulence. So I circled a couple of times to consider the situation, and decided to come in from the east. Back came the throttle, down went the nose of my DH.50 float-plane; a touch of aileron, a touch of opposite rudder, and we side-slipped neatly over Westminister Bridge and touched down on the water in front of St Thomas's Hospital."

Pl. 5.   Miller Gore Brittain's 1943 painting, *Night Target, Germany*. A bombardier with the Royal Canadian Air Force during the Second World War, Brittain remembered a German city while being bombed as looking like "a casket of jewels opening up."

whenever possible in the language of the persons about whom I am writing. I was further drawn to do this because aviation attracted many talented writers, whose style cannot easily be separated from content. When translating from foreign languages, I have remained as close to the original as I could without losing the meaning or the flavor of the text. During the writing of this book, I have gained an ever greater respect for the art of translation, which in the end is a Sisyphean task condemned to failure. The better the writer, the less the chance of rendering him or her effectively in another language. Translating Saint-Exupéry into English, as others discovered before me, is a humbling experience and a hopeless task.

For a cultural history of flight between 1920 and 1950, iconographic evidence is vital. It is one thing to read about people, another to see how they actually looked. And, then, it is essential too to see how aviators were represented in the visual media of the period. Hence the illustrations play a central role here. Though some of these pictures are well known, others are obscure, buried in now forgotten sources. Looked at carefully, they can yield fresh meanings. I would like them to be read with the same care as the words themselves. The relationship between aviation and photography and then, later, between aviation and film, is so close that in the twentieth century it would have been difficult to imagine flight without its photographic and cinematic representation. Nor should we forget the importance of the sound of the aircraft of the period, which has been captured in the films of the 1920s and 1940s. Accustomed to being surgically insulated from the planes on which most of us fly, we have forgotten the deafening growl of aircraft engines that provided such an important part of the sensory background for the stories that I tell.

This book is about a period in our not-too-distant past that now seems far away and is, in some respects, unthinkable. Already in 1939, Saint-Exupéry recognized himself as a pilot of another era and wrote with nostalgia of experiences that were forever gone and could only be recovered in memory. As we trudge through a crowded airport, full of disgruntled people, on our way to what we hope will be a routine and monotonous flight, we should remember that it was not always so. There was once a fleeting moment when flight was the greatest of adventures. As Sir Alan Cobham put it, it really *was* a romantic time.[11] And, for pilots and their passengers, a dangerous one.

I

The Ambassador of the Skies

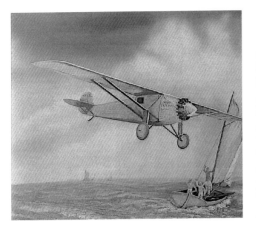

Abandon all suspicion,
Land of Cuauhtémoc,
Don festive clothes
And embrace him strongly with your heart,
For it is Lindbergh, the poet of the air
And prince of aviation,
Who like the spirits
That Dante placed in the Realm of God,
Comes flying through the ether
Like a flash of light,
To alight bonfires of enthusiasm in our bosom
And illuminate our minds with the light of hope.
Efrén Rebolledo, December 1927[1]

PARIS. Saturday, 21 May 1927. The low clouds and fog of the previous week had given way to brilliant sunshine and pleasantly balmy daytime air. Strolling Parisians crowded the sidewalks of the grand boulevards and filled the outdoor cafés. The previous afternoon the electric news sign at the Place de l'Opéra had flashed a bulletin, indicating that an "American aviator" had taken flight for the city of light. Yet sports fans, with the money and leisure to indulge their fancy, were not hovering anxiously over their wireless waiting for word of Charles Lindbergh's fate. They were instead gathered at the Stade Français in St. Cloud where Big Bill Tilden and Francis T. Hunter were scheduled to play the world's finest doubles team, the famous Musketeers Jean Borotra and Jacques Brugnon. Among the excited spectators was the American ambassador, Myron T. Herrick, the handsome, silver-haired former banker and politician from Cleveland, known for his unswerving attachment to France and the French.[2]

While the players were preparing to enter the court, a rumor spread throughout the stadium that Lindbergh had been sighted over the western coast of Ireland. At his present speed, he would reach Paris by 10:00 p.m. After a flutter of excitement and cheers for Herrick, who was sitting in a first-row box along the sidelines, the crowd settled down to watch the match. But their hearts were no longer in the tennis. They could think of nothing but the brave American making his lonely way toward Paris. Many had left the stadium long before the French team had won the match: 4–6, 6–2, 6–2.

Herrick was one of them. Suddenly rising from his seat in the middle of the third set after being handed a telegram confirming Lindbergh's successful crossing of the Atlantic, he returned to the embassy, ate a quick dinner, and set off in his chauffeur-driven limousine for the airdrome of Le Bourget, which lay a few miles to the northeast of Paris. Had he waited for the end of the match or tarried over dinner, he might never have reached the airfield, for the narrow two-lane road that led there was already filling with an unending stream of vehicles that would soon bring traffic to a halt.

Deeply dedicated to the cause of better Franco-American relations, Herrick must have felt some apprehension as he was being driven to Le Bourget.[3] It was not at all clear what

Pl. 7. The crowd glimpses Lindbergh as he arrives at Lambert Field in St. Louis following his record-breaking flight across the North Atlantic in May 1927.

Pl. 8. In this watercolor, Lindbergh's low-flying *Spirit of St. Louis* skims above the Atlantic, as it nears the Irish coast.

Pl. 9. The doubles match between the Americans and the French at the Stade Français in St. Cloud outside of Paris on 21 May 1927. The lifted leg of the player in the left foreground would not be recommended today.

attitude Parisians would take toward the arrival of an American aviator. Americans were no longer as popular as they had been ten years before when the United States had entered the war on the side of the Allies and helped to bring the German Empire to its knees. The American refusal to offer the French a military guarantee against a resurgent Germany was seen by many as a betrayal of Wilson's promises of a world made safe for democracy and free from imperialist threats. American isolationism had been accompanied in recent years by American demands for the repayment of debts incurred in the successful prosecution of a war in which both powers had a stake and in which the French had lost nearly one-and-a-half million men. The death sentence meted out to the American anarchists Sacco and Vanzetti enraged many in France, who identified themselves with parties and causes of the left. Passions rose so high that the American embassy had to be defended against angry demonstrators who threatened to storm the building. The fall of the franc against the dollar attracted a flood of free-spending and loud American visitors whose rowdy and sometimes drunken behavior irritated the Parisian population with which they came in contact. American tourist buses had been stoned by angry French crowds.[4]

French readers seeking reasons to dislike the Americans in 1927 could have chosen from a smorgasbord of recently published anti-American books.[5] French travelers to the United States found the Americans obsessed with the accumulation of money and impoverished in their culture. Some warned against following their example.[6] Even a political figure as knowledgeable about America as André Tardieu, former French High Commissioner in Washington during the Great War, had to admit that periods of cooperation between France and the United States had been based not on sympathy but on interest, and were, furthermore, few and far between. The war for the Americans, he noted bitterly, had been short indeed when compared with the fifty-two months endured by the French: thirty-two months of neutrality and twelve more of "military" abstention before the Americans had actually entered the fight.[7]

This smoldering resentment against Americans had recently flared up in French reactions to the disappearance of two famous French aviators, Captain Charles Nungesser and Captain François Coli, who had taken off from Paris just two weeks before in an attempt to achieve the first nonstop flight between Paris and New York. On Monday, 9 May, a rumor spread in Paris that Nungesser and Coli's plane, the *Oiseau Blanc* (the White Bird), had been sighted over Newfoundland. The afternoon newspapers, led by *L'Intransigeant*, reported that the French aviators had landed opposite the Battery in New York harbor at

4:35 p.m., Paris time. This triggered wild celebrations in Paris: cannons were fired at the military fort of Vincennes; a plane launched red rockets over the city; and in the cafés impromptu orchestras played the 'Marseillaise'. But then, as the afternoon gave way to the evening and no confirmation of the French pilots' arrival was received from Canada and the United States, the mood of the crowd turned to sadness and outrage at the newspapers held responsible for the false reports.[8] The offices of the American expatriot newspaper, the *Herald*, had to be given special police protection, and an angry crowd gathered before *Le Matin*, Paris's most air-minded daily, and insisted that the American flags intertwined with French ones across the front of the building be taken down.[9] Some French newspapers went so far as to accuse the American meteorological service of refusing to provide the French pilots with accurate reports of weather conditions over the North Atlantic; and Ambassador Herrick, always sensitive to French opinion, felt compelled to warn Washington against New York–Paris flights on the grounds that they might be misunderstood and misinterpreted in France "when the fate of the French aviators is still in doubt . . ."[10]

★   ★   ★

Whatever his thoughts en route to the airdrome, Herrick, like the hundred thousand others who had succeeded in reaching Le Bourget, was quickly swept into an unfolding drama that made all previous receptions given to aviators pale in comparison, as the nervously expectant crowd stomped their feet in the damp evening air and searched the illuminated sky for signs of Lindbergh's arrival.[11]

Hank Wales, a cigar-chomping, raspy-voiced, fast-talking reporter who would walk over his mother's cadaver for a scoop, was at that time head of the *Chicago Daily Tribune*'s foreign news service in Paris. Under instructions from the home office to cover Lindbergh's arrival, he cashed a check for 10,000 francs and headed for Le Bourget in a taxi, accompanied by two assistants. Caught in the huge traffic jam, the trio abandoned their cab and joined the army of people heading toward the airdrome on foot. Arriving at the small terminal, they went upstairs to the bar where a boisterous contingent of reporters from all over the world was gathered.[12] Among them, the famous American dancer Isadora Duncan, along with a

Russian friend, was drinking a glass of champagne. "How can a lone American in a ram-shackle plane make it," a Frenchman said to her with ill-concealed disdain, "when two great French pilots of much more experience and in a better plane – the best France could make – failed?"[13] This bitter thought lay buried in more than one French spectator's mind.[14]

Shortly after 10:00 p.m. a siren wailed and the crowd fell into a hushed silence. The sound of a steadily whirling engine could be made out in the distance. "Un moteur améri-cain," a mechanic standing close to Wales whispered. A small searchlight picked up a silver plane and silhouetted it against the night. Here is how Wales described the scene ten years later through the golden aura of Lindbergh's yet unblemished fame.

> Overhead the plane swept on. It veered off to the east, was lost a moment, then thread-ed its way back and glided lower over the field. Delicately, skillfully, it reconnoitred the drome, feeling out the terrain. It reminded me of a great eagle, tired, lost, circling about warily, seeking a place to perch in a strange country. It made another turn at the far end of the field, was lost to sight a few seconds, then back it came. It was lower now and dropping steadily. It entered the zone of darkness just above the ground and disappeared. The glare of the floodlights obliterated it. Through the tense silence came a light, muf-fled thud; then the roar of the motor as Lindbergh gave it the gun to taxi in. The crowd's pent-up feelings burst![15]

As Lindbergh taxied towards the terminal, the crowd trampled the wire fence that had been strung up to contain it and broke through the police cordon formed by gendarmes with interlocked arms. Men hurled their boaters into the air, where they were illuminated like shooting stars by the floodlights.[16] Somehow Lindbergh managed to shut down his engine before the propeller sliced the leaders of the onrushing cohort to pieces.[17] The wide grin he flashed upon first extending his head from the cockpit of the *Spirit of St. Louis* turned quickly to a frozen look of dismay and incomprehension as he watched the crowd attack his plane in search of souvenirs. Lindbergh heard wood crack and fabric tear and felt the *Spirit of St. Louis* bend beneath the weight of pressing bodies. Descending from the cockpit, he suddenly found himself prostrate, bobbing like a cork in a sea of human beings. Two French aviators quickly appeared and liberated him from the mob and, in the darkness, succeeded in spiriting him away in a small Renault to a darkened hangar from which he was later taken to an office on the other side of the field. In the confusion of the moment, Lindbergh's helmet had been ripped from his head and had ended up in the hands of an innocent young American university student who was mistaken for the aviator and carried in triumph to the terminal observation deck, where Herrick waved the helmet to mollify the cheering crowd. Meanwhile sitting on a simple camp bed and drinking water in the office of Major Pierre Weiss, commander of a fighter unit that was located across the field from the civilian air terminal, Lindbergh's first thoughts were for the safety of his plane and the letters of introduction he had brought with him. Little could he know that the journey he had started at Roosevelt Field in New York was just beginning. He was on the verge of passing from the ephemeral height of record-breaking aviator to the lasting Olympus of world-historical fame.[18]

★   ★   ★

Contrary to common opinion, Lindbergh was by no means the first aviator to cross the Atlantic by air. Indeed, it is some measure of the impact of Lindbergh's flight that the scores of persons who risked their lives and succeeded in flying the Atlantic before him are now all but forgotten. And yet they too had been acclaimed as heroes immediately following their exploits and given elaborate public celebrations of a sort normally extended only to royalty and military victors.

The Atlantic was first conquered in 1919, just ten years after Blériot had ventured out into the mists of the English Channel in his fragile flying machine. On 27 May, U.S. Navy Lieutenant Commander Albert "Putty" Read and his five-man crew landed their flying boat, the NC 4, in Lisbon, the first aviators to cross the Atlantic by air. Read's flight had taken eleven days and was broken by a stop in the Azores at Horta on the island of Fayal. The scale of the challenge that he and his men faced is suggested by the fact that he was supported by a fleet of sixty-six U.S. Navy warships strung out across the Atlantic.

Two weeks later, on 14 June, John Alcock and Arthur Brown achieved an even more impressive first when they flew their modified two-engine Vickers-Vimy bomber 1,890 miles from Newfoundland to Ireland in sixteen hours and twenty-eight minutes, thus completing the first nonstop flight across the North Atlantic. Hopelessly disoriented in a cloud bank, they miraculously survived a spiral dive that carried them from six thousand feet practically to the height of the ocean's spray. The next month, July 1919, yet another record was set when the giant British dirigible R34 overcame gale-force headwinds and thunderstorms to cross the Atlantic from east to west, landing in New York after a flight of one hundred and eight hours, twelve minutes. The R34 then returned to England, having made the first transatlantic round-trip by air. Seven more transatlantic flights were made by Zeppelins and seaplanes in as many years. By the spring of 1927, ninety-one men had successfully flown the Atlantic, including the brother of the future *caudillo* of Spain, Ramon Franco.[19]

None of these flights, however, was made in the atmosphere of high drama that existed in May 1927 when the public in both France and the United States waited anxiously to see who would be winner of what journalists liked to call the great transatlantic race. The

Pl. 12. The Curtiss NC-4 arrives in Lisbon.

VIEW OF THE GIANT FLYING N. C. 4. TAKEN AT THE INLET, ATLANTIC CITY, N. J.

Designed by J.C.H. 1919 — First Airplane to cross The Atlantic Ocean

story begins in the spring of 1919 when aviators were trying to make the difficult transition from war to peace. Just before Putty Read landed in the Azores, Raymond Orteig had posted a letter to the president of the Aero Club of America:

> Gentlemen: As a stimulus to the courageous aviators, I desire to offer, through the auspices and regulations of Aero Club of America, a prize of $25,000 to the first aviator of any Allied country crossing the Atlantic in one flight, from Paris to New York or New York to Paris, all other details in your care.[20]

A French emigrant to the United States who had worked his way from being a waiter to become the owner of two fashionable New York hotels, Orteig was concerned that there had been so much talk of flights from Canada to the Azores, Portugal, and England, but nothing about the country of his birth, where he regularly spent the summer. The prize he

Pl. 13. John Alcock and Arthur Brown pose jauntily before their flight from Newfoundland to Ireland.

Pl. 14. Alcock and Brown taking off from Newfoundland on 14 June 1919.

14

offered was meant to focus attention on the special relationship that existed between the United States and his beloved France.

Aviators knew that a flight between New York and Paris was not practicable at this time because no engine existed that was dependable enough to power such a long-distance undertaking. Thus no contenders presented themselves in the early 1920s. But Orteig renewed his offer for a second five-year period in 1924; by then new, more powerful and reliable engines had become available; and rumors began to circulate in 1925 that French aviators were determined to be the first to make the flight.[21]

One of these was the French "ace of aces," René Fonck, who had seventy-five official kills to his credit and claimed fifty-one more. Famous for his coolness and methodical approach to air fighting, Fonck was well aware that the flight between Paris and New York would be more assured of success if it were undertaken from west to east because of the prevailing winds, which tended to blow toward Europe. In late 1925 he traveled to New York to meet with a group of American aviation enthusiasts called the "Argonauts" who had been raising money to finance a New York–Paris flight. When the French ace arrived, the Argonauts had already entered into a contract with the Russian emigrant Ivan Sikorsky to construct a plane capable of flying the necessary distance with fuel to spare. Fonck must have been persuasive because the Argonauts agreed to engage him as their chief pilot at a salary of $250 a week, on the condition that he select an American as his copilot.

Pl. 15. The R34 after its transatlantic crossing in July 1919.

In consultation with Fonck, Sikorsky agreed to modify his original design for what he called the S-35 and produced a huge all-metal trimotor designed to carry the French pilot and a crew of three. The most expensive airplane yet built, the S-35's cabin was decorated like a drawing room with a sofa and chairs and a color scheme of red, gold, and silver, panels of Spanish leather, and a mahogany finish. On 21 September 1926, against the better instincts of Sikorsky who wanted to conduct further test flights, Fonck headed the heavily overloaded S-35 down the unpaved runway at Roosevelt Field and gave it full throttle; midway through its takeoff roll, as the spectators watched in horror, the huge plane lost one of its wheels and veered out of control, causing it to plunge into a gully and burst into flames.[22] Fonck and his American copilot somehow escaped from the burning aircraft, but his French radio operator and the Russian mechanic lent to him by Sikorsky perished in the blaze. Fonck's popularity in America was not enhanced by the fact that he insisted, defensively, that the accident was in no way his fault. "It is," he said in a phrase reminiscent of the casual attitude of First World War flying aces, "the fortune of the air."[23] Others were not so sure.[24]

After an inquiry into the accident, Fonck announced that he would try again, and Sikorsky agreed to build him another plane. But the publicity given to Fonck's flight and its disaster inspired other contenders who, like champions entering a tournament, indicated

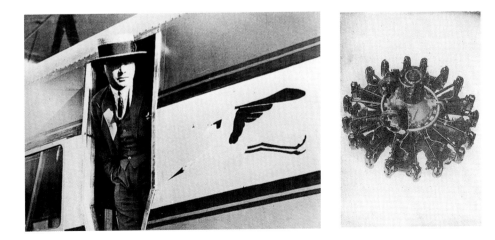

Pl. 16. A debonair René Fonck appears at the door of the huge and luxurious Sikorsky.

Pl. 17. The Wright Whirlwind engine that made possible the success of Lindbergh's flight.

15

Pl. 18.   The French ace
Nungesser displays the medals
he won in the First World War.

Pl. 19.   Nungesser and Coli
pose before the *Oiseau Blanc*,
which bears Nungesser's First
World War emblem of a casket
and a skull and bones.

their intention to compete. First to register for the Orteig Prize was U.S. Navy Lieutenant
Commander Noel Davis, commander of the Massachusetts Naval Reserve Station in
Boston, who obtained financial backing from the powerful veterans organization, the
American Legion. The Legion saw an opportunity to publicize the convention it was plan-
ning to hold in Paris in the summer of 1927 to commemorate America's entry into the
Great War. What better way to re-evoke the alliance between the two countries, which had
fought side by side in the First World War? Davis, though, was tragically eliminated from
the competition when his Keystone trimotor crashed in a bog at Langley Field, Virginia,
on 26 April, while taking off on a test flight. Both Davis and his navigator, Stanton H.
Wooster, suffocated before a rescue crew could reach them. The victims of the Orteig Prize
competition now stood at four.

Meanwhile, a new and formidable pair of French contenders had appeared. The one-
eyed former French ace Captain François Coli had been trying for years to organize an
east–west flight from Paris to New York. By May 1927 he had the kind of partner he sought
– the flamboyant and much decorated war ace Captain Charles Nungesser whose exploits
during the war exceeded his – and a plane: the Levasseur PL-8, whose builder Pierre
Levasseur had hopes of winning a profitable contract from the French government.

Nungesser and Coli baptized the PL-8 the *Oiseau Blanc*, and Nungesser affixed to it the
coat of arms he had painted on his pursuit planes during the war: a coffin, two burning can-
dles, a skull and crossbones, all placed within a large black heart – a reminder of a daring
escape from German troops he had made at the beginning of the war while still a cavalry officer.[25] The meaning of this symbol, Nungesser explained, was that "a strong heart doesn't fear
death, even in its most terrible aspects."[26]

By early May Nungesser and Coli had flight-tested their plane and were ready to leave at
the first indication of good weather and favorable easterly winds over the Atlantic. On
Saturday evening, 7 May, Coli was told by General Delcambre, director of the French
Meteorological Service, that conditions between the Irish coast and Newfoundland were as
good as they were likely to see in the foreseeable future. Coli immediately responded that he
would take the responsibility for their departure; on arriving at Le Bourget and being briefed
by Coli, Nungesser agreed. At daybreak the next morning, after an emotional farewell and a

spontaneous ovation by their friends and loved ones, the two pilots took their places in the cockpit, and Nungesser gave a signal to start the propeller. Two minutes later, satisfied that the powerful engine was running smoothly, he indicated with a gesture that the restraining blocks should be removed from the wheels. With agonizing slowness, the *Oiseau Blanc* picked up speed and laboriously rose from the unpaved field of Le Bourget, disappearing into the morning fog. Borne on its wings, according to Paris's leading morning newspaper *Le Matin*, was "the total admiration of France for two heroes whose goal was the triumph of French aviation and energy."[27] Once they left behind the coast of France and the escort of four planes that accompanied them, they were never seen again. It is difficult to imagine the anguish that the French felt when it became clear that they had definitively disappeared. French people who were teenagers in 1927 still sigh at the mention of Nungesser's name.

★   ★   ★

While the search for Nungesser and Coli went on amidst wildly conflicting reports that kept hope for their eventual rescue alive, the spotlight shifted to New York, where two Americans were making preparations to attempt the transatlantic flight, though neither had formally registered as contenders for the Orteig Prize. One was Commander Richard E. Byrd of the U.S. Navy, another certified hero, who had won renown the year before for a flight from Spitsbergen to the North Pole in a three-engined Fokker, for which he was awarded the National Geographic Society's prestigious Hubbard Gold Medal and the Congressional Medal of Honor and given a confetti-strewn New York parade.[28] Byrd was a meticulous organizer and proven fund-raiser who did not believe in leaving anything to chance. He was determined to make a flight that would be "scientific" and that would "point the way for the trans-Atlantic plane of the future." To accomplish this objective, he chose to fly a modified version of the large three-engined Fokker with which he had circumnavigated the North Pole, and found an enthusiastic and rich patron, Rodman Radamaker, who was willing to underwrite the considerable expenses such a flight would entail.[29] The *America*, as he christened his plane, would carry four crew members and eight hundred pounds of equipment, including a sophisticated radio, two lifeboats, and rations that would allow Byrd and his crew to subsist for at least three weeks if they were forced to make an emergency landing before reaching their destination.

The *America* was ready for a test flight by 16 April; but when Anthony Fokker, its designer and builder, took it up with Byrd and two of his crew members on board, he was unable to control the nose-heavy plane while landing and overturned it, severely injuring his passengers and effectively removing Byrd's chosen pilot, Floyd Bennett, from participation in a transatlantic flight that spring because of his broken leg and dislocated shoulder. Repairs to the Fokker, not to mention the mending of Byrd's broken left wrist, would take weeks and would further delay the *America*'s departure for Paris.

The other contender for the honor of organizing the first flight between New York and Paris was the entrepreneur Charles Levine, a stubborn and abrasive self-made millionaire, who had developed a passion for flying. Levine lacked credentials as a hero; but he had a talent for publicity in a decade that prized ballyhoo and had the cash to purchase a fast high-wing monoplane, designed by Giuseppe Bellanca and built by the Wright Corporation, that had already shown its ability to stay in the air for over fifty hours and was thus capable of reaching Paris in a nonstop flight.

Levine's problems began when the navigator he had chosen for the flight, Lloyd Bertaud, balked at the agreement Levine had convinced him and his pilot, Clarence Chamberlain,

Pl. 20. Lieutenant Commander Richard E. Byrd in a publicity shot made in 1927.

Pl. 21. Charles Levine (center) stands stiffly between his navigator Lloyd Bertaud (left) and his pilot Clarence Chamberlin.

to sign and then sought legal redress through an attorney. Levine was at first conciliatory and committed himself verbally to a contract that would provide insurance money for the wives of his crew, should they be lost; and in the case they were successful, Levine promised them the Orteig Prize money. But when the document was drawn up, the mercurial and unpredictable Levine refused to sign it. Bertaud then attempted to buy the *Columbia* from Levine who, after giving the impression that he might be amenable to the idea, suddenly announced that he intended to replace Bertaud with another navigator. Furious at being eliminated from an undertaking that he expected to bring him fame and fortune, Bertaud instructed his lawyer to obtain a temporary injunction restraining Levine from sending the Bellanca to Paris without him on board. After hearing arguments pro and con, a Brooklyn judge summarily dismissed the injunction on the morning of 20 May. The *Columbia* was now free to fly with any crew Levine chose to name.[30]

By then, however, Charles Lindbergh was well on his way toward Paris. Of all the contenders for "the transatlantic race," Lindbergh was the most obscure and the least well financed, hence ideally equipped to play a role for which Americans have traditionally shown a weakness, that of the dark horse and underdog.[31] An unknown airmail pilot, Lindbergh had convinced a syndicate of St. Louis businessmen to contribute $10,000 toward the purchase of an airplane for the New York–Paris flight.[32] Lindbergh's first inclination had been to purchase a Bellanca, but the Wright Corporation had turned him down, fearing that an unsuccessful transatlantic flight by an obscure pilot would reflect unfavorably on the company. Frustrated by the Wright Corporation's response, Lindbergh turned to Levine, who briefly gave Lindbergh the impression that he would sell him his Bellanca for $15,000; but then, when Lindbergh succeeded in raising the additional money,

Levine characteristically added at the last moment that he insisted on the right to decide who was going to fly the ship.

Unwilling to acknowledge defeat, Lindbergh turned to a small San Diego company called the Ryan Aircraft Corporation, which agreed to build a one-engine monoplane to his specifications in the record time of sixty days. With Lindbergh in San Diego overseeing every detail of the plane's construction and their personnel working overtime, the Ryan Corporation lived up to its commitment.[33] On the night of 10–11 May 1927, Lindbergh flew his plane, the *Spirit of St. Louis*, from San Diego to St. Louis; the following day he continued to New York, shaving five hours and thirty minutes from the existing record for a flight across the continental United States and demonstrating that he was now a serious candidate for the Orteig prize.[34] Eight days later, benefiting from the delays caused by Byrd's accident and Levine's legal problems with Bertaud, Lindbergh stole a march on his rivals, much as Blériot had done in 1909, and raised the *Spirit of St. Louis* from a muddy Roosevelt Field on Long Island, New York, with "disheartening slowness," barely clearing the telephone wires at the end of the runway.[35] Whether or not Lindbergh was lucky to survive his flight, he had indisputably benefited from the misfortune of his rivals.

★   ★   ★

The aura of wonder that Lindbergh's flight inspired, as he swooped out of the night to land at Le Bourget, was only enhanced by his behavior once he had arrived. To be sure, the young airman's easygoing charisma had already been revealed during his eight-day stay in New York. Newspaper reporters thrived on the interviews he graciously offered and marveled at his apparent indifference to the terrible risk that he was about to take; photographers and newsreel cameramen could not get enough pictures of his broad grin, tousled hair, and slim

Pl. 22.   Charles Lindbergh poses alongside the Spirit of St. Louis. Unlike Levine, Bertaud, and Chamberlin, he embodied the popular image of the aviator because of the flying suits he chose to wear, his bearing, and his irresistibly photogenic face.

silhouette; and, as his image became known through the power of the media, crowds gathered whenever he appeared, hoping to share vicariously in the awesome daring of his gesture. Women seemed to be particularly susceptible to his clean-cut and boyish good looks, and several sent him letters and telegrams, begging to make the flight with him.[36] When he took to the air from Roosevelt Field on 20 May, Lindbergh was already a celebrity.[37]

But no one could have predicted the success that lay ahead in a country where attitudes toward the United States were highly ambivalent, if not outright hostile. For someone who had dropped out of college after having obtained mediocre grades in mechanical engineering and who did not speak a word of French, Lindbergh showed himself to be surprisingly sensitive to French concerns and unusually adept at confirming French self-perceptions. Many have wondered, understandably, how in the circumstances of 1927 an obscure and uneducated American from the depths of the Middle West could have won the hearts of the skeptical Parisians, who prided themselves on their sophistication.

The argument that after arriving in Paris a young and naïve Lindbergh was coached and manipulated by Herrick for his own diplomatic ends fails to convince.[38] I am more inclined to believe Herrick's account: "I naturally told him who the people were we were going to see, what the occasion was about, and things of that sort. But I never told him what to say. He did not need to be told . . . Whenever he was called upon to reply to the really wonderful speeches that were made to him by the greatest orators in France, it seemed to me that he always said exactly the right thing in exactly the right way."[39]

Certainly, if there was ever a man who insisted on going his own way, it was Lindbergh. Stubbornness, as time would show, was one of his most salient characteristics. Though only twenty-five, he was remarkably self-assured and projected an aura of authority, especially when speaking about his flight and the future of aviation. He was also a fast learner and a man of great, if undeveloped, intelligence, who displayed in Paris an unexpected talent for diplomacy.[40] To be sure, contemporary newsreels show Lindbergh stiff and sometimes embarrassed; uncertain in his movements, he disguises his awkwardness by eagerly shaking the countless hands extended toward him. But an aura of dignity and an extraordinarily photogenic smile carried the young pilot through the most trying of ordeals. Even if "bewildered" during the first days and overwhelmed by his reception, Lindbergh rose to the occasion and intuitively made the most of opportunities created by the American ambassador and the French authorities.[41] The foreign correspondent and historian William Shirer, who accompanied Hank Wales to Le Bourget and was assigned by Wales to cover the Lindbergh story while the flyer was in Paris, later wrote that he had "never seen a man, let alone one so young, bear such fantastic adulation with such good grace and modesty."[42]

While still dazed by the ordeal of his flight and the frenzy of his reception, Lindbergh gave evidence of understanding the sensibility of the city whose honored guest he had become. Driven late in the night to Ambassador Herrick's residence at the Place d'Iéna by Major Weiss and two other French aviators, Lindbergh insisted on stopping at the Arc de Triomphe, where he stood in silence with bared head before the tomb of the Unknown Soldier. Weiss later wrote that "No spectacle of such solemn grandeur has been witnessed in this generation."[43] Weiss and his companions were deeply moved by this act of homage by one "conqueror" to another, and *Le Matin* featured this gesture of "the exhausted aviator" in one of its headlines, announcing Lindbergh's arrival in its edition of 22 May. For the French, it was vital that the United States not forget their sacrifices at a time when the question of French war debts and French security against a resurgent Germany had yet to be resolved.

And for the French it was vital too that Lindbergh's triumph should be understood in the proper aeronautical context as a glorious episode in a collective effort to conquer the air, an effort in which the French considered themselves to have played the leading role and in which they had recently lost two of their most famous aviators.[44] Whether coached or

Pl. 23. Nungesser's mother in her apartment, surrounded by mementos of her dead son.

not, the young American gave a convincing, and even moving, impression of relating his achievement to those of his French predecessors.

Lindbergh's first official visit, after awakening on the 22nd, was to the small apartment of the grieving mother of Charles Nungesser, who still clung stubbornly to the hope that her son was alive. With tears streaming down her deeply lined face, Madame Nungesser pleaded with Lindbergh to find him.[45] French newspapers were quick to feature photographs of this event that coincided with a cordial exchange of telegrams between the French president Gaston Doumergue and Calvin Coolidge, in which the American president recalled the major contributions "French genius" had made to the progress of aviation.[46] The next day, at a reception given for him by the Aéro-Club de France, Lindbergh won the hearts of his audience by saying that he wanted to express "America's sympathy for Captains Nungesser and Coli who were lost in a far greater attempt than mine." For the trip from Paris to New York, he explained, was a more daring project than his because of the prevailing western winds.[47] Upon hearing these words, those in attendance "broke into howls of approval." When toasted by French aeronautical enthusiasts as "the greatest aviator," he replied with a toast to "the nation of the greatest aviators." Shortly afterward, at a luncheon given for him by Louis Blériot, when the flying pioneer presented him with a fragment of the propeller of the monoplane with which he had crossed the Channel in July 1909 and lifted his glass to toast his "great exploit," Lindbergh rose quickly to his feet and replied: "That which I did, my dear Monsieur Blériot, is not to be compared with what you accomplished. So far as I am concerned, you will always remain my master."[48] Later that afternoon, presented with a letter of congratulations from the mother of Roland Garros, the first man to cross the Mediterranean by air, he commented to the well-known French aeronautical journalist Jacques Mortane with "touching sincerity": "Poor Garros,

Pl. 24. Louis Blériot, flanked by Lindbergh and Ambassador Herrick.

how I would have loved to see him. If he was still living, he would perhaps have been the one to make the first New York–Paris [flight]."[49] As far as the French aeronautical community was concerned, Lindbergh had risen to the challenge of understanding the historical meaning of his flight.

He had also done something else of equal, or even greater importance. He had reminded the French of American generosity and of the special relationship that existed between the United States and France. On 24 May, while addressing a luncheon of five thousand Americans at the American Club, Lindbergh disingenuously claimed that the name of his

Pl. 25. Lindbergh and Herrick wave an American and French flag from the balcony of the ambassador's residence the day after Lindbergh's arrival in Paris. Though few realized it at the time, gestures like these were embarrassing and even painful for Lindbergh. "I just stood there while my face got red and I said nothing. I realized it was a great honor, and I was deeply touched by the ovation; but I slipped in off the balcony as soon as I could with tact."

Pl. 26. Thirty-five thousand Parisians gathered in front of the Hôtel de Ville (City Hall) where a reception was held in honor of the young American pilot five days after his arrival. The crowds along the route he traversed in an open car down the Champs-Elysées and along the Rue de Rivoli were estimated at between five hundred thousand and a million people, testimony to the continuing fascination with Lindbergh's persona.

plane, the *Spirit of St. Louis* – which to the French suggested their medieval and saintly king – had been chosen to convey "a certain meaning to the people of France."[50] On the 25th, he took time from his busy schedule to draft a letter to the widow of the famous patron of French aviation, Henry Deutsch de la Meurthe, who had indicated her desire to contribute 150,000 francs ($5,850) toward a cup to be awarded to Lindbergh for "his glorious flight." He declared that he was unable to accept such a generous gift and instead asked that the money be used to create a fund for the families of French aviators who had laid down their lives in the cause of aviation. He ended by saying that he offered this sum "as an indication of my affection for France and my appreciation of her generous welcome."[51]

On 27 May Lindbergh was driven through cheering crowds, estimated at half a million people, to the Hôtel de Ville where he received the keys of the city and waved the flags of America and France from the balcony to cheers and delirious applause. The young aviator acknowledged the honor bestowed upon him with the following words that could only please his French admirers:

> I am not going to try to thank you for all the wonderful receptions you have given me, because I am too full of emotion to attempt it. However, there is one thought that I would like to leave with you; that is, that I believe my flight is the forerunner of a regular commercial air service uniting my country with yours in a manner in which they have never been united before, which I believe was the idea M. Blériot had in mind in 1909 when he flew the Channel . . . If those great heroes, Nungesser and Coli, had landed in New York, I believe they would have expressed a very similar thought.[52]

Leaving Paris for Brussels in the *Spirit of St. Louis*, Lindbergh paid homage to the Parisians by flying at low altitude over the Place de la Concorde in central Paris and dropping an American flag to which was attached a letter on which was written a message expressing his gratitude: "A thousand thanks for the kindness of Paris." Delighted at the rapidity with which Lindbergh's visit had swept away the storm clouds troubling Franco-American relations, Herrick dispatched a cable to Secretary of State Frank Kellogg, proclaiming the young flyer "a real ambassador to France"; and similar sentiments were expressed by a highly respected French aeronautical authority who wrote that in one day Lindbergh had succeeded in mending the diplomatic breach between France and the United States where innumerable diplomatic conferences had failed.[53]

★   ★   ★

23

Pl. 27. Lindbergh bids farewell to Paris by flying along the Seine. Note how low Lindbergh is flying, as he swoops pass the Alexander III bridge. The Grand Palais and Petit Palais are in the upper right hand corner.

The masses that flocked to Le Bourget and later crammed Parisian streets and squares in order to cheer Lindbergh doubtless did so because they were thrilled by the daring of his flight; because they wished to pay homage to the young man's courage; and, also, because they may have sensed that they were participating in a turning point of world history. But even in the emotional heat of the moment, some Frenchmen tried to give deeper meaning to the event and relate it to France's past and future. In a country that prided itself on its aesthetic sensibility, it was to be expected that some would try to understand the impact of Lindbergh's flight in France in terms of its poetic quality. Echoing the reaction to Wilbur Wright's flights in France in 1908–9, Paul Painlevé, the minister of war, who had made his first flight with Wright, proclaimed Lindbergh's flight "an aesthetic triumph, a thing so beautiful that it has gone straight to the heart of the world as only beauty and beauty alone can."[54]

General Duval, a high-ranking officer in the French Air Force, was less rhetorical and more troubled by the long-range consequences of Lindbergh's success for French aviation. Two weeks earlier, distressed by the recent disappearance of Nungesser and Coli and of three other French airmen who had attempted a nonstop South Atlantic crossing, Duval had written an article in the influential newspaper *Le Figaro*, denouncing the public passion for transatlantic flights as a perverted concept of sport reminiscent of the "barbarism" that prevailed during the contests of the ancient gladiators. It would be both "immoral" and "shameless" if the "crowd" were to become excited at the prospect of "spectacles" in which the cost of failure was almost certain death. Neither of the French planes recently lost, Duval argued, represented a technological breakthrough in terms of radio communication, navigational equipment, or physical comfort. They were nothing but flying "gas tanks." Enterprises of this sort would teach us nothing. They could succeed only through the lucky combination of favorable winds, clear weather, faultless navigation, and an engine that never failed. And even if they did succeed, they would have no scientific consequences and would only have the effect of encouraging dangerous illusions, which might lead to further useless deaths.[55]

Writing in *Le Figaro* on 23 May directly after Lindbergh's flight, Duval had obviously been touched by the general enthusiasm that had gripped Paris and seemed to have changed his mind about its potential meaning. He now conceded that it "incontestably marks a date in the history of the world." Indeed, Duval went on to take issue with those who had emphasized Lindbergh's luck in encountering favorable atmospheric conditions. "Is such an exploit only transitory? Certainly not. It's the exploit of a man who possesses extraordinary character and ability . . ." In Duval's view, Lindbergh had demonstrated an absolutely astounding "instinct" for navigation. The "worthless" compass he carried could not explain the accuracy of his flight.[56] And then there was his extraordinary force of character. "To listen thus to his motor over a period of thirty hours knowing that an irregularity in its humming was a signal of death; to remain untouched by this anguish and to preserve intact one's *sang-froid*; to maintain one's concentration at highest pitch without respite, and all that while completely deprived of sleep and more or less of food. And alone! To be alone! Do you have any idea what it means to feel oneself alone in such a trial?"[57] Yes, luck had favored Lindbergh, but luck favored those who deserved it, and Duval suspected that not only Lindbergh but also the engineers who had designed his plane had merited their success.

A week and a half later, while still recognizing the greatness of Lindbergh's exploit, Duval saw fit to downplay the young hero's personal role in order to emphasize the collective achievement of American technology and to contrast it, implicitly, with the French failure of Nungesser and Coli. The French had no shortage of men like Lindbergh, but they lacked airplanes of the quality of the *Spirit of St. Louis*, a design, Duval wrote fancifully, that had been perfected to carry mail between New York and San Francisco. Like the Germans, by whom they had been inspired in many respects, the Americans believed in experimenting; they did not concern themselves that much about immediate practical results. By contrast, the French bureaucrats who controlled aeronautical development did not believe in trial-and-error experiment and were enamored of pure science and abstract thinking. They had nothing but scorn for those who were active in the design and production of aircraft and the practice of commercial aviation. "They don't ever act as stimulants, rarely as collaborators; they generally put on the brakes." Duval concluded bitterly that Lindbergh's airplane could not have been built in France because its tubular steel structure violated existing bureaucratic guidelines.[58]

But the Frenchman who wrote with the greatest feeling and eloquence about Lindbergh and the meaning of his flight was Major Pierre Weiss, the air force officer to whose office at Le Bourget Lindbergh had been brought after having been rescued from the crowd. Himself a record-breaking aviator as well as a poet and a novelist, Weiss was sensitive to Lindbergh's "moral elegance" and "intellectual refinement," qualities he ascribed to the education he had received from an exceptional mother and the unquestioned "French affinities" of St. Louis. Meeting him face to face, Weiss found Lindbergh to be an "eminent

Pl. 28. Pierre Weiss photographed with Lindbergh (to his left) and other French airmen at Le Bourget.

Pl. 29. The famous Lindbergh smile that Weiss and the French found so captivating. Lindbergh's height also caused him to stand out. Here Ambassador Herrick is forced to stretch in order to strike a paternal pose.

Pl. 30. Lindbergh, accompanied by Herrick, salutes the standard of the 34th regiment of the French Air Force. On occasions like these, Lindbergh displayed a sensitivity and gravitas that won the hearts of the French people.

technician, a navigator and a mariner, a powerful individual as well as a sublime hero." Weiss made no effort to conceal that he was relieved to find in the young aviator a figure of exquisite sensibility – in other words, not the sort of person the French associated with Americans. "How sad it would have been to see emerge from the *Spirit of St. Louis* a second-class hero, with a cigarette hanging from his mouth! And what satisfaction to our desire for unity and our desire for plenitude in perfection that glory should have gone to this gentleman with light-blue eyes, a sign of the seal he bore of race and of tradition; he was valiant like [the First World War ace] Guynemer, shrewd like [the daring seaman] Surcouf, and more impressive looking than a portrait of [T. E.] Lawrence."[59]

Weiss admitted that, even when acclaiming Lindbergh, the crowd at Le Bourget could not help but think: "How sad that he's not one of ours!"[60] They wished him success but their feelings for him lacked conviction and fervor. All this changed, however, once he had arrived and the Parisians discovered his graciousness, simplicity, exquisite modesty, and sharp intelligence. At the Chamber of Deputies, the Senate, and the City Hall, Lindbergh imposed himself. "He was eloquent, and the maturity of his character and the seriousness of his physiognomy contrasted with the extreme youthfulness of his face. Racine would have written for him eternal verses: [He was] 'Young, charming, attracting all hearts toward him . . .'"[61]

According to Weiss, Lindbergh did more than charm the French; he helped them to rediscover themselves. "We believed ourselves to be inwardly turned, without strength or enthusiasm. Your miraculous appearance was enough – as the call to arms in 1914 had been enough – for the French masses to re-discover themselves . . . a people who bear in their hearts a desire for the infinite."[62] Then, continuing, Weiss sounded a theme that had appeared already in Edmond Rostand's 1911 poem *Le Cantique de l'aile*, with reference to Blériot. Lindbergh had exposed the mistake so commonly made of contrasting muscle to brain, action to spirit. "The conqueror, the aerial athlete, and the man who had triumphed over oceans was also a young sage . . . You were strong, Lindbergh, but you also had soul. And it's your soul that has conquered the French soul, which exists in each of us, the French soul that has saved us so many times. For, you should know this: you have placed us in a state of grace."[63]

Pl. 31. Lindbergh on the steps of the American Embassy with Ambassador Herrick and Gaston Doumergue, President of France (center), after receiving the Legion of Honor. Lindbergh was the first American ever to receive the Legion of Honor from the hands of a French President. Herrick is making no effort to conceal his contentment at the reconciliation of France and the United States.

Two years later, reflecting on the meaning of Lindbergh's flight, Weiss reached even higher levels of eloquence — and rhetoric — in trying to convey his point.

[His] exploit was prodigious. We lived it all in our imagination. It was an archangel who had done it . . . Never since the Armistice had the country been so moved. Paris knew itself to be the goal of the flight and of this herald with blue eyes — and blonde like Columbus! This event began to cure us of many maladies. There was something of the divine about it and it re-opened the era of chivalric exploits. It had the color of dawn and hope. By acclaiming Lindbergh, the [French] masses surrendered to their need for communication with the invisible. The *charmeur de nuages* [the man who charmed clouds] brought them a message from the place where dead gods and departed heroes sleep.[64]

★   ★   ★

During the week Lindbergh spent in Paris, there was much speculation about his immediate plans. He quickly put to rest any thought that he might want to repeat his transatlantic flight from east to west. On the other hand, he was clearly tempted by the idea of making an aerial tour of European cities, including Brussels, London, Copenhagen, Berlin, Vienna, Rome, Madrid, and Stockholm, where King Gustaf indicated his desire to give the most famous of Swedish-Americans a decoration and a gift of money as a reward for his exploit.[65] Like any tourist arriving in Europe for the first time and unsure of when he might return, Lindbergh hoped to make the most of the opportunity and yearned to see some of the sights. But the sights Lindbergh had in mind were primarily aeronautical: he wanted to go to all those countries that had "real aviation, study their ships, and fly them."[66]

Lindbergh soon discovered that he would not have the luxury of exploring Europe as an airborne tourist.[67] The American government had other plans for the young hero. This change in Lindbergh's plans, of course, had its advantages as well as its unpleasant features.

Pl. 32.   Lindbergh landing at Croydon airfield near London.

Pl. 33.   Lindbergh looking quite at ease with the air-minded Prince of Wales (right) and Lord Lonsdale.

Lindbergh first set off for Brussels, where he spent forty-eight hours as the guest of the air-minded Belgian King Albert at the Royal Palace and was presented with the decoration of Chevalier of the Order of Leopold. He then went to London where he was received by King George V at Buckingham Palace. The scene at Croydon airdrome, when he arrived, made his reception at Le Bourget appear a paragon of order. The police who had been assembled there were unable to restrain the hundred thousand people who swarmed over the field as Lindbergh attempted to land, forcing him to ascend again until the police had pushed the crowd back and made a clearing in which he could safely put down. Even then, he had to take refuge in a small building reserved for pilots and plead with the crowd to let the car through that had been sent to transport him from the field to the American Embassy in London. The press of crowds and the insistence of people on touching him were beginning to try the young aviator's patience. While in the British capital, during the intervals between banquets and other official events, Lindbergh reluctantly let himself be persuaded by Ambassador Alanson B. Houghton that he should cut short his European tour and return to the United States where his compatriots were eager to honor him. To transport him from Cherbourg to Washington, D.C. in a style worthy of his "marvelous achievement," President Calvin Coolidge sent nothing less than the flagship of the U.S. European fleet, the cruiser USS *Memphis*.[68]

But before embarking for the United States, Lindbergh insisted upon returning to Paris where he thanked Ambassador Herrick for his hospitality and was made an honorary member of the legendary Lafayette Escadrille, a squadron of American pilots who volunteered to fly for France before the United States entered the First World War. In the speech presenting this award, Edmund Gros said: "Our feeling for you has been summed up in the compliment paid you by a woman of the people, who seeing you land at Le Bourget, was heard to remark to a mother who had lost a son in the war: 'Do you know I believe he is the spirit of our sons coming back to us?' " Lindbergh replied that this honor, linking his exploit with the loss of human life in the Great War, meant more to him than any other he had received.[69] The next day he flew to Cherbourg where he set sail for Washington, D.C. and prepared himself to receive the adulation of his fellow citizens.

The receptions given to Lindbergh in the United States, first in Washington, then in New York and St. Louis, were among the most lavish that any human being in history had ever received. An unprecedented convoy of destroyers, dirigibles, and airplanes accompanied the *Memphis*, as it steamed up Chesapeake Bay. As the cruiser approached the Navy Yard on 11 June, a battery of large guns delivered a thunderous salute. During the ceremony held in front of the Washington Monument to honor Lindbergh the next day and broadcast by radio throughout the country, the usually taciturn president, Calvin Coolidge, was so moved that he carried on at what was for him remarkable length about the virtues that had earned Lindbergh his promotion to colonel in the Army Air Force Reserve and the Distinguished Flying Cross. Among them, he did not forget to mention Lindbergh's contribution to the world of "American genius and industry", a hundred American companies, he proudly recalled, had furnished materials, parts, or participated in some way in the construction of the *Spirit of St. Louis*.[70] Lindbergh, for his part, assured his audience of the affection the French and other Europeans felt for the United States.

On 13 June, four million people jammed the streets of New York to hurl eighteen tons of paper and confetti on Lindbergh's caravan, while three thousand seven hundred dignitaries attended a banquet given for the young aviator the following night. When Lindbergh arrived in the banquet hall, "dignified federal judges, elderly corporation leaders, black-garbed priests and clergymen, general officers of the army and admirals of the navy, nationally known men in many walks of life, climbed on top of chairs and pushed and fought with each other to catch a good view of the tall, slender, serious youth who was unknown to the world a month ago."[71] Five days later, five hundred thousand inhabitants of St. Louis threw paper and roses on Lindbergh, as he paraded through the city in an automobile on which "The Spirit of St. Louis" and "We" were written in violets. At a banquet given for Lindbergh, Secretary of War Davis did not hesitate to compare Lindbergh to Christopher Columbus and Lindbergh's St. Louis backers to Queen Isabella of Spain. It would be some

Pl. 34.   Lindbergh disembarks from the U.S.S Memphis in Washington, D.C.

Pl. 35.   Coolidge awards Lindbergh the Distinguished Flying Cross and announces his promotion to colonel in the United States Reserve Army Corps in front of a distinguished audience that included everyone who mattered in the capitol on a hot, humid Washington summer day.

Pl. 36.   New York Harbor on the day of Lindbergh's arrival. Lindbergh was flown to the harbor by an amphibious plane, then transferred to the Macom, the Mayor of New York's yacht, which transported him to a triumphant welcome in the Battery.

Pl. 37.   Lindbergh's caravan proceeds up Broadway in New York City, as confetti and ticker tape rain from the sky.

Pl. 38.   Lindbergh with his mother in New York before the Paris flight. Lindbergh adamantly refused all requests to be photographed kissing his mother, and here he steadfastly and stiffly maintains his distance, refusing to give the press the picture of a tearful farewell that they coveted.

time, he said, before air routes would connect America with Europe as sea routes did now. But when that time came, ". . . the name of Charles Lindbergh will be linked inevitably with those who have traversed the unknown sea, who have fought their way through the wilderness to open new worlds to men, who have placed the elements under man's control, men who have dared, and, in daring, have won imperishable fame."[72] It was as if Lindbergh had discovered Europe for the Americans.

It is impossible to know, of course, what was going through the minds of those millions who thronged the streets of Washington, New York, and St. Louis to celebrate Lindbergh's exploit. Many were, no doubt, simply thrilled by the immensity of the occasion and immersed themselves happily in the collective delirium of an unprecedented public celebration. But some ideas about the way people responded to Lindbergh and his deed can be gathered from the vast outpouring of verse produced by poets, some established, most obscure and deservedly destined to remain so.[73]

Almost all Lindbergh poets felt compelled to comment on the terrible loneliness of the flight, the dauntless courage of the pilot, the potentially fatal dangers of cloud, sleet, and fog he encountered, and the union of the plane and its pilot, "heart of youth and wings of steel."[74] But women poets, who dedicated poems to him in great profusion, were especially sensitive to his embodiment of values they admired, such as unspoiled youth, gleaming purity, untarnished idealism, unselfconscious modesty, and indifference to personal profit in an era they perceived as one of corruption, materialism, and moral decline. For many of them, he was the ideal son. As Josephine Burr put it in "We,"

He was youth's answer to the wail of those
Who mourn a world swift crumbling to decay.

He was the hope that every woman knows
But some may never say.

30

The son who died, or who was never born,
Who might have been like this. He was the bright
Indomitable breaking of the morn
After a weary night.[75]

There were naturally those who sounded a Promethean note:

Look on this hero risen
Up from our earthly star,
And know that men need hardly be
Less than the angels are.[76]

And there were also those who saw him as a poet whose plane's propeller spun new dreams for men:

He is the poet of the air. He writes
In verse immortal that all men may read.
His meter is a motor-measured beat;
His thought aspires through clouds to distant heights.
He spells in piston-power of strength and speed.
His is the courage that defeats defeat.[77]

Both of these poems could have been written about aviators before 1914. New, though, was the notion of the record-breaking pilot as a "gift-bearer" and a "prophet":

Gift to the future you have made
Your winged path o'er land and sea;
Your deed is like an eagle's quill
With which you write a prophecy.[78]

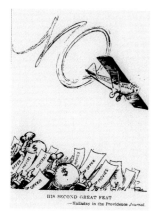

HIS SECOND GREAT FEAT
—Halladay in the Providence Journal.

Pl. 39. In this newspaper cartoon, republished in the *Literary Digest* on 9 July 1927, Lindbergh flies above the temptation to commercialize his exploit.

But a prophecy of what? Certainly not a prophecy of a technologically driven society, for technology seldom appears in these poems, which could not be less mechanistic or Futurist in inspiration. References are mostly to the past; Lindbergh is identified with "intrepid Marco Polo," "bold Columbus," and "Saint-Louis."[79] Nor are myth and chivalric legend neglected; Daedalus, Icarus, Apollo, Ulysses, Galahad, Bayard, and Lohengrin also make frequent appearances as earlier incarnations of Lindbergh's daring and nobility. But when the poets forget about poetic rhetoric and concentrate instead on what Lindbergh's flight meant to them, they are almost unanimous in viewing him as a redeemer who carried a message of liberation from the sordid materialism of an age "fat with glut of gold" and "untouched by finer dream or thought":[80]

A faithless generation asked a sign,
Some fresh and flaming proof of human worth,
Since youth could find no flavor in life's wine,
And there were no more giants in the earth.
Then out of gray obscurity he came
To laugh at space and thrust aside its bars;
To manifest the littleness of fame
To one who has companioned with the stars.
The drought of greed is broken, – fruitful streams
Of courage flow through fields long parched and dead;
Young men see visions now, old men dream dreams,
A world moves forward with uplifted head:
A lad with wings to dare had faith to rise
And carve proud arcs across uncharted skies.[81]

Redemption is identified with a nostalgic vision of America's past and a hopeful view of America's future:

Lithe stripling of the stock of pioneers,
You are that dream-self we all long to be,
Adventuring with purpose high and free,
Untouched by dross, untroubled by base fears.
Lead on! America's great future nears.
You are our pledge to all posterity,
A promise true, cloth'd in simplicity,
That we for history's finest can breed peers.[82]

Lindbergh's pink-cheeked Nordic looks were clearly part of his appeal to Anglo-Saxon women in a period when America was being invaded by swarthy immigrants from Mediterranean Europe and Jews from Eastern Europe. Many feminine poets see him as a worthy ancestor of the Vikings:

Blonde young Viking, flying, flying,
Like a sword that breaks the blue,
While the world remembers the men who made it,
It shall remember you.[83]

And, most of all perhaps, Lindbergh presented the writers of these poems with an incarnation of the sea-venturing, pioneering ideal with which they associated their past as a people; he was at the same time the "last frontiersman" and the "forerunner":

You symbolize our splendid, secret dreams;
Ideals of manhood, virtues we hold dear.[84]

These were the virtues of youth – purity, courage, sincerity, idealism, and "praise-proof modesty." And Lindbergh was thus, in the words of one woman poet, the "embodiment of all we've prayed America might be."[85]

★   ★   ★

During the months following the flight, the American public came to know in greater detail the hero they had so spectacularly anointed. There was no lack of journalists and self-appointed biographers eager to enlighten them. Lindbergh, they were told, was "clean, virile, and courteous, serving his country well, yielding his life to sport and to the conquest of the elements and throughout preserving his ideals untarnished, even in a moment of unique splendor."[86] Bashful, boyish, innocent, the young daredevil was totally unaware of the importance of what he was setting out to do when he undertook the flight to Paris.[87] He was what every mother wanted her son to be, and he had done what every man wished he had the nerve to do. The public learned that Lindbergh's father had served as a radical congressman from Minnesota for ten years, and that his widowed mother was a high school teacher of chemistry in Detroit; that he had dropped out of the University of Michigan's engineering school and spent a year in Army Air Force flight training where he had excelled and won his wings; and that before the flight he had earned his living flying the mail between St Louis and Chicago and was now a colonel and flight commander in the Missouri National Guard.

Yet the public wanted to know more, and America's journalists understood that "Lindy" sold newspapers as no hero (or villain) ever had before.[88] They would continue writing about him because it was their job to give the public what it wanted. What newspaper and magazine readers wanted was a hero who would reveal to them American virtues with which they could identify vicariously. In celebrating Lindbergh, they celebrated their country – and, by extension, themselves.

Lindbergh, however, had his own ideas about the meaning of his flight. From the moment of his triumph until his death in 1974, he would resist the attempt of others to

Pl. 40.   The cover of Richard J. Beamish's *The Boy's Story of Lindbergh: The Lone Eagle*. Lindbergh is attributed here with the virtues of an Eagle Scout in a period famous for its corruption and loose morals.

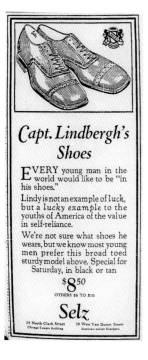

shape and control the narrative of his life. And this entailed developing a talent for which he had little preparation; he had to learn how to speak and write in such a way that he could reach large audiences. It is some measure of his self-confidence and the many facets of his complex character that he felt he could do what had to be done in order to become the master of his own story. Hence the failed university student and taciturn pilot became a public speaker and an author, who would one day win the Pulitzer Prize.[89]

During the week Lindbergh spent in New York before taking flight for Paris, he signed a number of contracts, including one with the *New York Times* for an exclusive interview and a series of articles, which appeared under Lindbergh's name between 23 May and 11 June in the *Times*, and also in other newspapers and magazines in the United States and abroad. Lindbergh later claimed in *The Spirit of St Louis*, published twenty-six years later, that these articles included many errors and that the "first several" were ghostwritten after short interviews. The demands on his time during this period, he said, were so great that he found "no opportunity to correct, or even read, the story which was cabled home."[90]

Yet even granting that these articles contained some inaccuracies and exaggerations that the twenty-five-year-old Lindbergh (and even more so the middle-aged man) might have found embarrassing and irresponsible, what emerges clearly is Lindbergh's determination to deny that there was anything accidental about the success of his flight. "If I have been lucky, it was because I got fitted out with a perfect ship, equipped by men who took every care and precaution. Nothing was overlooked, and from the first we never had any trouble or setback. I had the pick of everything in the way of equipment."[91]

In short, Lindbergh insisted that he had in no way been unprepared for the flight he made and that there was therefore nothing lucky about it.[92] The 33 hours he spent in the air between New York and Paris, he reminded his readers, was but a fraction of his total flying time during the past year, which amounted to 763 hours. "I have carried 5,951 passengers, and I am glad to say I have never had an accident either to any one of them or to myself."[93] And this message of self-assured professionalism, which reached millions of people at the time, came through unambiguously and was echoed in the admiring accounts of journalists and in the many advertisements that traded on Lindbergh's name and exploit.

Shortly after landing in Paris, Lindbergh signed yet one more contract – this one with G. P. Putnam's Sons for a book on his life and flight. The project must have had a strong attraction for him because he had been careful to emphasize while in Europe that he intended to make no commercial commitments before returning to the United States.

It was Lindbergh's understanding that the book to be published by Putnam would be written by a professional writer in the third person, based on interviews with him, and that he would be allowed to confirm its authenticity and contribute a foreword. A *New York Times* reporter, Carlyle MacDonald, was assigned to the task and accompanied Lindbergh during his return to the United States on the *Memphis*. During the nine-day journey, Lindbergh worked with MacDonald on the book. In less than two weeks of frantic writing after Lindbergh's arrival, MacDonald delivered a completed manuscript to his publisher. George Putnam was delighted with the result, and it's easy to see why; he had every reason to believe that he had a bestseller on his hands.

The trouble was that the man in whose name the book would be published thought differently. A stranger to the world of publishing and its imperatives, Lindbergh felt betrayed. He was being asked to affix his name to an overblown account of his life and flight written in the first person. What MacDonald had written represented everything he loathed about the newspaper coverage of his flight. Fully aware that a great deal of money was at stake, Lindbergh refused to authorize the publication of MacDonald's manuscript and instead announced that he intended to produce his own autobiography, which he did in a remarkable three-week period of intensive writing while staying at the Long Island estate of Harry and Carol Guggenheim. The book, entitled *We* and preceded by a hero-worshipping preface by Myron T. Herrick that compared Lindbergh with Joan of Arc, Lafayette, and the "Shepherd Boy David," was published in July 1927 and immediately became a bestseller.[94] Within one month of its publication, it had gone through six printings. It was the first of many attempts Lindbergh would make to shape and assert control over the narrative of his life.

We takes its title from the mode of narration that the *New York Times* chose for the ghostwritten first installment of Lindbergh's story: "As you know, we – that's my ship and I – took off rather suddenly."[95] But, curiously, at no time in *We* does Lindbergh use this phrase or develop the idea of union with his airplane, which was a popular theme of aviation writers during the period before 1914. On the contrary, in those sections of his book in which he reverts to the first person plural, it refers not to himself and his "ship" but to the Army Air Force cadets with whom he trained at Brooks and Kelly fields or the unnamed people who aided him to prepare his flight while in New York.[96] In the appendix to the book, however, which was written by Fitzhugh Green, the title takes on a new and distinctly different meaning. Green quotes at length from the speech given by Jimmy Walker, mayor of New York, at City Hall on 13 June:

> We have heard, and we are familiar with, the editorial "we," but not until you arrived in Paris did we learn of the aeronautical "we." Now you have given to the world a flying pronoun. That "we" that you used was perhaps the only word that would have suited the occasion and the great accomplishment that was yours. That all-inclusive word "we" was quite right, because you were not alone in the solitude of the sky and the sea, because every American heart, from the Atlantic to the Pacific, was beating for you. Every American, every soul throughout the world, was riding with you in spirit, urging you on and cheering you on to the great accomplishment that is yours.[97]

Lindbergh's flight thus became a triumph of all Americans, one that could be applauded by the entire world.

We has the quality of a Norman Rockwell painting. It is naïve, straightforward, chronological in its structure, flat in its prose, and at the same time aglow with self-confidence and faith in aviation's future. In the opening chapter, Lindbergh portrays himself as an inveterate wanderer and an intrepid adventurer drawn to aeronautics – a young man who walks on the wing of an airplane as it buzzes a small town and free falls hundreds of feet through the air before his parachute opens on his first jump. There is no trace of self-advertisement or bragging; no attempt to extract melodrama from what was clearly an extraordinary series of adventures; only a matter-of-fact and unadorned prose that records the exploits of a mechanically minded and self-reliant young man capable of fixing anything, whether it was a leaky boat he used to go down the Yellowstone River or the motorcycle, which he overhauled after a piston jammed while he was in Nebraska. The settings he evokes are small town America and the wilds beyond it, a world that has little to do with the country's quickly growing cities. We would not be far removed from the world of Tom Sawyer or Huckleberry Finn in these pages, were it not for the role that the internal combustion engine plays in making it possible for the young Lindbergh to explore the skies and to move quickly from one section of the country to another. *We* is from the beginning a story of locomotion and mobility in which immense distances are traversed in a few days.

We oscillates strangely between claims for the safety of commercial aviation and hair-raising accounts of Lindbergh's aerial adventures as an aspiring pilot during the early 1920s. This contradiction cannot escape even the most casual reader. Midway through the first chapter Lindbergh interrupts his narrative, almost as an afterthought, in order to insert a note into the middle of the text explaining that the experiences and incidents related in his book in no way describe modern commercial flying conditions. "Commercial air transport has developed rapidly during the last few years, until today it has reached a stage where the safety of properly operated airlines compares favorably with other means of travel." He adds that the more spectacular events described in his book ". . . took place in such a manner that all risk was taken by the pilots and by members of the aeronautical profession . . ."[98]

Yet Lindbergh's depiction of his experiences as a barnstormer in 1923, an air force cadet in 1924, and an airmail pilot in 1925–6, was anything but reassuring for those who had reservations about the future of aerial transportation. He describes a potentially fatal tailspin as he teaches himself to loop his Jenny with a frightened passenger aboard; a takeoff in which he cleared a railroad trestle by inches; a forced landing in a Minnesota swamp in which his plane nosed over, leaving him hanging by his safety belt upside down; a mid-air collision with another air force cadet from which he escaped by means of a parachute jump; a second jump from a plane he was testing, which had gone into an uncontrollable tailspin, from a height of 350 feet; and two perilous emergency parachute jumps at night while carrying the mail when lost in fog, in one of which he came close to being hit by his own airplane.

The reader can only conclude that flying was an exceedingly dangerous (if thrilling) enterprise, even when conducted by the world's most famous pilot. Yet Lindbergh is dismissive of newspapers that report such incidents, because of the ignorance of journalists and their tendency to dramatize what in his mind are banal and everyday occurrences in which the element of danger is minimal. Commenting on a story about his Minnesota crash, which appeared the next day in a Minneapolis newspaper and stated that he had been flying three hundred feet above the ground when his plane suddenly went into a nosedive and landed on its propeller in a swamp, Lindbergh observes rather disdainfully that it exemplifies "the average man's knowledge of aeronautics." Small wonder, he concludes, that "the average man would far rather watch some one else fly and read of the narrow escapes from death when some pilot has had a forced landing or blowout, than to ride himself."[99]

The truth, Lindbergh says, is that most serious accidents in the period of aviation he is describing were caused by inexperienced pilots who were allowed to fly without license and restriction and to carry anyone who might be beguiled into riding with them. But this is precisely the way that he has described his own adventures as a barnstormer – someone who taught himself to fly at the risk of others' lives and did not hesitate to subject his passengers to unnecessarily frightening and dangerous experiences. The reader again can only take away from such passages the conviction that Lindbergh was no average man, because average men were fearful even when they had no grounds for being so.

And this is indeed the way the book was interpreted by many, if not most, of those who read it. After recounting Lindbergh's marvelous adventures, Bruce Bliven concluded in the *New Republic*: "Grant that he uses all the science there is; grant that he now takes no more chances than he can avoid except by staying on the ground, still it is clear, I think, that this tall lad flies in answer to some deep-rooted demand of his inner nature, turns to the air as the moth to the candle, answers voices whose call his conscious mind does not even hear. He is the Flying Fool; a fact which the world instinctively recognized even through his hot denials – and loved him for it."[100]

★   ★   ★

Lindbergh was not satisfied to let *We* speak for him. To make the case for aviation, he clearly felt that his words had to be reinforced by deeds. People had to be convinced that flying was both dependable and safe. This could only be done by demonstrating that planes could perform on schedule regardless of weather conditions.

Thus Lindbergh responded enthusiastically when his newly made friend Harry Guggenheim, former naval aviator and heir to a vast fortune, suggested an aerial tour of the United States. The Daniel Guggenheim Fund for the Promotion of Aeronautics, of which Harry Guggenheim was president, would provide the funding and provide Lindbergh with a fee of $50,000, an immense amount of money for someone who not long before had been making $200 a month. With his customary decisiveness, Lindbergh quickly came to the conclusion that at least one stop should be made in every state of the union and that routes should be direct, even if it entailed flying over high mountains.[101] The assistant secretary of aeronautics, William P. MacCracken Jr., agreed to assign a Department of Commerce plane, piloted by Lindbergh's old army and airmail buddy Phil Love, to accompany Lindbergh, who would fly alone in the *Spirit of St. Louis*. MacCracken appointed Donald E. Kehoe, a publicist for the Department of Commerce and a retired Marine Corps officer and pilot, to serve as Lindbergh's aide. The Wright Corporation assigned a third man, Ted Sorenson, to act as mechanic for both planes.[102] Kehoe would fly with Love and be responsible for acting as a buffer between Lindbergh and the outside world. Kehoe was told by MacCracken that this meant, in effect, taking "all the knocks possible."[103] But what aviator wouldn't jump at the opportunity to fly with the world's most famous pilot? An advance man, traveling a zigzag course by train, prepared their stops and cooperated with local authorities in arranging the sequence of events.

The idea was to give the country a view of the "lone eagle" while at the same time providing a carefully organized setting in which Lindbergh could present his message to the public. Only a man with a mission (or an insatiable taste for public ceremonies) would have considered subjecting himself to such a punishing schedule: 82 stops and 22,000 miles of flying over a period of three months. It was estimated that 30 million people turned out to see him, one out of every four Americans – a figure all the more astonishing when one

Pl. 43. The route followed by
Lindbergh and his companion
plane during the American
tour between 20 July and 23
October 1927.

realizes that many must have traveled long distances and automobiles in some parts of the country remained a luxury. Perhaps the most astonishing statistic is that Lindbergh subjected himself to riding 1,285 miles in parades and delivering 147 speeches, activities for which he felt no fondness.[104]

The three-month tour began with a flight from New York's Mitchell Field to Hartford, Connecticut on 20 July and ended in Philadelphia on 23 October. The format for the stops seldom varied. An advance man, Milburn Kusterer, traveling by train, had the difficult responsibility of assuring that the local reception had been organized to fit Lindbergh's specifications. The escort plane, flown by Phil Love and carrying Donald Kehoe and the mechanic, would appear at the airport of the city or town to be visited around 1:30 in the afternoon and would check out landing conditions. Lindbergh himself would then approach at 2:00 in a fast glide under power after having circled the field once or twice. Instead of putting down immediately, however, he would pull up into a steep climb at an angle, a maneuver that thrilled the spectators and confirmed their belief that Lindbergh was a "flying fool" who could not resist "stunts." Only after ascertaining that the crowd was safely under control would he repeat his approach and land.[105] A motorcade would transport the hero past thousands of cheering spectators to grandstands where he would make a brief speech. Once in his hotel, he would give a press conference, during which he politely, but firmly, evaded all questions about his private life and his attitude toward girls, saying: "I shall be glad to tell you anything I know – on aviation," a word that he stubbornly pronounced with a short rather than a long "a," over the written protests of many of those who heard his speeches.[106] In the evening, local dignitaries would offer him a banquet between 7:00 and 9:00 p.m. at which his virtues would be recited, and he would respond by presenting his view of aviation's present situation and its future possibilities, emphasizing whenever possible the impact that commercial flight could have on the city's economy and relations with other sections of the country.

To drive home his message, Lindbergh emphasized the tremendous aeronautical progress that had been accomplished over the past twenty-five years. No other mode of transportation could boast of such rapid development. Problems of design, weight, and construction

Pl. 44. A remarkably boyish Lindbergh seizes a moment of relaxation near Butte, Montana, during his cross-country tour.

materials had all been overcome. Moreover, the safety record of commercial airlines – not to be confused with military and experimental aviation – equaled that of other types of transport while offering vastly greater speed in covering large distances. Lindbergh did not conceal that much remained to be done to improve the regularity of commercial flights and to limit the high costs of operating airplanes. The problem of landing in fog, for example, had not yet been resolved. Yet Lindbergh was certain that it soon would, and he believed that we were not far distant from the time when flying boats would offer regular service across the Atlantic, making it possible for people to travel to Europe by air. In the meantime, it was essential for Americans to be "awake to aviation" so that they would be in the forefront of aeronautical progress, moving ahead of the Europeans. The most immediate tasks were to construct commercial airports near the centers of cities and to standardize aviation laws and regulations.[107]

Lindbergh would recall many moments of his aerial tour with great pleasure, as he came to know the United States in a way that no other man before him ever had. He enjoyed meeting old flying friends from his days of barnstorming and cadet training from whom he had been separated for years and appreciated the warmth of the reception in cities and towns that had played important roles in his life, such as his birthplace Little Falls, Minnesota, San Diego where the *Spirit of St. Louis* had been built, and St. Louis whose businessmen had financed the purchase of his airplane. During a week's vacation at Elbow Lake near Butte, Montana, spent with his companions on the tour, he was able to give outlet to his love of wilderness and escape from the pressures of the tour by fishing, canoeing, and playing practical jokes on his friends.

Yet Lindbergh's happiest moments were spent in the air where he honed his already formidable navigational skills and played aerial tricks on his friends in the escort plane.[108] As the tour progressed, he mapped out long detours from his official route because it was the hours spent in flight that he found most restful and fulfilling.[109] Life on the ground, by contrast had become a burden that Lindbergh bore stoically and – externally, at least – with unfailing good humor, even though his tolerance for grasping crowds, intrusive journalists, and self-important politicians had been subjected to serious strain.

Pl. 45.   Sheet music for *Lucky Lindy*.

And who could blame him? People threw penknives and toy airplanes at his car during parades. They jostled and pulled at him in an attempt to touch him and shake his hand. They stole his laundry and his flying clothes. They claimed to be his friends or relatives in order to gain access to his hotel suite. Journalists insisted on asking him about his love life while ignoring the content of his speeches. Press photographers sneaked into private homes where he attempted to relax during his days off. Politicians used his presence in their cities as opportunities to bask in his reflected glory and engage in empty rhetoric that had nothing to do with the purpose of his visit. Welcoming committees insisted on playing popular songs inspired by his Paris flight which he endured with ill-concealed irritation. One can only guess at how many times he was subjected to the strains of "Lucky Lindy," a tune that he abhorred.

These ordeals brought into profile an aspect of Lindbergh's personality that, though crucial to the preparation and success of his flight, had earlier been concealed by his extraordinary courtesy and sensitivity to the feelings of his European hosts. Lindbergh refused to deviate from plans and commitments he had made and his sense of what was fitting and morally right. He balked at posing for photographs on the grounds that he was an aviator and not an actor. He refused to give journalists glimpses into his personal life or quotable statements that might have enlivened articles that were otherwise reduced to dry and dreary summaries of his predictions about the future of commercial aviation. And when local politicians and reception committee members tried to alter Lindbergh's schedule, he adamantly refused, even when such refusals meant that parades had to be abbreviated and many people disappointed. In at least one instance, Lindbergh's unwillingness to adjust his schedule inspired "a storm of criticism." "I was afraid this would happen," Lindbergh remarked when told of the reports. "But I couldn't see that there was anything else to do."[110]

Toward the end of the tour, Lindbergh uncharacteristically opened up to Kehoe and raised the question of his future plans. He spoke about his desire to return to private life. "Perhaps it might help aviation if I were to keep on visiting cities and talking about flying, but I think that there are more important things to be done. I'd like to be free to work out some of the scientific problems we ought to solve. Even though regular flying is quite dependable there is still a lot of research to be done."[111]

Several months after his flight to Paris, Lindbergh still does not appear to have grasped the nature of the Faustian bargain he had struck with the admiring multitudes following his arrival in Paris five months before.[112] A return to private life was not an option Lindbergh had. The world, and especially the Americans, had too much emotion invested in him. They could love him, as they did now; they could hate him, as many would later; but they could not leave him alone. Lindbergh would spend the rest of his life repaying the staggering price of fame.[113]

★　　★　　★

When in Paris in May 1927, Lindbergh was careful to present himself as the heir of Louis Blériot, and he was right to do so. Like Blériot, he had set out alone across a daunting body of water on a flight that could easily have cost him his life and that ordinary mortals could not conceive of having undertaken. Like Blériot, he was competing for a substantial monetary prize against formidable rivals and was not, at the beginning, the one thought most likely to succeed. And like Blériot also, he enjoyed, after his success, enormous public celebrations and an apotheosis that went far beyond his own assessment of the dimensions of his deed.

Lindbergh saw yet another connection between himself and the French pioneering pilot, which he emphasized at every opportunity. As he put it in his brief speech to the French Chamber of Deputies on 26 May 1927: "Less than twenty years ago, when I was not far advanced from infancy, M. Blériot, here beside me, flew across the English Channel, and he was asked: 'What good is your airplane? What will it accomplish?' Today those same skeptics might well ask me what good has been my flight from New York to Paris. My answer is that I believe it is the forerunner of a great air service from America to France, from America to Europe, which will bring our peoples together, nearer in understanding and in friendship than they have ever been."[114]

A brilliant stroke of diplomacy, and one that the French would have appreciated, Lindbergh's attempt to enlist the Blériot of 1909 among the prophets of commercial avia-

Pl. 46.　Blériot kisses Lindbergh. Lindbergh's smile seems forced, as befits a man who was uncomfortable being photographed while being kissed by his mother, not to mention a man.

41

tion was somewhat misplaced. When Blériot flew the Channel the airplane was viewed primarily as a high-speed sporting vehicle (like a race car) or a possible instrument of war rather than a means of transporting goods and people. In 1909, even aeronautical experts doubted that ordinary people could ever be convinced to travel by air. Lindbergh inhabited a quite different mental universe, which gives us some measure of the extraordinary progress that had occurred in aviation in less than twenty years. A professional airmail pilot who marveled at the passenger traffic departing from Le Bourget toward London and other European destinations, Lindbergh was persuaded that his flight was not the act of a daredevil, but a decisive step toward the establishment of regular commercial flights between the United States and Europe. With them, he believed, would come closer relations between the Americans and the Europeans. Implied, of course, was the optimistic assumption that the more people of different nationalities saw of one another the closer they would become.[115] This was a conviction that had been voiced by apostles of aviation ever since the achievement of powered flight, but no one articulated it with greater authority or reached such a wide audience as Lindbergh. For this he deserved the title conferred on him by the poet Virgila Stephens: "Ambassador of the Skies."[116]

One predecessor whom Lindbergh failed to mention while in Paris was Wilbur Wright, dead then for fifteen years and, if not forgotten, diminished in the public imagination. This was some indication of the extent to which collective memory of Wright's triumphant 1908 season of flights in France had faded over the past two decades. By 1927 Wright was remembered as an inventor rather than a record-breaking pilot, a turn of events that would have pleased him, had he still been alive.

Yet, superficially at least, Lindbergh had a great deal in common with Wright. Just as Wright had done in 1908, he had demonstrated to the French that they could no longer claim to be in the forefront of aeronautical progress. As much as the French might celebrate and honor Lindbergh, they could not forget that his success was a cruel reminder of Nungesser and Coli's tragic failure and of French aeronautical decline.[117] The lesson was further driven home when two more of France's most famous aviators, Dieudonné Costes and Rignot, failed in their attempt to set a new distance record shortly after Lindbergh's flight. American engines were evidently more reliable than French ones; American planes were

Pl. 47. A front-page cartoon of Lindbergh being courted by kings and presidents and entitled "An Ambassador of Good Will."

more resistant to storms; American instruments were more sophisticated; American pilots were more resourceful and possessed greater endurance; and America offered a better environment for the development of commercial aviation. All these were issues that gave the French aeronautical community grave cause for concern and made its members wonder if they were not destined to be left behind by the Americans. Gloomy thoughts like these arose within the larger context of general fears of French and European decline.[118]

Lindbergh also had in common with Wright his dedication to the principle of preparation. As risky as his enterprise was, he attempted to give himself the maximum chance of success by pre-testing his equipment and anticipating the emergencies he might have to face. Both men relied on their own intuition and were unmoved by general opinion. Just as Wright had refused to be forced into flying by the crowds that assembled at Hanaudières and Auvours in 1908, so Lindbergh bided his time after arriving in New York on 11 May 1927, refusing to take flight until he was convinced that the conditions were right. And, finally, like Wright, Lindbergh possessed a confidence in his own abilities so unshakeable that he never doubted that he would succeed where others had failed. The "calm assurance" and "controlled enthusiasm" that so impressed Harry Guggenheim when he met Lindbergh in New York before the flight derived in great part from the "faith absolute" that he had in his airplane, which, like Wright, he had helped to design and construct.[119] Known by others as daredevils – in Wright's case a "fanatic of flight," in Lindbergh's a "flying fool" – both men viewed themselves as twentieth-century men of science who prided themselves on never taking unnecessary risks.

The comparison could be extended. Both Lindbergh and Wright came from the American Middle West and had a strong sense of what was right and wrong. Eventually, this last quality would lead them into long and enervating struggles that would end by casting a shadow over their reputations. Both combined uncommon mechanical ability with technical imagination. Both were known in Europe for the brevity of their remarks and the austerity of their personal lives. Neither seemed susceptible to the charms of seductive women or the lure of fast living. The women who shared the spotlight of their fame were comfortingly asexual: Wright's sister, Lindbergh's mother. Cynical and hard-living journalists were both impressed and intimidated by the monk-like purity with which they pursued their aeronautical careers.

But Charles Lindbergh was a more complex figure than Wilbur Wright, and the mark he left on the sensibility of his time would be deeper than that of the man who, with his brother, claimed to have invented the airplane. This development requires some explaining. The Wrights had been the first to achieve controlled and powered flight. Lindbergh, by contrast, was only one of many talented and courageous pilots; and 1927 was a year of record flights. Lindbergh's nonstop crossing from New York to Paris was quickly followed by Chamberlain and Levine's to Germany and Byrd's to France. Yet these flights would soon be forgotten, just as Alcock and Brown's Atlantic crossing had been, and Lindbergh's would not. Why?

To begin with, Lindbergh's exploit was different in many easily identifiable respects. He flew alone in a small one-engined monoplane without a radio, leaving all hope of human contact behind him as he plunged into the double peril of the night and the fog and ice of the Atlantic Ocean after leaving Newfoundland. He piloted his plane while at the same time doing his own navigation, a feat that many aviation experts considered both foolhardy and impossible. He made no stops and was in the air alone for $33\frac{1}{2}$ hours, thus providing an example of what many people saw as superhuman endurance and unbelievable fortitude. And he linked together New York and Paris, the two preeminent symbols of urban modernity in the 1920s.

Pl. 48. Two pool players marvel at Lindbergh's clean-living habits in a cartoon published in the *Literary Digest* on 9 July 1927, p. 30.

This last achievement should not be underestimated. Unlike so many other transatlantic fliers, Lindbergh had taken off at one airdrome and landed at another, just as he had said that he would do. Alcock and Brown, by contrast, had crash-landed in a bog in a remote corner of western Ireland, hardly a reassuring demonstration that the age of transatlantic air travel was about to begin.[120] Even the flights of Chamberlain and Byrd in June 1927 ended in emergency landings: the first in a German wheat field in Mansfeld near Eisleben, the second more dangerously in the waters of the Atlantic not far from the Norman town of Caen.

It is also true that never before had such large masses of people on two widely separated continents been able to participate so intimately in a transatlantic flight. Indeed, never before had the pre-1914 Futurist ideal of a "simultaneous" event that united people living at great distances from one another been so fully realized. Lindbergh's flight was a dazzling demonstration of the magical powers of the new technologies of communication. News of his progress was circulated instantaneously by cable and wireless, then flashed on electric bulletin boards, broadcast over the radio, and diffused in special editions of newspapers whose headlines raised the hopes and anxieties of their readers to fever pitch. Motion pictures of his takeoff in New York and reception in Paris were seen in newsreels throughout the world. His image quickly became as familiar as Charlie Chaplin's. Lindbergh's celebrity was all the more impressive because it came into being with a rapidity that seemed to reflect the accelerated pace of life of modern times. On the night Lindbergh took off from New York, forty thousand people in Yankee Stadium assembled for a prize fight between Jimmy Maloney and Jack Sharkey rose in unison for a moment of prayer after they were informed by loudspeaker that Lindbergh was two hundred miles out at sea and well. As the hush finally fell over the crowd, one spectator shouted: "He's the greatest fighter of them all!"[121]

Lindbergh also showed himself much cleverer than Wright in separating himself from the commercial spirit that so dominated his time. Though by no means indifferent to the financial possibilities that his exploit opened and quick to integrate himself into the networks of corporate America, he did so in a way that avoided any suggestion of vulgarity or the pursuit of mean-spirited private gain. It helped also that even after his success in crossing the Atlantic, he continued to undertake dangerous flights that confirmed his dedication to aeronautical progress rather than personal profit. A wealthy man by any standard after 1927,

Pl. 49. Alcock and Brown's Vickers-Vimy ignominiously mired in an Irish bog. They crashed after completing their transatlantic flight in June 1919.

he maintained an image of irreproachable integrity and incorruptibility far removed from the world of the American Establishment in which he was, by means of personal relationships, thoroughly at home.[122]

In retrospect, it seems astonishing how effortlessly and smoothly Lindbergh transformed himself from an obscure airmail pilot into a public figure and semi-official representative of the United States. Already in his mid-twenties he radiated an unmistakable quality of dignity and *gravitas*, an aura of seriousness that he would retain for the rest of his life. After May 1927, Lindbergh moved among politicians, diplomats, corporate leaders, and distinguished scientists with the ease of a man born into a royal house. When he completed a 9,500 mile flight to the countries of Central and Latin America in 1928, the correspondent of the *New York Times* saluted it not only as a great aeronautical feat but as a triumph of diplomacy. Lindbergh, he wrote, had proved again that "as an ambassador of good-will he has no equal in the world. Lindbergh is Lindbergh to all people, whatever their speech or race, and his effect upon them is the same – an uplifting of the spirit which approaches a religious revival." The same correspondent then quoted a Mexican senator who had told him that "That boy has brought more happiness and joy to the world than any man who ever lived."[123]

But the explanation of the Lindbergh phenomenon goes even deeper. There was something in the Lindbergh personality and the Lindbergh appearance that mesmerized the peoples of the West.[124] He incarnated better than any other aviator the "celestial helmsmen" and "men-machines" that Gabriele D'Annunzio and F. T. Marinetti had imagined before 1914: a fearless master of technology, fused with his airplane, who was more at home in the sky than on the ground. In a time when people worried about the moral fiber of the younger generation and Freudian ideas had begun to make their way, Lindbergh's face projected a message of comforting stability and calm self-confidence far removed from the protean promiscuity of the jazz age. Here was a man of steely character whose technical ingenuity and unyielding determination were capable of overcoming any obstacle to progress the century might present. Untouched by doubt, unswerving in his resolution, indifferent to the threat of death, Lindbergh had challenged the vengeful powers of Nature and triumphed over human frailty as no one in history ever had.

Such a man might perhaps have arisen in other professions – in dangerous sports, for example, such as bullfighting, mountain climbing, or race-car driving. But only aviation allowed the hero to place himself above the common run of humankind that was condemned to live on the ground. To admire Lindbergh was to raise one's head from the tawdriness of everyday life in overcrowded cities toward the majesty of the sky, to glimpse the possibilities for transcendence that lay hidden in human beings, and in doing so to be exalted. The Superman had passed from the philosophical and literary imagination into technological fact, and every witness of Lindbergh's extraordinary achievement felt vicariously elevated by it.

R. Mahoney '56

BALBO E TRANSVOLATORI ITALIANI

2

Flying and Fascism

Not everyone can fly . . . Flying must remain the privilege of an aristocracy; but everyone must want to fly, everyone must regard flying with longing. All good citizens, all devoted citizens must follow with profound feeling the development of Italian wings.

Benito Mussolini, November 1923[1]

THE reasonable assumption would have been that Lindbergh's celebrity would lose its bloom and fade, as the public recovered from its infatuation and went in search of new heroes. After a few months, he should have receded from public view as other record-breaking aviators had done. Gene Tunney, heavy-weight champion of the world who knew something about the adulation of the masses, advised Lindbergh in a newspaper interview "to commercialize his stunt for every cent that's in it, for in a year from now he will be forgotten."[2] But Tunney was wrong. Lindbergh's six months of fame stretched into a lifetime of celebrity. Even when the public's admiration turned into hostility and Lindbergh tarnished his image with what appeared to be a flirtation with Nazi Germany and a damning expression of anti-Semitism, he was never forgotten. He looms large in the American imagination, a fallen but vividly remembered idol whose exploit symbolizes a moment in the life of the West. For aviators, he became the measure against which all fliers were measured. They understood that as an airman he was not an invention of the media but the real thing.

In the short term, Lindbergh's flight and his persona became a stimulus to an extraordinary range of cultural activity. There seemed to be no limit to the uses to which "Lucky Lindy" could be put. People sang songs about the "Eagle of the USA" and danced on into the 1930s to the Lindy Hop. In Walt Disney's first Mickey Mouse cartoon, *Plane Crazy*, screened in May 1928, the mischievous little rodent sets out to emulate Lindbergh, tousles his hair, studies a flight manual, transforms an automobile into a plane, and takes his girl friend Minnie for a perilous flight that ends when he crashes and a horseshoe drops on his head. This gives Disney's brilliant animator Ub Iwerks opportunities to devise visual effects not unlike the ones that Italian Futurist artists were trying contemporaneously to create. The French theatrical impresario Sacha Guitry was inspired a few months later to write a play based on the premise that Lindbergh's impeccable behavior while in Paris belied the French stereotype of the American as someone who was uncivilized, vain, vulgar, and interested only in financial gain. While praising Lindbergh, Guitry gave himself ample oppor-

Pl. 51. Giacomo Balla's 1931 painting, *Balbo e i trasvolatori italiani*, celebrates the transatlantic flight of Italo Balbo and his men to Rio de Janeiro.

Pl. 52. Benito Mussolini, "the first pilot of Italy."

49

Plate 53. Story boards for Plane Crazy. Mickey realizes the importance of Lindbergh's tousled hair as he sets out to emulate America's favorite hero.

tunity to reinforce French prejudices about the United States: "There's no more inhuman country on earth!"[3] The following year Bertold Brecht wrote a didactic radio play called *Der Lindberghflug* (The Lindbergh Flight) that was set to music by Kurt Weill and Paul Hindemith and performed at the Baden-Baden music festival in July. Lindbergh, a paragon of rugged individualism, was transformed by the Marxist Brecht into a Promethean symbol of collective action that held out hope for the eventual triumph of a liberated humankind over the primitive forces of nature and a naive belief in a hereafter.[4] A human being with remarkable virtues and serious defects, Lindbergh had become in one short year an icon worshipped through the West by people who did not know and had no wish to know what he was really like.

Plate 54. Rudolph Schlichter emphasizes Bertolt Brecht's defiance and proletarian dress in this 1926 portrait.

Though Lindbergh himself showed no interest in politics until he reluctantly and disastrously enlisted in the struggle against American intervention in the war against Nazi Germany, others were tempted by the prospect that aviators possessed qualities that might allow them to pilot to safety the societies in which they lived. Who better than the aviator could bring to bear on the problems of Western societies ". . . a different point of view, a new perspective, a more consistent aim, coordinating and correlating circumstances and conditions for the common good?"[5]

The idea of the aviator as a natural leader was one that Benito Mussolini seems to have grasped intuitively at an early point. In the introduction to a book entitled *Mussolini aviatore* first published in 1935, the Italian journalist Guido Mattioli explained why as a thinker, a man of action, and a political leader, Mussolini had no choice but to take up flying. "No other machine requires such a concentration of the human spirit, of man's will . . ." The pilot knows exactly what it means to "govern." Hence there was a "necessary and intimate spiritual connection" between aviation and fascism. Mussolini had understood this already, Mattioli said, when he flew for the first time in August 1915. He had grasped that to fly meant to raise one's body and one's spirit above mediocrity, and by doing so to give the lie to "the facile economic science of determinism." This was the symbolic meaning of Mussolini's decision to become an aviator. He maneuvered his airplane with the same "serene firmness" he applied to the guidance of the Italian people.[6]

To us the connection between flying and fascism may not seem so obvious. For Italians, however, by 1935 the relationship between their dynamic new regime and aeronautical pre-eminence was something they took for granted: during more than a decade it had been drummed into them by means of words, images, and spectacular demonstrations staged throughout the world. For Italians, fascism was synonymous with flying. "Every aviator," Mattioli said confidently, "is a born fascist."[7]

★　　★　　★

Pl. 55.   D'Annunzio writes at his villa outside Florence before the outbreak of the First World War. Before 1914, no one exemplified better than he did the image of an aesthete and dandy.

In this area of fascist rhetoric and symbolic practice, as in so many others, the poet and novelist Gabriele D'Annunzio could justifiably claim to be the prophet and the source. The author of one of the first and most influential aviation novels to be published before the outbreak of the Great War, *Forse che sì forse che no* (Perhaps Yes, Perhaps No), D'Annunzio had devoted himself to establishing the identification between the Italian people and aviation.[8] The very slogan by which Mattioli said that Mussolini lived – "never stop, always go beyond and higher" – had been coined (more elegantly) by D'Annunzio in 1917 when he admonished Italian aviators to fly *più alto e più oltre* – higher and ever further.[9] "Dare the undareable," was D'Annunzio's persistent advice. *Volare necesse est, vivere non est necesse* (To fly is necessary, living is not necessary).[10] Had not D'Annunzio already predicted in April 1910 that the flying machine would create a new civilization with new idols, new laws, and new rites. The "Republic of the Air," he told a French interviewer, would exile the wicked and open itself to men of good will. "The elect leave behind themselves the chrysalis of their weight, they soar, they fly. Their eternal dream becomes reality."[11]

Except on the level of rhetoric, D'Annunzio did little to indicate that he intended to participate actively in the creation of this new aerial civilization during the years that followed this interview. But when the war came and Italy's involvement in it on the side of the Allies became a reality in May 1915, he sensed a once-in-a-lifetime opportunity to exorcize his personal demons, escape his omnipresent creditors, and transform himself from an artist who celebrated fictional exploits into a flesh-and-blood hero. Though fifty-two years old and widely regarded as Italy's greatest living poet, he immediately volunteered for active service. The letter Italy's Chief of Staff, General Cadorna, wrote to D'Annunzio granting his request makes clear that he had in mind for this notoriously mercurial figure a primarily spectatorial role. Cadorna authorized d'Annunzio to attach himself to the commands of the various Italian armies in order "to be present at those acts that would be taking place on the entire front of the Army." Cadorna was already thinking of the inspiring narratives the Poet would write after having been in contact with the army in the field; his prose would represent a "most worthy exaltation of the magnanimous gesture which the Army was about to make . . ."[12]

D'Annunzio had very different plans. With the aid of highly placed officers in the navy, he began preparations for a flight across the Adriatic to drop leaflets and bombs on the

Austrian-held, but Italian-speaking, city of Trieste. When the Ministry of the Navy issued instructions forbidding D'Annunzio to participate in such a "dangerous undertaking," the Poet fired off a letter of protest to none other than the prime minister himself. Though this "volume" – as its recipient called it in a private letter to a friend – is full of the usual exaggerations and self-posturing that people had come to associate with D'Annunzio, it was also deeply felt. D'Annunzio had no intention of confining himself to *writing* about the war. He was determined to fight. D'Annunzio insisted that he had lived his entire life waiting for this moment. "I am not a man of letters of the old stamp in a skull cap and slippers. I am a soldier, I've always wanted to be a soldier . . ." To bar him from wartime operations on the grounds that he had the duty not to expose himself to danger was absurd. "If my life has been anything, it has been a game of risks . . . It's perhaps easier to protect the wind than me."[13]

Though Prime Minister Salandra grumbled in private about D'Annunzio's demands, calling him yet one more "misfortune" his government had to confront in difficult times, the veto on D'Annunzio's participation in combat operations was lifted; and on 7 August 1915 D'Annunzio carried out the flight over Trieste as he had planned. Flown by Lieutenant Giuseppe Miraglia, the Poet dropped patriotic leaflets over the city promising the citizens of Trieste that their liberation was close at hand and released eight bombs, one of which remained attached to the airplane despite D'Annnzio's desperate efforts to break it free. The incident might well have ended tragically for D'Annunzio and his pilot. D'Annunzio later wrote that he had been "tortured" by the fear that the bomb might explode over Venice. "Never in my life did I experience such anguish . . . with the left hand I continued to pump gas, with the right . . . I held on to the explosive with all the force of my redoubled will. Finally we passed over the Lido and the houses of Venice. Thanks to the incomparable ability of the pilot, we were able to descend quietly into the lagoon, protected from the winds. Everything was safe."[14]

It is hard to suppress a smile when reading about D'Annunzio's wartime exploits. How many combatants of the Great War had the opportunity to achieve the status of a hero while maintaining a luxurious residence on the Grand Canal in Venice and pursuing a successful and profitable literary career? D'Annunzio fought when and where he pleased, passing from torpedo boats to bombers and carrying on affairs with a series of women who followed him to one of Europe's favorite playgrounds. Yet the Austrians were not amused: after his flight over Trieste, they put a prize of 20,000 crowns on D'Annunzio's head. Several of the pilots who flew him during the war, including Giuseppe Miraglia, lost their lives. D'Annunzio himself was blinded in his right eye when pursuing Austrian aircraft forced his pilot to attempt an emergency landing on the sea at Grado. For months he lived in total darkness, uncertain as to whether doctors would be able to save the sight in his left eye. Thus D'Annunzio was not merely playing with words when he told the sailors of a shipwrecked cruiser that "the blood of the Patria gushes forth, flows, impregnates our liberated soil."[15] Looking at the enterprises he conceived, planned, and executed, no one can doubt that he was prepared to sacrifice his own life.[16] Indeed, D'Annunzio never felt more alive than when in the presence of death, and this was the secret of his love affair with the war.[17] Many aviators would come to feel the same way about flying.

Free to move about the Italian armed forces at will and well connected in the highest military circles, D'Annunzio was able to fight on land and sea as well as in the air. Yet there seems little doubt that, despite his long-standing reputation as a prophet of Italian sea power, he felt a special attachment to the nascent air arm. It was airpower, he insisted, that would decide Italy's fate.[18] Perhaps because D'Annunzio was not himself a pilot, his imagination gravitated more easily toward missions that involved the dropping of projectiles on enemy targets than reconnaissance flights or combat between pursuit planes. By May 1917

Pl. 56. D'Annunzio in 1916 after losing the sight in his right eye. The inscription, "L'Orbo veggente," can be translated as "The Blind Seer."

he had become a proponent of strategic bombing. As he explained to General Cadorna in a letter written at that time, a fleet of a hundred bombers could be sent to carry out a strike against the armament factories in Essen as a response to the German declaration of unrestricted submarine warfare.[19] One of his arguments in favor of investment in the air arm was the impact that "the protection that comes from their brothers, the dominators of the sky" would have on infantry morale. "Many times I have seen our soldiers regain their enthusiasm upon seeing a single Italian plane."[20]

In August 1917 D'Annunzio persuaded the Italian High Command to authorize a series of mass bombing raids against the ships and submarines moored in the Austrian port of Pola across the Adriatic Sea from Venice. The sight of turbid flames against the background of the "white hell" of Pola and "restless" searchlights stirred his imagination and produced a report the likes of which few flight commanders must have seen in this war or any other. After describing the places in which his plane had been hit by antiaircraft fire – the right wing next to the cockpit, the upper wing, the right motor, the cockpit next to the right gasoline tank, in the elevator and the rudder – D'Annunzio described the return flight: "We came back in the peace of the night, flying along the silent coast. The coast of Istria led us by force of love, known to us like the features of a loved one asleep. No light, no sign of life . . . The happy constellation of the Bear indicated the course, casting sparkling light over the dark coast."[21]

Never one to underestimate the symbolic aspect of warfare, D'Annunzio seized the opportunity of his third bombing raid on Pola to create a new battle cry for Italian aviators. Instead of shouting the barbaric "Ip, ip, urrah!" – a sound unfit for Latin mouths – D'Annunzio instructed his crew to shout "Eja! Eja! Alalà," the cry (according to him) with which Achilles had incited his horses to battle. "The command was executed with divine pride. The alalà was inaugurated at the summit of the most beautiful youthful virtue . . . On the way home it seemed to us as if we had conquered all the stars for Italy."[22] The Poet coined for his squadron a motto appropriate to the city where they were stationed – *Iterum rugit leo* (The lion roars again) – and affixed to his bomber the image of a winged lion – symbol of Venice – a practice that later bombing crews would imitate, though without the type of ancient historical reference that was D'Annuzio's stock-in-trade.

During the year that followed the bombing of Pola, D'Annunzio conceived and executed a series of raids, each one more spectacular than its predecessor, even if they were of minimal or uncertain military significance. On the night of 4–5 October 1917 he led a bombing raid on the Austrian naval and submarine bases near Cattaro. To reach these bases, the Italian planes had to traverse four hundred kilometers of open sea without any point of reference. After taking off and setting forth across the Adriatic, D'Annunzio noted: "My heart is traversed by a melodious current, as in the beginning of the creation of a poem. Am I not about to create my adventure?"[23] As he so often did, D'Annunzio was moved to associate war with literature and erotic pleasure. The "crafty and taciturn gaiety" he and his men felt at striking the enemy in their homeland could only be compared with the sentiments of Ulysses on returning to Ithaca; to glimpse the Italian coast on the return from Cattaro was an unforgettable experience, "like the rapture of love."[24] The bombing of Cattaro was followed by the "Beffa di Buccari" (The Jest of Buccari), in which D'Annunzio and twenty-nine companions – "thirty-one with death," as he was later to put it in the poem he wrote about the episode – slipped unnoticed through the Quanaro Straits just to the south of the large Austrian sea base of Fiume (Rijeka) with three torpedo boats and sank an Austrian warship in the bay of Buccari. Besides his role in planning it, D'Annunzio's contribution to the raid was to throw into the sea three bottles, decorated with the colors of Italy's flag, each of which contained a message taunting the Austrians with the fact that Austria's enemy number one – *fra tutti I nemici il nemecissimo* – had come with these heroic Italian sailors to

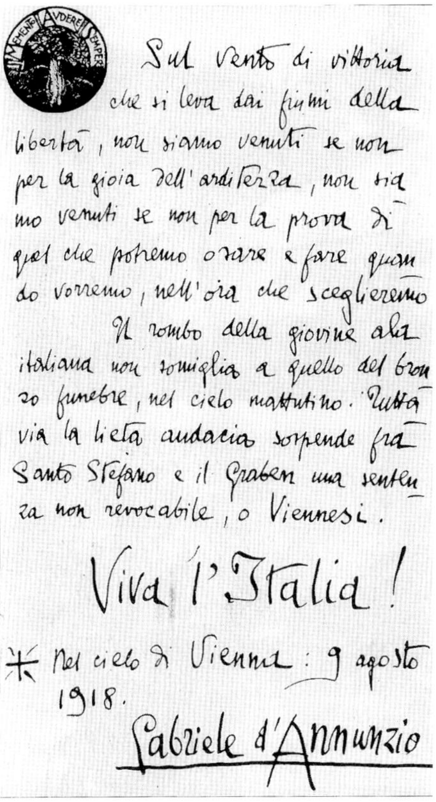

Sul vento di vittoria
che si leva dai fiumi della
libertà, non siamo venuti se non
per la gioia dell'arditezza, non sia
mo venuti se non per la prova di
quel che potremo osare e fare quan
do vorremo, nell'ora che sceglieremo.
Il rombo della giovine ala
italiana non somiglia a quello del bron
zo funebre, nel cielo mattutino. Tutta
via la lieta audacia sospende fra
Santo Stefano e il Graben una senten
za non revocabile, o Viennesi.

Viva l'Italia!

Nel cielo di Vienna: 9 agosto
1918.

Gabriele d'Annunzio

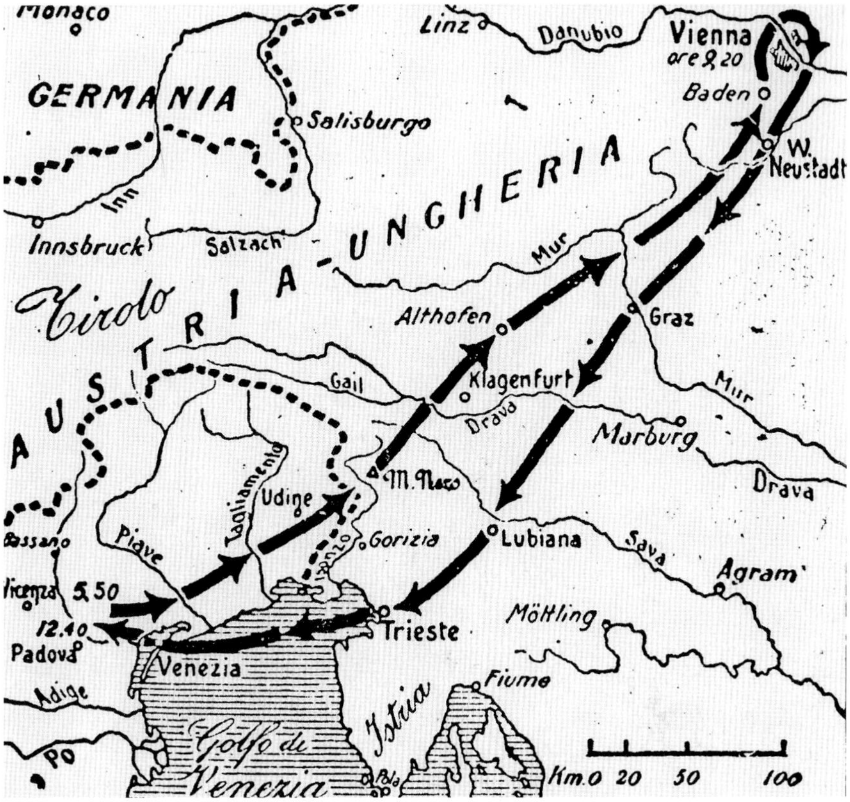

laugh at the price that the Austrians had put on his head.[25] And, finally, in August 1918 D'Annunzio carried out an enterprise that he had been contemplating ever since October 1915. With a squadron of eleven long-range SVA reconnaissance bombers, specially modified for the occasion with an additional fuel tank, he took off from the San Pelagio airfield near Padua for Vienna – a flight of one thousand kilometers – where he and his seven companions dropped half a million manifestoes on the Habsburg capital.[26] These manifestoes, written "on the wind of victory," reminded the Austrians that they were now at the mercy of Italian bombers "in the hour we will choose."[27] Though the raid on Vienna was discounted by Austrian officials as a harmless stunt, it was no insignificant aeronautical achievement and further consolidated D'Annunzio's reputation as an international celebrity. For the admiring *Times* of London, D'Annunzio's achievements outshone "in their poetic quality the legendary flights of Ruggiero and Astolfo on the Ippogrifo. What Ariosto sang, D'Annunzio has accomplished."[28] D'Annunzio would surely have appreciated the comparison with *Orlando Furioso*; and whatever its military value, D'Annunzio's Vienna flight would remain in the Italian collective memory a glorious moment in Italy's victorious war against the Austro-Hungarian Empire.

Pl. 57. The handwritten message D'Annunzio and his squadron dropped on Vienna. It begins with a typically D'Annunzian rhetorical flourish that defies translation into English because of its use of double negatives. "On the wind of victory that rises from the rivers of liberty, we only came for the sheer joy of the challenge, we only came to demonstrate what we can dare and do when we wish, in the hour we will choose."

Pl. 58. The route followed by D'Annunzio and his squadron during their flight to Vienna. The return to Italy took them over several major Austrian cities: Graz, Ljubliana, and Trieste.

Meanwhile D'Annunzio was organizing a squadron of torpedo-bearing seaplanes of which he had been given command – what would become known as the Squadron of San Marco or in D'Annunzio's more poetic version, "La Serenissima." He feared that flying at high altitudes in cold weather would damage his remaining eye. Hence, as he explained in a letter to the Air Force High Command his slogan *più alto e più oltre* (higher and further) would have to become *più basso e più oltre* (lower and further). To drop torpedoes effectively against enemy ships, he would have to descend to a height of less than four meters above the water.[29] His letters to the designer of the aircraft, Gianni Caproni, abound with pleas to hasten production and include detailed instructions regarding the painting of his emblem on

Pl. 59.   Alfredo Ambrosi's 1933 painting, *Il volo su Vienna* (The Flight over Vienna), was inspired by a Futurist school of artists who called themselves "air painters." The founder of Futurism, F. T. Marinetti, identified Ambrosi as one of the leading exponents of "a synthetic aeropainting, dynamic documentary of landscapes, and cityscapes seen from above and at speed."

Pl. 60.   The insignia of the 87a Squadron, "La Serenissima."

56

the fuselage of his planes. The job, D'Annunzio said, should be confided to a proper artist and not a mere house painter so that the design did not lose its "vigorous style."[30]

D'Annunzio was lavishly rewarded for his military adventures. Promoted from lieutenant to lieutenant colonel for service extending over a period of little more than three years, he received Italy's highest military decoration along with a chestful of lesser medals and orders, both Italian and foreign.[31] The citation awarding him the *medaglio d'oro* (Gold Medal) praised his "high intellect" and "tenacious will" which, in a pure spirit of duty and sacrifice he had dedicated entirely "to the sacred ideals of the Patria."[32] But the truth was that the motives driving him during the war were considerably more complicated. War for him, as he explained in his famous speech to the recruits of the class of 1899, was a "lyrical event, an enthusiastic explosion of the will to create."[33] As someone who confessed to "adoring" war, he could only view with "fright" the arrival of peace, even if it meant the victory of his country and the collapse of the hated enemy. On 14 October 1918, just two weeks before the armistice with Austria was signed, he wrote to Constanzo Ciano, who had commanded the raid on Buccari: "For me and for you, and for people like us, peace *today* is a disaster. I have to have at least the time to die as I deserve . . . Yes, Constanzo, let's attempt another great exploit before they *pacify* us by force. Better to be engulfed by our sea than by the shifting mud."[34]

What great enterprise? One possibility was a long-distance flight from Rome to Tokyo that D'Annunzio had conceived in 1918 and that the Italian government was now actively promoting.[35] Tempted by the possibility to demonstrate to the world Italy's preeminence in the field of aviation, D'Annunzio had agreed to become the organizer and *condottiere* of this raid. It suited his psychological need for a heroic venture that would allow him to continue the type of life he had come to love during the war: potentially deadly missions combined with war male comradeship in a spectacle played out before the admiring gaze of the masses that could later be narrated and celebrated in extravagant prose. As he wrote nostalgically, remembering the hours spent in the air with his pilot Natale Palli during the flight to Vienna: "What in the world equals the calm and strong glance exchanged between two faithful companions, three thousand meters above the earth?"[36]

The Italian government had agreed to invest 3,800,000 lire in the Rome–Tokyo flight on the grounds that it offered an opportunity to promote the Italian aviation industry and demonstrate Italian prowess in the air.[37] As important a motivation for the government's enthusiasm for this project, however, was the possibility it offered to distract D'Annunzio from his other, more political projects and to remove him from the Italian peninsula for an extended period of time.[38] By the summer of 1919, the Poet-Soldier, as he was now called, had emerged as a fierce and unsparing critic of the government's foreign policy and the chief spokesman for those groups in Italy who felt that their country had been cheated out of its rightful spoils along the Dalmatian Coast. Famous for his wartime exploits in these waters, D'Annunzio was coming under increasing pressure to organize a march on the city of Fiume, which was regarded by Nationalists as the symbolic center of Dalmatian *italianità* and which was now under Allied occupation while its fate was being decided.

The seizure of Fiume in defiance of the Italian government and their wartime allies and its transformation into a private fiefdom would be D'Annunzio's last and greatest adventure. In July 1919, however, the Poet-Soldier was still undecided about which course he should take.[39] On the 9th he went to Centocelle, an airfield on the outskirts of Rome, where he addressed a group of aviators and aviation specialists. His prestige in the aeronautical community was already such that it was being rumored that he was about to be appointed head of Italian civil aviation.[40] In this speech, D'Annunzio summed up brilliantly his wartime aviation rhetoric and formulated a program for Italian aviation and an image of the Italian aviator that the Fascist regime, with minor modifications, would later make its own.[41]

Pl. 61. D'Annunzio and Natale Palli pose jauntily arm-in-arm in front of their SVA-10 after the flight to Vienna.

Pl. 62. Having chosen to return to earth, D'Annunzio leads his legionnaires into Fiume on horseback.

Playing on the connotations of his given name – Gabriel, bringer of joyful tidings – D'Annunzio proclaimed himself the bearer of great news (*un grande annunzio*). The government had authorized Italy's aviators to fly once more; they were no longer required to confine their flying to a minimum. D'Annunzio presented this announcement as a victory of the aviation community over the cowardly *capi* who were afraid of risk and feared death – the same leaders who had tried to prevent the heroic acts of aviators during the war. Among the great mass of combatants now making the transition to civilian life, the aviators were the privileged ones: unlike the others, they would not be required to lay down their arms. ". . . we can still triumph, we can still die; we want to go on triumphing, we want to go on dying . . . Every day we can take off on a marvelous adventure, on the last adventure. Just as we gave our country heroes during the war . . . so will we give our country heroes during the peace. *Si vola! Si vola!* [We fly! We fly!] The wings of Italy are liberated."[42]

In order to render even starker the contrast he felt between the heroic exhilaration of war and the pusillanimous boredom of peace, D'Annunzio recalled repeatedly the wonders that the Italian aviation community had accomplished between 1915 and 1918. It had created elegant and graceful planes, such as the SVA-10 that D'Annunzio and his companions had flown to Vienna, a marvelous combination of beauty and utility, like "an object of Antique manufacture, like a Caparra lamp, like a violin made by Andrea Garnieri." It had produced the most heroic pilots, like Francesco Baracca, "the divine downer of enemy aircraft" (*il divino abattitore*), who lived and died fighting according to the (D'Annunzian) formula: "We have dared the undareable." And it had done all this alone, *against* Italy's governing class, "ill-concealed enemies of flight and flyers . . . tired old men or backward-looking opportunists, who lacked knowledge of the new machines and were opposed to the divine instinct, men incapable of understanding the genius of the race and unable to second and incite it."[43] Abandoned by their political leaders, Italy's aviators had built and maintained Italian wings against all odds, living according to the severe D'Annunzian commandment: *Più alto e più oltre.*

More and more openly hostile to the new government headed by Francesco Nitti that had just taken power, D'Annunzio emphasized that there were two Italies: the animal Italy that thought of nothing but its stomach and the spiritual Italy that gazed toward the sky. The aviators – and by extension, the entire aeronautical community – represented the "vigorous, spirited, adventurous" Italy. In no other country had the "Icarian instinct" taken such deep root. Go to the airfield at Cervetri, D'Annunzio said, and you will see wonders. "Miracles have become an easy game. Daring is an ingrained habit."[44] Italy was full of "wonderful human resources," men who yearned to fly away toward adventure and conquest. Let those fearless aviators have their way. "Let them go, let them dare. Let them follow our destiny, from goal to goal, from death to death, from glory to glory."[45] D'Annunzio called on Italian aviators to turn their backs on the degenerate West that had become "an immense Jewish bank in the service of a merciless transatlantic plutocracy."[99] They should instead look toward the East where Arabs and Indians were oppressed by the same Western powers that had snatched away Italy's Malta and Fiume. Recalling his service as the commander of Italy's first naval aviation squadron, D'Annunzio assured his audience that two hundred torpedo-bearing planes would be sufficient to blow the British fleet out of "our" Mediterranean.[46]

Then, evoking the matyrs of Italian aviation, D'Annunzio reminded his audience that the shadow of the "winged machine" was similar to the shadow made by the wooden cross, symbol of sacrifice and salvation.[47] "Thus [during the war] we carried with us a vial containing the blood of our matyrs that kept us warm against the ice; that lighted our way in darkness and in doubt; that cured us of every impure thought, that every hour revived our courage; that every hour inspired us to sacrifices; that every hour prepared us for a good death; that every dawn instilled us with new hope; and that every evening made demands on our suffering and fatigue as fragile sons of divine and eternal Italy!"[48]

As rhetorical and overblown as this speech may seem to us today, it would have been clear enough to those who heard or read it what D'Annunzio was proposing. The metaphor of the "wing" had both a specific and a more general meaning: it referred to the aviation industry and the air force while simultaneously suggesting a new and more heroic way of life for all Italians. The enemies of Italy's "wings" – namely, the liberals – must be removed from power. They must be replaced by leaders sensitive to the aeronautical community's needs. Just as Italy had given the world great naval captains in the past, so now she could give it planes and teach it how to fly.

For this to happen, however, the government must be prepared to offer credits for the expansion of the aircraft industry. Italian aircraft manufactuers, like Gianni Caproni, would have appreciated the way D'Annunzio combined a sensitivity to the aesthetics of their planes with down-to-earth economic proposals. So too would the Nationalists have applauded D'Annunzio's declaration that Italy's future lay in expansion toward the east and that airpower would make it possible for the Italians to chase the British out of the Mediterranean and take their place. D'Annunzio had voiced out loud what many of them privately thought: that the West was "decadent" and had become "an immense Jewish bank in the service of the pitiless transatlantic plutocracy."[49] Italy should heed the cry of the oppressed nationalities in the east waiting to rise against their Western rulers and become the leader of a great anti-Western crusade.

Who was capable of overseeing such an ambitious program? Obviously, no one better than the hero of Pola, Cattaro, Buccari, and Vienna – the author of *Forse che sì forse che no*, the prophet of Italy's wings. It can scarcely have been an accident that of many aviation heroes celebrated by D'Annunzio in this speech, all except himself were safely dead.

Remembering the pilot who had flown him to Vienna who had recently died of exposure after making a forced landing in the Alps, D'Annunzio romantically evoked the possibility of his own death en route to Tokyo in a Mesopotamian valley or on the left bank of the Ganges. "And in all of Italy there would not be a more Italian grave than that lonely heap of stones."[50] But instead of flying off toward Tokyo, D'Annunzio chose to march on Fiume.[51] For all his love of aviation, he could not forgo this dazzling opportunity to play out his political and military fantasies before an astonished world. What other poet had ever dared to seize and rule a city in flagrant violation of international law? D'Annunzio's Fiume adventure and the toll it took on him meant that it would fall to others to realize his dream of a "winged Italy."

★   ★   ★

D'Annunzio would continue to be an important force in aviation circles.[52] But his place of primacy in this domain, as in so many others, was increasingly challenged and eventually usurped by his ambitious but less famous rival, Benito Mussolini. Mussolini's passion for flight and his intuition into the wider significance of aviation went back to the years before 1914. On the eve of Latham's unsuccessful attempt to fly the English Channel in July 1909, Mussolini contributed an article to Cesare Battista's Trentine newspaper *Il Popolo* in which he expounded on the significance of the Channel flight. Unlike many other commentators at the time, Mussolini saw that aeronautical exploits could not be understood simply in terms of sport. For him they were an expression of the deepest tendencies of the new century. Latham, Mussolini said, was a hero. Our age was a heroic age, perhaps more heroic even than the Ancient World. The word that summed up the new century and gave it a unique character was *movement*. "Movement toward the icy solitude of the poles and toward the virgin peaks of the mountains, movement toward the stars and or toward the depths of the seas . . . Movement everywhere and acceleration in the rhythm of our lives."[53] And when Blériot succeeded in flying the Channel, Mussolini saluted him as one of the first champions of a new race of Nietzschean men of action destined to dominate others, one of those restless figures who give meaning to life through their realization of an ideal. The Channel flight was interpreted by Mussolini as a sign that Zarathustra's prophecies of the coming of the Superman were on the verge of being realized. Perhaps man's painful prehistory was over. Glory to the avant-gardes and "lost sentinels" who prepared the way and achieved the synthesis of thought and action. "No longer the fratricidal dominion of man over man, but the dominion of man over nature, over life, over the universe."[54]

Pl. 63. Mussolini as a bersagliere in 1917.

The war, which Mussolini experienced from the immobility of the trenches, only increased his reverence for aviators. What a difference between his inglorious earthbound war and the glamorous aerial exploits of D'Annunzio and others! Even before the war was over, he obtained permission from the military authorities to make some brief flights at the airdrome of Cascina Costa, close to the present Milanese airport of Malpensa. The ace Mario Stoppani, who took Mussolini up in an SVA at the Borzoli airfield, remembered him as being in a state of "enthusiastic delirium." Mussolini himself later wrote that when they reached seventeen hundred meters he urged Stoppiani to continue climbing. "*Ancora, ancora, più in alto*" (Go on, go on, higher), he urged with excited gestures. As the plane nosed up, Mussolini had the exhilarating sensation, shared by so many early aviators, of the earth receding into the distance. "What diaphanous serenity in the twilight sky!"[55] Driving away from the airfield with a group of aviators, it occurred to Mussolini that these men represented "the new Italian race of producers, builders, and creators." They were the Italians of the future who would conquer the land, the sea, and the sky.[56]

Mussolini understood, with his journalist's flair for the marketable image, that airplanes could be used symbolically and politically to enhance his popularity and to invest him and his newly formed Fascist movement with the cachet of modernity and glamour that aviation and aviators had acquired during the war. But aviation also had deeper meanings for him. It was a *sign* of national energy and vitality and a *means* of moving "the torpid soul of the masses."[57] It was also a *value* that must be defended against what D'Annunzio called its "ignorant" and "pusillanimous" adversaries, those skeptics who dismissed aviation as a destructive and frivolous game.[58] Quick to appropriate the Italian avant-garde's themes of the internal enemy and the two Italies – one decadent, the other vital, risk-taking, and creative – Mussolini glimpsed an opportunity in his embrace of aviation for mythmaking and the mobilization of the masses against Italy's governing elite in the name of this most modern of technologies.[59]

When fourteen people, among them five prominent Milanese aviation journalists, were killed in the crash of a Caproni biplane near Verona on 2 August 1919, Mussolini rose to the defense of aviation, whatever its costs in human lives. As a gesture of defiance he organized a flight of journalists from Milan to Mantova by way of Bergamo and Brescia to dramatize the necessity and safety of air transportation.[60] He had himself flown to Forlì where during the funeral of one of the pilots who had died in the accident he dropped copies of the speech D'Annunzio had given at Centocelle, proclaiming the determination of Italian aviators to fly at any cost.[61] He was quick to publish the text of D'Annunzio's Centocelle speech on the front page of his newspaper; and two weeks later, on 20 August, he initiated a *pagina dell'aviazione* in *Il Popolo d'Italia*, thus giving representatives of the Italian aviation community an opportunity to air their grievances against the liberal government.[62] In the brief insert with which Mussolini introduced the "aviation page," he expressed his enthusiasm for flight in terms that would have appealed to aviators, no matter what their political orientation:

> To fly! Always higher, in a prodigious tension of nerves, of will, of intelligence that only that little mortal body of man can give. To fly above all the petty struggles of this terrible, continuous trench that is present-day life.
>
> To fly! To fly for the beauty of flight; almost art for the sake of art – to fly so that tomorrow the collectivity possesses a new instrument, which will render easier, more rapid, and more frequent intellectual, moral, and commercial relations among the most distant peoples.[63]

Mussolini even played with the idea of participating in the Rome–Tokyo flight as a journalist and had himself flown to Fiume to consult with D'Annunzio – a fiasco that did little to improve his relationship with the Poet, now indulging his most wild fantasies of megalomania. This escapade ended badly with Mussolini's brief, but ignominious arrest by carabinieri after being forced by bad weather to land at Aiello, close to the headquarters of General Badaglio at Udine. But the fascist leader had nonetheless strengthened his credentials with the leaders of the Italian avaiation community.[64]

Unlike D'Annunzio, Mussolini was not satisfied to remain an aerial passenger; he wanted to experience the exhilaration and sense of domination that came with control of an aircraft; and he also understood that the full mystique of aviation would only adhere to those who learned how to pilot a plane. In March 1920, at the age of thirty-seven, he signed up for a course of flying lessons at Arcore near Milan. During the following year, he flew regularly with the good-natured director of the school Cesare Redaelli, a former wartime aviator, with a bushy mustache, a ready smile, and a knack for extracting himself and his impetuous student from hazardous situations.[65] Generally, Mussolini commuted Milan to Arcore by train, normally leaving Milan at 1:00 p.m., but sometimes he made the trip from the offices of *Il Popolo d'Italia* in Milan to the airdrome on his bicycle with a straw hat on his head and an evident eagerness to get down to the business of flying.[66] His determination to master the art of flight never blinded him to the potential political uses of his aeronautical passion; and when possible, he combined his training flights with dramatic gestures that conveyed his faith in aviation, as when he flew with Redaelli to Verona in August 1920 to throw flowers on the grave of one of the victims of the previous year's aviation accident or used an airplane to transport himself to the sites of his electoral speeches.

Pl. 64. A postcard Mussolini wrote to his "very dear" friend Attilio Longoni in 1918, expressing his envy of Longoni's service in the Air Force.

61

Pl. 65.   A balding and clearly middle-aged Mussolini projects determination in this 1921 photograph with his flying instructor, Cesare Redaelli.

Pl. 66.   A photograph that Mussolini dedicated to Radaelli shortly after having to come to power, "with fraternity and the fidelity of a pilot."

The notes Mussolini wrote to Redaelli from time to time, excusing his absences and reiterating his commitment to his lessons, show that he was having difficulty combining his political and journalistic responsibilities with his flight training. Then, in March 1921, as national elections neared, Mussolini and Redaelli had a potentially fatal accident when their Aviatik lost power shortly after takeoff and slipped laterally toward the ground from a height of 130 feet, as Redaelli tried in vain to bank toward the field.[67] Though Mussolini downplayed the seriousness of the incident, he was confined to bed for two weeks and his left knee, though not fractured, was battered to the point that he could walk only with extreme difficulty.[68] Soon afterwards the Fascist leader was elected to parliament, and he abandoned his flying lessons (if not his flying) as his political life became more intense.[69]

Yet if Mussolini spent less time practicing flight – and temporarily gave up the ambition to obtain his license – he continued to emphasize his commitment to the cause of aviation. He surrounded himself with war aces, like Aldo Finzi who had participated in D'Annunzio's raid to Vienna, and aviation personalities like Arturo Mercanti and the journalist and former syndicalist Attilio Longoni, founder and editor of *La Gazetta dell'Aviazione*, who put him into contact with the aviation manufacturers. He sponsored air races through his newspaper; he traveled by air whenever possible, especially when making public appearances; he played a prominent role at an aerounautical convention in Milan organized by Longoni in late March 1921, where he proposed measures designed to develop air-mindedness among Italian youth; and he became a fierce critic of the liberal government's negligence in aviation matters. Calling himself an "aviation fanatic" in private correspondence with Longoni, he proclaimed his faith in Italy's ability to regain its position of preeminence in aviation and proposed getting rid of the bureaucrats who stood in the way of Italy's aeronautical progress. It was obvious, he wrote to Longoni, that deskbound functionaries would never be able to understand the beauty and necessity of flight. "We'll cut off their heads with our propellers. A sure means of persuasion."[70] Upon being elected to parliament, one of Mussolini's first acts was to organize an aeronautical group to represent aviation interests. He even tried, in vain, to persuade the aeronautical branch of the industrial firm Ansaldo to provide him with an airplane for his political trips away from Rome, no doubt with a thought to ensuring his ability to move around the country at a time when railway strikes made travel by train an uncertain form of transport.[71]

Mussolini's overtures to the Italian aviation community, which reached their peak in 1921–2, had their effect. Though there is no evidence that the aircraft manufacturers provided major funding for Mussolini's movement, it is clear that they regarded him as being attentive to their needs and sympathetic to their aims.[72] Various groups of Fascist aviators were formed, including a paramilitary organization called the Gruppo Aviatori Fascisti Natale Palli – named for the pilot who had flown D'Annunzio to Vienna in 1918 – and in October 1922, when the Fascists threatened to march on Rome and overthrow the government, they occupied important airfields around Rome and overflew the city in planes painted partially in black.[73] They had hoped to fly Mussolini from Milan to Rome, when the king called him to form a government, but torrential rain made flying hazardous and Mussolini prudently chose to come to the capital by rail in a sleeping car used during the war by General Cadorna, commander-in-chief of the Italian Army. The Natale Palli Group had to be satisfied with providing Mussolini's train with an aeronautical escort during the last leg of its journey from Santa Marinella on the coast to Rome.[74]

Thus the Italian aviation community had every reason to regard with favor and keen anticipation the naming of Mussolini to the premiership; and Mussolini acted quickly and unambiguously to satisfy their demands. His aeronautical policy manifested itself simultaneously along four parallel and overlapping lines. It was based on his belief that aviation had a profound spiritual – hence political – meaning that went beyond technology, military strategy, or any utilitarian end that it might serve.[75] His goal was nothing less than the creation of an aviation culture.

While still on the train to Rome to accept the king's invitation to form a government, Mussolini charged Aldo Finzi with the task of organizing a separate air force and what would eventually become an independent ministry of aeronautics.[76] In doing so, he was moved not so much by the doctrine associated with Giulio Douhet that airpower would be decisive in coming wars as by the desire to create a military service dominated by Fascists and Fascist values that would symbolize the new regime's dynamism and modernity.[77] Though, like D'Annunzio, convinced that Italy had the elements necessary to achieve preeminence in aviation, Mussolini gave equal, if not greater, weight to the role that aviation could play *domestically* in forging a Fascist civilization.[78] Finzi moved quickly to establish a commissariat of aviation, which Mussolini himself headed in name but which was in reality administered by Finzi and his deputy Pier Ruggiero Piccio between January 1923 and June of 1924. In March 1923 the army and naval air forces were merged to form the *Regia Aeronautica*, an organization that brought together military, civilian, and colonial aviation. With this bold act, Italy joined Great Britain as the only major power to have an independent air force.

D'Annunzio and the Fascists had accused the liberal government of deliberately destroying Italian aviation by starving it of funds.[79] Mussolini authorized a rapid expansion of the air budget, which rose from 200 million lire for the year 1923/24 to 630 million for the year 1926/27, though even this sum represented only a seventh of Italy's military expenditures.[80] Mussolini also provided funds for the organization of long-distance flights, such as Francesco De Pinedo's to Melbourne and Tokyo in 1925 and Arturo Ferrarin and Carlo Del Prete's record-breaking 1928 flight to Brazil; and he made clear the Fascist state's commitment to Italian participation in such hotly contested international competitions as the Schneider Cup races, which against all odds the Italians won in 1926 at Hampton Roads, Virginia.[81] As he had promised, Mussolini set out to develop an aeronautical consciousness among the Italian people by publicizing Italian aviation exploits and staging spectacular displays of aircraft, as in October 1923 when 263 planes flew above the capital to commemorate the March on Rome and Italy's victory in the First World War. When De Pinedo returned to Rome from his epic-making 1925 flight, Mussolini proclaimed him to be the prototype of the new Fascist man, at once "serious, intrepid, tenacious."[82]

Mussolini explained his aeronautical policy in a speech to the Aero Club of Italy on 5 November 1923, the day on which the creation of an independent air force had been celebrated with the bestowing of a separate flag on the new service by a head of government

Il verme non può amare l'aquila

Pl. 67. A caricature of the liberal Prime Minister Francesco Nitti. The caption reads: "The worm can't love the eagle."

Pl. 68. Ugo di Lazzaro's poster for the the 1927 Schneider Cup race reminds Italians that the Fascist state is offering a fifty percent reduction in railway fares for those attending the event in Venice.

Pl. 69. In a pose that he would often repeat with famous aviators, a stern Mussolini turns to face the camera, as he congratulates De Pinedo.

who hastened to identify himself as an "aviator who has flown and will continue to fly." Introducing Mussolini, in whose honor the banquet had been organized, was Arturo Mercanti, a Fascist of the "first hour," president of the Aero Club, and a high-ranking official in the Commissariat of Aviation, a position he owed to the evening's honored guest. Mussolini began, typically, by pointing out that he had proven by his own example that it was possible to govern a nation without ceasing to fly because "life must be risked and risked daily, continually, demonstrating that one is ready to throw it away when necessary." Referring to the aeronautical progress made by his government in one brief year and the spiritual qualities of Italian pilots – "by unanimous opinion, even of the foreigners, they are among the best in the world" – he concluded by once again emphasizing the role the press must play in creating an Italian aeronautical consciousness. "Not everyone can fly. It's not even desirable that everyone should fly. Flying must remain the privilege of an aristocracy; but everyone must want to fly, everyone must regard flying with longing. All good citizens, all devoted citizens must follow with profound feeling the development of Italian wings."[83] This was the message that the Italian aviation community had been waiting to hear.

★   ★   ★

The full implementation of the aeronautical program Mussolini set forth in 1922–3 had to await Mussolini's consolidation of power and his selection of Italo Balbo in November 1926 as undersecretary of aviation. The thirty-year-old Balbo was not an obvious choice for this position. He was not a pilot; he had no standing in the aviation community; and, though the holder of one bronze and two silver medals for valor for his bravery during the Great War, he had fought an earthbound war in the alpine infantry rather than the air force.[84] While on active service in the army, Balbo had never risen above the rank of lieutenant, a detail bound to be remembered by the generals and colonels with whom he would have to collaborate and command. He was identified in the public mind primarily with the organization of the Fascist squads in central Italy, his leading role in the March on Rome

Pl. 70. Along with (from left to right) Michele Bianchi, Emilio De Bono, and Cesare Maria De Vecchi, a gaunt and very youthful Balbo flanks Mussolini as they review Fascist squadrists after the March on Rome in October 1923.

Pl. 71. In a photograph dedicated to the Italian engineer and aircraft designer Gianni Caproni, Balbo poses in his uniform as commander of the Fascist militia. There is little hint here of the good-natured charm he would later display as Italy's air-minded ambassador of good will.

in October 1922 as one of its four primary organizers, and his alleged involvement in the murder of a Catholic priest in his home town of Ferrara. Driven by the fanaticism of the recent convert who has no doubts of the righteousness of his cause and who is not averse to using violence, Balbo evoked memories of the worst moments of the civil war that had raged between the Fascists and their adversaries in central and northern Italy between 1921 and 1922 – memories that most Italians wanted to leave behind them.[85]

Yet though pursued by a shadowy past that invited unsavory comparisons with thuggery and gangsterism, Balbo turned out to be one of the most fascinating figures of aviation during the interwar period. He brought to his new post formidable qualities: youthful energy; unquestionable charisma; an unqualified love for aviation; a willingness to risk his own life in dangerous enterprises; the ability to inspire his subordinates; a talent for organization; and a flair for spectacle that he had developed during the battle for control of central Italy's cities in 1922. A ferocious political infighter who insisted on unqualified loyalty from those around him, generous to his friends and even to his enemies (once defeated), dashing in appearance, facile with a pen, at ease when speaking before large crowds, Balbo would brilliantly represent and embody the cause of the air-minded civilization that D'Annunzio had prophesied and whose political foundations Mussolini had laid.[86] Indeed, Balbo would embody this cause so brilliantly that Mussolini would one day feel the need to divest him of his position as the leader of the Italian Air Force and exile him to a faraway, if prestigious post.

Mussolini's reasons for choosing Balbo to head the Air Ministry remain obscure; the only certainty is that it was his decision and his alone, and that there is no evidence to suggest that it was determined by any passion Balbo might have shown for aviation prior to this date.[87] The first undersecretary, Aldo Finzi, acting through his deputy General Piccio, had demoralized the officer corps by a policy of promotion that violated military tradition and favored pilots over officers with administrative experience. Implicated in the cover-up of Fascist involvement in the assassination of the Socialist parliamentary deputy Giacomo Matteotti, Finzi had been forced to resign in June 1924.[88] His successor Alberto Bonzani, a drab army general, was unable to conceal the lack of enthusiasm he felt for flight and provoked the ire of the aviation community, who yearned after an undersecretary who would fight for their interests.[89] By November 1926, having survived the storm created by the Matteotti Affair and no longer as dependent on the goodwill of the Army as he had been at the height of the scandal that threatened to drive him from office, Mussolini was in a position to shape more actively the new service he had created. Known for his military expertise, Balbo was a man of energy and proven administrative abilities whose squadrist credentials were bound to please the Fascist militants on whom Mussolini depended as a counterweight to the conservatives who maintained reservations about the man who had saved them from a left-wing revolution.[90] He could be counted upon to implement Mussolini's policies; and should he fail, he could easily be replaced.

Ambitious and anxious to demonstrate to Mussolini that his choice had been a good one, Balbo acted quickly to impose himself on his subordinates and establish his authority over an Air Ministry whose equipment he found to be in questionable condition and whose mentality he found insufficiently "Fascist." On the 28 November, he ordered all the air force's planes to take flight: fighters for two hours and all others for three hours. Of these, only two hundred out of the sixteen hundred succeeded in passing the test of airworthiness; and even these, Balbo later wrote in a memorandum to Mussolini, had been incapable of engaging in combat.[91] Leaving aside the accuracy of this report on the situation Balbo had inherited from his predecessor, it had the happy result of providing the new undersecretary with a basis for requesting an immediate increase in the air force budget, a request Mussolini granted.[92] Less than a year after taking office, Balbo was quick to take credit for having turned around a dismal situation. He assured Mussolini that maneuvers conducted in the Veneto region under difficult weather conditions had been a splendid success. Italy, Balbo claimed, now had a perfectly trained air force ready for combat.[93] This was no doubt an exaggeration; but unlike his predecessors Balbo had actually made efforts to develop a realistic vision of aerial warfare based on technological realities and the resources available to him.[94]

A firm believer in an independent air force, Balbo asserted his control over aircraft that had formerly been under the command of the army and the navy, reminding Mussolini that neither of these services could compete with the air force in blood spilled nor "ardent faith in the destiny of Fascism."[95] And indeed, Balbo made it clear to his officers that he expected them to instill in their men an understanding of the political aims of Fascism, the liberal "abyss" from which it had saved Italy, and a "boundless pride in being Italian." "Aviation, which is the most powerful and superb instrument of force and domination, must be served by people permeated by pride in their race, which is a thoroughly fascist feeling." [96] By 1928 the Fascist emblem had been put on every air force plane; all aviators had been authorized to wear the *nastrino*, insignia of the March on Rome; and the Fascist *saluto romano* (Roman salute) was required of all aviators. As Balbo explained to the Chamber of Deputies, ". . . the war-like spirit of our aviators is one with their Fascist soul."[97]

A strong air force required a strong and disciplined aircraft industry. Balbo lost no time in serving notice on the aircraft manufacturers that he expected them to meet stringent deadlines for the delivery of their products. Those who failed to meet their commitments would pay heavy penalties and lose their contracts.[98] But Balbo also promised swifter payments from the government and state support for the sale of Italian aircraft abroad. War, he said, was possible at any moment; and the manufacturers must understand that their interests had to be subordinated to the needs of the nation.[99] And indeed, under Balbo's regime, the Italian aircraft industry thrived, despite the worldwide economic crisis that began in 1929. A steady flow of commissions from the Air Ministry provided the money necessary to keep Italian aircraft factories and their employees working, though never at the levels of production their owners would have liked. New flight schools were opened; novice pilots were awarded a prize of 1,000 lire upon receiving their licenses; new airports were built and older ones modernized; the miles flown by Italian airlines increased six-fold; and subsidies were offered to Italian civilians who wished to acquire planes.

★　　★　　★

Pl. 72.   Arturo Ferrarin appears almost dazzled by the wealth of medals, trophies, and gifts he received for his 1920 Rome–Tokyo flight.

Pl. 73.   Mario De Bernardi between Bruno (left) and Vittorio Mussolini (right). Both of Mussolini's sons became decorated military pilots, and Bruno was later killed in a flying accident.

It was one thing for Balbo to impose himself on military bureaucrats and aircraft manufacturers; it was another to win the respect of airmen whom he now commanded. Many had distinguished records in the Great War; others, like Francesco De Pinedo, Arturo Ferrarin, Mario De Bernardi, and Umberto Nobile had to their credit postwar aeronautical achievements that had gained them the status of celebrities and national heroes. Balbo's first inclination was not to risk the possible humiliation that trying to learn to fly might entail; he feared that in the eyes of the expert pilots who surrounded him he would always remain a "duffer." But within three months of assuming his duties as undersecretary Balbo changed his mind and quickly met the requirements for a military pilot, then went on to earn a seaplane rating. Before his death in 1940, he would log over three thousand hours in the air, though on hazardous flights he was always careful to be accompanied by a copilot, usually Stefano Cagni on whose brilliant flying skills he could always count.[100]

Francesco De Pinedo and Arturo Ferrarin were famous for their long-distance flights, individual enterprises carried out with a crew consisting of a mechanic and sometimes a navigator; Mario De Bernardi had won the Schneider Cup in November 1926 and shortly afterward set a new world speed record of 512 kilometers an hour; Umberto Nobile had piloted Amundsen across the North Pole in a dirigible of his design in May 1926. Balbo could not hope to equal achievements of this type. Nor did he try. His intuition, reinforced by his ambition and perhaps rationalized by official Fascist ideology, told him that the era of individual exploits was drawing to a close. For him, Lindbergh's flight from New York to Paris represented an end rather than a beginning. The next phase of aviation progress, he believed, would come about as a result of collective and carefully planned enterprises. Group flights represented the wave of the future. Thus he wasted no time in making clear that aviation celebrities unable to subordinate their own ambition to the common cause (as defined by Balbo) would have no place in the Italian Air Force.[101]

Hence while Balbo continued Mussolini's policy of sponsoring state-financed exploits aimed at setting distance, speed, endurance, and altitude records by Italian military aviators – initiatives that met with great success in the late 1920s and early 1930s – he devoted his own efforts to the organization of mass flights or *crociere* (cruises), which he justified on the military grounds that they gave the air force an opportunity to perfect their flying and navigational skills far from their Italian bases and under difficult weather conditions.[102] No less important, however, in the thinking of both Balbo and Mussolini were the display of Italian aviation prowess before an admiring foreign public, the resulting opportunities to publicize Italian international prestige domestically, and the possibility of selling Italian aircraft to foreign powers.[103]

The first and largest cruise took place in the western Mediterranean between 26 May and 2 June 1928. Sixty-one seaplanes – the majority of them S.59 reconnaissance and light bombers along with a squadron of S.55 bombers – flew from Orbetello on the Tuscan coast to Los Alcazares in southern Spain with stops in Sardinia and Majorca. They then returned by way of Puerto Alfaques in Catalonia and Berre in France. Lest there be any doubt that this enterprise had political aims that went beyond the military training of the crews, a large contingent of passengers, including the air attachés of the United States, England, France, Spain, and Romania and eleven Italian journalists, had been invited to participate in the cruise. A cinematographer was on board to capture the flight on film so that Italian movie audiences could participate vicariously in the event.

The stakes for Balbo were immense. No flight on this mass scale had ever been attempted before. Several of Balbo's technical advisers had warned him against undertaking such a foolhardy enterprise, predicting that five aircraft would be lost in every stage of the journey with the probability of fatal accidents.[104] And indeed a storm at the normally calm Spanish base of Los Alcazares near Cartagena nearly fulfilled their prophecies. Only after an Olympian struggle of nearly four hours were Balbo and his men able to secure their planes amidst swells that reached nine feet and winds of sixty miles per hour.[105] In retrospect, it seems almost miraculous that the inevitable collisions that took place between Italian aircraft, as they were tossed about like corks by the turbulent seas, did not result in greater damage – a fact that Balbo would later ascribe to the meticulous training of the crews.[106]

Balbo's awareness of his technical limitations is shown by the fact that he made no pretense to assuming the leadership of the enterprise. The uniform of a general in the Fascist militia that he donned for the occasion underlined his purely political role.[107] Planning and command were left to De Pinedo, who flew the lead aircraft and put on a spectacular show of tight formation flying. At Puerto Alfaques, all sixty-one aircraft took off simultaneously; lined up, wing tip to wing tip, the Italian air fleet extended over a distance of four kilometers.[108] In Marseilles crowds cheered as the Italian planes passed over the city, after taking off from the hydroport of Berre. From every point of view, the cruise was a huge success. Addressing Balbo's crews after their return to their base at Orbetello, Mussolini praised them for their achievement. "I consider the cruise a perfect work of art that bears the style of the new Italy: having left as a mass, you returned as a mass."[109] As a mark of his approval of Balbo's role in the organization of the cruise, Mussolini elevated him in August 1928 to the grade of reserve *generale di squadra aerea* and then recalled him to active service. This dramatic promotion made Balbo the highest-rank-

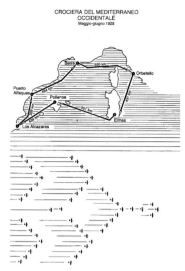

CROCIERA DEL MEDITERRANEO OCCIDENTALE
Maggio-giugno 1928

Pl. 74. The route followed during the Western Mediterranean cruise and the formation flown.

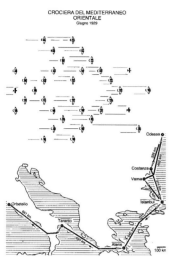

Pl. 75. The route followed during the Eastern Mediterraean cruise and the formation flown.

Pl. 76. Mussolini in aviator's garb reviews the officers who participated in the Western Mediterraean cruise. Balbo, still wearing his militia outfit, is to Mussolini's left and De Pinedo, in his Air Force uniform, to Mussolini's right.

ing officer in the air force and gave him an exalted military status that as a major in the army reserve he had hitherto lacked.[110] He would be quick to take advantage of it.

Elated by the success of his first cruise and clearly relishing his role as the roving ambassador of Italian aviation, Balbo instructed De Pinedo to plan a cruise to the eastern Mediterranean for the summer of 1929. He was under no illusions concerning the difficulties of such an enterprise nor his own ability to command it: a much less ambitious effort by him to lead a flight of twelve land planes in July 1928 on a cruise to London and Berlin had turned into a humiliating fiasco and brought home to him his pilots' lack of navigational skills and the importance of careful planning.[111]

The novelty of the eastern Mediterranean cruise, aside from its longer distance (4,700 kilometers as opposed to 2,800 kilometers for the cruise to Spain and France) and its smaller size (40 planes as opposed to 61) was its extension, by way of Taranto, Athens, Istanbul, and Varna in Bulgaria, to the Soviet city of Odessa, where Balbo had obtained permission from the Soviet authorities to land. In principle, the Soviet Union was the last place a Fascist leader, who had made his reputation as an implacable adversary of Communists, would want to visit and the last place, also, where he could expect to receive a warm reception. It is revealing of Balbo's ideological tendencies and intellectual curiosity that he wanted to see the home of Communism with his own eyes and sensed a possible bond between Fascist Italy and the Soviet Union in their hostility to the Western democracies, which he viewed as "rotten to the bone, lying and false . . ."[112]

Balbo approached the cruise in the spirit of an intrepid and enthusiastic boy embarking on a great adventure. Like other members of his generation and his class the product of a classical education, while flying from Athens to Constantinople Balbo could not prevent himself from thinking of Ulysses, Agamemnon, and Achilles. He scanned the horizon, unsuccessfully, for traces of Troy's Acropolis. How many students of the classics had been allowed to live a magical odyssey like this?[113]

Once more Balbo's aviators, flying S.55 seaplanes, displayed their skill at formation flying and were received enthusiastically everywhere along their route, especially Odessa. Whatever apprehensions he may have had about his reception in the land of the "reds," Balbo found that he got along famously with his Soviet hosts. Though appalled by the

Pl. 77.   A Savoia Marchetti S.55 prepares to take off from Taranto during the Eastern Mediterranean cruise.

Pl. 78.   Balbo, in the dress uniform that he would henceforth don for official receptions abroad, poses with his Soviet host, General Baranov.

poverty of the people he saw, he was careful to show respect for the Bolshevik convictions of the officials who entertained him. There must be some reason for a successful revolution, he later wrote, even if it struck a Westerner as a "collective aberration." The Soviets he met were far from being "stupid or crazy."[114] Like the Fascists, they were men of faith, real soldiers who were not lacking in chivalric spirit.[115] Comparing retrospectively the liberty with which he and his men could move about the Soviet city, Balbo remembered the constraints the French police imposed on the Italian aviators the previous year during their stay in Marseilles for fear of anti-Fascist demonstrations. Was this the result of a different type of "social discipline," he wondered ingenuously, justifying to himself the lack of civil liberties in Fascist Italy?[116] Ideological differences aside, the Soviets were impressed enough with what they saw of the Italians and their aircraft to order thirty S.55s.[117] And the cruise prompted the International League of Aviators to offer Balbo the 1929 Harmon Prize, which he prudently turned down on the grounds that his contributions to aviation had been more of an organizational nature than exploits of "personal daring."[118]

On Balbo's recommendation, the Harmon Prize instead was awarded to General Pellegrini – a slight deliberately meant to insult the cruise's organizer, chief pilot, and commander, General De Pinedo.[119] Balbo had been given reason to believe that his celebrated subordinate was scheming behind his back and lobbying for his position. The festering conflict between the two men came to a head during an otherwise unimportant incident at Odessa and exploded in a series of mutual accusations during the weeks following the completion of the eastern Mediterranean cruise.[120] Vastly overplaying what turned out to be a weak hand, De Pinedo went so far as to draw up a memorandum, calling into question Balbo's competence to administer the air force and accusing him of lacking any doctrine of aerial warfare.[121] In this document De Pinedo unambiguously put forward his candidacy for Balbo's post, emphasizing that as a military organization the air force needed to be led by a military man: someone "profoundly competent in its deployment and technology . . . who with constant, persevering, far-seeing action knows how to look ahead, maintain [the forces that exist in] the present and prepare for the future . . ."[122] Forced to choose between two competing egos of large proportions, Mussolini showed no sign of hesitation. As confirmation of his victory over his rival, Balbo was promoted to full-fledged minister of air in September 1929. Balbo immediately took advantage of his victory to remove De Pinedo from his position as undersecretary of the air force General Staff. De Pinedo was then exiled to Buenos Aires as Italian air attaché, an assignment unworthy of his elevated rank. Eventually, he was released from active service, a sad end to the career of Italy's most prestigious airman. As Balbo forthrightly acknowledged, there wasn't "room for both of us in the same cockpit," and Balbo possessed the Fascist credentials that De Pinedo lacked.[123]

★   ★   ★

The idea for the next cruise was born during a month-long trip Balbo took to the United States in December 1928. Like many Europeans, he was impressed by the raw vitality and brash modernity of American industrial civilization. He came away with the idea that, unlike in Europe, aviation had become an integral part of American life. Embarking for Italy from New York by ship as night began to fall, Balbo was suddenly seized by the vision of a squadron of Italian seaplanes trimphantly arriving in the skies over Manhattan after having crossed the Atlantic. What a "superb spectacle" it would be, Balbo thought to himself![124]

Discussions with other members of his delegation and the captain of his ship, however, forced him to face reality and convinced him that a collective crossing of the North Atlantic was impossible at the present time. Of the thirty-nine previous attempts to fly the North Atlantic, only nine had succeeded.[125] Why not then instead undertake a flight to Latin America? This, too, could have a major impact. "Even the greatest doubters would be convinced that aviation was revolutionizing the concepts we had of the world, of its inter-relationships and its distances, and opening unsuspected horizons."[126] Moreover, in the South Atlantic, the odds would be in the Italians' favor; six out of eight attempts had been successful. After careful study and consultation with Mussolini, Balbo decided on a flight of four squadrons of three planes each from Rome to Rio de Janeiro. The crossing of the Atlantic would take place between Bolama in Portuguese Guiana and Porto Natal in Northern Brazil, a flight of three thousand kilometers. There was a certain irony in this choice since De Pinedo, despite all his expertise and experience, had attempted and failed to make seven takeoffs from Bolama in February 1927 in an earlier version of the S.55 because of the sweltering heat, the heavy humidity, and lack of wind. Thus from the beginning, the South American flight implied a gamble.

Balbo was keenly aware of the tremendous risks involved in the Latin American cruise. In the eyes of the world and the stern judgment of the Duce, it would either make or break him. Preparations took a year, and the training of the air crews was conducted at Orbetello, a sea-plane base on the Tyrrhenian coast about 150 kilometers north of Rome, under the supervision of Umberto Maddalena, one of Italy's most famous aviators and holder of various records for

Pl. 79. The seaplane base at Orbetello. A French writer whose plane was forced by a storm to land at Orbetello in December 1931 commented admiringly on the monk-like discipline that Balbo had imposed on his men. ". . . it's a real monastery, like those on Rhodes and Malta . . . I don't need to add that fatalities are high in this heroic camp, but the rule is that the press is never informed [of these misfortunes]."

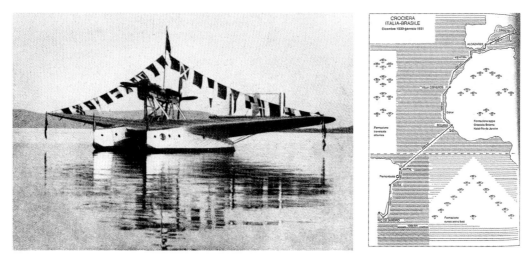

distance flights in closed circuit. The sixty-four aviators selected for training – "chosen by merit from the moral aristocracy of the Aeronautica" – were warned by Balbo that while at Orbetello nothing must distract them from the "ideal and moral" pursuit of their goal.[127] Married men, as well as bachelors, were allowed to leave the walled-in compound only one Sunday every two weeks. Looking back on these twelve months of "spiritual decimation" and "monk-like discipline," the Romantic in Balbo could not avoid pronouncing them to have been a "mystical" experience that only men of exceptional temperament could have survived.[128]

The aircraft chosen was a two-hulled seaplane of plywood-covered spruce and ash, the S.55 TA, with two six-hundred-horsepower Fiat engines mounted in tandem above the single cantelever wing. Even today photographs of this ship can stir an aviator's soul, and Balbo was deeply moved by its shape, more beautiful he thought than a Greek statue.[129] To further enhance their aesthetic distinctiveness, the twelve S.55 TAs were divided into four squadrons of three planes, each identified by a color: black for Fascism and red, white, and green for the colors of the Italian flag.

The S.55 TA's virtues were not confined to its appearance. A powerful but lightweight radio, specially developed for the cruise, gave it the capability of electronic communication across distances of thousands of kilometers, and the aircraft was outfitted with the equipment necessary to survive forced landings in high seas and towing by a rescue ship. Longer and wider hulls made it more maneuverable on water than the S.55s with which Balbo had made his earlier cruises.

Yet as elegant and seaworthy as the S.55 TA was in flight or moored and as much an improvement as it represented over its predecessor, as a transatlantic craft it possessed certain drawbacks: its ceiling was limited to fourteen thousand feet, which made it impossible for it to fly above bad weather; its cockpit lacked the artificial horizon and directional gyro necessary for instrument flight; and its radiators were subject to overheating and leaks. In conditions of mist, fog, and cloud, pilots had no choice but to reduce altitude in order to establish some point of visual reference.[130] A three-thousand kilometer flight across the South Atlantic therefore presented considerable dangers. In awareness of this, Balbo prudently arranged for eight Italian destroyers to be positioned along the cruise's route. Their mission was to offer navigational bearings and meteorological information, and assistance in the case of forced landings. As it turned out, they would be needed.[131]

After two days of delay owing to stormy conditions in the western Mediterranean, Balbo gave orders for departure on the morning of 17 December 1930. A few days before he had addressed his crews, reminding them that what they were about to accomplish would become of the most memorable displays of prowess in aviation history. "We will do our duty to the end and at any cost. Whatever surprise the future holds for us, we will know that we are serving a destiny greater than ourselves and of such a nature, in any case, to justify any sacrifice, even the supreme one [of our lives] . . . The blue soldiers of the sky do not fear death and are used to giving their lives generously in order to go *più oltre* [beyond the call of duty]."[132]

En route to their first stop, the bay of Los Alcazares near Cartagena, on the 17 December, the members of Balbo's squadrons had ample opportunity to ponder these words as they battled turbulent winds in conditions of thick cloud and heavy rain, which forced them to fly at ever lower altitudes. The formation had no choice but to break up, and Balbo's group of six planes put down in a small bay near Campos at the southern end of the island of Majorca, where violent winds and the heaving sea came close to destroying the S.55 TAs before they could be hauled up on the narrow beach. The squadrons were finally reunited at Los Alcazares on 19 December, but inspection of the planes showed that the wind, rain, and hail had taken a heavy toll on their wooden propellers, not all of which could be replaced in time to maintain the schedule. Those not replaced could not be properly balanced, thus producing vibration that would eventually undermine the performance of the engines. The determination to push ahead, no matter what the consequences, had seriously diminished the squadrons' chances of ultimate success.[133]

From the beginning, the flight was planned as a mass spectacle in which millions of persons would participate directly and vicariously. Three commemorative medals were struck in honor of the cruise and distributed in thousands of copies by local air clubs, along with models of the S.55 TA and other trinkets. Posters, portraying the cruise's route, were exhibited in every Italian town. In the tradition of D'Annunzio, three artists were commissioned to design distinctive mottoes for each squadron. Balbo chose for his own black squadron the verse taken from Dante's *Canto di Ulisse* (Song of Ulysses): "E misi me per l'alto mare aperto" (And I embarked upon the open sea). Special stamps were printed to mark the occasion. A cinematographer and five journalists, representing the major Italian newspapers, were dispatched by ship to Brazil to capture the "poetry" of the flight in their reports. While in the air, Balbo reported regularly by radio to the Duce in Rome regarding the squadron's progress. When tailwinds accelerated his arrival in Rio, Balbo did not hesitate to order his pilots to hold for an hour outside the bay so that the crowd could assemble to greet them, despite the danger of a mechanical failure after so many hours in the air.

Their arrival, Balbo later wrote, was an apotheosis in brilliant golden sunlight and an empyrian blue worthy of Dante: "a vast scenario of land and water that the divine sense of the bizarre possessed by the Creator disposed in a dazzling game of perspectives, of reliefs, of light, of shadows, and of color . . ." Balbo was so overcome by the spectacle of this "paradise on earth" that he felt it transcended the fantasy of the greatest painters and poets who had tried to imagine paradise in the world to come. "Perhaps in creating the bay of Rio, God wanted to demonstrate that all art derived from Him."[134]

The event was so carefully choreographed that the arrival of Balbo's airmen at 5:00 in the afternoon on 15 January was coordinated perfectly with the entry of the eight Italian destroyers into the resplendent bay. As Balbo's men stood at attention on the wings of their planes, the ships fired nineteen salvoes of forty-eight canon as a salute to the airmen and their triumphant flight of ten thousand four hundred kilometers over the seas of three continents, while a million Brazilians danced and cheered on the beach. The Brazilians responded with salvoes of their own. "The air vibrated and trembled, the sky was hightlighted with brief flashes and resonated with deep thunder. The surrounding mountains echoed the Cyclopean greeting with a long roar."[135]

Pl. 83.   Balbo's squadron moored in Rio de Janeiro's bay.

Pl. 84.   The S.55 TAs in tight formation as they cross the South Atlantic.

The flight was not without its victims. Two airmen were killed in training exercises before the departure from Orbetello. Five others died during the nightime takeoff from Bolama. These losses clearly anguished Balbo and threw a cloud over the triumph of the ocean crossing, no doubt in part because he feared, with some reason, that the Duce would hold him personally responsible for accidents that might have been avoided. Mussolini was pointedly not among those who rushed to congratulate Balbo by telegram upon his arrival in Natal.[136] But in his own mind Balbo came to justify these deaths with the thought that the sacrifice of these lives had not been in vain. These losses were tragic, but "sublime." They had demonstrated to the world the difficulty of the enterprise. Progress, of which aviation was the most potent weapon, required the sacrifice of individuals for the good of humanity. "The blue knights of the air serve humanity and their *patria* to the extreme limits of life, ready for the passage toward death when duty calls for it." A "breath of heroic love for the *patria*" dispelled the shadow cast by the death of his companions. The survivors of the flight were ready to die for Italy, which would be all the greater for the sacrifice of their dead companions.[137]

And indeed the achievement of Balbo and his men was a major one that redounded to the credit of Italian aviation. No group flight across the Atlantic had ever before been attempted. With the success of Balbo's cruise, the number of men who had crossed the South Atlantic by air had, in a single flight, leaped from twenty-four to sixty-four. Forty-four of these were Italian.[138] When news of Balbo's arrival in Brazil reached Italy, performances at both the theaters of La Scala in Milan and the Royal Theater of Opera in Rome were interrupted to make the announcement, followed by a long outburst of applause and the singing of the national anthem. The long telegram of congratulations from Mussolini that Balbo and his men eventually received in Rio must have come as a relief to the cruise's leader, even if it alluded specifically to the five comrades lost at Bolama.[139] In June 1931, Balbo was awarded the golden medal of the International Federation of Aviators, an honor that was reserved for the outstanding aeronautical exploit of the year. The Italian minister of air now joined the prestigious company of Lindbergh, Alan Cobham, Dieudonné Costes – and De Pinedo. One can only imagine how sweet this prize must have been for him; the neophyte, who once feared the disdain that other celebrated flyers would feel for him, had at last been admitted to the elite of the aviation world.

Balbo was not satisfied to rest on the laurels of his achievement. A man of intellectual ambitions, he quickly set out to transform his adventure into literature. And here, too, his efforts were crowned by popular success. The account Balbo wrote of his flight became a bestseller. Later, in excerpted form, it was required reading for Italian middle-school children.[140]

Like many aviation books, *Stormi in volo sull'oceano* (Squadrons in Flight over the Ocean) combines several genres: its main story line is a tale of exciting and dangerous adventures, interspersed with the type of description of exotic places and people one expects from travel literature and with some historical digressions thrown in for good measure. The whole is enveloped in a package of intense patriotism. There are remarkably few traces of official Fascist ideology, though Balbo is careful to note that the officers of the cruise are given Fascist Party membership cards before leaving Orbetello and the crews don black shirts for the Atlantic crossing, as a symbol of their "Fascist will" to conquer the ocean.[141]

Pl. 85. The cover of Balbo's account of the South American flight. Though Balbo stressed the collective nature of his exploit, this picture leaves no doubt about the man in charge.

The portrait Balbo gives us of himself is replete with revealing contradictions. He presents himself as an admirer of modesty in pilots; yet he cannot resist the temptation to put himself on center stage at every opportunity and gives detailed accounts of every social function given in his honor. He tells us that he is a man of poetic sensibility while emphasizing that he thinks of himself primarily as a soldier. He prides himself on being an austere disciplinarian; then he reveals to us that he chose not to share the monastic life of his men at Orbetello and instead installed himself in a campsite on the beach near Viareggio where he delights in rumors of his escapades with vacationing actresses.[142] He is a moist-eyed patriot of the nineteenth-century stamp, who thinks of himself as a modern man dedicated to the progress of humanity and the establishment of closer relations between distant peoples. In the end, Balbo emerges from his own account in much the same way that he does in the accounts of those who knew him: as an intensely likable man who was prey to the vice of vanity; as someone curious about other peoples and, at the same time, obsessed with his own; as a figure consumed with his own importance, yet, like a good commander, worried about the welfare of his men; and finally, as a talented author who had probably read too much D'Annunzio for his own good.[143]

The following passage from *Stormi in volo sull'oceano* highlights both Balbo's strengths and weaknesses as a writer. Describing the takeoff from Bolama, he succeeds in evoking the drama of the scene, then undermines the effect by surrendering to the lure of D'Annunzian rhetoric.

Pl. 86. Balbo listens attentively as D'Annunzio declaims during a visit to the Air Force's High Speed School at Desenzano on the Lake of Garda, not far from the Poet's villa.

The enormous seaplane, so heavy that its stern is entirely submerged in the water, departs with a rush that already causes it to rise suddenly above the dead and dense water. It has its nose slightly in the air; it cuts forward with ever greater decisiveness through the waves along an invisible straight line. It accelerates, runs, and devours distance, angrily and frenetically, jumping brusquely and jerkily, with rapid, sharp, and decisive movements, against the waves. We have to treat it brutally, we have to make it feel our uncompromising and dominating will, stronger than its own. Soon the nose is slanted upward; it grazes the water for a few instants. We pull the wheel toward our chests; I feel us leave behind the surface of the marina and sense the more rapid movement of the flying boat through the night air. We have to hold the wheel firmly with all the strength we have in our arms and give to the flight, in this dramatic moment, the greatest possible velocity. Woe to him who looks outside the cabin toward the skin of the water. Woe to him who looks for the horizon. The least indecision, the moment of doubt, the imponderable error – the fruit of blind instinct – means the sure loss of the aircraft and of our lives. Forward, forward, straight into the darkness.[144]

In this passage, one can feel across the chasm of seven decades what it meant in January 1931 to lift a plane weighing 5,148 kilos (11,440 lb), with a load of 4,700 kilos (including over 4,000 kilos of gasoline and oil) from a tropical sea in the murky depths of a foggy night in conditions of minimal visibility.[145] In Balbo's account, the aircraft has to be wrestled into the air, against its own desire to remain on the surface of the water; the indomitable will of the aviator overcomes the resistance of the machine. We recoil at what appears to us the filtering of a straightforward technological event through a Fascist imagination, and we are no doubt right to do so. But reading these pages today, it is easy to forget the degree of physical force necessary to lift these planes into the air and the fact that none of these airmen knew whether their planes would actually leave the water's surface at the moment when they began their takeoff run into a pitch-black sky and unforgiving ocean with no horizon by which to guide their flight. In this nocturnal struggle against "dead and dense water" and humid air, five Italians lost their lives.

★   ★   ★

A new and distinctive service of the sort Balbo was creating called for a building that would do it justice and express its values. Before Balbo's appointment, the employees of the Air Ministry had been dispersed throughout Rome in twelve sites, of which the most important had been on the Viminale hill next to the offices of Mussolini and the minister of the interior. This situation, which persisted during Balbo's first three years in office, suggested the ambiguous status of the air force as an independent branch of the armed services and clearly was incompatible with the new undersecretary's ambition. In the summer of 1929, after having consolidated his power, eliminated his rivals, and cleared the way toward his nomination as full-fledged minister of air, Balbo was authorized by Mussolini to begin construction of the Ministry of Air. Despite the onset of the Great Depression, it was finished in record time and inaugurated on the 28 October 1932, testimony to the high priority the government assigned to this project.[146] Working with plans originally drawn up by Colonel Adolfo Crugnola, who supervised the construction of the building, Roberto Marino, a young and relatively inexperienced architect on the teaching staff of the Roman School of Engineering, was responsible for its design and final shape. Nonetheless, there is every reason to believe that both Crugnola and Marino, along with the architect Meraviglia

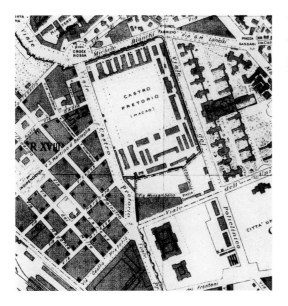

Pl. 87. The Ministry of Air was situated on a large parcel of land adjacent to the recently built Città Universitaria (University Campus) and close to the railway station, which can be glimpsed in the lower left hand corner of the picture.

Mantegazza, who contributed to the design and decoration of the interior spaces, were subjected to Balbo's desires and demands, often expressed in peremptory fashion. Thus the building, with all its virtues and its defects, must be regarded as corresponding to his aesthetic vision.[147] Both outside and inside, it was Balbo's ministry.

Located between the central train station and the then recently constructed University of Rome on the Viale Pretoriano, the eight-story rectangular structure is situated in a large and artfully landscaped park surrounded by walls. The central facade, surmounted by an eagle with wings modeled on those of the Savoia-Marchetti 55X with which Balbo had crossed the South Atlantic, is sober yet imposing, without being so monumental as to dwarf the human beings who work in it; its three arches, protruding entrances, columns, and cor-

Pl. 88. A frontal view of the Ministry of Air.

nices manage to express an aspiration toward neoclassic Italian tradition, promoted by the contemporary *Novento* movement; while at the same time the Ministry's self-conscious lack of adornment projects a sense of twentieth-century bureaucratic modernity and efficiency. This, the structure's graceful and well-proportioned yet austere exterior tells us, is a place where serious business is taking place.

Still, the overall effect is not intimidating or especially martial. While an immense Italian flag was unfurled every morning from the central balcony of the second story, to inspire feelings of national pride and *italianità* in those who entered, there was nothing threatening, sinister, or "totalitarian" about the appearance of this building. One has to stretch to find its "virile" or "Fascist" quality. The alternation of travertine marble and Roman brick, when viewed in the bright sunlight of Rome, blend together in a pleasing symphony of amber tones.[148] Though it has lost much of the impact it must have had in October 1931 when inaugurated, because of the buildings that press in upon it and the general congestion of the neighborhood now so typical of central Rome, it retains, even today, a great deal of its charm.

The real novelties of this building, however – and its aspiration toward a distinctive type of modernity – are only to be discovered upon entering it. After passing through one of the three arches and crossing a vestibule inscribed with the names of those who died while serving in the air force, one comes upon a wide and gracefully curving staircase, which leads to a vast rectangular space on the second floor, the Hall of Heroes, filled with busts and surrounded by portraits of Italy's greatest aviators, including the First World War ace Francesco Baracca and D'Annunzio. On this floor were located the offices of Balbo, the Chief of Staff of the air force, and other high-ranking officials. Frescoes, representing Balbo's aeroautical cruises and inscribed with D'Annunzian mottoes, adorned the walls. An

Pl. 89.   The entrance to the Ministry of Air on the Viale Pretoriana. The letters above the façade originally read: MINISTERO DELL'AERONAUTICA.

Pl. 90.   "The Staircase of Honor" leads to the upper floors.

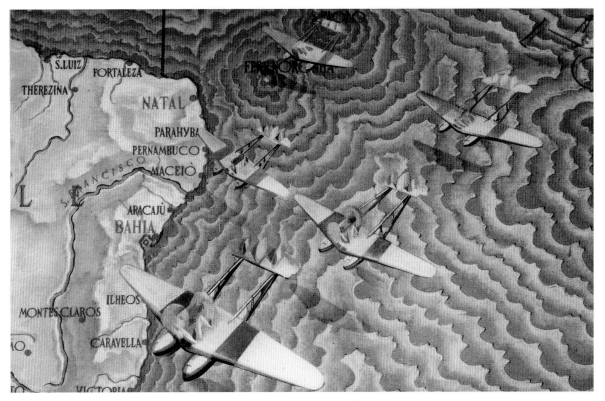

Pl. 91.   A fresco depicting the crossing of the South Atlantic by Balbo's squadron.

Pl. 92.   A fresco depicting the arrival of Balbo's squadron in Rio de Janeiro.

Pl. 93. Balbo's office with its original furnishings.

Pl. 94. This 1931 photograph of an office in the Air Ministry shows furniture that appears to be inspired by the modernist movement De Stijl.

eliptical portrait of the Madonna of Loreto, patron saint of aviators, hung on one wall. The furniture was austerely modern, inspired by the Austrian designer Josef Hoffmann and the Dutch modernists of De Stijl; the chairs, like the tables, were of wood, and rugs and tapestries were shunned in favor of bare but elegant parquet. The only concession to human frailty was a disappearing bed reserved for post-prandial naps. A messenger, stationed outside in the corridor, hastened to Balbo's office when he saw the red lamp outside it illuminated. Otherwise total silence was observed.

Less grand employees worked in offices, located along corridors that ran the length of the building. These spaces were separated by transparent glass walls so that their inhabitants would not be tempted to fritter away their time in nonproductive pursuits, such as chatting, reading newspapers, or snoozing. Communication between floors was by constantly circulating elevators without doors, called *paternoster*, onto which one jumped, a reminder of the dynamism and airborne qualities of the air arm. Memoranda, mail, and coffees circulated by means of an elaborate system of pneumatic tubes, thirty-six kilometers long. Movement between offices and idle conversation were not encouraged; the personnel were expected to remain at their desks, which were deprived of drawers to encourage order and neatness.

The emphasis everywhere in the building was on efficiency, rationality, and discipline. Unlike in other Roman ministries where employees worked from 8:00 a.m. to 12:00 and then, after lunch and a siesta, from 4:00 p.m. to 7:00, the schedule here was *unico* (continuous), beginning promptly at 8:00 and ending at 3:45 p.m. Anyone arriving after 8:00 was denied entrance and then, subsequently (in the case of military personnel), punished or (if civilian) deprived of his quarterly bonus. Lunch was served between 11:45 and 12:30 — outrageously early and short by Roman standards — and eaten in the Ministry's subterranean *aeromensa* (air mess) standing up before tables of aluminum and glass that had been especially designed for the purpose. The tables were numbered, and to save time the food was waiting when employees appeared. Meals were light, though filling, and accompanied by recorded music chosen to complement the dishes, such as "Va pensiero" from Verdi's *Nabucco* for *vitello tonnato* or the triumphal march from *Aida* on those rare occasions when venison from the king's hunting grounds was served. Though all personnel ate the same food, payment was proportional to rank, ranging from 5 lire for Balbo and higher ranking officers to 1.20 for those at the bottom of the scale. At Balbo's decree, the only bread served was soft *pane ferrarese* from his home town. After lunch,

everyone was expected to repair to washrooms where tooth brushes and tooth paste (at a price) were provided for the cleaning of teeth. Afterwards one went to the *Aerobar* for coffee and card games. Tennis courts were available on the terrace for those athletically inclined. Whimsical murals by Marcello Dudovich, mixing images of imperialist expansion in Africa and aviators cavorting in the clouds, adorned the walls of the common rooms and emphasized that special combination of lightheartedness and ever-present danger that aviators liked to affect.

In case there were doubts, Balbo circulated a brochure to all employees explaining in laborious detail how they were to comport themselves during and after lunch. They were told to keep their legs together while eating, maintain a distance of ten centimeters from the table, and to keep their conversations cheerful. Police reports record the personnel's complaints, ranging from alleged digestive problems to claims that the lack of the accustomed break between 12:00 and 4:00 p.m. was destroying family life; but morale in the Ministry was apparently high, and no one could deny that Balbo was creating a distinctive military service, even if it seems going a bit too far to compare life in the Ministry with that of a Benedictine monastery, as one Italian historian has done.[149]

Pl. 95.   A corridor running between offices in the Ministry.

Pl. 96.   A view of the constantly circulating elevators without doors, designed to maintain the agility of the Ministry's employees.

Pl. 97.   The Ministry's dining room. The mural by Marcello Dudovich in the upper right hand corner strikes an imperial note.

Pl. 98.   Employees at the Ministry consume their lunch in the forty-five minutes allotted to them and do their best to appear cheerful while eating on their feet, a situation that we do not ordinarily associate with Italians.

Contemporary critics praised the building's simplicity and modernity, and found it an impressive expression of the Fascist spirit. "It has emerged with a pure Fascist style, rapidly and in silence," one anonymous reviewer observed.[150] For the modernist architectural critic Pier Maria Bardi, writing in *L'Ala d'Italia*, it was the "ideal Fascist ministry."[151] Yet viewed from the perspective of the present, it appears not so much a "Fascist" building as a product of the Fascist period that sought to embody the values of aviation and, at the same time, connect itself with Italian architectural tradition.

To be sure, the murals in the offices of Balbo and other high-ranking officers portray the regime's imperialistic ambitions; but they do so in historical terms and are derived from fifteenth-century maps, principally those in the Belvedere Gallery of the Vatican.[152] Balbo's suite of offices is strikingly lacking in any kind of explicit Fascist imagery. The idea of glass partitions between offices – sometimes taken as a Fascist desire for control over workers – came to Balbo after his 1928 visit to the United States. The rigid hierarchy between various levels of bureaucracy could be found in any American corporation. The exaltation of technology, efficiency, and activism displayed throughout the Ministry seemed eminently American; and indeed a highly approximate painting of Manhattan, inspired by a contemporary aerial photograph, hung on a wall of the undersecretary's antechamber. Describing the building to the deputies of the Chamber of Deputies in April 1932, Balbo emphasized not its Fascism but its "simplicity," "its clarity," and its "speed," all "elements of the modern discipline of work." The dining hall, he said, was supposed to evoke "the healthy and sacred collectivism of wartime messes, a human memory of that irreplaceable period of our life that five million Italians led on the fronts of our tormented epoch; hours full of serene spiritual solidarity."[153]

★　　★　　★

Pl. 100.   This mural depicting the Mediterranean, identified in Latin as *Mare Internum Nostrum* (Our Internal Sea), portrays the power of Rome during the height of the Empire and suggests Fascist ambitions.

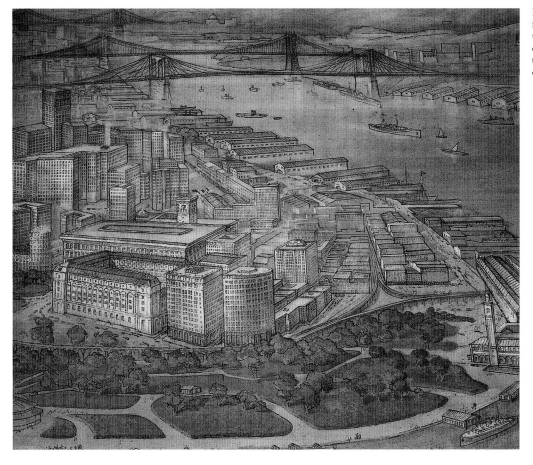

Pl. 101.   Manhattan, somewhat fancifully imagined by an unknown Italian artist, decorates one of the walls of the Undersecretary of State's office.

By November 1931, when the Palazzo dell'Aeronautica was inaugurated, Balbo had become a master of the media. As someone who had himself founded and run a newspaper, he was deeply conscious of the importance of the press. He cultivated aviation writers, gave them special privileges, and did not hesitate to rebuke them or even rewrite their stories when they produced copy that displeased him.[154] His aviation publishing center, the Editoriale Aeronautico, produced three journals – *L'Ala d'Italia*, *Le Vie dell'Aria*, and *L'Aquilone*, and the more specialized *Rivista aeronautica* – and sold them at its own kiosks.

Nor did Balbo overlook the importance of the cinema. His exploits and those of other Italian aviators were caught on film by the government-financed LUCE, which showed their newsreels and documentaries throughout the country. LUCE's 1932 documentary *Vertigine* (Vertigo), directed by Filippo Masoero, was an exhilarating and modernist hymn to the aesthetics of flight. Many of its scenes were taken from the spectacular air shows – the so-called "Days of the Wing" – that Balbo organized in Rome in the early 1930s to display the talent of his aviators and the power of his air force.

Mario Massai, an aviation reporter for the *Corriere della Sera* who was close to Balbo, evoked in excited prose what he had seen during the "Day of the Wing" on 8 June 1930. A squadron of five planes that had earlier astonished the crowd with their display of aer-

Pl. 102. Melchiorre Melis's poster for the *Day of Wings* of 8 June 1930. As in the case of the Schneider Cup race, people attending this event received a fifty percent reduction in railway fares.

Pl. 103. Some of the aviation magazines produced by the Editoriale Aeronautico (Air Publishing House) in the Ministry of Air, which ranged from technical journals such as *Aeronautica* to publications which stressed political and cultural issues (*L'Ala d'Italia*) or appealed to young people (*L'Aquilone*).

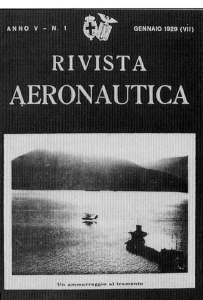

Pl. 104. A kiosk belonging to the Editoriale Aeronautico.

obatic maneuvers suddenly appeared at the extreme end of the field. They dived towards vehicles in flight from a simulated African village. One heard the crackling of machine-gun fire. In close formation the five planes pointed their noses toward the sky. They began to climb in vertical flight.

> And in this moment the unexpected happens, the incredible spectacle; it's enough to take away your breath! As if a bomb had exploded in the middle of the formation, the five planes take off in all directions, filling the sky with roaring airplanes that ascend and descend in apparent disorder in order to then pounce upon the same objective. It's a spectacle that is both terrifying and marvelous at the same time![155]

Yet the spectacle that obsessed Balbo still evaded him. Ever since December 1928, Balbo's dream had been to land in New York habor with a squadron of Italian seaplanes. The 1930–31 flight to Brazil was conceived as a prelude to this future enterprise, and indeed Mussolini had alluded to "an even greater aerial test" in his cable of congratulation when Balbo and his men arrived in Rio in January 1931.[156] Planning for the North American flight began already on the ship that took Balbo and his crew back to Italy from Brazil. The original idea was extraordinarily ambitious: following routes earlier traveled by Ferrarin and De Pinedo, the Italians would fly to the United States by way of India, China, Japan, and Alaska; they would then fly south to Panama and north to Newfoundland, before crossing the North Atlantic and returning to Italy by way of Ireland, thus completing an aerial circumnavigation of the earth. One of the most experienced pilots from the Brazilian cruise, Enea Recagno, was dispatched in May 1931 to the Aleutian Islands to scout possible harbors where the Italian squadron might land while making the crossing from Asia to Alaska. After a journey through northeast Asia worthy of his given name, he proposed the island of Atu as the most ideal base. But the Asian route had to be abandoned because of the outbreak of war between Japan and China and the worsening of the world economic crisis that began to affect Italy adversely in 1931.[157]

Expenses would have to be trimmed and a new, more direct route established. The announcement of a world's fair in Chicago in the summer of 1933 on the theme of a "century of progress" gave Balbo his destination: what better way to celebrate a "century of progress" than to fly to Chicago, a city that also had the advantage of being home to a considerable population of Italian immigrants, and then to return to Italy by way of New York, the quintessential twentieth-century city. Such a flight, if successful, would achieve various objectives of importance to Mussolini and his regime. It would highlight the revival of Italy under Mussolini's leadership in the aftermath of the First World War; it would reveal to the world the capabilities of Italian aviators and aircraft manufacturers; and it would cap with a dramatic flourish the elaborate celebrations planned for the tenth anniversary of the Fascist Revolution. Hence the name given to the flight: *Crociera del Decennale* (Cruise of the Decade), which carried heavy symbolic significance for all Italians, including those who had emigrated to foreign lands.

The flight was planned with even greater care than its predecessors. Wolfgang von Gronau, the famous German explorer of North Atlantic aerial routes whom Balbo had met at a meeting of transatlantic aviators held in Rome in the summer of 1932, left his Italian host in no doubt about the treacherous fogs he would encounter during the flights he projected from Ireland to Iceland, and then from Iceland to Labrador. Von Gronau put Balbo in contact with a German meteorologist – Professor Baumann – who agreed to provide him with weather reports from a station in Greenland.

A special school was created at Orbetello, the School of Aerial High Seas Navigation, to train the seventy aviators chosen from the pool of volunteers who responded to Balbo's announcement of the flight. Four-fifths of those selected from the hundreds of applicants had no experience with seaplanes – a deliberate decision on Balbo's part to extend the possibility of participation in the cruise to the air force as a whole rather than limiting it to the much narrower pool of those demonstrated experts in maritime aviation. Thirty-five of those originally selected would fail the course and be replaced. Instruction began already in late May 1931, only a few months after the completion of the Brazilian flight. Training was by no means limited to flying: in addition to studying mathematics, physics, aerodynamics, navigation, and English, the crews were taught to maneuver aircraft on water, to sail, and (considering their northerly route) even to ski. Their most important training, however, was in instrument flying, a practice still rare among Italian aviators.

Pl. 105. Balbo and his staff plan the North Atlantic flight beneath a fresco portraying Rio de Janeiro.

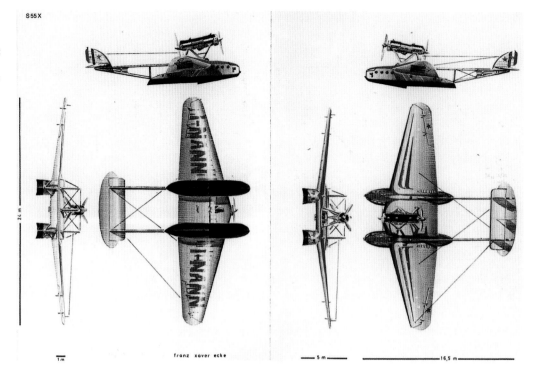

The plane to be used – a new and improved version of Balbo's beloved S. 55 – was fitted with Isotta-Fraschini Asso engines, capable a generating 750 horsepower; larger and smoother hulls; three-bladed metal propellers less susceptible to damage from inclement weather; larger fuel tanks; lighter and more reliable radiators; and a greater variety of instruments than the S. 55 TA had possessed, including a Sperry artificial horizon and a Sperry directional gyro that made possible flight under conditions of limited or non-existent visibility. Powered by its new engines, the new S. 55 – known as the S. 55X – was capable of transporting a load of 1,000 kilos more than 4,000 kilometers and could cruise at 225 kilometers per hour, while consuming less fuel than its predecessor.[158] Its normal crew consisted of four men: two pilots, a mechanic, and a radio operator. The S. 55X's designer, Marchetti, proclaimed it "all muscle, all power, all speed, like an Olympic athlete . . . Never have we looked forward with a firmer heart and calmer assurance to the wonderful adventure [that our aviators are about to undertake]".[159]

Testing the newly manufactured planes upon their delivery to Orbetello, the crews found them perfect mechanically as well as "shining" and "elegant" in their appearance.[160] To enhance the sleekness of their lines still further, the roof of the hulls had been given a trapezoidal shape. Each S. 55X was assigned a color – black (the color of Fascism) or red, white, or green (the colors of the Italian flag). These colors were used in a stylized design on the hulls and in the letters identifying the aircraft on the lower side of the wing. The squadrons, consisting of three planes, were further distinguished by either stars or circles on the two external rudders. The lead airplane had one star or circle; the right aircraft had two; the left three. Hence the two black squadrons were divided into one group of three that was starred and another that was identified by circles. The primary color of the S. 55X was aluminum, with the exception of the hulls, which were covered with shiny black varnish. Viewed individually and, even more so, when seen in mass, they were an impressive sight and a testimony to Italian aeronautical prowess and the Italian flair for industrial design.

Despite the Italian state's financial problems, it was decided that twenty-five S.55Xs would make the flight, twice the number of aircraft used in the South Atlantic cruise. One was to be held in reserve in the case of a mishap. Two Italian submarines, an Italian yacht owned by the air force, two smaller ships made available by the Italian Navy, and six leased English trawlers, commanded by Italian Air Force officers, would be stationed in the North Atlantic along Balbo's route to act as radio beacons, sources of weather reports, and to provide assistance in the case of forced landings. In addition, four Danish vessels were to provide meteorological information during the crossing of the North Atlantic. The extent of the infrastructure necessary for the flight's success and the substantial costs it entailed suggest the importance that Mussolini assigned to the cruise. In the end, according to official air force figures which were probably low, it would cost almost seven-and-a-half million lire.[161]

No less attention was devoted to publicizing the cruise and making certain it became an event of worldwide – or at least, Western – proportions. Five well-known Italian journalists and a cinematographer were sent ahead to Labrador on the air force yacht, the *Alice*, to report on the crossing of the Atlantic and the reception the Italians received while in America.[162] Balbo carried an additional cinematographer in his plane. Special stamps were printed in celebration of the cruise which Balbo optimistically hoped would offset some

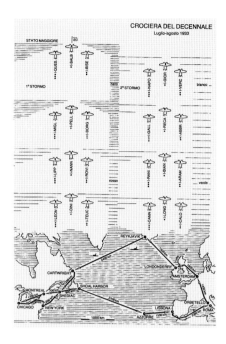

Pl. 108.   The route of the 1933 flight and the formations flown by the squadrons.

of the flight's cost.[163] Striking modernist posters were commissioned and displayed throughout the country.

Unseasonably cold weather off the coast of Labrador prevented the *Alice* from reaching Cartwright on schedule and establishing an Italian base there. An ice-breaking vessel had to be leased in order to open a way through the ice. It was not until 6 July that the base in Labrador was ready and the ships assigned to guide the squadron across the North Atlantic had been able to reach their positions. With the radio and navigational infrastructure finally in place, bad weather over the Alps and northern Europe further delayed the departure from Orbetello. Impatient to get under way, the crews can only have been reminded of the dangers they were about to face when on 20 June Balbo had a potentially serious accident when his S.55 trimotor hydroplane crashed into the sea after taking off from Punta Ala, where he and two other pilots had passed a pleasant Sunday with his family at his country house. Fortunately, the plane had risen to a height of only ten meters when it began to slip toward the left. It was later determined that the left aileron had broken under the strain of takeoff; had the S.55 reached a higher altitude, the accident would almost certainly have been fatal. It was not Balbo's first brush with aerial disaster.[164] Nor would it be his last.

Understandably, Balbo's first concern was to underplay the significance of the incident, so as not to worry still further the families of the men about to leave on a cruise that could result in the loss of lives.[165] Meanwhile, weather reports from northern Italy and Switzerland were not encouraging; they predicted thick fog along the route. Determined not to repeat the mistake he had made in December 1930 and urged by Mussolini to ignore his critics and not to leave until the time was right, Balbo waited until the weather along the first leg of the flight was unambiguously favorable.[166] News reports portrayed Balbo as looking "worn" and "nervous," with dark circles under his eyes.[167] At 4:00 a.m. on the morning of 1 July 1933, the minister had his crews awakened. The moment for departure had finally arrived. After his men had given the Roman salute to the flag, Balbo reminded them of their duty to triumph over the obstacles that awaited them for the sake of the *Patria*, even at the cost of their lives.[168] As the aviators boarded their planes, the coast was streaked with the red light of breaking dawn.

The cruise did not get off to an auspicious start. One of Balbo's planes capsized while landing in Amsterdam. The plane's engineer was fatally injured in the crash, and three of the other four occupants were severely injured, casting a cloud over what was supposed to be a triumphal arrival in the first city to be visited by the cruise.[169] Fortunately, there was a reserve S.55X to take its place. Storms in the North Atlantic delayed the departure from the second stop in Londonderry, Northern Ireland. Balbo was clearly feeling under pressure from Rome not to take any unnecessary risks.[170]

Flying between Londonderry and the Icelandic capital of Reykjavik on 5 July the squadrons had their first serious encounter with North Atlantic fog. For an hour and a half they were deprived of any visibility; nonetheless, with the radio assistance of the trawlers along their route they succeeded in maintaining their course. What was supposed to be a brief stop in Reykjavik turned into a stay of six days, while the squadrons waited for better weather. Not until 11 July – ten days after leaving Orbetello – did Balbo dare order his crews to take flight for what would be the longest and most dangerous leg of their flight: from Iceland to Cartwright in Labrador; and even then the takeoff had to be aborted for lack of wind. Always sensitive to the criticisms of the press, Balbo felt humiliated by his inability to take flight. The agument of his lieutenants that Providence must have intervened to save them from some frightful disaster did little to diminish his sense of failure.[171]

By 7:00 the next morning Balbo and his ninety-eight men were finally in the air and setting out across fifteen hundred miles of ocean. Twelve hours later, after having traversed banks of fog and patches of driving rain, they set down in Sandwich Bay outside Cartwright in North American waters. Not one of the forty-eight engines of Italian manufacture had faltered. The system of radio beacons and weather stations organized by the Italian Air Force had functioned perfectly. To appreciate the magnitude of the Italians' achievement, one must realize that before their flight, only five aircraft had succeeded in making the North Atlantic crossing from east to west.[172] That number now rose to twenty-nine, twenty-four of them Italian. Mussolini cabled to Balbo his satisfaction, carefully taking his share of the credit for the success of the North Atlantic crossing: "I see that you held fascistically to my orders: maximum discipline in the air, the minimal dispersion of energies on land. *A noi!* Mussolini."[173]

Once arrived safely at Cartwright, the Italian aviators could prepare to enjoy their triumph. Five journalists, two cinematographers, and seven other people, along with the crews' dress uniforms, were taken aboard for the remainder of the flight. Yet more passengers – including the journalist Nello Quilici and Balbo's nephew Lino – joined the group at Shediac in New Brunswick. The dangerous flying having been accomplished, the emphasis now would shift to public relations and image control.

The population of Montreal, their next stop, turned out in force to greet the Italian flyers; but the reception they received there paled before the ecstatic welcome they encountered in Chicago when the squadrons put down on Lake Michigan on 15 July before a cheering crowd of a hundred thousand onlookers. Over a period of four days, Balbo and his men were treated to a motorcade; a welcome at Soldiers' Field attended by more than sixty thousand persons at which Mayor Edward Kelly and the governor of Illinois compared their flight with Columbus's voyage; a series of elaborate banquets and receptions; a special tour of the world's fair; a solemn mass said in their honor, after which a telegram of congratulations and blessing from the Vatican, written by the future pope Pius XII, Cardinal Eugenio Pacelli, was read; and a farewell parade along Michigan Avenue, attended by crowds ten to fifteen deep. Seventh Street in downtown Chicago was renamed in Balbo's honor; he was made an honorary chieftain of the Sioux tribe under the name of "Flying

Pl. 109.   Balbo's planes moored on Lake Michigan during the stopover in Chicago.

Pl. 110.   A pretty Italo-American girl points to the sign, renaming Seventh Avenue in Chicago.

Eagle" and given an honorary degree by Loyola University. A monument to Columbus along the lakefront was inaugurated, which bore the inscription:

THIS

MONUMENT

HAS SEEN THE

GLORY OF THE

WINGS OF ITALY

LED BY

ITALO BALBO

JULY 15, 1933

Describing Balbo, the *Chicago Daily Tribune*'s reporter compared him with "Penelope's Ulysses come true."

Here is no routine Chicagoan of office or of bank but a Ferraran who puts his plane to bed on the bosom of an inland sea: a wanderer of the skies who on one day is in seven-hilled Rome, on another in diamond-cutting Amsterdam, on another in Londonderry of the ancient walls and the heroic siege, on another in fog-drenched Reykjavik, on another on the coasts of Canadian provinces, on another in high crowned Montreal of the royal hills, and who at the end of a fortnight charges courteously down upon the metropolis of middle America with his handkissing and his softly breathed "Grazia, signora, molta grazia!" A cavalier, then, from the skies.

And also a heartthrob. What did the women say as the "dark-eyed hero" rode by in his motorcade? According to the female correspondent of the *Tribune* who covered the event, she heard matrons saying, "'My dear, don't you love his beard!' and 'He's the most exciting man I've ever seen!,' and 'I think he's more romantic than Col. Lindergh ever thought of being,' and 'Did you ever *see* anyone so romantic looking? . . . He's as thrilling as the old Romans.'"[174] Even the *Tribune*'s male correspondent, while noting that Balbo was too stout

Pl. III.   Balbo being idolized
in Chicago.

for thirty-seven, was moved to call him "a D'Artagnan of the air – lacking only a Dumas
to immortalize him."[175]

Such adulation was enough to turn anyone's head, and it no doubt explains
why Mussolini felt it necessary to remind Balbo in a cable not to lose himself in the
American celebrations but to concentrate on preparing for the return to Rome where,
amidst the people of the capital, he and his men would bring to an end "the greatest aerial enterprise of modern times."[176]

Saluted by nineteen cannon shots fired from the warship *Wilmette* and escorted by thirty-six American fighters, the Italians took off for New York on the morning of the 19th.
Arriving in the city from the north and closely pursued by planes bearing newsreel cameramen, they were careful to follow the Hudson around Manhattan at an altitude of
approximately two thousand feet before heading eastward across Brooklyn and Coney
Island for their destination, the hydroport named after Floyd Bennett on Jamaica Bay.
Onlookers waved and cheered, while sirens and whistles from factories and ships in the
river and harbor blew a deafening welcome. Maintaining a perfect formation, the Italians
swooped around in a half-moon over the bay.

Suddenly, Balbo flight of three black-starred S.55Xs broke away from the formation and
began their gliding descent while the rest of the squadron continued their circular course
at the same altitude. "As thousands cheered, shouted 'Viva Generale Balbo!' at the top of
their lungs and thrust black-shirted arms into the air in the Fascist salute, General Balbo's
flight of three seaplanes gently descended to the water in a perfect landing and taxied to
the buoys provided for them in advance at the end of a line of twenty-four buoys spread
out fan-wise across the foot of the airport."[177] The remaining twenty-one planes descended gracefully in groups of three, while their companions continued circling, until the entire
squadron was spread across the bay and safely secured.

The Italians then proceeded to their Manhattan hotel, the Ambassador, where Balbo
gave a press conference in a suit of white pajamas, impressing the reporters with his
youthful vitality and affability. Asked what his flight had demonstrated, he responded in

Italian "with a shrug of his shoulders, and a jerk of his massive head": "The flight shows that aviation is always progressing. Instead of maneuvering over the Mediterranean we decided to take a stroll to America."[178] Coming from someone else these words might seem like bragging, but Balbo succeeded in saying them with a smile that disarmed his interlocutors.

The next morning, Balbo and twenty of his pilots were flown to Washington, D.C., where the most senior of them were invited to a luncheon at the White House hosted by President Roosevelt. Roosevelt attempted to persuade Balbo to extend his stay in the United States for a few months so that he could satisfy those cities whose officials had expressed a desire to receive the Italian aviators. Knowing that Mussolini would frown upon the idea, Balbo responded evasively by thanking Roosevelt for the unforgettable welcome the Italians had received from the American public and offered the FDR the gold medal that had been struck in honor of the cruise.[179] Balbo was impressed with Roosevelt's vivacious conversation, his "virile energy," and his "deep interest" in the Duce's efforts to resurrect Italy internally and restore its prestige abroad. Here was a statesman of "vast horizons," whose desire to empty the cities of their "exuberant population" seemed to Balbo to have much in common with Mussolini's urban projects. "I don't know if he is close to Fascism. In any case, he's a dictator."[180] It was probably for the best that Balbo didn't share these thoughts with his American hosts. After attending a dinner and a ball given in their honor at the Army and Navy Club, Balbo and his men returned to New York in a special train to enjoy the festivities the authorities in New York had planned for the following day.

No one could outdo New Yorkers when it came to celebrating people who had accomplished great deeds. As accustomed as he was to crowds, Balbo had never seen anything even faintly similar to the ticker-tape parade the city staged for him. "From every side the air was filled with an enormous concert of sounds: sirens, the raucous shout of horns, yells and whistles . . . Millions and millions of human voices were interwoven with the metallic din of noisy machines . . ." Pieces of paper and confetti rained from the sky. American and Italian flags waved from open windows. Resounding through the roar of the crowd was the refrain "Italia."[181] Balbo was especially moved by the sight of the thousands of Italo-Americans who turned out in mass to cheer him and his men. He sensed, quite rightly, that they saw in him not only a hero but a symbol of their homeland – a country that by this flight had gained the world's respect and cast Italians in a more positive light.[182]

That evening, in Madison Square Bowl in Long Island City before a crowd of sixty-five thousand Italo-Americans, Balbo gave an impassioned speech in which, to thunderous applause, he cleverly combined nationalistic allusions to the resurgence of Italy under the leadership of Mussolini with a pledge of friendship to the United States and a plea to those who had been born in Italy to respect the laws of their new country without ceasing to consider themselves Italians.[183] The next day Balbo and his men stood at attention during a mass of thanksgiving in St Patrick's Cathedral, as a bishop blessed them and the celebrant expressed his hope that "the new Italy from which these men bear greetings long live" and that "the generations yet unborn always keep in mind this contribution to the world's peace and progress."[184]

As spectacular as the Italians' triumph in the United States was, it coincided with a remarkable series of aeronautical stories that challenged its place of primacy on the front page of American newspapers. On 1 July 1933, the day that Balbo arrived in Amsterdam, the lead story in the *New York Times* was not the coming of the Italians but Roscoe Turner's record flight across the United States to win the Bendix Trophy. While Balbo waited for conditions to clear in Iceland on 10 July, Charles Lindbergh and his wife Anne departed in their Lockheed Sirius for their own crossing of the North Atlantic. As New York waited to

welcome Balbo on 19 July, Wiley Post was overflying Siberia on his way to a new record for a round-the-world solo flight. He arrived in New York in time to meet with Balbo before the Italian left. Shortly before Balbo left New York, James Mollison and his wife Amy Johnson took off from Croydon airdrome for a flight from London to New York that would end with a crash near Bridgeport, Connecticut.

The coincidence of these flights was not lost on contemporary observers. Writing on the aviation page of the *New York Times*, Lauren D. Lyman drew two conclusions. The success of the Balbo flight would give impetus to those who were supporting the government in its desire to increase the air armament of both the army and the navy; and the Balbo, Post, and Mollison flights had given the supporters of transatlantic airmail arguments for their cause. A period of spectacular aeronautical exploits was drawing to a close; Lyman could already foresee the day when what had been extraordinary would become routine.[185]

The return to Rome of Balbo and his men, though inevitably an anticlimax, reserved some unpleasant surprises. Two Italian planes were forced by mechanical problems to land during what should have been an uneventful flight from New York to Shediac, New Brunswick. Then, during the flight from Shediac to Shoal Harbour in Newfoundland, a third S.55X was forced to put down in the sea because of a broken water pump, prompting Balbo to wonder if the engines of his planes were beginning to show signs of wear after almost a hundred hours of flight. Was their luck beginning to run out? Perhaps the idea of returning by air to Italy had been overly presumptuous on his part.[186] The leg from Shoal Harbour to Valencia in Ireland, their next destination, would require a flight of eighteen hundred miles across the North Atlantic – three hundred miles further than the perilous crossing from Iceland to Labrador.

Winds of cyclone force in the North Atlantic prevented a takeoff from Shoal Harbour until 3 August when the weather along their route began to clear; then, just as Balbo was on the verge of ordering the departure, a telegram arrived from their meteorological station in Ireland announcing evening fog in Valencia. Tormented by the thought of a land-

Pl. 113. A huge crowd gathered in the Piazza Colonna in the center of Rome to greet the returning Italian flyers. A picture of Mussolini dominates the occasion and beside it a text, stating that Mussolini had proclaimed that the Atlantic would become for the Italian Air Force "a Mediterranean sea."

ing in a small and unknown harbor in conditions of minimal visibility – a recipe for sure disaster – Balbo ordered the trawlers in the North Atlantic southwards.[187] He did this against the advice of his metereological adviser, Professor Baumann, who predicted that the Irish fog would lift the next day, and knowing also that there were no harbors in the Azores capable of receiving the entire squadron. Given the stakes, he felt he had no other choice. Alas, as it turned out, Baumann was right; weather conditions in Ireland were ideal on 5 August; but by then it was too late to reverse course. The ships were already heading for their new positions. Suffering from the silent disapproval of his chief lieutenants, Balbo was cheered by an "affectionate" telegram from Mussolini, expressing his approval of the southern route and counseling patience. "No impatience and no hurry. The important thing is for you all to arrive safe and sound, and I'm sure that this will happen. *Ti abbraccio* [I embrace you]."[188]

On 8 August, at break of day the twenty-four S.55Xs rose from Shoal Habour in a murky haze that made it impossible to calculate distance; Balbo was surprised at how quickly his plane lifted from the water, despite its weight of four thousand kilos. Twenty minutes later, leaving Cape Split behind him as he headed into the Atlantic, he could see the red disk of the sun slowly rising. It cast a light on the sea and the sky that caused the clouds to take on the aspect of Byzantine cathedrals. He would remember it, romantically, as an occasion worthy of the celebration of a Roman conqueror or a mythic hero.[189] Classical educations leave their mark on even the most modern of men.

The plan was to fly in formation to the Azores and then to divide into two groups. Five squadrons would land at Ponta Delgada and the other three at Horta. The first four hours of the crossing proceeded routinely, as they overflew the thick fog banks off Newfoundland. But they soon found themselves in a zone of huge pitch-black storm clouds illuminated by flashes of lightning between forty degrees and thirty-five degrees latitude. Thinking the air would be calmer at lower altitudes, Balbo ordered the squadron to descend only to come up against another dark wall of clouds. Ascending and descending in a vain attempt to escape from this hellish nightmare of colossal clouds, they finally emerged into an open stretch of calm, blue sea.[190] Despite the dangerous ordeal, the squadron had somehow remained intact.

The landings at Horta and Ponta Delgada went smoothly, and Balbo could take heart from the fact that the most difficult part of the return flight had been accomplished without incident. But the takeoff the next morning for Lisbon from the small harbor of Ponta Delgada exposed the flat hulls of the S.55Xs to the long swells of open seas, and one of Balbo's planes crashed, fatally injuring a crew member, Lieutenant Enrico Squaglia. Watching the scene from the air and not yet aware of the seriousness of Lieutenant Squaglia's injuries, Balbo was overcome by a wave of sadness. How unjust fate was! His dream of arriving in Rome with his squadron of twenty-four planes intact was now dashed, and the wisdom of his decision to take the southern route seriously called into question. Not even his prudence, deemed excessive by some of his closest advisers, had been able to avoid disaster.[191]

Arriving in Lisbon, Balbo had the further blow of discovering that Squaglia had died. A depressing shadow now fell over Balbo's moment of triumph.[192] The ceremonies the Portuguese had planned were cancelled, and it was decided, in agreement with the authorities in Rome, to return directly from Lisbon rather than breaking the trip at Berre in France.

Departure was set for the early morning of 12 August. No one up to then had ever made the over eleven-hundred-mile flight from Lisbon to Rome nonstop. Fighting head winds and extremely high air temperatures that raised the temperature of their water and oil to dangerous levels, Balbo and his squadron reached Rome's hydroport at the Lido di Ostia at the mouth of the Tiber in the late afternoon, almost a month and a half after leaving Orbetello. There, dressed in black shirts inside their flying suits, they were met by Mussolini and his cabinet, members of the royal family, the Roman diplomatic corps, military authorities, Fascist dignitaries, and the aviators' families. They were then transported by car to Rome along a route lined with cheering onlookers that would culminate in the Piazza Colonna where a huge crowd of sixty thousand persons had gathered. Italy's capital had been transformed into "a mass of flags, flowers, banners, and flaming electric signs," while a barrage of publicity and special trains with discounted railway tickets had encouraged inhabitants of other cities and towns to make their way to Rome to celebrate what promised to be a historic occasion.[193]

The main festivities, however, were left for the following day, 13 August. The aviators' day began with a visit to the king in the Quirinale Palace, where Balbo was officially notified that he was to be promoted to air marshal. No airman had ever held that exalted rank, which had been reserved for the commanders of victorious armies. The Atlantic flyers, in resplendent white dress uniforms, then paraded to the Piazza Venezia and up the Via dell'Impero on a bed of oak and laurel branches, amidst fluttering and many-colored banners, through the Arch of Constantine to Domitian's Stadium on the Palatine Hill, as a half million spectators cheered and showered them with flowers. There Mussolini gave a speech in which he praised the contribution of Balbo and his men to Italy, to Fascism, and to aviation and announced their promotion to a higher rank. Mussolini embraced Balbo and gave him the air marshal's hat he had coveted for so long.[194]

But Balbo's happiness at his triumphal return to Italy can only have been clouded during the following months by his realization that Mussolini intended to divest him of his position as air minister, which he did officially at the end of October. Balbo's appointment as governor of Libya, which he made every effort publicly to accept with good grace, amounted to exile from the institution that he had built and deeply loved. Perhaps even more seriously, Balbo's new assignment dashed his hopes to be named head of the General Staff or minister of defense, a position that would have given him control over the army and navy as well as the air force and that would have made him, for all practical purposes, the second

Pl. 114. Balbo and his men march through the Arch of Constantine in central Rome.

Pl. 115. Mussolini addresses Balbo and his men from a commanding height.

most powerful person in the regime.[195] While putting the best possible face on his new appointment in public, Balbo bristled in private and admitted that it was "with death in his heart" that he was leaving "my house, my creature." [196] To his friend Emilio De Bono, he confessed that the real reason for his new appointment was Mussolini's envy of his success in the United States and the warmth of his reception when he returned to Italy. "When he saw the grandeur and, most of all, the spontaneity of the tributes given to us, he began to glower . . . If he thinks he can do with me as he does with the others, he's miscalculated."[197]

Yet whatever thoughts of resistance to Mussolini's action flashed through Balbo's mind during the first days after his discovery that he was being exiled to Libya, his natural optimism reasserted itself and he quickly pulled himself together, consoling himself with the thought, suggested by the king and other friends, that his new post could be a springboard to greater responsibilities.[198] Who could predict what the future held? Besides, he was not the kind of person who slammed doors because of an emotional blow.[199]

★   ★   ★

Balbo's feelings about Mussolini are hard to fathom. It seems extremely unlikely that even he understood them. One senses in Balbo moments of Oedipal revolt against a father figure from which he could never successfully separate himself. Giuseppe Bottai, a high-ranking Fascist leader who was fond of Balbo while also keenly aware of his faults, thought that his friend simultaneously loved the Duce and despised him. Yet Bottai was convinced that, deep within himself, Balbo longed after Mussolini's approval. "A gesture, a word, a hint of endearment was enough to send him into rapture or launch him upon the riskest of enterprises."[200]

If Bottai is right, this may explain the strange and dissatisfying account that Balbo wrote of his 1933 flight, *La centuria alata* (The Winged One Hundred). As in his early books, Balbo presents himself as a soldier and a person of poetic sensibility, who takes didactic delight in the geography and history of the territories he overflies and seizes every opportunity to show off his culture to his readers. There is the same irritating tension between his coy desire to portray himself as a modest and retiring member of a group of obedient airmen and his inability to withstand the temptation of vaunting before an admiring public the highly personal and extravagant honors he receives. But the real drama of the story Balbo had lived in July–August 1933 cannot be conveyed, because he is unable to be honest about the nature of his twisted relationship with Mussolini, an anguished combination of hostility, attraction, and a sense of grievance that causes him to oscillate uneasily between an attitude of filial rebellion and a sincere desire for Mussolini's approval. Balbo cannot admit that at every moment of the flight, from his departure from Orbetello to his return flight from Lisbon to Rome, he lived in constant fear of failure and doubted, with good reason, the Duce's confidence in his good judgment. Hence instead of portraying the conflict between himself and an insecure dictator, who envied his exploits and was determined to diminish the nature of his achievement, Balbo projects in his book an attitude of slavish dependence on his chief, taking refuge in his persona as a soldier who prides himself on his obedience to those of higher rank.

The result is a demeaning demonstration of the qualities that dictatorships nurture. Talking to the Duce by telephone after arriving in Montreal, Balbo suddenly realizes that he has been unwittingly standing at attention, a sign of his unlimited respect for his chief.[201] He writes that Mussolini is widely admired in the United States and reports that there are no signs of anti-Fascism along his route, though he is well aware that heavy security forces

Pl. 116. Balbo after being welcomed by Mussolini upon his return to Ostia, outside Rome.

had been mobilized in Chicago and New York to forestall the possibility of embarrassing anti-Fascist demonstrations.[202] When he anguishes over the loss of Enrico Squaglia's life on the takeoff from Ponta Delgada, he claims that he is relieved of all concern upon receiving a telegram from Mussolini, assuring him that he should not take this incident so seriously.[203] The reality was that Balbo was deeply depressed by an event that had seriously called into question his judgment in choosing the southern route against the opinion of his most trusted advisers. Shortly afterwards, describing his arrival at the hydroport outside Rome, Balbo lingers – in what may be an instance of wishful thinking and at the very least was an exercise in selective memory – over the spontaneous affection of his reception by Mussolini and gives the erroneous impression that he neglected to greet his family so that he could remain by the side of the Duce. News accounts instead describe him as first shaking hands with Crown Prince Umberto and other members of the House of Savoy and soon afterwards hugging and kissing his wife and children.[204]

In any case, Mussolini's embrace may not have been as warm as Balbo remembered. The welcoming ceremonies in Rome were designed to emphasize Balbo's role as the agent of Mussolini's will. As one of Balbo's biographers puts it, ". . . it was difficult to tell whether it was Balbo or Mussolini who had flown the Atlantic. Great posters displayed Mussolini in aviator's costume beside a squadron of planes, as if he had done the flying and Balbo had assisted him. The press referred to the 'Wings of Mussolini under the guidance of Balbo' and telegrams were published to show that Mussolini had directed the flight from day to day."[205] The truth was the Il Duce could not forgive his minion for having actually accomplished a feat of which he could only dream; and what better way to punish him than to exile him from the institution he loved, *questa mia casa, questa mia creatura*.[206]

★ ★ ★

In the early 1930s the leadership of the Fascist regime set out to narrate its history through the medium of elaborate exhibitions designed to reach a mass public and fix indelibly in the minds of the Italian people the historical role of Fascism and its leader Mussolini.[207] The narratives and aesthetics of these shows, directed toward a mass public, were complex, deriving ultimately from the different artistic agendas of the artists and architects involved and the unwillingness of Mussolini to impose on his regime a single style certified as being authentically "Fascist." One of the most spectacular of these exhibitions, which opened with great fanfare in the recently constructed Palazzo dell'Arte of Milan in June of 1934, was devoted to the history of Italian aviation. The crowds who flocked to see it exceeded expectations, forcing a two-month extension of its run. By the time the show closed at the end of the year over a million people had seen it.[208] Ten years of aeronautical propaganda and the intense publicity generated by Balbo's cruises had clearly had their effect.

Inspired aesthetically by the phenomenally successful *Mostra della rivoluzione fascista* (Exhibit of the Fascist Revolution) of 1932 and drawing on the talents of some of the same artists and architects, *L'Esposizione dell'aeronautica italiana* utilized modernist techniques of photomontage, bold colors, stark lettering, and dramatic lighting to draw the spectator into an emotionally charged journey that led from Leonardo da Vinci's studies of bird flight and designs for a flying machine to Balbo's 1933 "cruise of the decade."[209] As in the earlier exhibit, the aim was to break down the barrier between the spectator and the objects on display by creating environments that would give the visitor the sensation of participating actively, of actually being present, in the story that he or she was being told by means of visual representation.[210] Carefully chosen quotations, projecting aggressively from panels and temporary walls, stirred the viewer's emotions and imposed a coherent narrative on what might otherwise have appeared as a chaotic and haphazard array of documents and artifacts. Historic

Pl. 118. The façade of the building housing the *Mostra della rivoluzione fascista*.

Pl. 119. The redesigned façade for the *Esposizione dell'aeronautica italiana*.

Pl. 120. The entrance hall to the exhibit.

aircraft, such as the remains of the plane in which the ace Francesco Baracca had been shot down and killed in 1918, the SVA in which D'Annunzio had flown to Vienna the same year, and the S.55X with which Balbo had crossed the North Atlantic, were prominently exhibited – not merely as soulless machines but as sacred relics and "fragments of the *Patria*" that testified to the "impassioned grandeur" of Italian aviation. A solemn space in the center of the first floor of the exhibit, called the "Hall of Icarus," was set aside in which the visitor was invited to reflect on the cost in terms of human lives that humanity had paid for its present aeronautical prowess. Beneath the austere modernist sculpture of the first of flight's martyrs, visitors were invited to read D'Annunzio's defiant words: "A limit to our efforts? There is no limit to our efforts. A limit to our courage? There is no limit to our courage. A limit to our suffering? There is no limit to our suffering. I say that the refusal to *go beyond* [*non più oltre*] is the most insulting blasphemy one can make to God and man."[211]

The effect sought for, and achieved, in this carefully orchestrated show was an appreciation of the sequence of inventiveness, heroic action, martyrdom, and ultimate triumph that constituted the history of Italian aviation. Having passed through the exhibit's rooms, one could not help but feel a sense of national pride and a new appreciation of the role that the Fascist regime had played in transforming Italy into a state that exemplified the Promethean energies of modern times.

The organizers made no attempt to conceal that their intention in creating this exhibition was to pay tribute to the success of the Fascist regime in raising Italian aviation to its present position of power and prestige.[212] The Palazzo dell'Arte's redesigned façade, with a squadron of Italian planes against a blue background and the *fascio littorio*, symbol of Fascism, superimposed upon a map of Europe and Africa, suggested the inseparability of Mussolini's regime from Italy's aerial prowess and imperial future; as did the panel in the style of a photomosaic at the end of the entrance hall, which joined Mussolini's image in the act of addressing a crowd to a *fascio*, a blue wing, and the circular tricolor emblem borne by all

IL VELIVOLO DI BENITO MUSSOLINI

Pl. 121.   The plane in which Mussolini crashed in March 1921.

Italian military aircraft over the defiant words: "This wing that has resumed its flight will not again be broken." The message here was clear: Italian aviation had arisen like a phoenix from the ashes of its neglect by the liberal governing class in the aftermath of the war, and so long as the Fascists were in power it would continue to prosper and develop.

Visitors to the exhibit were also left in no doubt that Italians had been in the forefront of the development of military aviation: an entire room was devoted to the pioneering role that Italian aviators had played in the Libyan War of 1912–13, their heroic exploits, and their primitive experiments in strategic bombing. A painting at the end of the hall portrayed an Arab fleeing in horror at the sight of an Italian plane and contrasted his uncomprehending astonishment with a fragment of a Roman bas-relief that evoked the civilizing mission that Italy had undertaken with the conquest of Libya.[213] There followed a room on the aviators who had won the *medaglio d'oro*, Italy's highest military decoration, and featuring D'Annunzio's exploits; and yet another on the role of Italian aviation in the Great War, reinforcing the sense that no other country could pride itself on such valiant warriors and self-sacrificing martyrs.

As impressive as these early rooms were, however, they were only the prelude to a hall designed to remind visitors that it was Mussolini who was personally responsible for the resurgence of Italian aviation. After passing through the Hall of Icarus, visitors ascended a stairway to the exhibit's second floor where they were confronted by the plane in which Mussolini had crashed in March 1921. The visual logic here was inescapable. Like Icarus, Mussolini was a martyr to the cause of aviation, but one who had miraculously survived. Directly behind Mussolini's aircraft, they saw his words in sharp relief: "I can say with pride that I am an aviator, a title that I earned by flying at a time when few people flew and by crashing; because I was determined to be a pilot at 37 years of age, and, naturally, continuing to fly after having crashed."[214]

The visual narrative of Italian aeronautical triumphs that followed in the remaining rooms, including the one dedicated to Balbo's 1933 cruise, could only be interpreted by the visitor as the direct result of Mussolini's far-reaching vision and his unshakable will to dominate the air.[215] Having appropriated D'Annunzio's program of Italian aeronautical primacy and having disposed of the brilliant lieutenant who had presided over the triumphs of Italian wings and accomplished exploits of which his chief could only dream, Mussolini had no compunction about allowing himself to be put at the center of the story that the regime chose to tell about the history of Italian aviation. As Milan's leading newspaper pointed out, the head of the Fascist government was also the person entrusted with the "resurrection" of Italian wings.[216] Il Duce, Fascism, technology, modernity, and Italy's past grandeur and future imperial glory were all blended in this extraordinary exhibit visually and rhetorically into an indissoluble whole, of which Italian aviation was both an indispensable instrument and a resplendent manifestation. Fascism in the person of its leader had been fused indelibly with flying.

3

A Marriage Made
in Heaven

The sky looks sweet and wears a pretty blue dress, doesn't she, yeah. Well, don't kid yourself. She lives up there, and when she gets you up there, she knocks you down . . . . She sits in your lap and purrs, doesn't she? . . . The vicious, scheming, rotten . . . [bitch].
Clark Gable in *Test Pilot*, 1938

"You mean ground that kid? He'd rather be where he is [dead] than quit [flying]."
Cary Grant in *Only Angels Have Wings*, 1939

For Italians who followed movies, the great hit at the 1938 Venice Film Festival was a film called *Luciano Serra, pilota*. Along with Leni Riefenstahl's stunning documentary about the 1936 Berlin Olympic games, *Olympia*, it shared the Mussolini Cup for the best film and set a box office record for Italian motion pictures in the pre-1945 period, bringing in 7,720,000 lire in revenues at a time when the average Italian film cost a million and a half lire to produce. The film's plot was so popular that it became the basis for a comic strip that ran between January and June 1939 in *Paperino* (Donald Duck), a popular publication of the period issued by the publisher Alberto Mondadori.[1] This is but one of many signs that the campaign to create an aviation culture in Italy, first begun by D'Annunzio and continued by Mussolini and Balbo, had reached beyond the country's elite to achieve a resonance with the Italian masses. Of the many things that Fascism had come to mean to the Italian people, one was primacy in aviation.

To be sure, the success of *Luciano Serra* benefited from the circumstance that the driving force behind it was Vittorio Mussolini, the elder son of Il Duce. The young Mussolini combined an enthusiasm for aviation – at the time he took his license at the age of seventeen he was the youngest pilot in Italy – with an equally passionate love for cinema. Vittorio had recently spent nine months in East Africa as a volunteer airman, where he flew reconnaissance and bombing missions, returning with a silver medal for military valor.[2] Nor certainly did it hurt the film's commercial prospects that its leading actor was the handsome Amedeo Nazzari, a more slender and sensitive version of Errol Flynn, who with this picture would become Italy's preferred male star. An enthusiastic moviegoer and amateur critic, the Duce took a personal interest in the making of his son's film; he warned Vittorio against making it too openly propagandistic, reminding him of the negative precedent set by the Soviets; he visited the set escorted by uniformed and fawning officials; and while there he is even said to have suggested the title finally used – one in sharp contrast to the more poetic "Arriveremo al sole" (We'll make it to the sun) favored by the movie's young director Goffredo Alessandrini. Needless to say, Alessandrini was quick to accept the Duce's suggestion.[3]

Pl. 123. Clark Gable poses defiantly in front of the propeller and engine cowling of the Seversky-Special Two in a publicity photo for MGM's 1938 film *Test Pilot*. At one moment in the picture, Gable attempts to explain what leads test pilots to risk their lives. "We live to lay a floor up there so some day the world can go to sleep on it."

Pl. 124. Nazzari with Lilia Silvi in Nunzio Malasomma's 1940 film, *Dopo divorzieremo* (Later On We'll Get Divorced).

Pl. 125.   Mussolini poses proudly arm-in-arm with his pilot sons, Bruno (left) and Vittorio (right).

Pl. 126.   This poster for *Luciano Serra, pilota* emphasizes the difference between Italian modernity and Abyssinian barbarism.

Luciano Serra, as Vittorio Mussolini commented when giving the Mussolini Cup to Alessandrini at Venice, was indeed a "quintessentially Italian film."[4] It is hard to imagine it being made in any other country. The story of an Italian ace of the First World War who finds himself frustrated in his efforts to pursue a career in "the mortifying conditions" in which aviators found themselves in postwar Italy, *Luciano Serra* translated into cinematic images the main theme of the 1934 Milan aeronautical exhibition, namely the idea that the Fascist regime had rescued aviation from a neglect by the governing liberals that verged on criminality and anti-patriotism.

The beginning of *Luciano Serra* is carefully set in 1921, one year before the Fascists come to power. Its protagonist is "a born aviator, unwilling to tolerate any discipline, a dreamer whom the coming of peace has not demobilized."[5] Unable to make a living taking tourists for rides in the dilapidated seaplane he has managed to buy with money earned during the war and yet unwilling to give up flying in order to join his wealthy father-in-law's textile firm, Luciano is abandoned by his wife, who returns to her father's villa with their young son Aldo. With no prospects in Italy, Luciano emigrates to Latin America where he has been led to believe that he can find employment as an airmail pilot. There too he encounters humiliation, an experience with which the Italian film audience, many of whom had relatives living in the New World, could easily identify.

Ten years pass. Luciano has become a well-known aviator in Latin America, but he has never ceased yearning for Italy and his family. Offered an opportunity to make a nonstop flight from Rio to Rome by an unscrupulous newspaper man, Luciano leaps at the opportunity to return to his homeland and restore his honor. His self-esteem suffers a blow when he discovers that he is being used as a pawn by the newspaper syndicate to boost circulation; his cynical patrons have no real interest in him or his flight. Despite stormy conditions over the Atlantic and an aircraft that has not been properly prepared for the ordeal, Luciano insists on departing and disappears into the turbulent night. So far as his family and the world know, he has perished, yet another victim of the perilous South Atlantic.

Yet we soon discover that Luciano is not dead. He reappears five years later, under a false name, as a volunteer for service in the Italian East African Army. There, redeemed from his sordid life as an emigrant by the providential coming of the Abyssinian war, Luciano is able, as a result of an improbable coincidence, to save the life of his young son Aldo, who has become a pilot in the Italian Air Force. Luciano loses his own life in order to rescue his son and the film ends with a solemn ceremony in which Aldo's commanding officer and his father's old friend pins on Aldo's chest Italy's highest decoration, given posthumously to his father for his heroism and devotion to duty.

Italian critics were lavish in their praise for *Luciano Serra* and the group of young men who had made it. They appreciated its narrative style; the spontaneity with which its characters related to one another; the sensitivity and understatement with which Amedeo Nazzari had brought to life the appealing figure of Luciano Serra; and above all the sobriety with which the story of a believable Italian hero was told. "Here the hero is not an exceptional being, a knightly example, or a living allegory." He is instead a man of the people, "a child of the soil from which he comes and of his time." Like "the humble," he serves instinctively. It is because of this that he acts heroically.[6]

Some critics also went out of their way, either explicitly or implicitly, to distinguish *Luciano Serra* from American aviation films, of which a recent example, MGM's *Test Pilot*, was on display at the Venice Film Festival. As Vittorio Mussolini explained in an article he published in *L'Ala d'Italia* shortly before his film's premier, the Americans had provided the Italians with all kinds of aviation films, but "our intention has been to make something more serious and real . . . a strong human drama that will seize the spectator and move him, regardless of the class to which he belongs."[7] Asked by the editors of *L'Ala d'Italia* to compare *Luciano Serra* and *Test Pilot* after their screening in Venice, a well-known Italian filmmaker, Romolo Marcellini, suggested that the powerful emotions that *Test Pilot* had sought to evoke emerged more vividly in Vittorio Mussolini's film. In the end, Marcellini said, it was not *Test Pilot* that had captured the admiration of viewers at the Venice Festival but *Luciano Serra*, which reached its climax in "the skies of the Ethiopian War." This critic predicted that a new cycle of aviation films was beginning in which the Italians would take the lead.[8]

Yet this prediction turned out to be little more than wishful thinking. Leaving aside the impact that these two films may have had on the audiences that saw them and the very different type of messages they sent, no comparison of *Test Pilot* and *Luciano Serra* could fail to point out the immense lead the Americans held in the technique of making aviation films. Indeed, there were few flying scenes in the Italian film, and the most impressive one was taken from the Ministry of Aeronautics' documentary, *Vertigine*. In the fall of 1938, many of the greatest of American aviation films lay ahead; and the coming of the Second World War would open new perspectives on an already well-established genre in which Americans moviemakers had played a pioneering role and one that they would continue to dominate throughout the twentieth century.

★   ★   ★

Cinema and aviation – their marriage seemed made in heaven. Both technologies had been born in the belle époque, those years of extended serial innovation between 1895 and 1905 when the Western genii escaped from the bottle and the fantastic became part of the fabric of everyday life. Moreover, filmmaking and flying shared more than the accident of their simultaneous appearance; both aimed at nothing less than the liberation of humankind from the constraints of everyday reality, and both were forms of escape.[9]

And what better place for such a marriage to be consummated than in the fantasy land of Southern California. For flyers, Los Angeles was as close to paradise as they were likely to come. The center of a burgeoning aviation industry in the 1920s, the City of the Angels offered sunny skies and extended horizons, wide-open spaces in the case of forced landings, and more than fifty airfields, stretching from Venice in the west to March in the east and from Metropolitan (now Van Nuys) to the north to Long Beach in the south.[10] Like filmmakers, aviators came to Los Angeles for the weather, the variegated landscape, the freedom to do what they wanted, and the money that was there waiting to be made. Both Hollywood and the airplane were symbols of modernity: how could the first not embrace the second, and seek to translate the experience of flight to the screen?

But though Hollywood quickly learned how to exploit the airplane as a means of attracting audiences to its theaters and achieved a mastery of the technology required for photographing flight, what would become known as the aviation film during the 1930s only emerged slowly from its cocoon; and even when it did the genres that defined and confined filmmaking made it difficult for Hollywood to tell the aviation story as it developed between the wars. The result was a product that could dazzle and move the senses – a source of thrills as reviewers never tired of commenting; but also one that too often skated across the surface of events and trivialized motivations that were destined to transform the way that Americans and others lived their lives.

In the early 1920s, the inclination of the Hollywood studios was to use the airplane as a pretext for circus-like stunts or as the equivalent of an airborne horse. Action-filled pictures like *The Great Train Robbery* and *The Skyman*, which featured Ormer Locklear's wing walking and leaps from one aircraft to another, were guaranteed to keep audiences on the edge of their seat. Dozens of now forgotten aerial Westerns were made starring popular stars Tom Mix and Hoot Gibson.[11] The stories of these movies were so predictable that they understandably failed to attract the period's greatest actors. It's telling that even a comedian as

Pl. 127.   The powerful and flamboyant producer-director Cecil B. DeMille in 1919. DeMille learned how to fly during the First World War, built two airfields in West Los Angeles, and founded the Mercury Aviation Company, which offered a variety of services, including flying lessons, "advertising from the sky," and scheduled passenger flights between Los Angeles and Bakersfield, Fresno, Long Beach, Pasadena, and Catalina Island.

Pl. 128.   Lieutenant Ormer Locklear in a publicity photo for his first Hollywood picture, *The Great Air Robbery* (1919)

Pl. 129.   Locklear wing-walking. Locklear was killed in 1920 while doing a nighttime spin during the making of *The Skyman*, the second of his Hollywood films.

enamored of modern machinery as Buster Keaton was never tempted to take to the skies. Not until 1927 would the first real aviation film appear; and this was as a response to signs of a resurgence of interest in the First World War, and more specifically to the commercial success of two war films that appeared in 1925–6, *The Big Parade* and *What Price Glory?*

Made in 1926 but not put into general release until 1929, *Wings* was the first and certainly one of the greatest of aviation films, if one means by aviation film a motion picture that sets out to capture the experience of flight and communicate it to an audience. Though clearly a product of the silent era, it preserves a freshness, a sense of innocence, and a power to astonish and move that have only grown with the passage of time. It is a film that has aged like a great wine. To see it today is to be transported to a period when flying was still a miracle and a source of thrills, not yet an inescapable and troubling fact of modern life.

The story of the making of *Wings* reminds us of what a confluence of factors and talented people is necessary to create that rarest of occurrences: greatness in a work of entertainment aimed at a mass audience. The original idea for *Wings* sprang from the head of a clever and ambitious young journalist, John Monk Saunders, who would later go on to write many Hollywood aviation films. Handsome, athletic, and overly fond of drink, Saunders had left the University of Washington to join the Army Air Service in 1917. Assigned to teach aerobatics in Florida, he never saw action in France. He later told his wife, the actress Fay Wray, that on the night of the Armistice he went out to the airfield, leaned against the wing of his plane, and wept at the thought that he would never have the opportunity to fly in France and become an ace.[12]

Saunders's loss would be Hollywood's gain. With a sense of resignation to an unkind fate, the frustrated pilot returned to college, received his degree, and won a Rhodes Scholarship to Oxford, where he spent more time drinking and listening to the stories of returning war veterans than he did over his books. Consciously identifying himself with a "lost generation" unable to return to anything resembling normal life, he set out to make a career in New York. There he found a place on the editorial staff of the *New York Tribune* and then was appointed to an associate editorship on *American Magazine*. His first short story, listed as one of the best of 1923, was bought by Famous Players-Lasky and made into a film, *Too Many Kisses*. Through this picture, Saunders met Jesse Lasky and his wife Bessie, who was much taken by his charm; and she began what would become a lengthy affair with the dashing young writer. Lasky was at the time second in command at Paramount behind Adolph Zukor, hence a man of considerable wealth and power in the quickly expanding motion picture business. Saunders became a regular fixture in the Laskys' many households and was in a position to suggest to Jesse in 1926 the idea for a film that he promised would do for the air war what *The Big Parade* had done for the war in the trenches.[13]

Lasky sounded out his associates in Paramount's head office in New York and reported to Saunders that they were willing to proceed with the project, assuming that the Department of War would offer its full cooperation, as it had done in the case of *The Big Parade*. Saunders left that very night for Washington, where he succeeded in pitching the project to a trio of senior army generals whose support would be indispensable. Two weeks later, Secretary of War Dwight F. Davis offered the army's cooperation on several conditions. One was that Paramount would carry $10,000 worth of insurance on every army man who worked in the film. Another was that the army's role in the making of the picture would be kept out of the newspapers insofar as possible, so as not to suggest that it was being made to intimidate foreign countries. Still another was that the movie would not be released until the War Department had granted its approval.[14] Lasky convinced his associates in New York to accept these conditions, with the understanding that he would take full responsibility should the project fail.[15]

As the recently appointed head of the West Coast division of Paramount, B. P. Schulberg was put in charge of *Wings*. He chose as his producer Lucien Hubbard, an experienced studio supervisor and a veteran of making Westerns, who would be responsible for keeping

the film on track and within its budget. For his director, he turned to William Wellman, whose most important assets were the fact that Schulberg liked him and knew that Wellman had been an aviator who had flown combat missions in France during the final phase of the war. Wellman's obscurity is suggested by his salary: at a time when up-and-coming directors like John Ford and Victor Fleming were earning between $1,500 and $1,750 per week and established figures like Ernst Lubitsch were making $175,000 a picture, Wellman had only recently been raised to $250 per week.[16] Yet Wellman's low standing in the hierarchy of Hollywood directors does not seem to have given him pause in accepting a job that would require him to order about movie stars, studio executives, and army generals, and that was likely to make or break his film career. Tall and wiry with a shock of black hair, a short temper, and a salty tongue, Wellman was a tough guy who brooked no nonsense from anyone.

Today Schulberg's choice of the untested twenty-eight-year-old Wellman as the director of a two-million-dollar epic seems like a gigantic gamble. It was perhaps less so at the time when the directors were regarded more as technicians than as *auteurs*. Hubbard, after all, was presumably in charge of the movie. Nonetheless, Schulberg's decision to put the project in Wellman's hands would turn out, in retrospect, to be inspired. The young director brought to the task energy, unstoppable determination, unsuspected managerial skills, first-hand knowledge of what the Western Front had looked like from the ground and the air, and an uncompromising determination to recapture the experience of aerial combat during the final phase of the First World War. Even the financial people from New York, while grumbling at the budget overrun, came to recognize that Wellman was making a film unlike any other that had yet been released.[17] Events would prove them right. *Wings* became a huge box office success and won the first Academy Award for best picture, though the lowly Wellman would not be invited to the ceremony.

With the aid of the War Department, Wellman assembled the equivalent of a small army and a major air force at Old Camp Stanley, the Air Service Ground School at Brooks Field, and the advanced flying school at Kelly Field, all within easy striking distance of San Antonio, Texas. Wellman later claimed that the general in command of the army troops that had been put at his disposal had two "monumental hatreds": fliers and movie people.[18] He

qualified on both counts; but having served in the military Wellman realized that ultimately his highly ranked nemesis would have no choice but to follow the orders he received from his superiors in Washington, which were to offer Paramount the army's full cooperation. Nevertheless, the army airmen and the foot soldiers were soon at one another's throats, while Wellman tried to mediate their differences.

Wellman had other obstacles to overcome. Of the three leading actors assigned to the picture by Paramount, the two male leads, Buddy Rogers and Richard Arlen, were relatively unknown contract players who had yet to make their mark. Arlen had flown during the war with the Canadian Flying Corps; Rogers was eager to become a pilot. Beyond this, their qualifications for a major movie epic were yet to be established. Indeed, neither would go on to distinguished film careers. The one male actor in the film who would achieve stardom – Gary Cooper – made only a fleeting, if memorable, appearance. The feminine lead Clara Bow, the only member of the cast with demonstrated star power, presented Wellman with problems of her own. According to Wellman, all the young actors in the movie fell in love with her, not to mention Saunders and a couple of army flyers. Recalling the situation over three decades later, he added that: "if you had known her, you could understand why."[19]

Wellman had at his disposal the army's best fighter pilots from Selfridge Field in Michigan. Nonetheless, for the film's most dangerous flying scenes he turned to veteran professional Hollywood stunt pilots, like Frank Tomick, Ross Cooke, Frank Clarke, and Dick Grace. Tomick, a former Army Air Force instructor known for his precision, was in charge of the flying sequences; he was assisted by Sterling Campbell, who had flown with the Royal Flying Corps during the war. Seated in rear cockpits and not visible on the screen, Tomick and Cooke flew the planes in which Rogers and Arlen were photographed. A daredevil who prided himself on doing stunts that no one else was crazy enough to undertake, Grace's job was to stage several intentional crashes, critical to the movie's plot. Wellman had warned him that it wouldn't be easy because, among other stunts, he would have to do a dead stick landing within fifty feet of the cameramen, who would be dispersed and hidden in the area where he was supposed to come to rest.[20] In one sequence, he had to hit the ground in No Man's Land in such a way that his Spad would turn over on its back. He missed the balsam posts that had been placed strategically to ease the impact of the crash and two cedar posts pierced the fuselage, one passing eleven inches behind his head.[21] On another occasion, Grace crashed a D-7 Fokker into the ground with such force that his chest belt broke and his head broke through the instrument panel. It was not until the next day that he discov-

Pl. 132. A poster for *Wings* that features the charms of Clara Bow, the movie's only star.

Pl. 133.   Gary Cooper would quickly ascend to stardom after this brief scene. Wellman later wrote that to make that scene effective Cooper had to have "something unusual about him, that indescribable thing called motion picture personality . . . Gable had it, Colman, Tracy, Bogart . . . and there are a few more, but there are a lot of fine actors that haven't got it and never will have it. Cooper had it."

ered that he had broken his neck.[22] Dick Grace would survive a life of crashes and danger-ous stunts to die in bed. Not all the pilots who participated in the making of *Wings* were so lucky. At least one army pilot was killed while flying, and several others were badly injured.[23]

For all the risks taken by the stuntmen, the unsung heroes of *Wings* were the cine-matographers; it was they who captured the action in the air, and it is a miracle that none were killed or injured.[24] Wellman and Hubbard chose Harry Perry to serve as their director of photography. A veteran of Westerns, Perry was a master of the Akeley camera that had been designed by its inventor to capture the movement of African wild life. Its advantage lay in a gyroscopic system that allowed it to be panned and tilted in all directions without the blurring that was common in ordinary cameras.[25] Before production began, Perry made two trips to Texas during which he scouted locations and made tests in the air. He designed camera mounts to be placed on the planes and electrical devices, so that the stunt pilots could activate their battery-driven cameras when the moment for shooting came. Remote-controlled motor-driven cameras were installed in front of the cockpits, so that the faces of the pilots could be photographed in the course of aerial combat; or they were placed behind them, to give spectators the view that pilots had as they dived toward the ground. Nothing similar to it in its realism had ever been seen. As one young viewer of *Wings* later remembered, it was scenes like these that set his "blood racing" and "aircooled" his innards. "From 2,000 feet the theater nosed down in a steep dive toward a narrow bridge over which a regiment of infantry was straggling. The bridge swelled toward the edges of the screen, and details of the river, the bridge, and the panic-stricken soldiers rushed up at us while we held that plummeting dive. The theater 'pulled out' with what looked like inches to spare. The scene switched to a rear view past the tail, and that shrank the bridge once more to a speck."[26]

Perry recruited a group of talented cameramen that included veterans like his brother Paul Perry, Faxon M. Dean, Buddy Williams, and E. Burton Steene. Several youngsters, like Russell Harlan, Ernest Lazlo, and Bill Abbott, who would become among Hollywood's most famous cinematographers in coming years, also served on the camera crew.[27] The sto-ries these cinematographers later recounted are hair-raising. Burton Steene was assigned by Perry to photograph the bombing of a French village. Along with his Akeley and three Eyemo automatic cameras, he was placed in a small compartment that contained twelve one-hundred-pound bombs of TNT. Harry Perry, Faxon Dean, and Paul Perry were shoot-ing the scene in bombers from above. When the pilot was about the drop his bombs, he yanked on a thin rope that was attached to Steene's left arm, so that he would know that in fifteen seconds he should start cranking.

Pl. 134. Stunt pilot Frank Tomick enters the cockpit of a modified Fokker D.VIII during the filming of *Wings*.

Pl. 135. Dick Grace, the prince of Hollywood crash pilots in 1928.

Pl. 136. Wellman (third from the left) with his stunt flyers. Frank Tomick is on the left and Dick Grace is third from the right. John Monk Saunders is to the far right, dressed considerably more elegantly than the others.

Pl. 137. Harry Perry in the rear cockpit of the Martin bomber used as the camera plane in *Wings*.

Captain Stribling gave the two yanks . . . Looking through the finder, it was my job to grind and pick up the bombs as they dropped an inch or two from my cranking arm, keep them in the center of the picture until each one exploded. There was dynamite planted in the village to augment the explosions. Down they went, all in a row; they slipped out of the compartment like grease for I did not hear or see them until I picked them up in my finder. It was a wonderful sight to see these death-dealing messengers speeding down – the terrible explosions took place right on schedule . . . I do not know how far the concussion lifted the ship, but for several seconds it shook and trembled with

Pl. 138. Dick Grace crashes into a Texas farmhouse. This was one of several airplanes Grace destroyed during the making of *Wings*.

Pl. 139. Jack (Buddy Rogers) discovers that he has shot down his friend.

Pl. 140. Jack embraces his dead friend David (Richard Arlen) toward the end of *Wings*.

each explosion until I thought it might possibly be out of control. The sensation of being rocked and thrown about in the air in a giant bomber a scant 600 feet above the ground while dropping 1200 pounds of T.N.T. is a thrill not often given to a man. In my cramped quarters it would have been very difficult if not impossible to get away with my parachute, but my confidence in the pilot kept me in repose.[28]

Risky stunts like these produced unforgettable images. John Monk Saunders's story was another matter. If it seems familiar, it is because it falls neatly into the tripartite scheme that was characteristic of most of the war memoirs and autobiographies written in this period. The film begins in an unidentified small town in America where all is sun, innocence, and laughter. Two young men – David (Richard Arlen) and Jack (Buddy Rogers) – vie for the affection of the rich and spoiled Sylvia (Jobyna Ralston). The pretty and vivacious girl who lives next door to Jack, Mary (Clara Bow) tries in vain to attract his attention. America's entry into the war shatters the peace of this provincial paradise, and the action shifts to an army training camp where the two male protagonists begin their ordeal and, after a bracing fight, become fast friends. Assigned to flight school, they witness the death of a fellow cadet (played briefly but unforgettably by the young Gary Cooper).

Having survived their training, the two young aviators then find themselves in France, where they are put to the test of combat. Jack's friendship with David suffers a serious blow when the two fall out over a photograph that Sylvia gave Jack before his departure for military training; unknown to him, the photograph bears an inscription, stating Sylvia's love for David. To spare Jack's feelings, David destroys the photograph before his friend can see it. This act of generosity, however, has the effect of infuriating Jack who remains unaware of its motivation. Sent out on dawn patrol, David is shot down by the Germans and captured. Believing that David is dead, a repentant Jack goes forth to avenge him. In the meantime, David has escaped his captors and commandeered a German plane. Mistaking David for a German, Jack shoots him down and sends him spiraling to his death. The film ends with Jack's return to his hometown where he is given a hero's welcome and eventually forgiven by David's mother for having killed her son. Yet Jack has not escaped unscathed: now white-haired, he has lost his prewar innocence and will never be the same. The subtitles drive home the point, telling us that "He went to war a boy and returned a man." Yet the semblance of a happy ending is rescued when Jack is reunited with Mary and reciprocates the love that she has patiently nurtured for him.

In terms of its plot, *Wings* is only peripherally about aviation. There is no indication in the first part of the film that either David or Jack is affected by the flying craze that infected so many young Americans during the years before 1914. Nor is it their love for flight that binds David and Jack together; they become friends before learning how to fly. Forty minutes of *Wings* pass before the two protagonists get off the ground. Moreover, when Jack returns home, he gives no hint of wanting to continue his flying career. Now grounded, he drives off happily with Mary in his car, the "Shooting Star." To be grounded in later aviation films will be a fate worse than death.

Yet though the critics were unimpressed by Saunders's story, which they dismissed as no more than an "average tale" inferior to that of some of the war movies that had preceded it, *Wings* contained elements that anticipated what would become the dominating themes of the aviation movie. One was the danger represented to aviators by women. Through no intention of her own, Sylvia comes between Jack and David and indirectly causes David's death. The triad of two men and a woman would become a standard fixture of the Hollywood aviation film. The woman often adds to the perils the aviators must face. A decade later in *Test Pilot*, Clark Gable would be given dialogue that makes the equation between women and death explicit: "The sky looks sweet and wears a pretty dress, doesn't she, yeah. Well, don't kid yourself. She lives up there, and when she gets you up there, she knocks you down . . . She sits in your lap and purrs, doesn't she? . . . The vicious, scheming, rotten [bitch] . . ."

Fatal crashes of attractive characters for whom the audience has been made to feel sympathy are also central to the genre. After Cadet White (Gary Cooper) dies in a collision, David and Jack are assigned to pack up his belongings, including a chocolate bar he left behind. Later, after David dies, Jack must gather his things, including his stuffed bear, and carry them back to David's parents. Because of the violence of the impact when an airplane hits the ground and the fiery explosion with which so many crashes ends, often all that remains of the dead aviator are a few objects, usually of little if any value. These objects become sacred relics, to be treasured by those left behind, and reinforce the sense that the community of aviators is a quasi-religious brotherhood with its martyrs and its saints.

Most important of all, *Wings* sets a new standard for the realism and choreography of its aerial scenes. The airplanes themselves became protagonists of the picture, the performers of a deadly dance in the sky. Wellman was after authenticity, and he got it. Contrary to the usual practice, he insisted that all close-ups of pilots had to be shot in the air.[29] This meant placing heavy cameras behind the actors and throwing off the center of gravity of the planes. "There were many scenes," Lucien Hubbard remembered, "where we shot over Arlen's head, as he dived to earth. You put that much weight in an unaccustomed place, and you're courting a crash."[30] Even sophisticated reviewers wondered how Wellman had staged the scene in which Dick Grace, impersonating a German pilot, crashed his plane on takeoff, plowing into the ground after having risen to a height of twenty feet. Wellman himself did some of the stunts when his stuntmen and extras thought they were too dangerous.[31] For the scene of the final battle of St. Mihiel, while discharging a creeping artillery barrage from a hundred-foot tower, Wellman hit the wrong button by mistake and blew two men into the air. A few minutes later, a pursuit plane skimmed the helmets of the soldiers on the ground and crashed. When Wellman arrived at the scene, he saw the pilot leaning against an ambulance with a bandage around his head. "He was dazed, but not from the crash, and I suddenly realized that in all my planning I had forgotten one terribly important factor, the human element. This pilot had flown at the front. He had been decorated. He had flown missions just like this one. For five minutes it was not 1926 to him; it was 1918. He just stuck his hand out and said, 'I'm sorry.'"[32]

Paramount took its time in releasing *Wings* to the general public. The original fourteen reels shown at the premier in San Antonio in the spring of 1927 were cut to twelve before it opened in August at New York's Criterion Theater, with a dedication to Charles Lindbergh and "those young warriors of the sky whose wings are forever folded about them."[33] There it was shown in two parts, the first sixty-five minutes and the second seventy-four minutes in length. The aerial combat scenes were projected in a process called Magnascope, which increased the screen to four times its normal size.[34] A recording of sound effects played behind the screen provided an audio background to the dog fights, producing the drone of aircraft engines (one sound for the Allies, another for the Germans), the swish of propellers, the whirl of airplanes hurtling to the ground, the rat-a-tat-tat of machine-gun fire, the blast of exploding bombs and shells, and even the scream of a dying German pilot. A musical score for symphony orchestra was commissioned to accompany the film, and the individual prints were in part hand-colored, so that the sky was blue and machine-gun fire and bomb and artillery explosions appeared as red flashes. After a triumphant twelve-week run at the Criterion, the picture was shortened and supplied with an RCA sound track, incorporating the score but without dialogue. Not until January 1929, almost two years after its premier, was a silent version of *Wings* put into national release.[35] One measure of its popularity is that the sound craze, then sweeping through the film industry, did nothing to undermine its success.

Wings entered the select company of "road show films" that included *Birth of a Nation*, *Way Down East*, *The Ten Commandments*, *The Covered Wagon*, *The Big Parade*, and *Ben-Hur*. It was the highest-grossing film of 1928 and fully deserved its designation as "The Big Parade of the Air." Reviewers marveled at the realism of its crashes and thought that the scenes of aerial combat were "so magnificent, so impressive, so thrilling, that it is doubtful if one could feel more excited even if one were to watch actual aeroplane battles."[36]

This impression of having seen a true and thrilling re-creation of the war is no doubt what most viewers took away from *Wings*, and what kept the audiences coming and paying top dollar for over a year and a half. But from our perspective today, *Wings* has more to offer. While the last part of the picture lays bare the tragic side of war and the slaughter of innocent youth — and thus can be related to the literature of disillusionment that began to appear in the late 1920s — Wellman makes no attempt to hide the war's other aspects: the exhilaration of enlistment and training; the comradeship war inspires; the delight in downing other aircraft and killing the enemy; the fun of leave in Paris; the hero's welcome Jack receives when he returns to his home town. No sentimentalist, Wellman accepts war, without in any way romanticizing it. When David dies, a French officer comments fatalistically: "C'est la guerre," a phrase Wellman had heard frequently while in France. A sad French mother standing by with a child clinging to her dress, who witnesses the scene, suggests the likelihood that what has happened to David's mother may one day happen to her. It is this many-sided approach to war that gives the film its sense of reality. War is exciting. War is terrible. War makes fools of people. War ends in tragedy for some, in triumph for others. Those who triumph are not in any way better than those who die under absurd conditions, as David does, killed by his best friend. War will happen again. *C'est la guerre.*

★   ★   ★

There was one admirer of *Wings* whose reaction to the film went beyond the passive enjoyment of most viewers: he was rash enough to think that he could improve upon it and create an even more realistic version of aerial combat in the First World War. This might have remained nothing but a dream, had the person not been Howard Hughes, a very young man of unlimited ambition whose vast inherited fortune gave him the luxury of pursuing his fantasies, one of which was making movies, the other flying.

Tall, lanky, handsome, possessed of an offbeat charisma difficult to define, Hughes was not yet twenty years old when he arrived in Hollywood in the late summer of 1925 accompanied by his young bride, Ella.[37] With no background in the theater or cinema and an uneven education in a long series of private schools, he launched himself precipitously into the film business with predictable results. Hughes's first effort to produce a movie, *Swell Hogan*, ran far over budget and, when finished, was so bad that he wisely decided not to release it. But the young Texan refused to be discouraged. Determined to conquer Hollywood and egged on by the continuing opposition of his family who considered him irresponsible, Hughes hired a veteran filmmaker, Marshall Neilan, who provided him with a modest success.[38] The theme of *Everybody's Acting* – five actors who adopt a baby girl who grows up to be a beautiful woman – may not have excited Hughes, but it was distributed by Paramount, one of Hollywood's most prestigious studios, and compensated for the loss of $80,000 he had incurred in making *Swell Hogan*. Hughes had established a foothold in the Hollywood world where, then as now, success was measured by box office receipts.

A chance encounter at the Ambassador Hotel in early 1927 with Lewis Milestone, a talented young director who had served in the aerial camera section of the U.S. Army Signal Corps during the First World War, sent Hughes off on an even more promising trajectory. Taken by Milestone's charm, intrigued by his stories about his wartime service in the air arm, and aware that he had much to learn from him, Hughes signed the director to a three-year contract. The first product of their collaboration, *Two Arabian Knights*, was a comedy set during the First World War that delighted both audiences and critics because of its strong cast, consisting of William Boyd, Louis Wolheim, and Mary Astor, and its fanciful story, which reached its unlikely climax in the escape of the movie's protagonists from the Arabian peninsula. The film earned Hughes a handsome profit and won Milestone the first Academy Award for the best director of a comedy.[39]

By the time that *Two Arabian Knights* was released in October 1927, Hughes was already immersed in a new and immensely more ambitious project, a picture about aerial combat during the First World War that was meant not to equal, but to surpass the authenticity of *Wings*. Hughes was as fascinated by aviation as he was by motion pictures; but, curiously, he made no serious effort to learn to fly until the aftermath of the Lindbergh flight. Perhaps he was too busy with the refinement of his golf game, the pursuit of beautiful actresses, and his efforts to teach himself the movie business. Still, for someone who would develop such a passion for flight it is curious that he had made no effort to take to the air earlier.

For a man who later went on to become one of the most famous aviators of the 1930s, there is little known about Hughes's flight training; there is no doubt, however, that it coincided with his commitment to the making of *Hell's Angels*.[40] A man who did not believed in half-hearted enterprises, Hughes understood that he could not make the kind of picture he wanted without knowing how to fly. No one can accuse the young Hughes of a lack of ambition. It was in this period that he confessed to his business manager, accountant, and adviser Noah Dietrich that he intended to be "the greatest golfer in the world, the finest film producer in Hollywood, the greatest pilot in the world, the richest man in the world."[41]

The idea for the plot of *Hell's Angels* was given to Hughes by Marshall Neilan. Neilan also provided the initial treatment, which revolved around two brothers in the Royal Flying Corps who were rivals for the affection of a seductive and amoral English socialite.[42] It was understood from the beginning that Neilan would direct; one can only wonder what would have happened to the project had Hughes turned instead to Milestone, who went on in 1930 to direct one of the most memorable movies ever made about the First World War, *All Quiet on the Western Front*. It is hard to imagine two films that represented more radically different approaches to the memory and visual re-creation of the war.[43]

In any case, long before the movie was scheduled to go into production Neilan stormed off the set in protest against Hughes's interference. Dressed jauntily in riding breeches, a leather

Pl. 141. Howard Hughes at the premiere of *Two Arabian Knights* in 1927.

123

Pl. 142. Ben Lyon (left) and James Hall with Greta Nissen in the silent version of *Hell's Angels*.

Pl. 143. Harry Perry explains the choreography of a flying scene to Hughes' stunt pilots.

flight jacket, and shiny knee-high boots, the increasingly self-confident Hughes had made clear that he was no longer satisfied to finance pictures made by others; he intended to shape their content and their casting down to the most minute details. The next director Hughes chose, Luther Reed, though himself a novice, was no more willing to tolerate Hughes's meddling; he suggested, sarcastically, that if his employer knew so much, perhaps he should direct the "god damn thing" himself. To the surprise of Reed, Hughes called his bluff and said that he would.

From this point, everyone involved with the project realized that Hughes was the man in charge. Chosen to play the two brothers were Ben Lyon and James Hall, two popular stars of the period borrowed from Paramount and Warners respectively. The role of the sexy and promiscuous socialite was given to Greta Nissen, a statuesque Norwegian blonde whose limited English was heavily accented. At a time when movies had no spoken dialogue, Nissen's lack of English was more than counterbalanced by the aerodynamics of her figure. Hughes's wisest decision was to hire Harry Perry as his cinematographer. Perry brought with him E. Burton Steene, who had worked with him on *Wings*, and appointed as his chief assistant a young cameraman, Elmer Dyer, who would have a long and distinguished career in aviation films.

In view of the extraordinary number of people who were involved in making *Hell's Angels*, it is surprising how little we know about the details of the role that Hughes played in its production. There exists a rich photographic record of the making of the movie; but it consists mainly of shots of the stars, pilots, and photographers in high spirits and visibly enjoying their work. Hughes himself appears less often than one would expect in these photographs, and when we see him, he does not seem to be participating in the camaraderie of the crew. He looks aloof, distanced, and there is every reason to believe that he was. Certainly, he had ample reason for feeling distracted. He may have been worrying over his mounting bills or brooding over his disintegrating marriage with his wife Ella; or, in the later stages of *Hell's Angels*, he may have been thinking of the beautiful actress he had recently encountered and fallen in love with, the still married but very available and expensive Billie Dove. To the crew of *Hell's Angels*, Hughes appeared, in turn, a good sport who was willing to exchange practical jokes, and at the same time someone who was eccentric to the point of craziness and unreasonably demanding.[44]

A true son of Texas, everything Hughes did was on a grand scale. Drawing on the financial reserves of the Hughes Tool Company, he spent more than half a million dollars in assembling a fleet of over forty airplanes, including six authentic German Fokker D-7s, three British S. E. 5s, and five Thomas Morse Scouts, which were modified to look like British

Pl. 144.   Al Wilson (on the left), Roscoe Turner (second from left), and Ben Lyon (on the pony), along with other stunt pilots, have fun during the filming of *Hell's Angels*. Wilson would later be blamed for bailing out of Turner's Sikorsky and leaving his mechanic to die in the crash.

Pl. 145.   Hughes on the set of *Hell's Angels*.

Pl. 146.   Billie Dove in the late 1920s.

Pl. 147.   The Howard Hughes air force assembles for a publicity shot.

Pl. 148.   Hughes and other film personalities, including the MGM star Wallace Beery, himself a flyer (second from the left), greet Turner upon his arrival in Burbank with the Sikorsky. Like Beery, Greta Nissen (to the right of Turner) is careful to look at the camera. She would later be dropped from the film and replaced by Jean Harlow.

Sopwith Camels. To fly these planes and simulate aerial combat during the First World War, Hughes hired practically the entire corps of Hollywood stunt pilots at their going wage of $200 a week.[45] When his agents were unable to locate a German Gotha, necessary for one of the final flying scenes in which the two brothers attack a German ammunition dump, Hughes convinced the flamboyant aerial showman Roscoe Turner to fly his Sikorsky S-29A, then the largest plane flying in America, from the East Coast to California at a cost of over $10,000.[46] Whereas Wellman had used army pilots, aircraft, and airfields, Hughes set out to create his own infrastructure, at a cost of $400,000. To serve as his base of operations, he leased a tract of land in the San Fernando Valley, northwest of what is today Van Nuys Airport, and christened it Caddo Field, after his film company. A German air base was built further out in the Valley in Chatsworth; and a British flying school was simulated at the modest airfield in Inglewood that became the nucleus for what is now Los Angeles's principal airport, LAX. At various times, numerous other fields in California were used, ranging from

Pl. 149.   Hughes and Perry plan dogfight maneuvers.

San Diego in the south to Oakland in the north. A crew of thirty mechanics under Harry Reynolds was recruited to service the planes and keep them in the air. In October 1928, when cumulous clouds were lacking in the San Fernando Valley to serve as a backdrop for the culminating air battle between the British and the Germans, Hughes transported his crew of a hundred people and forty planes to Oakland where they spent four months at a cost of $5,000 per day in what would be remembered as one of the most expensive location shots in Hollywood history.[47] For what in retrospect appears *Hell's Angels'* most memorable sequence, a Zeppelin attack against London in which a huge airship is rammed and blown out of the sky by a British pursuit pilot, Hughes paid $460,000 to have two sixty-feet replicas built in a huge hangar on what is today the site of the Santa Anita Race Track in Arcadia, California under the guidance of a former Zeppelin engineer.[48]

The making of *Hell's Angels* brought out what was best and worst in Howard Hughes. His dedication to the project and the passion he felt for it were constantly in evidence; he worked day and night, gave unstintingly of himself, and expected his employees to do the same. Hughes was omnipresent: he oversaw the construction of the airfields and the hangars, supervised the pilots, helped to choreograph their dogfights, directed the camera planes from his own aircraft, participated in all the casting, wrote the checks, and found the money necessary to keep the film rolling, despite the mounting costs. One measure of his energy is that while making *Hell's Angels*, his film company released two other commercially successful movies, one of which, *The Racket*, a gangster movie directed by Milestone, was nominated for an Academy award as the most original and artistic production in 1927–8.

In the fall of 1929, when *Hell's Angels* was nearing completion, Hughes was forced to face an unpleasant fact: the era of silent films was over. He had invested millions of dollars in what was quickly becoming an obsolescent technology. Another producer might well have decided to cut his losses and release the film as it was, counting on the spectacular air sequences to attract audiences. Not Hughes: instead he resolved to re-shoot his picture in sound and took a huge gamble by replacing his leading lady, Greta Nissen, with an untested actress, the eighteen-year-old Jean Harlow. Sensing his own shortcomings as a director of actors as

Pl. 150. Harlow during the ball sequence with Lyon (left) and Hall (right). Though a novice actress, Harlow had already mastered the art of striking a provocative pose.

Pl. 151. Director James Whale in 1929. No one could ever accuse Whale of lacking style.

opposed to pilots, Hughes also brought in two new figures to ensure the successful transformation of *Hell's Angels* into a sound picture. In June 1929 Hughes hired Howard Esterbrook to write the dialogue for the new version of his picture. Realizing that he needed someone capable of directing actors who were going to be required to speak on the screen, Hughes was alerted to the availability of James Whale, an Englishman known for his success with the First World War play *Journey's End*. Whale accepted the assignment, though he did not conceal his dismay at the weakness of the script that Esterbrook had produced.

Whale was, in some respects, a strange choice as a director for an aviation picture. He feared flying and had a clause written into his contract that stipulated that he would under no circumstances be required to go up in an airplane during the shooting of the film. Whale also developed a visceral dislike of Jean Harlow, which shows on the screen. Yet he hit it off with Hughes, who uncharacteristically deferred to his judgment; and, enjoying Hughes's confidence, he persuaded his employer to bring on board Joseph Moncure March to rewrite Esterbrooke's material. March later confessed that, for the most part, he found the film "depressingly bad." "I had to contrive a story better than the one that Hughes had, but still manage to have it logically embrace the sequences which were good enough to keep . . ."[49]

No one who worked with Hughes on *Hell's Angels* doubted his brilliance. Yet his collaborators often found him stubborn, arrogant, and appallingly insensitive to the feelings of those around him, just as he had shown himself to be with his young wife who had returned to Houston in despair and was now resolved to seek a divorce. Everything had to be done Hughes's way and at his pace, even at the cost of the safety of those who were working for him. Even after two of his pilots had died in accidents, Hughes insisted on filming an unnecessarily dangerous scene in which Turner's Sikorsky S-29A, doubling for the German Gotha bomber, is shot down and spirals downward at full power toward a fiery crash. Turner, who had been flying the Sikorsky throughout the picture, refused to do the stunt unless Hughes agreed to have his plane checked thoroughly by a mechanic from head to tail.[50] Enraged at the idea that he should delay the shoot, Hughes then offered the job to the only pilot who might have pulled it off, Dick Grace, the ace of crashes. Grace was not unwilling, but he balked at the niggardly fee of $250 that Hughes was offering.[51]

Meanwhile, while Grace was dickering with Hughes for more money, Al Wilson agreed to take his place. With a young mechanic in the rear of the fuselage, Wilson climbed to seven thousand feet and then put the large ship into a spin. Realizing that the plane was out of control, he shouted twice to the mechanic to activate the lampblack and blowers and then jump. The pilot parachuted safely from the open cockpit, but his mechanic failed to hear Wilson's instructions and fell to a fiery death in the orange groves of Pacoima, not far from Burbank, California. Wilson's license was suspended by the Department of Commerce for three months, and he was expelled from the Professional Pilots Association after evidence surfaced that he had baled out only five seconds after starting the spin. A similar incident would play a prominent role in one of the most outstanding aviation pictures of the 1930s, *Only Angels Have Wings*.

If Joseph March improved the story of *Hell's Angels*, one can only wonder what it was like before he went to work on it. It depends for its effects on a series of coincidences that give new meaning to the term "suspension of disbelief." The film begins in prewar Germany, where one of two English brothers, Monte (Ben Lyon), reveals a weak and undependable character when he seduces the wife of a German aristocrat, General von Krantz, and then denies knowing the woman, leaving his brother Roy (James Hall) to fight a duel that should have been his responsibility. Action then shifts to England where the two brothers and a likable German friend, Karl, are portrayed, unconvincingly, as light-hearted Oxford undergraduates. The outbreak of war overtakes the three and finds them on different sides of the struggle. Both Roy and Monte join the Royal Flying Corps. Karl appears

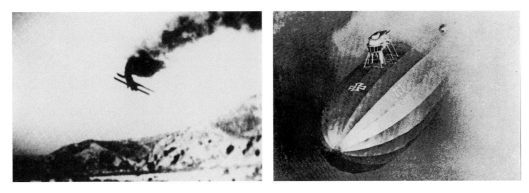

Pl. 152. The Sikorsky spirals to its destruction in the San Fernando Valley near Pacoima after Al Wilson successfully bales out.

Pl. 153. The Zeppelin just before its destruction.

as a member of a German Zeppelin crew whose objective is to bomb London's Trafalgar Square. Dropped in an observation car to guide the Zeppelin's bombs from above the cloud cover, Karl deliberately misdirects his commander so that the bombs are dropped harmlessly in Hyde Park. The Zeppelin is then set upon by four British pursuit planes, two flown by Monte and Roy. Desperate to gain altitude so that the airship can rise above its attackers, the Zeppelin's commander cuts Karl loose, thus sending him falling to his death, and orders several of his crew members to jump, which they obediently do, shouting "Für Kaiser und Vaterland." As the now lighter Zeppelin ascends, three of the pursuit planes, including those flown by the brothers, are forced to abandon the chase. Yet just when it appears that the Zeppelin might escape, it is rammed and destroyed by the fourth plane in a blast of fire that sends it plunging toward the earth.

An intermission followed this spectacular episode. Its equivalent in the second half was the dangerous mission Roy and Monte undertake when they volunteer to fly a captured German Gotha over the enemy lines in order to destroy an ammunition dump whose elimination is necessary before an Allied infantry attack can be launched. After destroying their target, the brothers are shot down over German territory in the midst of an epic aerial battle involving dozens of aircraft. Captured by enemy troops, the brothers are then delivered into the hands of the German general who appeared in the movie's opening scenes. Delighted to have the seducer of his wife in his hands and knowing Monte's cowardly character, Von Krantz offers the two brothers their lives in exchange for information about the British offensive. The weak-willed Monte cannot resist the chance to save himself, but before he can provide the information that the general seeks Roy pretends to agree to the general's request, tricks him into giving him a pistol, and shoots Monte to prevent him from telling what he knows. Roy is then put to death by a firing squadron, but not before shouting: "I'll be with you in just a moment, Monte." Running throughout the story is a silly and badly integrated subplot that features a British socialite, played by Jean Harlow, who pretends to love Roy; callously seduces his brother; then, after making her way to the front where she works in a canteen, cruelly abandons Roy for a drunken British officer.[52]

After months of speculation as to whether it would ever be released, *Hell's Angels* was finally unveiled to an elite audience at Grauman's Chinese Theater on Hollywood Boulevard on the evening of 7 June 1930. Hughes had prepared every detail of this event personally, down to the design of the movie's posters hanging in the lobby and publicity photographs of Harlow, emphasizing her plunging neckline and prominent breasts, which were then circulated to magazines and newspapers.[53] Far from concealing the costs of the film at a moment of economic distress when wasteful spending may have appeared in bad taste, Hughes's publicists vaunted their employer's extravagance, including the $40,000 that had been spent on the premiere.[54] Ten airplanes were ranged along the route leading to the theater. One hundred and eighty-five arc lights illuminated Hollywood Boulevard; a battery of searchlights dragged their beams across the sky as parachutists drift-

Pl. 154. A poster for *Hell's Angels* that makes the most of Jean Harlow's physical attributes.

Pl. 155. Grauman's Chinese Theatre on the night of the premiere of *Hell's Angels*.

ed downward toward the earth. A huge crowd, estimated at fifty thousand people and restrained by three hundred and fifty Los Angeles policemen and a hundred United States Marines, had gathered to observe the arrival of the crème of Hollywood's royalty, led by Douglas Fairbanks, Mary Pickford, Gloria Swanson, Charlie Chaplin, and Buster Keaton. When Hughes's motorcade was a mile from Grauman's he reached for the radiophone in his limousine and ordered a squadron of fifty vintage First World War aircraft to take off from their bases in the San Fernando Valley so that their flyover of Hollywood Boulevard would coincide with his arrival at the theater. They simulated aerial combat and emitted liquid smoke of red, gray, and ochre that, seen against the descending sun in a hazy sky, created an effect that Jean Harlow compared to "streaks of oil paint."[55]

As the thousand invited guests entered the forecourt of the theater, they passed under a Fokker D-7 biplane suspended in the air. Then at 10:00 p.m., when everyone was seated, the master of ceremonies, Frank Fay, invited the audience to applaud Roscoe Turner, who had just completed a record-breaking flight from New York to Los Angeles. Elegantly attired in a uniform of his own design, Turner was accompanied on the stage by his recently acquired pet lion cub Gilmore. Next came an elaborate vaudeville show, consisting of acrobats, ballet dancers, comedians, and a troupe of dancing poodles. Finally at 11:00 p.m., a curtain painted with scenes of First World War aircraft opened, followed by the projection of the film. Though there was tittering at the early scenes in Germany and Oxford, the audience followed with rapt attention the scenes portraying the Zeppelin attack on London and the climactic aerial battle between the British and the Germans. They were visibly moved by Roy's sacrifice of his brother and himself in order to make possible the victorious advance of the British Army with which the movie closed; and, being in the business of making motion pictures, they were no doubt impressed, as they were supposed to be, that Hughes had been willing to hire seventeen hundred uniformed extras for a battle scene that took up only twenty seconds of time on the screen.[56]

Pl. 156. The entrance to Grauman's Chinese Theatre during the showing of *Hell's Angels* in Hollywood.

Pl. 157. Turner poses with Gilmore in front of his Lockheed Air Express.

One can only guess what went through Howard Hughes's mind when, three hours after the film began, this crowd of veteran moviemakers leapt to their feet and gave him a standing ovation that lasted for twenty minutes. The suspicion that he would probably never make his money back must have paled before the exhilaration of his triumph in a town where hits of this magnitude were the province of studio bosses. In five short years he had conquered Hollywood and brought it to its feet. Hughes would remember this night as the happiest in his life.[57]

Though they were not unaware of *Hell's Angels'* defects, most critics could not resist the thrills and excitement it provided. It's not surprising that local papers like the *Los Angeles Times* would pronounce what had earlier been called Hughes's "folly" a "magnificent picture" and that the *Los Angeles Evening Herald* would claim that, compared with *Hell's Angels*, *Wings* was a "feeble thing." But even a critic as sophisticated as Mordaunt Hall of the *New York Times* declared himself to be full of admiration for the Zeppelin episode and thought that the aerial scenes portraying Richthofen's squadron pursuing the fleeing brothers in their Gotha bomber, with the crashing of flaming planes, had never been equaled on the screen.[58] Spectacle was what audiences wanted, and *Hell's Angels* provided that in strong, extended doses that took the viewers' breath away.

Hell's Angels will be remembered because Howard Hughes made it. The sheer megalomania of the enterprise inspires curiosity. Almost three years in production at a cost of close to $4 million, *Hell's Angels* consumed more than 3 million feet of film, of which only 15,000 were finally used. Hughes's pilots flew 227,000 miles; and the equivalent of a small army, estimated at over 20,000 people, had participated, in one way or another, in the movie's making.[59] Robert Sherwood may well have been right when he suggested that people had flocked to see it because they were fascinated by Hughes's extravagance and wanted to see what he had bought for all that money. Sherwood's answer – a sentiment not shared by many at the time – was that he had acquired "five cents' worth of plot, approximately thirty-eight cents' worth of acting, and a huge amount of dialogue, the total value of which may be estimated by the following specimen. Boy: 'What do you think of my new uniform?' Girl: 'Oh, it's ripping!' Boy: (nervously): 'Where?' "[60]

Writing in the *New Republic*, Malcolm Cowley was even more dismissive. One does not need to approve of Cowley's overheated rhetoric and Neronian analogies to think that he was on to something when he compared *Hell's Angels* with an automobile advertisement financed by a large corporation, and then went on to point out that this was a motion picture in which the "machines are the heroes and villains. Every expense is lavished upon them; their authenticity is guaranteed . . . But the actors themselves are false, puny, inadequate, the only real automatons in a world of vital speed . . . the people who enact these

Pl. 158.   The dogfight
sequence from the second
half of *Hell's Angels*.

simulacra [of death] are themselves only the simulacra of people."[61] Cowley was right. The
emptiness at the heart of the film, its lack of poetry and human values, its cardboard acting,
its parody of university life in England, its crude anti-German sentiments, and the vulgarity
with which Jean Harlow's sexuality was exploited all reflected the character of its maker.

Yet for all its defects, *Hell's Angels* marked a milestone in the history of the American
aviation film. Building on the example of *Wings*, it exploited the aesthetic possibilities of
flight as the real, if not the ostensible topic of a motion picture. The long sequence portraying the Zeppelin's raid on London and its destruction in a massive burst of flame
remains a haunting metaphor for the madness of the war and the perverse use of an invention that had captured the imagination of the masses. At the same time, *Hell's Angels'* flying scenes set a standard for authenticity, daring, and magnitude of aerial action that would
never be surpassed. Realizing that they would never be able to equal the resources that
Hughes had been able to bear, the makers of future aviation films would be inspired to
take more seriously the dramatic content of their pictures, while preserving the dimension of spectacle that by 1930 had become identified in the public mind with aircraft of
all kinds.

★   ★   ★

During the decade that followed the premiere of *Hell's Angels*, Hollywood took a crack at
many different types of flying stories, seeking to exploit the public's fascination with aviators and the planes they flew. Movies about aerial combat during the Great War remained
a favored topic; but the emphasis in these films shifted from the long balletic battle

sequences of *Wings* and *Hell's Angels* to the psychological stress and damage endured by hastily trained aviators who knew themselves condemned to die. The anti-heroic tenor of these pictures reflected a growing feeling, in the United States and elsewhere, that the war had been a futile undertaking and that those who survived were scarred in mind as well as in body. The explosion of war memoirs and fiction that began in 1928, most notably Erich Maria Remarque's international bestseller *All Quiet on the Western Front*, R. C. Sherriff's play *Journey's End*, and Ernest Hemingway's *Farewell to Arms*, had prepared the public for a less uplifting view of the life of young combatants during the war. Yet the inner life of pilots on the Western Front remained a relatively unknown story.

John Monk Saunders saw an opportunity here and was quick to exploit it. While a Rhodes Scholar at Oxford in 1919–21, the author of *Wings* had met flyers from the Canadian, British, and French air services and discussed with them "their own experiences and fears and hopes, adventures and activities while flying at the front during the war . . ." They had told him stories about "the terrific responsibility resting upon the squadron commanders, the excessive drinking of intoxicating liquors indulged in by the pilots at the front by reason of the nervous tension under which they operated and so many other phases of flying activities at the front . . ."[62] Though none of this material made its way into *Wings*, the post-1928 cultural climate was more receptive to it; and Saunders, with his Hollywood connections, was adept at selling his ideas to the studios.

Representative of the many pictures based on Saunders's stories was Paramount's *The Eagle and the Hawk*. This film, much admired for its realism when it was released in 1933 at the height of Anglo-Saxon reaction against the futility of the war, follows the career of an American ace in the Royal Flying Corps, played by Frederic March. Attracted by the "sport" of aerial combat and good at it, the initially carefree and fun-loving Jerry Young sees one after another of his observers killed. Eventually, he comes to see himself as a "chauffeur for a graveyard" and then, more ominously, as a heavily decorated killer of young boys. Unable to live with his conscience, he shoots himself rather than live with the memories of those for whose deaths he holds himself responsible. But his observer Henry Crocker – played by a young Cary Grant at the beginning of his film career – carries his body to their plane, takes off into the dawn light, and riddles the ship and Young with bullets from his own machine gun in order to ensure his pilot a hero's death. An ace cannot be allowed to die as a suicide; it would be a bad example to set for the legion of novice pilots needed to take his place and the place of the many others who had died, fighting in a futile and seemingly endless war. Though no friend of Jerry Young, Henry Crocker understood the function he performed as a model of heroic action. The image of a monument inscribed to March, with which the film ends, conveys its bitterly ironic message:

Pl. 159.   R. C. Sherriff's 1928 play Journey's End expressed the mood of disillusionment with the First World War that would soon make itself felt in aviation films, such as *The Eagle and the Hawk*.

Captain J. H. Young
Who
Gallantly Gave
His Life
In Aerial Combat
To Save the World
For Democracy
June 14, 1918

When not making aviation movies about the last war and the wounds borne by the aviators who had survived it, Hollywood discovered a new mission in dramatizing the training, equipment, and exploits of the air corps that would be expected to fight the wars of the future and defend the United States against possible air attack by unspecified enemies. What Hollywood insiders called the "service film" became one of the most favored forms of aviation movies during a decade when the world was edging toward war. With the encouragement and material help of the War Department, Hollywood made a series of films that were essentially recruiting vehicles for the navy and army air forces. These films disdained plot in favor of spectacle and sought to appeal to the public through a combination of exciting flying sequences, romantic subplots involving pretty girls, and charismatic leading men. Critics, both then and now, have found it difficult to take them seriously, dismissing them as "flag-wavers." But one should not underestimate the impact that they had on younger viewers, and they no doubt contributed to the mystique of flight and attracted countless young men to recruiting offices, as the threat to the country's security became more palpable.[63]

Among the many writers who made their living churning out service pictures about aviators, Lieutenant Frank "Spig" Wead quickly distinguished himself. Wead was a man of many talents. A graduate of Annapolis who served in the North Sea during the First World War, he had captained the United States team that won the 1923 Schneider Cup competition. The following year he broke five records for duration and speed in a single flight. Adding to his string of aeronautical achievements, he led a team of navy flyers to victory in an around-the-world race. Then, at the peak of his naval career in 1927, Wead fell down a flight of stairs in his home, broke his neck, and became completely paralyzed. By sheer force of will, he succeeded in getting himself back on his feet and regained partial use of his arms. Forced to retire from the navy, Wead took a small beach house in Santa Monica and began a new career as a writer, first of popular fiction, then of movie scripts. The world

Pl. 160.   Frank Wead (fourth from the right) poses with the triumphant 1923 Navy Schneider Cup Team.

he chose at first to write about was the one he knew best: that of naval aviation. A natural as an author of stories and scripts for naval service films, Wead co-wrote MGM's 1929 production of *The Flying Fleet* and then provided the stories on which Columbia's *Dirigible* and MGM's *Hell Divers* were based.

But Wead was not satisfied to limit himself to service films; and in 1932 he wrote a story that introduced a theme that would figure prominently in the aviation movies of the 1930s: the conflict between the daredevil pilots of the heroic period of flight and the businessmen, bureaucrats, and engineers who were increasingly coming to dominate the aviation industry.

During the First World War, the airplane had proved itself as an instrument of war; but once the war ended, it was not clear what its uses would be in time of peace. One possible use, of course, was to transport goods and people. But aircraft in the early 1920s were still extremely limited in their ability to carry cargo; they were slow, and their engines were unreliable to the point that choosing this mode of transportation as a passenger was almost as foolhardy an idea as becoming a pilot.[64]

Yet pilots and supporters of aviation were convinced that the obstacles to commercial success could be quickly overcome; and one of the ways to demonstrate the commercial possibilities of the airplane was to show that aircraft were capable of transporting mail more rapidly than the existing postal system, which depended on railways. This was difficult to do in Europe because distances between the major cities were relatively short and the railroad system was highly developed and efficient. The United States, however, offered greater possibilities because of the large distances between its major cities; already before the war ended, mail service had been initiated between Washington and New York.

To be profitable, mail service had to be fast, regular, and reliable; and this meant flying in bad weather as well as good. Mail pilots were therefore pushed to fly in marginal conditions when they lacked the instruments and the infrastructure that would have made such flights safe. The standing directive of the Air Mail Service was that pilots should fly by their compasses, even if visibility was minimal at the airport from which they were scheduled to depart.[65] The whole point of the operation was speed and reliability. Because the range of planes was limited, a system of interconnecting relay stations had to be created across the United States, establishing the equivalent of an aerial Pony Express. Thus one pilot landed; his plane was refueled; and a new pilot took his place. If for some reason the relieving pilot was absent or indisposed, the arriving pilot was expected to continue the journey. This was not a job for the faint-hearted, and it attracted the best and most daring pilots. Those who were not good enough simply did not last; and they were seldom mourned by their supervisors who were under pressure to get the mail through on time.[66]

Among the many pilots who passed through the Mail Service was Charles Lindbergh, who twice had to bail out of his De Havilland while flying the mail between St. Louis and Chicago, once in a harrowing situation in which his biplane spiraled around within a hundred yards of him as he drifted toward the ground. But by 1927, when Lindbergh left Robertson Aircraft Corporation to devote himself to the New York–Paris flight, a highway of beacons had been built across the United States and airmail service was prosperous enough so that the government could open up its routes to private bidders. The battle to demonstrate the commercial feasibility of airmail service had been won.

The story Frank Wead wrote in 1932, *Air Mail*, dramatized this achievement and the human costs it had entailed. Chosen by Universal's Carl Laemmle to direct the movie was John Ford, a veteran of dozens of short Westerns and the maker of a critically acclaimed and commercially successful film, *The Iron Horse* of 1924. There is no reason to believe that either Universal or Ford had a strong commitment to this project.[67] Like most of the movies churned out in this period, its sole purpose was to entertain at minimal cost.[68] Ford had no particular interest in aviation, nor any personal experience of flying; his passion was the sea. Yet his innate sense for the poetry of place and his quickly developing skill at cin-

Pl. 161. Director John Ford in the 1930s.

135

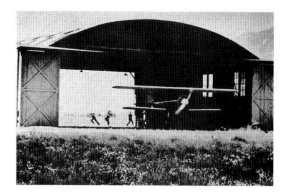

Pl. 162.   Paul Mantz flies through a small hangar in Bishop, California, where winds are notoriously unpredictable, and launches his career as Hollywood's leading stunt pilot.

ematographic composition give the setting of the picture – Desert Airport, a western relay stop in the network of coast-to-coast airmail service – a dark and haunting atmosphere, whose deadly dangers are signified visually by the relentless beating of rain, the fall of snow, and enveloping clouds of mist that reduce the visibility to zero.[69] The world of Desert Airport is divided into a warm and safe interior – an operations room barraged by radio messages from afar – and an outside where winter weather threatens human lives and air-craft engines throb relentlessly, signaling reassuring arrivals or ominous departures. The abyss between the inside and the outside is driven home with beautifully framed compositions shot through frost-covered windows that one remembers long after the details of the far-fetched and sometimes distasteful plot have faded.

Wead's story (co-written for the screen by Dale Van Every) establishes a conflict between the steady and responsible station chief, Mike Miller (Ralph Bellamy), and his nemesis, the brilliant pilot and ex-First World War ace, Duke Talbot (Pat O'Brien), who scoffs at all authority and lives to defy rules. Their characters are established early with the economy typical of this period of Hollywood filmmaking. Mike's dedication to duty is demonstrated when he insists on flying the mail himself after one of his pilots crashes while trying to land in conditions of impenetrable fog. Duke, played with self-important cockiness by Pat O'Brien, is the replacement for the lost pilot.

Talbot's arrival at Desert Airport takes the form of a series of dangerous stunts, capped by a series of passes through a hangar and the buzzing of the operations room.[70] Duke has nothing but scorn for Miller's dedication to the company's goal of getting the mail through under all conditions. He is a loner and grandstander in a world where corporations, such as the Federal Transcontinental Airways for which Mike works, are bound to dominate the future. When most needed by Mike to assure the continuation of mail service over the Christmas holiday, Duke nonchalantly announces his intention to quit his job and compounds his offense by taking with him the adulterous wife of a pilot who had recently died trying to reach Desert Airport in a driving snow storm.

Wead's ambivalence toward his own theme is shown by the film's denouement, when Duke saves Mike from certain death by means of a daring mountain landing in a narrow mountain ravine – not because of his affection for Mike or a conversion to Mike's values, but only in order to flaunt authority and show the world what a remarkable pilot he is. "You're a great guy, Duke," Mike says, making a mockery of everything he had earlier said about Talbot. The point seems driven home when Mike and his devoted fiancée Ruth are reconciled with Duke in an ambulance after he crashes "I walked away from that one, didn't I," Duke says self-complacently, thus sending the audience a mixed message. For the moment, the daredevil has the last word.[71]

★　　★　　★

Pl. 163.   The operations room at Newark airport, as Jake and his team witness Tex's crash.

Buoyed by his success in selling aviation stories to Hollywood, Frank Wead set his sights on an even more prestigious goal: Broadway. In the spring of 1935, a three-act play written by Wead opened at the Music Box Theater in New York to strong reviews. More complex than *Air Mail*, *Ceiling Zero* also deals with the changes taking place in commercial aviation; but here the conflict between the pioneers of the past and the profit-driven entrepreneurs and rule-oriented bureaucrats of the future is not just implied in rough brush strokes as background to an improbable plot, but instead carefully delineated and made the central focus of the story. Wead makes no effort to hide the camp with which his sympathies lie, but neither does he leave any doubt about the inevitability of the process he is describing. The pioneers must adapt themselves to change; otherwise, they will be swept aside by events they have no way of controlling. Their only consolation lies in the respect and admiration they can inspire in the younger men who are fated to replace them.

Wead's protagonist, Jake Lee, is the superintendent of the Eastern Division of Federal Air Lines based at Newark airport. A veteran of the First World War with eight thousand miles in the air to his credit, he is now a deskbound executive responsible for maintaining regular airmail and passenger service, dealing with government inspectors, and recommending the purchase of aircraft that Federal will need in order to become profitable. The operations office, from which Jake directs his flights, is brimming with a wealth of equipment meant to suggest the modernity of commercial aviation in 1935: radios capable of receiving and transmitting messages and sending navigational beams; a loudspeaker; microphones, a teletype machine; a telephone switchboard; telephones; a typewriter; weather maps; logbooks; and clipboards. The more recently hired pilots who work for Lee, like Tay Lawson, are college graduates, trained in aeronautical engineering, who know engines "like a book" and fly "like a hawk." Disciplined, uniformed, and at home with rules and regulations, Lawson represents the future of commercial aviation.

Yet though Jake Lee appreciates Lawson and gives him responsibility for the maintenance of the station's planes, his heart lies with the veteran pilots with whom he refuses to part, especially his old friends from the war, Tex Clark and Dizzy Davis. Dizzy is transferred to Newark after pioneering blind flying on the airmail route between Cheyenne, Wyoming, and Salt Lake City, Utah. Like *Air Mail*'s Duke Talbot, Dizzy is an inveterate ruler-breaker who buzzes the operations room in inverted flight on arriving at the field. Like Duke, too, Dizzy threatens to disrupt the harmony of Lee's team by relentlessly and successfully pursuing another man's woman, in this case the unmarried, nineteen-year-old Tommy.

The play thus begins on a note of lighthearted sexual innuendo, as Dizzy is revealed to be an inveterate and irresponsible womanizer; but toward the end of act two its mood switches suddenly to high-pitched melodrama when Tex is fatally injured attempting to land in conditions of low visibility after the failure of his radio.[72] Dizzy had originally been scheduled to make the flight; but he had lightheartedly persuaded Tex to take his place so that he could spend the evening with Tommy. Dizzy is devastated by Tex's death, and his gloom is only deepened when he discovers that his pilot's license has been revoked by the Bureau of Air Commerce as a result of his repeated violations of government regulations.

Jake's attempts to console Dizzy are in vain; but Tommy has greater success, especially when she indicates her willingness to yield to Dizzy's advances and abandon Lawson. Yet Dizzy's sense of shame is triggered when Lawson confesses the admiration that he and the other men at the base feel for him. Suddenly aware of the damage he will do in seducing Tommy, whom Lawson intends to marry, Dizzy seeks to redeem himself by an act of self-sacrifice. After knocking Lawson out and locking him in a storeroom, Dizzy takes the dangerous flight through driving sleet for which Lawson had originally been scheduled. As ice forms on his wings and Dizzy begins to lose control of the flying surfaces, he transmits instructions to Jake for improvements that have to be made in the new deicing equipment, with which the plane had been provided. Dizzy spins to his death while Jake participates impotently in the drama by means of radio. Jake's attempt to save Dizzy by ordering him to "hit the silk" is foiled by his friend's final act of disobedience; in violation of company regulations, he had refused to wear a parachute and thus, before crashing, can laugh at Jake's futile command to bail out.

Shaken but unbroken by the death of his closest friend, Jake seizes the opportunity of Dizzy's death to affirm his independence in the face of the executive from Federal Air Lines' New York office, who has been continually interfering in his management of the Eastern Division. And having obtained a promise to be allowed to run the operation as he wishes, he barks at his employees: "Well, what are you standing around for? We're still running an airline." Tex and Dizzy may be dead, but the weather is expected to improve and the mail has to be delivered.[73]

The manuscript of *Ceiling Zero* was brought to the attention of Hal Wallis, Jack Warner's second-in-command at Warner Brothers, well before the play opened on Broadway. The two readers to whom Wallis sent it for evaluation recommended it while warning that the figure of Dizzy Davis, as presently written, would cause problems with the censor because of his sexual amorality.[74] Warners nonetheless bought the rights from Wead for $21,000 and paid him another $6,750 to adapt it for the screen. When Wallis's first choices for director – William Wellman, Victor Fleming, and Tay Garnett – turned out to be unavailable, he reluctantly agreed with Jack Warner and the designated producer Harry Joe Brown that the best man for the job was an independently minded person with whom Wallis had a history of problems: Howard Hawks.[75]

Hawks is often likened by critics to John Ford, and in later life he did nothing to discourage the comparison.[76] Yet in the early 1930s, what Hawks had in common with Howard Hughes was a good deal more obvious than what he shared with Ford. Tall, thin, prematurely white-haired, with piercing light blue eyes, and sure of himself to the point of arrogance, Hawks had been born into affluence in Protestant mid-Western America. He would never know the stigma of being a first-generation Irish immigrant from which John Ford suffered, and which underlies even the least Irish of his films. Like Hughes, Hawks had been pampered as a child and brought up to believe that he was a member of a privileged class. Like Hughes, also, Hawks had spent part of his youth in upper-class Pasadena and attended a prestigious prep school in the East. Though almost a decade older than Hughes, Hawks shared with him a passion for golf, a yen for attractive actresses, and a fascination with airplanes. Hawks had learned to fly in the Army Air Corps in 1917 and served as an instructor in Texas before being sent to Ford Monroe, Virginia, where he was trained in reconnaissance and the spotting of big guns. He continued to fly throughout the 1920s and, like Hughes, sought out the company of aviators. Both Hughes and Hawks were notoriously laconic and famous for their ability to remain silent for extended periods of time. But, perhaps most important of all, what bound the two men together was their status as Hollywood mavericks: Hughes because he produced films outside the studio system; Hawks because, despite the fact that he made films for the studios, he refused to commit himself to a long-term contract with any of them and fought for personal control over the movies he made.

Hawks would make one of his most memorable films for Hughes in 1932, the gangster movie *Scarface*, but their relationship got off to a shaky start. When *Hell's Angels* was about to be released in early 1930, Hughes discovered that First National, a subsidiary of Warner Brothers, was shooting a film about the Royal Flying Corps during the First World War whose climactic aerial scene – an attack on a German ammunition dump – bore alarming similarities to his own *Hell's Angels*. The film was *Dawn Patrol*; its director was Hawks. Displaying signs of the paranoia that would become ever more pronounced as he grew older, Hughes attempted to obtain a script of First National's film by instructing one of his writers to bribe Hawks's secretary. When this resulted in the arrest of the writer for theft, Hughes sued First National for plagiarism in a desperate effort to postpone the opening of *Dawn Patrol* until *Hell's Angels* had completed its run. After viewing the two films, the presiding judge was unconvinced and Hughes's suit was dismissed as being without merit.[77]

Pl. 164. Hawks in 1935. Actors found him intimidating, but they nonetheless loved to work with him. Anyone who has seen the best of his pictures will understand why.

Sheerly on aesthetic grounds, Hughes had reason for concern. Based on a gripping and authentic story by John Monk Saunders, *Dawn Patrol* contained none of the distracting subplots that had marred Howard Hughes's film.[78] Its story of the British aviators who flew against the Germans in the late fall of 1915 when German aerial supremacy was at its height, the sense of futility they felt, the comradeship they shared, and the terrible burden of responsibility borne by their commanders was translated to the screen by Hawks with an economy of expression and a lack of sentimentality that set a new standard for aviation films. Watched today, the scenes of aerial combat, shot by Elmer Dyer, are every bit as stunning as those of *Hell's Angels*, despite the fact that Hawks was operating with a severely restricted budget and his flotilla of aircraft was necessarily smaller. Premiered on 10 July 1930 in New York to excellent reviews, *Dawn Patrol* played to standing room only during its first week and became one of the biggest hits of the year, despite the publicity blitz that Hughes and his minions mounted for *Hell's Angels*.[79]

As an aviator and proven director of aviation films, Hawks, then, was a natural choice to make the film version of *Ceiling Zero*; and he did nothing to disappoint Warner's expectations, though Wallis characteristically grumbled at the slowness of Hawks's start and the length of the shooting script.[80] Wallis need not have worried; Hawks shot the entire film in six weeks. Indeed, only four months passed between his signing on as director and the film's release in New York, an impressive example of Hollywood's factory system running at full throttle.[81]

The story told by the film follows closely the narrative sequence of the play. The mood that Hawks establishes from the beginning is oppressive. We are seldom allowed outside the operations room, and the few glimpses we get of airmail pilots in their enclosed cockpits seem equally claustrophobic. Unlike Ford in *Air Mail*, Hawks seldom takes us outside the setting of the action in order to view the inside from without; nor, more surprisingly, does he let his camera linger much over the sophisticated electronic equipment with which Wead carefully surrounded his protagonists. The sense of a new world where machinery dominates the lives of individuals, and where the most important messages are transmitted through the magic of radio, is not nearly so emphasized in Hawks's film as it is in Wead's play.

Though the outside world in *Ceiling Zero* is as full of perils as it was in *Air Mail*, Hawks keeps our attention focused on the characters and the relationships they establish with one another. The figures that pass through the operations room of Federal Air Lines are clearly divided into insiders and outsiders. Always inclined to strip a story to its essentials when translating it to film, Hawks eliminated several marginal figures that appear in Wead's play and clutter up the action; the result is to heighten the sense of drama and quicken the pace of the narrative.

Hawks made other changes, some subtle, others less so. The reasons for Dizzy's suicidal flight at the end are even more ambiguous in the movie than they are in the play. True,

Pl. 165. Dizzy (James Cagney) and Tommy (June Travis) are distressed as they wait for news of Tex.

Dizzy is indirectly responsible for Tex's fatal accident, but the real culprit is Tex's radio; and – what is all-important to Dizzy – Jake absolves him, commenting that once Tex agreed to do the run it was "his show." The implication is that another pilot in Tex's situation might have found a way to survive: Dizzy knows that Tex's nerves were fraying, and Jake suspects that he simply wasn't good enough to handle an unexpectedly tough situation. Almost as traumatic for Dizzy as Tex's death, however, is the loss of his pilot license, which symbolizes his *raison d'être*. When Jake offers to arrange for its renewal by turning to the airplane builder Fred Adams for help, Dizzy refuses on the grounds that in return for the favor Jake will have to buy Adams's less rapid and economically profitable planes. Dizzy warns Jake against his "silly sentimentality." "Let the oldtimers go. I won't be missed and neither will Tex . . . Our work is done. The pioneering's over."

Still, Dizzy's zest for life remains strong enough to accept Tommy's offer to spend the night with him, thus jeopardizing her relationship with Lawson. Why would Dizzy give her the key to his apartment and risk her reputation if he intended to die? Dizzy's encounter in the operations room with Lawson, after Jake has gone to comfort Tex's wife, becomes the catalyst for what appears an unplanned and gratuitous act of self-sacrifice. But even this event loses the meaning it had in the play because Hawks deprives Lawson of the line in which he assures Dizzy of the respect that every man at Newark Airfield has for him. This has the effect of undermining the play's point that Dizzy no longer feels entitled to live after having betrayed the only community that matters to him, the fraternity of flyers.[82] The information that Dizzy calmly transmits about the improvements that need to be made in the deicing equipment before his plane crashes cannot conceal the nihilistic and destructive nature of his act.[83]

The figure of Jake Lee stands at the center of Wead's play. Jake has learned to fill out forms and play by the new bureaucratic rules that are coming to dominate the world of commercial aviation; but he can still "fly with the best of them," and he continues to have fantasies of abandoning his desk, getting back into the cockpit, and perhaps starting a flying school with Tex and Dizzy or even going abroad to serve as a mercenary. Once a star of James Cagney's magnitude had been cast as Dizzy, however, it was inevitable that the center of gravity would shift from Jake's ambivalent feelings about his job to the high-octane antics of his rule-defying friend. From the moment when Dizzy's cocky voice is heard over the loud-speaker to the final scene in which Jake pieces together the torn bits of Dizzy's pilot license to form his likeness after his death, Cagney dominates the film with his charisma and intensity. Hawks was not responsible for the relative demotion of Jake Lee's part, but as an experienced Hollywood director who understood the imperatives of stardom, he did nothing to prevent it. Pat O'Brien, in the role of Jake, struggles to right the balance, but one can feel him reaching as he oscillates between machine-gun-like bursts of barking and sheepishly ingratiating smiles. Having acted with his ebullient co-star before, he knew that this was bound to be a Cagney film.[84] The respective size of their names on the titles leaves no doubt about the person on whom audiences should focus their attention.

Without ever rising to the level of greatness, *Ceiling Zero* dramatized, as no previous movie had been able to do, the moment in the mid-1930s when the fledgling industry of aviation was beginning to emerge from the era of barnstormers, racers, and record-breaking aviators who risked their lives for celebrity, thrills, and the sheer fun of flying. Aviation was becoming a business, as Dizzy explains to Jake. Flyers were no longer leather-helmeted pilots; they were now uniformed engineers. Aviation was becoming a "college-man's game." The age of pioneers was over.[85]

Indeed, United Airlines was so sensitive to public concerns about the safety of air travel that it persuaded Warner Brothers to shift the setting of the movie from the mid-1930s, where the action of Wead's play takes place, into the 1920s. At the request of the Aeronautical Chamber of Commerce of America, a trade organization that represented the

aircraft industry, Warner Brothers and Hawks also agreed to provide *Ceiling Zero* with a prologue, explaining that the phase of commercial aviation it describes is now ancient history.[86] "Today's lighted runways, expert radio and weather service, deicers and other safety devices enable the large passenger liners to give safe and dependable transportation which speed mail and passengers along the skyways and are a fitting memorial to the vision and courage of those pioneers who gave their lives in the early history of this industry to complete the mastery of the air."[87] Yet a nation that still remembered vividly the 1931 crash of the Fokker Trimotor that carried Knute Rokne, the well-known coach of the celebrated Notre Dame football team, may well still have had its doubts about the safety of the airlines when *Ceiling Zero* arrived in movie theaters in January 1936 to enthusiastic reviews.[88]

★ ★ ★

Ceiling Zero pointed the way toward the making of movies that would capture and dramatize the changes that were taking place in the American aviation industry. The Hollywood studios were quick to take up the challenge. They were limited, however, by the constraints of their own commercial success and the formulas with which they had achieved it.

Perhaps the best example is MGM's 1938 production of *Test Pilot*, a film that found great favor with the public and the critics and was nominated for three Academy Awards, including best picture. Its success, no doubt, was due to the star power it brought to bear in the trio of Clark Gable, Spencer Tracy, and Myrna Loy, the fluidity of Victor Fleming's directing, and the frequent thrills generated by its flight scenes.[89] But the picture's sentimental ending sequence in which Clark Gable survives what appears to be a fatal crash and then abandons testing aircraft in favor of a ground job in the army air force and domestic bliss with Myrna Loy and their young child was more a surrender to the rules of Hollywood moviemaking than a convincing portrait of the aviation world in 1938.

Pl. 167. MGM's three reigning stars of 1938 – Clark Gable, Myrna Loy, and Spencer Tracy – pose against the background of Alexander de Seversky's new long-range racing plane, the SEV-S2.

Pl. 168. Jules Furthman. Hawks claimed that he, Josef von Sternberg, and Victor Fleming were the only directors who could put up with him. "Everybody hated him. He was such a mean guy that we thought he was just great. He was bright, and he was short. He'd say 'You stupid guy' to somebody who wasn't as smart as him. He needed help, but when he got help he was awful good."

Given Hawks's sense of rivalry with his friend Victor Fleming and whatever involvement he may have had in writing the script on which Test Pilot was based, it may be that the success of that picture inspired him to go Fleming one better in a genre for which he felt, quite rightly, that he had a special feeling. If this is so – and there is reason to think that it might be – then he certainly succeeded.[90] *Only Angels Have Wings*, a movie Hawks directed in 1939 for Columbia, carried the aviation film to a new level.[91] Taken on its own terms, it has no peer among the aviation pictures of the 1930s, including the previous ones that Hawks himself had made. It was almost as if Hawks had set out to close the chapter on a genre that he had done so much to create.

The story of *Only Angels* is credited to Hawks and bears his stamp throughout. He always claimed that the script was based on people he had known and incidents that had actually taken place.[92] "There wasn't one single scene in the whole picture that wasn't real," he wrote

Pl. 169. Lionel Banks' set for *Only Angels Have Wings*.

to a critic who complained that for once Hawks had gone too far and strained the bounds of credibility. No one disputes that Hawks may have witnessed some of these scenes, perhaps in fundamentally different contexts; but it is clear that, not uncharacteristically, in memory he simplified and distorted the complex process by which the story took its final shape.[93]

To make the picture, Hawks assembled a formidable team. Jules Furthman, a veteran of Josef von Sternberg's best Marlene Dietrich films, was brought in to add his particular brand of cynicism, razor-sharp dialogue, and sense for exotic locales to a script to which at least three other writers also made important contributions. The similarity between the characters the writers created and those of Joseph Conrad was too great to go unnoticed by the many critics who have been drawn to a close analysis of Hawks's film.[94] This is a film very much set in Conrad's type of imperialist world where men carry heavy burdens from their past and strange things can be expected to happen.

The people responsible for the look of the film could not have been more qualified. Paul Mantz served as technical adviser and did the dangerous flying; Elmer Dyer handled the aerial photography; Joseph Walker, the brilliant and innovative cinematographer of Frank Capra's best films, shot the interiors; and Lionel Banks designed the elaborate sixty-foot high set on the Columbia Ranch in North Hollywood. A zoo-full of seagulls, condors, parrots, macaws, parakeets, desert eagles, and buzzards, authentic South American Chihuahuas, and a talented five-year-old mule were recruited to give authenticity to the setting and ministered to by the superintendent of Columbia livestock department.[95] Dmitri Tiomkin, who would later join the pantheon of Hollywood composers, was in charge of underlining swings of mood with music inspired by throbbing Latin American rhythms and elegiac themes.

The casting brought together a group of talented players. Taking on the role of Geoff Carter, Cary Grant reveals a darker and more sensitive side of himself than audiences were accustomed to seeing in the leading man of the recently made comedies, *The Awful Truth* and *Bringing Up Baby*. Jean Arthur, the reigning female star at Columbia, was also cast against type. While not the sexy, taunting siren Hawks would have liked, Jean Arthur is quirky and convincingly perplexed as the chorus girl Bonnie Lee who suddenly finds herself amid this strange band of men. Independent yet understanding and loving, Arthur is able to bring out Grant's sensitivity in a way that a tougher, more aggressive woman would never have been able to do. Thomas Mitchell plays the faithful friend and mediator Kid, without the self-conscious mannerisms that Walter Brennan would bring to this type of role in Hawks's later films. A visibly aging Richard Barthelmess takes on the role of Bat McPherson, a pilot ostracized because he parachuted out of an airplane leaving his mechanic behind to die. His presence in the picture is a reminder of one of the accidents

Pl. 170. Hawks directs Cary Grant and Jean Arthur on the set of *Only Angels Have Wings*. Asked to compare Grant with other actors with whom he had worked, Hawks commented: ". . . you have to watch out for Grant being oversensitive. You had to watch our for Bogart being insensitive. You're on a tighrope with a lot of those things — but they're all so good that it isn't much of a problem."

that occurred during the making of *Hell's Angels* and, at the same time, a reference to the grim world of the 1930 *Dawn Patrol* in which he had played the leading role. The memory of his past roles was such that the audience at the premier at Radio City Musical Hall broke out into applause when he was first seen on the screen.[96] Sultry but at the same time vulnerable, Rita Hayworth appears as Barthelmess's wife, Judy. As was often true of pictures in this period, even the minor parts were carefully developed. Aliyn Joslyn as Les Peters, Sig Rumann as Dutchy, Victor Kilian as Sparks, John Carroll as Gent Shelton, and Noah Berry, Jr. as Joe all make strong impressions in the short time they have on screen.

As in *Dawn Patrol* and *Ceiling Zero*, Hawks takes us inside the severely circumscribed world of a band of marginal men who face daily dangers that may result in their death. When watching the film, it is easy to forget how compressed the time frame is – less than forty-eight hours from beginning to end. The action is set in Barranca, a banana port in Ecuador whose swampy mists, waterlogged fields, and pounding rains suggest that it may not be the healthiest place for a flyer. We come to know this world through the eyes of an outsider, Bonnie Lee, a fetching young woman of dubious background, who arrives in Barranca by chance, misses her ship, and finds herself the object of two young aviators' attentions, Joe Souther and Les Peters. Through them she is introduced to Dutchy's place, a rundown and somewhat sleazy combination of general store, restaurant, bar, and hotel. It is also, as Bonnie soon discovers, the headquarters of a bush air service, owned by Dutchy and run by Geoff Carter, that carries the mail inland through a mountain pass. As the movie progresses, we come to recognize and share the pilots' view of Dutchy's as a welcoming and warmly lighted refuge against the natural dangers that lurk outside, a place where the aviators gather to celebrate the good luck of their survival with cigarettes and ceremonial drinks.[97]

Bonnie is soon introduced to the harsh realities of life at Dutchy's airfield when Joe crashes, trying to return to the field after a bank of impenetrable fog cuts off the pass. Geoff and the other pilots go on with their evening as if nothing out of the ordinary had happened. Bonnie is horrified when Geoff begins to eat a steak that Joe had ordered by radio and planned to share with Bonnie. "Don't you realize he's dead?" "Who's dead?" Geoff asks, cutting into the steak. "Joe," she replies. "Who's Joe?" Geoff replies, proceeding nonchalantly with his dinner.[98]

Repelled while at the same time fascinated by Geoff and his friends, Bonnie seeks insight into their strange behavior from the Kid. She wonders why Geoff and the others are so taken with flying? "They must love it." The Kid confesses that after twenty-two years as a pilot he can't give her an answer that would make any sense. Sensing that Bonnie's interest in Geoff goes beyond mere curiosity, he issues a kindly warning: "He's a good guy for gals to stay away from."

Ignoring the Kid's advice, Bonnie learns from Geoff that he once thought he loved a woman who couldn't stand "the gaffe" of seeing him risk his life constantly in an airplane. His code now is to live for the moment; he doesn't believe in laying in a store of anything: not matches, marbles, money and, least of all, women. What, Bonnie asks, would Geoff do if he found a woman who was willing to live on his terms. "That's what they all say. Women think they can take it, but they can't. The minute you get up in the air they start calling the airport. And when you get down, they hate your insides." "What if she were the type who doesn't scare so easily?" "There's no such animal." Soon afterwards, hearing that the weather has cleared over the pass through which they fly the mail, Geoff takes off into the night, certain that Bonnie will be gone when he returns. Against the Kid's advice, she decides to stay.

What happens next revolves around a series of coincidences and freak accidents. The next day a new pilot arrives. Geoff quickly recognizes Bat MacPherson, played by Barthelmess, to be Kilgallen, the notorious flyer who bailed out, leaving the Kid's younger brother behind to die. Having discovered MacPherson's identity, Geoff's men quickly ostra-

cize him. Accompanying MacPherson is his wife Judy, who, it turns out, is Geoff's former flame. Judy doesn't understand why other pilots shun her husband; but neither does the husband know about her affair with Geoff. Short of pilots now that Joe has died, Geoff offers MacPherson a dangerous flight to airlift the injured son of the owner of the San Felipe mine from a site that is accessible only by landing on a small mesa. MacPherson accepts the assignment and carries it out under exceedingly difficult conditions. Meanwhile, the Kid has failed an eye test administered by Geoff. Knowing the danger the Kid represents to himself and others, Geoff has no alternative but to ground him. Geoff's pool of pilots is diminished still further when Les Peters has his arm broken in a fight, triggered by the frustration the Kid feels after learning that he can no longer fly.

Under pressure to deliver the mail on time in order to meet the terms of Dutchy's contract, Geoff decides to attempt a flight in treacherous weather. Despite the Kid's defective vision, Geoff agrees to let him come along as copilot. His only hope is that the new, more powerful trimotor that Dutchy has acquired will allow him to fly above the fourteen-thousand foot pass. Before he can leave, however, the distraught Bonnie, in fear for Geoff's life, pulls his revolver from its holster, tries to stop him from leaving, and accidentally shoots him in the shoulder. MacPherson volunteers to take Geoff's place, and he and the Kid take off in driving rain. Unable to reach the necessary altitude before icing sets in, they turn back but are hit by a flight of condors while trying to traverse the pass. Disregarding the badly injured Kid's plea for him to bail out and abandon him while there's still time, MacPherson succeeds in returning to the field and extracting the Kid from the plane before it explodes after landing. As the others watch, surrounding the table on which the Kid has been placed, Geoff quickly comes to the point: "Your neck's broken, Kid." Demonstrating a sensitivity that he had been unwilling to show with Bonnie or Judy, Geoff pays the Kid the final compliment of leaving him alone "to take off" on what will be his last flight.

Amid the general atmosphere of gloom, Bonnie goes to Geoff's office in order to bid him farewell. Trying to push Geoff to admit that he wants her to stay, she is dismayed when he suggests that her staying or leaving should be decided by the flipping of a coin: heads she stays, tails she leaves. Only when Geoff has run off with Les Peters to board their plane for a trip through the pass does she stop to look at the coin that Geoff has tossed. A relic belonging to the Kid that Geoff had set aside for himself, it has heads on both sides. Beaming with happiness, Bonnie watches the two injured aviators take off. Brimming with high spirits, though each reduced to the use of one arm, they show every sign of being happy to return to the element in which they belong.

Though Paul Mantz does some fancy flying in Utah, dipping beneath the edge of a canyon on takeoff and then scaling the face of a mountain in a desperate attempt to gain altitude, the focus in *Only Angels* is only marginally on what happens in the air.[99] To that extent, it represents the culmination of a trend in aviation movies that began with Hawks's *Dawn Patrol*. Using Hawks's usual binary opposition of insiders versus outsiders, *Only Angels* dramatizes a theme that other aviation films had generally touched upon superficially and without conviction: the emotional world in which aviators lived, the bonds that attached them to one another, and the rites and rituals by which they lived and died. Though it contains elements that had appeared in *Wings*, Hawks's own *Dawn Patrol*, and many other aviation movies about the First World War, it is all the more powerful because it is not about men caught up in an inexorable clash of nations. Instead of diminishing the tragic dimension of his film, this shift paradoxically has the effect of enhancing it. These men are not the pawns of a fate over which they have no control, as in *Dawn Patrol*; they risk their lives not because they have to, not out of patriotism, not because they feel duty-bound to defend their country at the risk of their own lives, but out of some kind of existential need to prove themselves and create a bond with others like themselves. Unable to articulate their motivations, they cannot imagine any other way of living, even if it means dying. When Dutchy asks Geoff why he allowed Joe to go on flying when he was bound to die sooner or later, his reply is: "You mean ground that kid? He'd sooner be where he is than quit." Whether or not this applies to Joe, it certainly does to Geoff.

If Hawks's film retains our interest, it is certainly not because of the plot, but because of the success with which he brought his characters to life. And this, in turn, was possible because of Hawks's familiarity with the way the aviators of the period spoke, his understanding of their mentality, and his instinctive empathy for the stoic fatalism with which they reacted to the perils that they faced.[100] The situation he chose offered an ideal setting for the exploration of the type of values and human relationships that fascinated him and brought out the best in his filmmaking. The affection between Geoff and the Kid goes beyond mere friendship or camaraderie: the trust and respect they feel for each other as fellow aviators, ultimately indicated by Geoff's sensitivity to the way the Kid wishes to die, seem to exist in a realm removed from the more superficial attachments that draw the men and women in the film together. The Kid loves Geoff for what he is; Bonnie cannot help imagining another life for him.

The subplot involving Bat MacPherson gives Hawks an opportunity to present his own version of secular redemption. Guilty of the worst of sins for an aviator – leaving his mechanic to die when he baled out to save himself – MacPherson starts out as the consummate outsider, banished from the bar where shared cigarettes and drink unite Geoff's men. His salvation and integration into the group, after the demonstration of his adherence to its values, is signaled by Geoff's announcement that, before dying, the Kid had asked him to buy MacPherson a drink. As the brother of MacPherson's victim, only the Kid can forgive him, and, as Geoff realizes, the Kid's absolution disposes of any reservations the other members of the group might retain. Holding the glass with bandaged hands, MacPherson moves toward a distant table; Geoff consecrates his inclusion in the group by inviting him to have it here "with us" and by lighting his cigarette. By contrast, another pilot is fired curtly by Geoff and banished because he refuses to fly a load of nitroglycerin at the risk of his life. When he protests that flying explosives was not in his contract, Geoff dismisses him

Pl. 172. Geoff lights
MacPherson's cigarette.

with a disdainful glance and doesn't even bother to reply. Hawksian heroes do not live by scraps of paper. MacPherson had understood this; Gent Shelton had not.

Bonnie can also – provisionally – be integrated into the group at the end because she has made up her mind to love Geoff the way the Kid did.[101] She will try to live by the Kid's code: she will swear when Geoff tries to kill himself, be proud of him when he doesn't, and be there when he comes back. The one thing that she won't do is to try to prevent him from flying. But, of course, who can tell what will happen in the future? Geoff already suspects that she's "just like all the rest." The prospects for a happy coexistence between these two strong-willed persons seem distinctly unpromising. How different the ending here is than the one in *Test Pilot*, when Gable, improbably, gives up dangerous flying after his close friend, the mechanic, dies. No Hawksian hero would ever do that. Hawks believed firmly that nobody causes anything; things are destined to happen; when people get killed, it's generally because they're not good enough at their job; and when that happens, there's no point in moping around.[102]

Judged against other examples of the genre, *Only Angels Have Wings* is an aviation film that manages to be distinctive while at the same time incorporating many elements with which audiences would have been familiar. Though Hawks is careful to offer the thrilling flying scenes that viewers of these type of films would have expected, his real interest is in the rites and rituals of aviators – in what separates them from people who do not fly, and in the talk with which they fend off the constantly present chance of death. He makes us come to like these men, just as Bonnie does, overcoming our initial revulsion against the harsh and seemingly absurd code of "useless service" by which they live; but we do so only at a certain price by overlooking the lack of motivation for their actions, their idiosyncratic values, and their tendency to view women as potentially destructive figures whose main function in the movie seems to be to obstruct the heroic work of men.[103]

If Hawks is a modernist, then, as some have argued, I would submit that it is not because of his love for fast machines, still less because of the remote setting he chose for *Only Angels*, or the type of pilots he portrays, but rather because of the way he chooses to tell his story.[104] Through the use of multiple perspectives Hawks forces us to revise our understanding of characters we thought we knew.[105] Geoff is not the "hard man, much too hard" that Dutchy takes him for in one of the picture's early scenes. MacPherson is not a coward, as Geoff helps his wife to understand. And even Bonnie turns out to be somewhat different from what she at first appears; as the daughter of a trapeze artist who insisted on working without a net and was killed while exercising his craft, she is no stranger to danger. The lesson of the movie, then, is that no one can be taken at face value; everyone, including MacPherson's wife, is capable of becoming something else.

Hawks also shares the modernist belief that less can be more. Though it may be excessive to call Hawks the "Le Courbusier of the sound film," he certainly understood that stripping a film of its ornament and reducing it to its narrative skeleton could actually increase its impact.[106] Economy of expression was his goal; and this was related to his growing realization that the coherence and believability of a story is less important than the interaction between the characters and the impact of individual scenes. Hence though the entire plot of *Only Angels Have Wings* hangs upon the fulfillment of a six-month mail contract, we are never given a glimpse of the agents who represent the ghostly entity that will decide the fate of Dutchy's air service; nor do we have any reason to believe at the end of the picture that there is any realistic possibility of meeting its terms. All these characteristics of Hawks's style as a filmmaker identify him as a contemporary of the modernist novelists of the 1920s, like Hemingway and Faulkner, whose writings he knew and with whom he sometimes worked.[107]

Critics who reviewed *Only Angels Have Wings* when it first appeared found its flying scenes exciting, but were inclined to discount its story as "regulation muddle" and "routine" fare.[108] Hawks's later admirers have been less troubled by its lack of coherence and reliance on coincidence and have argued that the suspension of disbelief it requires is well worth the price of admission to the multitude of delights it offers. One has gone so far as to call *Only Angels* a "completely achieved masterpiece" that draws "together the main thematic threads of Hawks's work into a single complex web."[109] Few, I think, would share Frank Nugent's harsh judgment that the whole came to nothing but "an overly familiar total. It's fairly good melodrama, nothing more."[110]

On the contrary, from my perspective what is striking about *Only Angels Have Wings*, is how, for all its similarities to the aviation films that had preceded it – the dedicated leader determined to get the mail through on time, the aviator with a tainted past who goes under a new name, the veteran flyer who is grounded, the solemn gathering of the relics of pilots who have died – Hawks's picture actually differed from these earlier pictures in the way it uses this material and above all in its characterizations. Geoff, as portrayed by Cary Grant, is far more complex than his equivalents in *Air Mail* and *Ceiling Zero*. Though he loves flying, he has little in common with the likes of Pat O'Brien's Duke Talbot or Cagney's Dizzy Davis. While not averse to taking risks, he is no grandstander, and he prides himself on his professionalism: one cannot imagine Geoff embarking on a suicidal flight. On three occasions in the picture, he commands his pilots to return to base rather than to risk unnecessarily their lives. Bonnie fits into neither of the categories of the women one usually finds in aviation films; she is not the good girl who stands passively by, supporting her man in the sky through thick and thin, nor is she a non-comprehending complainer who threatens to pull him down to earth. Bonnie loves Geoff, but she is also a survivor who has the guts to leave him if she perceives him as being unable or unwilling to reciprocate her love.

The lifting of gloom at the end of the movie cannot conceal that the outcome of the story is ambiguous. Geoff is in high spirits not because Bonnie is staying, but because he is about to leave the ground. And who can predict what will happen when and if Geoff returns? Who knows whether Bonnie will be able to endure life with an aviator, or whether she will crack under the pressure of living with a man who puts his passion for flying above all other values, certainly domestic ones. The message of *Only Angels* seems to be that the past need not pursue us like an albatross; that the future is unknowable, hence not worth worrying about; and that all that matters is the present that has to be lived intensely, even at the risk of death.[111] Whether or not one regards this as subversive of the dominant Hollywood ideology that emphasized happy endings and rose-tinged domestic futures, it shows how a talented director, inspired by his material and assisted by an able group of people, could take a well-worn genre and stretch and refine it to fit his own sensibility.

★   ★   ★

I willingly confess my admiration for *Only Angels Have Wings*; I expect to go on enjoying its pleasures. But I am not unaware of the superficiality of its exploration of the aviator's psyche. It was as if Hawks set out to say something profound about the motives that led men to fly and then realized he did not really know what it was that he wanted to tell us. Was it not Hawks himself speaking when the Kid confesses to Bonnie that after flying for twenty-two years he cannot explain to her why men do it? Frank Nugent was on to something when he wrote in his review of *Test Pilot* that "risk, adventure, and dogged courage are the elements that have made flying dramatic. And so dramatic have they made it that no film of aviation can be as interesting on the ground as it becomes the moment a motor roars and a man and a plane take off into the blue unknown."[112] This no doubt explains why the only parts of *Only Angels Have Wings* that Nugent could appreciate were when the "plot's wheels leave the ground and take off over the Andes. Few things, after all, are as exciting as a plane in flames, or the metallic voices of a pilot in a fog-shrouded plane and the chap in the radio room, or a screaming power dive, or the wild downward swoop of a plane taking off from a canyon's rim."[113]

Nugent found Hawks's picture "very exciting and juvenile." Its dialogue, he thought, tended toward "silly romanticism." But judged by this standard, what Hollywood aviation movie could pass muster? Was there not something inherently exciting, juvenile, and romantic about flight? And was it not these qualities that appealed to the audiences that went to see these films, not to mention the men and women who chose to fly?

The Hollywood studios seemed to think so; by 1940 they had ground out hundreds of aviation films. Though surveys have been done, no one has calculated the exact number.[114] As early as 1933, critics had begun to complain that the "mass of earlier flight pictures" might undermine the enthusiasm of the public for this sort of production.[115] But the studios were undeterred. Audiences, particularly young men, continued to respond to these pictures. And there is every reason to believe that the people who made them enjoyed their work and believed that they were doing something worthwhile. Actors, cameramen, and directors found it "thrilling" to watch expert and daring pilots perform outside loops, fly upside down ten feet above the ground, and roll their ships with the wing tips almost touching the field. It made them feel that they were living a great adventure. In the film guide prepared for his 1938 epic of the history of flight, Wellman confessed that he believed that his picture had caught the spirit of "the greatest story ever told – the story of men with wings. If it tells only a part of what they dreamed, then my dream has been recaptured."[116]

By the mid-1930s, work on aviation films had become highly specialized. Paul Mantz was the stunt pilot of choice, his title elevated to "technical adviser."[118] Though other pilots, like

Pl. 173. Mantz, inverted, flies within inches of Frank Clarke during the National Air Races of 1936 at Mines Field (now LAX).

Frank Clarke and Tex Rankin, might have been his equal in executing difficult and dangerous aerobatics, none had his knack for flying the camera plane and obtaining the kind of footage that directors needed. He approached stunt flying as a business and by the late 1930s had achieved a quasi-monopoly over the aerial phases of the most prestigious aviation films.[118] Elmer Dyer and Charles Marshall brought the same kind of expertise to aerial photography that Mantz had in his flying, and they often worked together. Saunders and Wead were the writers whose names among the titles guaranteed the authenticity of a flying picture; they faced no serious competition, and when Saunders committed suicide in 1940, Wead reigned unchallenged as the dean of aviation writers. Many of Hollywood's leading male actors (and some of its leading ladies) had donned goggles and a scarf and climbed into a cockpit on more than one occasion. Several, such as Wallace Beery, Richard Arlen, and Ray Milland, learned how to fly and owned their own airplanes. Still others, such as Jimmy Stewart, Tyrone Power, Wayne Morris, Robert Taylor, and Clark Gable, would serve with distinction in the air services during the Second World War. David Niven was so taken by his role in the 1938 version of *Dawn Patrol* that he tried, unsuccessfully, to enlist in the RAF.[119]

The Hollywood studios cannot be faulted for failing to tackle a variety of aviation stories. On the contrary, they tried everything from adventure serials aimed at adolescents to movies that featured air hostesses. They were alert to the latest aviation headlines and were quick to dramatize Pan American's opening up of a trans-Pacific route (*China Clipper*), the army's development of the B-17 Bomber (*Men With Wings*), the 1936 record-breaking flight of Alexander de Seversky's SEV-S2 fighter (*Test Pilot*), and the excitement generated by the Bendix Air Race from Los Angeles to New York, the National Air Races in Cleveland, and the Powder Puff Derby (*Tail Spin*).[120] If the plot lines of these pictures often seemed to resemble one another, it was because so many of them were written, or based on stories, by Frank Wead. In the world of his imagination, the airplane was a metaphor for fun, freedom, and escape from the realm of adults and, above all, from the domestic sphere of women. It was a fast and expensive toy for the man who wanted to remain an adolescent and avoid entangling domestic alliances. Think, for example, of the scene toward the end of *Air Mail* when Duke Talbot decides on the spur of the moment to abandon the woman with whom he has run off to a Los Angeles hotel room, presumably with thoughts of a lasting relationship. Peering through the hotel window and seeing biplanes flying in formation, his priorities fall quickly into place. Duke slaps the woman on the behind, mutters a vague farewell, and rushes off to save Mike Miller, a man for whom he has up to this point only expressed disdain.

Pl. 174.   Myrna Loy as an aviatrix in Paramount's 1935 production of *Wings in the Dark*, which costarred Cary Grant.

Pl. 175.   Elmer Dyer beside his camera.

One could argue, of course, that Hollywood filmmakers were simply responding to the market and providing the public with what they expected and wanted to see. Still, it is impressive how homogeneous the message of Hollywood's major aviation pictures was. The vision they projected was of a male elite in love with a new technology. Women who threaten the fraternity of flyers must be expelled from their self-contained world, as is the sophisticated New York socialite, played by Rosalind Russell, in MGM's 1935 service film, *West Point of the Air*. Even when the protagonists were women aviators, as in RKO's 1938 *Tail Spin*, also written by Wead, no doubt is left that the women choose to fly in order to get closer to the men they love. Aviation remains a man's world, and women approach it at their peril. If they move from being spectators to participants, they risk losing both their lives and their femininity. The spoiled rich girl, played by Constance Bennett in *Tail Spin*, is reconciled with the flyer she loves only because she deliberately loses an air race that she would otherwise have won. She had trespassed upon a space that belongs to men and must pay the price of an accident that brings her back to earth. Movies that appear to be of pacifist inspiration, like *Dawn Patrol* in both its 1930 and 1938 versions, turn out on closer scrutiny to send a more complex message. While not concealing the terrible loss of life taken by aerial combat, at the same time they celebrate the fun of flight and the sense of fraternity it creates among the males who have mastered it. And perhaps this is the story that Americans wanted to tell themselves about aviation: that flying was essentially a form of masculine escape from the bonds of earth, humdrum existence, and the constraining responsibilities of everyday life, especially the demands of nagging women.[121]

Thus those Italian critics who detected a difference between *Luciano Serra, pilota* and the American aviation films of the past decade were not wrong, and the contrast would have been even sharper had they seen *Only Angels Have Wings*, which appeared the following year. The aviator portrayed by Cary Grant in *Only Angels* is a man outside society, a loner and individualist of a sort not easily conceivable in Europe. The only loyalty he has is to a highly personal code and a circle of friends he has chosen. His goal – to meet the deadline

Pl. 176.   This advertisement for *Men With Wings* leaves no doubt that flying is a man's business.

Pl. 177.   Of these three aviatrixes pictured in this poster for *Tail Spin*, two confess that they fly because it brings them closer to the men they love.

Pl. 178.   Constance Bennett contemplates her fate in *Tail Spin*.

Pl. 179.   Luciano Serra
rescues his injured son.

Pl. 180.   The pilots of the
Mary Ann receive their orders
prior to take off from Hickam
Field, Hawaii.

for a mail contract – seems to be more of a pretext for action that he enjoys than a rational motivation that justifies the sacrifice of men's lives. He wants to be beholden to no one; and in turn, he wants no one to be beholden to him.

The aviator, as he is interpreted by Amedeo Nazzari in *Luciano Serra*, could not be more different. He too finds himself an exile in Latin America; but unlike the bachelor Geoff Carter, the husband, father, and patriot Luciano Serra suffers from his estrangement from family and his *patria*. His ambition is to return covered with the glory of a successful transatlantic flight so that his family and his country can once again feel pride in him. *Luciano Serra* is not about flight as escape, but about flight as a means of reestablishing social and generational bonds, undermined by the weak and corrupt liberal regime and now restored by Fascism. Luciano's son becomes an aviator in emulation of his father, who had distinguished himself during the First World War, thus cementing the connection between the war and postwar generations. But the air force into which Aldo integrates himself has been rebuilt according to the Fascist principle that individualist action must be subordinated to the needs of the community. He becomes a member of a disciplined collective body into whose ranks he melts at the end of the picture. It would take the trauma of war to move the Hollywood aviation movie from its obsession with individual exploits, a lingering echo of the immense resonance of Lindbergh's flight, to a celebration of collective action in which the individual learns how to subordinate himself to the group. Paradoxically, it would be the supreme individualist, Howard Hawks – maker of *Dawn Patrol, Ceiling Zero*, and *Only Angels Have Wings* – who most successfully made this transition in his 1943 picture, *Air Force*, the very title with its collective connotation suggesting that the days of Dizzy Davis and Geoff Carter were now long gone.

4

Knights of the Air

The adventures of the air are the supreme *chanson de geste* of our time.

Joseph Kessel, 1933[1]

HOLLYWOOD was unequaled in its ability to capture the ludic dimension of aviation. In approaching the making of flying films, the studios might well have chosen as their motto the title Amelia Earhart chose to give to her 1932 book of memoirs: *The Fun of It.*[2] But for deeper reflections on the motivations of aviators and the meanings that people gave to flight, one has to turn to French writers of the period, who were able to connect aeronautical exploits to a tradition that would have struck most Americans as far-fetched and distinctly unmodern.

In November 1929, Maurice Martin du Gard, editor of the prestigious literary journal *Les Nouvelles Littéraires*, devoted a long article to a recently published book entitled *L'Espace*. Who, he asked rhetorically, was the author of this work; and quickly answered: "a knight in the best tradition of finesse, audacity, and the novel of adventures. How wonderful it was to escape from the world while setting such an example?"[3] Though it remained unspecified, readers would have understood that the tradition Martin du Gard referred to was French.

The man to whom the editor of the *Nouvelles Littéraires* dedicated these extravagant lines was indeed a remarkable figure. Pierre Weiss, scion of a cultured and accomplished Jewish family from Nancy, was a major in the French Air Force with a distinguished war record, 3,600 hours of flight time, and many notable aeronautical exploits to his credit. We first encountered him on the night that Lindbergh landed at Le Bourget. It was Weiss who organized Lindbergh's rescue from the crowd, then sheltered him in his office, and later drove him to the American Embassy in Paris. En route to the embassy, Weiss was at Lindbergh's side when he stopped at the Arc de Triomphe to pay homage to France's unknown soldier. In the same year that *L'Espace* appeared, Weiss, along with a companion, had broken the world speed record for a closed circuit of five thousand kilometers in a flight of twenty-seven hours.[4] Six years before he had been the first pilot in Europe to execute the refueling of an airplane in flight. There were few capitals in Europe he had not

Pl. 181. A 1929 poster for Aéropostale that has been adapted for a German clientele, emphasizing the international reach of the famous French airmail service.

Pl. 182. The cover of Bordeaux's biography of Guynemer. The book's super title, *Le Chevalier de l'Air* (Knight of the Air), conveys its theme.

Pl. 183. Captain Pierre Weiss in the early 1920s. Weiss would end his career as a general in the French Air Force.

visited by air. The "sweetness of perpetual danger" was, for him, an integral component of the profession he loved. "Born to die quickly and soon, we speak everyday to the invisible. Carry us away this evening if it pleases you, oh destiny!"[5]

As these lines suggest, what singled Weiss out from the majority of record-breaking aviators was his literary aspirations. His previous collections of poems and aviation books, inspired by his idol, friend, and fellow Lorrainer Maurice Barrès, had been published in small editions and directed toward a narrow circle of fellow aesthetes and aeronautical admirers. Martin du Gard made no effort to conceal the limitations he found in those earlier works; but in *L'Espace* he felt that for the first time Weiss had realized his literary talent and found his own distinctive "music." In this work, a "voluptuous painter" had teamed up with a "philosopher" to evoke the changing seasons viewed from the cockpit of an airplane.

Martin du Gard was especially moved by the way that Weiss had brought his deep culture to bear in filtering his impressions of flight through a refined poetic sensibility. "In autumn, in winter, Weiss achieves the same level of painterly perfection when he captures for us the long scarves of fog, the clusters of snow and of smoke." What reader, he asked, will not be enchanted when Weiss reflects on the *Nymphéas* of Monet while flying over the countryside surrounding the painter's home at Giverny? Who will be able to resist his description of a routine flying maneuver as "the delicious destiny of being endlessly able to efface all internal suffering . . . by a turn above a transparent object in which the world was nothing but a reflection of itself?"

Martin du Gard was struck by the paradox that Weiss had only realized himself as a poet when he abandoned verse in favor of prose. But wasn't every real aviator also a poet?[6] Martin du Gard ended his account of Weiss's book by hoping that when advancing years had robbed the pilot of the youth that daily flying required, he would continue to pursue his vocation as a writer and add many "vivid and golden pages" to the literature about the "new knighthood" of the air.[7]

The praise Martin du Gard lavished on Weiss contrasted with the dim view he took of earlier aviation literature. Since man had conquered his fear of the "infinite spaces" of the air and learned how to move about in it at will, the literary benefits of this achievement struck Martin du Gard as "meager." Where was the Pierre Loti, the Balzac, the Victor Hugo who would reveal to us life in the sky? So many rich secrets were there to be revealed by a writer who could combine the role of psychologist and moralist.

An innocent reader might easily have taken away from Martin du Gard's article the impression that hitherto few French writers of substance had responded to the new technology of flight. But this was not the case. Indeed, in no other Western country had highly regarded writers taken aviation and airmen as seriously as they had in France.

In 1911 Edmond Rostand, one of France's most highly esteemed playwrights, had dedicated a long poem to the heroism of French aviators who risked their lives in their pursuit of the domination of the skies.[8] During the same period, Emile Driant, a candidate for Alfred de Mun's chair in the French Academy, produced a series of popular novels that dramatized the potential of the flying machine for the bloody wars of conquest and empire-building that he foresaw in the near future.[9] Even Marcel Proust, France's greatest twentieth-century writer, had not been indifferent to the charms of flight and the power of aviation imagery. In *La Prisonnière*, the narrator confesses the envy that he and Albertine had felt for a returning aviator, "this stroller who had gone up to savor, in the distant expanses of the lonely horizon, the calm and clarity of the evening."[10] Nearing the end of the novel in *Le Temps retrouvé*, Proust used the metaphor of an aviator's takeoff from the ground to express his own ascension toward "the silent heights of memory."[11]

During the war the emphasis in aviation writing naturally shifted to the heroism of the airmen who were sacrificing their lives for the defense of France. Henry Bordeaux, a future member of the French Academy, devoted a widely read volume to the "heroic life" of the

GUYNEMER appartient désormais à la légende. Ne voulut-on pas donner son nom à un groupe d'étoiles? Pâle comme un ange du Greco, le jeune homme au grand cœur traverse le ciel de France. Les étendards s'inclinent sur son passage.

ace Georges Guynemer, who received credit for fifty-three victories before himself being shot down and killed in September 1917. Bordeaux's biography was quickly translated into dozens of languages, with prefaces by well-known personalities, such as Rudyard Kipling in England and Theodore Roosevelt in the United States. Its theme – that Guynemer had been the Roland of his time, "the last of the knight-errants, the first of the knights of the air" – would have a long life in French aviation literature.[12]

Even a writer as determined as Jean Cocteau was to establish his credentials as a champion of the avant-garde had no hesitations about celebrating Guynemer's glory during the Great War. "Henceforth Guynemer belongs to the realm of legend. Isn't there talk of giving his name to a group of stars? As pale as one of El Greco's angels, the young man with his generous heart streaks across the sky of France. Standards are lowered as he passes." The long poem Cocteau dedicated to his friend Roland Garros – at that time a German prisoner-of-war – suggests the power that aviation metaphors had come to have for serious writers. A famous pilot, Garros had taken Cocteau up for his "baptism of the air"; now Cocteau reciprocated in his poetry:

> I, in turn, take you up
> An aviator of ink
> me
> And here are my loops
> And my altitude records.[13]

The tendency to celebrate fallen French aces continued after the war and even reached the theater with Maurice Rostand's 1925 play based on Guynemer's life entitled *L'Archange*

(The Archangel), another term that French aviation writers would find irresistible.[14] But the French could not live indefinitely on the exploits of the past.[15] And, as Sacha Guitry's 1928 play and Pierre Weiss's books reminded them, a young American, Charles Lindbergh, was the hero of the moment. It was Lindbergh, as Weiss explained to his French readers, who had opened the way to a new era of chivalric exploits. Indeed, it was Lindbergh's flight that had rescued the French from the state of lassitude into which they had fallen.[16] It appeared that the flame of aeronautical prowess had passed from the French to the Americans. Where would the next Garros and Guynemer be found? And who would find them?

★   ★   ★

Not Pierre Weiss, as it turned out. Weiss certainly did his best to meet Martin du Gard's expectations by producing many more "vivid and golden pages" celebrating the new knighthood of the air. He went on to publish a series of aviation books during the 1930s, some of which, like *Le Portrait bleu du Sagittaire*, deserve to be rescued from the unjustified oblivion into which they have fallen. The best of them reflected the wide-ranging culture that his education in an elite French secondary school and university had given him, his wonderful (if sometimes overly precious) way with words, and his knack for conveying the sensations of an aviator during an adventurous flight.[17] In comparison to Balbo, the accounts he provides of his own flights seem self-effacing. He seems more at ease describing the exploits of other aviators (including Balbo's) than going on about his own considerable achievements.[18] No one wrote with more passion of aviation, whose "profane beauty" was, for him, the truest and most indisputable manifestation of a chivalric elite.[19] In his view, aviation was "a vast feast of the intelligence as well as a practical force." "It will dispose for a long time to come of a secret power . . . Its tide has not yet ebbed."[20]

But Weiss's cult of Maurice Barrès, his position as a career officer in the French Air Force, his deeply felt patriotism, and his willingness to sing uncritically the praises of French aviation figures, whether military or civil, deprived his writing of the edgy cynicism and the Nietzschean sense of the abyss that French critics responded to in the late 1920s and early 1930s.[21] He could not have been more removed from the nihilist sensibility of Henry de Montherlant, Pierre Drieu la Rochelle, and André Malraux, the rising literary stars of the period. As Weiss himself recognized, he was out of step with the "agitated, complicated, and hatred-inclined Europe" of the 1930s.[22]

Leaving aside his traditional values and old-fashioned style, Weiss lacked a compelling narrative capable of galvanizing the French public. Where was such a story to be found? The writer who happened across it and possessed the insight to intuit its importance was Joseph Kessel, an immensely prolific author whose fame as a writer of *grands reportages*, penchant for fast publications, and lack of philosophical pretensions has long obscured the important role he played in French literary life during the years between the wars.[23]

Built like a boxer, bull-necked yet with feline eyes and a gentle look that many found seductive, Kessel broke upon the French literary scene in 1923 with a novel entitled *L'Équipage* (The Air Crew). The great success of the French literary scene that year, Kessel's novel went through eighty-two editions in thirty months and was proclaimed by Léon Daudet in the monarchist and anti-Semitic newspaper *L'Action Française* to herald the advent of "a powerful literary personality." Indeed, Daudet, whose authority among the readers of the *Action Française* was unquestioned, went further and predicted that Kessel would go on to produce a body of great work.[24] Daudet was not mistaken in anticipating

a brilliant career for Kessel; four decades later, this Argentinian-born son of Russian Jewish émigrés would be elected to the French Academy.

Though in appearance nothing but one more in the long stream of memoir-novels recounting the war experiences of its author, *L'Équipage* stood out from its predecessors, and not only by the natural storytelling talent of its author. To begin with, it portrayed in muscular and hard-hitting prose a different type of war than the depressing hell of the trenches to which the French reading public was accustomed by novels like Henri Barbusse's *Le Feu* and Roland Dorgelès's *Les Croix de bois*. Kessel wrote of the world of wartime aviation that its author had experienced as a young observer in 1917–18 during the decisive battles of that year. Kessel made no attempt to hide the unsavory aspects of the life that he and his fellow flyers led. In his novel, they seem more preoccupied with their pleasures and rituals than with the winning of the war.[25] They drink heavily, play cards, gamble beyond their means, frequent the local cabaret – a "vulgar and ill-smelling place" – and couple with unwashed and unattractive local girls when withdrawn behind the lines to rest. Medals are easily come by and toasted by unending flows of wine and champagne. When not flying because of bad weather, they indulge themselves in "deliciously lazy pursuits" and while away the "nonchalant mornings" in comfortable circumstances that make them feel guilty when they encounter infantrymen on their way up to the trenches.[26] They can be noisy, crude, and juvenile and amuse themselves at the expense of the young recruits who come to fill the places of those who have died. Their mess is reminiscent of life in a disreputable American fraternity.

Yet the tenderness and deep affection with which Kessel described these men raised them to the level of mythical heroes. The "haggard brightness in their eyes" and the "fever-

ish light" that hovered over their faces were like a "sort of offering that elevated these men who cared so little about their death."[27] Daudet found Kessel's description of these airmen "unforgettable." Writing in the *Nouvelle Revue Française*, a literary journal where reputations could be made or broken, the aviator and writer Roger Allard went even further. Kessel's portrait of his squadron leader Gabriel Thélis, Allard claimed, was "worthy of Plutarch" and the account he had written of his death was reminiscent of the *Song of Roland*.[28] Though he expressed reservations about Kessel's style, Allard went on to say that he possessed something vastly more important: "the magic ability to give passions a memorable face, and to lend to the humblest human words the heroic accent of the epoch."[29]

As adept as Kessel's "rapid and flaming" prose was in evoking "the intoxication of flight," what impressed the most sensitive readers of this first novel was the moral context in which the author had set his tale.[30] Kessel presented the air war as an arena in which new values of fraternity and comradeship were being forged. What drove Kessel's protagonists to risk their lives was not some abstract notion of patriotism, nor even a Nietzschean will to transcend themselves in an act of self-overcoming, but a common commitment to a male brotherhood, in Kessel's view the highest form of human love. The pilot Claude Maury and the young observer Jean Herbillon, who form the aircrew that gives Kessel's novel its title, are transformed by their combat experience into "a single moral entity, a cell with two souls that beat with a similar rhythm . . . They did not merely love each other; they completed each other."[31]

The power this aspect of Kessel's novel exercised on his contemporaries is displayed in a letter that the already renowned Catholic novelist François Mauriac wrote him after reading *L'Équipage*. Confessing that he had at first been suspicious of the theme of Kessel's novel – during a leave in Paris Jean Herbillon discovers to his horror that his young mistress is his pilot's wife – Mauriac went on to say what a surprise he had felt to find himself in the midst of a true human drama. There he was "en pleine verité!" (in the midst of living truth). He especially admired the way Kessel portrayed the friendship between the two men. Kessel, he said, was the first novelist to have captured the nature of "the heroic camaraderie that it was women's mission to destroy . . ."[32] "But will those who read you in 1980 suspect that *L'Équipage* is an historical document and that such young men existed? And yet who among us does not carry in his heart the memory of a Thélis?"[33]

Mauriac was perceptive in underlining the truth of Kessel's improbable story.[34] The striking figures with which Kessel had peopled his novel had all been members of his squadron; the prototype of Gabriel Thélis, Thélis Vachon, had died the hero's death that Kessel described so eloquently in the last chapter of his novel; and while Jean Herbillon was, in most respects, a faithful portrayal of the young airman Kessel had been in 1917–18, it was in fact he, Kessel, who had been betrayed while at the front – only by a mistress rather than a wife, a young actress with a husband under arms whom he had innocently left in the care of his beloved younger brother.[35] The bitter misogyny given expression by Jean Herbillon no doubt reflects feelings that Kessel still harbored in 1923.[36]

★　　★　　★

L'Équipage launched Kessel's career. Money, mistresses, the Légion d'honneur, and the literary Grand Prix of the French Academy soon came his way. Kessel's bouts of drinking in gypsy cafés and the colorful company he kept made his life as famous as his work. His sense for books and articles that would appeal both to demanding critics and the reading public seemed infallible; his touch seemed made of gold. But despite the trappings of success and the prospect of a brilliant career, Kessel was tortured by the knowledge of his moral failings, made even more unbearable by the premature death in 1928 of his young wife from tuberculosis. As André Gide intuited, *Belle de jour*, the highly acclaimed and widely read novel Kessel published that year, projected onto a woman the self-destructive, yet insuperable conflict its author felt between his love for his adoring and ailing wife and his inability to withstand the pleasures of the flesh.[37] A man as pursued by internal demons and as in love with exotic settings as Kessel was, would always be tempted by escape. Thus when two aviators regaled him in December 1928 with stories about the airline for which they flew and invited him to share the dangers of a flight from Casablanca to Dakar, Kessel could hardly refuse – especially since he was in search of fresh material for the newly created weekly *Gringoire* that he had agreed to edit.

The two aviators were Marcel Reine and Eduard Serre. The cocktails they shared with Kessel at Chez Francis on the Place d'Alma ignited in short order a sense of comradeship, facilitated by the presence of the famous flyer Joseph Le Brix and the awareness of the three airmen that Kessel, author of *L'Équipage*, had flown during the war. They quickly treated the celebrated journalist and novelist as one of theirs. The evening they spent together would forever remain engraved in Kessel's memory.

Reine was twenty-seven years old, short, charming, and earthy. A master of Parisian slang whose language was unprintable in 1929, he overflowed with *joie de vivre* and was inclined to take regulations lightly. "I have aviation in my blood," he confided to Kessel.[38] Reine came as close as you could imagine to a French version of Cagney's Dizzy Davis in *Ceiling Zero*. Serre was thin, frail, intellectual, and a graduate of France's finest engineering school, Polytéchnique – the type of highly educated technician that civil aviation could no longer do without.[39] Eternally dressed in a blue three-piece suit with a lorgnon and a briefcase, his look was "a little distant and full of reflection and gentleness, as if fixed on new problems that he wished to resolve."[40] Serre could not have been further removed from Reine, though he shared with him a love of flight and a taste for adventure. An observer during the war, a pilot in peacetime, Serre's job was to oversee radio and electrical equipment, essential for the tasks that lay ahead. Reine and Serre represented, in reality, the contrast between the past and the future of aviation that appeared so often in the Hollywood aviation pictures of the 1930s. For all their differences, however, what united them were their proven courage and their dedication to the cause of civil aviation. Both of them would die in its service.

Pl. 189.   A caricature of Marcel Reine. The men of Aéropostale adored him, and so did Kessel who wrote about him with deep affection more than four decades after their first meeting.

Pl. 190.   A caricature of Eduard Serre. Serre was respected more than liked.

Pl. 191. Latécoère in a photographic portrait by Nadar.

Pl. 192. The cover of a brochure depicting the Latécoère line's route from its base in Toulouse to Casablanca. The plane portrayed is a good deal more advanced than the ones Latécoère's lines were using in the late 1920s.

Reine and Serre worked for an airline, founded by the engineer and industrialist Pierre-Georges Latécoère. Even before the war had ended, Latécoère had conceived the extraordinary idea of creating an aerial network of some twelve to thirteen thousand kilometers that would extend southward from his base in Toulouse along the Spanish coast to Algeria and Morocco, continue down the African coast to the French colony of Senegal, then at the narrowest point between Africa and Latin America, overfly the Atlantic, thus making it possible to unite by air the cities of Europe with faraway Rio de Janeiro, Buenos Aires, and Santiago de Chile. Latécoère's vision was extraordinary – some might say mad – because in 1918 the radius of aircraft was extremely limited, the unreliability of aircraft engines predictable, navigational instruments limited to a compass, flight by night inconceivable, low ceilings an invitation to gamble with one's life, the dangers of forced landings in areas of Africa not under European control daunting, and the ability to negotiate the right to overfly foreign territories uncertain. Given these circumstances, the only cargo Latécoère could consider transporting was mail; and even this would have to be heavily subsidized by the French state.

By January 1929, when Kessel arrived at Toulouse to catch his plane to Casablanca, Latécoère's dream was well on its way to realization, though the cost in human lives had been heavy and control of his airline had slipped from his hands and passed to a financial group headed by the Latin-American based financier, Marcel Bouilloux-Laffont. Toulouse–Casablanca was now considered a routine, if often bumpy journey. Casablanca–Dakar was another story: the fact that Reine and Serre had just spent four months in captivity after a forced landing that resulted in their capture by a dissident Moorish tribe was a reminder that the flight down the west African coast was not for the faint-hearted.[41]

Accompanied by Serre, Kessel left Paris on 2 January 1929. During the next three weeks he lived with some of the men who, by dint of determination, discipline, and dedication were creating an airmail service that would stretch from Toulouse to Santiago. Known to the general public by its new name – Aéropostale – it was to the men who built it simply *La Ligne* (The Line). It became, and remained for the rest of his life, one of Kessel's great passions. Among its members, he rediscovered to his delight the community and type of male comradeship he had known during the war in his squadron; only now "the sign that death puts on the men it stalks" and "the dim flame" that alternately clouded and illuminated these aviators' faces were the product, not of a catastrophic war, but of an unambiguously admirable effort to conquer nature and, in so doing, to bring humanity closer together. For Kessel, *La Ligne* was not merely an airline but "a gigantic organization with its leaders, its discipline, its engineers, its ships, its aerial fleet, its creators in the desert, its adventurers, and its mystique . . . " In short, it was one of the most beautiful creations of the human spirit that one could hope to encounter. Yet for all his enthusiasm, Kessel did not conceal his realization that, while now still in the full bloom of youth, *La Ligne*'s definitive success would mean "mechanization and death." Risk and danger were the soil preconditions for *La Ligne*'s grandeur. Once their route was safe, the men who flew it would be nothing but technicians. Fortunately, that moment lay far away in the future.[42]

Kessel's account of his African adventure, first published as articles in *Gringoire*, then as a book under the title *Vent de sable* (Sand Storm), was a powerfully written epic, dedicated to the men of *La Ligne*.[43] The title that preceded its beginning chapter – "Documentary" – was meant to remind the reader that nothing in these pages had been invented. The series of adventures he would relate had been his own.[44] Though *Vent de sable* bore signs of the rapidity with which it had been written, it was one more demonstration that Kessel had a way of making topics his own. Banality was not one of his defects.

Despite his title, Kessel's theme was not the landscapes he had seen but the aviators and mechanics whose lives he had briefly shared. Taken together, they represented "a national and human treasure worth more than the majority of politicians, generals, and men of letters whose names and photographs clutter the newspapers."[45] Kessel wrote that he had glimpsed in the eyes of these simple and carefree men an elusive quality that one sometimes saw in the eyes of lovers, mystics, vagabonds, and mariners. Through their perilous work they had achieved "a fusion of sensual and spiritual forces, a tension in which each individual takes part, which is almost invincible."[46] When Kessel fell in love, he fell in love hard.

For Kessel the miracle of *La Ligne* was that though products of a technological civilization, servants of metal and matter, these men had been able to give their machines a soul – a soul that was often more beautiful and purer than their own. Here, as in *L'Équipage*, Kessel was fascinated by the way that aviation possessed the ability to transform men and raise them above themselves; for, in his view, the soul of *La Ligne* was not an amalgam of the individual souls of the aviators who composed it but the soul of aviation itself.[47] Though unable to formulate it in these words, the men of *La Ligne* lived for an abstraction that they prized more highly than their lives.

Kessel was at first puzzled by the willingness of these aviators to risk their lives for the cause of a business letter or a tourist's postcard. Why not delay rather than running the risk of flying in dangerously inclement weather? Why was *le courrier* (the mail) such a sacred word? The answer he came to understand was that these men were mystics, driven by a faith. "Without any doubt, I found myself in the presence of one of these cases of invincible human dedication – to an emblem, a symbol, an idol – that overcomes man's most violent instinct: that of self-preservation. I was confronted with a beautiful mystery."[48]

The idol to which these men were devoted was speed. In an age of railways and ocean liners, this was the only reason for being of an airline. Without the rationale of a more rapid form of transportation, there would be no Aéropostale. Thus when the pilots of *La Ligne* deified the mail, they were actually defending their life as "men with wings" and all the possibilities that aviation offered them, even if they lacked a clear conception of their own motives. Kessel had no doubt that they were right in doing so. "For without this interior flame that overcomes and transcends him . . . man is nothing but an unworthy or desperate mechanic."[49] No one could read *Vent de sable* without feeling that the best, the noblest, the most selfless, and the most generous sons of France were to be found aloft among the desert winds that blew between Casablanca and Dakar.

The nobility and sense of self-sacrifice of the men whose collective praises Kessel had sung throughout his book could only be enhanced by the author's revelation that the pilot who had flown him from Casablanca to Dakar, Émile Lécrivain, disappeared in the Atlantic on a routine flight between Agadir and Cap Juby only fifteen days after having delivered Kessel safely back to Casablanca. The first to fly the mail between Casablanca and Dakar, Lécrivain was unknown by the French public. Indeed, he suffered from the fact that the French government had yet to award him the Légion d'honneur. "I hope that they hurry . . . One never knows."[50] During the three weeks they spent together, Kessel had developed a deep affection for Mimile, as he was known among his many friends. This affection was elevated to respect and admiration when Mimile, during a superhuman struggle, saved Kessel, Serre, his radio operator, and another passenger from what seemed certain death when flying through a blinding sandstorm between Cap Juby and Villa Cisneros. It was this experience that had provided Kessel with the title for his book and its most enthralling pages.

Flying Kessel and three other men to Villa Cisneros, Mimile had lost his way in the "yellow prison" of the sandstorm and wandered out to sea. Long overdue at his destination and desperate to find land, he set a course of due east, only to find himself faced with cliffs along

Pl. 193. "Mimile" Lécrivain in 1926, looking anything but a hero.

166

the coast. An already dangerous situation became potentially fatal when Mimile's overheated engine refused to respond to his controls when he tried to ascend. As he struggled to avoid the cliffs, he entered a dangerous zone known by the pilots of *La Ligne* for its turbulence at lower altitudes. Their plane was buffeted with hammer-like blows; Kessel's head banged repeatedly against the wing above him. "Blown toward the sea, hurled into the air, the airplane cracked in every joint." The blows were followed by sudden dives; the plane seemed hopelessly out of control. "From its propeller to its tail, it was nothing but a trembling mass."[51] Kessel and his companions sensed that the end was near. They watched in a combination of fascination and fear as Mimile waged deadly battle with winds of hurricane force. "It was then," wrote Kessel, "that I saw him in all his grandeur. Torn from his seat by the battering ram-like blows, hunched over the pedals and the wheel, he worked with all his muscles, all his intelligence, and all his intuition. I don't know with which sense he guessed in advance the gusts of wind and took action to avoid them, to soften their blows." The destiny of four men lay in his hands. Suddenly the weary pilot's face broke into a smile "contracted by effort and paled by the sand." "A few seconds later, my eyes which were less practiced than Mimile's, distinguished at the end of a promontory drowned in yellow fog the faint lines of a building: Villa Cisneros."[52] A man who avidly sought out danger and had more than once faced death, Kessel had never before felt so afraid.[53]

Mimile represented everything that Kessel loved and admired in *La Ligne*: warmth, simplicity, comradeship, boundless *joie de vivre* and gaiety combined with generosity, courage, indifference to death, and dedication to the unwritten code of an organization that consisted solely of males.[54] The humility, innocence, and lack of heroic pretensions that emerge in Kessel's portrait of him only serve to reinforce Kessel's point that *La Ligne* constituted a fraternity that was greater than the sum of the individuals who belonged to it. It was *La Ligne* that had given Lécrivain, an ordinary person, the opportunity to become the great man he was. "How can I leave an airline like this," Mimile once asked Kessel. How could I abandon "the sea, my mechanics who expect everything from me, and then, the bases in the desert?" How many flights similar to his, Kessel thought, must Mimile have made during his forty months of service on the route between Casablanca and Dakar? How many epic battles with the elements must he have fought? "He didn't count them, and I believe he loved them. Besides, he felt for these flights, combined with sun, hurricanes, and fog, an almost sensual tenderness . . . He was a mystic. 'Aviation,' he told me, 'is my real mistress.' "[55]

Writing in 1929 on the eve of the breakthrough of civil aviation, Kessel was aware that before many years had passed the story he told would seem improbable. "Flying machines will soon be so rapid and so safe, their instruments and their use so perfected, that flight will become a tranquil way of traveling." But he allowed himself to hope that the men who were the first to carry the mail across the skies of the desert would not be completely forgotten. "Those who placed the first sails on hollow hulls did not have more heart or more daring."[56] *Vent de sable* would be Kessel's first hymn to the heroes of *La Ligne*, but not his last.

★　　★　　★

While on his three-week journey from Paris to Dakar and back, Kessel heard many stories about the adventures of the men who worked for *La Ligne*, some of whom had already been transferred to Latin America. One name that came up frequently was that of Antoine de Saint-Exupéry, the former chief of Aéropostale's airfield at the isolated and depressing Spanish fort of Cap Juby, which lay due east of the Canary Islands. It was Lécrivain

Pl. 194. L'Aéropostale's facilities at Cap Juby. The Spanish fort and prison are in the upper left hand corner.

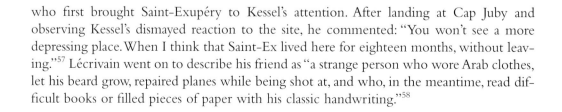

Pl. 195. Saint-Exupéry seems very much in his element in this photograph taken at Cap Juby in 1927.

who first brought Saint-Exupéry to Kessel's attention. After landing at Cap Juby and observing Kessel's dismayed reaction to the site, he commented: "You won't see a more depressing place. When I think that Saint-Ex lived here for eighteen months, without leaving."[57] Lécrivain went on to describe his friend as "a strange person who wore Arab clothes, let his beard grow, repaired planes while being shot at, and who, in the meantime, read difficult books or filled pieces of paper with his classic handwriting."[58]

168

Pl. 196. Saint-Exupéry in 1938, looking uncharacteristically elegant. He rarely allowed himself to be photographed smiling.

Though Saint-Exupéry was on leave in early 1929 when Kessel traveled from Casablanca to Dakar, what he heard from his newly made friends was enough to inspire him in *Vent de sable* to single out Saint-Exupéry for his eccentricity, his intellectual curiosity, his intellectual depth, and above all his courage. How often during the captivity of Reine and Serre, Kessel wrote, had Saint-Exupéry landed in the desert to leave a message, an interpreter, or a spy, perhaps with the secret hope of being captured himself so that he could locate them? "For this dreamer, who has just published a wonderful book . . . is as taken by the taste for adventure as the most down-to-earth of his comrades."[59] The pieces of the legend – the unpredictable and absent-minded eccentric, the dreamer, the adventurer, the philosopher – were already in place.[60]

The "wonderful book" to which Kessel referred was *Courrier-Sud* (Southern Mail), a short novel that appeared a few months before *Vent de sable*. Its author was a twenty-nine-year-old airmail pilot with an aristocratic name and a scorn for "literary men" – an unusual curriculum vitae for an aspiring writer in the world of Parisian letters.[61] Saint-Exupéry was a person people did not easily forget. Tall, thickly built, physically awkward, prematurely balding, careless in his dress to the point of shabbiness, eternally short of money, frequently absent-minded, often late to important appointments, he had a face that sparkled with intelligence and he loved to talk about an astonishing variety of topics. "He seemed," one of his friends said, "to hold a degree in all subjects."[62]

Saint-Exupéry's intellectual curiosity, however, was accompanied by a low level of tolerance for what he perceived to be intellectual pretentiousness. Complexity and paradox for their own sake infuriated him. Too many people, he thought, were attracted to ideas not because they led to understanding but because they produced strong emotions. "I can't consider ideas like tennis balls or a currency designed for fashionable conversation."[63]

Saint-Exupéry realized that his resistance to fashionable intellectual trends or much admired works of art often made him appear difficult or unreasonable. "I'm a bear who isn't particularly likable and that gives me the appearance of being melancholy," he wrote to one of his closest female friends in 1926.[64] And indeed there was something bumbling and sad about him. Still, Saint-Exupéry possessed a rare capacity for establishing intimate connections with other human beings when he cared to make the effort. Friendship was, for him, a sacrament. For many who crossed his path, his charm, sincerity, and scintillating conversation were irresistible.[65] "He left permanent wounds in the hearts of those who saw him smile even once."[66]

For all his advantages and qualities, Saint-Exupéry's course in life had not been smooth. In a country that put a high value on test-taking, he was unable to pass the examination that granted admission to the *École Navale*, the French equivalent of Annapolis. The beautiful fiancée he pursued in the early 1920s, Louise de Vilmorin, played with his affection before rejecting him, a bitter blow to someone already self-conscious about his appearance and his lack of prospects. Plagued by persistent financial problems and dependent on money from his mother, Saint-Exupéry fought off bouts of depression and the feeling that he was misunderstood, even by those closest to him.[67] Half-hearted attempts at a business career, including a job as an itinerant truck salesman, led nowhere, though they may have confirmed him in his contempt for commercial values and his scorn for the provincial bourgeoisie.[68] Then, in October 1926, capitalizing on his ability to fly, a skill he had learned during his military service five years earlier, Saint-Exupéry landed a job with *La Ligne*. This was to be his salvation and would provide the inspiration for many of his most successful literary works. At the time, however, his ambitions were more modest: he hoped to become financially independent and return to his mother "a marriageable man."[69]

All *La Ligne*'s newly recruited pilots went through a period of initiation at the company's Toulouse headquarters where they were required to pass a period of apprenticeship as a mechanic before being entrusted with the mail. Saint-Exupéry found his "comrades" there "delightful" and was flattered to be so quickly accepted in their group. Among the men towards whom he was drawn was Henri Guillaumet, whose friendship would become one of Saint-Exupéry's most treasured possessions.[70] Guillaumet sat Saint-Exupéry down before a map and gave him tips about the aerial route between Toulouse and Alicante that he would soon be asked to fly. His advice: "don't let yourself be intimidated. If the veterans have gotten through, so will you." A letter Saint-Exupéry wrote soon after arriving in Toulouse expresses what for him was a rare message of contentment. "You can't imagine how much I like these guys." To which he characteristically added, introducing a theme that would become central to his writing: "And how manual labor bestows intelligence on people."[71]

Unlike other pilots with greater experience and larger egos, Saint-Exupéry thrived under the harsh regime of *La Ligne*'s legendary director of operations, Didier Daurat.[72] Instead of rebelling against Daurat's unforgiving policy of sanctions for the infraction of company rules that other pilots considered unreasonable, Saint-Exupéry transformed him in his imagination into a tortured hero who through the power of the young author's pen would be awarded a privileged place in French literary history. Saint-Exupéry's appointment as chief of the airfield at Cap Juby in October 1927 was a reward for his successful service on the desolate and dangerous Dakar–Casablanca route. Daurat had recognized in him not just another courageous pilot but a potential leader of other men.[73]

The year the young aristocrat spent at Cap Juby represented a critical turning point in his life. It was in this lonely and dangerous setting that he discovered what would become one of his central literary themes: that men learned to communicate with one another by making a "gratuitous sacrifice."[74] He was also thrilled to be living amidst the Moors – such

Pl. 197. Louise de Vilmorin. De Vilmorin was herself an aspiring writer and had a knack for associating herself with men who left their mark on French letters, including André Malraux with whom she spent her last years. Jean Cocteau described her as a tall and delightful young woman with "a deep voice and the awkward gestures of a high school girl, a laugh that wrinkles her nose and raises a cruel lip above sparkling teeth, a perfect, confident, uneducated simplicity – and genius."

Pl. 198. Didier Daurat, exhibiting the unforgiving look that struck fear and respect into the hearts of his pilots.

a "lovely race." "Imagine the Moors dressed in blue with curly hair that floats and never separating themselves from their rifles. It's splendid." Life in the desert was *wonderful*. True, it was also dangerous, but it "*was well worth the risk*" (Saint-Exupéry's italics). Don't feel sorry for me, he told his most intimate correspondent. Life here was "so unimaginable."[75] The young aviator considered himself extraordinarily lucky to have escaped from the "stupid" Negroes and the even worse French colonials in "disgusting" Dakar.[76] He relished and retold his extraordinary adventures, such as the occasion when he spent two days and two nights in dissident territory with eleven Moors and a mechanic in order to save a friend; or another when he had walked sixty kilometers in the desert with the mail after having been forced by engine failure to land. Yet despite a sense of achievement, Saint-Exupéry also experienced moments of loneliness and melancholy when he confessed that he "was disgusted with himself."[77]

By 1929 Saint-Exupéry had moved from being an unemployed aristocrat with a dismal future to a respected figure among the pilots who worked for France's most famous airline. No longer a loner with a suspicious pedigree and intellectual pretensions, to the men with whom he worked he was now a "comrade" who was commonly referred to as "Saint-Ex." Daurat thought highly enough of him to send him to navigational school at the academy in Brest, the same institution that he had failed to enter ten years before. His future on *La Ligne* now seemed assured.

Saint-Exupéry's literary future, however, was less certain than his prospects on *La Ligne*. Though he had been dabbling at poetry and fiction since the age of six, he was slow to

Pl. 199. Yvonne de Lestrange's apartment on the Quai Malaquais (opposite the Louvre) was a meeting place for the writers of Gaston Gallimard's publishing house.

win recognition in the fiercely competitive Parisian literary world. Judged by Kessel's meteoric standard and that of many of his own coevals, Saint-Exupéry was a late bloomer. He was keenly aware of his lack of publications, and on more than one occasion he claimed that he had lost his zest for writing.[78] When *Courrier-Sud* appeared in 1929, he had in print only one short sketch, "The Aviator," published in a journal that was on the verge of disappearing.[79]

Still, as an aspiring literary figure Saint-Exupéry was not without advantages. He benefited from excellent connections through an aristocratic relative in Paris, who relished his company and encouraged his intellectual ambitions. At the elegant *hotel particulier* of his mother's worldly and cultivated second cousin, Yvonne de Lestrange, the Duchess of Trévise, the young aviator met the leading lights and rising stars of Gaston Gallimard's prestigious publishing house, which was located just a few steps away.[80] Gallimard agreed to publish *Courrier-Sud* and the remainder of Saint-Exupéry's *oeuvre*, a guarantee that his writings would be taken seriously by the critics who mattered.

Furthermore, as a chronicler of *La Ligne* Saint-Exupéry enjoyed an indisputable advantage over Kessel: he wrote from the vantage point of an insider. He was a pilot and a full-fledged member of the daring fraternity whose praises the older writer had sung. As the station chief at Cap Juby, Saint-Exupéry knew from firsthand experience the feelings and ordeals of the men of *La Ligne*. He had survived numerous crashes and forced landings in dissident territory; for him the sandstorm that formed the centerpiece of Kessel's reportage was not an extreme situation but a fact of everyday life and work.[81] As Kessel himself later admitted, Saint-Exupéry succeeded in fusing his activities as a flyer and a writer as none of his predecessors had been able to do.[82]

Then there was Saint-Exupéry's style and his literary voice. A gifted storyteller, who regaled his friends with his tales before consigning them to paper, Saint-Exupéry also possessed a flair for philosophical generalization, a talent much appreciated by the French. His use of language was musical and lyrical, yet strikingly concrete. A dedicated literary craftsman whose manuscripts had to be wrested from him by his publishers, he believed that a grammatical mistake was preferable to a defect in rhythm and that perfection in a work was achieved when there was nothing that remained to be removed.[83] One cannot imagine a literary sensibility more distant from Kessel's. Indeed, Saint-Exupéry's imagination was so distinctly *his* that it sometimes seemed to come from a literary landscape divorced from the one in which he lived. He was at the same time a poet, a philosopher, and a *moraliste*. One of his most sensitive readers believed that he could sense in Saint-Exupéry's pages "the ghost of Pascal."[84]

These qualities did not yet come into clear focus in *Courrier-Sud*. Although Saint-Exupéry's novel was praised for the vividness of its flying scenes and the grace of its style, its narrative and characterizations seemed derivative, self-indulgent, and dismayingly reminiscent of the novels of anxiety [*inquiètude*] so popular among the young writers of the late 1920s.[85] "Quite literary and quite superficial," was the disdainful verdict of the influential critic Edmond Jaloux, who seized the opportunity to express his skepticism about the future of the aviation novel. "M. de Saint-Exupéry, like M. J. Kessel in *L'Équipage*, borrows his novelistic themes from the same emotional sources that writers always have. Only the picturesque elements in the world change – and the picturesque becomes outmoded."[86]

Jean Prévost, a slightly younger friend of Saint-Exupéry's who had already fallen beneath his spell, was more indulgent. Writing in the prestigious *Nouvelle Revue Française* – a literary journal that was, not coincidentally, published by Saint-Exupéry's publisher, Gaston Gallimard – Prévost confessed that he found it difficult not to like this first novel. The author, he thought, had described marvelously the distance that the use of a powerful machine created between an aviator and the world. Reading *Courrier-Sud*, Prévost sometimes felt as if he had been struck by "a blast of strong wind" that stunned and at the same time excited him. He especially admired a passage in which the protagonist confessed that "I have enjoyed a life I never quite understood, a life of imperfect fidelity. I don't even know exactly what it is I needed. I felt a vague sense of yearning." For lines like these, that achieved "a grandeur and a truth beyond time," Prévost was willing to pardon a certain awkwardness in the sentimental plot and a few overly facile sentences that strove too hard toward lyricism.[87]

The problem was that in *Courrier-Sud* Saint-Exupéry told two stories that, as Prévost admitted, were badly interwoven.[88] One was a refreshingly original description of the life of the Aéropostale pilots who flew the mail between Toulouse and Dakar and carried in their fragile planes what Saint-Exupéry rather grandiloquently called the "meditations of a people." The young author was at his best when evoking the slang these pilots used; the bulky clothes they wore; the nomadic existence they led; their sense of isolation from the world they had left behind; the dangers they faced; the bonds of comradeship that united them; the moments of fear they experienced; the look of the mountains and desert they overflew; the isolation of the lonely outposts where they landed; the anguished wait for news of a lost comrade; and above all, the telegraphic language they used on the radio network that magically united them along a route of five thousand kilometers, ending with the dramatic message:

> From Saint-Louis du Sénégal for Toulouse: France-Amérique found east of Timeris. Stop. An enemy party in the vicinity. Stop. Pilot killed plane smashed up mail intact. Stop. Continue to Dakar.[89]

Saint-Exupéry conveyed a sense for the discipline and intercontinental scope of the peerless flying organization that Latécoère and his lieutenant Didier Daurat had created. How could readers in 1929 resist the excitement of the passage that described the protagonist's takeoff from Toulouse? In this stripped down prose, which my translation captures only approximately, nature is portrayed as being subjected magically to the control of well-trained technicians who brook no errors. One can easily imagine it as the voice-over in a documentary film.

> The runway chief takes a last look: absolute order of things; studied gestures as if for a ballet. This plane has its exact place in this hangar, just as it will have its exact place five minutes from now in the sky. This flight as well organized as the launching of a ship. This missing bolt: an egregious error. These five-hundred watt bulbs, these penetrating looks, this iron discipline, all aimed toward making this flight, launched from stop to stop until it reaches Buenos-Aires or Santiago de Chile, a matter of ballistics rather than an accident. So that, in spite of storms, fogs, tornados, in spite of the thousand traps of valve-springs, rocker-arms, and matter, distances are overcome and effaced: express trains, cargo-boats, and steamships! And Buenos-Aires or Santiago de Chile will be reached in record time.
> Start her up!
> A slip of paper is handed to the pilot Bernis: the battle plan.
> Bernis reads:
> "Perpignan indicates clear skies, no wind. Barcelona: storm. Alicante . . ."[90]

The other story Saint-Exupéry told was an extraordinarily complex lament for a woman and a world that the protagonist had lost, a story that the author's contemporaries had no hope of understanding and hence found confusing or badly constructed. Its narrative was presented in the form of flashbacks and rapid shifts of time and place in a language that was often more like poetry than prose. Reading it today, one cannot help but think of *Mrs. Dalloway*, another novel of nostalgia and lost opportunities, published five years earlier. But unlike Virginia Woolf's novel, here there is only one voice, that of Saint-Exupéry himself; a voice, moreover, coded in such a way as to throw his readers off the track of his deepest feelings. He is eager to confess, yet unwilling to be known. The weakness and vulnerability of his male characters, Jean Bernis and the narrator, seem in stark contradiction with the heroic actions they undertake; the female protagonist, Geneviève, is a fantasy rather than a human being.

The misinterpretation of the novel was all the more inevitable in view of the preface that Gaston Gallimard commissioned from André Beucler.[91] Beucler dwelt on Saint-Exupéry's heroism and soldierly qualities; he stated unequivocally that he was not a writer; he forewarned the reader not to expect the type of novel to which the public was accustomed but a more direct – read naïve – account. *Courrier-Sud*'s author, Beucler said, had no other style than that "of a sensibility and a sincerity subjected to energy and born from a magnificent profession."[92] Small wonder that this preface was not reproduced in future editions of this strangely captivating yet uneven work.

★   ★   ★

Gaston Gallimard was anxious to capitalize on the interest that Saint-Exupéry's first book had aroused, and his new author was understandably eager to oblige him. Yet Saint-Exupéry's first responsibility was to *La Ligne*. Two months after *Courrier-Sud* was published, he was informed by the Toulouse office of Aéropostale that he was being transferred to Latin America where the company's ambitious new owner, Marcel Bouilloux-Laffont, was creating a French-dominated network of airlines aimed at connecting the Latin American countries by air. Upon arriving in Buenos Aires, Saint-Exupéry discovered

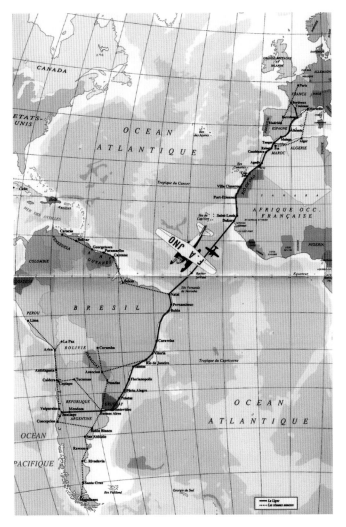

Pl. 201. A map of Aéropostale's expanded operations when Saint-Exupéry arrived in Argentina. The red line indicates existing routes, the dotted lines projected ones.

that he would be director of Aeroposta Argentina, an affiliate of Aéropostale; his charge was to create an airline that would extend from Buenos Aires down the coast of Argentina to Rio Gallegos, just to the north of the Strait of Magellan and the Tierra del Fuego. For the first time in his life, he enjoyed a generous salary of 25,000 francs per month (about $10,000 in today's currency) and had the luxury of indulging himself while at the same time helping his mother with monthly infusions of cash. Small wonder that he felt vindicated after his earlier setbacks. *La belle vie!*[93]

Saint-Exupéry's new assignment offered ample opportunity for new adventures that would find their way into his future works. Much of his time was spent in the air under conditions for which not even the perils of the Casablanca–Dakar route had prepared him. Flying in an area where winds could reach a velocity of 125 miles an hour in airplanes whose cruising speed was considerably lower, he and the pilots who worked for him were often forced to recognize their inability to overcome a headwind and retreat. The friendship Saint-Exupéry had forged with Henri Guillaumet in Toulouse was further deepened when in June 1930 Saint-Exupéry spent five days flying in the Andes vainly searching for his missing friend, only to discover to his immense relief that Guillaumet had improbably been found walking in the mountains seven days after crashing. Three months later Saint-Exupéry was introduced to the woman who would become his wife, Consuelo Gómez Catrillo, the seductive and mercurial widow of a Guatemalan journalist who had moved in the same orbit as such avant-garde literary figures as Paul Verlaine, Oscar Wilde, and

Pl. 202.   A relieved Saint-Exupéry greets his friend Henri Guillaumet after his escape from the Andes.

Pl. 203.   Consuelo looks uncharacteristically demure. She and Saint-Exupéry would have a tumultuous marriage characterized by long absences. Consuelo later wrote of their first conversation: "What charm in his images, what a fierce accent of reality combined with the improbable!"

Maurice Maeterlinck. Somehow in the midst of his event-filled life, Saint-Exupéry found the time to write. When he returned to France in February 1931 for a two-month leave, he brought with him a four-hundred-page manuscript that he would strip down by more than half before giving it to André Gide to read.

The title of Saint-Exupéry's novel, *Vol de nuit* (Night Flight), cannot possibly have the resonance for us today that it had for him and his readers when he wrote it. Who among us today regards "the conquest of the night by the airplane" as a manifestation of "the grandeur of the modern world?" And yet one of the most perceptive reviewers of *Vol de nuit* dwelt on this aspect of the book. "Flying by night without access to brightly lighted airfields means death. To be lost in the clouds during a night flight means the risk of running into a cliff or a mountain, to crash. To find yourself in a storm means being destroyed. And in both cases to lose your way. And all these risks are terribly multiplied and rendered more urgent by limitations of fuel. The fact is that no plane can carry enough fuel to fly by night: it has to land one or two times to refuel. Either you reach your destination or you die."[94]

Well aware that he had tried to put too much of himself and his own life into *Courrier-Sud*, Saint-Exupéry was careful to avoid this temptation in his second novel. The action is compressed into a single night. At its center is the company's Director of Operations in Buenos Aires, Rivière, whose age of fifty, menacing illness, weariness, and aura of authority, all distance him from the still youthful Saint-Exupéry. The story is so straightforward and tersely narrated that it reads more like a play or a screenplay than a more complexly structured novel.

Pellerin, the pilot entrusted with flying the mail from Chile, arrives safely in Buenos Aires after surviving an epic battle with a storm over the Andes. He agrees to have dinner with a company inspector, Robineau, whose charge it is to enforce Rivière's strict rules that often result in penalties against the company's personnel or sometimes the loss of jobs. Another pilot, Fabien, and his radio operator, are lost in the storm Pellerin survived; they are carrying the mail northward from Patagonia. In an emotionally charged scene, Rivière is forced to confront Fabien's distraught wife. She realizes that Rivière perceives her as a threat to his mission; she represents the "truth" of marriage, but this goes against his truth – the truth of duty to his chosen craft – and in that sense she is inevitably his "enemy."[95] Refusing to yield to defeat and the specter of fear that would undermine the courage of his men, Rivière orders a third pilot to depart for Brazil with the European-bound mail that has now arrived from Chile and Paraguay. Though he is aware of Fabien's fate, the third pilot feels a tremendous surge of power and pleasure at the thought of his flight, as his plane is prepared for takeoff.

Skillfully interwoven with this deceptively simple narrative is a meditation on the meaning of life organized around a series of contrasts: the contrast between day and night; between people on the ground pursuing their humdrum routines and aviators in the air risking their lives; between bureaucrats like Robineau and visionaries like Rivière; between women who live for individual happiness and men who live for collective action; and, above all, the contrast between triumph and defeat.

Vol de nuit proposes no simple solutions to these conflicts. Night can be both welcoming and deadly. Fabien is no D'Annunzian hero who looks down with scorn on those below. On the contrary, weary from his daily battle with the sky Fabien feels the need to lay down his arms and enjoy the kind of uncomplicated life led by peasants whose villages he overflies. A Hamlet-like figure, Rivière is hounded by doubts. He recognizes that the war he wages can never be definitively won. He loves his men not because they are heroes but because they speak of their craft in the same way that a blacksmith speaks of his anvil.

Still, it is clear that Rivière is delivering Saint-Exupéry's message when he thinks that ". . . we always act as if something was more valuable than human life." To the question of how he could justify depriving men of lives that might be happy, Rivière replies that even the most golden of sanctuaries are destroyed by age and death. Perhaps there was something more lasting than individual happiness? "Perhaps it was to save this part of men that Rivière was working? If not, there was no justification for action."[96] Rivière's harshness and inflexibility in applying a set of rules are justified in the end by Saint-Exupéry's belief that his aim was to give a soul to their bodies, to create in them a will to transcend themselves, to "launch them beyond themselves."[97] Life for its own sake was not a worthy objective; what mattered above all was to give meaning to one's acts; and, paradoxically, potentially fatal actions had the effect of delivering men from death – the death of a life without meaning.[98]

For André Gide, who volunteered to provide *Vol de nuit* with a preface, its central message was ". . . that man's happiness is not to be found in liberty but in the acceptance of a duty." What Gide liked best about the novel was its "nobility." "We know all too well the weaknesses, the surrenders, the downfall of man, and the literature of our days is only too good at denouncing these; but what we need is someone who can show us that transcendence of self that an iron will achieves." With war discredited as a means of transcendence after the senseless carnage of the Western Front, Gide was prepared to believe that the theater of life within which courage could most admirably be deployed was the world of aviation.[99]

In explaining the "exceptional importance" of *Vol de nuit*, Gide drew attention to its value as a historical document. There is no doubt that the impact of the book, and its durability, gained from its aura of authenticity; and the articles that accompanied its publication made it clear that Saint-Exupéry was a veteran of *La Ligne* and had himself faced perils similar to the ones experienced by the pilots depicted in *Vol de nuit*.[100] The chapters devoted to Fabien's ill-fated flight up the Patagonian coast do not have the ring of fiction.

Yet, at the same time, as one of Saint-Exupéry's most perceptive reviewers pointed out, *Vol de nuit* is intensely subjective; the emphasis throughout the novel is on introspection. Despite its careful description of contempotary aeronautical technology – airplanes, instruments, radio messages – the most important action takes place in the minds of the characters. The effort throughout is to raise the modern world to the level of poetry.[101] The repetition of words, like "night," "weary," "heavy," "eternal voyager," "watchman," "conquest," "triumph," and "defeat," give the book the quality of an incantation. And though Saint-Exupéry sometimes overreaches in his search for the lyrical phrase, he often achieves a level of poetic expression of rare beauty, as when the pilot Fabien, hopelessly lost in the storm, bursts through the cloud cover and ascends until he reaches a beautiful calm sky illuminated by brightly shining stars. Fabien and his radio operator were bathed in a "milky light," reflected from the clouds below as they wandered among the stars with no hope of ever returning to earth alive. "They were like those thieves in fabled cities, immured in a chamber full of treasures from which they would never be able to escape. Among the iced jewels, they wandered, infinitely rich, but condemned."[102]

In the wake of Gide's enthusiasm, critics were inclined to overlook *Vol de nuit*'s defects in favor of its virtues. They praised Saint-Exupéry's sober lyricism, his "muscular and rapid" prose, and his "austere and sad" reflection on action and its meaning.[103] Edmond Jaloux, writing in *Les Nouvelles Littéraires*, concluded that *Vol de nuit* was more than a "beautiful literary work"; it also contained "a moral beauty that we find rarely in contemporary literature."[104] Robert de Saint Jean agreed, but he insisted that *Vol de nuit* should not be thought

of as a novel, but as an epic poem on the theme of aviation – and beyond that, "a message and a meditation." Beneath the novel's apparent simplicity, he found complexity; beneath its apparent "hymn to human prowess" a strain of pessimism that made this book "one of the most significant expressions of modern anxiety [*inquiètude*]."[105] Other critics were no less enthusiastic. They praised *Vol de nuit*'s "tragic beauty" and the austerity of its author's style. "No unnecessary words, no artifice, no ornamentation. But notes of simple grandeur that reduce grandiloquence to silence."[106] No one seemed troubled by the similarities between the portrait of Rivière and the contemporary cult of the leader or the implication that death was a precondition for a fulfilled life.

When Saint-Exupéry received the coveted Prix Fémina in December 1931, Maurice Martin du Gard consecrated his literary fame by devoting to him a long article in *Les Nouvelles Littéraires* – the third inspired in that journal by the publication of *Vol de nuit* – in which he certified Saint-Exupéry's nobility, generosity of spirit, and courage and returned to a comparison that had occurred to other reviewers.[107] The plunge of Fabien and his radio operator into a "nest of storms" had been described by Saint-Exupéry "with a miraculous pen, a dramatic plenitude that makes one think of Conrad."[108] Given the reverence with which Conrad was viewed in France, this was high praise indeed: *La Ligne* had found its epic poet.

★　　★　　★

Vol de nuit ends on a note of triumph. "Rivière the Great, Rivière the Conqueror, who shoulders [the burden of] his heavy victory."[109] Yet Aéropostale was anything but triumphant when Saint-Exupéry's novel appeared. The company was in bankruptcy; its assets had been taken out of the control of its former owner Marcel Bouilloux-Laffont; its management had been handed over to a three-man committee of liquidation headed by Raoul Dautry, a railway man; and its ambitious network of services in Latin America had been reduced to the route leading from Brazil to Buenos Aires and then on to Santiago de Chile. Didier Daurat, the figure on whom Rivière was based and to whom Saint-Exupéry dedicated the novel, had been sacked under humiliating conditions on a trumped up charge of having tampered with the mail when it passed through Toulouse. Though no one could have been certain of the company's future, the process was well under way that would lead to Aéropostale's disappearance as an independent entity and its incorporation into the state-owned company that would become Air France in August 1933.[110]

The heated debate over the future of Aéropostale took place behind closed doors, on the floor and in the corridors of the Chamber of Deputies, and in the public press, where accusations of shady and criminal behavior were brought against Marcel Bouilloux-Laffont and his son André. They were accused of having drawn on the government subventions given to Aéropostale in order to cover a cash shortfall in their other enterprises caused by the onset of the Depression and held responsible for bad financial management. Defenders of *La Ligne* replied that Bouilloux-Laffont had risked his fortune in a patriotically motivated effort to win the French aeronautical dominance in Latin America. They accused the government of setting out to destroy a valuable and unique French institution, the greatest airline in the world.[111] What was at stake, they insisted, was something that went far beyond money. For them, this was a conflict between tawdry commercial and materialistic values on the one hand and lofty ideals on the other. "The 'mail,'" wrote one well-known defender of Aéropostale. "Listen to the pilots of Aéropostale speak about it, and speak about it with an irresistible and mystical conviction. They have for it an invincible collective dedication to a symbol, an idol. The 'mail is sacred' . . ."[112] For the protagonists of this increasingly politicized struggle, there could be no possible compromise between economic considerations, aggravated by the Great Depression, and the sacred cause of Aéropostale.

By 1933, *La Ligne* was foundering, its liquidation only a matter of time. Yet paradoxically, as the organization went under, its story began to take on mythical proportions, as could be seen in a reportage that first appeared in the right-wing newspaper *Le Petit Journal* and then was later published in 1933 as a book under the title *Les Chemins du ciel*. Its author, Jean-Gérard Fleury, was a young journalist, with a law degree and a zest for faraway lands, who had been engaged in 1931 by Dautry, the new administrator of Aéropostale, to write articles favorable to the organization that he was charged to reorganize.[113] With Dautry's encouragement and assistance, Fleury was allowed to travel as a passenger on the fourteen-thousand-kilometer route that began in Toulouse, snaked down the Spanish and African coasts to Dakar, continued after the four-and-a-half-day crossing of the Atlantic by ship from Natal to Rio, then to Buenos Aires, and finally across the Andes to Chile. Fleury left Paris on a summer night in August 1931, accompanied by Parisians hurrying off to enjoy their vacations; he arrived in Santiago in the midst of winter. The trip had taken what in 1931 seemed a miraculously brief period of time: nine days. It seemed a dramatic example of the way the world was shrinking because of the rapid progress of commercial aviation.

Fleury was an inspired choice for the assignment Dautry had in mind. Intelligent and gifted with a facile pen, likeable, sensitive to the mystique of Aéropostale and anxious to publicize the achievements of its personnel, he quickly won entry to the fellowship of *La Ligne*, and this in turn led to a deep and lasting friendship with Kessel.[114] Though Fleury lacked the literary ambitions and talent of Kessel and Saint-Exupéry, he would nonetheless become one of the most faithful defenders of Aéropostale's legacy and eventually its first historian.[115]

Fleury's quest for historical accuracy, however, lay in the future. His task in 1931 was to burnish Aéropostale's tarnished public image, and he went about his work with an unabashed enthusiasm that sometimes verged on hero worship. Yet how things had changed in the two and a half years since Kessel's reportage! In *Vent de sable*, Kessel had lingered over the figure of Didier Daurat, widely recognized at that time as the force behind Aéropostale's success. It was this former squadron leader of the First World War, Kessel said, who maintained "the

Pl. 206.   Jean-Gérard Fleury in the early 1930s.

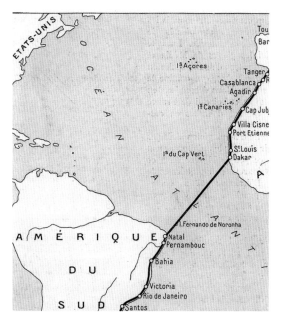

Pl. 207. The itinerary followed by Fleury in his 1930 flight from Toulouse to Santiago de Chile.

sacred flame" of the company's aircrews by means of his "crushing labor, his authority, his inflexible demands, and his contagious faith."[116] In *Les Chemins du ciel*, Fleury does not mention Daurat by name, and his role is reduced to that of an administrator at Toulouse – an aviation fanatic with a willful look in his face – who sees Fleury off and warns him gruffly that his flight will not be pleasant.[117] Careful not to burn his hands in the debate over Daurat's role in the Aéropostale scandal, Fleury prudently saves his most fulsome praise in the early pages of his book for his patron Dautry and Dautry's lieutenant Abel Verdurand.[118] It was to these two men that *Les Chemins du ciel* was dedicated because it was they who had permitted Fleury "to live this beautiful adventure." No fool, Fleury knew how to play by the rules of Parisian journalism in the 1930s; he danced happily to the tune of his masters.

Enclosed in his fur-lined flying suit (under which he would insert newspaper to fend off the cold) and coiffed with a leather helmet, Fleury crammed himself into a space behind the navigator and radio operator where the mail was ordinarily stored. Ten hours later, after a cold and bumpy ride down the Spanish coast and across the Strait of Gibraltar, his plane arrived in Casablanca. His next pilot for the stretch between Morocco and Port-Etienne would be none other than Saint-Exupéry himself, who had been transferred a few months earlier from Latin America to the African run. Fleury knew him only as the author of *Courrier-Sud*, since *Vol de nuit*, though completed, had yet to appear. Though dimly aware of Aéropostale's political problems at this time, Saint-Exupéry had no idea that his relationship with *La Ligne* was nearing its end.

The usually congenial Saint-Exupéry did not hesitate to communicate to Fleury that he was far from delighted at the thought of having a passenger. Fleury's weight meant losing a hundred liters of gasoline – one hour less of flying time – and the weather report for the flight was not encouraging. But used to executing the director's orders, Saint-Exupéry resigned himself to the situation and concentrated on the business at hand.[119]

As Fleury understood from having read *Vent de sable*, a series of articles about Aéropostale derived much of its interest from the dangers to which the author had willingly subjected himself. The journey must be raised from the level of a tourist's excursion to an adventure. Nor could an account that would first be published in installments in a newspaper delay in generating excitement.

Fleury follows Kessel's model so closely that even one of the pilots to whom he had become most attached perishes soon after flying him up the coast of Brazil, much as Lécrivain had in *Vent de sable*.[120] Fleury's first brush with danger comes when Saint-

Pl. 208. The illustrator Géo Ham [Georges Hamel] retraced the itinerary of Fleury's flight in 1932. He recorded some of its moments in the following drawings, accompanied by a colorful commentary, which he published in *L'Illustration* on 19 November. This one shows the improvised passenger compartment, which Ham shared with the mail and a hooded Arab interpreter between Agadir and Cap Juby. The flame of the exhaust, in the far right hand corner, adds drama to the scene, as they fly above a cloud layer in moonlight.

Pl. 209. The arrival at Cap Juby. " . . . only an encirclement of barbed wire separated us from the camps of dissident Arabs who kept us under surveillance."

Exupéry is forced to make an instrument landing in fog at Agadir. The weather report from Cap Juby is bad. "Violent storms – Ceiling 200 meters – Bad visibility." Fleury asks whether they will remain at Agadir. Saint-Exupéry responds indignantly. "What do you mean? Never! We'll try to get through. You must understand, the mail doesn't wait."[121]

The flight to Juby passes without incident. Saint-Exupéry and Fleury continue on in clear weather to Villa Cisneros and Port-Etienne. Nonetheless, Fleury dwells on the perils of the flight, neglecting to mention that the plane that was transporting him – a Laté 26 – was a much more powerful and reliable aircraft than the equipment available to the aviators of Aéropostale in the period when Kessel had made the flight. Flown to Dakar by another pilot, Fleury is whisked off, along with the mail, to the small steamship that will take him to Brazil. Here also the emphasis is on the courage of the crews that make this dangerous crossing. Just two years before, Fleury recalls, an Aéropostale ship had gone down in the Atlantic.

At Natal, the port of disembarkation in Brazil, Fleury seizes the opportunity to alert his readers to the dangers posed by foreign competition. His attention has been brought by one of the officers of his ship to the presence of the all-metal airliner of the German Kondor Line, the rival of Aéropostale. Fleury visits the "magnificent" French seaplane base – created by Marcel Bouilloux-Laffont's now bankrupt South American holding company – but worries that the transatlantic Zeppelin service that the Germans had recently inaugurated will deprive the French of the monopoly they enjoyed in mail service between Europe and Latin America. The Germans were investing nothing yet, simply waiting patiently in the hope that the French, unaware of the value of their bases, would abandon an infrastructure that had not only cost a great deal of money but countless human effort and heroism.[122]

From Natal's port Fleury is driven at breakneck speed by his pilot to the airfield where their plane's engine has already been warmed up. "Like knights of old, we don our leather armor and our flying helmets."[123] They reach Recife where Fleury glimpses beneath them a large circular field with a pylon in the middle. The pilot passes him a note: "It's the base of the Graf Zeppelin . . ." One more reminder that the Germans are omnipresent in Latin America and waiting to take the place of the French.

When they arrive at Maceio on their way southwards toward Rio, the weather report is threatening. Storms are predicted in the area of their next stop, Bahia. The ceiling is low. There's no moon, hence no light by means of which to navigate. They're advised to wait for daybreak to continue their flight. But the pilot replies: "You must be joking." Fleury adds: "I discerned a secret anger in Dupont's sarcasm. He's a fanatical believer in night flights, a slave to the mail. What do clouds, squalls, storms, and even deadly fog mean to him . . . He has received an order: carry the mail to Rio without delay. *Il faut partir* [We have to leave]."[124]

Having slipped through a hole in the clouds to land at Caravellas and refuel, they are forced to halt their night flight temporarily. To the south, visibility is zero. The manager of the field quickly quashes any idea the pilot might have of continuing. "*Mon vieux*, I have my

Pl. 212.   The Aéropostale mail plane approaches the bay of Rio de Janeiro.

Pl. 213.   Aéropostale's Laté 26 is guided by a beacon to a night landing in Mendoza. Fuses attached to the plane's wheels illuminate its descent.

Pl. 214. A Potez 25, with a higher ceiling, traverses the Andes on the final leg of the journey to Santiago. "…we graze the mountains while performing a crazy dance: taken by the down drafts, blown around in every direction, whipped by a wind that raises the snow from the peaks, I stiffen myself against the fuselage despite my numb fingers. The thermometer registers 35 degrees Celsius below zero; my ears hum; it seems to me that my head will burst."

orders. When you can't see anything, you don't fly unless you want to kill yourself." The next morning, before dawn breaks, they are in the air. After a brief stop in Victoria, they push on to Rio de Janeiro. "We've flown twenty hours since leaving Natal! Almost an entire day."

From Rio, Fleury is flown by yet another legendary figure on *La Ligne*: Marcel Reine. Captured three times by the Moors, he epitomizes for Fleury the courage of the aviators of Aéropostale. During the flight Reine more than lives up to his reputation. Going against the advice of the head of the airfield at Florianpolis, he continues his flight through fierce storms and minimal visibility toward the south. Flying a few meters above the beach through thick fog and fading light, Reine glimpses the lights of Porto-Alegre and sets down on a field soaked by relentless rain, just when Fleury has been warned by the radio operator that they are about to crash. Informed by the head of the field that he will not be cleared for departure because of the weather conditions to the south, the frustrated Reine agrees to delay the departure from Porto-Alegre until the fog lifts. They are in the air again before dawn, heading for Montevideo and freezing in the Latin American winter. Finally, from Montevideo to Buenos Aires, they enjoy the luxury of a closed cockpit.

Fleury flies the final leg of his journey from Buenos Aires to Santiago with a new crew. After a brief stop in Mendoza, they change from the Laté 26 they have been flying to a lighter Potez 25 biplane that is capable of climbing to seven thousand meters, necessary in order to cross the Andes. The final flight provides its share of thrills. Fleury is instructed to be ready to bail out at a moment's notice. They are tossed about like a fragile toy by the violent up- and down-drafts that blow through the passes on the Argentine slopes of the

Cordillera and threaten to hurl them against the menacing rock walls. They are numb from the freezing cold and short of breath, for the plane lacks oxygen masks. Fleury feels light-headed and wonders how the pilot can go on flying. Finally they break through the clouds and see the snowy peaks of the Chilean side of the Andes glistening in beautiful sunlight. Santiago, with its beautiful avenues and gardens, lies before them at the end of a valley.

Throughout his book Fleury took every opportunity to emphasize the dedication of the aviators who worked for *La Ligne*: their courage, their heroism, their high level of technological expertise, their efficiency, and the prestige they had won for France throughout Latin America.[125] Over a course of fourteen thousand kilometers, there were forty-six airfields and forty-three radio stations that monitored the progress of the mail. But even more important than the material infrastructure that Aéropostale had created, Fleury urged, was the "moral capital" represented by its outstanding personnel. "Fanatics of the mail, our pilots refuse to let themselves be stopped by any storm, by any fog."[126]

Fleury found it sad that the French were so unaware of the achievements of these magnificent men for whom aviation was less a job than a religion.[127] Their passion had given rise to the creation of "knightly and magnificent values." Fleury lamented that all that so many French people knew about Aéropostale were the machinations and the scandals associated with the directors of the company. But if you went to Latin America, you discovered that people there recognized in the aviators of *La Ligne* a new French knighthood. "The glory of our aviators, so pure and so disinterested, reflects on us, because we are French as they are . . ."[128] The practical lesson Fleury drew from his adventure was that this was not the moment for the French to abandon their Latin American airlines to the Germans. The French government must continue its support for Aéropostale and provide it with planes capable of flying the South Atlantic. Otherwise the Zeppelins would take the place of French planes, and the heroic efforts and sacrifices of *La Ligne* would have been in vain.[129]

Alas, Fleury should have been less concerned about the Germans. It was the Yankee airline Pan American that was France's most dangerous rival. As Paul Morand explained soberly in a book he wrote about his travels through South and North America that appeared shortly before Fleury's *Les Chemins du ciel*, the French were ten years behind the Americans in the quality of their aircraft and their infrastructure and the efficiency of their management. The American approach to commercial aviation, he said, could not be more different than that of the French. "No heroic deeds. Metal aircraft, trimotors endowed with an excess of power that makes it possible to lift twenty persons to an altitude of twenty-four thousand feet, along with their baggage and the mail. When the weather is bad, no take-offs . . . *Safety first*: thus the greatest respect for the life of travelers, and to boot the comfort of the best trains. No loss of personnel and never a delay during the more than two years the line has been open. For them, two hundred miles an hour is not viewed as a record, and it's at this commercial speed that I will cross all of Latin America." Morand added sardonically that "the travelers of 1932 have no interest in running the risks of Guynemer and Garros."[130]

★　　★　　★

Fleury devoted much of the second part of *Les Chemins du ciel* to stories he had been told about the extraordinary exploits of the aviators of Aéropostale in Latin America during the years between 1928 and 1931. Among the pilots he singled out for praise, one stood out above the rest: Jean Mermoz. Fleury met Mermoz only after having returned to Paris and published his articles in *Le Petit Journal*. But the charisma of his newly found friend shaped the ending of *Les Chemins du ciel*. "Rarely have I seen a man so devoted to an ideal . . . The profound influence that he exercises over his comrades and his tenacious will have allowed

Pl. 215.   A photograph taken in the early 1930s that captures Mermoz's charisma and his charm.

Pl. 216.   The Comte de la Vaulx (Laté 28-3) about to depart from Saint-Louis du Sénégal for Brazil on 13 May 1930.

him to protect the growing Line against discouragement and defections."[131] Fleury's admiration for Mermoz was so great that he closed his book with a chapter devoted to a flight he took with Mermoz from Toulouse to Alicante entitled "The Spirit of *La Ligne.*" In this chapter Mermoz recounts his life to Fleury and tells him his disdain for the dangers that he faces daily. "To perish at the controls of an airplane does not seem to me a pitiful, nor even a sad fate. We accept an end that we dearly seek. Sickness would be the real defeat." Fleury claims to see in Mermoz's face the reflection of the faces he saw during his trip to Latin America. "And their passion brought to bloom in their exalted souls knightly and magnificent virtues: indomitable courage, fraternal and generous camaraderie, and a firm feeling of duty."[132]

In 1932, when Fleury first met him, Mermoz was already an international celebrity, the French equivalent of Lindbergh. Like Lindbergh, he had the looks necessary for a period that idolized the image and had discovered the means for circulating the likenesses of the famous quickly to millions of people. His exploits were legendary among the men of *La Ligne,* who repeated among themselves the stories of his adventures. A veteran of the Casablanca–Dakar run, he had twice been captured and held for ransom by dissident tribesmen. The initiator of night flights between Rio and Buenos Aires at a time when the intervening airfields were lighted only by bonfires, he was also the first Aéropostale pilot to chart the path across the mountains from Argentina to Chile. The survivor of a crash in the Andes from which he escaped by means of a superhuman effort, Mermoz became a French national hero in May 1930 when he succeeded in flying the mail across the South Atlantic from Saint-Louis in Senegal to Natal, Brazil, in twenty-one hours and thirty-eight minutes.

When Mermoz returned to France in July 1930, he had an encounter that would have important literary implications. In a small Montmartre restaurant that specialized in south-

Pl. 217.   Mermoz relaxes on the Côte-d'Azur in the 1930s.

Pl. 218.   Mermoz is identified as a "popular hero" on the cover of the magazine *Voilà*.

western cuisine frequented by men of *La Ligne*, he met Joseph Kessel. The attraction between the two was immediate. Mermoz had every quality needed to inflame Kessel's imagination and inspire in him feelings of deep friendship. Handsome and athletic, a *bon vivant* whose feats at table and in bed were as fabled among his intimates as his achievements in the air, Mermoz could match Kessel in his favored excesses. Taken with his new friend, Kessel lost no time in introducing him to the gypsy café where he loved to pass his nights. Kessel later remembered that evening as a revelation for Mermoz. It was "a dazzling descent into a radiant hell whose delights were forbidden . . . He needed air, space . . . He tore off his tie, threw down his jacket. The column of his neck burst forth from his open shirt. His bronze muscles rippled on his chest. His hair was intertwined like snakes on ancient sculptures. Overcome by emotion, I thought I saw Dionysus . . . We were terribly happy and drank endlessly from breaking crystal glasses to celebrate our intimacy."[133] Henceforth, whenever Mermoz was on leave in Paris or on the Côte d'Azur, he could be seen at Kessel's side.

By December 1936 Mermoz was the most famous man in France: only thirty-five years of age, he had already been elevated to the rank of Commander of the Legion of Honor. Air France had recognized his primacy among their pilots by promoting him to the position of "general inspector" and rewarding him with a princely salary of more than 200,000 francs a year, the equivalent of an ambassador or a large factory manager's compensation.[134] Mermoz's image was as well known as that of any movie star; his lectures in 1934 at the Petit Palais and the Theâtre des Ambassadeurs about his famous flights drew overflowing and enthusiastic audiences; his appeal cut across social classes and political alignments at a time when French society was becoming more and more politically polarized.

This is all the more surprising because Mermoz himself had made the decision to enter the political arena and lend his prestige to an explicitly antiparliamentary organization that was being denounced by the left-wing parties as fascist. Disgusted with the government's aban-

Pl. 219.   Mermoz marches next to La Rocque in 1933 in a homage to Joan of Arc.

donment of the air routes that he had risked his life opening in Latin America, Mermoz joined Colonel de la Rocque's right-wing Croix de Feu and quickly became a member of La Rocque's inner circle. Mermoz's commitment to La Rocque's "National Volunteers" was not casual, nor did it lack ideological motivation. Mermoz considered himself a national socialist and hated the conservative right (*la droite bien pensante*) that he held responsible for the present situation in France.[135] He was convinced that his appreciation for hierarchy, his nationalism, and his disdain for parliamentary intrigue corresponded to the values defended by the man he now deemed to be his "leader" in the struggle against the decadent Third Republic.[136] La Rocque knew an opportunity when he saw it. He reciprocated Mermoz's unquestioning devotion by offering him the position of vice-president in his newly formed Parti Social Français, a post the pilot willingly accepted.

Mermoz threw himself heart and soul into La Roque's crusade against the Third Republic. Speaking before the constituent assembly of the PSF in July 1936 after having made a difficult South Atlantic crossing, he defended La Roque against the accusations that had been made against him, dismissed any rumors that he considered himself the Colonel's rival, and declared his unbounded faith in the new party's leader. In an airplane, Mermoz explained, the captain was a quasi-god. His orders were never criticized or questioned by his crew. Nobody could give a damn about politics. "We know that there are 12,000 kilometers to go before we reach our destination. That means sixty hours. It's a goal that is perhaps faraway, but for us it's close because it's achieved through the good intentions and courage of every one of us." The same principle applied to politics. "In France we're dying because of the lack of a leader and when we have one we spend our time criticizing and judging him." As for himself, Mermoz left no doubt that, like a good crew member, he had found his captain and intended to follow him. "The moment will come when we have to act, I'm sure that this moment in near, I'm telling you what I believe. We aren't finished yet; we've been through worse moments. Before long, we'll prevail and we'll have our enemies where we want them."[137]

For Mermoz, then, the *La Ligne* had become a model for the rebuilding of the French nation. He had no doubt that the values that had inspired his comrades and himself could be transferred to the nation as a whole, and especially to French youth. Aviation was more than a profession; it was a mystique, a "sort of social religion." It could also become a school aimed at the creation of leaders. If they submitted themselves to the "social school of aviation," French young people would find physical equilibrium and mental health; they

189

would develop a feeling for collective discipline in the service of an "ideal task"; and they would come to understand that it was possible to create a healthy atmosphere in which harmony could be achieved between those "satisfactions we derive through effort and the disappointments of our petty failures in the daily struggle of our human existence."[138]

On 7 December 1936, just as his politics were beginning to put strains on his closest friendships, Mermoz took off in the early morning from Dakar with the mail in a transatlantic flight that by then had become routine. Four hours later, he and his four companions disappeared into the sea after having sent a brief radio message reporting a problem with one of their engines. No trace of them was ever found.

★　　★　　★

During the months before Mermoz died, Kessel had been urging his friend to collaborate with him on a book about his life. In August 1936, while sharing a villa with Kessel at Saint-Tropez, Mermoz had spoken freely about his experiences before joining *La Ligne*. Now that Mermoz was dead, the need for a biography seemed even more pressing. The man of flesh and blood needed to be rescued before he was transformed into an "apostle" and "an archangel" by writers who were quick to exploit the occasion and enshrine Mermoz in myth "more tomb-like than death itself."[139] And who was better suited for that task than Kessel?

In August 1937 Kessel left France for Latin America to research that part of Mermoz's career that he knew least well. Never before had Kessel taken such care with a book. Not until March 1938 was he willing to hand over the manuscript to the editors of *Paris-Soir*,

Pl. 220.　The Laté 300, *Croix du Sud*, which Mermoz was piloting across the South Atlantic when he disappeared in December 1936. Compare it to the much smaller Laté 28-3 (Pl. 216) in which Mermoz and his two companions had crossed the South Atlantic in 1930.

Pl. 221.　The cover of Jacques Mortane's 1937 book, *Deux Archanges de l'air* (*Two Archangels of the Air*). From this point on the association of Mermoz with Guynemer would become a favored theme of the French right.

who devoted the first page of the edition of 2 April to the initial installment of Kessel's biography and then continued publication over a period of weeks. When Gallimard published the book version at the end of the summer, despite its relatively high price it sold more than seventy-five thousand copies within a few months. By chance, the book appeared during the Munich crisis at a moment when war with Germany seemed imminent and the French had every reason to believe that their future might soon depend on the prowess and courage of their aviators.

Though Kessel had missed few opportunities to exalt Mermoz's reputation when he was alive and after he died, he was in no mood for hagiography when he set out to write Mermoz's life.[140] What he grieved was not the passing of the hero but the loss of a friend with whom he had spent some of his most cherished moments. Beginning his book on the ship that would take him to Latin America, Kessel addressed an emotional letter to Mermoz, which he would later use as the introduction. In it he wondered whether he would have the necessary inner resources "to tear you from the robe of glory, to dissipate the icy incense, and bring you to life in your flesh and blood, in your heart, in your violence and your humanity, in your perpetual conquest and victory over yourself." To rescue and recreate the man he had known and loved Kessel confessed that he would have to expose aspects of his friend's life that only he knew. "No matter how violent they might be, no matter how sensual or shocking they might seem in the eyes of the vulgar, they seem to me to depict you as well as your exploits. You were a man and not a statue. And that was the source of your grandeur and your example."

Would he be capable of making others understand and accept the man he had known? Calling on Mermoz himself for inspiration and help, Kessel confessed that, despite all his doubts, he had accepted the challenge and taken up "the quiet battle that every man has to lead against himself, until the moment of his death."[141] Whether Kessel realized it or not, in writing those words he had revealed his central theme: the terrible struggle Mermoz had waged against himself to achieve the grandeur that led others to admire him and pronounce him to be a "sublime figure" without equal from both a moral and professional point of view.[142]

Pl. 222. A teen-aged Mermoz with his mother after they were reunited in 1917.

A master storyteller, Kessel made the most of Mermoz's many exploits and close scrapes with death. But for him, these deeds, which had won Mermoz fame with the public, were nothing but the outer shell that surrounded a complex and tormented inner life. The key to Mermoz's psychology, he thought, was his need for self-transcendence in the name of a cause that went beyond himself and that was ultimately unattainable. This was the cause of his greatness, but it was also the cause of his "mortal sadness." "In order to live, he had to escape from everyday life."[143]

With the cooperation of Mermoz's mother, Kessel revealed that the future pilot had been the offspring of a broken marriage. After his mother abandoned her husband taking along her son, Mermoz lived with his grandfather and his second wife under repressive and unpleasant conditions. Then, when the war broke out, the twelve-year-old boy was separated from his mother for three years, before she could be repatriated from German-occupied France. Reunited in 1917, the two had moved to Paris where the mother had been promised a post as a nurse and her son a scholarship at the Lycée Voltaire.

Jean's hopes of pursuing engineering studies at the École Central were dashed when he failed the oral exam for his secondary degree in science. Devastated, he volunteered in 1920 for military service, with the intention of becoming an aviator. Yet though Mermoz enjoyed flying and was good at it, he hated life in the bombing squadron in Metz to which he was assigned. While waiting for a reassignment to Syria, which he had requested out of a sense of desperate boredom and disgust with what seemed to him pointless discipline, he lapsed into dangerous habits that called his future into question. "For a few months, Mermoz was an aimless corporal who, when not engaged in dubious street fights and bat-

Pl. 223. Mermoz as a decorated military aviator in the early 1920s.

tles without glory against his superiors, found his form of escape in a furnished room next to a girl who was a cocaine addict, whose bed and artificial paradise he shared."[144]

Though Mermoz won the respect and admiration of his fellow aviators and commanding officers for his courage and dedication to duty while in Syria, he quickly found himself in serious trouble after returning to France. Unwilling to tolerate abusive superiors, he rebelled and barely escaped being court-martialed before he was released from the army in 1924. The period that followed was one of the darkest of his life; down-and-out in Paris, he lived a tawdry life of poverty, squalor, humiliation, and moral degradation. Then, in September 1924, there arrived a letter from Didier Daurat, inviting him to Toulouse to try out for a job with the Latécoère airlines. It held out a glimmer of hope and promised to rescue him, at least temporarily, from the hell into which he had fallen.

Now, said Kessel, would begin the process leading to the emergence of the heroic figure the world would know as Jean Mermoz. The embryo of the pure and poetic youth Mermoz once was had been buried beneath the sordid experiences of his years in the army and the six months spent as a penniless tramp in Paris. The road he would now follow, marked by exploits, triumphs, and miracles, would lead not only to the conquest of the world but more importantly to the "reconquest" of himself.[145]

Yet Kessel's portrait of Mermoz's career was far from one of uninterrupted ascent. Kessel revealed that Mermoz had resented Daurat's harsh discipline; that he had more than once felt the lash of Daurat's tongue; and that even after he had been elevated from the status of a mechanic to a pilot and allowed to fly the mail on the Spanish route between Toulouse and Alicante, he had complained about being exploited and secretly applied for a job with a rival airline in the hope of making more money. Mermoz had not yet become the person he was capable of being. Fortunately, Daurat understood this. In claiming that Aéropostale's director glimpsed in the young pilot something that Mermoz did not yet see in himself, Kessel returns to the argument he had made in *Vent de sable*: namely, that the collective enterprise, dangers, and discipline of *La Ligne* brought out qualities in its members of which they themselves were unaware and which they would never have developed under different circumstances.

Mermoz was transferred to the Casablanca–Dakar route in March 1926. He soon realized that it was very different from the type of flying he had been doing in Spain. Because of the unreliability of the planes the Line was flying, the difficult weather conditions, and the lack of inhabited towns in a desert landscape dominated by hostile tribes, the Latécoère pilots never flew the mail alone; they were always accompanied by another plane whose mission it was to make certain that the mail got through, no matter what happened to the pilot whose aircraft had been forced to land and the interpreter who accompanied him. It was under these conditions, Kessel wrote, that Mermoz's latent nobility came to the fore; it was in Africa that he began to single himself out among the other pilots of the Line. He shared their pleasures and their debauches, but they sensed that there was something different, something special about him. He had a "spiritual density" that the other pilots lacked. Though his comrades on the Line found it difficult to formulate in words what was distinctive about Mermoz, Kessel was convinced that whereas for the other pilots aviation was an end in itself, for Mermoz it was "a simple instrument, a sign." He cherished flying as "a unique means of grandeur and escape." "And Mermoz's comrades unknowingly admired in him the ideal personification of their acts and their sacrifices. On the forehead of their companion, they saw the poetry of their lives shine."[146]

By late 1927, Mermoz was looking for new challenges. Not surprisingly, given Lindbergh's recent success, he thought of a transatlantic flight between Paris and New York, a feat that no one yet had accomplished. Then, against his own inclinations, Mermoz was persuaded to assume responsibility for the creation of the infrastructure necessary for a mail service between Natal in northern Brazil and Buenos Aires.[147] This was in one sense a

defeat. An administrative position in faraway Latin America hardly appeared to offer possibilities for glory. For an ambitious aviator anxious to make his mark, it was a form of exile. But Mermoz transformed what might have been a desk job into a platform for heroic action. He discharged his administrative tasks while at the same time throwing himself into a frenzy of flying. Calling on the testimony of former Aéropostale pilots he met during his trip to Latin America, Kessel explained how, by sheer force of will and example, Mermoz succeeded in imposing his authority on aviators older and more experienced than himself.

As he neared the end of his book, Kessel wrestled uneasily with the contrast between the public image of Mermoz and the man he had known. His conclusion was that even toward the end of his short life, when he had reached the apogee of success, Mermoz was a bundle of contradictions. A kind and gentle man by nature, he was capable of violent outbursts. A person who overflowed with *joie de vivre*, Mermoz thought frequently of death. While brought up outside the Church by a mother and grandfather who were atheists, Mermoz had a "yearning for the infinite" and a "profound sense of the sacred," feelings that were essentially "mystic."[148] An example of focused concentration when flying, on the ground he was distant and a dreamer. A fearless hero in the public's eyes, he was privately consumed by doubts and mourned the passing of the heroic age of aviation. Henceforth, he lamented, pilots would be nothing but bus drivers. "Glorious archangel, profound neurasthenic, resigned mystic, dazzling pagan, in love with life, inclined toward death, child-like and sage, all these things were true of Mermoz, but all were false if one isolated any of these elements. For they all came together in an extraordinary unity."[149]

The most difficult aspect of Mermoz's life for Kessel to confront and explain was his friend's involvement in the right-wing, proto-fascist Croix de Feu. Here Kessel confessed that Mermoz's passionate commitment to this organization had created a strain between them; but he insisted that Mermoz's engagement had been pure, disinterested, and ultimately inspired by his disgust at the way the government had abandoned *La Ligne*. And here also, Kessel admitted, Mermoz found himself caught in a terrible contradiction: the antiparliamentary league he had joined because of its opposition to politics, deputies, and capitalists became a party that engaged in politics, had its own deputies, and was forced to ask for money from the very capitalists they pretended to despise and combat. Kessel claimed that Mermoz suffered from this contradiction, but had convinced himself that these compromises with principle were necessary in order to achieve the goal of a new, revived France. Later everything would change.[150]

Pl. 224.   Mermoz looking quite dandyish in comparison to his fellow mechanics in Toulouse during his apprenticeship with the Latécoère Line.

Pl. 225.   Mermoz stands out among his comrades. Mermoz is to the far right, Henri Guillaumet third from the left.

Pl. 226.   Mermoz delivers a speech at the Salle Wagram on 30 March 1936. La Rocque is seated directly behind him.

Pl. 227.   Mermoz relaxes with his wife Gilberte. He had already begun to take his distance from a relationship that was becoming painful for both.

Kessel put so much of himself into this book that at times it is difficult to know whether it was Mermoz or himself he was describing. Indeed, Fleury, a close friend of both, complained that Kessel had projected into his image of Mermoz far too much of his own Dostoevskian character.[151] Kessel's Mermoz is often sad, brooding, and given to excesses and violent outbursts; he is self-destructive, subject to depression, and incapable of happiness. Kessel concluded that only an extraordinary act of will had allowed Mermoz to exorcise his demons and overcome his Bacchic side.[152] He conceded, however, that to a much greater extent than himself Mermoz had forged a discipline over the years that kept his powerful instincts under control.[153]

Kessel's Mermoz was also deeply misogynist – like Kessel himself. His relationship with women other than his mother, as reconstructed and related by Kessel, revealed a lack of consideration that bordered on cruelty. His consorts were more often than not prostitutes or women of easy virtue; and when he married, he found he was confronted with a choice between flying and domestic peace. For those who knew Kessel well, it could have come as no surprise that he should present Mermoz's eventual separation from his wife as the triumph of his idealism and spirituality over the more materialistic and selfish attractions of a conventional family life.[154] Or as Kessel put it: "He understood once and for all that he had been born to worship at only one altar [aviation]. He blamed himself for being tough [with her]. And at the same time, he didn't want to give up his toughness."[155]

Having reached the end of his book, Kessel confessed his anxieties about the result. Though he had poured into these pages everything he had learned about the craft of writing, in the end Mermoz had escaped him. "Nothing succeeds in reproducing the luxuriant vibration of life."[156] Just as he could find no photograph of Mermoz that captured the man he had known, so he found his own literary portrait wanting. Others at the time agreed.[157] Over six decades later, a reader of Mermoz's published correspondence cannot help but notice that, for all his good intentions, Kessel could not escape the temptation to idealize a friend whose concerns were often more mundane than he made them out to be. Once launched on the orbit of his career as a famous flyer, Mermoz allowed nothing and nobody to stand in his way. Nor can his involvement in radical right-wing politics be dismissed as mere naïveté. He consciously sought the radical transformation, if not the outright over-throw, of the Third Republic.

Still, no aviator has ever received such a literary monument by a writer of such power and facility of expression. Part adventure tale and history of the men of the *La Ligne*, part psychological portrait, part story of a quest for a lost friend, Kessel's book is unique; no biography, no matter how skillfully done, will ever replace it.[158]

★   ★   ★

It was typical of Kessel's acute sense for friendship that he lingered in his biography over the relationship that Saint-Exupéry developed with Mermoz when both were assigned to the African route. Saint-Exupéry had quickly seen in Mermoz an "exceptional being" because of his vitality, his warmth, and his sensitivity. Mermoz had been drawn to Saint-Exupéry because of his extraordinary culture, his sharp wit, and his inclination toward philosophical generalizations. They treated each other with a deference, Kessel wrote, that was unusual among the men of the Line. Only a decade after meeting did they begin to address each other with the familiar "*tu*." When Saint-Exupéry was forced to come to grips with the disappearance of Mermoz in the South Atlantic, he wrote of him with deep affec-tion. He had given us, Saint-Exupéry wrote, the example not of work but of love. He had shown us how the smile of a man could light up his face after a struggle and victory against the overwhelming odds. "He was the salt of the earth: the type of man who throws him-self into life heart and soul. He never spared any effort; he never shrank before any adver-sary. He put all of himself into his acts. He was the image of plenitude: Jean Mermoz offered himself to the blowing wind like a tree."[159]

Kessel tried to imagine the scene when Saint-Exupéry had read passages of his first novel to Mermoz at Cap Juby. It was, he said, a meeting between "the greatest poet of wings" and "the most beautiful gladiator of the sky."[160] But when Kessel wrote these generous lines, "the greatest poet of wings" had not produced a book for seven years.

The period following the publication of *Vol de nuit* had not been a happy one for Saint-Exupéry. He had parted company with Aéropostale under unpleasant circumstances after having published an article in Gaston Gallimard's left-leaning weekly magazine, *Marianne*, that annoyed the company's new director.[161] The success of *Vol de nuit* and the celebrity it brought its author had the paradoxical effect of alienating some of his fellow aviators on the Line, who felt that the stories of their adventures were for them alone and not to be shared with the general public.[162] Some may have disliked the heroic portrait of the administrator Rivière, thinking that Saint-Exupéry had elevated Daurat at the expense of the flyers who risked their lives on a daily basis carrying out orders that he issued from behind a desk. Others may have been privately annoyed that Saint-Exupéry was profiting financially from their efforts. Whether justifiably or not, Saint-Exupéry was convinced that he was being boycotted by his former friends and protested that he had been reduced to poverty because of writing "this ill-fated book."[163] In a self-pitying letter written to his friend Henri Guillaumet toward the end of 1933, Saint-Exupéry lamented that he no longer had the courage to go to the airport at Le Bourget. "I would have been afraid of crying. You don't know, you can't imagine how much I've suffered during the last two years . . . Life is indeed pitiless."[164]

Saint-Exupéry's bitterness when he wrote this letter was exacerbated by his awareness that his life as an aviator was essentially over. His efforts to win a place as a pilot on the newly created Air France in 1933 had been ignored, a rebuff that he understandably took badly.[165] A post with Latécoère's Toulouse aircraft factory as a test pilot that Didier Daurat arranged in early 1933 came to a nearly fatal end when in December Saint-Exupéry, carrying three passengers, botched a landing in the Laté 293 seaplane he was putting down in the bay of Saint-Raphaël. Miraculously, no one was killed, but a rumor began to spread that the author *Vol de nuit* was a better writer than pilot. It would never be dispelled.

Saint-Exupéry was finally offered a largely symbolic position by Air France in early 1934, but it was not as a pilot but a publicist, implicit recognition that he was now viewed more as a man of letters than an aviator. Anxious to get back into the air, constrained by his life in the Parisian literary world, and eager to escape from what had become an unhappy marriage, Saint-Exupéry attempted two long-distance flights, one in 1935 and another in 1938; but though both would contribute to the advancement of his literary career, they ended ingloriously, the first in a forced landing in the Libyan desert and the second in a crash while taking off from Guatemala City. The Guatemala debacle, from which Saint-Exupéry and his mechanic escaped with their lives by a miracle, cast further doubts on his reliability as a pilot, for he had failed to verify that the fuel load had been reduced sufficiently to account for the high altitude of the La Aurora airfield, as he had been advised to do by Pan Am officials stationed there.[166]

Aside from his Air France salary of 3,000 francs a month, Saint-Exupéry earned his living during the 1930s by writing screenplays and articles for newspapers and magazines, assignments that he accepted out of financial necessity rather than desire. When given the opportunity, he continued to memorialize the men of *La Ligne*; but he also revealed an unsuspected talent as a writer of *grands reportages* – accounts he produced on commission for large circulation newspapers recounting his ordeal in the Libyan desert and visits to Moscow and Spain after the beginning of the Civil War. The articles that were extracted from him by editors, eager to capitalize on his celebrity, no doubt meant less to him than the deeply felt and elusive prose "poem" he had begun in 1936 that would be published posthumously under the title *Citadelle*; yet carefully screened and painstakingly revised, the occasional pieces Saint-Exupéry wrote during the 1930s were nonetheless to provide the foundation for the book that Gaston Gallimard awaited impatiently.[167]

Despite the long period of gestation, the work that Saint-Exupéry produced in the last six months of 1938 was a work of circumstance, patched together rapidly under pressure. It bore the mark of disparate figures with very different agendas and was also clearly influenced by the deteriorating political situation in Europe. Eager to hatch the book that he knew Saint-Exupéry had within him and perhaps acting as an intermediary for Gallimard, André Gide had counseled his friend to attempt a collection of chapters that would capture the sensations, emotions, and reflections of the aviator, something along the lines of Conrad's *Mirror of the Sea*.[168] This suggestion could not have left Saint-Exupéry indifferent since, aside from the fact that it came from the most influential figure in French letters, he was not unaware that he had already been referred to by some of his admirers as the "Conrad of the air."[169]

The immediate incentive to the production of *Terre des hommes*, however, was less literary in nature: it came from Eugene Reynal and Curtice Hitchcock, the American publishers of *Vol de nuit*, whom Saint-Exupéry met while stopping in New York before embarking on his ill-fated flight to Latin America. Perennially short of money, he was in no position to refuse the substantial advance of $2,500 that they offered him for a book based on the

Pl. 228. Saint-Exupéry's career as a test pilot came to an ignominious end in this potentially accident in the bay of Saint-Raphaël.

ANNABELLA
PIERRE RICHARD-WILLM
JEAN MURAT

anne marie

Scénario original de
ANTOINE DE SAINT-EXUPÉRY
Un Film de RAYMOND BERNARD

Pl. 229. A poster for *Anne Marie*.

numerous articles he had written during the past six years.[170] The translator that Reynal and Hitchcock assigned to the project, Lewis Galantière, struggled with the nuances and lyricism of the Frenchman's prose and pushed him to produce a series of sketches about his flying adventures to which Galantière suggested the title: *Wind, Sand and Stars*. Saint-Exupéry had in mind something more ambitious: a book of philosophical reflections that would go far beyond flying. In a strange inversion of the usual relationship between an author and his publishing house, Galantière resisted Saint-Exupéry's attempts to tighten his book and eliminate whole sections.[171] The result was that the Americans would get one version of Saint-Exupéry in the late 1930s and the French another. The differences were subtle, but revealing.

The untranslatable title that Saint-Exupéry finally gave the French version of his book is a strange one for an aviator. *Terre des hommes* – Land of Men – alerts the reader that the emphasis is not going to be on escape from the earth, a favored theme of aviation literature. And this is reinforced by the book's prologue, omitted from the American translation, in which Saint-Exupéry, remembering his first night in Argentina and the sparse lights he saw on the plain below, concludes that he must try to establish some connection with people on the ground. "I must try to communicate with some of these lights that burn at distant intervals in the countryside."[172] The emphasis from the beginning is on the isolation of men and the quest for a means of overcoming it.

Terre des hommes is a book that evades characterization; it belongs to no recognizable genre. Its reception reflects the confusion of its readers. A work based on Saint-Exupéry's experiences and those of his friends, *Terre des hommes* nonetheless received the French Academy's highest prize for *fiction*, the Grand Prix du Roman. Written in prose, it was praised for its poetry.[173] Paradoxically, though it is one of the most famous flying books ever published, it is only secondarily about aviation. Most of the action occurs on the ground. The first chapter, "La Ligne," is an intensely moving account of the events preceding Saint-Exupéry's first mail flight from Toulouse to Alicante. The flight itself is not described. *Terre des hommes*'s longest chapter is primarily devoted to the author's ordeal in the Libyan desert when he and his mechanic wandered for three days without food or water after Saint-Exupéry ploughed his recently acquired Simoun into a sand dune while trying to set a record for a flight between Paris and Saigon. The period in the air before the crash is treated as a prologue.

When the airplane appears in *Terre des hommes*, Saint-Exupéry takes pains to present it as a tool, a means rather than an end.[174] The justifications he gives for it seem far removed from the world of commercial aviation in which he made his early career. The airplane, he tells us, offers a way of fleeing from cities where authentic human life is impossible; it opens up a fairy land of visual sights; it puts us into contact with nature; it can take us to strange places and plunge us into the "heart of mystery"; it enables us to see the earth in a new way; and it inspires deep relationships of trust and fidelity among the men who use it. It is a "foot bridge," launched in the night, capable of uniting men across vast distances.[175] There is no mention of the charms of speed or the Promethean conquest of distance. The airplane's novelty – a persistent theme in aviation literature from the earliest days of flight – is immediately undermined by Saint-Exupéry's comparison of it with a peasant's plough and his claim that it puts us into contact with "all the old problems," by which he means the age-old struggle between man and the obstacles that nature presents to his survival.[176] The two principal heroes of the book – Mermoz and Guillaumet – are great not because of their aeronautical exploits but because of the universal human qualities they exemplify. The group he associates them with – the comrades of *La Ligne* – is at times replaced by a broader one that includes surgeons, physicists, astronomers, and poets.

In a book that was aimed toward a public that relished aerial adventure, Saint-Exupéry goes out of his way to express his disdain for men who risk their lives out of love of danger.[177] *La Ligne*, he claims, is not important because of the heroic acts its discipline produced but because it was the soil – *le terrain* – that makes possible the emergence of men like Mermoz and Guillaumet.[178] We are thus very far away from the world of Kessel and Fleury where the men of *La Ligne* are compared with medieval knights or members of a religious order. They are instead equivalent to rural laborers – *défricheurs* – whose virtue derives from their close contact with nature. When Mermoz disappears in the South Atlantic, he is compared with a peasant who, having harvested his wheat and tied it in bundles, goes to sleep in his field.[179] The Hamlet-like hero of *Vol de nuit* – Rivière – here is reduced to a small walk-on role as "the Director."[180] What matters are "the comrades," the title of the second chapter. They represent a closed community – "a large professional family" – who live by a different code and experience the world differently than ordinary men.[181]

Reading *Terre des hommes*, one is often reminded of the immense literary shadow cast by Proust in interwar France. Like Proust's novel, this is a book about memory – Saint-Exupéry's memories, of course, but also the memories of others. But these are not just any memories; they are, for the most part, memories of *La Ligne*. They are also generally memories of a world that no longer exists. Yet this remembered world, though now gone, is more real to Saint-Exupéry than the barren and threatening world in which he lives. Hence on one level, *Terre des hommes* is a book that seeks to recapture a past that is now lost along with many of the persons who inhabited it, such as Jean Mermoz whose exemplary life and death are remembered in order to drive home the point that the grandeur of a craft lies above all in its ability to unite human beings in a struggle towards a common goal.[182]

The memories of Saint-Exupéry's friends are also passed through the filter of his imagination. The exciting and well-known story of Guillaumet's escape from the Andes is used to illustrate the point that the quality that distinguishes Saint-Exupéry's friend (to whom

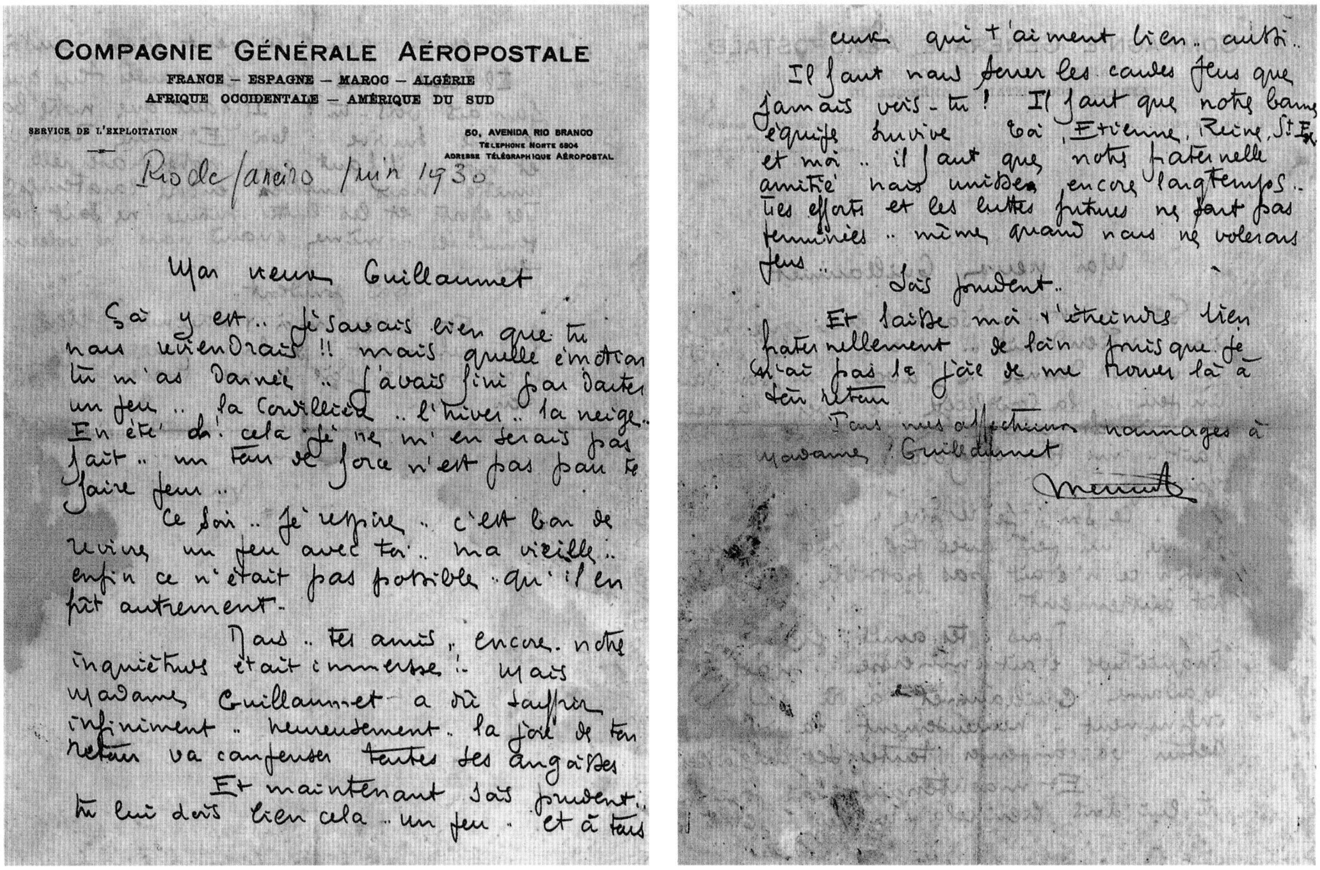

COMPAGNIE GÉNÉRALE AÉROPOSTALE
FRANCE — ESPAGNE — MAROC — ALGÉRIE
AFRIQUE OCCIDENTALE — AMÉRIQUE DU SUD

SERVICE DE L'EXPLOITATION

50, AVENIDA RIO BRANCO
TELEPHONE NORTE 5604
ADRESSE TÉLÉGRAPHIQUE AÉROPOSTAL

Rio de Janeiro Juin 1930

Terre des hommes is dedicated) is not his courage, but his sense of responsibility: to himself, to the mail, and to the comrades who are hoping for his safe return.[183] This then leads us to what Saint-Exupéry considers to be the profound moral meaning of what others had trivialized as an exploit. "To be a man is to be responsible . . . It's to be proud of a victory that the comrades have achieved. It's to feel that in laying down one's stone, one is contributing to the building of the world."[184]

Saint-Exupéry is aware that some experiences cannot be recaptured because their drama, when recounted, is untrue to what the participant of the incident actually felt at the time. In a chapter written for the American edition of *Wind, Sand and Stars* but published in France separately after the publication of *Terre des hommes*, he recalls a terrifying flight in Patagonia. Caught in a hurricane, Saint-Exupéry is too busy coping with turbulence to feel fear. Winds of up to 240 kilometers per hour hurled him toward the ground and made it impossible for him to control his plane. Blown out to sea, he felt as if he were affixed "to the end of a monstrous whip that cracked above the sea."[185] Fighting against torrential winds, he was only able to cover ten kilometers in one hour of flight. Yet when he escapes from his terrible ordeal and lands he has nothing to say to the comrades awaiting him. "I'm sleepy. I slowly move fingers that I am unable to bring back to life. It scarcely seems to me that not long ago I was afraid. Was I afraid? I was involved in a strange spectacle. What strange spectacle? I don't know." To be sure, tomorrow he may be moved by his experience; but it will only be in memory and in imagination. Physical dramas, he concludes, do not touch us unless someone is able to disengage from them their spiritual meaning.[186] Attempting to do that, in fact, is what *Terre des hommes* is all about.

The specter of Nietzsche hovers over these pages, even if, like that of Proust, his name goes unmentioned.[187] The prophecy of the "last man," Nietzsche's scorn for conformity, and

Pl. 230.   In this letter of June 1930, written from Rio de Janeiro on Aéropostale stationery and using the familiar *tu* (you), Mermoz expressed his relief at the news of Guillaumet's rescue after having been lost in the Andes. "I was certain that you would come back to us!! but you've really given me a scare . . . Tonight . . . I can breathe again." Mermoz goes on to urge Guillaumet to be careful for the sake of his wife and all his friends. "We have to tighten our ranks more than ever . . . Our good old team [équipe] has to survive . . . our comradeship (*fraternelle amitié*) must unite us for a long time to come." Mermoz foresees the end of their adventure when he says that "Our efforts and future struggles are not over . . . even when we won't fly any more."

199

his admonition to live dangerously and to be without pity have all left their mark on *Terre des hommes*. Much of the book represents a meditation on the conditions that produce greatness. Saint-Exupéry expresses disdain for the provincial bureaucrat with whom he shares an omnibus in Toulouse on the way to the airfield. "You have achieved peace, like the termites, by covering over with cement every escape toward the light. In your island of bourgeois safety, you have rolled into a ball your routines and the stifling rites of your provincial life; you have erected this humble rampart against the winds and the tides and the stars. You don't want to worry about the pressing problems; you've had enough trouble forgetting what it means to be a man."[188] Saint-Exupéry later tells us that the appearance of a poor Pascal means more than the birth of several nobodies destined to riches.[189] Reading this passage, which begins the concluding chapter of *Terre des hommes*, one cannot help but think of Nietzsche's remark that the only thing that justifies the murderous chaos of history is the emergence of great individuals.

In a remarkable closing section, Saint-Exupéry recalls a scene when he observed a Polish family on a train from Paris taking them back to their native country. Noting the poverty, filth, and ugliness of the father and mother, he wonders how they were transformed into these "packages of clay." Through what sausage factory had they passed? Then he observes their son, a marvel of charm and grace, whom he compares with a "golden fruit." "Here is a musician's face, here is Mozart as a child . . ." Had he been a rose in a garden, gardeners would have rushed to cultivate him. But there are no gardeners to care for men. "The child Mozart will be marked like the others by the sausage factory . . . Mozart is condemned."

What depresses Saint-Exupéry is not the plight of these miserable people, but its implications for the human race. "I'm no great believer in compassion. What torments me is the point of view of the gardener. What torments me is not their poverty . . . Generations of Orientals have lived in filth and enjoyed it. Soup kitchens will not cure what torments me. What torments me is not these humps nor these hollows nor this ugliness. It's a bit, in each of these men, the Mozart who has been murdered."[190] Nietzsche could not have said it better, nor felt more deeply the mediocrity of the masses above which superior men must struggle to raise themselves.

Though the tableaux that make up *Terre des hommes* clearly come from different periods of Saint-Exupéry's life and were written for very different audiences, ranging from mass circulation magazines and newspapers such as *Marianne* and *L'Intransigeant* to journals aimed at more sophisticated readers such as the *Nouvelle Revue Française* and the Surrealist *Minotaure*, they are effectively held together by an ongoing meditation on life in a barren civilization where men in suburban trains are reduced, like ants, to the use that is being made of them.[191] Communism and fascism are never mentioned by name; but as the book progresses they emerge, implicitly, as challenges to a decadent and desolate world that Saint-Exupéry seeks to understand.[192] He discerns beneath their deadly conflict a common yearning toward spiritual values.[193] Men cannot reveal their innate grandeur unless they have a goal beyond themselves the pursuit of which may cost them their lives. Take Mermoz for example, Saint-Exupéry says. If you had claimed that the letters he was carrying across the Andes when he risked his life to open up the route between Santiago and Buenos Aires were not worthy of this sacrifice, he would have laughed in your face. What mattered was the man who was born in him when he crossed the Andes. It was the action, not the ostensible purpose, that produced the extraordinary man he became. "The truth for a man is what makes him a man."[194]

Saint-Exupéry was assembling and revising *Terre des hommes* during the months directly preceding and following the Munich crisis of August–September 1938. Though he was aware that many of the values he was proposing were values that flourished in times of conflict, he rejects war as a solution to the problems that Europeans face. Saint-Exupéry had no illusions about what such a war would mean, nor was he impressed by the arguments that Nazis and fascists were using to justify it. Since the introduction of the airplane and poison gas, war was nothing but a form of "bloody surgery." "Each side takes refuge behind a cement wall; night after night it launches squadrons that torpedo the adversary in his entrails, blows up his vital centers, and paralyzes his production and commerce. Victory belongs to the side that rots first. And the two adversaries rot together."[195]

Terre des hommes is ultimately about the mysterious process by which apparently ordinary men are transformed into something higher. *La Ligne* becomes the prototype for such a transformation. In Saint-Exupéry's memory, the rickety old omnibus that took Aéropostale's pilots to the airfield at Montaudran outside Toulouse from which they flew the mail to Spain became the "gray chrysalis from which a transfigured man would emerge."[196] It had also been for many men of *La Ligne* a "last refuge" and a "final procession" on their way to death.[197] In Saint-Exupéry's mind these two metaphors were closely connected. The willingness to risk one's life was a prerequisite for rebirth and transfiguration.

Saint-Exupéry was not unaware of the paradoxes involved in his choice of *La Ligne* as a model for the way in which men should live their lives. The precondition for transcendence was the embracing of values normally associated with war by men living in a world at peace. Walking in the frozen streets of Toulouse before his first mail flight at Christmas time, the young Saint-Exupéry feels like "a threatened warrior" and scrutinizes the sky for signs of an approaching storm. The stars disappeared one by one, communicating to him "the positions of the enemy before the battle." Though a form of work like any other, flying set the men who did it apart from other human beings. How could these city strollers, these "barbarians," react to the possibility of snow as he did? How could they receive from the night the messages that he received? Looking at the brightly lighted store windows full of Christmas presents, Saint-Exupéry experiences a feeling of "proud intoxication" at the thought of the material world he is giving up. "What did I care about these shimmering crystal glasses designed for evening parties, these lamp shades, these books. An airline pilot, I was already bathing in the spray of the wind, I was already sinking my teeth into the bitter pulp of night flights."[198]

Flying, then, was a means of escape from the commercial spirit in an age of base materialism; but the end toward which even the most quixotic of aviators was contributing was a world in which airplanes could safely transport people and goods, thus facilitating the exchanges on which capitalism thrived. Progress in aeronautical technology would inevitably undermine and destroy the moral universe of *La Ligne*. Once flying was no longer dangerous, the soul of *La Ligne* would be dead.[199]

The messages conveyed by *Terre des hommes* were appealing, even stirring; but they were also contradictory and maddeningly elusive. They expressed the confusion that many people felt as the 1930s drew to an end and Europe prepared to go to war and resume the conflict that had ended two decades earlier. There would be no winners in a war, and thus every effort should be made to avoid it; but war brought out the grandeur in men and rescued them from the mediocrity of their peacetime lives. Under their differences, men everywhere had the same needs and contained the same potential; but some had taken refuge in islands of bourgeois safety while others elevated themselves above the mass by dedicating their lives to a cause that extended beyond their own self-interest. Europeans yearned for a spiritual meaning they could give to their lives; but, sadly, few were capable of forsaking materialism and liberating themselves from the miserable bourgeois conventions by which they lived. Men like Mermoz and Guillaumet were great because they were responsible to their comrades; but toward which ends should comrades dedicate their sense of responsibility? *Terre des hommes* poses this question, but its author is incapable of answering it in a way that avoids relativism and the doctrine of action for action's sake.[200] No matter how rhetorically reassuring and inspired by a humanism whose sincerity no one can doubt, the central insight that Saint-Exupéry derives from his reflections was hardly one that could guide decisions in the difficult circumstances of 1939: "Bound to our brothers by a common goal that is situated outside of ourselves, only then do we truly breathe; and our experience shows us that to love is not to look at each other but to look in the same direction."[201]

In a country where political animosities ran deep and had become visceral, personally dividing former friends, Saint-Exupéry could only have been pleased, and perhaps a bit surprised, by the unanimous praise that *Terre des hommes* enjoyed. Critics across the political spectrum praised the lyricism of his prose, his modesty, his personal courage, and the humanist values he embraced. Indeed, it was sometimes difficult to know whether it was the book or the man that most attracted *Terre des hommes*'s reviewers. The Communist Paul Nizan wrote that Saint-Exupéry's account of his experiences as an airline pilot was "composed with a precision, a sense of proportion, and a dignity that inspires admiration and friendship." He found the heart of the philosophy of this "peasant of the sky" in a passage where Saint-Exupéry exclaims: "I don't like anything that degrades men."[202]

Many reviewers seized the occasion of *Terre des hommes*'s publication to promote Saint-Exupéry in the hierarchy of French letters. Saint-Exupéry was no longer compared with the English author Conrad, as he had been after publishing *Vol de nuit*, but to monuments of French literature, like Chateaubriand. He was now not just a promising talent; he had been elevated to the status of a "very great writer."[203] Henry Bordeaux, the biographer of Guynemer, later compared the excitement that came over him on reading *Terre des hommes* with the feelings that must have been aroused in the first readers of Descartes's *Méditations* or the first persons to see Racine's *Le Cid*. What impressed Bordeaux above all was the novelty of Saint-Exupéry's literary voice. The author of *Terre des hommes* used images that were either unfamiliar, or else employed established images in an unexpected way. "He saw people and things in a different way than we did." Bordeaux could already imagine Saint-Exupéry's future election to the French Academy, where he would represent "the new knighthood of the air." In the meantime, Bordeaux was instrumental in persuading his fellow academicians to award Saint-Exupéry's memoir the Academy's prize for the best novel of the year.[204]

André Gide's unqualified and growing admiration for the author of *Vol de nuit* was also helpful in rallying support for Saint-Exupéry's new book. The younger man frequently sought Gide's counsel when their paths crossed at the chateau of his mother's cousin Yvonne de Lestrange. Not known for his generosity in judging others, Gide let his friends know that he enjoyed Saint-Exupéry's company, was confounded by his card tricks, and found him to be "extraordinarily intelligent" and possessed with a "prodigious talent for invention."[205] The pages of *Terre des hommes* that Saint-Exupéry read to him surpassed his "wishes, hope, and expectation."[206] With patrons like Bordeaux and Gide, the success of *Terre des hommes* was assured.

As may have been expected, Maurice Martin du Gard's *Les Nouvelles Littéraires* led the charge on Saint-Exupéry's behalf.[207] Even before its first review of *Terre des hommes* appeared, the magazine ran an interview with its author in which the interviewer confessed that it had been moving to have the opportunity to speak on familiar terms with a man "who has so often played with death."[208] The following week, in a rubric named "The Book of the Week," René Lalou, warned readers not to approach the *Terre des hommes* only as a "magnificent aviation poem." Its import, he said, was far greater. All the stories Saint-Exupéry told and all his meditations on their meaning testified to "the glory of the Spirit."[209] Two weeks later, *Les Nouvelles Littéraires* printed a more extensive review by Edmond Jaloux. Jaloux explained that *Terre des hommes* was, in its core, not the work of a

Pl. 231.   In this 1938 photograph of André Gide, there is little doubt of his profession.

Pl. 232.   A poster publicizing the prize that Saint-Exupéry received from the French Academy.

writer of adventure stories but the meditations of a moralist. Reading Saint-Exupéry's account of the night before his first mail flight from Toulouse, Jaloux was reminded of the eve that young French knights of the thirteenth century were required to pass before receiving their arms. As a moralist, Jaloux placed Saint-Exupéry in the elevated company of Nietzsche, Carlyle, and Emerson. His "firm and concise" style allowed him to project on the stories he told a stark and lively light. How many pages there were in this marvelous book that one would like to remember! Jaloux confessed that *Terre des hommes* was one of the most delightful books he had read in a very long time.[210]

When *Terre des hommes* won the Grand Prix of the French Academy for the novel in late May, the *Nouvelles Littéraires* seized the opportunity to publish yet another article about Saint-Exupéry, this one on its front page. Jeanine Delpech explained that "Like the Greek heroes, he is as shrewd as he is brave. He knows how to outwit winds, deceive downdrafts, sidestep thunder, and outrun lightening. He knows also how to cheat fear, the requirements of the body, and the failings of instinct . . . Saint-Exupéry's name is one of the few that the wives of marquises and café waiters utter with equal admiration."[211]

In this torrent of praise, one of the only dissenting voices was Saint-Exupéry's friend Benjamin Crémieux. A great admirer of *Vol de nuit*, Crémieux was by no means insensitive to the charms of *Terre des hommes*. He established the close connection between the two books by pointing out that *Terre des hommes* set out to define that elusive quality in man that Saint-Exupéry had identified in *Vol de nuit* as being more valuable than happiness. But Crémieux found the connection between the various sections forced and sometimes awkward; and he felt that the juxtaposition of poetic passages and abstract philosophical formulas sometimes verged on affectation and a search for beauty as an end in itself.[212]

Crémieux's real objection to *Terre des hommes*, however, went far beyond the defects of its form: he was primarily concerned about its philosophical dimension, the version of humanism that had so attracted other reviewers. Crémieux understood that Saint-Exupéry was proposing a form of pragmatism, a doctrine of action for its own sake; and he saw the connection between his friend's acceptance of the superiority of soldierly virtues and the dangerous myths that the totalitarian regimes were propagating in order to justify their assault on individual freedom.[213] Crémieux was quick to recognize that Saint-Exupéry opposed war, hate, servitude, and hereditary aristocracy. But he rejected out of hand as seductive but utopian the solution Saint-Exupéry had offered in his concluding section on the Polish family. "One doesn't cultivate a genius like a rose. One gives to all children the possibility to become geniuses if they can." Crémieux was willing to accept the primacy of actions that were idealistically motivated over those inspired by materialistic greed; but he balked at what he perceived as Saint-Exupéry's willingness to give priority to action over thought and a life dedicated to conflict over a life conducted in peace.[214] "Nothing," he concluded, "indicates that human life is made for heroism rather than for peace and order in a world of justice."[215]

Reading this review that appeared in André Gide's *Nouvelle Revue Française*, one can sense that Crémieux expressed his reservations about his friend's book with reluctance. His criticisms are carefully balanced with praise. But one has to wonder whether the Jewish and staunchly Republican Crémieux was also troubled by the memory of articles, published by Saint-Exupéry in the newspaper *Paris-Soir* in October 1938, that provided confused but seductively sophisticated reasons to justify the abandonment by France of Czechoslovakia at the Munich Conference of September 1938. That series of articles had ended with a nostalgic hymn to the virtues of peasant France that echoed many of the sentiments dear to the anti-Republican Right.[216] In 1939, *Terre des homme*'s themes of antirationalism, antiurbanism, and scorn for bourgeois values, combined with the exaltation of heroic and fraternal action whatever its motivation, put its author in dangerous company.[217]

★   ★   ★

On 7 December 1937, to commemorate the first anniversary of Jean Mermoz's disappearance in the South Atlantic, Joseph Kessel contributed an article about his friend to the mass circulation newspaper *Paris-Soir*. Its theme was that Mermoz was in the process of ceasing to be a man and well on his way to becoming a myth. This development depressed Kessel, though he recognized its inevitability. But reflecting on its implications led Kessel to a larger thought. "Our time is beginning to construct its own legend . . . No one is consciously working toward this end, yet everyone contributes to it. Love, hate, fear, admiration, envy, and this profound and eternal need that peoples have to forge myths that transcend themselves are already transforming men familiar to us into figures larger than life."[218]

In making this statement in an article very consciously designed to shape the French collective memory of Mermoz as a pilot who had been "so great," "so courageous," and "so gentle," Kessel was being disingenuous. He himself had missed few opportunities to glorify the exploits of the men of *La Ligne*; he was well aware of his friend Jean-Gérard Fleury's book and newspaper articles devoted to their cause; he was close to Saint-Exupéry and an admirer of *Courrier-Sud* and *Vol de nuit*, which he had recently praised for its literary innovations; and, even if he hadn't read them, he would have known the general tenor of the accounts of Mermoz and his comrades in books by Maurice Bourdet, René Chambe, and Jacques Morane.[219] If any myth had been consciously constructed, it was the myth of *La Ligne*.

Kessel was right, however, in predicting that when the French did get around to constructing their twentieth-century pantheon, Mermoz would be reserved an honored place. This was in part because aviation had a privileged place in French conceptions of their national identity. Already before the Great War, the French had been told that they were the people best suited to locomotion in the air; they were "the winged nation" par excellence. To fly required imagination, valor, daring, elegance, subtlety, élan, and a sense of adventure: were these not quintessentially French qualities? As heirs of classical antiquity, did it not make sense that the French should be in the forefront of those determined to avenge the defeat of Icarus, a prolific French novelist asked in 1914?[220] Drawing on a well-established self-image that had long been used to justify the production of luxury goods and an aversion to the kind of heavy industry cultivated by the British and the Germans, French writers had convinced themselves that being "the most refined and intellectual nation in the world," all Frenchmen have aviation in their blood.[221] Can one imagine another Western country in which a government agency would proclaim, as the Under Secretariat of Aviation did in a brochure prepared for an airplane exhibition in December 1924, that "With a prestigious beating of its wings, the airplane has returned Poetry to its place in the skies after it had been chased away by factory smoke"![222]

To be sure, France had many famous flyers during the interwar years who enjoyed moments of popularity and mass adulation; one thinks of Charles Nungesser, Dieudonné Costes, Joseph Le Brix, and Hélène Boucher. But the aviation story the French preferred, and the one they chose to remember, was that of Aéropostale. And among the pilots of Aéropostale, as Kessel foresaw, Mermoz has a privileged place.

Pl. 233.   The French aviatrix Hélène Boucher. Admired for her 1929 Paris-Saigon flight and other exploits, she died in a flying accident in 1934.

Since 1939, the French have told and retold themselves the saga of Aéropostale in the form of histories, biographies, autobiographies, articles and entire issues of the magazine *Icare*, which is devoted to the history of aviation, with an understandable emphasis on the experience of the French. They have made movies on the topic, produced television documentaries and a six-part fictionalized television series, children's books, and even comics.[223] A major composer, Arthur Honneger, composed a suite for orchestra based on his music for the 1937 film *Mermoz*. Moreover, there is no indication that the French were losing interest in the adventures of Aéropostale as the century turned.[224] In 1999 the French astronaut Patrick Baudry and two other pilots, accompanied by three journalists and a mechanic, retraced the thirteen-thousand kilometer route flown by Aéropostale from Toulouse to Santiago in a restored Catalina amphibious aircraft that dated from the 1930s. The book that Baudry and his photographer later assembled, documenting this exploit, bore the title: *A Legendary Flight on the Path of Aéropostale: Mermoz Still Lives.*[225]

The primacy the Aéropostale story has come to occupy in the French collective memory is due to a constellation of factors. The saga of Aéropostale has a complex narrative structure and a cast of colorful characters that cannot be matched by discrete aeronautical exploits or even an individual aviator's life, no matter how heroic or tragic. Moreover, the achievements of Aéropostale represent a crucial bridge between the now fading memory of France's aeronautical prowess in the pre-1914 period and the resurgence of its aircraft industry after the Second World War. The line from Louis Blériot to the Concorde passes through Aéropostale.

Having said this, however, it is clear that in a country that defines itself in terms of the high points of its literary tradition, the works that Saint-Exupéry devoted to Aéropostale's memory have ensured that the achievements of the men of *La Ligne* would not be forgotten. Many French writers were drawn to aviation; in the decade of the 1930s alone, one thinks of Paul Morand, Jérôme and Jean Thauraud, Anne de Noailles, and above all André Malraux.[226] But no one invested as much of himself in this theme as Saint-Exupéry; no other French writer of his stature was capable of bringing to bear on his writing the experience of a veteran pilot; and none was more skillful at drawing larger moral lessons from

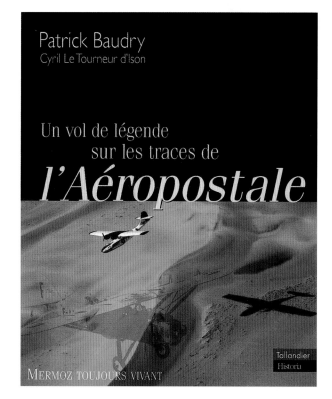

Pl. 234.   The jacket of *Un Vol de légende sur les traces de l'Aéropostale. Mermoz toujours vivant* by Patrick Baudry and Cyril Le Tourneur d'Ison.

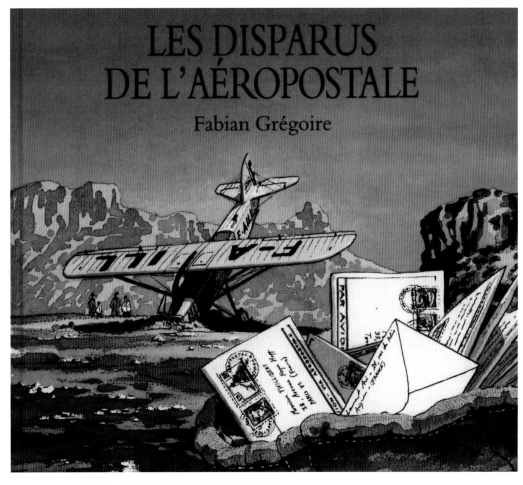

Pl. 235. The cover of Fabian Grégoire's 1999 children's book, *Les Disparus de l'Aéropostale*.

Pl. 236. Mermoz, played here by the actor Robert Hughes-Lambert, seeks to free his plane from the snow after crashing in the Andes in a scene from the 1937 movie *Mermoz*.

Pl. 237. This 1970 Mermoz/Saint-Exupéry 10 franc stamp links Aéropostale with the Concorde, a symbol of continuing leadership in aviation by the French.

what might have appeared with time a chapter in the decline of French imperialism or mere adventures in the air.

The range of Saint-Exupéry's influence is sometimes surprising. In the fall of 1939 Jean-Paul Sartre was called up for military service. While awaiting the outbreak of armed conflict with Germany in eastern France, he confessed to Simone de Beauvoir that reading *Terre des hommes* had inspired him to imagine another life than the one he had and to which he was otherwise happily attached. "For the first time I didn't long for my real and past life, you, Paris, my period, the places I've known. It was something else, much more tender and resigned: I longed for Argentina, Brazil, the Sahara, a world that I don't know, an entire life in which neither you or anyone else had any place . . . I felt lonely and childish, moved like a very young man envisaging a future − and at the same time knowing that it would not be my future. It was metaphysical and lacking any jealousy . . ."[227]

A decade later, Sartre would write that Saint-Exupéry's had been a model for the literature of extreme situations that his time required: after his example, how could the writers of his generation be satisfied with mere description, as their predecessors had been? Things had to be steeped in action, as Saint-Exupéry had done with the airplane by making it an organ of perception for the pilot. It was Saint-Exupéry who in *Terre des hommes* had shown the way that Sartre's generation of writers would follow.[228] And certainly Saint-Exupéry's disappearance in the Mediterranean while making a reconnaissance flight in 1944 gave to his life and work an aura of authenticity that they might not have had if he had lived on into the fractious postwar period. Henry Bordeaux was not alone in noticing that Saint-Exupéry, like Guynemer, Nungesser, and Mermoz, had disappeared without leaving a trace. This elevated him from a pilot and writer to the status of an "archangel of the air."[229] Saint-Exupéry's death, Bordeaux wrote in 1948, would be, from a literary point of view, "the most memorable and most painful loss" of the Second World War.[230]

Pl. 238. Sartre about the time he read *Terre des hommes* after having been mobilized in 1939.

Pl. 239. An airmail envelope commemorating the fiftieth anniversary of Saint-Exupéry's death.

I suspect also that since the Second World War the Aéropostale story has derived part of its fascination for the French from its entanglement with the politics of the Third Republic during the 1930s. Aéropostale's great achievements in the 1920s were followed by its collapse in early 1933. Its bankruptcy and abandonment by the government seemed to many at the time as a metaphor for the rot at the core of the Third Republic. Yet even as it foundered, Aéropostale stood as a reminder that France was capable of producing heroic and self-sacrificing figures, worthy of her knights of old, men cut of different cloth than the corrupt and contentious politicians running the country.

This was the lesson that the Catholic novelist François Mauriac drew from Mermoz's death in an article he contributed to Colonel de la Rocque's right-wing newspaper, *Le Flambeau*, in January 1937. In sacrificing himself for an ideal, Mermoz had understood the Christian precept that there were some things more valuable than life itself. No lover of risk for its own sake, Mermoz took every precaution that his bold enterprises permitted. But having done so, he did not hesitate to depart and take his chances. Aviation, Mauriac conceded, had much to account for. It had "extended the empire of death to the stars" and had "disturbed with its machine guns the eternal silence of [Pascal's] infinite spaces." Yet it had one excuse before God, "one magnificent reason for being." It had opened up a new road "toward that impatience to transcend oneself that constitutes the grandeur of God's creatures." When a nation began to lose faith in itself and doubt its mission, as France was doing now, aviation had produced a Mermoz – a man in whom the French nation had recognized her highest virtue and her "vocation as a Daughter of God."[231~]

In the dark days of the 1930s and the even darker ones that were soon to follow, it was comforting to remember that France's aviators had redeemed her honor and represented the promise of a renewed and revitalized France that would once again achieve the grandeur of the past. Contributing a preface for a new and revised Latin American edition

Pl. 240. These images from a Vichy brochure link French aviation heroes – Clément Ader, Georges Guynemer, and Jean Mermoz – with Marshal Pétain.

of his history of *La Ligne* in 1942, Jean-Gérard Fleury compared the greatness of Mermoz and his companions – men of the race of Bayard, Jean d'Arc, and Guynemer – with the pettiness of the politicians who had consigned France to catastrophe and ruin during the previous fifteen years. "The majority of [the aviators of Aéropostale] have given up their lives on the winged road of honor and virile virtues. If their sacrifice has failed to bring dividends to the capitalists, we cannot complain, for it has bequeathed to their country a much more lasting legacy: an authentic glory, still warm and shining, that bears witness to the eternal vitality of France. The example of Mermoz, of Guillaumet, of Reine, and of a hundred other heroes smolders discretely in the hearts of thousands of young Frenchmen, like an ever-burning fire beneath the ash of misfortune. One day the flame will once again burst forth."[232]

221

5

Bombs Away!

Our civilization is dying. It *must* be dying. But it isn't going to die in its bed. Presently the aeroplanes are coming. Zoom – whizz – crash! The whole western world going up in a roar of high explosives.

George Orwell, 1936[1]

THE nostalgic memories of flying for Aéropostale that Saint-Exupéry evoked for the readers of *Terre des hommes* were overwhelmingly positive. But not all French intellectuals were so sanguine about flight in the 1930s. In January 1936, Paul Claudel, acclaimed poet and dramatist, deeply pious Catholic, and recently retired ambassador of France, wrote an essay that gave voice in heavily ironic tones to some of his anxieties about the present state of European and world politics. Claudel had been one of the thousands who had made his way to Le Bourget to witness Charles Lindbergh's arrival in May 1927 "under the great starred sky."[2] A practiced and enthusiastic air traveler, he understood the "poetry" and "art" of flight.[3] He could be moved by the departure of an airplane in the rising sun and feel admiration for aviators like Dieudonné Costes and Joseph Le Brix who had carried off a difficult long-distance flight.[4] Now, however, Claudel's mood was more somber.

The development of new technologies, like radio and the airplane, Claudel observed, had brought peoples closer together physically but had had the effect of increasing their moral distance and diminishing their mutual sympathy. It was hard to escape the conclusion that the more people came to know their neighbors, the less they liked them. An exasperated nationalism had coincided with the development and acceleration of new means of communication. Everywhere one looked, one saw totalitarian masses marching to a single tune. Even the democracies – the United States, Australia, Canada – had shut their doors to emigration, hoping that legislation could preserve them from the contagion of outsiders who might dilute their tribal uniqueness. "Statist and stagnant seas had taken the place of human streams."[5]

Claudel's ruminations on the rampant nationalism of his time suddenly gave way to the evocation of a scene that at first appears a surprising and unmotivated digression. Caught unawares, the reader hesitates, uncertain how to respond. High in the sky, Claudel writes, one hears a buzzing, almost like that of a bumblebee. A small dark cross appears above, in the blue. It's the airmail plane passing by. Then Claudel produces a series of simple, but highly evocative, sentences that seem to celebrate the conquest of the air. That man in the air was very different from us; he was truly free. All alone with his wings, he depended on

Pl. 242.   British children in a trench watch in a mixture of fascination and awe as British fighters engage attacking German bombers over Kent in September 1940.

Pl. 243.   General Giulio Douhet.

213

nothing more than his motor and his propeller. He was capable of going anywhere. Nothing blocked his way. He sustained himself in flight by means of nothing but the movement that he himself created. For the airmail pilot, the earth was a patch of ground on which he alighted in order to exchange his postal sack for another and to take on fuel. Then, amidst the roar of his throbbing engine, he took off again and ascended toward infinity, while we, mere earthlings, were left behind on the ground. "Bon voyage!"[6]

These thoughts might easily have been produced before 1914. They suggest the boundless freedom of flight and the mixture of envy and awe that spectators felt for the fearless men and women who had learned how to dominate flying machines and navigate the air. Yet Claudel's mood turned darker, as he reflected on the deeper meanings of this "great mosquito" whose buzzing sound refused to leave his ear. This airplane in the sky, whose daily visit was as predictable as the postman's, represented a threat. It reminded Claudel that we were no longer the masters of our own territory. The shadow cast by the wings of the airplane reminds us that there is a breach in our sense of security, an irritation, a malaise that refuses to go away. There is something above us that exists without our permission; something that hangs over our head.[7]

The sky had suddenly become omnipresent and dangerous. One lived in a continual state of alert. It was impossible to open a newspaper without being reminded of one's vulnerability to attack from the air. "Germany has 2,600 airplanes. England has 2,400. France . . . Italy . . . America . . . The theories of General Douhet. The remarkable development of Soviet aviation." The result, Claudel said, was that everyone reached involuntarily for some device to protect him or herself from falling projectiles, a weapon, a shield, an air raid shelter, even an umbrella.[8]

Claudel ended by warning that the next war would be different from the one that had begun in 1914. Then the public had followed the conflict vicariously through communiqués, "artistically" prepared by the specialists of the General Staff. If war were to break out now, it was the airplane that would deliver news of the war. And its messages would be delivered "red hot" in Europe's cities. Soldiers at the front would not be alone to enjoy the benefits of high explosives and mustard gas. On the contrary, well equipped with a sophisticated gas mask and protected by thirty meters of reinforced concrete, the soldier's fate would be enviable, compared with what Parisians could look forward to experiencing. Claudel's advice to them was to read the *Apocalypse* – or more to the point, the air raid instructions posted in the entrance to their building. "Oh earth, open thyself to receive us! For it is the moment when the stars are going to fall, or lacking this, something even more explosive and stinging! Beware down below!"[9]

Among the disquieting aeronautical messages with which the French public was being bombarded by the newspapers in 1936, Claudel included in his list "the theories of General Douhet." When the decade began, Guilio Douhet was relatively unknown in France, except in narrowly circumscribed aeronautical and military circles. But in February 1932, his most influential book, *Il dominio dell'aria* (The Command of the Air), was published in French translation and his ideas were summarized and debated in specialized journals and circulated throughout the popular press.[10] The Geneva Disarmament Conference, which met that month to discuss means of banning the bomber or limiting its use against civilian targets, combined with newsreel images of Japanese planes bombarding Chinese cities, had clearly given Douhet's theories a relevance that they had lacked in 1921 when *Il dominio dell'aria* had first appeared.

If Douhet's book received so much attention in the early 1930s, it was because his central argument had such frightening implications and also because, from a technological point of view, it no longer seemed as improbable and far-fetched as it had ten years before.[11] Douhet's central theme was that the invention of the airplane had revolutionized warfare. It was now possible to fly over fortified lines of defense without first breaking through them. Consequently, in the next war there would be no distinction between soldiers and civilians, because all citizens of a state would be subject to aerial attack. The only sure defense against mass destruction from the air was the ability to destroy the enemy's air force with a knockout blow before it had the chance to strike. Command of the air meant victory; to be beaten in the air meant defeat and the acceptance of whatever terms the enemy chose to impose. And command of the air could be achieved only if the air force was made independent of the army and the navy and given the necessary resources to develop a striking force of heavy bombers. Douhet had no doubt that an independent air force, properly equipped and trained, could inflict upon an unprepared enemy sufficient damage to bring about the collapse of its forces in a matter of days. Since no adequate defense against aerial attack was possible, it was necessary to resign oneself to whatever damage the enemy was able to inflict before the end of the conflict.

This was a disconcerting thought, especially for civilians. But disciples of Douhet could take heart from his assurance that, once command of the air had been won, the dominant air force would be free to bomb its enemy at will. Major cities would naturally become targets because it was here that the nation's morale and will to fight could be broken. Douhet evoked the vision of an attack on a large city by a single bombing unit. "Within a few minutes some 20 tons of high-explosive, incendiary, and gas bombs would rain down. First would come explosions, then fires, then deadly gases floating on the surface and preventing any approach to the stricken area. As the hours passed and night advanced, the fires would spread while the poison gas paralyzed all life. By the following day the life of the city would be suspended . . ."[12] And what, Douhet asked, would be the effect of such bombings upon the inhabitants of cities not yet subjected to attack? His answer was that, driven by the instinct of self-preservation, they would rise up and demand an end to the war. This would happen, he predicted, long before their army and navy had time to mobilize. "A complete breakdown of the social structure," he concluded, "cannot but take place in a country subjected to this kind of merciless pounding from the air."[13]

Douhet warned against the illusion that international agreements could prevent the use of bombers against civilians. Even if negotiated and duly signed and ratified, they were "fated to be swept away like dried leaves on the winds of war. A man who is fighting a life-and-death fight — as all wars are nowadays — has the right to use any means to keep his life." Wars could not be classified as human or inhuman. The purpose of war was to harm the enemy as much as possible, and all means would (and should) be employed to achieve this end, no matter how destructive they were. "The limitations applied to the so-called inhuman and atrocious means of war are nothing but international demagogic hypocrisies."[14] Hence, like many military figures writing during the interwar period, Douhet took it for granted that airplanes would be used to drop poison gas on cities during the coming war.

Douhet conceded that it was tragic that success in war now depended on smashing the material and moral resources of a people to the point where social order collapsed in the midst of a frightful cataclysm. But he concluded cheerfully that the wars of the future would be mercifully short because the decisive blows would be struck against that sector of the population least able to sustain them – civilians living in cities. These wars, he said, might thus turn out to be more humane than wars in the past because in the long run they might shed less blood. Fear, rather than destruction, would be decisive in determining the outcome of wars. The massive bloodletting of the last war would thus be avoided.[15] Nonetheless, despite this optimistic conclusion, Douhet left his readers in no doubt that those peoples who were unprepared to fight the air wars of the future and survive them would be doomed to defeat.[16]

★   ★   ★

By 1936, it was by no means necessary to read Douhet in order to appreciate the terrible threat that hung over the heads of Europeans and other peoples throughout the world. Appeals circulated in France by the pacifist organization, the Ligue Internationale des Combatants de la Paix (The International League of Fighters for Peace), evoked the specter of "cities destined to incendiary bombs, deadly gases, and annihilation" and of civilians succumbing to "mortal panic, terror, and misery."[17] An anonymous article that appeared during the Paris Air Show of 1932 described in frightening detail the imagined destruction of Paris in a single night by German bombers and concluded that those people who survived the poison gas the planes had dropped would be like "a herd of animals gone

Pl. 245. Everytown under bombardment in *Things To Come*. This was one of the film's many striking images that would not be easily forgotten by its viewers.

insane."[18] And in England, where apocalyptic fears of a "bolt from the blue" and the "savaging" of London had weighed heavily on Britain's leaders for years, a report from the Chiefs of Staff in November 1935 considered the possibility that Britain might be subjected to an "air attack so continuous and concentrated and on such a scale that a few weeks of such an experience might so undermine the morale of any civilian population as to make it difficult for the Government to continue the War."[19]

Documents such as these, of course, were circulated only to high-ranking government officials who generally kept such gloomy forecasts to themselves; but in 1936 the British moviegoing public could see a frightening feature film entitled *Things To Come*, written by H. G. Wells, produced by Alexander Korda, and directed by William Cameron Menzies, that graphically depicted an aerial attack launched during the Christmas holidays of 1940 against a city called "Everytown" but disturbingly similar to London.[20] The scene is one of darkness, screeching sirens, ineffectual antiaircraft fire, and ambulances careening through the streets. Gas bombs are dropped; pedestrians rush about in all directions, their eyes filled with panic; buildings crumble; masses of people force their way into a tube station, like frightened animals taking refuge in their burrows in the ground; the face of a dead boy is glimpsed among the rubble. Audiences could hardly have been reassured by the film's optimistic ending, in which, after the collapse of civilization, a deadly plague, and reversion to the equivalent of the Dark Ages, two young members of a new technological elite, led by aviators, are hurtled into outer space on their way to explore and colonize the moon. The images of *Things To Come* that would stick in the mind were of "Everytown" in ruins and of innocent children crushed beneath collapsed masonry.

When *Things To Come* was released, Europeans had already grown accustomed to seeing newsreels of bombs being dropped on Chinese cities and Abyssinian civilians. But the nightmare of cataclysm launched from the air edged closer to the European heartland when Spain, an economically backward and militarily weak country far removed from the central power struggles of the interwar years in Europe, plunged into civil war in July 1936. After months of uncontrolled street violence and political instability following the victory of a coalition of left-wing liberals, socialists, and communists in February 1936, a number of high-ranking military officers organized a simultaneous rising against the government which left the country divided between supporters and opponents of the rebellion. Though neither the Loyalists nor the Nationalists possessed sufficient airplanes or trained aviators to carry out the type of massive air raids that Douhet had called for and that British and French leaders feared, many of Spain's cities were bombed during the first months of the conflict, most notably Madrid where 133 people died during four days of bombing between 19 and 22 November 1936.[21] By that time, Francisco Franco had been anointed *Generalísimo* and Head of State of the Nationalist forces; the small stock of Spanish aircraft had been augmented by shipments of planes from France, the United States, Germany, Italy, and the Soviet Union; and pilots and ground crews from those countries had become active participants in what began as a narrowly Spanish struggle.[22] Through photographs published in newspapers and illustrated magazines and newsreels shown in movie theaters, Europeans outside of Spain could view the shattered buildings and mangled bodies that were the result of bombing raids and wonder when their turn would come.

The Spanish generals' coup d'état failed initially because of unexpectedly stiff resistance by hastily formed militias in Spain's major cities and the unwillingness of many officers and military personnel to join the rebellion. But so too did the government's attempt to restore its authority throughout the country fail, and Spain settled down into a long and bloody civil war. In late October 1936, fearing Soviet intervention and influence over the Republican government, Hitler decided to step up German support for the Nationalist rebels. He authorized the creation of an expeditionary force of airmen, drawn

Pl. 246. General Hugo von Sperrle on his flight to Spain in 1936.

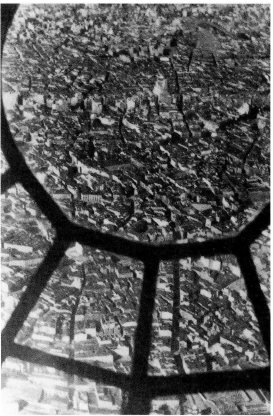

Pl. 247. Central Madrid as it appeared to a German bombardier in a Condor Legion Fornier 17 around November 1936.

from the German Luftwaffe, to be named the Condor Legion. This group of German volunteers was equipped with some of the Third Reich's most advanced aircraft. To command it, Hitler's Minister of Air, Hermann Göring, chose General Hugo von Sperrle, a physically imposing and pleasure-loving man. Sperrle was instructed that the objective of the Condor Legion was to be the "quick occupation of the harbors important for Russian supplies."[23]

Frustrated in his attempt to take Madrid and under pressure by the increasingly impatient Sperrle, Franco ordered the rebel forces to undertake an offensive toward the Basque provinces in the north, with the objective of eliminating this enclave of Republican resistance and capturing the important industrial center and seaport of Bilbao. The Condor Legion and its planes were transferred to the cities of Burgos and Vitoria, within easy flying distance of the front. Commanding the day-to-day operations of the Legion was Sperrle's Chief of Staff, Lieutenant Colonel Wolfram von Richthofen, a cousin of the famous German ace, who himself had been given credit for shooting down eight enemy planes during the Great War.

Richthofen was an ambitious man, demanding of himself and others, keenly aware of the aristocratic name he bore, and with definite ideas when it came to modern warfare. Even more irritated than Sperrle with the indecisiveness and unsoldierly qualities of the Nationalist troops, Richthofen had become a dedicated believer in the need to coordinate air and ground attacks.[24] Bombers and fighters, he thought, could best be used to disrupt the enemy's communications and demoralize his troops, thus clearing the way for the rapid deployment of ground forces. Like Sperrle, Richthofen resisted the demands of General Emilio Mola Vidal, the Nationalist commander of the northern offensive, that he organize bombing raids against Basque factories in Bilbao, for the purpose of cleansing Spain of the poisonous contagion of the industrial proletariat. Why destroy factories that would soon be in Nationalist hands?[25]

Views like these appear to run directly counter to the theories of General Douhet, who in his last writings had unambiguously rejected out of hand an auxiliary role for the air force. Yet Richthofen shared with Douhet, whose book *The Command of the Air* he kept in the hotel suite he occupied in Vitoria, the belief that air operations would inevitably result in civilian casualties. A memo posted in the operations room of the Condor Legion and dated 31 March reminded his crews that, although they would be dispatched only against military targets, they should pursue their attack "without regard for the civilian population." And, indeed, that very day the Legion bombed the town of Durango with the loss of hundreds of civilian lives.[26]

Early in the morning of 26 April 1937, after consultation with Colonel Juan Vigón Suerodíaz, Chief of Staff of the Nationalist forces leading the offensive against the Basque Loyalists in the north, Richthofen planned a bombing raid aimed at cutting off, or at least disrupting, the retreat of the enemy's troops. The target was a bridge over the Mundaca river that lay just outside Guernica, a small market town fifteen miles from the coast that had played a special role in the history of Basque liberties and independence from the centralizing authority of the Spanish crown. Richthofen personally chose the mix of heavy explosive bombs, anti-personnel shrapnel bombs, incendiaries, and grenades his pilots would carry. His objective was to demoralize the Basque forces and to block their retreat toward the north. In planning this operation, he seems to have been unconcerned about the fate of the civilians, who could be expected to be flocking into town from the surrounding countryside on a market day. This, after all, was not his responsibility. To monitor the operation more closely, Richthofen left his base at Vitoria and raced in his Mercedes sports car to a vantage point on Monte Oiz, from which he had a view down the wide valley that led toward Guernica.

What happened that afternoon and early evening between 4:40 and 7:45 is still the subject of acrimonious and partisan debate.[27] Yet most historians agree that, whatever the motivation for the raid, the nationality of the planes taking part, the tonnage and type of bomb load, and the duration of the bombing runs, 70 percent of Guernica's center was destroyed and hundreds of civilians, including many women and children, were torn to pieces by shrapnel bombs, crushed under collapsing buildings, incinerated by fires, or strafed by fight-

Pl. 248. Lieutenant Colonel Wolfram von Richthofen observes the bombing of Guernica from Monte Oiz.

Pl. 249. Guernica burns after the air attack, throwing up a thick blanket of smoke.

ers as they tried to flee the town. Photographs taken after the raid portray a scene of apocalyptic destruction; Guernica burned for days, as the survivors struggled to put out the fires; yet, ironically, the ostensible target of the operation, the bridge over the tiny Mundaca river, survived intact, despite the fact that Richthofen's most experienced bombing crew led the attack. The smoke caused by the first bombing run, it appears, had obscured the target, and Richthofen's fliers were under explicit instructions to drop their bombs, even if they were unable to locate their objective.[28]

Visiting the town on 30 April after it had been occupied by Nationalist troops, Richthofen noted that the effect of the incendiary bombs used in the raid had been enhanced by the type of wooden construction common in Guernica. He was apparently untroubled by the fact that his pilots had failed to destroy the bridge, since the damage to buildings, water lines, and streets had been so great that the town had been closed off for at least twenty-four hours, thus offering the possibility for the bottling up of the retreating Republican troops. Though annoyed by the failure of Mola's troops to exploit the situation, Richthofen considered the effects of the one-kilo I. G. Farben incendiary bombs a "complete technical success." The destruction they had wrought had created the preconditions for a major breakthrough.[29] Yet if in military terms the bombing of Guernica was a triumph, in the war of words and images that the Spanish Civil War was generating, Guernica turned out to be a propaganda disaster for the Nationalist camp.

★　　★　　★

This may have been something of an accident. On the evening of 26 April, the South African-born but Oxford-educated journalist George Steer was having dinner in the Torrontegui Hotel in Bilbao when at 10:00 someone phoned to say that Guernica was in flames. Steer had come to Spain after witnessing in Ethiopia the effects that bombing could have on an ill-trained and ill-equipped army and a civilian population. Rightly suspected of a lack of admiration for Mussolini and Fascism, he had been expelled from their new colony by the triumphant Italian forces.[30] In the war between Franco's Nationalists and the Republicans, Steer had no doubt about the side with which he stood. He showed a particular weakness for the cause of Basque autonomy, an idea that was anathema to the Nationalist forces.

Upon receiving news of the bombing of Guernica, Steer rushed by automobile to the town along with four other foreign journalists. Once there, he surveyed the damage and interviewed survivors; most were women, whom he found sitting on broken chairs and lying on wet mattresses with dirty pillows in the central plaza. Beyond this open and heavily bombed space, in what had once been the town, "the streets were a royal carpet of live coals; blocks of wreckage slithered and crashed from the houses, and from their sides that were still erect the polished heat struck at our cheeks and eyes." Before returning to Bilbao, Steer chain-smoked and "wondered why on earth the world was so mad and warfare become so easy." "Between cigarettes I played with three silver tubes picked up that evening in Gernika.[31] The argent thermite distilled itself slowly from their bases; they came from the German RhS factory in 1936, said their stamp. And over the legend stood a symbol in miniature, the [German] Imperial eagle with scarecrow wings spread."[32] When Steer left Guernica that night, he had no doubt who had dropped the bombs.

The story Steer wrote for *The Times* of London, which appeared on 28 April under the title "The Tragedy of Guernica" and was also printed on the front page of the *New York*

Pl. 250. George Steer displays his bag of wildfowl after hunting in Ethiopia in 1935, where he was reporting for the London *Times*.

Times, sent a shudder through the Western world and reminded the British of their own vulnerability to aerial attack.[33] Affecting a tone of historical distance that he scarcely felt, Steer noted that the raid on Guernica by a powerful fleet of German airplanes was unparalleled in history because of the form of its execution, the scale of the destruction it wrought, and the selection of its target. Its aim had been nothing less than "the demoralization of the civil population and the destruction of the cradle of the Basque race." The tactic of the German bombers was first to stampede the population from their shelters with grenades and heavy bombs; then to machine-gun those who ran in panic through the streets and attempted to escape the town; and finally, by means of more heavy bombs and incendiaries, to wreck the houses and burn them on top of their victims. The bombing went on for over three hours until the entire city and its hospital were "glowing heaps of embers." The result had been the total destruction of an "open town far behind the lines" that had no value as a military objective.[34]

Following Steer's article was a statement by José Antonio de Aguirre, president of the Basque Republic, that blamed the bombing on "German airmen" and called on the Basques to "react with violence" against this attempt "to wound us in the most sensitive of our patriotic sentiments" by destroying "the very sanctuary which records the centuries of our liberty and our democracy."

Franco's foreign press agency in Salamanca at first denied that the bombing had taken place and that any German military forces were in Spain, insisting through their radio service in Salamanca that Aguirre's accusations were "lies, lies, lies." Then, when confronted with the evidence of Guernica's destruction, Franco's representatives shifted their ground, arguing that it had been the work of the Basque militia, who they claimed had dynamited the town before retreating toward Bilbao in order to deny it to the Nationalist liberators as part of their scorched earth policy. Besides, Franco's press agency added, Aguirre's claims were further belied by news that had just arrived from the Basque front, indicating that Nationalist planes had been grounded by bad weather on 27 April and therefore could scarcely have bombed Guernica.[35]

In Paris, the press was bitterly divided, as was to be expected in a country where feelings about the Spanish Civil War were running high and political camps were becoming increasingly polarized around a Marxist left and an anti-Marxist right. The conservative newspapers, hostile to the Republican government, at first tended to downplay the story, stressing its impact on British public opinion rather than its possible implications for France, whereas the Communist newspaper *L'Humanité* translated Steer's article in its entirety and declared in its headlines that "A Thousand Incendiary Bombs Dropped by the Planes of Hitler and Mussolini Reduce the City of Guernica to Cinders."[36] Yet during the last days of April evidence mounted that the Germans were indeed in Spain and that it had been their bombers that had destroyed "the holy city of the Basques." On 5 May, *L'Illustration*, a magazine that no one could accuse of radical leanings, published five large photographs of Guernica in flames that spoke more eloquently of the town's martyrdom than any written text could ever do.

★   ★   ★

Among those Parisians with left-wing sympathies who were horrified by the slaughter of Guernica's civilian population and the destruction of the city was Pablo Picasso, a Spanish expatriot and Europe's leading modernist artist. In January 1937, Picasso had been approached by a group of Spanish friends who, in the name of the Spanish ambassador to France, had asked him to contribute a large mural to the pavilion they were planning for the approaching World's Fair. The theme of the fair was the rapid advance in modern technologies, among them aviation; but the occasion also offered an opportunity for Fascist Italy and Nazi Germany to display their superiority to the decadent Western democracies and for the Soviet Union to celebrate the achievements of the world's first worker state. Uncomfortable with openly political art and not one who painted on commission, Picasso had at first been evasive. His distaste for the leader of the Spanish rebellion and his desire to show his solidarity with the Republic were such, however, that he reluctantly agreed to provide them with the work they sought.[37]

Some of Picasso's closest friends doubted that he would ever do the promised painting, to which the organizers of the Spanish pavilion had assigned a large wall not far from the entrance on the ground floor. But the events at Guernica fired Picasso's imagination and gave him the incentive to set to work. He made the first sketches for the mural five days after the bombing, on 1 May 1937, the date of a huge left-wing demonstration whose main theme was a protest against the moral outrage of Guernica and a plea for aid for its victims. Six weeks later he notified his friend Josep Lluis Sert, the young Catalan architect of the pavilion, that it was ready to be hung. In this relatively short period of time, Picasso's original conception for the painting had gone through a remarkable series of transformations.[38] What had begun as an intensely private composition, with roots in his previous art and personal relationships with women, had become a public statement about the times in which he and his contemporaries lived.[39]

An immense canvas over eleven feet high and almost twenty-six feet long, Picasso's painting contained no obvious visual references to the events of 26 April in Guernica. There were no symbols of Basque identity; no attempt to evoke, even indirectly, the central plaza that had been so heavily bombed; no sign of the sacred Basque oak that had miraculously survived the bombing intact. There were no demolished buildings, no threatening German bombers; indeed, there was no sky. The electric light to the left of center in the upper border of the mural suggested the inside of an air raid shelter; but the building to the right, from which an outstretched arm with a lamp and a female face emerged, encouraged the

Pl. 252.   Picasso in 1937.

Pl. 253.   The Palais de l'Air at the Universal Exhibition of 1937 in Paris.

Pl. 254.   Robert and Sonia Delaunay's mural for the Palais de l'Air. It features the bright colors and circles and propeller shapes so dear to Robert Delaunay. One can glimpse it in the background in Pl. 253.

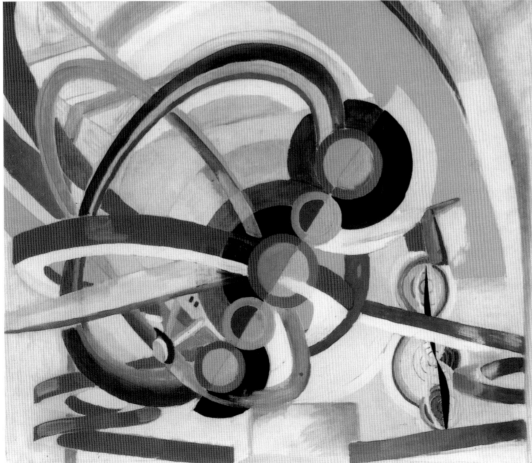

EXPOSITION INTERNATIONALE
PARIS 1937

Pl. 255 The German pavilion (to the left) and Soviet
pavilion (to the right) face each other against the backdrop
of the Eiffel Tower at the 1937 Universal Exhibition.

Pl. 256. The Spanish pavilion was designed by Picasso's
friend Josep Lluís Sert and Luis Lacasa. The letters on the
façade read: "There are more than a half million Spaniards
with bayonets in the trenches, who will not let themselves
be trodden underfoot."

viewer to interpret the scene as taking place outside. The starkness of the setting, the flatness of the space, and the theatricality of the gestures portrayed are reminiscent of the modernist stage decors that Picasso had designed twenty years earlier for *Parade* and *Antigone*.[40]

Though highly stylized, disproportioned, and placed in unnatural positions, the nine figures depicted in the painting were by no means abstract. To the left a screaming woman carries in her arms a dead child. Above her hovers a defiant bull with oddly placed human eyes and a tail waving in the air like a flag. Immediately to the bull's right, the open beak of a darkly outlined bird, bifurcated by a triangle of light, emits a cry of horror vertically toward a non-existent sky. Beneath the bull a dead warrior lies, clutching in the stiffened fingers of his extended right arm a broken sword. Above and to the right of him an impaled horse, his tongue in the shape of a dagger, emits a cry of unbearable pain. The two female figures to the right of the horse express horror and disbelief at the scene they are witnessing. A kneeling woman at the extreme right, with her face extended vertically upward toward the sky, stretches out her arms in a gesture of supplication, while flames lick at the building's roof. The effect is one of claustrophobic containment, desperate supplication, and inescapable destruction, underlined by the black, gray, and white coloring that gives the scene the look of newsreel images projected on a screen and, in its central section, a Cubist collage.[41]

Looking at the painting today and knowing that it has become one of the best-known icons of the twentieth century, it is difficult to grasp the hostility with which it was viewed when the Spanish pavilion opened its doors in July 1937.[42] Left-wing critics frowned on its somber colors, its formalist language, and its lack of an unambiguous message of resistance to fascist oppression; and even some of Picasso's friends had doubts about its appropriateness for a site that was designed to appeal to the masses. During the course of the fair, efforts behind the scenes were made to remove it from its place of honor on the ground floor and to replace it with a work that would be more immediately accessible to the pavilion's visitors.[43]

Friends of the Republic and partisans of the Left searched the painting in vain for a clear message. Did the bull represent brutal fascism or the defiant Spanish people? Was he responsible for the stricken horse's agony or was he the weeping mother's benevolent pro-

Pl. 257. A photograph of Picasso's *Guernica*, as it was exhibited in the Spanish pavilion in 1937.

225

tector? And why was the bull given human eyes and a human face?[44] Was *Guernica* meant to be an expression of grief or a call to action?[45]

The truth was that not even Picasso himself could answer these questions satisfactorily.[46] Yet over time the power of the painting and its strikingly original aesthetic qualities proved capable of overcoming the ambiguity of its symbols. Indeed, the mural's very unspecificity – its lack of clear referents – helped to ensure its survival as a universal icon representing the horror of war and facilitated its interpretation not so much as an evocation of what had happened at Guernica but as an anticipation of events to come. No one understood this better than Picasso's friend Michel Leiris who, defending the painting in the *Cahiers d'Art*, wrote: "Picasso sends us our letter of doom: all that we love is going to die, and that is why it is necessary that we gather up all that we love, like the emotion of great farewells, in something of unforgettable beauty."[47]

★　　★　　★

In the early 1930s European fears of bombing had the quality of a general anxiety that was all the more frightening because one could never be quite sure from what corner the danger would come. The Japanese had bombed Shanghai in 1932; the Italians had attacked Abyssinian villagers from the air in 1935. The knockout blow that Douhet had predicted could conceivably come from many quarters. In the late 1920s, the British air force developed contingency plans for a war with its ally, France. Robert Knauss's 1932 novel, *Luftkrieg 1936* (War in the Air 1936), described in graphic detail the destruction of Paris by a British air fleet.[48] The plot of *Idiot's Delight*, a 1936 Broadway hit starring Alfred Lunt and Lynn Fontaine, also revolved around an air strike against the French capital; yet in Robert Sherwood's political comedy, the bombers were Italian, an echo of the publicity that Mussolini's air force had received in the United States because of Balbo's 1933 flight. But after the bombing of Guernica and the popular outcry that its destruction provoked, fears about death raining from the sky became increasingly directed toward the German Luftwaffe and its leader, the flamboyant and unpredictable General Hermann Göring.

During the 1914–18 war, Göring had risen into the pantheon of German aces, with twenty-two credited victories. As a reward for his service to the Fatherland, he had received the coveted Ordre pour le mérite from the hands of the Kaiser himself. In July of 1918, as the war entered its final phase, he was given the honor of commanding Manfred von Richthofen's famous "Flying Circus" squadron, where he succeeded in imposing his authority on Germany's most highly publicized group of combat flyers – men whose combat record in several cases outshone his own. Yet though some of his pilots might excel Göring in aerobatic skills or in the number of enemy aircraft shot down, none possessed his flair for drama or his gift for cultivating his own myth. When commanded to surrender his planes to the nearest Allied troops in November 1918, he instead ordered that five of them should be flown to Darmstadt, and took care to see when landing that his own machine was smashed beyond repair. At a farewell dinner honoring the Richthofen squadron before it was disbanded, he spoke emotionally of the group's achievements and promised his men that "the forces of freedom and right and morality" would win through in the end against the revolutionaries who were dragging the record of Germany's war heroes through the mud. "Our time," he said, "will come again."[49]

During the decade and a half following the war, Göring proved his unswerving loyalty to Hitler, his dedication to the Nazi program of German revival and expansion, and his talents as a dynamic organizer and shrewd political infighter who seldom allowed himself to be outflanked. With his flying credentials, it was thus to be expected that when Adolf Hitler

Pl. 258. Horacio Ferrer's *Madrid 1937, aviones negros* (Madrid 1937, Black Airplanes) corresponded more closely to what many supporters of the Spanish Republic thought a painting protesting the bombing of innocent civilians should be than Picasso's *Guernica*. There is no doubt here about the victims of Franco's Nationalists and their German and Italian allies.

Pl. 259.   A French illustrator imagines an air attack against Paris. The large plane, guided by radio waves emanating from a faraway central – "for example, Berlin" – directs unmanned aircraft that are essentially "flying torpedoes."

Pl. 260.   Hermann Göring at the end of World War One. Note the coveted Ordre pour le mérite decoration, which he proudly displays beneath his collar.

became chancellor of Germany in 1933, one of his first acts would be to appoint Göring Reich commissioner of aviation, a title that would later in 1935 be changed to minister and commander-in-chief of an independent air force. Göring took full advantage of the assignment. Vain, self-indulgent, constantly struggling against his expanding waistline and an addiction to pain-killing drugs, yet at the same time charismatic, charming when it served his interests, and capable of sustained bursts of energetic activity, the new commissioner of aviation grasped, as no one else in the Nazi regime did, the symbolic power and the political uses of aircraft. His intention, under the camouflage of expanding Germany's civil aviation fleet, was to embark on the creation of an air arm that would be the strongest in the world, an objective for which he had Hitler's unconditional support.

To assist him, Göring chose as his deputy the chief executive officer of the German airline Lufthansa, Ernst Milch, a man noted for his ambition, ruthless efficiency, rude manners, and determination to achieve his goals. Göring told Milch that "I collect planes like others collect postage stamps" and "Money is no object."[50] Milch took Göring at his word: four months later he issued contracts for the building of one thousand planes. By the end of 1933 the Luftwaffe was employing two million workers in the construction of airfields and aircraft factories. During the next six years the Luftwaffe would dispose of an average annual budget of 3,000 million Reichmarks.[51]

Milch wanted ten years to build the Luftwaffe into an efficient fighting force that could deliver successful air strikes against the British Isles. Hitler had no intention of waiting so long: inspired by the writings of Douhet, he believed that the Luftwaffe could be used as an instrument of terror and intimidation to obtain concessions from the British and the French and the governments of Central Europe, whose territories he coveted as part of his plan for expansion toward the east.[52] Always the faithful disciple, Göring agreed. Thus in May 1938, when Hitler revealed to his commanders-in-chief his intention to make war against Czechoslovakia, Göring suspected that the British and the French would find reasons not to come to the defense of their ally. One of the many motivations pressing them to seek a diplomatic solution for the crisis, he believed, would be their fear that their air forces would not be able to stand up to the new Luftwaffe and that their cities would be subjected to deadly bombing attacks by German aircraft.

Göring was not a man who left things to chance. He carefully cultivated the young aide to the French air attaché in Berlin and arranged for the commander of the French Air Force, General Joseph Vuillemin, to visit selected Luftwaffe air bases and German aircraft factories in August 1938, just as Hitler began to threaten war against Czechoslovakia if its leaders refused to meet his terms. At Augsburg, Vuillemin was shown the latest Messerschmitt fighters and then was taken to the Luftwaffe's experimental center at Barth on the Baltic coast where, under an intense blue sky, bombing runs were staged by the Luftwaffe's new Stuka dive bombers, the Ju-88. In the process of touring the recently constructed Heinkel aircraft factory at Oranienburg, the French general was treated to a display of the extraordinary maneuverability of the He 111 bomber and deliberately buzzed, while landing, by the experimental Heinkel 100 fighter in which the former ace and present Luftwaffe general Ernst Udet had recently broken the world speed record. Visibly shaken by the strides the Germans had made in aviation technology and under the impression that the experimental aircraft he had seen were pouring off the production lines in great numbers, on returning to Paris Vuillemin notified his government that the Luftwaffe was a force of "truly devastating power" against which the French Air Force would have no chance of prevailing.[53]

This gloomy message was only reinforced by Charles Lindbergh. Passing through Paris after having visited the Soviet Union and Czechoslovakia, he dined with Guy La Chambre, the French minister of aviation, at the country house of the American ambassador to France and shared with him his impressions of German air power. Lindbergh estimated that the German air fleet was "stronger than that of all other European countries combined." The Germans were building as many planes every three or four months as the French hoped to have in April 1940. Lindbergh came away from this encounter convinced that the French situation was "desperate." He noted in his journal that La Chambre "apparently realizes this fact."[54]

A month later, as the Czechoslovakian situation deteriorated and Hitler's rhetoric became more inflammatory, the British ambassador to Berlin, Sir Nevile Henderson, met with Göring at his palatial villa outside Berlin, Karinhall. Henderson was concerned that Hitler might rush into war before the British prime minister could return to Munich to pursue a peaceful solution to the Czechoslovakian crisis. Göring downplayed the imminence of war, but warned Henderson in no uncertain terms that if Britain was determined to go to war in order to save the integrity of Czechoslovakia the results would be devastating for both the Czechoslovaks and the British. "Before the war is over, there will be very few Czechs alive, and little of London left standing either."[55]

The truth was that the Luftwaffe had no aircraft capable of threatening London. Their existing bombers were confined to a range of no more than 430 miles with a half-ton load. The general charged with exploring Germany's options in the case of a war with England, Helmuth Felmy, reported on 22 September 1938 that with the aircraft presently available "a war of annihilation against Britain appears out of the question . . ." The most the Luftwaffe could hope for with its existing equipment was a "disruptive effect." "Whether this will lead to an erosion of the British will to fight is something that depends on imponderable and certainly unpredictable factors."[56]

But Hitler was undeterred by such considerations. The immediate objective, after all, was not London but Prague, which lay well within the range of German bombers, as did Paris

Pl. 261. Two decades later, Göring's girth was larger, his uniform less austere, and his marshal's baton a symbol of his power and prestige in Hitler's Third Reich.

Pl. 262. Göring's deputy, Erhard Milch (third from the left) in a procession of high-ranking Luftwaffe officers.

and other French cities. When the time to deal with England came, new aircraft would be available. On 23 September the Führer issued his ultimatum to Czechoslovakia; and the British and the French, anxious to avoid war at any cost and mindful of the damage the Luftwaffe could do, signed an agreement that gave Hitler the Sudetenland and effectively deprived what remained of Czechoslovakia of the ability to defend itself.[57] Five months later, after Göring had described the Luftwaffe's plans for the destruction of Prague in a face-to-face meeting in Berlin, the president of Czechoslovakia, Emil Hacha, fainted; then, upon regaining consciousness, he capitulated to a new set of Hitler's demands and agreed to the occupation of his country by German troops.

Next came Poland. Dazzled by a show of technological wizardry that the Luftwaffe had staged for him on 3 July 1939, Hitler resolved to go to war against the Poles, despite the fact that the British and the French had guaranteed the territorial integrity of Poland and made it clear that they would regard a German invasion as an act of war. On 22 August Hitler assembled fifty of his senior commanders and assured them that the technical superiority of the Luftwaffe would "mangle every Polish nerve" and "grind away" the enemy.[58] And indeed the Luftwaffe with its four thousand aircraft quickly achieved command of the air against the vastly outnumbered Polish air force and destroyed the Polish army's transportation and communication systems. Meanwhile, the inhabitants of Paris and London braced themselves for German air raids that never came and the Royal Air Force confined itself to ineffectual attacks on German ships and dropping propaganda leaflets over Germany.

In line with his conviction that the Luftwaffe could be used to intimidate civilian populations, Göring had planned a show of massive German airpower over Warsaw for the first day of the war on 1 September, but bad weather forced the cancellation of Operation Seaside and when the weather lifted the force of one hundred fighters and bombers Göring sent over the city encountered fierce resistance and succeeded in doing little damage. This, however, was only a brief respite. By 13 September, the Polish government had fled Warsaw and the hundred thousand soldiers in the city were encircled. Despite their hopeless situation and repeated German demands that they surrender, they continued to resist. Göring seized the opportunity to display the firepower of the Luftwaffe, and during the last week of September Warsaw was incessantly shelled and bombed, though Wolfram von Richthofen's "urgent" request on 22 September to "eradicate" the city by conducting a "large-scale experiment" in terror bombing was rejected.[59] Even if Warsaw was not reduced to a customs office at the border between Germany and the Soviet Union, as Richthofen thought it should be, the damage wrought by the Luftwaffe was impressive. By the time that Polish negotiators signaled their willingness to surrender on 31 September, the city's services had ceased to function and almost thirty thousand people had died, the great majority of them civilians.[60]

★ ★ ★

To commemorate the achievement of the Luftwaffe in Poland, the Propaganda Ministry commissioned from Tobis, one of the major German production companies, a feature-length film called *Feuertaufe* (Baptism of Fire), which interwove numbing scenes of destruction with exhilarating representations of a nation arisen like a phoenix from the ashes of defeat and literally soaring above its adversaries.[61] *Feuertaufe* was written and directed by Hans Bertram, an aviator with several long-distance flights to his credit and the author of a best-selling book, *Flug in die Hölle*, an account of his ill-fated 1932 flight around the world. An aspiring moviemaker, Bertram had both scripted and directed the aerial scenes

Pl. 263.   Shortly after the Munich agreement of September 1938, Géo Ham imagines a surprise air attack against a large European city and subtitles his water color *The Nightmare of a Europe in Arms.*

Pl. 264.   German Stukas diving over Poland.

for the popular 1939 aviation film *D 111 88,* commissioned by Goebbels to promote the Luftwaffe among young viewers.

Bertram was a dedicated believer in the Luftwaffe and its mission. Commenting on the origins of *Feuertaufe* when it was released in April 1940, Bertram wrote enthusiastically that the most "unforgettable experience" of his life was a flight he took in September 1939 over the battlefield along the Bzura river, just to the west of Warsaw, ". . . where the encircled Polish troops made desperate and futile attempts to break out [of their encirclement] and the Luftwaffe dropped its bombs on a thirty square kilometer area . . . Through this fiery curtain, which our fliers laid in front of the river bank no one slipped through alive . . ."[62] Bertram set out to recapture the emotions he had felt, as he watched the destruction of Poland from the air. From 230,000 feet of newsreel footage, he produced a propaganda film whose intimidating force can still be felt today.

The picture begins with titles that appear against a background of moving clouds that signal that its action will take place in the sky. A written prologue assures the audience that the images they are about to see are "genuine and straightforward, harsh and pitiless, like war itself."[63] A list of the seven cameramen who died in the making of *Feuertaufe,* accompanied by funereal music, offers a further gauge of its authenticity. This film, the prologue tells us, was meant to serve to document for living and coming generations of Germans the struggle for freedom and a greater Germany.

And, indeed, the first part of *Feuertaufe* is devoted to justifying the attack on Poland and its destruction as a sovereign state. With the aid of animated maps, Poland is shown expanding toward the west and driven by evil designs on German territories, while plutocratic England with its *Kriegspolitik* (policy of war) encourages Poland's imperialistic ambitions in order to weaken Germany and eliminate it as a Great Power. The effect of these early scenes is to present the German attack on Poland as a necessary defensive action to save Germans from Polish aggression and Germans living in Polish territory from maltreatment; they culminate in Hitler's declaration to the Reichstag on 1 September 1939 denouncing Polish aggression and vowing that: "From now on we shall retaliate bomb for bomb."[64] In a rhetorical operation of extraordinary cynicism, Neville Chamberlain is personally held responsible for the terrible suffering of the Poles. "What do you say now, Herr Chamberlain?" the narrator defiantly asks after we have been saturated with scenes of Poland's devastation and Polish civilians and soldiers with downcast eyes. "This is your work."

Once the responsibility of the Poles and the English has been established, *Feuertaufe* goes on to its real purpose, which is to celebrate the Luftwaffe and to display its awesome power. The images chosen and the music that accompanied them, composed by Norbert Schultze, were designed to emphasize the Luftwaffe's mastery of the air, its pinpoint bombing of military targets, its enthusiastic, youthful, and well-trained personnel, and its unlimited supply of aircraft and bombs. The Luftwaffe is portrayed as a smoothly functioning machine whose elements – airmen and ground crews – meshed together in radiant camaraderie to create a force that no enemy could resist. German bombers fly in perfect formation, reinforcing the feeling of an unstoppable juggernaut on the move. We dive with a screaming Stuka toward a military target that reconnaissance photos had earlier identified; we watch bombs being released from within a Heinkel 111 bomber with deadly accuracy. And all the while, in the background, an exuberant airmen's choir sings the battle song "We fly against the East!":

> We flew to the Vistula and Warthe
> We flew into the Polish land.
> We hit it hard
> The enemy army
> With thunder and bombs and flame.[65]

Polish aircraft, when shown at all, are pictured on the ground as they are being attacked and destroyed, never in the air, a realm reserved for the victorious Luftwaffe. War, for the Germans, seems more like good-natured sport, and without serious risks. After a bombing raid, the narrator comments:

> In a shower of missiles, the concerted and invincible might of the Luftwaffe had unleashed its fury. Mission over. Back home to base. Like noble greyhounds, our pursuit planes gambol over the conquered areas.[66]

Still, the images the viewers of the film were most likely to carry with them from the cinema were of the Dantesque scenes of Warsaw reduced to rubble with its railroad station and railway system destroyed, its shops and apartment buildings in ruins, its streets full of bomb craters, and fires burning out of control throughout the city. A thick blanket of smoke envelopes the city in a suffocating embrace. As the background music alternates between the tragic moaning of violins and Mahler-like tones of doom, the survivors of the ordeal wander about the streets with glazed eyes, totally dependent on their attackers for the necessities of life. After scenes of a victory march in Pilsudski Square in which Hitler reviews his troops and airplanes roar overhead, a stern Göring appeared to explain the indispensable contribution of the Luftwaffe to the German victory. It was mainly owing to the Luftwaffe, he said, that Germany owed its defeat and annihilation of Poland. France and England's turn would come next. And in the film's final frames, German bombers are pictured heading westward from Koblenz, across the Rhine, and flying out over water through banks of clouds. The clouds suddenly open to reveal a map of England on whose vital center a massive load of bombs is dropped. The film ends in a thundering explosion that throws up immense clouds of smoke and leaves no doubt about the fate that now awaited Herr Chamberlain and his people, as an airmen's chorus sings triumphantly "Bombs, bombs, bombs on England!" and the scene disappears behind a black curtain.[67]

In the autumn of 1939, Albert Speer watched a private screening of *Feuertaufe* in Berlin with Hitler and Josef Goebbels. Decades later he recalled the response of the Führer; one can only marvel at the precision of his memory. It must have been a dramatic occasion.

> Clouds of smoke darkened the sky; dive bombers tilted and hurtled toward their goal; we could watch the flight of the released bombs, the pull-out of the planes and the cloud from the explosions expanding gigantically. The effect was enhanced by running the film in slow motion. Hitler was fascinated. The film ended with a montage showing a plane diving toward the outlines of the British Isles. A burst of flame followed, and the island flew into the air in tatters. Hitler's enthusiasm was unbounded. "That is what will happen to them!" he cried out, carried away. "That is how we will annihilate them."[68]

Feuertaufe was premiered with great fanfare in Berlin at the Ufa Palade theater before an audience that numbered Göring, Generals von Brauchitsch and Milch, eight Reich minis-

Pl. 265. *Feuertapfe* lingered over scenes like this photograph of the Warsaw gasworks in flames.

Pl. 266. In this advertisement for the opening of *Feuertapfe* at one of Berlin's leading cinemas, the UFA Palace, the harshness and authenticity of the film is stressed. It is presented as a document to be studied by coming generations who wish to understand the history of the German struggle for freedom against their oppressors.

233

ters, and hundreds of lesser officials in dress uniform. All foreign military attachés, leading journalists, and other prominent foreigners were invited to participate in the event; among them were Count Ciano and several Italian ministers and generals, who had been invited for the occasion by the German ambassador to Rome. At the end of April the film was released to a thousand German cinemas, and edited versions in eighteen languages were prepared with special emphasis on those countries in Western Europe that might soon be presented with German ultimatums.[69] Yet though Nazi police reports emphasize the enthusiasm with which *Feuertaufe* was received by some sections of the audience, they also acknowledge that there were spectators, especially women, who expressed sympathy for the Poles. For these viewers, ". . . faced with the sight of Warsaw in ruins, the feeling was one of depression and anxiety about the 'horrors of war' rather than one of heroic pride."[70] It did not take extraordinary imagination to realize that what had happened to Poland could also one day happen to Germany.

★　　★　　★

Within days of the surrender of Poland, Hitler issued a directive for an attack in the west. Its purpose was ". . . to defeat as much as possible of the French army and of the forces of the Allies fighting on their side, and at the same time to win as much territory as possible in Holland, Belgium and northern France to serve as a base for the successful prosecution of the air and sea war against England and as a wide protective area for the economically vital Ruhr."[71]

Fall Gelb (Case Yellow), as the plan of attack was codenamed, was delayed for months, as Hitler's generals haggled over its details and sought to avoid a winter offensive in the soggy soil of northwestern Europe that so many of them had experienced during the 1914–18 war. But Hitler was not to be denied the victory in the West that he sensed now lay within his grasp. With the aid of his more imaginative generals, he devised a plan, codenamed *Sichelschnitt* (Sickle Stroke), that was aimed at drawing the French and British armies into a pocket in Belgium and northern France where they could be surrounded by German armies attacking from the north, east, and south. The key to the success of the plan was a lightening blow across the central region of northern France, which the Germans would enter through the narrow roads and heavily wooded terrain of the Ardennes Forest. On 10 May the German army struck simultaneously against the Netherlands, Belgium, Luxemburg, and France. Within three days their armies had overrun the Dutch and Belgian defenses and had reached the banks of the Meuse, which they succeeded in crossing, thus opening a corridor into northern France and offering an opportunity to realize their plan.

At the heart of the German success on the Meuse was the coordination of quickly moving armored panzer units with heavily concentrated bomber attacks from the air. Between them, Generals Bruno Loerzer and Wolfram von Richthofen, commanders of the two air fleets assigned to provide air support for the crossing of the Meuse, disposed of twelve hundred aircraft, a number sufficient to guarantee German command of the skies above the battlefield. Especially devastating to French morale were Richthofen's Ju-87 Stuka dive-bombers.[72] Equipped with screeching sirens and in their shape distressingly evocative of birds of prey, the Stukas dived from great heights in endless waves, dropping their five-hundred-pound bombs on the French infantry and artillery, who had taken refuge in hastily dug trenches and bunkers. The effect of this bombardment was out of all proportion to the number of casualties it caused. French wounded complained in the field ambulances of "the noise, the horrible noise!" "You feel the bomb coming, even if it falls 50 or 100 yards away. You throw yourself to the ground, certain of being blown into thirty pieces. And when you realize it was only a miss, the noise of this shrieking takes the ground right out from underneath your feet."[73] Five hours of this relentless pounding sufficed to panic the French troops and break their resistance to the German attack. "The gunners stopped firing and went to ground, the infantry cowered in their trenches, dazed by the crash of bombs and the shriek of dive-bombers . . ."[74]

The day after they succeeded in crossing the Meuse, 14 May, the Germans encountered unexpected opposition in the Dutch city of Rotterdam, a secondary objective to the northwest of the Meuse battlefield. Frustrated in his attempt to secure the immediate surrender of the city, the German general directing the attack requested a "short but devastating air raid" to demonstrate the uselessness of continued fighting by the Dutch forces that had taken refuge in the northern part of the city. By the time the German Heinkel III bombers had taken off, the Dutch were in the process of negotiating their surrender and the German authorities in Rotterdam had sent an urgent message to call off the attack; but the red flares they fired to warn off the bombers were apparently not seen by one wave of fifty Heinkels that dropped their bomb load in the center of the city, killing 980 people, igniting fires, causing widespread destruction, and leaving over 78,000 people homeless. In the confusion of the moment, the Dutch foreign minister declared that 30,000 people had died in the German attack, victims of a deliberate attempt to use bombers in order to terrify civilian populations and intimidate their leaders.[75] Later that afternoon the Dutch commander-in-chief, General Winkelmann capitulated, appealing to the civilian population "to secure the respect of

Pl. 267. Rotterdam after the German bombardment of 14 May 1940. As devasated as the Dutch city was by German bombing, it seems relatively intact in comparison to the appearance of German cities during the last years of the war.

the enemy by the maintenance of a worthy, earnest, and peaceful attitude during the occupation which is in prospect."[76]

The lesson was not lost on the French. On 3 June, as the last British and French troops were being evacuated by ship from the pocket around Dunkirk where they had been surrounded by the advancing German armies, the Luftwaffe staged a massive raid on Paris, concentrating their efforts on the airfields and factories circling the city and killing two hundred and fifty people. One bomb actually hit the Ministry of Air, landing in the middle of a ministerial reception. It was fortunately a dud, but the Germans had made their point.[77] A week later, on 11 June, after a tense meeting with the British prime minister Winston Churchill who urged in vain that Paris be defended from "house to house," the French commander-in-chief Maxime Weygand proclaimed the French capital an open city. By that time the French premier, Paul Reynaud, and his cabinet had already fled southward to Tours. For all practical purposes, the war in the west was over. In the minds of many Parisians the bitter humiliation of the defeat may have been mitigated by the thought that the city of light had at least been spared the terrible destruction by air that so many writers had imagined and others predicted.

★　　★　　★

London would not be so lucky. German propagandists had dwelt relentlessly on the responsibility of the British for the outbreak of war in Europe in 1939. Their logic ran that by guaranteeing the integrity of Poland against legitimate German demands for Danzig, the British had encouraged Polish resistance and condemned Europe to unnecessary bloodshed. The British soon gave the German leadership additional reasons for exasperation. On 15 May, the day after the German air raid on Rotterdam, the British War Cabinet decided to "take off its gloves" and authorized an aerial attack against oil and railway targets in the Ruhr. The Luftwaffe, at that time preoccupied with the drive against northern France, did not respond with a reprisal raid against Britain, as the leaders of the RAF had predicted they might; but nine days later Hitler issued a directive stipulating that: "Independently of the operations in France, the Luftwaffe is to undertake a full-scale offensive against the British homeland as soon as sufficient forces are available. It is to initiate a devastating reprisal raid in response to the English attacks on the Ruhr area."[78]

By 16 July 1940, after savoring and celebrating his victory over France, Hitler was ready to turn his attention to Britain. He ordered that preparations be gotten under way for an invasion of England and charged the Luftwaffe with the task of achieving command of the air over the Channel, destroying British costal defenses, and breaking the resistance of the enemy's land forces. In the euphoria of his recent victory, however, Hitler seems to have doubted that Operation Sea Lion – as he codenamed his invasion plans – would be necessary. It only stood to reason that the British, like the French, would seek an accommodation with the Germans and abandon all thought of continuing the war. Why would a decadent race, once so soundly defeated, choose to carry on the fight? When it became clear that the British had no intention of laying down their arms, the angry Führer ordered the Luftwaffe "to overpower the English air force with all the forces at its command in the shortest possible time."

Ever the faithful disciple, Göring expressed confidence that Hitler's goal could be achieved. On 1 August he assured his generals that he intended to bring the British to their knees "in the nearest future, so that an occupation of the island by our troops can proceed without any risk."[79] Privately, however, the commander of the Luftwaffe took a more cautious view. Attempting to disabuse Hans Jeschonnek, his chief of staff, of his optimistic hopes for a quick and relatively painless victory over England, Göring asked sarcastically:

"Do you think that Germany would give in if Berlin was in ruins?"

"Of course not," replied Jeschonnek.

"Then you think the British are different? That is where you are wrong . . ."[80]

Göring's doubts about the chances for a rapid air victory over England were not shared, however, by other high-ranking German air force officers. Carried away by the swiftness of their successes in Norway and France, they underestimated the adversary they now faced. Equipped with Hurricane and Spitfire fighters that were the equal of the German Messerschmitt 109 and 110s, operating from their own bases and having the advantage of fighting close to England's shores, and guided to their targets by a recently developed radar system that the Germans had failed to destroy, the British Royal Air Force defeated the Luftwaffe by refusing to be beaten. The fighting was fierce; losses in aircraft and pilots heavy on both sides; but despite their success in destroying British planes, the leaders of the Luftwaffe were all too aware by late August 1940 that they had failed to achieve air superiority over the waters surrounding England. To that extent, their campaign had failed, and they knew it.

It was at this point that Hitler made a fateful decision. Convinced that time was running out and that the weather would soon turn to the advantage of the defenders, he authorized the bombing of London and other British cities. Central to his shift in strategy was his Douhettian belief that the bombing of London would inspire panic among the population, bring essential services to a standstill, and possibly cause an uprising of the working classes against their upper-class masters, thus forcing the British governing elite to sue for peace.[81] Toward the achievement of this last goal, he ordered the Luftwaffe to concentrate its bombing in the East End of London where the poorer sectors of the population lived and worked.[82] Transported by righteous indignation at the crimes of the "night pirates" of the RAF, Hitler seized the opportunity to pit the hardened will of the German people against what he perceived to be the flabby resolve of British civilians. Douhet's theories would now be put to the test. In a speech on 4 September, the Führer assured his audience that: ". . . if the British air force drops two or three or four thousand kilograms of bombs, then we will drop in a single night 150,000, 180,000, 230,000, 300,000, 400,000, a million kilograms. If they announce that they will attack our cities on a large scale, then we shall wipe their cities out!"[83] In this war of people against people, he promised, it would not be National Socialist Germany that would be the first to crack.[84]

The first blow against London came on 7 September at five o'clock in the afternoon when a wave of three hundred German bombers initiated an attack that would last for twelve hours and leave over three hundred people dead and the docks along the Thames ablaze with a thousand fires, many of which were still burning the next day. When daytime bombing proved too costly in planes lost to RAF fighters, the Germans shifted to night raids, which in turn increased the number of wayward bombs that fell on nonmilitary targets, thus accentuating the haphazard and terrorist aspect of the German bombing campaign. The attacks continued with only brief respites until mid-November when the Germans began to devote their attention to other provincial cities, most notably the industrial city of Coventry whose center they destroyed under the full moon of 14 November. By the end of November 12,696 civilians in the London region had been killed and another 20,000 seriously wounded by 36,000 bombs.[85] The bombing would continue until 10 May 1941 when the Luftwaffe staged another major raid on London, killing almost 1,500 people and damaging or destroying many historic buildings.[86] Thus ended what had come to be known as the Blitz.

Pl. 268. In this 1941 painting, *Bomben über England* (Bombs over England), Georg Lebrecht portrays a German bombing raid on London. Fortunately for the city's inhabitants, the Stukas were not as unopposed as they appear here.

Pl. 269. London's St. Paul's Cathedral in the midst of a German bombing attack on 29 December 1940. The photograph by Herbert Mason became a metaphor for London's miraculous survival during the Blitz.

Pl. 270. This photograph, taken from St. Paul's Cathedral on the day following the German bombing attack of 29-30 December 1940, gives eloquent testimony to the devastation caused by the raid in the neighborhood surrounding St. Paul's.

The British struggle against the German aerial offensive took place on many levels, ranging from the young men who flew the Spitfires and Hurricanes to the volunteer wardens, firefighters, and ambulance drivers, who labored to limit the damage caused by the bombers that got through. But another type of combat took place on the cultural front in the world of film, where the battle was fought with images and the objectives were the hearts and minds of the British people – and even more so, perhaps, those of their potential American allies.[87]

Long before the war began, the Committee of Imperial Defence, gravely concerned about the ability of the British people to sustain the rigors of a war against Germany, had recommended the creation of a Ministry of Information, one of whose functions should be the maintenance of morale.[88] Underlying the creation of this bureaucracy, which became a haven for unemployed middle- and upper-class intellectuals, was the assumption that the British working masses would have to be inspired to fulfill their responsibilities in a situation of total war. Though no one could define it with any precision, morale was perceived to be a precarious state of mind that might easily collapse under pressure. The underclasses, this argument went, were Britain's Achilles heel, for unlike the middle and upper classes they might not understand why they were being asked to fight, to suffer, and possibly to die in a war that Hitler insisted was unnecessary.[89] Motion pictures were the most obvious means of reaching the less educated and less privileged classes, for it was they who frequented the cinemas most regularly; and in 1940 the Crown Film Unit was formed under the direction of Ian Dalrymple, who recruited his staff largely from within a group of talented documentary filmmakers who had been working for the General Post Office. During the course of the war they would produce almost two thousand films, which by 1942 were being shown to between twenty and thirty million filmgoers weekly.[90]

One of their first and most successful efforts was a short but stirring film called *London Can Take It*, specially shot for exhibition in the United States. The purpose of this documentary was to turn the devastation of the Blitz to the advantage of the British and to win the sympathy of American audiences. Originally, the picture was supposed to have been made by Movietone News. Harry Watt of the Crown Film Unit was assigned to advise the Movietone crew. But when Watt saw the footage Movietone had shot, he was appalled. It gave the impression that London had been flattened. Watt succeeded in convincing the Ministry that the Crown Film Unit should make the film and managed to negotiate a contract with Movietone according to which he would pay them a pound for every foot of their material he used, which as it turned out was almost nothing.

After five days and nights of hectic filming where "the action was thickest," Watt had some spectacular footage of London and the Londoners under attack by German bombers. What he needed now was a narrator capable of writing his own commentary. The American Division of the Ministry suggested Mary Walsh, an ambitious young journalist who would later become Ernest Hemingway's fourth wife. But Watt was convinced that a woman narrator would undermine the effect of his film. He pleaded with Sidney Bernstein, deputy director of the Film Division of the Ministry of Information, to suggest someone else; and Bernstein came up with the name of Quentin Reynolds, a reporter for *Colliers* magazine who was staying at the Savoy Hotel.[91]

Quent Reynolds was an inspired choice. A hard-drinking New Yorker with a love for yarns, a fast and loose way with facts, and a terminal case of Anglophilia, Reynolds felt that everyone you saw in London was "pulsating with life."[92] When initially contacted by his

Pl. 271. Quentin Reynolds improbably became the spokesman for embattled Britain during the Blitz.

friend Sidney Bernstein, Reynolds was told that the Ministry of Information wanted a film that would show London as it is today. "Show the damage no matter how bad it is. Don't minimize the suffering which the people are undergoing. Just a stark realistic picture of London as it is – no frills, no propaganda."[93] Watt showed Reynolds the footage that he and his crew had shot and set him to work writing in the underground Grill at the Savoy, from which (according to Watt) Reynolds "steadfastly refused" to come out at night.[94] Watt encouraged Reynolds to tighten his script and later succeeded, with some difficulty, in extracting from him the slow, growled narration that gave the film much of its effect.[95]

London Can Take It is set five weeks after the onset of the bombing, in mid-October of 1940.[96] We first see the Londoners during the late afternoon rush hour, chasing buses and scurrying toward their homes. Reynolds tells us that they are hastening to reach their homes before their "nightly visitors" arrive. These people you see, the narrator explains, are members of the greatest civilian army every assembled; it is they who are really fighting this war. Many of them are returning to their homes to don the uniforms of their special service after spending a day at work. We are shown civilians lining up, like the "good soldiers" they are, before the entrance to shelters. The assumption is that every Londoner, no matter how young or old, is mobilized in this war that is being fought by night. Sirens screech. The engines of approaching bombers drone. Searchlights sweep the sky. Antiaircraft guns explode in gusts of rapid fire. This, says Reynolds ominously, is the "symphony of war."

The spectacle of the Blitz is about to begin. The "People's Army" of air-raid wardens, firemen, and ambulance drivers is ready. A bomb falls. The sky is illuminated in sudden flashes of light. We see a young girl and an older man soundly sleeping side by side in a shelter. "Do you see any signs of fear on these faces?" Reynolds asks us.[97] The People's Army now swings into action. They fight fires, rescue the injured from burning buildings, attend to their wounds. They ignore the bombs and the shrapnel. "Brokers, clerks, peddlers, merchants by day – they are heroes by night."

Morning comes. The all-clear signal announces that the bombers have gone. London takes stock of the damage done to its buildings and its people and prepares to go back to work. The shops are all open – some a bit more open, Reynolds says with dark humor, than they had been before the bombing. Identifying himself as a "neutral reporter," Reynolds assures the audience that there is no panic, no fear, no despair in "London town"; there is nothing but determination, confidence, and high courage among the people of "Churchill's island." A bomb, Reynolds tells us, has its limitations. It can destroy buildings and kill people, but it cannot kill "the unquenchable spirit of the people of London. London can take it!"

Central to the film is the message that England is fighting back, that its people are united as never before, and that they are defending "the frontiers of freedom" – read the freedom not just of the British but also that of the other peoples, like the Americans who had not yet entered the war. We are told grimly that some of the people we have seen in this film will perish before the night's attack is over; but the cause of freedom will prevail in the end. *London Can Take It* was a great success in Britain and the United States, where it was distributed by Warner Brothers; and it transformed Reynolds into an international celebrity, whose ensuing lecture tour in the United States fetched the princely sum of $750 an appearance. To the great amusement of Watt and his fellow filmmakers, Reynolds returned to London with a poster depicting him "gazing defiantly at the skies in a British tin-hat, and warding off, with his strong right arm, a five-hundred-pound bomb!" Watt concluded, sardonically that "It must have been a lot tougher in the Savoy Grill than we thought."[98]

★   ★   ★

Pl. 272. Londoners sleep peacefully. "Do you see any signs of fear in these faces?" Reynolds asked during his narration.

Pl. 273. A shattered store front.

Pl. 274. Londoners make their way to work through the rubble after a German raid.

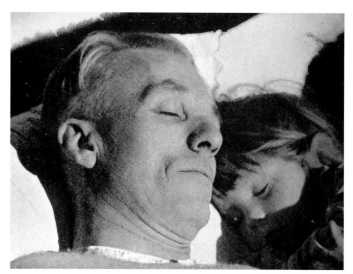

Pl. 275. London buildings burn during a raid.

Pl. 276. Quentin Reynolds: "And they know that every night the R.A.F. bombers fly deep into the heart of Germany, bombing munitions works, aeroplane factories, canals; cutting the arteries which keep the heart of Germany alive."

As propaganda, *London Can Take It* ran a risk. It portrayed Britain as a country under siege – admirable to be sure, bravely carrying on, but still perilously close to defeat. The ruins and rubble the film showed in central London could hardly be reassuring to Britons or their friends. Aware of this, Reynolds was careful to explain that one of the reasons why the morale of the Londoners remained so high was because they knew that every night the RAF was striking back and flying deep into the heart of Germany, where they bombed munitions works, airplane factories, and canals, cutting the arteries that kept Germany alive. The British were not only taking it; they were also dishing it out.

This was a message the British people were anxious to hear, and the Crown Film Unit made it the theme of their most successful production of 1941, *Target for Tonight*. Directed by Harry Watt and portraying RAF personnel rather than professional actors, this feature-length film ingeniously blurs the boundary between the documentary and cinematic fiction. Before shooting it, Watt had spent a month at Bomber Headquarters, talking to people, reading reports of bombing missions, and waiting for the crews to come back. "The ones who didn't," he later remembered, "were almost always the newcomers."[99]

Target for Tonight tells the story of the planning, organization, and execution of a night-time bombing raid over a German city identified as Freihausen; the objective is an oil reservoir, which the Wellington crew we follow throughout the film destroys with their last bomb, a thousand-pounder. In his search for authenticity, Watts even succeeded in persuading the commander-in-chief of the RAF's Bomber Command, Sir Richard Pearse, to appear in a scene in which he looked at aerial reconnaissance photographs and, turning to his second in command, said: "Yes, I agree these are interesting. Put a squadron on to bomb it tonight." Watt's job was then to show what "those few casual words meant to six ordinary Air Force bods."[100]

The emphasis throughout the fifty-minute film is on the efficiency of the RAF, the skill and understated confidence with which its members go about their jobs, and the deadly accuracy of their bombs. High technology is omnipresent: in the telephones with which the officers communicate at the base; the precise aerial photographs they analyze before deciding to bomb Freihausen; the meteorological equipment they use to determine the weather; the radios with which they guide the planes; the bombsight with which they locate the target; and the ability of the plane itself to withstand German fire and return to England safely, despite thick fog surrounding its base. Neither German flak nor impenetrable weather can shake the crew's faith in their aircraft and their pilot. One leaves the film certain that Britain is firmly in control of its destiny: nothing has been left to chance. The only Germans we glimpse on the ground are hard-faced soldiers, preparing to respond to the attack with antiaircraft guns. Our sympathies are totally with the bomber crew who, matter-of-factly and good-humoredly, go about their duties. When *Target for Tonight* was released in the United States in November 1941, *Time* praised it for its authenticity and pronounced it "far & away the best picture that has come out of World War II."[101] Fifty million people are estimated to have seen it in twelve thousand theaters throughout the United States, Canada, and Latin America. This figure does not include Britain where *Target* ran at three West End cinemas simultaneously, while its story was serialized in the *Daily Express* under the title "The Greatest Story of the War."[102] One can only conclude that the sight of British bombs falling on Germany had a popular appeal that was by no means confined to the British themselves.

The irony is that at the very moment when *Target for Tonight* was enjoying its success as a triumph of realistic filmmaking, Bomber Command was undergoing a serious crisis. A secret report presented to Churchill in August 1941 concluded that of those crews who claimed to have attacked their primary target — two-thirds of the bombers sent out on any given night — only one-third had come within five miles of their aiming point. In the case of the Ruhr, a frequent objective of bombing raids because of its concentration of heavy industry, the figure was even lower, one aircraft out of ten. When moonlight was lacking, these figures dropped to one in fifteen.[103] And this at a time when Bomber Command's

Pl. 278. Eric Kennington's 1940 portrait of Harris before he was appointed head of Bomber Command. He appears less menacing here than he did in later photographs.

losses had begun to rise to unacceptable levels. On the night of 7 November 1941, thirty-seven aircraft out of four hundred dispatched over Germany were lost. One out of five of the planes sent to the Ruhr failed to return.[104] Alarmed by these losses, the Air Ministry instructed Bomber Command to curtail its operations, especially in bad weather. By the end of 1941, even some high-ranking Air Ministry officials had begun to have doubts about the efficacy of the RAF's precision bombing campaign against German military targets.[105]

The fact remained, however, that bombing raids were the only means the British possessed to bring the war home to the Germans, and Churchill never swerved in his belief that "an absolutely devastating, exterminating attack by very heavy bombers from this country upon the Nazi homeland" was essential if the British were to win the war.[106] Hence on Valentine's Day 1942, after months of debate within the government, the Air Ministry issued a directive to Bomber Command, removing all constraints on bombing policy. Operations "should now be focused on the morale of the enemy civil population and in particular, of industrial workers." Among the targets listed were Berlin, Düsseldorf, Cologne, Lübeck, Rostock, Bremen, Kiel, Hanover, Frankfurt, Mannheim, and Stuttgart.[107] In effect, the decision had been made to abandon the precision bombing of military targets in favor of the bombing of civilians. To remove any possible ambiguity about the objectives of the new policy, the Chief of Air Staff specified that the aiming points were not to be dockyards or aircraft factories but the built-up areas, with the objective of rendering the German workers homeless and putting their cities to the torch with incendiary bombs.[108]

The man chosen to implement this policy, as commander-in-chief of Bomber Command, was Arthur Harris, who replaced Sir Richard Pearse in February 1942. Harris remains as controversial today as he was when he left the RAF under stormy and obscure circumstances in 1945. He has never been without his steadfast admirers just as he has never lacked implacable critics.[109] No one has ever disputed his dedication or abilities; it is his temperament and judgment that are at issue. Perceived by some as domineering, direct to the point of rudeness, driven by an obsessive vision that no accumulation of countervailing facts could ever shake, Harris was convinced that, if supplied with the necessary

British Bombers now attack Germany a thousand at a time!

equipment, Bomber Command could bring Germany to its knees. Having watched the bombing of London and observed the strain to which the city's inhabitants had been put, he believed that no country could endure a protracted bombing offensive, if it were continued long enough and carried out by a sufficient number of heavy bombers and the right kind of bombs.[110] No one would ever convince him that he was wrong.

In the spring of 1942, as an indication of the type of campaign that he intended to conduct, Harris fire-bombed the old Baltic cities of Lübeck and Rostock to the ground and sent a force of a thousand bombers to attack Cologne in a raid that destroyed six hundred acres of the city and left four hundred and seventy-four civilians dead and forty-five thousand people homeless.[111] Though war production quickly returned to normal levels, Harris obtained the publicity he craved for Bomber Command and offered a beacon of hope to a nation still traumatized by the experience of the Blitz and now demoralized by a series of humiliating defeats in the Middle and Far East. In the midst of otherwise gloomy news, Harris's voice rang out proudly and defiantly. "We are going to scourge the Third Reich from end to end. We are bombing Germany city by city and ever more terribly in order to make it impossible for her to go on with the war. That is our object; we shall pursue it relentlessly."[112]

★ ★ ★

Less than two months after *Target for Tonight* was released in the United States, Japanese carrier-based aircraft attacked the American fleet at Pearl Harbor. Six of eight battleships in harbor were sunk, and the remaining two badly damaged. Ten other small vessels were sunk or damaged; one hundred and sixty-four planes were destroyed on the ground. Over two thousand servicemen and civilians were killed, and another thousand wounded. Yet as serious as these military losses were, the damage done to the American psyche was even greater. Suddenly, war no longer appeared as something that was happening to people in faraway lands. Americans, especially those living on the West Coast, suddenly felt themselves vulnerable to air attack. If the Japanese had been able to penetrate the formidable defenses of Hawaii, what was to prevent them from striking Seattle, San Francisco, or Los Angeles? And how could America strike back?

Stepping forward to help the American public answer these questions was Alexander de Seversky, whose book *Victory Through Air Power* appeared in April 1942.[113] Slightly built, kinky-haired, and articulate, Seversky was one of a number of colorful and talented European émigrés who made careers in American aviation after the First World War. A Russian naval pilot who had lost a leg when his plane was shot down in 1915 during a bombing mission, the young Seversky had equipped himself with an artificial limb, obtained a special decree from the Tsar that permitted him to return to combat, and gone on to shoot down thirteen German planes and win a slew of decorations, including the Gold Sword and the Order of St. George, Russia's highest military award. In 1918, when the Bolshevik government withdrew from the war and signed a separate peace with Germany, Seversky was in the United States as a member of the Russian Naval Aviation Mission. He immediately offered his services to the American government and was appointed a test pilot and aeronautical engineer. Having no desire to return to Bolshevik Russia when the war ended, Seversky stayed on in America, married an attractive society girl, and worked with General Billy Mitchell between 1921 and 1924 to develop a new and more accurate bombsight during Mitchell's attempts to demonstrate the ability of aircraft to sink battleships. With $50,000 paid to him by the American government in return for

Pl. 279. A British poster depicting a thousand-bomber raid over Germany by Bomber Command. Such images were considered good for British morale.

247

his patent claims, he went on to found his own aircraft company. Although this company failed in the stock market crash of 1929, he organized another in 1931 which specialized in long-range pursuit planes. Despite government contracts, this company also lost money; by 1940 the disgruntled investors had removed Seversky from the board of directors and changed the name of the organization to Republic Aviation Corporation, a company that would prosper during the Second World War.[114]

Yet if Seversky was down, he was by no means out. A better designer, pilot, and writer than businessman, Seversky was responsible for dozens of technical innovations, broke several world speed records, and had emerged by 1939 as an eloquent and widely read expert on the tactics and strategy of aerial warfare. In May 1941, shortly after having been awarded the Harmon Trophy for his aeronautical achievements, Seversky did not hesitate to take on Charles Lindbergh himself and explain, in an article published in the *American Mercury*, why the conqueror of the Atlantic and the world's most famous pilot was wrong in urging a policy of noninterventionist neutrality and isolation for the United States in the face of the German conquest of Europe.[115]

The views he presented in the *American Mercury* and in other articles written in 1940–41 were expanded and presented with even greater force after Pearl Harbor in *Victory Through Air Power*, the most influential work on aviation published during the Second World War. At least 350,000 copies of Seversky's book were sold in hard cover and paperback and it has been estimated that five million people read some portion of it in book form, its condensation in the *Reader's Digest*, or syndicated newspaper articles.[116] Walt Disney was so taken by its argument that he transformed it into an animated motion picture in 1943 and allowed Seversky to explain his theories on the screen, an unprecedented honor for an aviation theorist and a testimony to Disney's determination to contribute to the war effort, even at the cost of losing his audience.[117]

Isolationism, Seversky pointed out, was not a realistic option for the United States because there was no longer any place on earth that could be considered safe from air attack. In the tradition of H. G. Wells, Seversky imagined a devastating air attack against the United States:

> From every point of the compass – across the two oceans and across the two Poles – giant bombers, each protected by its convoy of deadly fighter planes, converge upon the United States of America. There are thousands of these dreadnoughts of the skies. Each of them carries at least fifty tons of streamlined explosives and a hailstorm of light incendiary bombs. Wave after wave they come – openly, in broad daylight, magnificently armored and

Pl. 280. Alexander de Seversky exudes authority, as he explains the role that strategic bombing could have in winning the war in Walt Disney's 1943 film, *Victory Through Air Power*.

Pl. 281. Seversky's hero, General Billy Mitchell, an unrelenting advocate of strategic bombing. Mitchell was court-martialed in 1925 criticizing his superiors for their neglect of air power. Seversky thought so highly of Mitchell that he chose this photograph as the frontispiece for his 1942 best-seller, *Victory Through Air Power*.

armed, surrounded by protective aircraft and equipped to fight their way through to their appointed targets. Aerial armadas now battle boldly and fiercely, just as great naval armadas used to do in the past, only with a destructive fury infinitely more terrifying.[118]

The result of such an attack, Seversky predicted, would be ". . . to break our strength, destroy our civilization, lay low our cities, decimate our population, and leave us to dig out of the debris slowly and painfully."[119] The United States would be eliminated as a world power economically and politically for generations to come.[120]

Seversky insisted that there was nothing fanciful about this nightmarish scenario. Technically, it had been feasible for some time. Only "psychological meekness" and "deficient military imagination" had prevented the creation of "aerial armadas" capable of carrying the war to the enemy's heartland. Moreover, contrary to the belief of the isolationists, the United States was more susceptible to bombing than any other country because it was the most industrialized nation in the world. Here an enemy could hope to achieve more destruction per ton of explosive than in almost any other part of the world.[121] The only sure defense against such a devastating attack was to build a giant long-distance air striking force that was capable of hitting the enemy in its heartland and its cities. The main investment of American wealth and energy should therefore be put into aviation. "We can assume a defensive strategy on the sea, hold our land forces in abeyance for the issue, while air power takes the initiative and batters through to a victorious conclusion."[122]

In making the case for airpower as the decisive factor in the world war now under way, Seversky appeared to be following in the footsteps of Douhet. A more immediate influence, however, was Seversky's early patron and mentor, Billy Mitchell, who had campaigned in the 1920s for an independent and vastly expanded air force. Indeed, drawing on the experience of the British during the Blitz, Seversky argued against the "haphazard destruction of cities" in favor of the precision bombing of military targets, such as electric power installations, aviation plants, docks, and essential public utilities. "The 'panic' that was expected to spread through a city or even a nation as bombs began to fall has turned out to be a myth."[123] Only by carrying the war to the enemy's heartland could we hope to obtain victory; and this could be achieved only through airpower. In Disney's film, the book's central message was illustrated brilliantly by animated sequences in which American bombers pulverized the heartland of Nazism and an American eagle alighted from the sky to squelch the Japanese octopus, whose tentacles had extended menacingly throughout the Pacific and the Far East.

Pl. 282. American bombers cast their ominous shadow over the Third Reich in this still from *Victory Through Air Power.*

One might imagine that the leaders of the U.S. Army Air Force would privately appreciate Seversky's campaign in favor of an independent strategic bombing force. The fact is that they didn't. General Hap Arnold, Commanding General of the USAAF, feared that Seversky's withering criticism of American air force leadership for its lack of imagination and daring would undermine public confidence in his organization and its equipment, precisely at the moment when he was preparing to expand the USAAF to a force of two million men. Working behind the scenes, Arnold and his aides orchestrated a campaign in the press against Seversky toward the end of undermining his credibility as an expert on military aviation and grand strategy.[124]

Yet despite Arnold's personal hostility to Seversky and his conviction that the Russian was acting irresponsibly, the leaders of the USAAF soon found themselves moving quickly to create a gigantic strategic bombing force not unlike the one conceived by Seversky. This was because their civilian commander-in-chief, President Franklin Roosevelt, had become a believer in the virtues of strategic bombing and had no qualms about the bombing of German civilians. Even before the United States entered the war, Roosevelt had ordered the production of five hundred heavy bombers a month, at a time when the British, with their backs against the wall, were manufacturing that number in a year.[125] Roosevelt was as anxious as Churchill to carry the war to the Nazi homeland long before any invasion of Europe could seriously be contemplated.

The result was the creation of the Eighth Air Force. Conceived originally for the purpose of supporting a projected invasion of northwest Africa urged by Churchill, its commanding officers were instead sent to England where, under the command of Carl Spaatz and later Ira Eaker, it grew from six men and no airplanes in February 1942 to a huge force of four hundred thousand officers and men and eight thousand aircraft by June 1944.[126] Unimpressed by the results the British had achieved with nighttime bombing, the Americans were determined to demonstrate that their B-17s were capable of hitting precision military targets during daytime raids and protecting themselves against the attacks of German fighters. Before they prevailed, they would endure terrible losses, along with the skepticism of their British allies.

Pl. 283. William Wyler directs Bette Davis and Teresa Wright during the making of *The Little Foxes* in 1941. Wright also played a major role in Wyler's *Mrs. Miniver*.

Losses needed to be justified, especially when the outcome of a long war still hung in the balance. The American government, no less than its British counterpart, felt the need to maintain the morale of the civilian population. And in the meeting of this challenge, experienced filmmakers could prove invaluable. Most were more than willing to serve their country, though their contributions to the war effort took a variety of forms, some more courageous (or more foolhardy) than others.

For reasons that are unclear, William Wyler, a well-established and stylish Hollywood director, was drawn toward the coming bombing campaign in Europe. Wyler had never made an aviation movie; his specialty was melodrama, in which he had excelled as a director of the temperamental Bette Davis. Yet it turned out that he was made of stronger stuff than some of Hollywood's most macho actors and directors. An Alsatian Jew who cared deeply about the Nazis and anti-Semitism, he was not satisfied to make flag-waving films from the safety and comfort of the Southern California studios.

Introduced to Carl Spaatz at a cocktail party by his friend Sy Bartlett, Wyler convinced the general that he should be allowed to make a documentary about the Eighth Air Force. Instantaneously elevated to the rank of major in the air force without a day of basic training, Wyler assembled a team, consisting of three cameramen (William Clothier, Harold Tannenbaum, and William Skall) and a writer (Jerry Chodorow). While his crew remained in the States trying to acquire equipment for shipment by sea, Wyler set off on 6 August 1942 for London in a PBY flying boat with a hand-held, sixteen-millimeter camera and only the vaguest of notions of how he was going to go about his task of capturing on film the experiences of the Eighth Air Force's bombing crews.

When Wyler arrived in England, he already possessed impressive credentials as an Anglophile and propagandist. Indeed, his most recent picture, the extravagantly praised and commercially successful *Mrs. Miniver* released by MGM in July 1942, was a sterling example of the kind of morale-building movies that the American government wanted Hollywood to make.[127] Set in an idyllic English village during the Blitz, *Mrs. Miniver* had taken the themes of *London Can Take It* and transformed them into a highly sentimental melodrama that managed to suggest simultaneously the bestiality of the bombing campaign that the Germans had ruthlessly launched against innocent civilians, the unbreakable spirit of resistance in Britain, and the essential similarity between the American and British peoples. From the sensitive and compassionate performance of Greer Garson to the symbol of the English rose – the master metaphor that bound the disparate parts of the film together – everything in *Mrs. Miniver* suggested the inevitability of the alliance between Britain and the United States. President Roosevelt was so impressed by the stirring speech with which the film ended, in which the village vicar played by Henry Wilcoxon set forth his vision of the "People's War," that he ordered the text to be translated and dropped in leaflet form over German occupied Europe and read over the Voice of America.[128] Churchill reportedly claimed that *Mrs. Miniver* did more to help the British cause than a fleet of destroyers.

For all the success of *Mrs. Miniver*, once in England Wyler encountered nothing but frustration. Unlike in Hollywood, where the pressure had been to make films quickly, the American military bureaucracy seemed determined to do everything possible to slow Wyler down. One disappointment followed another; a few months after arriving in London, Wyler discovered that the sophisticated cameras he would need for aerial photography had been "lost in transit" from the United States. Refusing to be defeated, he rounded up forty hand-held sixteen-millimeter cameras, some of which he distributed to American aircrews in the hope that they would provide him with combat footage he could use. But nothing could substitute for a firsthand experience of the drama he had come to

A Speech from "Mrs. Miniver"

Toward the end of the recent moving-picture version of *Mrs. Miniver*, the Rector talks to his congregation following a ghastly bombing of their little English town. The Editors of Good Housekeeping, who thought the picture a great one, think, too, that the Rector's simple words should be printed and reprinted, many times in many places

Pl. 284. Within a bombed-out village church, the vicar (Henry Wilcoxon) delivers a stirring sermon toward the end of *Mrs. Miniver*.

Pl. 285. The editors of *Good Housekeeping* magazine thought so highly of the vicar's speech (and Wyler's picture) that they published the text in its entirety in their issue of August 1942.

England to film. Finally, in December 1942, Wyler succeeded in convincing General Ira Eaker, who had replaced Spaatz as commander of the Eighth Air Force, that he should be allowed to participate in bombing raids. Wyler's mission, as now defined by Eaker, was ". . . to portray the U.S. Army Air Force carrying the air war to the enemy. These films are conceived as documentary motion picture stories exploiting the human element, as contrasted to factual and newsreel material."[129] The phrase, "exploiting the human element," reveals the opportunity that Eaker saw to utilize Wyler's talent to dramatize the contribution the Army Air Force was making to the winning of the war. An expert in public relations, Eaker knew that it was not enough to drop bombs on enemy targets; it was also essential to tell the story of the Eighth Air Force to the American public. Who could do this better than the director of *Mrs. Miniver*?

Wyler would not let Eaker down. Armed with Eaker's authorization, on 26 February 1943 Wyler embarked on his first mission out of Bassingbourn, a former RAF airfield southwest of Cambridge. The crew with which he flew was normally assigned to a B-17 named *Memphis Belle*. On this raid they were flying another bomber, the *Jersey Bounce*, because the *Belle* was being repaired after having been badly shot up on a raid against the submarine pens at Saint-Nazaire on the west coast of France. The pilot was Robert K. Morgan.[130] The primary target was the harbor facilities in Bremen, but when they arrived there clouds obscured the harbor. With German fighters in close pursuit, the force diverted toward the secondary objective, the naval base at Wilhelmshaven. American losses were heavy and the bombing ineffective because of bad visibility over the target. Walter Cronkite, another non-combatant who was authorized to go on the raid as a special cor-

Pl. 286.   The crew of the *Memphis Belle*. The crew's pilot, Robert Morgan, is standing fourth from the left with Wyler to his immediate right.

respondent for the British United Press, described the scene he witnessed as "a hell of burning tracers and bursting flak; of crippled Fortresses and burning German fighters; of men going down in parachutes and other men not so lucky."[131]

The spunky Hollywood director surprised Morgan and his crew by his calmness under fire. The bombardier, Vince Evans, later recalled Wyler "walking the open catwalk of the bomb bay five miles above Germany, breathing out of a walk-around oxygen bottle." Evans was fascinated by the single-mindedness with which Wyler pursued his filming while flak burst around them and German fighters attempted to break their formation. "We could hear him cuss over the intercom . . . By the time he'd swung his camera over to a flak burst, it was lost. Then he'd see another burst, try to get it, miss, see another, try that, miss, try, miss. Then we'd hear him over the intercom, asking if [Morgan] couldn't possibly get the plane closer to the flak."[132]

Wyler would go on four more raids, two with Morgan and his crew in the *Memphis Belle*. Despite the danger and discomfort, he found the experience strangely exhilarating. "Aerial warfare," he wrote to a friend in Hollywood, "takes place in altitudes where the oil in your camera freezes, where you have to wear oxygen masks or die, where you can't move around too much and keep conscious, where the world below you looks like the map of another planet, where human resistance and wit are taxed to the maximum, where things happen faster than any man can think. These and many other conditions are far removed from the comforts of Stage 18 in Burbank or Culver City. This is life at its fullest. With these experiences, I could make a dozen *Mrs. Minivers* – only much better."[133]

By May 1943 Wyler knew that he had the makings of a picture; he decided to organize it around the *Memphis Belle* after Morgan and his crew successfully completed their twenty-fifth mission and were greeted with a reception at their base that had been carefully staged by their commanding officer, Colonel Stanley Wray, to achieve the maximum effect for Wyler's waiting camera crew.[134] With the encouragement of General Eaker, Wyler returned to Hollywood to edit his nineteen thousand feet of color film and to provide it with sound effects, a narrative, and a musical score. Wyler had at first intended to make a two-reel documentary along the lines of *Target for Tonight*, emphasizing the American approach to daylight precision bombing.[135] But the authenticity of the film he had shot and the publicity that the *Memphis Belle*'s crew and their pilot attracted when they returned to the United States and went on a carefully organized public relations tour convinced Wyler that he should aim instead for a feature picture that would be shown at theaters throughout the country.[136] Always alert to possibilities for drama, Wyler convinced the air force to send the crew of the *Memphis Belle* to Hollywood to do dialogue voice-overs for the section of the film that dealt with its defense against attacking enemy fighters after

delivering its bombs. This turned out to be an inspired idea and became one of the most impressive and commented on aspects of the forty-three minute documentary that Wyler completed in early 1944.

Memphis Belle is organized around the story of its crew's twenty-fifth and final mission. Its narration, written by Lester Koenig, a protégé of Paramount studio head B. P. Schulberg, is spare yet eloquent, poetic yet lacking any trace of sentimentality.[137] As Anglophile as *London Can Take It* and *Mrs. Miniver* – with lovely pastoral scenes of an ancient island that has been transformed into "a battlefront like no other" – Wyler's film succeeds in making the case for bombing Germany while at the same time shifting the emphasis away from those on the ground who are being bombed toward the terrible ordeal of those who are dropping the bombs. One would never guess from Koenig's narration that the "deadly cargo" the Flying Fortresses carried often fell not on armament factories and submarine pens but on innocent civilians. Though *Memphis Belle* in no way glamorizes the air war, it nonetheless conveys a sense for the massive effort the Americans were mounting and their determination to carry the campaign through to victory, no matter what the cost. The crewmen it depicts are not superhuman heroes, but members of a smoothly functioning team. They come from every walk of life and every corner of the United States. All-American young men, it is impossible not to like them. They never doubt the justice of their cause because, as the narrator reminds us, the German houses and fields over which they fly belong to a people "who twice in one generation have flooded the world with suffering." Wyler's Technicolor images of bombers sailing through blue sky toward their target have an eerie beauty that is juxtaposed to great effect with the fear of men who know that they can fall to a fiery death at any time. And when the *Memphis Belle* returns safely to Bassingbourn and a member of its crew kisses the ground in thanksgiving, we heave a sigh of relief.

Having edited the film, Wyler flew to Washington where he ran it for General Arnold, the supreme commander of the Army Air Force, and President Roosevelt in a private screening in the White House basement. Roosevelt, Wyler later remembered, "was very enthusiastic . . . He said it had to be shown right away, everywhere." Arnold thought that it was "an important piece of documentary history which has caught the spirit of our air and ground personnel in true and memorable fashion," and wrote as much to Barney Balaban, president of Paramount Pictures, who agreed to distribute *Memphis Belle* free and exhibit it in three-quarters of the nation's sixteen thousand movie theaters.[138]

When *Memphis Belle* was released on 15 April 1944, the critics were universal in praising the illusion that Wyler's documentary gave of immediacy and personal experience.[139] Even James Agee, who had disliked *Mrs. Miniver*, felt that "everything is seen, done, and experienced as if from inside one or another of the men in the plane."[140] But perhaps the most interesting testimony comes from the French writer Jules Roy, who was at that time flying bombing missions with the RAF over Germany. Roy saw the film on 14 November 1944 and was impressed with its "admirable restraint." "I don't know if we [French] would have been able . . . to describe the business with such a true simplicity. Above all, I was touched by the absence of affectation in the characters; they don't view themselves as heroes, they make no theatrical gestures when departing, but on returning they abandon themselves to their joy and one of them, who is perhaps the commander of the crew, kisses the ground on jumping out of the airplane."[141] Had he known Roy's reaction, Wyler would have been delighted, for the understated heroism of the bomber crews was exactly the impression he hoped to convey.

★   ★   ★

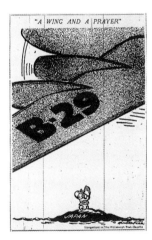

Pl. 289. A newspaper cartoon from the *New York Times* on 26 November 1944 that suggests the popularity in the United States of the bombing campaign against Japan.

While Wyler was shooting *Memphis Belle*, the Hollywood studios were in the process of discovering the charms of the heavy bomber as a subject for feature films. But reflecting the fierce anti-Japanese sentiment in the United States, the theater of war they chose to represent was not Europe but the Pacific and the city whose destruction they preferred to imagine was not Berlin or Hamburg but Tokyo, origin of the nefarious attack against Pearl Harbor that had brought America into the war.[142] In March 1943, Warner Brothers released Howard Hawks's *Air Force*, a highly praised picture about the odyssey of a B-17 bomber crew across the Pacific during the days immediately following Pearl Harbor; and the following July RKO's *Bombardier* made the Army Air Force's case for precision bombing, ending in a spectacular scene in which the captured Randolph Scott guided Pat O'Brien's bombers to their military target in Tokyo, gladly sacrificing himself for the pleasure of seeing the city go up in flames.[143]

Yet the bombing story that most caught the fancy of Hollywood producers and their audiences in 1943–4 was an event that now lay in what seemed the distant past. Two weeks after Pearl Harbor, President Roosevelt had gathered his highest military advisers and told them that he wanted to stage a bombing raid on the home islands of Japan as soon as possible to bolster the morale of America and her allies.[144] General Hap Arnold, the Army Air Force Chief of Staff, directed the War Plans Division of the Air Staff to draft plans for retaliatory air strikes against Japan.

The plans for an air attack on Tokyo, however, came not from the air force but from the navy. Captain Donald Duncan, a staff officer known for his perfectionism, prepared a detailed report in which he concluded that, if suitably modified and transported to within five hundred miles of Japan, sixteen North American B-25 bombers could take off from a carrier carrying two thousand pounds of bombs, hit selected targets in Japan, and continue on to China, where they would land at Chinese-controlled airfields. The secret to the operation's success would be total surprise. At stake would be the lives of thousands of men and over a dozen ships, for the carrier would have to be accompanied by a substantial task force. With the support of the Navy Chief of Staff, Admiral Ernest J. King, Duncan then approached Arnold, who responded enthusiastically to the proposal. He and King decided that Duncan would coordinate the naval side of the mission, and that Arnold would appoint someone under his command to oversee the modification of the planes and the training of the crews.[145]

A "nearly suicidal" job like this required a leader of exceptional ability and a man of demonstrated courage. The man Arnold selected to organize and lead the raid was Lieutenant-Colonel Jimmy Doolittle, after Lindbergh the most famous aviator in the United States. It was, Arnold later wrote, the "natural choice." Forty-five years old, short, wiry, and feisty, Doolittle was an independent type who loved challenges and thrived on high-risk operations. As far as he was concerned, the tougher the job, the more he liked it. For a famous aviator, Doolittle possessed unusual credentials: the winner of the 1925 Schneider Cup Trophy and numerous other races and at the same time the holder of a doctorate in Aeronautical Sciences from M.I.T., Doolittle combined technical brilliance and fearlessness with the ability to inspire others to perform dangerous and exacting tasks.[146]

Pl. 290. Jimmy Doolittle during the Second World War.

Given his new assignment by Arnold in January 1942, Doolittle quickly took charge. After assembling a group of volunteers, he oversaw their training in B-25 bombers. The pilots were taught how to make short-field takeoffs, necessary for raising their planes from the deck of a carrier in a fraction of the distance they were used to having at their disposal on the ground. The crews were trained in day and night navigation, gunnery, and precision bombing. Doolittle himself oversaw every detail of the preparation of the B-25s and their armament, including the removal of the lower gun turrets, the design of a new bombsight for use at low altitudes, the manufacture of special incendiary bombs, and the modification of the bomb racks.[147] Meanwhile, Doolittle's men could only speculate about their destination. Ignorance was the price that had to be paid for protection against a possible security leak.

In late March, Doolittle received orders to fly to Sacramento, where the B-25s would receive a final check before being loaded on the *Hornet*, a recently constructed carrier. On 2 April, he and his men boarded the huge ship and, accompanied by two cruisers, four destroyers, and a tanker, the *Hornet* steamed out of San Francisco Bay into the Pacific, its destination latitude 38 degrees north, longitude 180 degrees west, where it was scheduled to rendezvous on 13 April with another task force commanded by Admiral William F. Halsey. From there the two fleets – henceforth to be called Task Force Sixteen – would merge and proceed together to a point four hundred miles off the coast of Japan from which the B-25s would be launched.

As they made their way westward, the pilots were briefed on their objectives by the *Hornet*'s intelligence officer, Lieutenant Commander Stephen Jurika, who had served as naval attaché at the American embassy in Tokyo before the outbreak of the war. He was not encouraging about their prospects if they fell into the hands of the Japanese. For his part, Doolittle stressed repeatedly that his crews were to confine themselves to military targets and became annoyed when he heard talk of bombing the emperor's palace. "I told them about my visit to Britain in 1940 when the German Luftwaffe had bombed Buckingham Palace, a useless attack that only served to bring the British even more closely together. Attacking the Temple of Heaven, the home of Japan's venerated spiritual leader, would unite the Japanese people as much, if not more so."[148]

The first cloud over the mission appeared on 18 April when Task Force Sixteen began to sight Japanese vessels, one of which it sank. Convinced that his sixteen-ship fleet had been spotted and was at risk, Halsey ordered Doolittle to take off and wished him and his "gallant command" good luck and God bless. The *Hornet* was 220 miles to the east of the point from which the attack was supposed to be launched. The ability of the B-25s to reach their Chinese bases would now be threatened; the shift in plans would also mean that Doolittle's force would have to attack in broad daylight instead of at night. Nonetheless, despite the cramped conditions on the carrier deck and heavily cresting seas, all sixteen bombers got into the air and most succeeded in dropping their bombs on Tokyo and other Japanese cities.

Pl. 291. Doolittle is the first to take off from the *Hornet* en route to Tokyo.

The Doolittle raid is a sterling example of how an operation of limited military significance can be turned into a major public relations success. Though the bombs of Doolittle and his flyers did little damage to Tokyo, they did provide a gleam of good news at a moment when the military situation of the United States and its allies was otherwise gloomy.[149] The Americans had served notice on the Japanese that they intended to attack them at home on their islands and were capable of doing so. Roosevelt was especially delighted at the inability of the Japanese to determine where the planes had originated and, acting on a suggestion by one of his speech writers, declared that they had come from Shangri-La, the mythical land in Tibet imagined by James Hilton, in his widely read novel *Lost Horizon*.[150]

Doolittle himself was able to fly his B-25 to safety on the Chinese mainland. After bailing out, he and his crew were rescued by Chinese soldiers and decorated by the Chinese government; Doolittle then returned to the United States to a triumphant welcome. President Roosevelt personally decorated him with the Congressional Medal of Honor, and he was elevated to the rank of brigadier general, skipping the rank of colonel. At first disconsolate about the loss of his B-25 and what he perceived to be the failure of his mission – the sixteen bombers were supposed to be delivered to the Tenth Air Force in China for use against the Japanese – Doolittle did not believe that he had merited America's highest military honor and vowed that he would spend the rest of his life trying to earn it.[151]

Not all the participants in the raid were as lucky. Several were severely wounded; one was killed parachuting out over China; two drowned after their pilot ditched the plane near the China Coast, and the remaining three crew members, in addition to the crew of another B-25, fell into the hands of the Japanese. Of these three were tried, convicted, and executed by a firing squad, and a fourth died in captivity of malnutrition. Yet another crew headed northwards against orders and landed at a field near Vladivostock. To their surprise, they were treated as prisoners of war and interned in the Soviet Union for fourteen months before escaping into Iran. With the aid of Chinese guerillas and civilians, the remainder of the survivors made their way to Chinese-controlled territory and freedom.

The Doolittle raid was the sort of story made for Hollywood. It was based on real events, hence safely removed from the kind of fictional propaganda movies that film critics disdained; its protagonist was a certified American hero whose exploits went far beyond anything that Hollywood scriptwriters would dare imagine; the experience of the downed airmen could be used to drive home to the American public the virtues of the Chinese and the bestiality of the enemy they were facing in the Pacific; and there were few spectacles that gave so much satisfaction to American audiences as the sight of Tokyo in flames. The Hollywood studios were quick to rise to the challenge. RKO's *Behind the Rising Sun* (1943), Warner Brothers' *Destination Tokyo* (1943), and Twentieth-Century's *The Purple Heart* all drew on certain aspects of the Doolittle raid. It was not, however, until November 1944, when the bombing campaign against Japan was about to move into high gear, that the American moviegoing public was treated to a full-blown version of the raid's preparation, execution, and aftermath, with one of America's most admired film heroes, Spencer Tracy, in the role of Jimmy Doolittle.

Pl. 292.   Ted Lawson in pilot garb.

MGM's *Thirty Seconds Over Tokyo* was based on the bestselling book by Air Force Captain Ted Lawson and edited by Bob Considine, a well-known journalist.[152] One of the sixteen pilots who had taken off from the *Hornet*, Lawson had bombed Tokyo, then crashlanded on Nantien island along the Chinese coast in an area patrolled by the Japanese. Severely wounded, he, along with his crew, had been rescued by Chinese guerillas and transported by litter, a canal boat, and junk to a village on the Chinese mainland. Because his wounds had not been properly cared for immediately following the crash of the B-25, Lawson's left leg became infected and had to be amputated by an army doctor, a member of one of Doolittle's crews who by chance had been taken by Chinese guerrillas to the hospital where Lawson was being treated. On the brink of death from infection, Lawson somehow survived his ordeal. On 16 June, two months after taking off from the *Hornet*, he arrived at Bolling Field, outside Washington D.C., "the end of a trip nearly all the way around the world by plane, ship, stretcher, flat-boat, junk, stretcher again, sedan chair, truck, bus, station wagon, train and plane again."[153]

Thirty Seconds Over Tokyo was proudly presented by MGM as a "true story." The producer, Sam Zimbalist, went to extravagant lengths to obtain the permission of the film's protagonists to use their names. Yet in 1944 even true stories had to be adapted to Hollywood conventions and the psychological imperatives of a war that was now drawing ineluctably toward its end. Dalton Trumbo, a skilled scriptwriter and quirky figure who could have stepped out of a 1930s' screwball comedy, was given the assignment. In order to ensure the film's authenticity, he spent several days in Washington, D.C. with Lawson before writing his script. Reading it today, one would never guess that Trumbo was known at the time as the author of an antiwar novel and that he had recently joined the American Communist Party. Nor that six years later he would be in federal prison for contempt of Congress and forbidden to write for Hollywood under his own name.

Trumbo's screenplay was generally faithful to Lawson and Considine's book, but it differed from it in some significant ways. Lawson tells us that his great ambition in life was to become an aeronautical engineer. He loved airplanes and joined the Army Air Force Reserve in March 1940 because he wanted to get his "fingers into different types of planes and see how they worked. The Army had those planes."[154] After winning his wings and receiving further training at Kelly Field, he was assigned to bombers and sent to McChord Field, near Tacoma, Washington. There, in April 1941, he saw his first B-25. He couldn't wait to get a crack at it. "You just had to stand there and look at them, and breathe heavily. We were learning a lot from the war abroad. The B-25 proved that at first sight. My hands itched to unroll the blueprints on this job. The work that must have gone into it – from the bottom of its tricky tri-cycle landing gear to the tip of its double rudders high in

Pl. 293.   Dalton Trumbo with Bette Davis at the Warner Brothers studio in 1935.

Pl. 294.   The B-25 so beloved by Lawson.

back!"[155] Lawson later claimed that it was his love for the B-25 that persuaded him to try to land on a Chinese beach rather than to continue on instruments as far west as his fuel would take him. "To desert it in the air, coughing and preparing to nose over for its final plunge, was beyond endurance."[156]

For understandable reasons, Trumbo's script de-emphasized Lawson's love affair with airplanes in favor of his relationship with his wife Ellen, played sweetly and sentimentally by newcomer Phyllis Thaxter. Van Johnson brought to the part of Lawson an almost feminine sensitivity and ingratiating innocence that contrasts sharply with the prewar image of the aviator, as it had been embodied in men like Lindbergh, Mermoz, and Doolittle and portrayed on the screen by actors like Jimmy Cagney, Pat O'Brien, Clark Gable, and Cary Grant. Ellen becomes the model serviceman's wife, stoically and patriotically resigned to the possible loss of her husband's life. As she explains to the wife of another member of the mission, even if Ted fails to return, she can console herself with the thought of the baby she bears within her. "If anything happened to Ted, I'd still have the baby." Lawson's vocation for aeronautical research is transformed into a pastoral yearning for a ranch with eighty head of cattle and a little hunting. The America that Doolittle's raiders were fighting to preserve had to be represented as rural, a point that is emphasized musically by a scene in which they entertain themselves by singing "Deep in the Heart of Texas."

To judge by Lawson's own account, there is no reason to assume that he ever questioned the morality of what he was being asked to do. He notes Doolittle's order not to bomb the imperial palace, but goes on to say that Doolittle justified this prohibition on the grounds of military efficiency. "He said it wasn't worth a plane factory or a steel smelter or a tank farm."[157] Nor, apparently, was Lawson very concerned about sparing the lives of civilians. Heading southward after bombing Tokyo, Lawson saw an opportunity for his rear gunner to get some target practice. "A big yacht loomed up ahead of us and, figuring it must be armed, I told [Sergeant David] Thatcher to give it a burst. We went over it, lifted our nose to put the tail down and Thatcher sprayed its decks with our 50-calibre stingers."[158] Lamenting the reprisals the Japanese had carried out against the Chinese who had helped the Americans to escape, he suggested that they had been meant as ". . . a warning to Chinese who might be thinking of helping other American aviators who, inevitably, will land in China in the series of future raids which, I pray, will blow Japan off the map of the world."[159] Lawson concludes that Lieutenant Commander Jurika had been right when on the *Hornet* he had told Doolittle's men that the Japanese were "inhuman."[160]

By contrast, Trumbo evidently felt the need to probe more deeply into the psychology of Doolittle and his raiders. It perhaps struck him as odd that they would not be troubled by the inevitable civilian casualties their bombing would entail. To explain the frame of mind in which they approached their mission, he invented a scene in which Doolittle

Pl. 295. Doolittle, played by Spencer Tracy, addresses his pilots aboard the *Hornet*.

sternly addressed his men on the nature of their targets. Trumbo has Doolittle stress that they were to bomb military objectives and nothing else. The lines he inserted into his script follow closely Army Air Force doctrine of the time and the historical record, as we know it.[161] But in Trumbo's screenplay, Doolittle goes on to concede that even military targets, like aircraft factories, have civilian workers, who may fall victims to their bombs. "If you have any moral feelings about this necessary killing, you should drop out. No one will blame you." The operative adjective here is "necessary"; Douhet himself would not have put it differently. Civilians would have to die so the war could be brought to a speedier end. In the long run, bombing was a more humane form of warfare – so long as it was properly done and was precise.

Trumbo added another scene that did not appear in the book. The night before the planes take off, Lawson and his friend Bob Gray (played by Robert Mitchum in his first movie role) have a conversation in which their attitude toward the people they are about to bomb arises. Lawson remembers that his mother once had a Jap gardener. "He seemed like a nice little guy." Gray continues: "I don't hate the Japs *yet* [my italics. but emphasized by Mitcham]. It's a funny thing. I don't like them. I don't hate them." Lawson agrees: "I guess I don't either. You get kind of mixed up. It's hard to figure. I don't pretend to like the idea of dropping a ton of explosives on someone. But if we don't, they'll be dropping bombs on Ellen." The effect of this line is heightened by the fact that it is pronounced by Van Johnson, whose all-American looks and air of innocence guarantee its sincerity. We know that this clean-cut young man could never do anything intentionally evil to anyone.[162] By this down-to-earth representation of what the best of Americans are fighting for, an offensive operation of dubious military value is transformed into a defensive action. If we don't do it to them, they'll do it to us – or worse, to our women. And, besides, they started it with the treacherous and dirty attack on Pearl Harbor. They wanted the war; now they would get it.[163]

The significance of the Doolittle raid in April 1942, Lawson thought in retrospect, was that it gave the American people a "lift" and "made them sure that we could go to work on the Japs, no matter how far away they were."[164] A feeling of invulnerability in Japan had turned to fear.[165] This was what made the raid worthwhile, despite the deaths of six men, the internment of ten others, the loss of sixteen airplanes, untold suffering and carnage on the Chinese mainland, several disabling injuries, and (in Lawson's case) an amputated leg.

Dalton Trumbo's script made no attempt to engage these issues. Its purpose was to entertain a mass audience, while remaining as faithful as Hollywood conventions permitted to

Lawson's story, and in these two respects it was judged to have succeeded brilliantly. Bosley Crowther of the *New York Times* thought that "as the recreated picture of one of the boldest blows in this war and as a drama of personal heroism, it is nigh the best yet made in Hollywood."[166] He was so impressed with its "magnificent integrity and dramatic eloquence" that he devoted another article to it a week later, defending the romance between Van Johnson and Phyllis Thaxter, scarcely mentioned in the book, on the grounds that it made all the more vivid and inspiring Lawson's courage and sacrifice.[167]

Even critics with reservations about war movies praised *Thirty Seconds Over Tokyo* for its lack of pretentiousness, its "dogged sincerity," and "documentary realism."[168] The gripping re-creation of the hedge-hopping flight over Japan and the bombing of Tokyo was "one of the outstanding thrills of cinema history."[169] MGM's technicians had "reproduced the face of Tokyo and the sight and sounds of the five-hundred-pound bombs striking the city from a plane that you see at the same time, with its bomb-bay doors ajar and its fuselage shaking from the concussion." There had been "few better artificial representations of air war, or any kind of war, than this."[170]

The extent to which Douhettian values had triumphed and been accepted by the American public as natural and even self-evident seven years after Guernica was revealed by the fact that no critic seemed troubled by the notion of dropping five-hundred-pound incendiary bombs on Tokyo or questioned the ability of American bombing crews to hit military targets with precision while skimming over the city at a speed of three hundred miles an hour. The "necessary killing" of civilians entailed in a serious bombing campaign, such as the one now under way, in Japan, was generally accepted. For those with doubts or "moral feelings" about civilian deaths, *Thirty Seconds Over Tokyo* enjoined them to toughen themselves, as Spencer Tracy/Jimmy Doolittle had, and to accept the human costs of war. As Spencer Tracy reminded his men repeatedly, those who felt uncomfortable or squeamish had the right to "drop out." America, after all, was a democracy and hence incapable of forcing its citizens to sacrifice themselves for the good of the state.

But the assurance that "No one will blame you" was of course absurd, and every member of the audience who watched this film in 1944–5 – including the seven-year-old I was – knew it. This would have been tantamount to dropping out of the national consensus: there were few Americans in 1944 who did not believe that doing anything necessary to win the war was justified.

The point was made even more starkly in another Doolittle raid film that had been released in February 1944. *The Purple Heart*, said to have been written by its producer Darryl Zanuck, complemented Lawson's story in that it sought to reconstruct imaginatively the "fate of the heroic American aviators forced to earth in the bombing of Tokyo."[171] Rather than reveal any details about the raid that might be of use to the Japanese, eight captured airmen endure torture and calmly embrace their death before a military court in Japan while singing defiantly "Mine eyes have seen the glory of the coming of the Lord." Before being marched off to a military prison to await their execution, Captain Ross, played by Dana Andrews, addresses the presiding judge:

> It's true we Americans don't know very much about you Japanese, and never did – and now I realize you know even less about us. You can kill us – all of us, or part of us. But, if you think that's going to put the fear of God into the United States of America and stop them from sending other fliers to bomb you, you're wrong – dead wrong. They'll blacken your skies and burn your cities to the ground and make you get down on your knees and beg for mercy. This is your war – you wanted it – you asked for it. And now you're going to get it – and it won't be finished until your dirty little empire is wiped off the face of the earth![172]

A little over a year after *The Purple Heart* was released, an American armada of three hundred and thirty-four B-29s dropped two thousand tons of bombs, in great part incendiaries and napalm canisters, on a twelve-square-mile area of central Tokyo where population density averaged a hundred and thirty-five thousand persons per square mile. It was the most destructive air raid in history, greater in its effects even than the later atomic bomb attacks against Hiroshima and Nagasaki. Between ninety and a hundred thousand people died; a quarter of the buildings in Tokyo were destroyed; over a million people lost their homes; almost sixteen square miles of the city were reduced to cinders.[173] Because the Akukaze or "Red Wind" was blowing that night, a tidal wave of fire swept across the city that asphyxiated people before they could be incinerated and sucked people out of canals in which they had taken refuge.[174] Robert Morgan, pilot of the *Memphis Belle*, participated in that raid. His B-29, the *Dauntless Dotti*, was flying at seven thousand five hundred feet. He remembered the updrafts bringing with them "the smell of roasting human flesh," a sickening odor that he would never be able to get completely out of his nostrils.[175] Though Tokyo had not been wiped off the face of the earth, it had been effectively burnt to the ground. During the months to come, other Japanese cities would suffer the same destiny.

★   ★   ★

While MGM was re-creating the bombing of Tokyo and imagining its future destruction, the Allied air forces and the Luftwaffe were staging a spectacle over Europe that any Hollywood producer would have envied. Every day and every night when weather permitted, Allied bombers swarmed through the skies over Germany and occupied Europe in tight formation, their bomb bays bursting with high explosives and incendiary shells. Deep in bunkers familiarly called "battle opera houses," Luftwaffe personnel of both sexes charted the progress of the Allied planes on a huge panel of frosted glass, while from the box before the stage Luftwaffe officers dispatched fighters to intercept them.[176] As the bombers neared their targets, searchlights lit up the heavens and hundreds of flak batteries provided a musical accompaniment to this deadly aerial ballet. On a given day or night, dozens of these metallic monsters might plummet flaming through the sky, as a few lucky men managed to escape and leaped into the void, entrusting themselves to parachutes and the unknown attitudes of people on the ground whom they had been sent to kill. In their wake, the bombers that got through left fire storms, collapsed buildings, rubble, smoldering ash, and heaps of cremated corpses. No prewar novelist, not even H. G. Wells at his most apocalyptic, had come close to imagining the extent and frequency of destruction to which the inhabitants of German cities were becoming accustomed in 1944.[177]

The men who flew these raids passed through a sea of fire, flame, phosphorus, and smoke that far surpassed Dante's most inspired imaginings of hell, not knowing whether they would ever emerge from the experience alive. They watched helplessly as the flak burst around their planes; some were mesmerized by the sight even as they quivered with fear and prepared to die. A British copilot recalled his emotions while flying through a flak barrage over Kiel in the winter of 1940.

Almost instantaneously black puffs of smoke materialized around us. Plainly visible, like clenched fists against the faint light of the night sky, they crowded in upon the aeroplane from all the sides. I had just time to think that this was how the hero comes in to bomb on the films, before fear broke its dams and swept over me in an almost irresistible flood. Concentrating all my energies, I forced myself to sit motionless in my seat next to the

Pl. 296.   By 1944 the
Germans had assembled 55,000
of these deadly 88-millimeter
anti-aircraft guns to ward off
Allied bombers. They set up a
wall of fire in the sky which
bombers had no choice but to
traverse if they persevered in
reaching their targets.

Pl. 297.   Flares and flack light
up the Berlin sky in January
1945, as Allied bombers begin
their bombing runs.

Pl. 298.   Corpses in Dresden
after the firebombing of the
city in February 1945.

pilot, fighting back an insane impulse to run, despite the fact that in an aircraft you cannot run because there is nowhere you can run to, unless you decide to take it with you.
As the gunfire got heavier, light flak joined in and I gazed fascinated, as if at a deadly
snake, when a stream of incendiary shells came up in a lazy red arch which rapidly
increased speed as it got nearer and at last flashed past a few inches above the wing on
my side, two feet from the window. As the shells went by, they seemed to be deflected
by the air flow over the wing and to curve round it, describing a fiery red line round its
upper contour. By now the aircraft was becoming filled with the fumes of cordite from
the bursting flak shells. It seemed each second must be our last, and that we must surely disintegrate in a blinding flash at any moment, or come tumbling down flaming from
a direct hit. We sat the aircraft in that box barrage for ten minutes, and did not get out
of it until we had flown out of range.[178]

By any imaginable standard, these men displayed extraordinary courage. Anyone who
reads their story must wonder what he or she would have done in their place. Yet for all
their heroism, the exploits of the bombing crews of the Second World War failed to give
rise to the kind of myth that developed around the aces of the First World War. Everyone
knows of Manfred von Richthofen, but who remembers his equivalents among the
bomber pilots?

In Britain, to be sure, there are Guy Gibson and Leonard Cheshire, but they achieved
celebrity for engaging in operations quite untypical of the war that most bomber crews
knew: in Gibson's case, because of the high-risk dam-bursting raid in the Ruhr that he led

in 1944; in the case of Cheshire, who inherited Gibson's elite 617 Squadron, because of his success in the precision bombing of French factories and German industrial targets by low-level marking, a practice at odds with the approach of Harris and his closest advisers.[179] With the years, even Gibson and Cheshire have come to fade in our collective memory. Paul Tibbets, the commander of the plane that dropped the first atomic bomb and considered by many to be the greatest American bombing pilot of the war, remains a darkly ambiguous figure. Why did the bombing war fail to leave behind a more enduring myth?

True, the memory of swarms of heavy bombers, "black as vermin . . . carrying harm in their wombs that ache to be rid of death," lacked chivalry and romance.[180] It was not an exception to the mechanized slaughter on the ground, as had appeared to be the case with the air war between 1914 and 1918, but its ultimate exacerbation. Those bombed responded angrily. They could not understand the rationale behind the destruction, which often appeared from the perspective of the ground to be willfully haphazard, deliberately cruel, and counterproductive.[181] Downed airmen were sometimes shot or beaten to death by enraged civilians who came across them as they were descending or after they reached the ground.[182]

For most members of the bombing crews, fear predominated over fun and exhilaration. Their goal was to complete their missions and get home in one piece. The experience of flight in a bomber, while exciting, was also oppressive. Bomber crews were incarcerated in the equivalent of a narrow box car rather than flying in an open biplane with a silk scarf flapping romantically around their necks and the rushing wind giving them a sense of liberation from the earth. Instead the dominant feeling was one of no possible escape from the fiery fate that struck haphazardly and that no amount of skill could avoid.

Pl. 299.   British and American bombers over Hamburg in July 1943. On 29 July 1943, Ernst Jünger recorded in his diary: "Frightening news from Hamburg and Hanover. During the phosphorous bomb attacks, the asphalt began to burn so that persons fleeing [the bombing] sank into it and were carbonized."

Pl. 300. Guy Gibson in flying gear.

Pl. 301. Leonard Cheshire and his wife Constance in September 1944.

Pl. 302. Paul Tibbets (right) salutes after being decorated by General Spaatz.

Pl. 303. A Vichy poster denouncing the murder of innocent French children by Roosevelt's bombers.

Aircrews also suffered from a further disadvantage when compared with First World War pursuit pilots. Subject to a factory-like discipline, they were technicians, the prototypical figures of a democratic and industrial war. The qualities demanded of them did not easily blend with traditional concepts of heroism.[183] Their training was long; the skills required of them exacting; their role in the airplane highly specialized; their reliance upon one another total. The mistake of one could lead to the death of all. They flew in huge formations and obeyed commands issued by superiors whom they seldom, if ever, saw. Members of an immense force, they were easily replaceable, like the spare parts of the airplanes they flew. The Futurist Marinetti, who lived to suffer their attacks in Milan, should have approved.[184] This was the kind of truly mechanized war that he had imagined before 1914.

Yet perhaps the real reason why no lasting myth of the bomber could take hold was the realization, the full implications of which did not become clear until after the war had ended, that the primary job of the bombing crews was not to engage the enemy in combat – even though surviving the attack of flak batteries on the ground and fighters in the air was a prerequisite to performing their mission – but rather to drop tons of high explosives and incendiary shells on cities where they were bound to kill civilians, as it turned out principally women and children. Certainly, this did not disturb the aircrews during the war itself; they understandably were too concerned with their own survival to worry about

266

Pl. 304. Laura Knight's *Take Off* shows the cramped quarters endured by a bombing crew during hours of flight.

Pl. 305. The eight-man crew of a British Stirling bomber and the small army of supporting ground personnel needed to keep it flying.

their victims and were almost universally convinced of the justice of their cause.[185] But it did somehow tarnish retrospectively the image of these men for the generations who came after theirs and had to contemplate the death and destruction they had wrought. The image the bombers left behind was thus ambiguous: they were both self-sacrificing saviors and angels of death. With time, the second image has come to cloud, if not efface, the first.

There were, of course, marked differences in the way the belligerent countries have remembered the bombing. During and immediately after the war, many Germans, especially those with religious inclinations, may have regarded the bombing of German cities as a form of divine retribution for German crimes against humanity.[186] Hans Carossa captured these feelings in verse inspired by an incendiary raid on Munich in September 1944:

> In ruthlessness we sought the light,
> Which should illuminate our path,
> And we wondered why the sky grew darker still.
> It was we ourselves who summoned the gray choir of furies,
> Which now hunt through the heavens of our homeland,
> Spreading terror: city after city falling victim.[187]

With time, some German historians came to deny that Germany had initiated the terror bombing of civilians. At the same time, they put the blame on Hitler and Göring for not having provided them with a fleet of effective strategic bombers capable of knocking England out of the war. It was not the Luftwaffe that had failed, they argued, but its Nazi leadership.[188] Not until 2002 would a comprehensive history of the bombing war against Germany be written by a German; upon appearing, it would become a bestseller, suggesting that this was a story that the Germans were now prepared to confront.[189]

The British preferred to concentrate on the glamour and heroism of the fighter pilots who had saved them from the German onslaught in 1940. The television mini-series the BBC has mounted about the air war have dealt with Fighter Command and the tragic life

Pl. 306. Paul Nash's painting, *The Battle of Britain*. In his 1942 article, "The Personality of Planes," Nash wrote: "I first became interested in them pictorially when I realized the machines were the real protagonists. Although vast human forces were involved, their operations were directed mechanically, and they themselves assumed increasingly a mechanical appearance. Pictorially, they seemed to be unimportant compared with the personality of the machines they employed as weapons, for, so powerful were these agents of war, that once set in motion they soon dominated the immense stage."

Pl. 307. Eric Kennington's 1943 portrait of Richard Hillary.

Pl. 308. Sir Arthur Harris and his family leave England after the war.

of Richard Hillary, whose Oxford education, disfiguring burns suffered while flying a Spitfire, and complicated personality make him a more attractive topic for dramatization than the more ordinary blokes who flew Lancasters over Germany. The one exception is Guy Gibson whose extraordinary fame guaranteed the popular success of his posthumous memoir *Enemy Coast Ahead* and the book and the 1954 film, titled *The Dam Busters*, that his exploits inspired.[190] Two recent biographers acknowledge that the story of the breaching of the Ruhr dams by Gibson and his 617 squadron in May 1944 has ". . . joined that group of historically based tales – like King Arthur, or Robin Hood – which defy all efforts at scholarly revision."[191]

Sir Arthur Harris has fared much less well than Gibson. Harris was shocked when, in his speech of 13 May 1945, Churchill neglected to mention the contribution of Bomber Command to the Allied victory. The sense of injury was then further deepened when the British government declined to reward Harris's aircrews with a campaign medal to commemorate their services and sacrifices. Harris went into a self-imposed exile in South Africa without the peerage that would have seemed to be his due and that the outgoing Churchill had recommended.[192] The British happily forgot him and the destruction he had wrought, symbolized by the February 1945 raid on Dresden that remains difficult to justify on purely military grounds, except perhaps by the desire of Churchill to impress Stalin with the efforts the British were making to bring the war to a speedy close. Noting that "by the spring of 1944 it was quite clear that Harris's area bombing offensive had failed to bring Germany even within distant sight of defeat," Max Hastings concluded in his 1979 history of Bomber Command that "The obliteration of Germany's cities in the spring of 1945, when all possible strategic justification had vanished, is a lasting blot on the Allied conduct of the war and on the judgement of senior Allied airmen."[193]

There are certainly many who dissent from this view and their arguments are persuasive; but Harris remains a controversial figure whose obsession with the bombing of German

Pl. 309.   The statue of Harris
in front of St. Clement Danes
Church in London.

civilians has clouded his unquestionable contribution to the winning of the war.[194] The decision of the Bomber Association to erect a statue to Harris beside St. Clement Danes church in London's Strand provoked sharp criticism in the British press, letters of protest from the mayors of Dresden and Cologne, and an angry demonstration when it was unveiled in May 1992, almost a half century after Harris had relinquished his command.[195] In the mind of many, Harris's name continues to suggest those "bombing zealots" whose determination to raze Germany's cities to the ground was "a prescription for massacre, nothing more nor less."[196] During the three decades he lived after the end of the war, Harris never faltered in his belief that Bomber Command had failed to receive the recognition it deserved for what he considered to be its decisive role in the defeat of Germany. Today we know to what lengths Harris and other leaders of Bomber Command went to prevent the publication of the British government's official history of the strategic air offensive against Germany.[197] Ironically, that history concludes that, despite early failures, Bomber Command made a substantial contribution to the Allies' victory. For Harris, this was insufficient.[198]

The American case is somewhat more complicated. Again Hollywood is a useful, if not infallible, guide to American attitudes. During the war, bomber movies had invariably dealt with Japan. Only after the war did Hollywood take up the theme of the extensive and costly bombing campaign waged against Germany by the British-based Eighth Air Force. When it did, the emphasis was on the tremendous psychological burden carried by American group commanders. Hollywood's most successful postwar Eighth Air Force movie was, in fact, an adaptation of the plot of Howard Hawks and John Monk Saunders's *Dawn Patrol* with a psychological twist inconceivable in 1930. In *Twelve O'Clock High*, released in 1949 by Twentieth-Century Fox, General Frank Savage (Gregory Peck) replaces his friend Colonel Keith Davenport (Gary Merrill) as Commanding Officer of the 918th Bomb Group and tries to restore the group's morale, undermined by the high losses they have been suffering in daylight bombing raids. But General Savage is, in turn, traumatized by the crews who fail to return and has a nervous breakdown, which leads to his own replacement.

The film's co-scriptwriter, Colonel Beirne Lay, knew the bombing war at first hand. He had participated in the devastating Regensburg raid of 17 August 1943, when 24 of 146 B-17s had failed to return to their bases. The report he wrote for his commander on 25 August 1943 captures the sense of helplessness and terror that bomber crews experienced when attacked by German fighters:

A shining silver object sailed past over our right wing. I recognized it as a main exit door. Seconds later, a dark object came hurtling through the formation, barely missing several props. It was a man, clasping his knees to his head, revolving like a diver in a triple somersault. I didn't see his chute open.

A B-17 turned gradually out of the formation to the right, maintaining altitude. In a split second, the B-17 completely disappeared in a brilliant explosion from which the only remains were four balls of fire, the fuel tanks, which were quickly consumed as they fell earthward.

Our airplane was endangered by various debris. Emergency hatches, exit doors, prematurely opened parachutes, bodies, and assorted fragments of B-17's and Hun fighters breezed past us in the slip-stream.

I watched two fighters explode not far beneath, disappearing in sheets of orange flame, B-17's dropping out in every state of distress, from engines on fire to control surfaces shot away, friendly and enemy parachutes floating down, and, on the green carpet far behind us, numerous funeral pyres of smoke from fallen fighters marking our trail.[199]

Lay and his cowriter Sy Bartlett, who had also been with the Eighth Air Force, were able to convey the unbearable emotional pressure that experiences like these put on the crew

Pl. 310. General Frank Savage (Gregory Peck) cracks under the pressure of sending his crews to die in *Twelve O'Clock High*.

members who survived them. But by placing its emphasis on the men who commanded and the terrible strain they underwent, *Twelve O'Clock High* fails to engage the most disturbing questions posed by the bombing campaign, as have the less distinguished Second World War bombing films that followed it.[200] The message the film sends is that the bombing war must go on, even if the individuals who wage it falter and fall by the wayside. Once set in motion, the machine of war cannot be stopped. The atmosphere of nostalgia for these awful yet thrilling days, evoked at the beginning of the film when Major Harvey Stovall (played by Dean Jagger) decides to revisit the 918th's old base while on a trip to London, precludes any examination of the meaning of the raids which the Davenports and the Savages are organizing and leading. The past is now past and can be revisited only in fond memory; it cannot be interrogated.

In retrospect, what seems curious is how difficult Americans have found it to rethink the bombing war. By this, I do not mean to suggest that no one made the case in favor of or against strategic bombing. This is obviously not true. Anyone could read for themselves the ten-volume *United States Strategic Bombing Survey*, which concluded that bombing had failed to halt the growth of German industrial production; or the four volumes of the British study on the effectiveness of Bomber Command's operations, which praised Bomber Command's "decisive" contribution to victory but acknowledged somewhat cryptically that it had been "long delayed."[201] Still, despite the thousands of pages written on the topic, the debate was never truly joined. The opponents of strategic bombing claim that the slaughter of civilians failed to halt German military production or force the German government to lay down its arms. Its proponents respond that in a multitude of ways the bombing campaign played an invaluable role in winning the war. Since both camps are right, neither has felt the need to engage seriously the arguments of its adversary. The shrill reaction to the 1994 attempt to mount an exhibit at the National Air and Space Museum on the dropping of the atomic bombs on Hiroshima and Nagasaki only shows that bombing in the Second World War is an issue that Americans are reluctant to face, not to mention debate. Our national dialogue on this question continues to be one of the deaf, *un dialogue des sourds*.

Pl. 311.   A magazine cover from 1940, depicting British bombers attacking German factories.

Pl. 312.   This drawing by A. Leydenfrost that appeared on the cover of *Life* on 20 August 1945 depicts the destruction of Hiroshima, as the Enola Gay flies off into the distance. The scene is portrayed from such a distance that one could easily suppose that no human beings were present when the city was incinerated.

Perhaps this is because we are hesitant to admit that the bombing campaigns against Germany and Japan were conducted with such ferocity, at the cost of millions of civilian lives, not because they could be counted upon to be militarily decisive – until late in the war no one could know that this would be the case, and in fact the contribution of bombing to victory is still debated by historians today – but because they were popular with the public and politically expedient. The news of bombing raids raised the morale of the home front by demonstrating that "we were carrying the war into the heart of the enemy," and incidentally also made the air force case for producing more bombers and training more crews.[202] Civilian casualties could easily be justified by the unknown number of Allied lives that would be saved by shortening the conflict; and there was the deep satisfaction that came at the thought that the enemy was paying dearly for its evil deeds. Moreover, bombing shifted the emphasis from the expenditure of manpower to capital investment and advanced technology, areas in which the United States was clearly dominant over its adversaries.[203] Thus *Time* magazine greeted the March 1945 fire raid on Tokyo as a "dream come true," which showed that "properly kindled, Japanese cities will burn like autumn leaves"; and 85 percent of Americans (and 72 percent of Britons) polled in August 1945 approved of the use of atomic bombs against Japan.[204] Douhet, who was so wrong in his assessment of the ability of civilians to withstand protracted bombing, proved to be correct in his paradoxical prediction, made in the direct aftermath of the massive carnage of the Great War, that nations would use the most destructive of weapons once they possessed them on the humanitarian grounds that their employment would save lives and shorten the agony of war.[205]

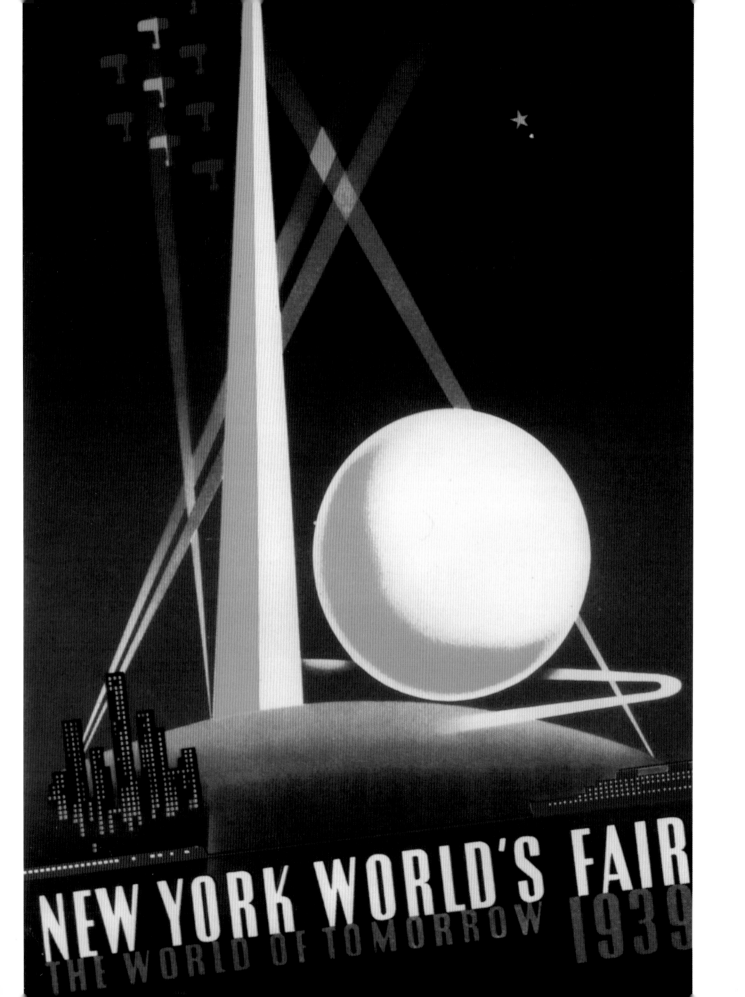

6
A New Civilization

The airplane, advance guard of the conquering armies of the New Age, the airplane arouses our energies and our faith.

Le Corbusier, 1935[1]

How quickly has flight, this age-old and precious dream, lost every charm, lost every meaning, lost its soul. Thus one after another of our dreams are realized to death. Can you have a new dream?

Elias Canetti, 1942[2]

IN 1928 Ernst Jünger, one of the leading spokesmen for the German Radical Right and an acclaimed portrayer of the war experience, wrote the preface to a collaborative and densely illustrated book entitled *Luftfahrt ist not!* (Flight Is Necessary). As might be expected from a relentless critic of the Weimar Republic and a highly visible proponent of nationalist revival, Jünger gave his argument a strongly political twist. The "free and hard life" of Germany's young glider pilots was, he said, the best refutation of the claim, made by some, that our race is declining. They were a symbol of the best and most valuable resources that Germany possessed. Their "soaring flights" staked out the precincts of "a magical world." At a time when it appeared questionable whether Germany still belonged to the ranks of the Great Powers, "what are armies and fleets against the secret conviction that a people possesses of its calling?"[3]

For some time, Jünger had proposed a new synthesis of men and machines, based on the interpretation he had developed of his experience on the battlefields of the Western Front. His generation, he said, had been the first to reconcile itself to the machine and to grasp its aesthetic possibilities. It was the war experience that had made it possible for them to escape from "that gray, frightening world of utilitarianism and from that Manchester landscape in which coal dust veils all values, that same world that drove men with diabolical logic into the hell of the battlefields of the Great War. What would these iron weapons with which we fought have been if our nerves had not been intertwined with them and if our blood didn't flow around every axle?"[4] Anyone who loved life in all its fullness and power could not be indifferent to the beauty of the machine. Central to Jünger's thought was the idea that the machine could not be reduced to a means of production whose only purpose was the satisfaction of our miserable material necessities.

Pl. 313. Ascending airplanes lead the way into "the world of tomorrow" in Joseph Binder's prize-winning poster for the 1939–1940 New York World's Fair.

Pl. 314. Ernst Jünger in 1918, after receiving Germany's highest military decoration, Pour le mérite.

277

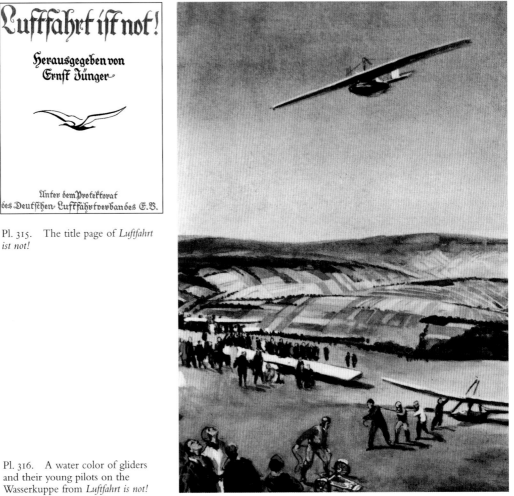

Pl. 315. The title page of *Luftfahrt ist not!*

Pl. 316. A water color of gliders and their young pilots on the Wasserkuppe from *Luftfahrt is not!*

Rather, it ought to bestow on us "higher and deeper satisfaction." The machine was a means of reaching those "higher and deeper goals" that Nietzsche had placed above the Darwinian struggle for existence as a motive for human life and effort.[5]

In his foreword to *Luftfahrt ist not!*, Jünger applies this idea to aviation. Flight was not merely useful; it was necessary. If one wanted to understand it, one had to free oneself from the misconception that it could be grasped exclusively in terms of technological progress, improvements in transportation, or an enhancement of our economic life. To be sure, it was all these things – *also*; but its essence and its meaning lay elsewhere. Flight was more than an activity aimed at practical or economically motivated results. It was "the living expression of a powerful life feeling [*Lebensgefühl*], a moral endeavor, to which the question of utility is unconditionally subordinated, and next to which it plays a minor role." Whether flight is profitable, he concluded, is immaterial to those who practice it. Jünger had no doubt that the "flying man" was "the sharpest manifestation" of a new model of male humanity. He represents a new type, one that was already foreshadowed on the battlefields of the First World War.[6]

When Jünger wrote these lines about the aviator as an exemplar for his time, he was already a highly controversial figure; he would remain so to the end of his long life. Yet whatever one thinks about Jünger's political agenda and his hopes for a "flying generation" of Germans that would express "the best forces that live in the *Volk*," it is hard to deny the truth of Jünger's central theme: that aviation during the period following the First World

War cannot be understood solely in terms of technological innovations or economic considerations. Building on Jünger's argument but broadening it, I should like to explore some of the meanings that flight had for the peoples of the West during the years between 1920 and 1950.

★   ★   ★

Accustomed as we are to considering all parts of the globe within our reach by air, we might think that one of the primary attractions of flight in this period was its ability to achieve great speed and hence to diminish the importance of distance. In making this assumption, we would be right. Before 1914, the Futurist Marinetti had welcomed the coming of the airplane because it promised to eliminate the importance of space and time as limitations on human existence. By shortening the time required to traverse long distances, Marinetti thought, the airplane would have the effect of lengthening the life span, if not in quantitative certainly in qualitative terms. Air travel held special promise for Europeans living in far-flung corners of their country's empire. Air races, like the Schneider Cup, the Bendix Cup, and the Powder Puff Derby, attracted large audiences and were followed and appreciated by millions through newpapers, radio, and newsreels. The airplane could easily be conceived within the framework of a twentieth-century cult of speed that prized the increased velocities of automobiles, trains, motorboats, and steamships.[7] Aviators were prominent participants in the pursuit of records that seems, in retrospect, such an important feature of life during the 1920s. Increased speed made possible longer nonstop flights to destinations that had formerly been beyond reach.[8] The prospect of faster communication among peoples was the precondition for the existence of all airlines, including Aéropostale.

Yet to recognize that speed was the rationale of aviation's existence is only to scratch the surface of its mystique. To begin with, what was distinctive about flight during the 1920s was not the rapidity with which it could transport people from one place to another. Weather and night remained daunting and sometimes insuperable obstacles. Alan Cobham defeated a steamship captain by only two days on his return from his record-breaking flight to Cape Town in 1925.[9] The defeat of distance was a promise and a challenge rather than a reality for aviators at this time. In both Europe and the United States, traveling by train was a surer way of arriving at one's destination on time.[10] Transoceanic flight with passengers in airplanes became practicable only in the late 1930s, but the number of people who availed themselves of this expensive and potentially dangerous option remained extremely limited.

No, I would argue that the charm of flight lay not in its speed but in the ability of aircraft to transport people to a realm fundamentally different from the one in which they lived. For those who practiced it as well as those who followed it from the ground, flight was regarded as one of the greatest adventures within the grasp of human beings. Those who flew considered themselves privileged beings. In *L'Espace*, Pierre Weiss gave voice to a feeling that most aviators had, even if they would have been unable or reluctant to express it in the lyrical terms that Weiss chose. "To have space as a field for work, to have in exchange for our pains its delights. To fight in space for a goal that is not materialistic. Let's thank our lucky stars [*Mesurons bien notre bonheur*]."[11]

Weiss wrote in 1929 when the "tide" of aviation had yet to "ebb."[12] Looking back at her career over four decades later, the record-breaking aviatrix Louise Thaden found herself groping for words to convey her feelings about what it was like to fly in the late 1920s and early 1930s. She begins by distinguishing between flying and flight. Flying was "factual, often sensuous, tangible. At its highest peaks we feel truly 'masters of our fate, captains of our destiny.'" By contrast, flight was "the essence of the spirit. It nutures the soul. It is awesome. Often ethereal. Glorious. Emotionally wondrous and all-pervading. Intangible." But Thaden quickly added that flying and flight were no longer synonymous in the way they had been when she had first taken to the air in the late 1920s. In her view, that era had ended for the civilian pilot with the entry of the United States into the Second World War. "We knew the ecstasy of discovery. Adventure – a part of every flight – was spine-tingling, inspiring."[13] If the loss of a flight certificate was tantamount to a death sentence, as it was represented in so many Hollywood movies of the 1930s, it was because it closed off access to a magical world of unlimited and unpredictable adventure.

The adventure of flight could be experienced in different forms. Flight brought with it an extraordinary sense of freedom, an awareness of having broken through boundaries, a sense of escape and liberation from earthbound existence, the exhilaration that comes with transgression, a passport to a fairy-tale world not accessible to other human beings, and sometimes a feeling of quasi-divinity.

Viewed from the ground, aviators seemed to be free of earthly constraints. Seeing his first airplane while riding horseback in the country near Balbec, its sparkling metallic wings a mere fifty meters above his head, the narrator of Proust's novel is reduced to tears. "I was as moved as a Greek would be who saw for the first time a demi-god . . . The aviator seemed to hesitate in choosing his way; I felt there lay open before him – before me, if habit had not held me prisoner – all the routes of space, of life; he flew away, glided for a few instants above the sea, then brusquely making his decision, seeming to surrender to an attraction the opposite of that of gravity, as if returning to his homeland, with a light movement of his golden wings, he ascended straight up toward the sky."[14]

Aviators themselves experienced such feelings, though few sought to express them with such elevated and poetic prose. Explaining why he had abandoned his engineering courses at the University of Wisconsin at Madison in order to pursue pilot training in the early 1920s, Lindbergh wrote matter-of-factly: "The life of an aviator seemed to me ideal. It involved skill. It commanded adventure . . . I was glad that I had failed my college courses. Mechanical engineers were fettered to factories and drafting boards, while pilots had the freedom of wind in the expanse of sky. I could spiral the desolation of a mountain peak, explore caverns of a cloud, or land on a city's flying field and convince others of aviation's future. There were times in an airplane when it seemed I had partially escaped mortality, to look down on earth like a god."[15] His wife, Anne Morrow Lindbergh, also assigns such feelings to Eve, her fictional alter ego in the novella she published in 1945 called *The Steep Ascent*. Flying over the Alps with her aviator husband, she thinks: "With such height one was free, all-powerful, all-seeing. One felt oneself a god."[16]

Meditating on the transformation that flight brought about in the men who practiced it, the French aviator and writer Jules Roy was careful to avoid the heresy of divinity, but claimed that takeoff from the ground produced a state of grace that conferred on the pilot "a sort of supernatural power" because of the superiority he felt to those men who remained "stuck like an insect to the earth's bark."[17] The airplane, he said, had not changed man's nature but had returned him to a simpler life of mind and muscle. The aviator "sees clearly the essential, he discovers his lost treasure. His eyes are turned toward the sky, towards its snares and its promises, in the contemplation of a purified world. He looks endlessly upwards; his slave's look having become the look of a king."[18]

Such sentiments, and even the language in which they are expressed with its references to the "essential" seen by aviators and the "purified world" they contemplate, are reminiscent of Saint-Exupéry's *Terre des hommes*, a book Roy knew and admired. The disdain Roy feels for those who remain stuck to earth's bark like "insects" echoes D'Annunzio and pre-1914 Futurist poetry. One naturally approaches with caution what appears to be a literary and highly ideological filtering of the aviation experience. But one should not forget that while flying in the 1920s and 1930s, aviators had access to a realm that still remained largely unregulated. The freedom of flight was real. As Louise Thaden, who cannot be accused of literary pretensions, remembered: "We tightened the seat belt in the open cockpit and, in the doing, buckled on the wings of flight. Unshackled. Unfettered. Free to soar as never bird had soared, pinioned only by the motor's throaty roar, its glad prisoner of sound – drinking deeply of the cool, clear air, alone in an untrammeled sky."[19] Aside from its emphasis on the freedom and the "untrammeled sky," perhaps what we should retain from this recollection is the total immersion in the "throaty roar" of the engine that the pilots of this era experienced. They were the "glad prisoners" of deafening sound.

★   ★   ★

One of the words that appear most frequently in the writings of aviators and their passengers in this period when describing the charms of flight is that of escape. The first lines of John Gillespie Magee's poem *High Flight* remains the best-known expression of this feeling:

> Oh! I have slipped the surly bonds of earth
> And danced the skies on laughter-silvered wings;
> Sunward I've climbed and joined the tumbling mirth
> Of sun-split clouds – and done a hundred things
> You have not dreamed of – wheeled and soared and swung
> High in the sunlight silence. Hov'ring there,
> I've chased the shouting wind along and flung
> My eager craft through footless halls of air.[20]

Pl. 317.   Beryl Markham shortly after she learned how to fly in 1931.

Countless variations on this theme can be found throughout the literature on aviation. Remembering her mood after taking off from England on her transatlantic flight in September 1936 the aviatrix Beryl Markham wrote: "I feel the security of solitude, the exhilaration of escape. So long as I can see the lights and imagine the people walking under them, I feel selfishly triumphant, as if I have eluded care and left even the small sorrow of rain in other hands." Yet aviators were intensely aware that their escape from the pettiness of earthly concerns was temporary. "Flight," Markham wrote with a touch of sadness, "is but momentary escape from the eternal custody of earth."[21]

The escape made possible by flight is often conceived, as it was by Mermoz and Saint-Exupéry, in terms of a distinction between the sordidness and materialism of everyday earthly life and the purity and idealism of the sky. One of Mermoz's earliest biographers, René Chambe, developed this idea at length in his 1928 novel, *Sous le casque de cuir* (Underneath the Leather Helmet):

> For us [aviators], flight is a refuge. It's our cocaine, our opium, our sense of vertigo. Up above, problems, annoyances, the greatest sorrows disappear for a few hours. What pilot hasn't known this impression of deliverance, this kind of victory of the spirit at that moment when, enveloped in the glorious thunder of the motor, the airplane leaves the ground . . . The life on the ground remains below, far below, further and further below, with all its banalities, its anxieties, its vileness, its ignominy. One forgets it. One no longer belongs to it. One is torn away from it.[22]

Pl. 318.   The last picture taken of Markham as she headed for the Atlantic bound for New York.

Pl. 319.   After twenty-one hours and twenty-five minutes of solitary flight, she crashed in a bog on Cape Breton Island in Nova Scotia. She later wrote that "We fly, but we have not 'conquered' the air. Nature presides in all her dignity, permitting us the study and the use of such of her forces as we may understand."

THE GREAT ADVENTURE

"I was the last to wave good-bye to Mrs. Markham," writes Henry How, "Daily Mirror" photographer, who in a 'plane escorted her for the first few miles and took this farewell picture. "As our 'plane drew close to hers, we could see her studying maps. Our machines drew closer. I waved my hand, wishing her God-speed. She waved back—and headed for the Atlantic at 130 m.p.h."

Why this need to escape? The answer is not obvious. Kessel, of course, was persuaded that the key to Mermoz's character and his life was his need to escape from his own demons and passions in an impossible search for a transcendence that was destined to elude him. Mermoz himself contrasted the purity of life in the air to the sordidness of everyday life on the ground in a speech he gave to an assembly of the Croix de Feu. Saint-Exupéry believed that the certification of Mermoz's greatness was his indifference to all material concerns and his success in rising above them. Somehow flight had become identified in the minds of some influential aviators with the triumph of the spirit over vulgar gain and selfish domestic happiness. And lest we think that such ideas were confined to French intellectuals, let us remember Louise Thaden: "Flight [in contrast to mere flying] is the essence of the spirit. It nurtures the soul."[23]

★   ★   ★

Adventure, freedom, escape – all these implied transgression, a breaking of the rules by which ordinary human beings lived. Hollywood was quick to exploit this aspect of aviation. The characters played by Pat O'Brien in *Air Mail*, James Cagney in *Devil Dogs of the Air*, *Ceiling Zero*, and *Captain of the Clouds*, Fred MacMurray in *Men With Wings*, and Errol Flynn in the 1938 version of *Dawn Patrol* all derive much of their charm from their quality as men outside the pale of ordinary society. Many believed that there was something crazy or unbalanced about a man who was prepared to dedicate his life to aviation. For months after his Paris flight, Lindbergh had to see himself referred to in the media as "the flying fool." It was a term he found particularly offensive, but it was taken up and repeated because it corresponded to a widely diffused image of the aviator. As if recklessness and lack of responsibility were not bad enough, in both fiction and films male pilots were often portrayed as womanizers who lacked respect for social conventions and the sanctity of the family. The protagonist of Louise Faure-Favier's 1923 novel, *Les Chevaliers de l'air* (Knights of the

Air), is an airline pilot who has a girl in every major city along his flight path. "Bertrand Darbois had made for himself an international harem of whom he was the aerial sultan."[24] Because of these images, fathers understandably often disapproved of flyers as husbands for their daughters. In *Luciano Serra, pilota*, the protagonist is abandoned by his wife, loses his beloved child, and is forced to go into exile because he refuses to give up flying.

It is easy to understand why flight was often identified with transgression, both by those who practiced it and those who followed it from the ground. To fly was to enter a forbidden realm that had formerly been reserved for birds, angels, and God. It brought with it feelings of exhilaration and a sense of breaking boundaries that hemmed in and limited ordinary human beings. This was especially true for those few women who chose to fly and succeeded. The term used to describe them in the 1920s and 1930s – "aviatrix" – suggests the exoticism of the phenomenon and its distance from us today.[25] For a woman to learn to fly was to demand entry to a world reserved for men; for a woman to fly professionally – and thus to compete with men – was to throw down the gauntlet and challenge the principles on which contemporary society was based. Women who did persevere and insisted on flying were well aware of the obstacles they faced. As Amelia Earhart explained to Louise Thaden, "Men do not believe us capable . . . Manufacturers refuse us planes, the public have no confidence in our ability . . . Thank heaven, we continue willingly fighting a losing battle . . ."[26]

This is not to say that the efforts of women aviators were not supported by men; nor that the achievements of women aviators went unappreciated. On the contrary, the handful of aviatrixes that succeeded in distinguishing themselves were idolized. Less intent on promoting herself than some of her colleagues, Louise Thaden was frank about the disadvantages and advantages of being a woman pilot. Women were held to a high standard by male pilots and were always in danger of being dismissed by the press as incom-

Pl. 320. The photogenic Jean Batten is featured among a group of record-breaking aviators, most of them males, in a composite drawing that appeared in a London newspaper in the 1930s. Amy Johnson is consigned to a supporting role.

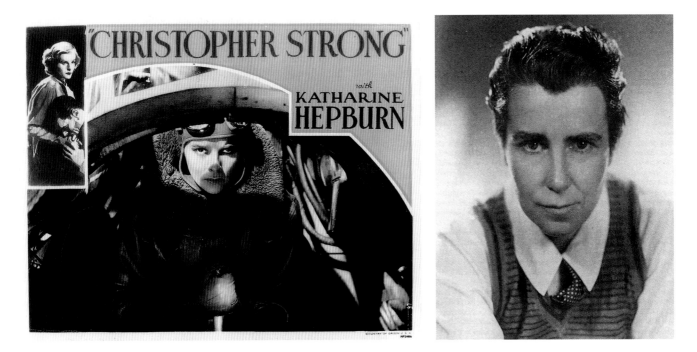

petent amateurs who represented a danger to themselves and others. "Basically we were usurpers in a man's exclusive world. The penalties were severe in the never-ending struggle to accumulate the flying time which alone could develop piloting skills. There were also advantages. Women pilots were oddities and therefore more 'newsworthy' than were the male counterparts."[27] What Thaden neglects to say is that women could become famous, and even rich, for exploits that had already been achieved by men.[28]

Nonetheless, regardless of the fame and fortune they attained, by definition aviatrixes were marginal figures who failed to fit into the roles that women were expected to play. Their celebrity was a confirmation of the norm that consigned the majority of women to another realm. No one could be surprised if the life of such women had a tragic end. They were courting disaster by failing to respect established social boundaries.

A noteworthy attempt to explore this issue is the 1933 RKO movie *Christopher Strong*, starring the young and vibrant Katharine Hepburn in her second appearance on the screen. Like so many Hollywood films of the period dealing with women, this picture sends conflicting messages and ultimately surrenders to the wisdom of convention. In the process of providing the resolution that Hollywood's moral code demanded, however, the female writer and director of this unusual film found ample occasion to call into question the prevailing social and sexual practices of the time.

Adapted by the well-known Broadway playwright Zoë Akins from a best-selling novel by Gilbert Frankau and directed by Dorothy Arzner, *Christopher Strong* is the story of a virginal and independent-minded young English aviatrix – Lady Cynthia Darrington – who falls in love with a rich and successful married man; enters into an affair with him; and then, finding herself pregnant, commits suicide in her plane after setting a new altitude record for women. The plot, put in this simplified form, could not be more banal, and one respected film critic has dismissed the picture as "silly"; yet it is fascinating to follow the way that director Dorothy Arzner and her writer reshaped Frankau's novel, itself a complex and densely textured work.[29]

Though convention triumphs in the movie, as it did in Frankau's novel, the impression the film leaves is that of a highly unconventional woman, played in a thoroughly unconventional way by a woman of ambiguous sexual identity, who is devoted to the "god of speed" and lives according to the non-female principle that courage conquers everything, even love. Lady Cynthia chooses to commit suicide by ripping off her oxygen mask after breaking the alti-

tude record. She realizes that, as a man of duty, her lover would be miserable if he left his wife to marry his pregnant mistress. The critical moments of her relationship with Sir Christopher flash before her eyes on her altimeter, as she spins downward toward her fatal crash. The film leaves no doubt that her romance was doomed from the start.

The social order is thus restored. Sir Christopher's marriage is happily reconstituted; a monument is erected to the courage of the daring aviatrix. Melodrama is well served. But there is something dissonant about the *way* the story is told. Despite the reassuring ending, no one leaving the movie theater could have any doubt that Lady Cynthia was made of stronger stuff than the effete conformist for whom she had given up her life. And one could reasonably have doubts also about Lady Cynthia's desire for a conventional married life. The way Katharine Hepburn moves, the mannish clothes she wears, the provocative looks she gives, and her evident love of flying all seem to contradict the picture's ending. Why should Lady Cynthia die for a man so clearly inferior to herself?

Critics have been tempted to see in Lady Cynthia reflections of Amelia Earhart.[30] It is true that Earhart became the first woman to fly the Atlantic in May 1932 and was very much in the news during the making of *Christopher Strong*; it is also true that Earhart received the sort of welcome in New York that Lady Cynthia enjoys in Arzner's picture after, fictionally, flying around the world. Newsreel footage from that event may very well have been used in Arzner's film. But there is no need to go beyond Britain's shores to find a figure on which Frankau's heroine might have been based.[31] Though no aristocrat, the twenty-six-year-old Amy Johnson had made a daring solo flight from London to Darwin, Australia in May 1930 – the first woman to do so – and won the hearts of the British and Australian people with her courage, modesty, and dogged determination.[32] Nor did Johnson rest long on her laurels. The same year that *Christopher Strong* was released, she and her husband Jim Mollison – himself a record-breaking aviator – took off from South Wales in a round-the-world flight. That it ended with a forced landing outside Bridgeport, Connecticut did nothing to diminish Johnson's fame nor discourage her from further exploits. Lady Cynthia was not as fanciful a figure as some movie critics may think.

Pl. 323.   In this still from *Christopher Strong*, Katharine Hepburn displays her knack for appearing both beautiful and provocative.

Pl. 324.   Amy Johnson (left) with Amelia Earhart in 1933 around the time of Italo Balbo's flight to New York. Though we take women in slacks for granted, those who chose to wear them in the early 1930s, like Johnson, Earhart, and Katharine Hepburn, were making a statement.

★　★　★

If flight was so often experienced as an adventure, it was also because it offered extraordinary sights not available to ordinary human beings. Saint-Exupéry captured this aspect of flight in one of the most charming tableaux of *Terre des hommes*. One of the miracles of the airplane, he said, was that it plunged you directly into the heart of mystery. "You were a biologist, studying the human anthill from behind a porthole . . ." Then, suddenly, your engine faltered and you found yourself "the prisoner of a lawn in a sleepy hollow."[33] The airplane took you to unexpected places; and in a period when engines were still notoriously undependable, you might suddenly find yourself on the ground in an unexpected and wondrous place.

Recalling the motivations that drew them to flight and drove them to persist in a "business that offered so few financial rewards and took lives at such a cruel rate," both Elinor Smith and Ruth Nichols emphasized the aesthetics of flight. All Smith could remember of her first flight was the view. "It was totally unobstructed and its beauty was breathtaking. Shafts of sunlight streamed down through broken clouds, turning the drab truck farms below into a fairyland of gilded greens and golds. Constantly changing cloud patterns were seemingly painted on a vast blue canvas by an unseen artist who directed the wind to air-brush his designs."[34] Nichols also introduced the trope of a "Master Artist" when describing a flight across the Arizona desert in 1929. "I will never forget the savage magnificence of flying across the desert at sundown, seeing the jagged mountain peaks change slowly from rose quartz to cobalt blue and violet, with the desert sands stretching in yellow waves at their bases in startling contrast to the blackened lava flows. At such a time one stands in awe at the power of the Master Artist whose invisible hand paints a landscape of such bold and primitive color."[35] It was moments like these, she thought, that kept pilots in the air.[36]

Early air travelers differed over the view from above in a quickly moving airplane. Some thought that it rendered the earth monotonous and robbed it of its colors and variety.[37] Others were impressed by the larger panorama that flight offered: "By flying over countries," the American journalist Lowell Thomas pointed out in 1929, "you get an impression of them as a whole . . ."[38] Most writers who recorded their impressions in the 1920s and 1930s agreed that the earth looked very different from aloft, though they often groped for words with which to express the images they had seen while flying. In 1932, after making a flight from Paris to Bucharest, Paul Morand, a bestselling French author known for the exotic settings of his books, attempted in a work of fiction to explain the difference between what he saw while looking down and moving through the air at great velocity as opposed to traveling at a more leisurely pace along the ground. He began by observing that when in a plane all those objects we are used to focusing on – the blue bottoms of leaves, the stratified façades of mountains, the colonnade formed by a forest, the dark pockets of valleys, and human beings – disappear or become unrecognizable.

> The landscape no longer presents itself like a sequence of pictures, of green curtains, of plaster props, of earthy screens, of stone corridors, that are constantly interfering with one's view. The world, seen from above looking down, is like a painting that has been freed from the old perspective and yesterday's colors . . . The snake-like rivers show their solidified depths; the lakes their dark volumes; the empty roads gloriously crown cities like the wheels of a lottery. It's in this way that the squared, compartmentalized, and geometrical universe down below offers itself to the gaze of the aerial surveyor.[39]

Not surprisingly, some air travelers who were familiar with European avant-garde art made the connection between what they saw from an airplane and the cubist aesthetic. Traveling through the United States by air in the 1930s, Gertrude Stein "saw all the lines of cubism made at a time when not any painter had ever gone up in an airplane. I saw there on the earth the mingling lines of Picasso, coming and going, developing and destroying themselves. I saw the simple solutions of Braque, I saw the wandering lines of Masson, yes I saw and once more I knew that a creator is contemporary, he understands what is con-

temporary when the contemporaries do not yet know it, but he is contemporary and as the twentieth century is a century which sees the earth as none has ever seen it, the earth has a splendor that it never has had . . ."[40] Thus for Stein, avant-garde painters had conceived the world as it was seen from above before any had actually flown.

Ernest Hemingway had similar thoughts when flying from Paris to Strasbourg in 1922:

> We headed almost straight east of Paris, rising in the air as though we were sitting inside a boat that was being lifted by some giant, and the ground began to flatten out beneath us. It looked cut into brown squares, yellow squares, green squares and big flat blotches of green where there was a forest. I began to understand cubist painting.[41]

Among aviators who became authors, Anne Morrow Lindbergh was especially sensitive to the way flight changed our visual perception of the world and returned to it frequently in her writing. Indeed, though she had not yet met Saint-Exupéry when she wrote these lines, she used the same word he did in explaining one of the appeals of flying: its ability to transport one to an unfamiliar world of "mystery." Introducing the book that she wrote about the flight that she and her husband took to the Orient by the northern route, she emphasized its "quality of magic – a quality that belongs to fairy tales."[42] Asked why they made their flight, she said that their immediate response would be the indisputable importance of prospecting future air routes between America, Japan, China, and Siberia. But to this must be added, she went on, "other small, personal and trivial reasons" that are difficult to imprison with a name. Reasons such as "*color, glamour, curiosity, magic*, or *mystery*."[43] Then several years after they returned to the United States, while being flown from New York to Washington by her husband, she looks down toward the ground and thinks:

> One could sit still and look at life from the air; that was it. And I was conscious again of the fundamental magic of flying, a miracle that has nothing to do with its practical purposes – purposes of speed, accessibility, and convenience – and will not change as they change. It is a magic that has more kinship with what one experiences standing in front of serene madonnas or listening to cool chorales, or even reading one of those clear passages in a book – so clear and so illuminating that one feels the writer has given the reader a glass-bottomed bucket with which to look through the ruffled surface of life far down to that still permanent world below. For not only is life put into new patterns from the air, but is somehow arrested into form . . . And if flying, like a glass-bottomed buck-

Pl. 325. This view of the French countryside from a plane tracking Charles Lindbergh on his flight to Brussels in May 1927 is not unlike the scene that Ernest Hemingway described when he flew from Paris to Strasbourg in 1922.

Pl. 326. Charles and Anne Morrow Lindbergh pose before the Lockheed Sirius, with which they flew to the Orient in 1931. The Sirius had just been outfitted with aluminum floats necessary for landing on water in remote locations.

et, can give you that vision, that seeing eye, which peers down to the still world below the choppy waves – it will always remain magic.[44]

Though a spectator in the scene she is describing, Anne Morrow Lindbergh was herself a pilot. But in the early days of commercial air travel, passengers had similar experiences because the planes in which they flew remained at lower altitudes and provided them with experiences that few air travelers have today. As one of the first persons invited to fly from Marseille to Saigon, the French writer Jérôme Tharaud experienced an epiphany when being flown over the ruins at Angkor in Cambodia. As a well-known writer traveling at the invitation of the airline, Tharaud was permitted privileges not available to the normal passenger; but the account he provides of his impressions demonstrates the way that flight could transform a normally earthbound person's vision of the world.

Tharaud has no doubt that what he sees from aloft is fundamentally different from what he would have seen had he approached these ruins from the perspective of the ground. Instead of being overwhelmed by the chaos of heaps of stones and details, as he would have been had he visited the site on foot or by vehicle, he is treated from his aerial perch to a grandiose ensemble of stones, trees, and water, spread out across the ground in geometrical patterns, with beautiful staggered towers, that lift themselves toward the sky. His perspective, he concludes, is the same as that of the gods to which these ruined monuments were once dedicated:

> The pilot goes out of his way to make me admire Angkor in the detail of its sculptures. We almost touch the foliage; we graze the gods with our wings. Their enormous faces, that form the facades of the towers, contemplate serenely the flight of this enormous

Pl. 327. Géo Ham depicts a scene not unlike the one that Jérôme Tharaud experienced and later described.

bumble bee that envelopes them in its roar. When we charge through the air on top of these colossal figures, they appear to us like the images of a film that, from the depths of the screen, pursue you, become larger, then recede and vanish in the same fantasy. Following the stages of the flight, one by one the temples and the gods are reduced to the scale of a postcard, or a simple stamp, only to reassume a moment later their supernatural dimensions. Has any other human being (I mean the crew and myself) gotten closer to these eyes, these smiles? In order to see them better, I kneel down before the window of the cockpit. Who, before me, has ever traveled on his knees around these gods?[45]

★   ★   ★

The perception of flight as an adventure was certified by its connection with risk, danger, and possible death. This was the price that aviators paid for the rewards of their profession. Ernst Jünger was convinced that one of the sources of the attraction of the airplane was "a very modern feeling that sensed in the contest with material objects the charm of dangerous games."[46] Jünger was right: flight attracted men and women in search of challenges, danger, and intense emotions; people who felt the need to live on the edge of the abyss and feel the precipice beneath them; persons who longed after a faster pace of life and were willing to pay the price. When friends urged Jean Batten to give up dangerous flying after she had set a solo record for flying from England to Australia and then become the first woman to fly from Australia to New Zealand across the twelve hundred-mile-wide Tasman Sea, she demurred, thinking: "I wanted very much to settle down in my own country and lead a calm peaceful life, but in my heart I knew only too well that I was destined to be a wanderer. I seemed born to travel and, in flying, I found the combination of the two things which meant everything to me: the intoxicating drug of speed and freedom to roam the earth. In my innermost thoughts I knew the fire of adventure that burned within me was not yet quenched, and that urge was drawing me on – to what?"[47] A reader of her biography might reply: to tragic death or public adulation.

Excitement and the exhilaration came from escaping death after having deliberately put oneself in situations of peril. Everywhere you found wings and growling motors, René Chambe wrote, the rhythm of life accelerated and intensified. The eyes of flyers were brighter, their voices more distinct, their laughter brighter, their handshakes more forceful.[48] In *The Steep Ascent*, a novella that reaches its climax in a dangerous flight across the Alps, Anne Morrow Lindbergh also dwelt on the paradox that by bringing one close to death flight enhanced one's sense of life. "The nearness to death made life more alive, and beauty more beautiful."[49]

It was their close commerce with death that set aviators apart from ordinary people, as the English poet Stephen Spender sought to convey in these lines:

> This aristocrat, superb of all instinct.
>   With death close-linked
> Has paced the enormous cloud, almost had won
>   War on the sun;
> Till now, like Icarus mid-oceaned drowned,
>   Hands, wings, are found.[50]

There are few aviators of the period who do not confess that they were alive to tell their story by chance. In this respect, Lindbergh was an exception; the fear of death is almost totally absent from the accounts he has left of his flights. Alan Cobham is more typical. He admitted to having been terrified on some of the long flights he made in the 1920s, such as the one in 1924 on which he transported the British director of civil aviation, Sir Sefton

Brancker, from London to Karachi.[51] They had made their way, with many difficulties and delays, to Poix in northeastern France, then to Berlin, Warsaw, Lvov, Bucharest, Constantinople, and Konya in central Anatolia. The next leg of their journey to Iskenderun (then called Alexandretta) required crossing the Taurus Mountains, which rose to twelve thousand feet and which Cobham's De Havilland 50 was incapable of overflying.

> I threaded my way between them by way of a pass that would lead to the head of a river, and then I could follow its valley down to the coast. But I soon found myself in trouble. I was flying in effect through a tunnel, an extremely narrow one, which twisted and turned at every point; there were jagged mountainsides to left and right, disappearing overhead into a ceiling of low cloud, into which I could not climb without the near-certainty of hitting one of them. I could not turn back either. There was not enough lateral room for even the steepest turn, nor was there any possibility of landing among the crags and pinnacles below me. I had no alternative but to press on, and to be frank, I was terrified. Again and again, as I made my way down that winding ravine, I would find myself in an apparent cul-de-sac, heading straight for a vertical rock face with no possible way out. There always *was* a way out: it appeared at the very last minute, unexpectedly, perhaps on the left and perhaps on the right, and I then had to fling the aircraft into an immediate steep turn, squeezing through with just a few feet to spare, and then needing to repeat this hair-raising performance only seconds later.

Cobham survived this ordeal, which he remembered as a "real nightmare," but only after an hour and a half of struggle during which he felt his strength failing and, with it, the kind of judgment required for split-second flying in this kind of life-or-death situation.[52] Though Cobham tells the story in an understated way, he leaves no doubt that professional aviators in the 1920s were accustomed to coming face to face with death.

Most aviators thought of flight as a Faustian bargain. The "sweetness of perpetual danger" was an integral part of their profession. "Born to die quickly and soon," Pierre Weiss wrote, "we speak everyday to the invisible."[53] Amelia Earhart thought that:

> Courage is the price that life exacts for granting peace.
> The soul that knows it not, knows no release
> From little things.
> Knows not the livid loneliness of fear
> Nor mountain heights, where bitter joy can hear
> The sound of wings.[54]

Earhart went on to ask how life could "compensate for dull gray ugliness and pregnant hate unless we dare." Mermoz would have agreed. Pilots, he explained in a funeral oration he gave after the death of one of his comrades in a commercial flight, did not have the fear of death that makes ordinary people so attached to earthly existence that they fear risking and losing it. "Who among us . . . does not have this secret ambition, this legitimate pride in an end worthy of our efforts, of our struggles, and our sacrifices to which we have freely and ardently consented?"[55] Mermoz would have the end he secretly desired.

Lindbergh also confessed that as a young man he looked down condescendingly upon "the skeptics on the ground," who were unwilling to assume the risks of flight. His life, he thought, was "richer because of its very association with the element of danger they dreaded, because it was freer of the earth to which they were bound. In flying, I tasted a wine of the gods of which they could know nothing. Who valued life more highly, the aviators who spent it on the art they loved, or those misers who doled it out like pennies through their antlike days? I decided that if I could fly for ten years before I was killed in a crash, it would be a worthwhile trade for an ordinary lifetime."[56]

★   ★   ★

If many, like Lindbergh, were drawn to aviation because of its dimension of freedom, beauty, and adventure, others were attracted because it seemed to represent the triumph of Western technology, rationality, and the domination of nature. Flight was one of the most visible examples of the inexorable advance of Western science; it promised to break through many of the boundaries that for millennia had consigned men to the earth. To see an airplane in the sky was to be reminded of the modernity of the age in which people were now living. In Virginia Woolf's 1925 novel *Mrs. Dalloway*, the appearance of an airplane over London sets into motion the imagination of her characters strolling through the city's streets. "Away and away the aeroplane shot, till it was nothing but a bright spark; an aspiration; a concentration; a symbol (so it seemed to Mr. Bentley, vigorously rolling his strip of turf at Greenwich) of man's soul; of his determination, thought Mr. Bentley, sweeping round the cedar tree, to get outside his body, beyond his house, by means of thought, Einstein, speculation, mathematics, the Mendelian theory – away the aeroplane shot . . . Unguided it seemed; sped of its own free will. And now, curving up and up, straight up, like something mounting in ectasy, in pure delight, out from behind poured white smoke looping, writing a T, an O, an F."[57]

For pilots, the machines they flew were almost living beings capable of exercising a sensual and aesthetic attraction. To survive, they had to know them inside out. When Jean Batten arrived at the Lympne Airdrome to begin her 1935 South American flight, she was dazzled by the sight of her newly acquired Percival Gull 6: "The big hangar doors swung back, revealing a low-wing monoplane. Its silver surface, glistening and gleaming under the powerful electric lights, made it look like some lovely thoroughbred groomed and polished in readiness for some great race and straining to be away."[58]

During the 1920s and early 1930s there was no necessary contradiction between flight as adventure and flight as a means of technological advance. Aeronautical progress could be achieved only at the cost of great risk and the sacrifice of lives. More than a hundred men lost their lives flying for Aéropostale between 1919 and 1933. The goal of dominating the sky seemed worth the price. Airplanes in flight inspired a sense of wonder, awe, and pride. Every technical breakthrough was viewed as a step closer to the goals of total dependability and

Pl. 329. Jean Batten with her
beloved Percival Gull 6.

safety. After having accomplished the greatest adventure in the history of flight, Lindbergh
transformed himself into the paladin, pioneer, and prophet of the development of commercial aviation. He later confessed that flight had always attracted him because of its connection with progress. Explaining his fascination with technology as a young man, he echoes
the Futurist Marinetti's hope that men would one day fuse with machines. "I grew up as a
disciple of science. I know its fascination. I have felt the godlike power man derives from his
machines – the strength of a thousand horses at one's fingertips; the conquest of distance
through mercurial speed; the immortal viewpoint of the higher air. I have sensed the harmony of muscle, mind, and mechanism which gives the illusion of life to substance until
levers move with thought as hand or foot, until the rhythm of an engine is geared to the
beat of one's own heart, and wing in turning flight seems an extension of one's own body."[59]

For three exciting decades, it was possible to combine adventure and scientific innovation; but the clock was ticking and the day of the adventurer was drawing to an end.
Writing the introduction in 1938 to the account his wife had written of a long-distance
flight they had made five years before, Lindbergh commented:

Our flight lasted for nearly six months. This book covers only ten days of that time. It is
about a period in aviation which is now gone, but which was probably more interesting
than any that the future will bring. As time passes, the perfection of machinery tends to
insulate man from contact with the elements in which he lives. The "stratosphere" planes
of the future will cross the ocean without any sense of the water below. Like a train tun-
nelling through a mountain, they will be aloof from both the problems and the beauty
of the earth's surface. Only the vibration from the engines will impress the senses of the
traveller with his movement through the air. Wind and heat and moonlight take-offs will
be of no concern to the transatlantic passenger. His only contact with these elements will
lie in accounts such as this book contains.[60]

Pl. 330.   H. Raymond Bishop's drawing shows Lindbergh leading the way into the new aerial age.

Later, writing *The Spirit of St. Louis*, an imaginative reconstruction of his early life, Lindbergh returned to this topic; but the way he poses the question shows a remarkable evolution in his conception of aviation and a shift away from the scientific materialism to which he had earlier been so attached:

> Is aviation too arrogant? I don't know. Sometimes, flying feels too godlike to be attained by man. Sometimes, the world from above seems too beautiful, too wonderful, too distant for human eyes to see, like a vision at the end of life forming a bridge to death. Can that be why so many pilots lose their lives? Is man encroaching on a forbidden realm? Is aviation dangerous because the sky was never meant for him? When one obtains too great a vision is there some power that draws one from mortal life forever?

But then Lindbergh poses an even more disturbing question. Will the power of this forbidden realm "smite down pilot after pilot until man loses his will to fly?"

> Or, still worse, will it deaden his senses and let him fly on without the vision? In developing aviation, in making it a form of commerce, in replacing the wild freedom of danger with the civilized bonds of safety, must we give up this miracle of air? Will men fly through the sky in the future without seeing what I have seen, without feeling what I have felt? Is that true of all things we call human progress – do the gods retire as commerce and science advance?[61]

Like Lindbergh, Mermoz, Saint-Exupéry, and their comrades on *La Ligne* were keenly aware in the 1930s that the adventure they were living was reaching its end. Essential to the charm of aviation in its early phase was its danger; once flight became safer and more predictable, it was inevitable that it would lose its reason for being for those who had been drawn to the sky as a great adventure. Kessel had understood this as early as 1929, when he wrote *Vent de sable*. The success of Aéropostale, he observed sadly, would mean "mechanization and death."[62]

Paradoxically, then, aeronautical progress came to be perceived by some aviators as a threat to what they understood as "the soul" of aviation. Dizzy Davis, in *Ceiling Zero*, commits suicide in the air, testing an anti-icing device, because there will be no place in the coming aviation world for men like him. By 1938 the French aviator Robert de Marolles, looking back over his twenty-five-year career as a pilot with undisguised nostalgia, could lament that flight had ceased to be "an exceptional domain, accessible as in the past only to a few of the predestined, who seemed marked by a supernatural sign and destined sooner or later to a brutal end."[63]

Thus aviators in the 1930s devoted themselves to aeronautical progress and at the same time anticipated with foreboding their success because safety in flight could be arrived at only through rules and regulations and the replacement of human perception by instruments. They knew these changes to be necessary; yet, deep down within, they regretted them because they knew that they were bound to destroy the freedom of flight that they associated with memories of their youth. How, asked Marolles, does one explain the attraction of flight? He answered that it was "a complex feeling" made up of various components: "the obscure desire to escape from the constraints of the earth, an almost sensual joy in unleashing a speed that is forbidden almost everywhere else, and at the same time a feeling of profound intellectual satisfaction."[64]

★　　★　　★

Between 1920 and 1935, most people no doubt thought of flight primarily in terms of adventure and technological advance. No one made the connection between the airplane and the new times more forcefully than the modernist architect and urban planner Le Corbusier. The airplane, he wrote in 1935 in the introduction to a book of photographs, was "the symbol of the new age. At the apex of the immense pyramid of mechanical progress, it opens the NEW AGE; it wings its way into it. The mechanical improvements of the fierce preparatory epoch – a hundred year's blind groping to discovery – have overthrown the basis of a civilization thousands of years old."[65] The airplane, in Le Corbusier's mind, represented clearness of function and the daring required to break with the past. "New machines, new men. They [the aviators] are filled with enthusiasm, the pleasures of daring, of breaking with current stupidities . . . In aviation everything is scrapped in a year."[66] Le Corbusier accompanied bold statements like these with an ambitious program for rebuilding many of the world's major cities.

> Being indissolubly connected in all the fibers of my being with the essential human affairs which architecture regulates; having waged for a long time, without fear of hatred or ambush, a loyal crusade of material liberation by the all-powerful influence of architecture, it is as an architect and town-planner – and therefore as a man essentially occupied with the welfare of his species – that I let myself be carried off on the wings of an airplane, make use of the bird's-eye view, of the view from the air, to which end I directed the pilot to steer over cities. And, justly stirred . . . I have added my own [sub]title [to this book]: "The airplane indicts [*L'avion accuse*]."[67]

The view from above, made possible by the airplane, had revealed the scandal of nineteenth-century cities: "bustling, cruel, heartless, and money grubbing." They must now be destroyed and fresh cities built to replace them.[68]

Because of its connection in people's minds with modernity and a technologically altered future full of unsuspected marvels, flight was a source of endless cultural stimulation during the years between 1920 and 1950. The most popular exhibit at the 1939–40 New

294

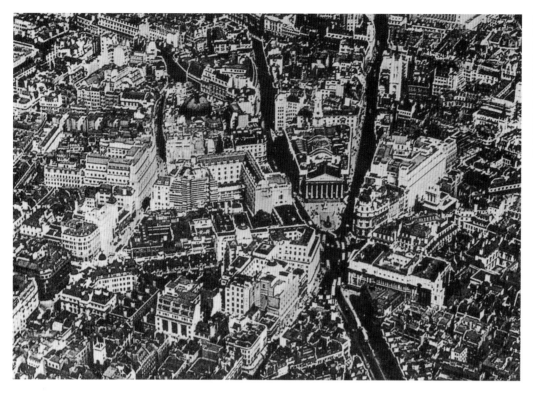

York World's Fair portrayed the imagined future of America in 1960, seen from the air. Designed by Norman Bel Geddes and financed by General Motors, the *Futurama* was at that time the largest animated model ever made. After a long wait that sometimes extended to two hours as they made their way along serpentine ramps on the outside of the building, spectators were seated in luxurious six-feet-high armchairs contained within compartments that held two people. They were then moved along a conveyer of over a third of a mile through different levels of the building that gave the illusion of flying over the land and cityscapes of the future at low altitude. A sixteen-minute recorded narration, synchronized with the movement of the chairs, described the wonders that awaited them in the world of tomorrow.

> A transcontinental flight over America in 1960. What will we see? What changes will transpire? . . . Sunshine, trees, hills and valleys, flowers and flowing streams . . . the world of tomorrow is a world of beauty . . . here are the fine farm-roads of the community . . . Here we see one of our 1960 express motorways . . .[69]

The thrills that the twenty-five million people who visited it derived from this spectacle were enhanced by the fact – almost unimaginable for us today – that few of them had traveled in an airplane, not to mention traversed the country by air. The scale of different sections of the display varied between a few inches to ten feet, giving the spectators of the *Futurama* the impression that the plane in which they were flying had descended for a closer look at some of the objects on the ground.[70] Among other novelties – modernist skyscrapers widely spaced from one another rather than clustered so as to create an impression of light and freedom, super highway interchanges with scarcely perceptible traffic, and double-decked bridges – the spectators were treated to the sight of a circular airport, located across the river from an imagined city center, viewed from the perspective of an incoming airliner, with terminals and hangars arranged along the circumference of a circle whose diameter contained the runways. An exciting glimpse into America's future, the *Futurama* also was a testimony to the way that the airplane was transforming people's vision of the world.

Pl. 332.   Norman Bel Geddes.

Pl. 333.   Bel Geddes overflowed with ideas as to how the objects in our increasingly technological world could be redesigned to make them both more efficient and more beautiful. In 1932 he published drawings of a floating airport in New York Harbor southwest of Battery Park meant to accommodate land planes. The weight of this floating airport would be supported by columns placed upon ballasted buoyancy tanks.

Pl. 334.   The General Motors building at the 1939–1940 New York World's Fair.

Pl. 335.   A long line of people waits to gain access to the *Futurama*.

Pl. 336.   Spectators seated in the *Futurama* observe Bel Geddes' vision of America in the 1960s.

Pl. 337.   Among the futuristic sights a visitor to the *Futurama* would see was this depiction of a university. The narrative explained: "Now we approach a modern university center. Here, in buildings of simple but functional architecture, the youth of 1960 study for their future in a world of still greater progress and achievement."

Pl. 338.   As befitted an exhibit installed in the General Motors building, there was a great deal of emphasis in the *Futurama* on the highways of the future. "Looming ahead is a 1960 Motorway intersection. By means of ramped loops, cars may make right and left turns at rates of speed up to 50 miles per hour. The turning-off lanes are elevated and depressed. There is no interference from the straight ahead traffic in the higher speed lanes."

★   ★   ★

A survey of cultural responses to aviation during the three decades between 1920 and 1950 would have to cast its net to include works as different as the aerial paintings and sculpture of the second wave of Italian Futurists; the beginnings of airport architecture; the murals with which they were provided; the countless novels aimed toward a public eager for adventure tales set in the air; comic books like *Tale Spin Tommy* and *Ace Drummond*; and musical compositions like George Antheil's airplane sonatas and Marc Blitzstein's originally acclaimed but now forgotten *Airborne Symphony*.[71] Yet what interests me more here in this concluding chapter are the traces aviation left on cultural works that are not ostensibly about flight. One small, but revealing, example can be found in the opening pages of F. Scott Fitzgerald's unfinished novel, *The Last Tycoon*, written in 1939–40 just before his death from a heart attack at the age of forty-four.

The Last Tycoon is about Hollywood during the mid-1930s when the studios were at the height of their influence and power. Some consider it the finest novel written on this topic.

Pl. 339.   Tullio Crali portrays a city as it appears to a pilot who initiates a dive in this 1939 air painting.

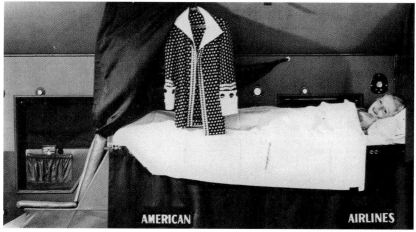

Pl. 340. F. Scott Fitzgerald in 1937 shortly before his death. The actress Fay Wray called him "an almost too-beautiful man."

Pl. 341. A sleeping birth on American Airlines in 1933. Seven decades later, American Airlines passengers would not be so pampered.

It opens, however, not in Hollywood but on a cross-country flight from New York to Los Angeles. The narrator Cecilia Brady is returning home in June after completing her junior year at Bennington, a fashionable women's college in Vermont. Traveling by air and provided with a sleeping compartment, Cecilia knows herself to be a member of the elite, her status made possible by her father's affluence as a Hollywood producer. Ordinary people in this period travel by train, car, or bus. When her plane is forced to land in the middle of the night in Nashville because of a storm, Cecilia reflects on the peculiarities of airports:

Pl. 342. The waiting room at the Washington, D.C. airport in the 1930s. The furniture (or lack of it) speaks eloquently of the small pool of air travelers in this period.

I suppose that there has been nothing like airports since the days of the stage-stops – nothing quite as lonely, as somber-silent. The old red-brick depots were built right into the towns they marked – people didn't get off at those isolated stations unless they lived there. But airports lead you way back in history like oases, like the stops on the great trade routes. The sight of air travelers strolling in ones and twos into midnight airports will draw a small crowd any night up to two. The young people look at the planes, the older ones at the passengers with a watchful incredulity. In the big transcontinental planes we were the costal rich, who casually alighted from our cloud in mid-America. High adventure might be among us, disguised as a movie star.[72]

When the storm weakens, the sleepy-eyed passengers, several bound for Hollywood, gather in the airport, waiting for the call to board their flight. Cecilia thinks: "Slowly the idea of a perilous journey was recreated out of the debris of our failure."[73] Flying by commercial airliner, we are led to understand, is still not without its dangers.

Cecilia is infatuated with one of the passengers – Monroe Stahr, modeled after the famous chief of production at MGM, Irving Thalberg. Thalberg had overseen the production of many of the early aviation movies made at MGM. When reflecting on Stahr's meteoric career, Cecilia turns to the metaphor of flight. "He had flown up very high to see, on strong wings when he was young. And while he was up there he had looked on all the kingdoms, with the kind of eyes that can stare straight into the sun. Beating his wings tenaciously – finally frantically – and keeping on beating them he had stayed up there longer than most of us, and then, remembering all he had seen from his great height of how things were, he had settled gradually to earth."[74]

The chapter ends as the plane approaches Glendale Airport. Cecilia sees their landing through the prism of Stahr's settling into Hollywood:

The motors were off and all our five senses began to readjust themselves for landing. I could see a line of lights for the Long Beach Naval Station ahead and to the left, and on the right a twinkling blur for Santa Monica. The California moon was out, huge and orange over the Pacific. However I happened to feel about these things – and they were home after all – I knew that Stahr must have felt much more. These were the things I had first opened my eyes on, like the sheep on the back lot of the old Laemmle studio; but this was where Stahr had come to earth after that extraordinary illuminating flight where he saw which way we were going, and how we looked doing it, and how much

Pl. 343.   Glendale Airport in the 1930s seen from the sky. The mountains in the background added to the drama of an arrival in Los Angeles by air.

of it mattered. You could say that this was where an accidental wind blew him but I don't think so. I would rather think that in a "long shot" he saw a new way of measuring our jerky hopes and graceful rogueries and awkward sorrows, and that he came here from choice to be with us to the end. Like the plane coming down into the Glendale Airport, into the warm darkness.[75]

Fitzgerald planned to bring the novel to a climax in which Stahr and two other major characters would be killed when a plane, bearing them back to Hollywood, crashes in the Rocky Mountains and their possessions are plundered by two boys and a girl whose lives would be shaped inexorably by the objects they had stolen.[76] Just as Stahr's triumph in Hollywood had earlier been compared to that of a "high flyer," so his final defeat would be suggested through the falling of his plane from the sky.[77]

Fitzgerald's novel gives a fascinating glimpse into the way that images of flight had infiltrated the imagination of one of the period's most important American novelists. Flight meant adventure, privilege, power, spectacle, and death. Indeed, in Fitzgerald's notes for the landing scene at Glendale Airport, the element of spectacle is even further emphasized. Now the scene is described not from Cecilia's but Stahr's perspective; he sees the city below as a movie set and imagines himself adjusting its lights to heighten the dramatic effect: "I shall take these lights in my fingers. I shall make them bright . . . The plane bumped lower, lower; the engines stopped breathing – then round softly and down. It was always very exciting to get there."[78]

There was Hollywood; and for those who want to understand what flight had come to mean for ordinary people Hollywood remains the best source, if only because Hollywood reached a larger and more international audience than any other form of culture. The traces of flight are to be found not only in the aviation films I have discussed, but also in pictures that belong to very different genres. The unmistakable message of all these movies was that the airplane was transforming the world and the way that some people lived. Though still exotic and distant from the lives of ordinary human beings, it represented the future and modern times. Perhaps the most dramatic example (because the most outrageous) is the first Fred Astaire and Ginger Rogers musical, *Flying Down to Rio*, released in 1933. The protagonist of the movie, played by Gene Raymond, is a band leader who thinks nothing of flying his small biplane from Florida to Rio, a major feat at that time; the film's two most spectacular dance sequences take place in an modernistic aviators' club, where uninhibited Brazilians dance the Carioca, and on the wings of biplanes where chorus girls perform their act as they overfly the city; the marriage of the two principals occurs unexpectedly in an

Pl. 344. The Grand Central Terminal, Glendale Airport, in 1928.

Pl. 345.   The creator of this poster for Casablanca grasps the importance of the airplane, which in the picture itself could barely be seen through the mist of the final scene.

Pl. 346.   A poster for *Flying Down to Rio*.

Pl. 347.   A squadron of biplanes attacks King Kong atop the Empire State Building.

Pl. 348.   Plane crashes in Hollywood movies were not always fatal, as can be seen in this scene from *Lost Horizon*, which sets the stage for the unfolding of the story. The reality was somewhat different.

airplane from which the female star's resigned fiancé then proceeds to bail out, leaving the newly weds to fly off to marital bliss.

What impresses is the *variety* of ways in which the imagery of flight was being used in some of the movies that we remember most vividly from the thirties and the forties. In *King Kong* (1933), it is only the devastating firepower and maneuverability of the airplane that can vanquish the monster that has established himself on the summit of yet another symbol of modernity, the Empire State Building. By juxtaposing the snail-like pace of Clark Gable and Claudette Colbert by bus and the rapid flight of Colbert's father, *It Happened One Night* (1934) suggests that the sky belongs to the rich and powerful. Ordinary folk are consigned to the ground. The risks and excitement of air travel are suggested by another Frank Capra film, *Lost Horizon* (1937), that delivers its protagonists to the utopian society of Shangri-La by means of a dramatic plane crash in the Himalayas after they have been kidnapped by their treacherous Mongolian pilot and diverted from their original destination in Shanghai. The message here seems to be that once you have consigned yourself to an airplane anything can happen. *Flying Deuces* (1939) uses the airplane for comic purposes and exposes the incapacity of normal earthbound creatures like Laurel and Hardy to master its controls, thus underlining the arcane skills possessed by aviators. The Hitchcock suspense drama and propaganda film *Foreign Correspondent* (1940) reaches its climax during a flight across the North Atlantic that signals the beginning of a new era in transatlantic travel. The final scene of the most emblematic movie of the early 1940s, *Casablanca* (1942), is played against the backdrop of an airfield tarmac, the exciting growl of aircraft engines, and the whirring of propeller blades. Frank Capra's *State of the Union* (1948) contrasts the purity of aviation with the corruption of American politics; the protagonist's fall from grace is conveyed by his alienation from flying, the profession that had made his fortune and set him off from other men.

By 1950, Joseph Mankiewicz's *All About Eve* makes it clear that a stage director invited to make a movie in Hollywood would take it for granted that the only respectable way to make the trip would be by air. Flying to the coast had ceased to be exotic. There would be no local people hanging around the airport in hopes of glimpsing a celebrity. When the film's protagonist, played by Bette Davis, wants to indicate her intention to make a scene she tells her guests: "Fasten your seat belts. It's going to be a bumpy night!" This was no mere metaphor, but a reminder that before the introduction of jets heavy turbulence (especially when crossing the Rocky Mountains) remained an expected and predictable aspect of commercial air travel.

★   ★   ★

Aviators who wrote often commented on the privileges that mastery of the air bestowed on them. "Is not to fly," Robert de Marolles asked in a book significantly entitled *Aviation, école de l'homme* (Aviation, School of Man), "to achieve a synthesis whose exact parallel is not provided by any other human activity? Is not to fly to be exposed to unexpected and unforgettable impressions that no one can imagine if he has not experienced them?"[79] And indeed, the author of this work ended his book by reflecting on the paradox that aviation, the most recently born product of technological progress and, superficially, an invention designed to sweep its practitioners into a dizzying vortex that left little time for thought, sometimes offered opportunities for spiritual transcendence without which life would not be worth living. The airplane, he insisted, should not be included among those many machines that had contributed to the degradation of thought and undermined the notion of a hierarchy of values. It had not contributed to the creation of a more artificial,

Pl. 349. Ernst Jünger chose this photograph of a German ace to illustrate his point about the look of aviators in *Luftfahrt ist not!*

mechanized, and mindless civilization. Though the "vulgar" might see in it nothing but an instrument for racing through the world at a speed not attainable in other vehicles, the airplane revealed itself upon reflection to be also "the most extraordinary means of escaping from ourselves and from the existence that oppresses us."[80]

Some aviators were moved to see in flight something more than a magic carpet that led to marvelous adventures, an escape from the banality of earthly existence, or a manifestation of the power of modernity: they sought in their experiences in the air lessons that could be applied to society as a whole. Mermoz believed that having been born from an act of faith – the need to escape from ourselves, the will to raise ourselves above the contingences of a constricting earthly life, and the desire to break with the monotony of a regime that had become too egotistical – aviation was destined to become "a sort of social religion, which is going to serve as the basis for the profound evolution of the spirit of the new generations." Like other religions, aviation would have its own mystique, its own apostles, and its own martyrs.[81]

For Ernst Jünger, the flyer was the prototype of "the new man, the man of the twentieth century," who would combine the characteristics of the soldier and the worker. Some artists, he thought, had captured the ideal image of aviators in their flying garb with faces under leather helmets that looked as if they had been carved out of stone. "Duty and service, intelligence and ability, character and heart gave these young faces at an early point their form . . . They are an expression of the best forces that are living in the *Volk*."[82]

The next year, in his book *Das abenteulicher Herz* (The Adventurous Heart), Jünger reported that he had spent a fair amount of time during the previous two years in the company of

flyers, going so far as to live on an airfield for two weeks. Aviators were such good company, he said, because they represented an intensification of the qualities of the worker and the soldier. They bore the stamp of good metal; they had dedicated their intellect to service; and at the same they had a devil-may-care attitude and a sense of aristocratic lightheartedness. "Again I discovered what had been clear to me earlier, namely that the decisive endowment necessary for the domination of a form of life that is lived under conditions of intense danger, is not "nerves of steel." Struggle in the civilized world requires, on the contrary, a high degree of sensibility . . ."[83] Aviators possessed this quality; and this, together with their other attributes, set them apart and above ordinary human beings.

The mention of names like Mermoz and Jünger raises a delicate question: the relationship between aviation and fascism during the interwar years. Already in 1909, pondering the meaning of Louis Blériot's Channel flight, H. G. Wells had predicted that the flying machine would bring an end to "the days of natural bureaucracy." The time was coming when men would be sorted out into "those who will have the knowledge, nerve, and courage to do these splendid, dangerous things, and those who will prefer the humbler level."[84] Gabriele D'Annunzio, considered by some to be a precursor of fascism, had also predicted that aviation would produce a new elite. Had he not written in his 1910 novel *Forse che sì forse che no* (Perhaps Yes, Perhaps No) that the earthbound would be reduced to settling for the vicarious identification they could feel with the "celestial helmsmen" who looked down on those below with a scornful smile?[85] In the 1930s the two Fascist governments – Italy and Germany – paraded the achievements of their air forces; both were led by flamboyant and powerful figures within the regime; and both built imposing palaces dedicated to airpower in Rome and Berlin. America's most famous airman, Charles Lindbergh, was accused of harboring pro-Nazi sympathies after a series of visits he made to Germany to report to the American government on the threat represented by the Luftwaffe. Though he was repelled by Nazi anti-Semitism and Hitler's demagoguery, Lindbergh did not conceal his admiration for the achievements of the German aircraft industry and the vitality of the Third Reich.[86] His wife wrote a book in which she imprudently dared to suggest that the Fascists and Nazis might, with all their barbaric acts, represent the "wave of the future."[87] Benjamin Crémieux was not alone in discovering dis-

Pl. 351.   Ernst Sagebield's
Reich Air Ministry in Berlin,
1935.

turbing echoes of fascist ideology in Saint-Exupéry's *Terre des hommes*, a book that com-
memorated the heroic deeds of Aéropostale. And who can forget Hitler, in Leni
Riefenstahl's *Triumph of the Will*, descending from the sky in an airplane like a Wagnerian
god, in order to receive the accolade of a waiting crowd of Nazis?

Curiously, the only person I know who pursued the question of the relationship
between aviation and fascism in depth was a minor British writer – and one, moreover,
who had no personal experience of aviation during a decade – the 1930s – when aviation
was an irresistible topic among British authors and some had taken up flying.[88] Rex
Warner's 1941 novel, *The Aerodrome*, is not explicitly about fascism – indeed, the term is
never mentioned; yet it explores the chasm separating the values of aviators from those of
ordinary people in such a way as to question whether they can easily be reconciled with
those of liberalism and democracy.

A highly autobiographical work, *The Aerodrome* is the story of Roy, adopted son of the
vicar of a small village located in the environs of a military airfield, who, betrayed by his
fiancée, agrees to join the Air Force and falls beneath the influence and power of the base's
commander, identified only as the Air Vice-Marshal. The airmen being trained there are
taught by the Air Vice-Marshal to view all civilians with disdain.

It is against the souls of the people themselves that we are fighting. It is each and every
one of their ideas that we must detest. Think of them as earthbound, grovelling from one
piece of mud to another, and feebly imagining distinctions between the two, incapable
of envisaging a distant objective, tied up for ever in their miserable and unimportant histories, indeed in the whole wretched and blind history of man on earth . . . The race
which we, of all people, are now required to protect is a race of money-makers and sen-
timentalists, undisciplined except by forces which they do not understand, insensitive to
all except the lowest, the most ordinary, the most mechanical stimuli. Protect it! We shall
destroy what we cannot change."[89]

The Air Vice-Marshal thinks of himself as creating a "new race of men" that would dominate their inferiors because they had subjected themselves to a higher discipline. Roy

Pl. 352. The German ace Ernst Udet, now a general in the newly constituted Luftwaffe, entertains Charles Lindbergh in Potsdam in October 1938. Udet displays his Pour le mérite, won during the First World War.

quickly comes see the world through the eyes of the Air Vice-Marshal. Viewed from the air, he agrees, people below appeared "both defenceless and ridiculous, as though infinite trouble had been taken to secure a result that has little of no significance. I began to think now in the same way of those inhabitants of the earth who had never risen above it, never submitted their lives to a discipline like ours, a discipline that was unconnected with the acquisition of money or foodstuffs."[90]

Like Jünger, Marolles, and others, Roy recognizes that aviators are set apart from other men through their unique combination of intellectual and physical skills exercised under conditions of great danger. In exchange for the risks they run, they enjoy an exhilarating feeling of domination not accessible to ordinary earthbound human beings who dedicate themselves to the satisfaction of material and emotional needs. "We were set to exercise our brains, our nerves, our muscles, and our desires towards one end, and to back the force of our will we possessed the most powerful machines that have been invented by man. It was not only our dexterity with these machines, but the whole spirit of our training which cut us off from the mass of men; and to be so cut off was, whether we realized it or not, our greatest pleasure and our chief article of pride."[91]

Roy comes to realize that the Air Vice-Marshal's aim is nothing less than to seize control of an unspecified country, which is unmistakably England.

As I began gradually to understand the grandeur of the Air Vice-Marshal's plans, I realized that already we were equipped at any moment to take over the direction of the country whose servants nominally we were . . . I did not think of our purpose as a con-

307

spiracy, but rather as a necessary and exciting operation. We constituted no revolution-ary party actuated by humanitarian ideals, but seemed to be an organization manifestly entitled by its own discipline, efficiency, and will to assume supreme power. Outside us I could see nothing that was not incompetent or corrupt, and I remember as on various occasions I piloted the Air Vice-Marshal's plane from one aerodrome to another I would look down on the hills and forests, the coal mines and factory towns over which we flew, and would wonder with a kind of joyful trepidation how much longer we would have to wait before the word was given to us to seize into our own hands all the resources and all the power that we traversed with our wings.[92]

Toward the end of *The Aerodrome*, Roy begins to regret everything he has given up for the Air Force. He realizes that he has lost touch with the country in which he has been bred and the people who cared for him; he develops a longing for the countryside he had given up in exchange for the sky; and he dedicates himself to the physical recovery of the girl who had betrayed him. He suddenly understands that in abolishing inefficiency and hypocrisy, the Air Force had also destroyed "the spirit of adventure, inquiry, the sweet and terrifying sympathy of love that can acknowledge mystery, danger, and dependence."[93] He feels "the full inhumanity of the organization which he [the Air Vice-Marshal] had con-structed with such an expense of will and which seemed to me now, not only in this instance, to be designed to stifle life which, however misused, was richer in everything but determination than our order."[94]

There was, of course, nothing inherently fascist about flying; but in the atmosphere of the 1930s it is easy to see how people could make the connection. The transparently false state-ment that "every aviator is a born fascist" contained within it the embryo of a truth that Warner had partially grasped.[95] To be sure, the scorn of flyers for earthlings and the identi-fication of men with powerful machines that the author of *The Aerodrome* ascribes to the Air Vice-Marshal and his program for the creation of a "new and more adequate race of men" were prewar literary themes, almost as old as aviation itself; but Warner points to three new elements more typical of the thirties and the ideologies of fascist regimes: the cult of the leader (or, by metaphorical extension, the pilot in command); the subjection of the individ-ual to the collectivity or organization; and the free acceptance of an ascetic discipline that was spiritual in nature rather than oriented toward petty material concerns, such as "the acquisition by cunning and hypocrisy of large or small sums of money."[96] To these poten-tially fascist themes we can add the privileging of risk and danger over the preservation of life and its corollary: the neo-Romantic celebration of death and the worship of martyrs.[97] This conjunctural and coincidental overlapping between the ideology of fascism and the way aviation was practiced in the 1920s and 1930s explains why aviators were peculiarly sub-ject to "the fascist temptation" and why even those who resisted it, like Lindbergh and Saint-Exupéry, found reasons to understand, and even admire, those who did not.

★   ★   ★

By the time that Warner wrote *The Aerodrome*, the sound of wings and growling motors overhead had become for millions of Westerners a symbol not of adventure or the prom-ise of modernity but instead a portent of what Ernest Hemingway called "mechanized doom."[98] Warner himself was nearly hit by a bomb when crossing the street in London in the summer of 1940. On 5 October 1940 he wrote to a friend that "we had about 200 incendiaries round us the other night, one of which bounced off the roof into the garden, where we shoveled wall flowers + earth over it. It was an incredible sight at first, though in about 20 minutes nearly all the fires were out."[99]

Of course, the theme of death dripping from the sky had been developed in a literary work three decades before in H. G. Wells's *The War in the Air*. Both Londoners and Parisians experienced bombing raids during the First World War. Saint-Exupéry, then a young secondary student in Paris, had described the excitement he and a schoolmate experienced while watching Paris being bombed by the Germans in 1918. He warned his mother not to believe what she read in the newspapers; the reality had been much worse.

> The sky was riddled with airplanes caught in searchlights; flairs lighted up the sky; it was like a fairy tale. One could hear the machine guns and above all the anti-aircraft guns that didn't stop for a second, pan . . . panpan . . . panpan . . . panpan . . . and from time to time we saw a flash and heard the noise of bombs "that was some kind of rumpus, old man – you bet your life!" I saw a French plane fall in flames (for the Germans shot down *several*), it was like a great torch. I saw an oil depot explode that illuminated the entire sky with an intense red light – One has no idea how much damage they did and above all how many people they killed: it's fantastic.[100]

Saint-Exupéry made no effort to dissipate whatever fears his mother may have had for the safety of her son in a city under air attack. "I was very well situated and was in a state of enthusiastic delirium, I would have enjoyed seeing five or six [German bombers] go down in flames."[101] A few days later he returned to what had become his favorite theme: "The weather is good tonight, thus one can infallibly predict: Gothas [German bombers], being awakened, the basement. I wish that you were here to listen once to anti-aircraft fire. You would think yourself in the middle of a veritable hurricane, of a storm at sea, it's magnificent."[102]

Yet two decades later, when he wrote *Terre des Hommes* and the outbreak of war in Europe threatened, the thought of war in the air had lost whatever romance it had once held for the young Saint-Exupéry. All the airplane and the explosives it carried promised now was "a bloody slaughter." "Each side takes refuge behind a cement wall; night after night it launches squadrons that torpedo the adversary in his entrails, blow up his vital centers, and paralyze his production and commerce. Victory belongs to the side that rots last. And the two adversaries rot together."[103]

By the time that Saint-Exupéry made his way to Algeria in the summer of 1943, he had become deeply pessimistic about the coming postwar world.[104] In a letter that was probably addressed to his fellow aviation writer René Chambe but never sent, he spat out at great length his disgust at the contemporary world. Under a form of "universal totalitarianism" – and Saint-Exupéry had in mind the Western democracies as well as the fascist countries and the Soviet Union – man was becoming "soft, polite, and docile lifestock." "I hate my epoch with all my heart. Man is dying out of [spiritual] thirst . . . One can't live any more on refrigerators, politics, games, and cross-word puzzles, you know! One can't go on this way. One can't live without poetry, color, or love . . . Why did Mermoz follow a clown like the colonel [La Rocque], if not out of longing . . . It's all the same to me if I'm killed in the war. What will survive of everything I've loved?"[105]

Somewhat more surprising in this letter was Saint-Exupéry's confession that he had lost his zest for flying. Not even a few turns at the controls of the powerful and super fast P-38 had overcome his depression. He now wondered if his earlier enthusiasm for aviation had been misplaced. "I observe with melancholy that today, at forty-three years of age after six thousand, five hundred hours of flight everywhere in the world, I can't find great pleasure in these sorts of games. The airplane is no longer anything but a means of transportation – here [in North Africa] of war – and if I submit myself to speed and altitude at a patriarchal

Pl. 353. Saint-Exupéry at the controls of the P-38 Lightning. He had to be assisted with his flying suit and lifted into the cockpit.

Pl. 354. Jules Roy's fierce sense of determination is captured in this portrait.

age for this profession, it is much more in order not to refuse any of the messes of my generation than out of a hope to rediscover the satisfactions of the past. This is perhaps sad – but perhaps it isn't. It's no doubt because I was wrong at twenty."[106] Wrong, that is, in loving flight as much as he did.

One wonders what Saint-Exupéry would have written about aviation had he lived to see Europe's cities in ruins and photographs of incinerated Japanese cities. How remote all this would have seemed from the heroic days of Aéropostale in the late 1920s and early 1930s when he and his comrades were building an airline whose goal it was to bring distant peoples together. "Aéropostale," he wrote nostalgically in a bitter letter of December 1943 in which he recalled the brief periods of happiness in his life, "was sheer joy. And nonetheless, how great it was!"[107]

Had he survived the war, Saint-Exupéry certainly would have read with sympathy the works of his young friend and literary disciple, Jules Roy.[108] A career officer in the French Air Force, Roy had first met Saint-Exupéry in 1939; then, to his delight, he rediscovered him in Algeria at Laghouat where Saint Exupéry was being taught to fly the Bloch 175, a three-seat reconnaissance plane.[109] By an extraordinary coincidence, Saint-Exupéry had been assigned an adjoining room in Roy's hotel. Roy made no secret of his admiration for the older man's works and gave him a copy of a small volume of recently published poems that Saint-Exupéry agreed to read and then went on to praise.[110] Saint-Exupéry confided in Roy the anguish that he felt for the future of France. "Everything that he cherished and that gave value to his life was in danger of disappearing, and he had agreed to go down with the ship."[111] Roy's "integrity and youngness of heart" touched Saint-Exupéry; he was prepared to mentor him as a writer; and he offered him the precious "gift of his friendship."[112] Roy responded with hero worship.[113] Seeing Saint-Exupéry off on a flight to Algiers to visit some friends, among them André Gide, Roy was impressed by the way the writer's face changed once he had donned his pilot's gear. Stripped of its earthly appearance, his visage took on a "kind of supernatural virtue." "At the controls of the plane that shook and growled, he had suddenly become a god, and the most powerful god of all, the thundering Jupiter, his eye on the world and his hand on the lightning."[114]

When Saint-Exupéry disappeared over southern France in July 1944, Roy was flying missions over Europe as a bombardier in British Wellingtons. His path to England had by no means been straight or easy. An early admirer and supporter of Pétain after the fall of France, Roy was disgusted by the facility with which so many French officers changed sides in 1942 after the Allied invasion of North Africa. He later described himself in March 1943 as one of those who were lost "in the muddle of influences"; among the die-hard supporters of Pétain, the admirers of General Henri Giraud, and the converts to de Gaulle, he felt marginalized, like a beast of burden that finds no buyer at a country fair. Yet he yearned to get in the thick of things and test himself against God, the devil, and death to see what he was worth. The question was: where?[115] Unable to obtain a posting to the RAF as a pilot, Roy resigned himself to becoming a bombardier. "Was I thus destined to destroy? Did the peace of my conscience come at this price? I resigned myself to my fate."[116] On 26 October 1943, with nine hundred other Frenchmen recruited for the RAF, he embarked on a Dutch ship bound for Liverpool where he would become the unhappy guest of a people he confessed to both hating and admiring; a people he no doubt also envied for their freedom from German occupation.[117]

Roy's first days in England were anything but pleasant. Shortly after arriving there, he would write a bitter letter to Saint-Exupéry in which he expressed his disillusionment. "From here France seems to me even further away than it did from Algiers . . . It's this weight of the unknown that is so difficult to bear. Our uncertainty is such that we can't get it off our shoulders; it weighs on us like a monstrous hump that spoils our life . . . Even if I hadn't been caged in by barbed wire, I would have been the prisoner of my own impatience and my own demons. The wind that blows through the barracks will have frozen whatever remains of my youth; the winter that descends on the countryside doesn't hold within it spring . . ."[118]

And yet Roy persevered; he successfully completed his long training as a bombardier; and he was given command of a Handley Page Halifax with a French crew.[119] Despite the terrible fear that he experienced before taking off on missions and whatever secret pity he may have felt for his victims, Roy came to know a "barbarous happiness" that derived from his belief in the justness of his cause.[120] When he and his crew returned from a bombing raid, they had "the serenity of judges, for they were the instrument of the defense of a people, of a continent, of a mystique."[121]

Before Roy had finished his tour of thirty-seven missions, he had learned what it meant to participate in a terror raid against a German city. He confessed that deep down inside, he was overjoyed when he saw the conflagration that reduced the enemy's cities to cinders and the bones of their inhabitants to dust. He had the right to massacre people on the ground, he wrote, because at any moment he could fall in flames.[122] Roy knew himself and his crewmates to be "the delivery men of death, industrial killers, the elite of destruction." But dropping his bombs on Leipzig on the night of 13 February 1945, he didn't give a thought to the carnage they were causing on the ground but only to the difficulties of the flight.[123] He longed for that moment when he could announce to the crew "bombs away." So what if the bombs fell on the inhabitants of Leipzig cowering in their shelters. When they emerged from their rat holes – if they did – they would only find ruins and the smoke of incendiary bombs. But did he and his crewmates have any other choice? "True, we were also barbarians, criminals of war, but what if Hitler had perfected the atomic bomb before the Americans, Great Britain would have been destroyed and we with it."

What did Roy take away from the Leipzig raid in the form of memory? "A fantastic fireworks display, the crackling of guns, and, below, a golden lake that came close to becoming a sea. Think about it: a city of six hundred thousand inhabitants, the homeland of Richard Wagner, the leading German university, a library unlike any other in the world, an academy of fine arts, all that in flames, and an idiot [another bomber] who got in our way that [the pilot] Gronier jumped over in the light of the firestorm, a formidable explosion that lit up the sky for a few moments. After which, we had a snack . . ."[124]

In 1947 Roy set out in a short but moving essay to explore the world of the "secret society" of aviators, whose obligations, work, games, and rites were unknown to the understanding of ordinary men. He gave to this lyrical ode a curious title, *Comme un mauvais ange* (Like A Fallen Angel), whose meaning was not immediately clear. No one, I think, has written with greater passion about the sensual pleasures of flight:

> Every take-off is the revelation of a mystery. As soon as the plane leaves the ground, a mechanic raises the curtain on a magical scene and the prodigious gift of the world is bestowed upon the pilot. He leaves behind him a narrow horizon in order to gain by means of his view little by little the mist of the dawn on the plain, mountains whose flanks are eaten by forests, farms still full of sleep, villages similar to islands, orange groves, the dark and garnet-colored checkerboard of cultivated fields. A spectacle begins. Slowly and subtly, the regions give way to one another on the earth and in the clouds; they yield their flocks, their fields of snow, and their fabulous fortified cities.[125]

Once in the air, Roy tells us, the pilot's soul is magically transformed. Grace is conferred upon him in a peculiar state of ecstasy, reminiscent of the innocence of childhood. He is humbled and prepared to love the sky and the earth in a state of inner silence that is untroubled by the deafening noise of the aircraft's motors.[126]

And then inevitably comes the dispiriting return to earth when the pilot has to surrender his kingdom and all the beauties of its gardens and singing waters and become a man like any other:

> The airfield appears. He calms the growling of the motors, descends slowly. Little by little, things resume their appearance, the villages their low houses and their inhabited streets. The stage shrinks. On making his last bank, the pilot sees before him nothing but a depressing and empty wasteland with a décor of hangars. The curtain falls. The pilot reassumes the proportions of a man, and in the bus that drives him back to town he breaks out in a cold sweat when the driver approaches a turn at fifty kilometers per hour.[127]

In this passage, Roy captures a feeling that many pilots have experienced, but few have been willing to describe: the loss of the god-like sense of power and freedom that comes upon descending to earth.

Roy believed that, for pilots, their relationship to the airplane was the only love affair of which they would never tire.[128] Over forty years later, writing his memoirs, he reaffirmed that the airplane had been his only real passion.[129] Remembering his first encounters with the DC 3 in Morocco in March 1943, he recalled the pleasure that this powerful airplane gave him when he first was allowed to fly it. ". . . it ran with a wheel in the front, it took off like a flaming flower, and landed like a laundry iron, boum!, provided that one knew how to maneuver the upper flaps of the engine housing. Every flight resembled a rape . . . I dreamed of ripping open the sky, I was in love with the Douglases that tore apart the immense violet tapestry of the clouds."[130]

Still, for all his love of flight and desire to sing its delights, Roy brought himself to confess that he was struck by "the lack of fruit" that man had harvested in the "fields of clouds and orchards of stars." Those who sought in the skies the inner face of man had discovered to their horror that of Satan "in a red sky filled with the terrible combat of the fallen angels."[131] Such an admission could not have come easily for Roy. Like others, he had welcomed the dropping of the atomic bomb on Japan because it hastened the coming of peace.

It may be that the doubts expressed by his friend Albert Camus about Hiroshima and Nagasaki shook his certainty about the need to end the war at any cost; possible, also, that the ruins he saw in Germany soon after the end of the war caused him to have second thoughts about the devastation that aviators like himself had wreaked.[132] In any case, midway through *Comme un mauvais ange*, Roy moved abruptly from evoking the wonders of aviation to reflecting on its destructive power. The history he sketched was one of disenchantment. When Blériot flew the Channel in 1909 he believed that he was serving the union of humanity. When Mermoz opened the first mail routes in Latin America, he could justify the risks he took and asked others to assume in thinking that they carried in their planes the letters of businessmen, anxious mothers, and lovers. The truth was, however, that the mountains, the ocean, the clouds, and the night had only been conquered for a "satanic triumph."[133] Roy pondered the strange paradox that aviation – "a school of courage and virtue" – had become "one of the ten plagues of Egypt." "So many efforts, so many dead subordinated to the development of air power . . . have led to the mockery of a machine invented by man for his happiness and only working toward his destruction." The plague of aerial war held the planet in its tight grasp. "There are no more happy islands; it has rained steel in Tahiti, and the enchanted beaches are covered with fall-out [from atomic bomb tests]."[134] Years would pass, Roy thought, before the airplane would regain its role as an instrument of peace.[135] Still, Roy retained the hope in 1947 that military aviation would age and die with him. "It is only right that it should disappear in its turn beneath the weight of massacred children and cities in ruins, or that it should agree to finally serve the cause of peace alone."[136]

★   ★   ★

In 1910, soon after taking his first flight, Gabriele D'Annunzio confided to a French interviewer that aviation carried within itself "the promise of a profound metamorphosis of civic life" that would have far-reaching consequences for aesthetics as well as for war and peace. New idols would appear; new laws would have to be written; relations among nations would be transformed. High in the sky, above the clouds, customs barriers, property rights, and frontiers would lose their meaning. Aviation would create a new civilization, a new way of life, and a new elite. The "Republic of the Air" would exile the wicked and the parasites and would open itself to "men of good will." The "elect" would abandon the "chrysalis of weight" and would take flight.[137]

Forty years later, it was clear that D'Annunzio had been right in predicting important changes as a result of the invention of the airplane, even if his vague references to the emergence of an aristocracy of the air had failed to materialize, except in literature and film.

Flight changed warfare, turning the battlefield from a two-dimensional into a three-dimensional space and making it possible to transport troops long distances in short periods of time. It produced a new form of transport that, by the end of the 1940s, had already left its mark on the practice of politics, diplomacy, business, and commerce. Neville Chamberlain introduced "shuttle diplomacy" during the Munich crisis of 1938; Franklin Roosevelt would follow in his footsteps, flying to Teheran in 1944 and Yalta in 1945. Businessmen could meet their counterparts on other continents face to face. Perishable goods could be imported from anywhere in the world. In short order, flight would change the way that ordinary people used their leisure time and related to their families. Distance became a nuisance to be endured rather than an obstacle not easily overcome.

Flight had many other effects, some ephemeral, others more lasting.[138] It gave the West a new variant on the theme of the hero and a new type of entertainment in the form of air shows, air races, and the vicarious experience of hazardous long-distance flights followed by means of newspapers, radio announcers, and newsreels. It is difficult for us to grasp the frenetic enthusiasm these feats inspired, all the more so because space flight in our time has failed to unleash the outbreak of such spontaneous feeling. For whatever reason, this moment was actually quite fleeting; its greatest intensity extended only from 1927 to 1933. Amelia Earhart's fatal round-the-world flight of 1937 was undertaken in keen awareness that the period of record-breaking exploits was drawing to an end. She felt under pressure to defend her position as "the foremost woman pilot in the world."[139] Ironically, Earhart's flight attracted so much attention from the media only because it had a tragic end.

Flight also provided a new aesthetic object that had far-reaching effects on design. The streamlined shape of 1930s' aircraft would influence the look of trains, cars, clothes, and even household objects. It is difficult for us today to appreciate the passion that aircraft could inspire in an age whose most inventive minds were consciously seeking to liberate themselves from the forms of the past. The airplane seemed to many the purest product of the machine age. Balbo was not alone in thinking that the Savoia-Marchetti flying boat that he used in his *crociere* was more beautiful than a Greek statue. "All you need to do is to look at the S.55, whether it's flying in the air like a white heron with its wings outspread,

with its almost diaphanous lightness under the kiss of the sun , whether it's swaying atop the water, on its twin hulls, like a sea bird that puts down on the water after a long voyage and is liberated in midair from the effort of the flight. Nothing is more beautiful in the classical sense of the term than the profile that it displays in the lightly ascending line of its delicate ribbing, from the hulls to its streamlined wings, with its powerful motor hoisted on top like the head of an eagle on the lookout for its prey."[140] As late as 1950, the Lockheed Constellation produced similar feelings in some of the passengers who were fortunate enough to fly it.

The need for larger and larger airfields transformed the physical environment in which people lived and called forth a new form of architecture – the airport with its terminals, hangars, and ever more complex dependencies – whose imperatives would leave a lasting imprint on the form of the urban environment. The view from above in a fast-moving airplane added a new dimension to the way that people perceived the earth and, above all, its cities. The sight of skyscrapers and caverns of Manhattan from the sky became as common as the image of Times Square. How many Hollywood movies of the 1930s and 1940s begin with a panorama of New York City from the air? Meanwhile, the airplane was shrinking the globe and accelerating the interdependence of peoples long before anyone had uttered the word "globalization." By 1950 trips that had earlier required days and sometimes weeks could be accomplished in the space of twenty-four hours. As Richard Byrd had shown in 1929 with his flight over the South Pole, no place on earth was unreachable by plane.

In Marc Blitzstein's *Airborne Symphony*, the Narrator expresses his sense of wonder at a world that has been shrunk by the conquest of the air as a realm of transportation:

Pl. 356. Readers of popular magazines in the 1930s found the sleek lines of racing seaplanes irresistible.

Pl. 357. The Lockheed Super Constellation in flight. This one contains under its fuselage a container for freight, which suggests that its elegant lines had become a constraint on the cargo that it carried.

Pl. 358. A 1925 Renault advertisement for air travel and motoring. Only a privileged few in France in this period traveled by either airplane or car.

314

RENAULT

AVIATION   1925   AUTOMOBILE

Record du Monde de distance sans escale (Étampes-Villa-Cisneros - 3 Février)
Record du Monde des 24 heures, toutes catégories (Montlhéry - 3 Juin)

Pl. 359.   La Guardia Airport, 1937–1939.

Pl. 360.   Downtown Man-hattan in a wide-angle lens photograph by Charles Rotskin.

Pl. 361.   The Pan-American Sikorsky S-40 Clipper over Manhattan, 19 October 1931.

Laugh it off.
This little thought knocks out a mountain range,
Tears up the jungle. This notion eats oceans,
Puts the desert in its vest pocket,
Has geography for tea.
The barriers to the other side of the world –
They can pack it up now, and call it a day.[141]

Fairy-tale achievements like these, however, were not obtained without paying a price. It was true that in flying over countries one got a better sense for them as a whole than one did while traveling on the ground. Rivers, lakes, villages, towns, foothills, and mountain ranges appeared in a more panoramic setting and in sharper definition.[142] The airplane, Saint-Exupéry claimed in *Terre des hommes*, had made it possible to discover the true face of the earth. For the first time in history, man was in a position to judge human life on a cosmic scale, from the heights of the open sky and to see the world for what it really was.[143]

But even Saint-Exupéry confessed that the airplane's ability to travel in a straight line, avoiding obstacles on the ground, had been a "cruel" form of progress. The civilized world consisted of isolated islands spread throughout the planet; surrounding these islands existed a foundation of rocks, sand, and salt on which, here and there, life flourished "like a bit of moss in the hollows of ruins." Human beings, Saint-Exupéry concluded, had lived for centuries in ignorance of what the planet was really like. Thus deceived by so many self-indulgent lies, having seen in the course of their travels so many well-irrigated lands, so many orchards, so many meadows, earth dwellers had "embellished the image of their prison." Then came the airplane that revealed that the planet was not the temperate and welcoming place that they had believed it to be.[144]

Le Corbusier had similar thoughts six years earlier in a flight across the Atlas Mountains from Algiers to Ghardaïa in March 1933 and expressed them at the end of a book that was meant to celebrate the aesthetics of flight and the insights to be had from the perspective of the air. Le Corbusier complained that whereas from the ground landscape presented "a delight of the senses," from the air there remained only "a spectacle with a lesson – a philosophy." Abstraction triumphed over the human view.

> When the eye is five feet or so above the ground, flowers and trees have
>   dimension: a measure relative to human activity, proportion.
> In the air, from above? It is a wilderness, indifferent to our thousand-year-
>   old ideas, a fatality of cosmic elements and events.
> The huts of the Arab shepherds, clinging to the awesome heights of the
>   Atlas, terribly isolated in a strange game, are in their starkness a revelation
>   of natural violence.
> The elements are a frightening incubus.
> From the plane: there is no pleasure . . . but a long, concentrated, mournful
>   meditation.
> I feel myself unapt at this sort of unattainable delight.
> I understand and ponder, I do not love; I feel I am not attuned to the
>   enjoyment of these spectacles from above.[145]

Hence, for some at least, the world seen from above lost its human dimensions and took on an air of brutality. But beyond this introduction to an "unrelenting, impassive, careless game of gigantic forces out of all proportion" to humankind, flight brought with it other losses; because in exchange for diminishing the factor of distance and making possible a dazzling series of rapidly changing impressions, travel by air had the effect of blurring the sense of transition from one place to another. As early as 1935, Anne Morrow Lindbergh noticed that the rapid trip in her husband's powerful aircraft, *Sirius*, from New York to North Haven, Maine – the site of her family's vacation home – had lessened the joy of arrival. "I have had this sensation in flying many times before – this lack of synchronization of the speeds of mind and body. Pessimistically I have wondered if rapid transportation is not robbing us of the realization of life and therefore much of its joy." Acknowledging, however, that the feeling of loss she described might not be felt by others in the future, she added that she had decided that she was like the near-sighted man who is not yet used to his spectacles. "We are still trying to look at the stamen of a flower with spectacles made to look at horizons. Our children will measure their distances not by steeples and pine trees but by mountains and rivers."[146] She was right in predicting that the next generations would quickly become accustomed to covering vast distances in short periods of time; but one can argue that in doing so they lost that gradual sense of transition and joy of arrival that people had experienced in the past. Those who had the privilege of crossing the Atlantic by ship often have moments of nostalgia when being flown across the ocean at thirty-three thousand feet.

And though the airplane may have brought humanity closer together – what Saint-Exupéry proclaimed as the central struggle of humankind: "to understand one another, to join together for the common weal" – it also seriously undermined the sense of security that people had earlier felt.[147] Being able to be anywhere in the world within a matter of hours meant that distance was no longer a guarantee of difference nor of safety. As Douhet had predicted, no place in the world, no matter how remote or heavily defended, could be made safe from air attack. Boundaries and fortifications could be overflown; the bomber would always get through.[148] Though generally triumphant in its tone, the *Airborne Symphony* Marc Blitzstein wrote to celebrate the Eighth Air Force ended on a pessimistic note; victory had not been "without grief, not without warning. Warning!" Airpower remained a potentially destructive force:

> Watch this victory:
> Whose victory? Whose glory?
> Shall men, once again ready to resume the conquest of the skies,
> Once again be stopped?
> Once again – create
> The enemy?[149]

Just as Charles Lindbergh had served as the most eloquent prophet of the coming air age, so he was among the first to express his disillusionment with the development of aviation and to denounce its consequences. In the first days of the Second World War, after attending a meeting of the National Advisory Committee for Aeronautics, he confided to his diary that aviation had begun to lose its interest for him. "Now it is better for men of a different temperament to carry it into the routine place it will hold in commerce and life in the future. There is still romance in aviation, but of a different type. I shall always be interested in it, probably much as one loves and is interested in a grown child. But I realize, and have for a long time realized, that my mind is turning to a diverging path. Where it will lead I do not yet know."[150] In 1942, after taking a rating test in a B-24 bomber at Henry Ford's Willow Run aircraft complex where he was working as a consultant, Lindbergh reflected on how flying had changed since his early days as a pilot. "Flying was at first more an art than a science. Now it is more a science than an art. It has passed from the era of the pioneer to the era of the routine operator, from the time when a 'good pilot' forgot his instruments in an emergency to the time when a 'good pilot' turns to his instruments in an emergency." Lindbergh had no doubts about his ability to fly the B-24, but he was by no means certain that he could fly it "according to the ideas of the inspector whose entire life is wound around regulations and conventional airways procedures."[151] One would have expected to hear these sentiments from someone like Dizzy Davis in *Ceiling Zero*, but not from a man who had dedicated so much of his life in the 1930s to the development of commercial aviation. Was Lindbergh, like Saint-Exupéry, beginning to have doubts about his earlier love affair with flight?

Already before the outbreak of war, Lindbergh's discussions with Luftwaffe officers during his trips to Germany had brought home to him the potential horrors of aerial war. "I knew theoretically what modern bombs could do to cities. At the same time, experiences in war games had convinced me that claims for the effectiveness of both ground and air defense were tremendously exaggerated." What he saw and heard in Nazi Germany gave Lindbergh "a sense of blood and bullets, and I realized how destructive my profession of aviation might become."[152]

Lindbergh's experiences flying combat missions in the South Pacific in 1944, where he strafed and bombed Japanese positions, caused him to reflect on the god-like position of the aviator and his distance from the people he was killing on the ground:

> I don't like this bombing and machine-gunning of unknown targets. You press a button and death flies down. One second the bomb is hanging harmlessly in your racks, completely under your control. The next it is hurtling down the air, and nothing in your power can revoke what you have done. The cards are dealt. If there is life where that

Pl. 362.   Lindbergh on Bial Island in 1944 with Major Thomas B. McGuire.

bomb will hit, you have taken it. Yet it is still living, still breathing; the bomb is still falling; there are still seconds before it will hit . . . You bank your plane over a bit to see better. A column of black smoke and debris rises from the ground below – small – insignificant, like the houses. The world is the same. The sky is the same. Only that column of smoke, settling now, dissipating. How can there be death down there? How can there be writhing, mangled bodies? How can this air around you be filled with unseen projectiles? It is like listening to a radio account of a battle on the other side of the earth. It is too far away, too separated to hold reality.[153]

Pl. 363.   Nurenberg in ruins in the summer of 1945.

320

A trip to Germany to gather information about German aeronautical technology, immediately following the end of the European war in the summer of 1945, forced Lindbergh to face the terrible atrocities committed by the Nazis and, at the same time, put him in the midst of the ruins of German cities created by the Allied bombing campaign. When he arrives in Nuremberg, as night has begun to fall, what he finds is a "dead city; heavily bombed; piles of rubble; gutted buildings; ruined walls; a few lights here and there where a livable room is left. We drive for blocks without seeing a sign of life . . ." From the window of the room he is assigned, he can see "one spire of the cathedral, gutted, but still beautiful, dimly silhouetted in the night. Above, there are broken clouds, and stars are coming out. I feel surrounded by death. Only in the sky is there hope; only in that which man has never touched and which God forbid he ever will."[154]

By 1948, Lindbergh's disillusionment with flight had deepened. After making a long polar flight with the Strategic Air Command to which had been appointed a consultant by the newly created Department of the Air Force, he confessed to his wife that people no longer flew planes; it was the planes that flew people. "It's no longer an effort – Pole – equator – oceans – continents – it's just a question of which way you point the nose of the plane." "The pure joy of flight as an art has given way to the pure efficiency of flight as a science . . . Science is insulating man from life – separating his mind from his senses. The worst of it is that it soon anaesthetizes his senses so that he doesn't know what he's missing."[155]

That same year Lindbergh felt the need to sum up his concerns about the unchecked spread of scientific materialism and his fear that Americans were caught in a vicious circle in which our security today demanded regimentation and the development of weapons that would ruin us tomorrow. He did so in a short but deeply personal book called *Of Flight and Life*. Those who remembered the boundless optimism of Lindbergh's first book, *We*, could only have been shocked by what they found here. It was hard to believe that the two works had been written by the same person. Had Saint-Exupéry lived to read it, he would have been surprised to see how close the trajectory of Lindbergh's thinking had paralleled his own. Both men were deeply pessimistic about the prospects for the postwar world and considered it essential to fill what they considered to be a spiritual void.

Of Flight and Life began with an apocalyptic introduction. The values that we Americans were creating and the standards we were following, Lindbergh claimed, would lead to the end of our civilization. If we did not discover some way to control science by a higher moral force, it would destroy us "with its materialistic values, its rocket aircraft, and its atomic bombs – as it has already destroyed large parts of Europe."[156] Lindbergh confessed that happy memories of his early career as a pilot were now clouded by his experiences during the Second World War:

> I have seen the science I worshipped, and the aircraft I loved, destroying the civilization I expected them to serve, and which I thought as permanent as earth itself. In memory, the vision of my mail plane boring northward over moonlit clouds is now mingled with the streaks of tracers from my fighter, flaming comets, and bombs falling irretrievably through air. Why work for the idol of science when it demands the sacrifice of cities full of children; when it makes robots out of men and blinds their eyes to God? What artificial gift is worth the dulling of senses, the morbid destructiveness that modern industry has brought? What military victory can pay for a civilization's lost? To survive, on more than a temporary time scale, one must look beyond the speed and power of aircraft – beyond the material strength of science.[157]

The irony, of course, was that when Lindbergh wrote these lines flight was on the verge of becoming a mass phenomenon – the obligatory, if not preferred, form of transportation for most people compelled to traverse long distances. Travel and transport by air would become a formidable factor driving globalization. Though it would by no means make all people alike, as some feared, it would play its part in reducing the variety of the world. The "one world" that the former Republican presidential candidate Wendell Wilkie enthusiastically looked forward to in a bestselling 1943 book would have consequences that he did not foresee. Marveling at the fact that he had traveled 31,000 miles in only 160 hours of flight, Wilkie concluded that there were no longer any distant points in the world. "I learned by this trip that the myriad millions of human beings of the Far East are as close to us as Los Angeles is to New York by the fastest trains. I cannot escape the conviction that in the future what concerns them must concern us, almost as much as the problems of the people of California concern the people of New York."[158]

Wilkie was right, of course; but as flight became less exotic, it would lose much of its glamour and allure, and ultimately much of its power as a source of cultural inspiration. One of the cruelest paradoxes of flight is that its relentless progress would dilute the charm of travel. In 1950 that lay in the future; but the aviators of Lindbergh's generation already understood that the breathtaking technological advance of flight, to which they had dedicated their lives and which they could only applaud (if they lived to see it), was bringing to an end the passion for wings that had inspired so many vocations during the first third of the twentieth century. In winning its struggle with the elements and in transforming itself into a business and an indispensable means of making war, aviation may not have lost its appeal and its meaning as a form of adventure for a privileged few; but it had indisputably lost the soul that some had seen in it, that ability to transform men and women and raise them above themselves. Who could write today, with the same conviction Saint-Exupéry did in *Terre des hommes*, that the airplane, which seemed at first to separate the pilot from nature, in fact brings him closer to it?[159] Such is the price of progress. None of us, I suspect, would wish to give it up.

322

Notes

Introduction

1 Ruth Nichols, *Wings for Life* (Philadelphia and New York: Lippincott, 1957), p. 26.

2 One notable exception was Felix Philipp Ingold's *Literatur und Aviatik. Europäische Flugdichtung 1909–1927* (Basle and Stuttgart: Birhäuser Verlag, 1978). I later benefited from Joseph Corn's *The Winged Gospel. America's Romance with Aviation, 1900–1950* (New York: Oxford University Press, 1983); Laurence Goldstein's *The Flying Machine and Modern Literature* (Bloomington: Indiana University Press, 1986); and Peter Fritzsche's *A Nation of Fliers. German Aviation and the Popular Imagination* (Cambridge, Mass., and London: Harvard University Press, 1992).

3 (New Haven and London: Yale University Press, 1994).

4 See Norman Bel Geddes, *Horizons* (Boston: Little, Brown, 1932), p. 20 and Le Corbusier (Charles Jeannenet-Gris), *Aircraft* (Milan: Editrice Abitare Segesta, 1996 reprint; orig. ed. 1935), plates 8 and 61.

5 Antoine de Saint-Exupéry, *Oeuvres complètes* (Paris: Gallimard, 1994), Vol. I, p. 302.

6 Lindbergh also casts a long shadow over the American psyche, as shown by the reception of Philip Roth's novel, *The Plot Against America* (Boston: Houghton Mifflin, 2004). Almost eight decades after his famous slight and three decades after his death, Americans seem to be prepared to denounce him as an enthusiastic Nazi sympathizer and vicious anti-Semite as they were earlier to anoint him as their favorite hero and the embodiment of the values they most admired.

7 Daniele Del Giudice's meditation on flying, *Staccando l'ombra da terra* (Turin: Einaudi, 1994), ends with a chapter on Saint-Exupéry's last flight, but does not even mention Balbo.

8 "My name and presence had an electrifying effect. I was a national hero, a public figure with a record of dramatic achievement." Seeking to exploit his popularity and develop airmindedness in the British public, Cobham organized an air show called "National Aviation Day" that toured the British Isles during a period of four years in the early 1930s and attracted between three and four million spectators. Among these, almost a million people were taken up for brief flights, most certainly for the first time in their lives. Alan Cobham, *A Time To Fly* (London: Shepheard-Walwyn, 1986; orig. ed. 1978), pp. 124, 159.

9 Charles A. Lindbergh, *The Wartime Journals of Charles A. Lindbergh* (New York: Harcourt Brace Jovanovich, 1970), p. 222.

10 Albert Speer, *Inside the Third Reich*, trans. by Richard and Clara Winston (New York: Collier Books, 1970), p. 288.

11 Cobham, *A Time To Fly*, p. 167.

1. The Ambassador of the Skies

1 Efrén Rebolledo, "Ave, Lindbergh!," in *Obras completas* (Mexico City: Ediciones de bellas artes, 1968), p. 131.

2 When the French government and the diplomatic corps left Paris on 2 September 1914 to avoid what seemed an inevitable German occupation of the capital, Herrick refused to leave and, by doing so, won the admiration of the French authorities, including the personal thanks of President Poincaré. See T. Bentley Mott, *Myron T. Herrick. Friend of France* (Garden City, N.Y.: Doubleday, Doran, 1930), pp. 156–8.

3 T. Bentley Mott's "autobiographical biography" understates the American ambassador's concerns when he quotes Herrick as saying: "There was also another consideration which soon became apparent to my mind [after Lindbergh's arrival in Paris]. At the very moment Lindbergh started from America, we were in one of those periods of petulant nagging and quarreling between the French and ourselves which have flared up and died down more than once since the Armistice. I have lived through enough of these nasty equinoctial storms not to let them worry me very much, for not all the newspapers on both sides of the Atlantic can ever seriously affect the solid basis of our mutual feelings. But I hate this bad weather and like to see it clear up." Mott, *Herrick*, p. 352.

4 According to William Shirer in *Twentieth-Century Journey. The Start 1904–1930* (New York: Simon & Schuster, 1976), p. 328.

5 See Philippe Roger, *L'Ennemi américain. Généologie de l'anti-américanisme français* (Paris: Seuil, 2002), pp. 357–8. Roger's book suggests that French anti-Americanism was of long standing and not nearly as superficial as Herrick seemed to think.

6 Luc Durtain, *Quarantième étage* (Paris: Gallimard, 1927), pp. 51, 77; André Siegried, *Les États-Unis d'aujourd'hui* (Paris: Armand Colin, 1928).

7 André Tardieu, *Devant l'obstacle. L'Amérique et nous* (Paris: Émile-Paul Frères, 1927), pp. 6, 295, quoted by Roger, *L'Ennemi américain*, p. 346.

8 *Le Matin*, 10 May 1927.

9 Al Laney, *Paris Herald. The Incredible Newspaper* (New York and London: D. Appleton-Century Co., 1947), pp. 213–16. Laney insists that the source of the original rumor that the *Oiseau Blanc* had been seen over Newfoundland was Ambassador Herrick who innocently reported a rumor that he had heard to a group of French and Americans gathered to celebrate the event (p. 216). See also Charles L. Robertson, *The International Herald Tribune. The First Hundred Years* (New York: Columbia University Press, 1987), pp. 140–42. William Shirer claims that the rumor of the *Oiseau Blanc* being reported over Newfoundland was first circulated by an American news agency. "This report, broadcast over the radio and in special editions of the newspapers, set off a wild celebration in Paris." *Twentieth-Century Journey. The Start*, p. 326.

10 Quoted by Shirer in *Twentieth-Century Journey. The Start*, p. 327.

11 Willy Coppens de Houthulst, the Belgian air attaché in Paris, remembered Herrick looking concerned, as he waited for Lindbergh's arrival in the office of the director of Le Bourget. He gave the impression, Coppens de Houthulst wrote, of fearing that the United States would appear ridiculous if Lindbergh didn't satisfy the huge crowd by landing at Le Bourget. "La véridique histoire de l'arrivée de Charles Lindbergh au Bourget," *Icare*, no. 81 (Summer 1977), p. 67.

12 Henry Wales, "Formidable!," *Atlantic Monthly*, June 1937, pp. 671–2; Shirer, *Twentieth-Century Journey. The Start*, pp. 33–4. Shirer claims to have accompanied Wales and Jay Allen on the trip from Paris, though Wales nowhere mentions him in his account.

13 Quoted by Shirer, who was present at the exchange, in *Twentieth-Century Journey. The Start*, p. 315.

14 The fashion journalist Lillian Farley, who was at Le Bourget that night, recalled forty years later that "There was a strange but very distinct atmosphere of hostility around us . . . It seemed to be a mélange of resentment, envy and a certain sadness. Now and then they [the crowd] would start up with a chant, 'Nungesser – Nungesser – Nungesser; Coli – Coli – Coli.'" *Insight*, April–May 1967, pp. 92–3.

15 Wales, "Formidable!," p. 674.

16 One of the most detailed descriptions of the scene at Le Bourget is by Willy Coppens de Houthulst, who observed it from a privileged position in the office of the director of the airport. See "La véridique histoire de l'arrivée de Charles Lindbergh au Bourget," pp. 65–75.

17 Edwin James, head of the *New York Times* bureau in Paris, who had been instructed to spirit Lindbergh away after his landing before he could speak to other reporters, later wrote that he and two other *Times* reporters were standing about five hundred yards from where Lindbergh landed. "Suddenly we found ourselves confronting the whirring propeller bearing straight at us. We tried to halt. Good Lord! That crowd hit us like a shot out of a cannon. The propeller stopped turning when MacDonald [one of his *Times* colleagues] was six feet from it." From an article James wrote for the *Times* on 27 May 1927, reprinted in Meyer Berger, *The Story of the New York Times 1851–1951* (New York: Simon & Schuster, 1951), pp. 300–01.

18 The most reliable account of what happened to Lindbergh at Le Bourget when he landed remains Charles A. Lindbergh, *The Spirit of St Louis* (New York: Charles Scribner's Sons, 1953), pp. 495–501. Lindbergh had no way of knowing everything that went on at Le Bourget that night, and thus his memoir needs to be supplemented by Pierre Weiss, *La Bataille de l'Atlantique* (Paris: Euqene Fiquière, 1928), pp. 50–51; Jacques Mortane, "La merveilleuse aventure de l'Atlantique," in *L'Air*, 1 June 1927, p. 14; T. Bentley Mott, *Myron T. Herrick. Friend of France* (London: William Heinemann, 1930), pp. 340–44; Wales, "Formidable!," pp. 673–6; Edwin L. James, "Lindbergh Does It!," *New York Times*, 22 May 1927; Coppens de Houthulst, "La véridique histoire de l'arrivée de Charles Lindbergh au Bourget," pp. 65–75; and Shirer, *Twentieth-Century Journey. The Start*, pp. 334–6. Raymond H. Fredette has done a valiant job of trying to reconstruct the confused scene at Le Bourget at the time of Lindbergh's arrival in "The Making of a Hero: What Really Happened Seventy-Five Years Ago, after Lindbergh Landed at Le Bourget," *Air Power History*, 49, no. 2 (Summer 2002), pp. 1–32.

19 For a straightforward and useful account of these flights, see Peter Allen, *The 91 Before Lindbergh* (Eagan, Minn.: Flying Books, 1985). Allen acknowledges that if you eliminate airships and count only direct flights across the North Atlantic, then Lindbergh had been preceded only by Alcock and Brown (p. 174). For Franco's flight across the South Atlantic, see Lowell Thomas and Lowell Thomas, Jr., *Famous First Flights That Changed History* (Garden City, N.Y.: Doubleday, 1968), pp. 100–15.

20 Quoted by Cecil R. Roseberry in *The Challenging Skies. The Colorful Story of Aviation's Most Exciting Years 1919–1939* (Garden City, N.Y.: Doubleday, 1966), p. 26.

21 Of these new engines, the most important was the Wright Whirlwind radial engine, designed by Charles Lawrance, which made possible flights of much longer distance than had earlier been possible. Von Hardesty, *Lindbergh: Flight's Enigmatic Hero* (New York: Harcourt, 2002), pp. 20, 47.

22 According to Sikorsky's biographer, Frank J. Delear, "Igor believed the S-35 to be fully capable of a New York to Paris flight, but he wanted, particularly, to make gradual trials of its performance with heavier and heavier loads up to the heaviest which would be required for the transatlantic flight. This would have meant filling some of the fuel tanks with water as ballast and later steam-cleaning them and disassembling parts of the fuel system, and that would have brought further delays. He also wanted to test the plane's auxiliary landing gear in a series of take-off runs. The gear was intended to help support the fuel-heavy ship during its take-off run and was to be dropped when the ship became airborne. There was no time for these vital tests." *Igor Sikorsky. His Three Careers in Aviation* (New York: Dodd, Mead & Co., 1969), p. 125.

23 *New York Times*, 22 September 1916. According to Frank Delear, "Igor Sikorsky refused to blame Fonck, and years later would say only that 'some poor judgment was used.'" *Igor Sikorsky*, p. 128. In retrospect, Sikorsky believed that a crew of two would

have been sufficient to fly the plane to Paris, and Delear concedes that there was probably some unnecessary weight aboard.

24 In France, aeronautical experts attributed the crash to the faulty construction of the plane, which in their view did not possess sufficient lifting capacity. *New York Times*, 22 September 1926.

25 *Le Matin*, 7 May 1927.

26 Roseberry, *The Challenging Skies*, p. 87.

27 *Le Matin*, 9 May 1927.

28 Only six other men had received the Hubbard Medal: Admiral Robert E. Peary, Captain Roald Amundsen, Vilhalmur Stefansson, Captain Ernest H. Shackleton, Grove Karl Gilbert, and Captain Robert A. Bartlett. Richard E. Byrd, *Skyward* (New York: Halcyon House, 1928), p. 204. When presenting the Hubbard Medal to Byrd, President Coolidge commented on the extraordinary technological progress that had taken place during the previous seventeen years. According to Richard Montague in *Oceans, Poles and Airmen* (New York: Random House, 1971), Byrd's pilot, Floyd Bennett, later told Bernt Balchen that he and Byrd had never reached the North Pole. "We were just north of Spitsbergen when the commander [Byrd] discovered that oil leak. He became quite concerned about it and ordered me to fly back to the north coast of Spitsbergen – fifteen or twenty miles away. We flew back and forth for a while and the leak stopped. We discussed the possibility of flying over to East Greenland . . . but he finally ordered me to fly back and forth and this is what we did till he told me to return to Kings Bay. We flew back and forth for fourteen hours" (p. 48). Basing his account largely on Bernt Balchen's testimony, Montague himself concludes that "Byrd's claim to have reached the Pole *was* a fraud . . . In fact, it seems to have been the biggest and most successful fraud in the history of polar exploration" (p. 283). Commenting on Byrd's diary, which he edited for publication, Raimund E. Goerler concludes that whether he was right or not, Byrd "really thought he had been at the pole." *To the Pole. The Diary and Notebook of Richard E. Byrd, 1925–1927* (Columbus: Ohio State University Press, 1998), p. 56.

29 The plane with which Byrd reached the North Pole had been powered by three Wright Whirlwind engines. Byrd thus had reason to believe in his ability to make the New York–Paris flight. According to Von Hardesty, it was with Byrd's North Pole exploit that long-distance flying entered a new era. *Lindbergh*, p. 20. For Byrd's careful attention to the details of the New York–Paris flight and the innovations he made in the interests of safety, see Goerler, ed., *To the Pole*, pp. 100–02.

30 Clarence D. Chamberlain, *Record Flights* (Philadelphia: Dorrance & Co., 1928), pp. 35–41.

31 Writing in 1929, Bruce Gould recalled the obscurity of Lindbergh when he arrived in New York in May 1927. "He was then an almost ridiculously unknown youngster out of the west . . . Lloyd Bertaud . . . was rated a much finer airmail pilot than Lindbergh. And it would have been only to Lindbergh's discredit to compare any of his achievements with the fine flight to the North Pole made by Byrd. Acosta [who had replaced the injured Floyd Bennett on Byrd's transatlantic flight in Late June 1927] had been a well-known pilot while Lindbergh was still playing mumblety-peg, and Chamberlain, though not as famous as the others, had a reputation among pilots which any one might envy." *Sky Larking* (New York: Horace Liveright, 1929), pp. 74–5.

32 Anyone seeking to understand Lindbergh should begin with the books he wrote about himself: *We: The Famous Flier's Own Story of His Life and Transatlantic Flight* (New York: G. P. Putnam's Sons, 1927); *Of Flight and Life* (New York: Charles Scribner's Sons, 1948); *The Spirit of St. Louis*; *The Wartime Journals of Charles A. Lindbergh* (New York: Harcourt Brace Jovanovich, 1970); *Boyhood on the Upper Mississippi: A Reminiscent Letter* (St. Paul: Minnesota Historical Society, 1972); and *An Autobiography of Values* (New York: Harcourt Brace Jovanovich, 1978). The complexity of Lindbergh and the variety of his activities are suggested by the range of books and articles that have been written about him. A good starting point is Perry D.

Luckett, *Charles A. Lindbergh. A Bio-Bibliography* (New York: Greenwood Press, 1986). Luckett rightly emphasizes the continuing relevance of the early biographies by Kenneth S. Davis, *The Hero: Charles A. Lindbergh and the American Dream* (Garden City, N.Y.: Doubleday, 1959), and Walter S. Ross, *The Last Hero: Charles A. Lindbergh* (New York: Harper & Row, 1976). Among the biographies that have appeared since the publication of Luckett's book, Joyce Milton's *Loss of Eden* (New York: HarperCollins, 1993) and A. Scott Berg's *Lindbergh* (New York: G. P. Putnam's Sons, 1998) stand out. Hardesty's *Lindbergh* contains many rare photographs and provides the best account now available of Lindbergh's aeronautical achievements.

33 For a detailed account of the construction of the *Spirit of St. Louis* and the equipment with which it was provided, see Hardesty, *Lindbergh*, pp. 48–50.

34 Russell Owen in *Current History*, July 1927, 509.

35 The *New York Times* quoted in *Current History*, July 1927, p. 510.

36 Gould comments on this point. "Motherly old women, whose austere composure had given no signs of cracking in the presence of other pilots around the [Garden City] hotel, suddenly, and probably not a little to their astonishment afterwards, when they fell to thinking about it, stepped up to Lindbergh for the sole purpose of telling him that they had a boy like him once. Then, they would retreat hastily, but a little reluctantly, too, as though unwilling to leave him unprotected in a dangerous world." *Sky Larking*, p. 80.

37 Walter Hyams & Co., a newspaper clipping agency, reported on 22 May that Lindbergh had commanded more than twenty-seven thousand columns of newspaper space since leaving San Diego on 11 May. Quoted by the *Chicago Daily Tribune*, 23 May 1927.

38 Fredette comes close to endorsing this claim when he writes that "the ambassador [Herrick] effectively became the architect of the flier's celebration both official and personal." "Without Ambassador Herrick," Fredette concludes, "it is highly questionable whether Lindbergh would have become an American icon with the status of near royalty, the closest thing the country ever had to a Prince of Wales." "The Making of a Hero," pp. 24, 26.

39 Mott, *Herrick*, pp. 347–8. Herrick went on to say that "Providence had interposed in the shape of this boy, and if I did not seize the occasion offered I was not worth my salt. But I did not make the opportunity; I only took advantage of it. Lindbergh made it." Ibid., p. 352.

40 See Herrick's reported account in Mott, *Herrick*, pp. 348–9, of how quick Lindbergh was to seize upon an anecdote told to him by Herrick and adapt it to his own purposes when addressing the French Chamber of Deputies.

41 Waverly Root, an American journalist in Paris working for the *Chicago Daily Tribune* who attended Lindbergh's press conferences, remembered him as a "bewildered boy who had been promenaded helplessly [like a puppet] through meaningless ceremonies . . ." He added, however, that at a small luncheon given in Lindbergh's honor by the Anglo-American Press Association of Paris, he quickly impressed his audience as "a technician who knew precisely what he had done and why he had done it." *The Paris Edition. The Autobiography of Waverly Root, 1927–1934* (San Francisco: North Point Press, 1987), p. 37.

42 Shirer, *Twentieth-Century Journey. The Start*, p. 340.

43 "That night we understood of what stuff a nation's glory is made. The America pictured by novelists with its factories, monster cities, banks, subsoil coal, buildings of steel, was all fiction. The reality was the man who discovered within himself the strength, courage and skill to mock earthly slavishness and conquer the immensities of time and space." *Paris Herald*, 19 May 1928.

44 Though the attention of the French people had been focused on the disappearance of Nungesser and Coli and the search for their plane, three other French aviators had perished when they sought to cross the South Atlantic nonstop from Dakar on 4 May in a Farman Goliath. The wreckage of their plane was found off the coast of Brazil.

45 According to Henry Wales in the *Chicago Daily Tribune*, 23 May 1927.

46 *Le Matin*, 23 May 1927.

47 Reported by Henry Wales in the *Chicago Daily Tribune*, 24 May 1927.

48 *Literary Digest*, 11 June, 1927, p. 42.

49 Reported by Jacques Mortane in *L'Air*, 1 June 1927, p. 15.

50 *Current History*, July 1927, p. 523.

51 Quoted by Henry Wales in the *Chicago Daily Tribune*, 26 May 1927.

52 *Current History*, July 1927, p. 524.

53 For Herrick's use of the imagery of storm clouds to describe Franco-American relations before Lindbergh's arrival, see Mott, *Herrick*, p. 352; for Herrick's cable to Washington, Fredette, "The Making of a Hero," p. 26; for the view of a highly respected French aeronautical authority, Laurent Eynac, "Lindbergh ou l'ambassadeur d'aujourd'hui," *L'Air*, 1 June 1927.

54 Quoted by Henry Wales in the *Chicago Daily Tribune*, 24 May 1927, from remarks made by Painlevé at a reception given for Lindbergh at the Aéro-Club de France. For flight as an aesthetic phenomenon, see Robert Wohl, *A Passion for Wings: Aviation and the Western Imagination, 1908–1918* (New Haven and London: Yale University Press, 1994).

55 *Le Figaro*, 16 May 1927.

56 According to Von Hardesty, the Earth Inductor Compass and magnetic compass with which Lindbergh equipped the *Spirit of St. Louis* were far from being worthless. *Lindbergh*, p. 49.

57 *Le Figaro*, 23 May 1927.

58 *Le Figaro*, 3 June 1927.

59 Pierre Weiss, "Lindbergh," in *L'Aérophile*, 1–15 June 1927, p. 163. Weiss was not alone in making the connection between Lindbergh and T. E. Lawrence. Defending Lindbergh against his critics in the American press corps, Bruce Gould wrote: "And it seems to me Lindbergh should not be blamed because he cares nothing for publicity and refuses to stub his toe to provide a newspaper sensation. Like Colonel T. E. Lawrence, as sophisticated and erudite as Colonel Lindbergh is naive and practical, Lindbergh is not unduly impressed by the current huzzah. He is, in short, a man sufficient unto himself." *Sky Larking*, pp. 73–4.

60 Weiss, *La Bataille de l'Atlantique*, p. 37.

61 Weiss, "Lindbergh," p. 163.

62 Weiss, *La Bataille de l'Atlantique*, pp. 63–4.

63 Ibid., pp. 64–5.

64 Pierre Weiss, *L'Espace* (Paris: Louis Querelle, 1929), pp. 170–71.

65 According to Henry Wales in the *Chicago Daily Tribune*, 26 May 1927.

66 Lindbergh quoted by Henry Wales in the *Chicago Daily Tribune*, 31 May 1927.

67 Fredette claims that it was Herrick who dissuaded Lindbergh from undertaking a tour of European cities. This seems likely, although Fredette produces no evidence to support it. "The Making of a Hero," p. 25. According to Lindbergh, it was the American ambassador to Great Britain, Alanson B. Houghton, who informed him that President Coolidge had offered to send a warship to transport him back to the United States. "Such an offer," Lindbergh later wrote, "was practically an order." *Autobiography of Values*, p. 315.

68 President Coolidge quoted in the *Chicago Daily Tribune*, 1 June 1927.

69 *Current History*, July 1927, p. 526.

70 Ibid., p. 530.

71 Ibid., p. 534.

72 Ibid., p. 538.

73 A sample of this poetry can be found in *The Spirit of St Louis. One Hundred Poems*, ed. Charles Vale [Arthur Hooley] (New York: Charles H. Doran, 1927). These poems were selected from more than four thousand submitted in the Spirit of St Louis competition for a first prize of $500 and second and third prizes of $250. The competition, on the theme of Lindbergh's flight, was sponsored by Mitchell Kennerley, and the first prize was won by a girl of fourteen, Nathalia Crane.

74 From "To the Ambassador of the Skies – Captain Charles A.

Lindbergh," in the Lindbergh biographical file, National Air and Space Museum, Washington, D.C.

75 Josephine Burr, "We" in *The Spirit of St Louis. One Hundred Poems*, pp. 33–4.

76 Jean M. Batchelor, "Ad Astra" in ibid., p. 14.

77 E. R. Coe, "Lindbergh," in ibid., p. 48.

78 Edna Stimson, "Lindbergh. May 1927," in ibid., p. 225.

79 Alethea Todd Alderson, "The Spirit of St Louis" in ibid., p. 11.

80 The words just quoted are from Mary Gregory Hume Mills, "Lindbergh," in ibid., p. 176.

81 Molly Anderson Haley, "A Faithless Generation Asked a Sign," in ibid., p. 121.

82 Gladys M. Cripps, "To C.A.L.," in ibid., p. 73.

83 Mary Carolyn Davies, "Lindbergh," in ibid., p. 74.

84 Elizabeth Sampson, "The American Eagle," in ibid., p. 210. See also Marion Lockwood Ferguson, "The Last Frontiersman" in ibid., pp. 93–5; and Marion Thornton, "The Forerunner" in ibid., p. 230.

85 Edna Stimson, "Lindbergh. May 1927," in ibid., p. 225.

86 The Troy *Record* quoted in the *Literary Digest*, 9 July 1927.

87 Dale Van Every and Morris DeHaven Tracy, *Charles Lindbergh. His Life* (New York: Appleton, 1927), p. 2.

88 According to the *Magazine of Business*, September 1927, 245, newsprint interests had estimated that Lindbergh's flight was responsible for an added consumption of ten thousand tons of newsprint.

89 In *Lindbergh Alone* (New York: Harcourt Brace Jovanovich, 1977), an admiring book that raises many interesting questions about the formation of Lindbergh's character, Brendan Gill suggests that Lindbergh was an accomplished writer, even before the Paris flight (pp. 122–3). Anyone who compares *We* (1927) to *The Spirit of St. Louis* (1953), however, must come to the conclusion that, whatever his innate talent and the virtues of the short reports of his flights that Lindbergh wrote before his breakthrough to fame, Lindbergh transformed himself into a skillful writer of longer narratives through hard work and sheer will to excel. This, it seems to me, is even more impressive and some measure of Lindbergh's intellectual growth in later life.

90 Lindbergh, *The Spirit of St. Louis*, p. 548. According to Meyer Berger, Lindbergh eventually received $42,000 for the stories about his flight published by the *New York Times*. *The Story of the New York Times 1851–1951*, p. 305.

91 Lindbergh, "My Flight to Paris," reprinted in the *Aero Digest*, June 1927, pp. 520–22. A recent account of Lindbergh's career concurs with this claim. "Navigation would be a critical factor, and Lindbergh insisted on the best, an Earth Inductor Compass linked to a rotor and generator mounted on top of the fuselage [of the *Spirit of St. Louis*]. Space was also allotted for a magnetic compass. By modern standards, the instrumentation was minimal: an air speed indicator, an eight-day clock, an inclinometer (for the angle of attack of nose), an altimeter, two gauges for the measurement of oil pressure and oil temperature (key devices to monitor the condition of the engine while in flight), a turn-and-bank indicator, a fuel-pressure gauge, a magneto switch, and a mirror – all situated on a thin plywood dash of lightweight construction. A dunnage bag for maps, charts, and Lindbergh's minimal survival gear (a hunting knife and fishing tackle) was fitted behind the pilot's seat. Flares and water canteens, deemed essential, were given a place in the tightly designed cockpit area." Hardesty, *Lindbergh*, p. 49.

92 John Heinmuller, a student of aeronautical instruments and meteorology, came to a very different conclusion. "I consulted with Lindbergh before his great transatlantic flight, and I was fortunate in being able to stand at Le Bourget airfield on the dramatic night when he came winging in out of the darkness . . . At the time, I made a study of the weather conditions he faced; and some years later it was again possible for me to make further researches on this subject. I became convinced that Lindbergh was favored with weather conditions that were so perfect for his purposes as to be almost freakish . . . In any event it does not detract in any sense from his achievement in May, 1927, to say that no aviator within my knowledge was ever

blessed at a crucial hour by such a broad and generous smile on fortune's face." *Man's Fight To Fly* (New York and London: Funk & Wagnalls, 1944), p. 69. Fernand Sazarin, the chief mechanic for the French airline CIDNA at the time of Lindbergh's flight, examined *The Spirit of St. Louis* and discovered a leak of about twenty centimeters in the upper part of the oil tank. "If this leak had been located in the lower part, it's certain that Lindbergh would never have gotten to Le Bourget and his exploit would have ended in a catastrophe." "J'ai accueilli Lindbergh," *Icare*, no. 81 (Summer 1977), pp. 81–2.

93 *Chicago Daily Tribune*, 28 May 1927.

94 Lindbergh, *The Spirit of St. Louis*, p. 547.

95 *New York Times*, 23 May 1927.

96 See, for example, Chapter X, which begins "At New York we checked over the plane, engine and instruments, which required several short flights over the field." *We*, p. 213.

97 Lindbergh, *We*, pp. 302–3.

98 Ibid., p. 26.

99 Ibid., pp. 75–6.

100 *The New Republic*, 26 October 1927, p. 261. Bliven was speculating; but had he known how Lindbergh had behaved while in Paris, he would have had ample evidence for his claim that "this tall lad flies in answer to some deep-rooted demand of his inner nature . . ." Michel Détroyat, one of the French military aviators who rescued Lindbergh from the crowd at Le Bourget and was widely recognized as France's greatest aerobatic pilot in the 1930s, was assigned to escort the American while he took a "little stroll" early one morning aboard a powerful French pursuit plane. Détroyat was told by his superior to prevent Lindbergh from doing any stupid things. After a rapid briefing about the peculiarities of the Nieuport, Lindbergh gestured to Détroyat that he was ready to take off. "Gaining altitude while making a vertiginous chandelle, my companion headed at full speed for Paris . . . He moved through the sky like a colt who had suddenly been freed. After overflying the Arch of Triumph, he headed for the Eiffel Tower, which he circled at the height of the third floor." Even after Détroyat signaled to Lindbergh that it might be wise to return to Le Bourget, the American insisted on doing fifteen minutes of barrel turns, loops, and inverted flight above the airfield while Détroyat's superior looked on in horror, convinced that he was going to be held responsible for Lindbergh's death. Michel Détroyat, *Tu seras aviateur* (Paris: Les Éditions de France, 1938), pp. 190–93.

101 Donald E. Kehoe, *Flying with Lindbergh* (New York and London: G. P. Putnam's Sons, 1928), p. 6.

102 Donald E. Keyhoe, "Seeing America with Lindbergh," *National Geographic Magazine*, 53, no. 1, 2. Kehoe had participated in the Byrd Polar Plane Tour, sponsored by the Guggenheim Fund in 1926 and featuring Floyd Bennett. The mechanic, Sorenson, was later replaced by C. C. ("Doc") Maidment.

103 Kehoe, *Flying with Lindbergh*, p. 12.

104 Berg, *Lindbergh*, pp. 169–70.

105 Kehoe, *Flying with Lindbergh*, p. 71.

106 Ibid., pp. 18, 246.

107 Bruce L. Larson, "Lindbergh's Return to Minnesota, 1927," *Minnesota History*, Winter 1970, p. 147.

108 "When he sighted us cruising leisurely along, he [Lindbergh] would frequently come up straight behind to avoid being seen. Then, with wide open throttle, he would pull out to one side and dash by as though we were standing still. Before we had time to realize what happened, he would idle his engine, drop back and get in a position where his plane was hidden. From this point of vantage he would parallel each movement of the advance plane, probably laughing to himself at Phil's endeavors to locate him. At last, when we had finally decided that he had dropped down to explore the country below, he would shoot beneath us at a safe distance and tear away in the lead, leaning out to wave us a mocking farewell." Kehoe, *Flying with Lindbergh*, p. 68.

109 Larson, "Lindbergh's Return to Minnesota, 1927," p. 145. Larson's source for Lindbergh's feelings is a letter to him from Lindbergh, dated 24 June 1967. According to Kehoe, Lindbergh

told his companions the following story about one of his flying detours: "I was flying low around the side of a mountain when I saw an Indian village ahead. It was the only sign of life I had seen for a hundred miles, I was heading into a stiff wind so the Indians didn't hear the noise of my engine. I dropped down to see what they would do when they saw the *Spirit of St Louis*, but I was almost on top of them before they looked up. At that second about 25 Indians were in sight. The next second they were streaking for their huts, falling into them headfirst, all but one old fat squaw. She was scared to death and was doing her best, but she couldn't waddle any faster. Finally she dropped down, as I flew over her, and crawled on her hands and knees for the nearest tent. I circled around for five minutes but not one of them even peeked out. I suppose they thought I was some kind of a flying devil." *Flying with Lindbergh*, pp. 196–7.

110 According to Kehoe in ibid., p. 257.

111 Ibid., p. 290. Yet nonetheless Lindbergh embarked on a two-month Goodwill Tour of the Caribbean and Latin America on 13 December 1927. For a man who was fleeing the limelight, this seems like a strange choice.

112 Many biographers have tried to explain Lindbergh's character and motivations. For one of the most ambitious of such efforts, see Berg, *Lindbergh*, a widely admired biography that leaves one wondering how such an emotionally crippled man could have achieved such remarkable feats.

113 By the end of the tour, some journalists had lost their enthusiasm for Lindbergh, even if they were still reluctant to express their doubts about the hero in print. In 1928 Bruce Gould wrote: "From the first moment I saw him, I liked him. Unlike a number of newspapermen, I still do. Lindbergh has quite naturally resented the grosser importunities of the press, and with good reason has shown his dislike of various unwarranted invasions into his privacy. That has made him unpopular among a certain group of newspapermen. An almost equally large number are frankly bored by him. The journalistic mind is attuned to change, and Lindbergh, by remaining unspoiled through all the world's adulation, gives this group no opportunity to indulge in its customary practice of tearing down the idol it helped to erect." *Sky Larking*, p. 73. For a penetrating examination of Lindbergh's celebrity that puts his fame in historical perspective and explains the reasons for the turn against him by the American press, see Charles L. Ponce de Leon, "The Man Nobody Knows: Charles A. Lindbergh and the Culture of Celebrity," in Dominick A. Pisano, ed., *The Airplane in American Culture* (Ann Arbor: University of Michigan Press, 2003), pp. 75–101.

114 *Literary Digest*, 11 June 1927, p. 43.

115 Lindbergh's patron, Harry Guggenheim, shared this vision. "The airplane knows no barrier of river, sea, mountain, desert, or even distance, which have in the past isolated peoples. These physical barriers have set people apart until through this separation the centuries have moulded them by climate, laws, customs, language, religions, trade and tradition into distinguishable races, fundamentally alike but superficially very different. By the contact that communication creates these differences gradually disappear." Harry F. Guggenheim, *The Seven Skies* (New York and London: G. P. Putnam's Sons, 1930), pp. 90–91.

116 A copy of this poem is contained in the Lindbergh file at the National Air and Space Museum in Washington, D.C.

117 The stakes of the Nungesser–Coli flight had been brought out very clearly by Frantz Reichel in an article he had written just before their departure. Commenting on the technological marvels of the *Oiseau Blanc*, he wrote: "One sees in fact how important it is, from every point of view, that our aviation industry should be up to the task of achieving a quasi-monopoly over the lines between Europe and the United States, a privilege for which it is geographically well endowed." *Le Figaro*, 4 May 1927.

118 For an interpretation of French anti-Americanism within the context of fears of French and European decline, see Roger, *L'Ennemi américain*, pp. 363–91.

119 Guggenheim, *The Seven Skies*, p. 74.

120 According to Arthur Brown's account, the soldiers who were the first to reach him and Alcock after their potentially disastrous landing responded with incredulity when they announced that they had just come from America. "Somebody laughed politely, as if in answer to an attempt at facetiousness that did not amount to much, but that ought to be taken notice of, anyhow, for the sake of courtesy. Quite evidently nobody received the statement seriously at first. Even a mention of our names meant nothing to them, and they remained unconvinced until Alcock showed them the mail-bag from St. John's. Then they relieved their surprised feelings by cheers and painful hand-shakes." Sir John Alcock and Sir Arthur Whitten Brown, *Our Transatlantic Flight* (London: William Kimber, 1969), pp. 101–2. Both of Lindbergh's competitors for the Orteig Prize were forced to crash-land their planes in Europe, Chamberlain and Levine in a grain field near Eisleben, Germany and then, after a second takeoff, outside the village of Klinge, seventy miles southeast of Berlin; Richard Byrd's *America*, flown by Bert Acosta and Bernt Balchen, went down near a fishing village along the Normandy coast, named Ver-sur-Mer. The *America*'s crew arrived in Paris by train on 2 July 1927.

121 *New York Times*, 21 May 1927.

122 *We* alone earned Lindbergh royalties of over a quarter of a million dollars. For the many enticing offers that Lindbergh received and turned down after returning to the United States in June 1927, see Berg, *Lindbergh*, pp. 162–3. Lindbergh later claimed that he rejected one of the most profitable of these proposals – a motion picture contract from William Randolph Hearst that would have guaranteed him at least half a million dollars – because he disagreed with the values represented in Hearst's chain of newspapers. "They seemed to me overly sensational, inexcusably inaccurate, and excessively occupied with the troubles and vices of mankind. I disliked most of the men I had met who represented him, and I did not want to become associated with the organization he had built." *Autobiography of Values*, p. 317. Charles L. Ponce de Leon emphasizes the extent to which Lindbergh was manipulated by rich and powerful figures in the aviation industry, such as Harry Guggenheim, Harry Davison, Jr., Henry Breckinridge, and Dwight Morrow, all "Wall Street insiders who envisioned an [aeronautical] industry dominated by large corporations . . . For these Americans, Lindbergh was a godsend, a popular idol who shared their professed disdain for publicity and the tawdry lures of the entertainment industry. From the moment he landed in Paris, they began to use him as a weapon in their campaign against what they perceived as the 'excesses' of 1920s America. In their hands, he was transformed into a symbol of modesty, dignity, and youthful idealism – values that were antithetical to the avarice, ballyhoo, and cynicism of the 'jazz age.' " "The Man Nobody Knows," in Pisano, ed., *The Airplane in American Culture*, pp. 82–3. No one would deny that Lindbergh was a "godsend" for businessmen hoping to develop the aviation industry in the United States; but it was Lindbergh's qualities and personal integrity – not the manipulation of others – that made possible the emergence of his public image in the weeks and months following his flight.

123 Russell Owen quoted in *Current History*, 28, no. 1 (April 1928), p. 89.

124 In 1958 John W. Ward of Princeton University published an article in which he tried to decipher the "Meaning of Lindbergh's Flight." *American Quarterly*, 10 (Spring 1958), pp. 3–16. Ward's essay brims with insights on the response to Lindbergh's flight in the United States. But in focusing on the American public's division between viewing Lindbergh as an exemplar of the pioneering individualist who looked toward the past and a prophet of the industrial future, Ward overlooked the larger impact that Lindbergh had outside of the United States. Europeans were just as taken by Lindbergh as Americans, and I have found no evidence that they were drawn to his pioneering image.

2. Flying and Fascism

1 Quoted by Guido Mattioli, *Mussolini aviatore* (Rome: Aviazione, 3rd ed., 1938), p. 167.

2 Quoted by Brendan Gill in *Lindbergh Alone* (New York: Harcourt Brace Jovanovich, 1977), p. 174.

3 Guitry's play, *Charles Lindbergh*, which opened on 29 November 1928, was about a young French count who wished to marry a lovely and rich young woman. The problem is that the count's father opposes his marriage on the grounds that Florence Madison is an American. The count's father is no fan of Americans. "To be sure, the Americans have their qualities, but they have something uncivilized about them . . . Lacking ideals and a past, they despise the old Europe, as they call it, and treat us pitilessly, like poor relatives . . . They adore money! They put self-interest first." But after meeting Florence, whom he finds exquisite and observing Lindbergh in a parade, the father agrees to the marriage. Given its plot, it is not surprising that *Charles Lindbergh* did not turn out to be one of Guitry's triumphs. Nonetheless, it had a respectable run of eighty-eight performances. See Jacques Lorcey, *Sacha Guitry* (Paris: Éditions Pac, 1982), pp. 322–4.

4 At one point in the cantata, Lindbergh describes his flight as "a battle against the primitive/And a striving toward an improvement of the planet/similar to dialectical economics/which seeks to change the world from its foundations." Bertolt Brecht, *Versuche 1–3* (Berlin: Gustav Kipenheuer Verlag, 1930), p. 10. Following the performance in Baden-Baden, the entire text of *Der Lindberghflug* was scored by Weill alone and then conducted in Berlin by Otto von Klemperer and in the United States by Leopold Stowkowski. Two decades later, in response to what he perceived as the pro-Nazi attitudes of Lindbergh, Brecht removed every reference to the flyer and renamed his cantata *Der Ozeanflug*. See Kim H. Kowalke, "Der Lindberghflug: Kurt Weill's Musical Tribute to Lindbergh," *The Bulletin of the Missouri Historical Society*, April 1977, pp. 193–6. For the text of *Der Lindberghflug*, see Brecht, *Versuche 1–3*, pp. 2–19. For the context in which it was written and performed, see Jürgen Schebera, *Kurt Weill. An Illustrated Life*, trans. Caroline Murphy (New Haven and London: Yale University Press, 1995), pp. 132–8.

5 Cecil Lewis, *Sagittarius Rising* (London: Penguin, 1977 ed., first published in 1936), p. 83.

6 Mattioli, *Mussolini aviatore*, pp. 15–16.

7 Ibid., p. 15.

8 For a discussion of D'Annunzio's novel and the context in which it was written, see Robert Wohl, *A Passion for Wings: Aviation and the Western Imagination 1908–1918* (New Haven and London: Yale University Press, 1994), pp. 97–122.

9 Gabriele D'Annunzio, *Taccuini*. Ed. Enrica Bianchetti and Robert Forcella (Milan: Mondadori, 1965), p. 1342.

10 *Opere*, 41 (Verona: Mondadori, 1931), p. 87.

11 *Le Matin*, 30 April 1910, quoted in Saverio Laredo de Mendoza, *Gabriele D'Annunzio. Aviatore di guerra* (Milan: Impresa editoriale italiana, 1930), p. 90.

12 Cadorna's letter is reprinted in Saverio Laredo de Mendoza, *Gabriele D'Annunzio. Marinaio e aviatore navale* (Milan: Impresa editoriale italiana, 1936), pp. 117–18.

13 D'Annunzio to Antonio Salandra, 30 July 1915, in Laredo de Mendoza, *Gabriele D'Annunzio. Aviatore di guerra*, pp. 99–104.

14 Laredo de Mendoza, *Gabriele D'Annunzio. Marinaio e aviatore navale*, p. 279. See also D'Annunzio, *Taccuini*, pp. 740–45. A few months later Giuseppe Miraglia died in an accident while testing a plane that was going to be used by D'Annunzio in a similar flight over the Dalamatian city of Zara. Paolo Alatri, *D'Annunzio* (Turin: UTET, 1983), p. 368. Alfredo Bonadeo argues that it was with Miraglia that D'Annunzio translated into reality the fictional relationship between Paolo Tarsis and Giulio Combiaso that he had created in *Forse che sì forse che no*. *D'Annunzio and the Great War* (London: Associated University Presses, 1995), p. 99.

15 Quoted by Alatri in *D'Annunzio*, p. 367. In *D'Annunzio and the Great War*, Bonadeo locates D'Annunzio's passion for risk-taking in his attempt to escape from carnal lust and achieve a form of spiritual transcendence. Purity of soul could only be experienced in the act of risking one's life. "Contempt for physical safety, living beyond the limit, were the symptoms of a body that, having undergone that sublimating process that D'Annunzio, after Dante, styled *trasumanare*, has become more than human. And the body that has found the strength and secret to *trasumanare*, is a body that has gained freedom from the tyranny and misery of lust" (p. 85).

16 Even Romain Rolland, a fierce critic of the role that most European intellectuals played in legitimizing the war, was forced to acknowledge that D'Annunzio ". . . had given the world proof . . . of his burning courage. He alone among the rhetoricians of the war paid with his own person; he signed his rhetoric with his own blood." Quoted by Bonadeo, *D'Annunzio and the Great War*, p. 14.

17 "Even if this immense war did nothing but give back to man familiarity with death, abolishing that false limit that seemed to separate it from life and light, it deserves our praise and our blessing." Quoted by Bonadeo, *D'Annunzio and the Great War*, p. 103.

18 "I tell you that the newest arm, the most recent, will decide our fate; it will cut the tremendous knot [of stalemate]." From a speech given on the occasion of the "festa del nastro azzurro" on 22 July 1917, in Laredo de Mendoza, *Gabriele D'Annunzio. Aviatore di guerra*, p. 258. On 9 February 1917, D'Annunzio wrote to his friend Ugo Ojetti: "What is happening today in Italian aviation is vile. We have an admirable arm *with which to win the war*, with which to destroy the instruments of the enemy offensive, and we don't adopt it." By an "admirable arm," D'Annunzio was referring to the Caproni triplane. From Cosimo Ceccuti, ed., *Carteggio d'Annunzio-Ojetti (1894–1937)* (Florence: Felice Le Monnier, 1979), p. 168.

19 Alatri, *D'Annunzio*, p. 390.

20 Laredo de Mendoza, *Gabriele D'Annunzio. Aviatore di guerra*, p. 163.

21 Ibid., pp. 183–4.

22 Ibid., p. 186.

23 D'Annunzio, *Taccuini*, p. 1038.

24 Laredo de Mendoza, *Gabriele D'Annunzio. Aviatore di guerra*, p. 209.

25 Laredo de Mendoza, *Gabriele D'Annunzio. Marinaio e aviatore navale*, pp. 197–8.

26 The best account of the Vienna flight is Baldassare Catalanotto's "Il volo su Vienna" in *In volo per Vienna* (Milan: Giorgio Apostolo, 1993), pp. 77–83.

27 Laredo de Mendoza, *Gabriele D'Annunzio. Aviatore di guerra*, p. 283. D'Annunzio and his disciples later gave the impression that he alone organized the Vienna flight and was responsible for the messages that were dropped over the Austrian capital. This was clearly not the case. The High Command and the government maintained control over the content of these messages. The one calling upon the Austrians to surrender and translated into German was written by D'Annunzio's close friend, Ugo Ogetti. See Ceccuti, ed., *Carteggio D'Annunzio-Ojetti (1894–1937)*, p. 195, n. 88 and pp. 195–6.

28 *The Times*, 12 August 1918, quoted by John Woodhouse, *Gabriele D'Annunzio* (Oxford: Clarendon Press, 1998), p. 310.

29 See his February 1918 letter to Colonel Ernesto La Polla in Laredo de Mendoza, *D'Annunzio. Aviatore di guerra*, p. 224.

30 See, in particular, his letter of 1 June 1918 to Gianni Caproni, in Mendoza, *D'Annunzio. Aviatore di guerra*, p. 231.

31 By contrast, Francesco Baracca, a professional army officer and Italy's highest scoring ace, was promoted to captain after three years of wartime service.

32 Alatri, *D'Annunzio*, p. 400.

33 Quoted by Ettore Cozzani in *Gabriele D'Annunzio* (Piacenza: La società tipografica 1923), p. 82.

34 Quoted by Alatri in *D'Annunzio*, p. 399.

35 During his speech to the aviators at Centocelle in July 1919, D'Annunzio recalled the evening at the airfield of San Pelagio when he first proposed a raid to Tokyo in ten or twelve stages.

"Everyone was excited, everyone was ready. It seemed that they all were possessed by the same dream, and that I was only their seer and unexpected interpreter . . . And everyone wanted to leave immediately, as when the condottiere gives the signal to a flock of migrating birds and the air is moved by a unanimous beating of wings." D'Annunzio, *Opere*, 41 (Verona: Mondadori, 1931), p. 89. See also Attilio Longoni, *Fascismo ed aviazione* (Milan: Edizioni azzure, 1931), pp. 124–6. D'Annunzio's original intention was to make the flight with five SVAs, three Caproni triplanes, and one Caproni 450. He envisaged, in addition to himself, seven passengers, including the Japanese poet Haru Kichi Shimoi, five journalists, and, naturally, a cinematographer.

36 D'Annunzio, *L'Ala d'Italia è liberata*, p. 72.

37 For details, see ACS (Archivo Centrale dello Stato), Presidenza del Consiglio dei Ministri, 1920, Fasc 1/1, p. 1054. According to Gregory Alegi, "Italo Balbo, stato della ricerca e ipotesi di lavoro," in *Storia contemporanea*, October 1989, p. 1071, n. 44, the flight, when made in 1920, eventually cost the Giolitti government 20 million lire.

38 John Woodhouse claims that Nitti had tried to neutralize D'Annunzio politically in 1919 by offering him a commissariat in charge of the Italian Air Force or some other ministerial office of his choice. *Gabriele D'Annunzio*, p. 329. D'Annunzio's hostility to the liberal government ruling Italy was no secret. Already in October 1918 he had written to Major Armando Armani, in response to the latter's comments about the Italian domestic situation: "A bombing squadron over Montecitorio [seat of the Italian Parliament] in one of its next sessions would resolve all questions and liberate the Patria from every disgusting infection." In Laredo de Mendoza, *D'Annunzio. Aviatore di guerra*, p. 217.

39 In September 1919 the British ambassador to Rome, Sir Rennell Rodd, sent a dispatch to the Foreign Office in London, in which he expressed the fear that D'Annunzio's interest in the Rome–Tokyo flight was a feint in order to conceal his intention to march on Fiume. But there is no reason to believe that this was the case earlier in the summer. Carlo Ghisalberti argues that until late August 1919 D'Annunzio had shown no interest in the fate of Fiume, although he had mentioned practically every other Dalmatian town in his speeches. Woodhouse, *Gabriele D'Annunzio*, p. 330.

40 *Il Cielo*, 25 July 1919.

41 The speech is reprinted in D'Annunzio, "Primavere sacre dell'Italia alata e ripudio dell'Occidente," *Opere*, 41, pp. 73–95.

42 *Opere*, 41, p. 74.

43 Ibid., p. 75.

44 Ibid., p. 78.

45 Ibid., p. 88.

46 Ibid., p. 87.

47 Ibid., p. 94.

48 Ibid., pp. 94–5.

49 Ibid., p. 85.

50 Ibid., p. 93.

51 For a history of the 1920 Rome–Tokyo flight, see Domenico Ludovico, *Italian Aviators from Rome to Tokyo in 1920* (Rome: Etas Kompass, 1970).

52 In June 1922, D'Annunzio presided over a meeting of the Italian aviation community that took place in Milan. The motion voted by those in attendance and written by D'Annunzio could easily be interpreted as his bid to head some kind of civil aviation agency. "We need to create a Commissariat of Civil Aviation with young men of ardent and active faith, who have already proved themselves assiduously in war or office work. We need to put at the head of this new institution a deserving person, designated by the aviation community, someone who will be capable of dedicating himself, most efficiently and most devotedly, to the solution of the mountain of national problems [that we face]." Reproduced in Saverio Laredo de Mendoza, *La Carlinga armoniosa* (Milan: Ceschina, 1929), p. 37.

53 Quoted in Mattioli, *Mussolini aviatore*, pp. 20–21.

54 Quoted in ibid., p. 23.

55 *L'Ala d'Italia*, January–February 1923.

56 Ibid., 4.

57 *Il Popolo d'Italia*, 3 August 1919.

58 See D'Annunzio's statement in *Il Popolo d'Italia* on 5 August 1919, following the accident in Verona.

59 For the theme of the two Italies, as it was developed by the intellectuals of the Italian avant-garde magazine *La Voce* and its appropriation by Mussolini, see Walter L. Adamson, *Avant-Garde Florence. From Modernism to Fascism* (Cambridge, Mass.: Harvard University Press, 1993), pp. 86–7, 257–8.

60 Gregory Alegi claims that seventeen people were killed. See his article "Italo Balbo, stato del ricerca e ipotesi di lavoro," in *Storia contemporanea*, October 1989, p. 1071.

61 Longoni, *Fascismo ed aviazione*, pp. 50–51.

62 Yet *Il Popolo d'Italia* also praised aeronautical ventures sponsored by the government, such as the delegation of Italian aviators sent to Argentina and the Rome–Tokyo flight. See "Torino-Madrid-Roma in diciassette ore" (10 August 1919) and "L'aviazione italiana nell'Argentina" (12 August 1919). This may have reflected Mussolini's uncertainty in 1919 as to whether he was going to overthrow the liberal government or reform it from within.

63 *Il Popolo d'Italia*, 20 August 1919.

64 On 9 October 1919, Mussolini sent Michele Bianchi, an editor on *Il Popolo d'Italia*, to deliver a letter to Giuseppe Brezzi of Ansaldo, requesting an airplane for the Rome–Tokyo flight. "I don't believe it necessary to emphasize that my participation in this enterprise would have a modest, but nonetheless notable significance." On 15 October, Brezzi responded putting Mussolini off and warning him of the risks involved. "The fact is, as the Commandante [D'Annunzio] has indicated, that I'm talking to the governmental authorities [the Direzione di Aeronautica] about the preparation of some special SVA that would be appropriate for the Rome–Tokyo flight. I greatly fear that in Rome they don't have a clear understanding of the difficulties that this aerial exploit represents." Mussolini nonetheless insisted, writing Brezzi on 20 October that he would go "at his own risk and peril." Mattioli reproduces the Mussolini–Brezzi correspondence in *Mussolini aviatore*, pp. 50–54. For Mussolini's flight to Fiume and his detention at Aiello, see Renzo de Felice, *Mussolini il rivoluzionario 1883–1920* (Turin: Einaudi, 1965), pp. 567–8. Mussolini's own description of this adventure, originally published in *Il Popolo d'Italia*, is reprinted by Mattioli in *Mussolini aviatore*, p. 49.

65 The term "regularly" may be misleading. According to his instructor, between 20 July 1920 and 12 May 1921 Mussolini made eighteen flights for a total of seven hours and twenty-eight minutes. Some of these flights were extremely short, lasting only five or six minutes. See Cesare Redaelli, *Iniziando Mussolini alle vie del cielo* (Milan: Magnani, 1933), p. 46.

66 Jotti da Badia Polesine, "Mussolini aviatore" in Saverio Laredo de Mendoza, *Ali e squadriglie* (Milan: Impresa editoriale italiane, 1933), p. 224.

67 For Redaelli's account of the accident, see *Iniziando Mussolini alle vie del cielo*, p. 78, which suggests Mussolini's unawareness of the seriousness of the situation in which they found themselves when their engine began to fail.

68 According to his wife, Mussolini returned home after the accident supported by a doctor Binda. His head was bandaged and he limped. Rachele Mussolini, *Benito il mio uomo* (Milan: Rizzoli, 1958), p. 68. She claims that he suffered a great deal. The account of the accident published in *Il Popolo d'Italia* is more understated, but it acknowledged that, in addition to injuries in the face, Mussolini had suffered fairly painful blows in the legs and arms. Reproduced in Jotti da Badia Polesine, "Mussolini aviatore" in Laredo de Mendoza, *Ali e squadriglie*, p. 226.

69 It was not until 1933 that Mussolini would resume his training, with the object of certifying himself as a military pilot in multi-engine aircraft, which he did without subjecting himself to the requirement of solo flight, presumably in view of his position as

Duce and his importance to the nation. The pilots who flew with him testified after the Second World War that he was capable of maneuvering safely the three-engined military planes in use by the Italian Air Force in the 1930s; and there is no doubt that he logged hundreds of hours in flight, if not the seventeen thousand hours that some overly enthusiastic hagiographers claimed. Giuseppe D'Avanzo, *Ali e poltrone* (Rome: Ciarrapico, 1981), p. 50.

70 In a letter to Atillio Longoni, undated, reproduced in Mattioli, *Mussolini aviatore*, p. 58.

71 His correspondence with Giuseppe Brezzi in June and December of 1921 is reproduced in Mattioli, *Mussolini aviatore*, pp. 82–4.

72 On 27 October, Gianni Caproni, the proprietor of one of Italy's most important aircraft factories, proclaimed that "Mussolini will save Italy." Quoted by D'Avanzo in *Ali e poltrone*, p. 65.

73 Attilio Longoni later claimed that a battalion of pilots and aviation mechanics, along with volunteers from the other services, had formed the nucleus of the first Fascist squads. In Longoni, *Fascismo ed aviazione*, p. 11.

74 D'Avanzo, *Ali e poltrone*, p. 66; and Mattioli, *Mussolini aviatore*, pp. 109–11.

75 Mattioli, *Mussolini aviatore*, p. 95.

76 D'Avanzo, *Ali e poltrone*, p. 66. Finzi had piloted one of the planes that accompanied D'Annunzio during the Vienna flight.

77 For a summary of Douhet's ideas, see Chapter 5, pp. 215–16. Giorgio Rochat is persuaded that the creation of an independent air force was also intended to counterbalance in the eyes of Fascist militants Mussolini's decision to leave the army and the navy in the hands of the traditionalists Diaz and Thaon di Revel who set out to restore order and reestablish the principle of military hierarchy. *Italo Balbo. Aviatore e ministro dell'aeronautica 1926–1933* (Ferrara: Italo Bovolenta, 1979), pp. 19–20. Douhet was close to the group of Fascist aviators in Milan and contributed a series of articles to *Il Popolo d'Italia* in the autumn of 1922, just before Mussolini was called to power. Mussolini intended to appoint Douhet commissar of military aviation, but was forced to withdraw his name because of protests by high-ranking military (and especially naval) officials. See Rochat, *Balbo. Aviatore*, pp. 20–21, n. 22. Though Finzi was clearly influenced by Douhet (see his article "Riorganizzazione aeronautica," in *Gerarchia*, December 1923, 1389–90), the Fascist regime never committed itself to the creation of a large strategic bombing force and Finzi's successor as undersecretary of the commissariat of aviation, General Bonzani, lacked enthusiasm for Douhet's ideas and ensured that the army and navy's need for aerial support was assigned priority. Rochat, *Balbo. Aviatore*, pp. 39–40.

78 "Italy can, therefore must, achieve aeronautical preeminence. The material, the elements necessary for achieving preeminence exist . . ." Mussolini to Attilio Longoni in Mattioli, *Mussolini aviatore*, p. 62. For Mussolini's belief in the domestic political uses of aviation, see Rochat, *Balbo. Aviatore*, p. 34.

79 The claim that postwar Italian governments had deliberately set out to destroy Italian aviation was clearly untrue. For a more balanced account of Italian aviation policy between the Armistice and the coming to power of Mussolini in October 1922, see D'Avanzo, *Ali e poltrone*, p. 57; and Rochat, *Balbo. Aviatore*, pp. 11–17.

80 Rochat, *Balbo. Aviatore*, pp. 41–2.

81 Arturo Ferrarin claimed that Mussolini himself had intervened to make possible his 1928 flight to Brazil with Carlo Del Prete, after General Bonzani had expressed doubts about his ability to find the necessary funds. Arturo Ferrarin, *Voli per il mondo* (Milan: Mondadori, 1929), p. 167. For an account of the 1926 Schneider Cup race that emphasizes Mussolini's personal commitment to assuring Italian victory, see Ralph Barker, *The Schneider Trophy Races* (Shrewsbury: Airlife Publishing, 1981), pp. 123–49.

82 From Mussolini's speech of 7 November 1925 in Paolo Orano, ed., *L'Aviazione fascista* (Rome: Pinciana, 1937), p. 106.

83 Mattioli, *Mussolini aviatore*, p. 167.

84 Balbo was transferred from the Alpini to an air force base in Turin for flight training on 22 October 1917, just two days before the beginning of the battle of Caporetto. He was then evidently recalled in an attempt to reinforce the Alpini troops in the sector of Monte Altissimo. See Giordano Bruno Guerri, *Italo Balbo* (Milano: Garzanti, 1984), p. 37. In April 1918, Balbo was given command of an assault group, whose actions earned him his three medals.

85 For Balbo's life, see Guerri, *Italo Balbo*; Giorgio Rochat, *Italo Balbo* (Turin: UTET, 1986); and Claudio Segre, *Italo Balbo. A Fascist Life* (Berkeley and Los Angeles: University of California Press, 1987). For an attempt to put Balbo's conversion to Fascism in broader context, see Robert Wohl, *The Generation of 1914* (Cambridge, Mass.: Harvard University Press, 1979), pp. 175–6. The most important source for Balbo's values during the years immediately following the First World War remains his *Diario 1922* (Milan: Mondadori, 1932). Carlo Maria Santoro, ed., *Italo Balbo: Aviazione e potere aereo* (Rome: Aeronautica militare, 1998), contains valuable essays on various aspects of Balbo's contribution to Italian aviation.

86 Giuseppe Bottai has left a penetrating description of his friend and fellow Fascist leader, written in June 1940 after hearing that Balbo had died in Libya. "He only knew how to live like a partisan; he was always on the qui vive, in the forefront of the battle, and thriving on argument; the world for him was divided into two opposing camps; he was incapable of objectivity and a sense of proportion, always ready to defend and attack, generous and impatient with his supporters and unable to bear contradictions. But always deeply human." *Diario 1935–1944*, ed. by Giordano Bruno Guerri (Milan: Rizzoli, 1982), p. 206.

87 For a careful assessment of the evidence bearing on the reasons for Mussolini's selection of Balbo, see Alegi, "Italo Balbo, stato della ricerca e ipotesi di lavoro," pp. 1075–8. Alegi concludes that "The weight of Balbo's passion for aviation in Mussolini's decision [to appoint him] remains nonetheless an unknown" (pp. 1077–8).

88 For a useful overview of what is known of Aldo Finzi's career, see Gregory Alegi, "Il Sottosegretario Aldo Finzi e il caso Matteotti," in *Giacomo Matteotti. La vita per la democrazia* (Rovigo: Associazione Culturale Minelliana editrice, 1993), pp. 161–76.

89 Relations between General Bonzani and General Piccio were evidently bad and having a negative effect on air force morale, and Gregory Alegi speculates that Mussolini may have wanted to make a sharp distinction between the political post of undersecretary, which he gave to Balbo, and that of that of air force Chief of Staff, which continued to be held by Piccio. See his article, "Italo Balbo, stato della ricerca e ipotesi di lavoro," p. 1077, n. 65.

90 Rochat, *Italo Balbo*, pp. 116–22.

91 Quoted by Guerri in *Italo Balbo*, p. 204.

92 The air force budget rose from 558 million lire in 1925–26 to 754 million lire in 1926–27. It remained at this level throughout Balbo's tenure, making it roughly half the navy's and one-quarter of what the army received. See Guerri, *Italo Balbo*, p. 207. For Balbo's yearly reports on the state of Italian aviation, see the collection of his speeches, *Sette anni di politica aeronautica* (Milan: Mondadori, 1935).

93 Rochat, *Italo Balbo*, p. 123.

94 Alegi, "Italo Balbo, stato della ricerca e ipotesi de lavoro," p. 1080; and Balbo's article "Guerra aerea," in *Enciclopedia Italiana*, Appendice I (Rome: 1938), pp. 699–701, where he expresses skepticism about Douhet's theories and warns against the notion that the army and navy will be superseded by the air force in the next war.

95 Guerri, *Italo Balbo*, p. 211. During Balbo's seven years at the Air Ministry, 560 Italian pilots would die while flying, three-fifths of them pilots (p. 204). In his yearly speech to the Chamber of Deputies, given on 23 March 1928, Balbo argued vigorously in favor of the independence of the air force and the concentration of all its forces under a single command. See Balbo, *Sette anni di political aeronautica*, p. 109. In this speech he was clearly

under the influence of Douhettian ideas. See in particular pp. 110, 114–15, where he argues that nations will use all means at their disposal to win a war and that priority must be given to offense over defense.

96 Quoted from a circular of 6 December 1927, directed to all air force officers, and quoted by Rochat in *Italo Balbo*, pp. 124–5.

97 Balbo, *Sette anni di politica aeronautica*, p. 115.

98 Reviewing the available evidence, Alegi concludes that "With the [aircraft] industry Balbo was frank to the point of toughness." In "Italo Balbo, stato della ricerca e ipotesi di lavoro," p. 1085.

99 "Verbale della reunione degli industriali tenuta da S. E. Balbo il 19 novembre 1926," in the Balbo Archive. I am indebted to Gregory Alegi for access to this document.

100 For Balbo's initial hesitations about learning to fly, see Alberto Briganti, *Oltre le nubi il sereno* (Rome: Nuovo Studio Tecna, 2nd ed., 1994), pp. 90–91.

101 In a circular to air force officers of 6 December 1927, Balbo announced unambiguously his intention to eradicate all tendencies toward the singling out of aviation celebrities for special honors and privileges. "An officer selected to carry out an exploit beyond the range of his usual duties must not forget that, if the confidence of his superiors singles him out as the person best suited to a specialized task, he nonetheless can realize it only because the state has given him the means, which are the result in turn of the obscure work of many people. He must consider himself the anonymous agent of the organism to which he belongs. On occasions when honors are conferred on him, he must not lose control of himself and overestimate his own importance. He must then have a keen sense for the moment in which it is necessary for him to leave the limelight in order to resume quietly his own post." Quoted by Rochat in *Italo Balbo*, pp. 125–6. One wonders whether Balbo remembered these lines when he was removed from his post as Minister of Air in October 1933.

102 See Balbo, *Setti anni di politica aeronautica*, p. 113.

103 Rochat, *Italo Balbo*, p. 130.

104 See Balbo's speech on 2 June 1928 to the journalists who had participated in the cruise, reproduced in *Passeggiate aeree sul Mediterraneo* (Milan: Treves, 1929), p. 1.

105 According to the journalist Michele Intaglietta in ibid., p. 137.

106 Ibid., p. 4.

107 Rochat, *Italo Balbo*, p. 130.

108 Segre, *Italo Balbo*, pp. 195–7.

109 *Passeggiate aeree sul Mediterraneo*, p. 207.

110 Rochat, *Italo Balbo*, pp. 130–31. De Pinedo was also rewarded richly during the coming months: Mussolini promoted him to *generale di divisione aerea*; appointed him air force Chief of Staff; and bestowed upon him the title of *marchese*. These honors no doubt aroused Balbo's jealousy and contributed to the smoldering conflict that erupted during the summer of 1929.

111 For a detailed account by Balbo's adjutant, see Briganti, *Oltre le nubi il sereno*, pp. 95–9. Segre, *Italo Balbo*, p. 201.

112 Italo Balbo, *Da Roma a Odessa* (Milan: Treves, 1929), p. 150.

113 Ibid., p. 62.

114 Ibid., p. 119.

115 Ibid., p. 149.

116 Ibid., p. 131.

117 Ranieri Cupini, *Cieli e mari. Le grandi crociere degli idrovolanti italiani (1925–1933)* (Milan: Mursia, 1973), p. 81; Guerri, *Italo Balbo*, p. 241.

118 Cupini, *Cieli e mari*, p. 100.

119 Pellegrini, a colonel at the time of the cruise, acted as De Pinedo's assistant and copilot. Balbo's plane did not participate in the formation. See Cupini, *Cieli e mari*, p. 64. According to Cupini, De Pinedo's rank, responsibilities, and experienced conferred on him "an absolute preeminence in the direction and leadership of the flight" (p. 66).

120 Alberto Briganti, who participated in the cruise, claims that Balbo and De Pinedo fell out over a punishment imposed on a cinematographer from the Istituto Luce for impersonating a non-commissioned officer and failing to observe military discipline. *Oltre le nubi il sereno*, pp. 108–9.

121 De Pinedo's memorandum to Mussolini of August 1929 is reproduced in its entirety by Rochat in *Balbo. Aviatore*, pp. 189–207.

122 Quoted in ibid., p. 192.

123 Quoted by Segre, *Italo Balbo*, p. 212.

124 Italo Balbo, *Stormi in volo sull'oceano* (Milan: Mondadori, 1931), p. 15.

125 Cupini, *Cieli e mari*, p. 106.

126 Balbo, *Stormi in volo sull'oceano*, p. 19.

127 Ibid., p. 28; Cupini, *Cieli e mari*, p. 114.

128 Balbo, *Stormi in volo sull'oceano*, p. 31.

129 Ibid., p. 50.

130 Cupini, *Cieli e mari*, p. 117.

131 Two S.55 TAs went down during the Atlantic crossing. Both were located by Italians ships, but only one was successfully towed to the Brazilian island of Fernando di Norohna where it was repaired and refueled. It then rejoined the other ten planes in Porto Natal.

132 Balbo, *Stormi in volo sull'oceano*, p. 90.

133 Cupini criticizes in detail the decision to leave on 17 December, given the available weather reports, and Balbo and his lieutenant Umberto Maddalena's refusal to change course once they encountered stormy weather. See *Cieli e mari*, pp. 126–33.

134 Balbo, *Stormi in volo sull'oceano*, pp. 250–51.

135 Ibid., p. 254.

136 Cupini, *Cieli e mari*, p. 156.

137 Balbo, *Stormi in volo sull'oceano*, p. 220.

138 Cupini, *Cieli e mari*, p. 153. Cupini's count rises to forty-five Italians, but he counts Carlo Del Prete twice.

139 Balbo, *Stormi in volo sull'oceano*, pp. 256–8. Mussolini had pointedly not sent Balbo a telegram of congratulations when he reached Natal, thus signaling his displeasure at the losses suffered in the takeoff from Bolama. As he wrote in the order of the day, which he instructed Balbo to read to his men: "Until everything is finished, nothing is finished" (p. 257).

140 In 1934, Balbo published an anthology of his aviation writings, entitled *Stormi d'Italia sul mondo* (Milan: Mondadori), aimed at middle-school students. The editor of this volume, V. Veonio-Brocchieri, declared, with some hyperbole, that if Balbo's first book on the cruise to Odessa was the work of "an elegant reporter" and a "felicitous narrator," the last – *La centuria alata* – was "worthy of entering in the canon of our best literary monuments" (p. 6).

141 Balbo, *Stormi in volo sull'oceano*, p. 185.

142 In fact, Balbo was denounced in a police report to Mussolini for having spent state money during his vacation in order to entertain a mistress, the Countess S. S. Balbo denied having misused state money, but his biographer, Giordano Bruno Guerri, claims that it was well known that he was carrying on an affair with the Countess, whose husband was involved in the aviation world. *Italo Balbo*, p. 277.

143 After making the Atlantic crossing, Balbo received a cable from D'Annunzio, who characteristically seized the occasion to speak about himself, reminding Balbo and his men that "no one today merits the joy of your victory as I merit it as recompense for so many years of fearless faith, initiated and preached long before our admirable war." D'Annunzio's only regret, he wrote, was that he had not been able to accompany Balbo and his men on their flight. These impassioned words inspired Balbo to rise to the heights of D'Annunzian rhetoric in his cable of reply. "We felt the presence of the Poet-Soldier during our entire transatlantic flight, which was carried out by Italian soldiers with their hearts full of the winged poetry of the faraway Patria." He ended by assuring D'Annunzio that his words would propel the transatlantic flyers "always higher and further," an echo in slightly modified form of one of D'Annunzio most famous mottoes. Balbo, *Stormi in volo sull'oceano*, p. 216.

144 Ibid., pp. 189–90.

145 Claudio Segre estimates that if one takes into account the amount of water Balbo's wooden aircraft had absorbed after

three weeks of being soaked with water the actual weight of planes was over 9,900 kilos. *Italo Balbo*, p. 224.

146 According to Gabriele Morolli, a building of this magnitude would normally have taken eight years to complete. "L'area urbana e il Palazzo dell'Aeronautica," in Gabriele Morolli, Daniela Fonti, and Giuseppe Pesce, *Il Palazzo dell'Aeronautica* (Rome: Editalia, 1989), p. 38.

147 See Morolli, Fonti, and Pesce, *Il Palazzo dell'Aeronautica*, pp. 71, 118; and Mariano Marisi, "Il Palazzo dell'Aeronautica ha mezzo secolo," *Rivista Aeronautica*, no. 4 (1981), p. 40.

148 Marisi, "Il Palazzo dell'Aeronautica ha mezzo secolo," p. 42.

149 Francesco Stippelli, "Immagini del Ministero dell'Aeronautica," in *Rivista Aeronautica*, no. 4 (1981), p. 40. I am indebted to Stippelli's excellent article for many of the details of life within the Air Ministry. For a summary of police reports on morale in the Ministry of Air, see Guerri, *Italo Balbo*, pp. 230–31.

150 Quoted by Morolli in *Il Palazzo dell'Aeronautica*, p. 104.

151 *L'Ala d'Italia*, no. 4, April 1933, quoted by Morolli in *Il Palazo dell'Aeronautica*, p. 110.

152 Fonti, "Lo Stile 'Novecento' nelle pitture e negli arredi," in *Il Palazzo dell'Aeronautica*, p. 154.

153 Balbo, *Setti anni di politica aeronautica*, p. 220.

154 For a brief and preliminary approach to a topic that would bear closer study, see Massimo Ferrari, "Italo Balbo et la stampa aeronautica," in Santoro, ed., *Italo Balbo: aviazione e potere aereo*, pp. 461–6.

155 Quoted by Adriano Caperdoni in *Il volo e l'immaginario* (Florence: Firenze Libri, Atheneum, 1997), p. 189.

156 Balbo, *Stormi in volo sull'oceano*, pp. 257–8; Italo Balbo, *La centuria alata* (Milan: Mondadori, 1934), p. 13.

157 Balbo, *La centuria alata*, pp. 22–3.

158 Cupini, *Cieli e mari*, pp. 198–9.

159 Quoted in ibid., p. 199.

160 Ibid., p. 200.

161 Ibid., p. 280.

162 Adone Nosari of the *Giornale d'Italia*; Mario Massai of the *Corriere della Sera*; Mario Bassi of *La Stampa*; Paolo Monelli of the *Gazzetta del Popolo*; Luigi Freddi of *Il Popolo d'Italia*. The cinematographer was Mario Craveri.

163 Balbo, *La centuria alata*, p. 72.

164 On 5 July 1931, while taking off from Capri in an S.59bis, Balbo hit a submerged object and only escaped with great difficulty from the cockpit after the plane had sunk beneath the surface of the water.

165 Balbo, *La centuria alata*, pp. 85–9.

166 Cupini, *Cieli e mari*, p. 217.

167 *Chicago Daily Tribune*, 1 July 1933.

168 Cupini, *Cieli e mari*, p. 218.

169 The plane was piloted by Mario Baldini, a veteran of two previous cruises and a passenger in the S.55 that Balbo almost fatally crashed on 20 June, only two weeks earlier.

170 The *Chicago Daily Tribune* reported on 5 July 1933 that Mussolini had telephoned Balbo ". . . advising him not to take any risks and pointing out the folly of proceeding in the face of unfavorable weather conditions. The premier expressed the hope that all 24 of the planes could finish the trip to Chicago. He explained that it would not be to the credit of Italy to lose any of the ships through taking unnecessary chances."

171 Balbo, *La centuria alata*, p. 187. According to David Darah, writing in the *Chicago Daily Tribune* on 1 July 1933, at the time of his departure from Orbetello Balbo hoped to reach Chicago in six days.

172 Cupini, *Cieli e mari*, p. 153.

173 Ibid., p. 234.

174 *Chicago Daily Tribune*, 19 July 1933.

175 *Chicago Daily Tribune*, 17 July 1933.

176 Quoted by Cupini in *Cieli e mari*, p. 241.

177 *New York Times*, 20 July 1933.

178 Ibid.

179 For the confidential messages Mussolini sent Balbo during the cruise, see Guerri, *Italo Balbo*, pp. 260–64.

180 Balbo, *La centuria alata*, p. 284.

181 Ibid., pp. 289–90. The *New York Times* described the same scene as a "hurricane of sound." "As General Balbo stepped from his car the noise was deafening. Thousands of hands were raised in the Fascist salute." 22 July 1933.

182 Balbo, *La centuria alata*, 292. In the early 1930s the best-known Italian in America was the gangster Al Capone. Fiorello LaGuardia was elected mayor of New York in 1933 and began to turn that image around with a bold program of reform.

183 Ibid., p. 298.

184 *New York Times*, 24 July 1933.

185 *New York Times*, 30 July 1933.

186 Balbo, *La centuria alata*, p. 316.

187 In making this decision, Balbo may also have been influenced by his well-grounded suspicion that Mussolini preferred him to return by way of the Azores. While at Shediac, Balbo had received a cable from Mussolini, instructing him to take southern route if he was compelled to leave Shoal Harbour after 10 August. Cupini, *Cieli e mari*, p. 259.

188 Balbo, *La centuria alata*, p. 332.

189 Ibid., p. 341.

190 Ibid., p. 345.

191 Ibid., pp. 352–3.

192 Ibid., p. 359.

193 *Chicago Daily Tribune*, 11 August 1933; 12 August 1933.

194 For Balbo's long-standing ambition to be promoted to air marshal, see Emilio De Bono's diary entries of 27 February 1931 and 1 July 1933, quoted by Rochat in *Italo Balbo*, pp. 215, 216.

195 Segre, *Italo Balbo*, pp. 279–81; but also see Rochat, who argues that Balbo's removal from the Ministry of Aeronautics should not be interpreted as punishment or a demotion (p. 222).

196 In an intercepted telephone conversation with Renzo Chierici, federal secretary of the Fascist Party in Ferrara. Quoted by Guerri, *Italo Balbo*, p. 287.

197 Quoted and translated by Segre in *Italo Balbo*, p. 282.

198 Ibid., p. 283.

199 Reported by Guerri, *Italo Balbo*, p. 287.

200 Bottai, *Diario 1935–1944*, p. 207.

201 Balbo, *La centuria alata*, p. 234.

202 Ibid., pp. 252, 300.

203 Ibid., p. 360.

204 Ibid., pp. 372–4. According to the *New York Times*, 18 August 1933, Balbo first shook hands with Crown Prince Umberto and other members of the House of Savoy. He then ". . . turned toward the Premier, saluting his chief. Il Duce, however, instead of returning the salute, embraced his Air Minister and kissed him on both cheeks. A moment later the General was affectionately hugging and kissing his wife and two children." See also the *Chicago Daily Tribune*, which correctly reported that Balbo had three children. 13 August 1933.

205 Segre, *Italo Balbo*, p. 257.

206 As Balbo referred to the Ministry of Aeronautics in an intercepted telephone conversation with a friend after he received the letter from Mussolini appointing him governor of Libya. In Guerri, *Italo Balbo*, p. 287.

207 On these exhibitions and the aesthetics underlying them, see Jeffrey Schnapp, "Epic Demonstrations: Fascist Modernity and the 1932 Exhibition of the Fascist Revolution," in Richard Golsan, ed., *Fascism, Aesthetics, and Culture* (Hanover, N.H.: University Press of New England, 1992), pp. 1–33; Marla Susan Stone, *The Patron State: Culture & Politics in Fascist Italy* (Princeton: Princeton University Press, 1998); and Claudio Fogu, *The Historic Imaginary: Politics of History in Fascist Italy* (Toronto: University of Toronto Press, 2003).

208 According to Colonel Franceso Cutry, head of the Ufficio Storico of the Ministry of Air and one of the organizers of the exhibit. In *L'Ala d'Italia*, January 1935, p. 16.

209 According to Mario Massai, in *L'Esposizione dell'aernautica italiana* (Milan: Edizioni d'arte Emilio Bestetti, 1931), p. 177. For the 1932 Mostra della rivoluzione fascista and its relationship to the Esposizione dell'aeronautica italiana, see Stone, *The Patron State*, pp. 128–76, 222–6 and Schnapp, "Epic Demonstrations," pp. 1–33.

210 Stone, *The Patron State*, p. 131.

211 *Esposizione dell'aeronautica italiana*, n. p.

212 Marcello Visconti in his introduction to the exhibit's official catalogue, ibid., p. 17.

213 According to Antonio Monti, one of the organizers of the exhibit, in ibid., p. 86.

214 Ibid., p. 137.

215 The point was made more explicitly in the exhibition catalogue by Mario Massai, a friend and admirer of Balbo, who explained that: ". . . in a particularly delicate political moment that requires a single commander of Italy's armed services, Balbo can, with infinite pride, return to the Great Chief's hands, the kind of winged army that the Duce wanted, mighty and docile, aggressive and tenacious, sure of its power, and already put to the test in exploits no one else has ever attempted." Ibid., p. 177.

216 *Il Corriere della Sera*, 8 June 1934. The term in Italian is "*Partefice della resurrezione.*" "*Partefice*" is an archaic term used in Boccaccio's *Decamerone* to refer to someone entrusted with sacred relics.

3. A Marriage Made in Heaven

1 Giuseppe Gubitosi, *Amedeo Nazzari* (Bologna: Il Mulino, 1998), p. 25–6.

2 Of his experiences in East Africa, Vittorio Mussolini wrote that every flight was "a new fascinating undertaking in which the danger of dying excited the senses like a supreme sport." *Voli sulle Ambe* (Florence: Sansoni, 2nd ed., 1937), p. 28.

3 Mussolini evidently warned his son against an openly Fascist film that would fail to engage the public. "I think that not even the Russians are entertained when they see on the screen a Stakhanovite hero who is producing tons of steel ingots instead of kissing his fiancée." Quoted by Franca Faldini and Goffredo Fofi, eds., *L'Avventurosa storia del cinema italiano. Raccontata dai suoi protagonisti 1935–1959* (Milan: Feltrinelli, 1979), pp. 21–2. For the change in the film's title, see the interview with Alessandrini in Francesco Savio, *Cinecittà anni trenta* (Rome: Bulzoni, 1979), ed. Tullio Kezich, Vol. I, p. 56. "Arriveremo al sole" was the answer given by Luciano Serra to his young son Aldo when asked at the beginning of the film where they would go with the plane he had built.

4 Gubitosi, *Nazzari*, p. 34.

5 From Vittorio Mussolini's summary of the plot in "Luciano Serra, Pilota," *L'Ala d'Italia*, June 1937, p. 15.

6 Mario Gromo in his review for *La Stampa*, 29 October 1938, reproduced in Mario Gromo, *Davanti allo schermo. Cinema italiano 1931–43* (Turin: La Stampa, 1992), p. 99. Commenting on the sensitivity and understatement of Nazzari's performance in the *Corriere della Sera*, Filippo Sacchi concluded: "With this performance, Amedeo Nazzari emerges clearly as the most complete and robust young actor of our cinema." 29 August 1938.

7 *L'Ala d'Italia*, June 1937, p. 14.

8 Romolo Marcellini, "Aviazione e Cinema," *L'Ala d'Italia*, 1 September 1939, pp. 22–4.

9 Luigi Freddi, *Il Cinema* (Rome: L'Arnia, 1949), Vol. I, pp. 24–5.

10 Acknowledging the realities of flight in the early 1920s, a Chamber of Commerce report on aviation facilities in the Los Angeles area stated that ". . . there are hundreds of acres of level ground where emergency landings may be made in safety. An emergency landing may be made practically any place in the great Los Angeles Valley from the mountains to the sea." Quoted by Art Ronnie in *Locklear: The Man Who Walked On Wings* (South Brunswick and New York: A. S. Barnes, 1973), p. 105. How different things are today!

11 For a list of these films and plot summaries, see Stephen Pendo, *Aviation in the Cinema* (Metuchen, N.J., and London: The Scarecrow Press, 1985), pp. 7–11.

12 Fay Wray, *On The Other Hand: A Life Story* (New York: St. Martin's Press, 1989), p. 86.

13 This account of Saunders's life is based heavily, although not exclusively, on the testimony of his wife Fay Wray in *On the Other Hand*, pp. 86–7. Saunders evidently spoke quite candidly to Wray about his affair with Bessie Lasky and expected her to

tolerate their relationship, even after Wray and Saunders married in June 1928.

14 Kevin Brownlow, *The War, The West, and The Wilderness* (London: Secker & Warburg, 1978), p. 206.

15 George Turner, "Wings: Epic of the Air," *American Cinematographer*, 66, no. 4, p. 35.

16 For a list of directors' salaries in 1926, see Richard Koszarski, *An Evening's Entertainment. The Age of the Silent Feature Picture, 1915–1928* (Berkeley and Los Angeles: University of California Press, 1990), pp. 212–13.

17 For Wellman's account of his encounter with the "three great magicians of the buck" – Otto Kahn, Sir William Wiseman, and William Stralem – see his autobiography *A Short Time for Insanity* (New York: Hawthorn, 1974), pp. 171–6. There is a slightly more restrained version in Kevin Brownlow, *The Parade's Gone By . . .* (London: Secker & Warburg, 1968), pp. 176–7. According to Wellman, Schulberg was mad at him for having gone over budget while waiting for clouds against which he could shoot a dogfight scene. Then Kahn, Wiseman, and Stralem appeared when they were finally doing the scene. That night the three money men came up to Wellman's suite. He emerged from the shower and confessed that he was drunk. "What do you want," he asked? 'Nothing . . . We just want to tell you that you can have anything you want. The whole thing is yours. You're one hell of a man.' Then they shook my hand, and left. I waited till the door closed, then I fell down and cried."

18 Wellman, *A Short Time for Insanity*, p. 164.

19 Ibid., p. 164. Bow's biographer, David Stenn, disputes Wellman's account. He points out that Clara and the director Victor Fleming announced their engagement the day after her arrival in San Antonio for the filming of *Wings. Clara Bow. Runnin' Wild* (New York City: Cooper Square Press, 2000), pp. 74–5. Of course, one thing doesn't exclude the other.

20 Dick Grace, *Squadron of Death. The True Adventure of a Movie Plane-Crasher* (Garden City, N.Y.: Doubleday, Doran, 1929), p. 229.

21 Ibid., p. 248.

22 Ibid., pp. 260–66.

23 According to George Turner, Buddy Rogers believed there had been three fatal crashes during production, all involving military pilots. When Hubbard and Wellman saw an army plane crash, they were told by a field operations officer to think nothing of it, since pilots were often killed in training. "Wings: Epic of the Air," *American Cinematographer*, 66, no. 4, p. 40.

24 Dick Grace himself later paid homage to the courage of the cinematographers who worked on *Wings*. After crashing the Spad, he climbed out of the plane and was astonished to see how close he had come to the cameramen. "The nearest one was seventeen feet from the wrecked plane. What kind of nerves must a cameraman have to see an airplane traveling at a hundred miles an hour crashing into the ground so close to him that he can almost reach out and touch it?" *Squadron of Death*, p. 247.

25 Turner, "Wings: Epic of the Air," p. 36.

26 Beirne Lay, Jr., quoted in James H. Farmer, *Celluloid Wings* (Blue Ridge Summit, Pa.: Tab Books, 1984), p. 41. Richard Arlen later explained how these scenes were shot. "We were using the first motor-driven cameras which were mounted a little in front of the cockpit. The 400-foot reels ran off at about 90 feet a minute which gave us only a little more than four minutes of picture. Bill Wellman would tell us on the ground what he wanted us to do in the air. We would waggle our wings when ready and then take over as producer, director and actor. We would hold up the proper number of fingers for takes one, two or three. If we thought the scene was bad we would run a finger across our throats for a cut. That was why Wellman wanted actors for *Wings* who could fly. 'Buddy' [Rogers] couldn't, but he learned damn quick!" Quoted by Farmer in *Celluloid Wings*, p. 36.

27 Russell Harlan would photograph many of Howard Hawks's later films, including *Red River*, *I Was A Male War Bride*, *The Thing From Another World*, *The Big Sky*, *Land of the Pharaohs*, *Rio Bravo*, and *Hatari!*

28 Quoted by Turner in "Wings: Epic of the Air," p. 39.

29 *Variety*, 17 August 1927.

30 Quoted by Brownlow in *The War, the West, and the Wilderness*, p. 206.

31 Brownlow, *The Parade's Gone By . . .* , pp. 174–5.

32 Wellman, *A Short Time for Insanity*, pp. 72–174. According to Wellman, the two men blown into the air by the artillery blast survived, though one was badly injured.

33 Brownlow, *The West, the War, and the Wilderness*, p. 211.

34 Wellman took credit for the idea, though he acknowledged that the person who made it work was Ray Pomroy, head of Paramount's special effects department. Wellman, *A Short Time for Insanity*, p. 178.

35 Turner, "Wings: Epic of the Air," p. 41.

36 *Harrison's Reports*, 27 August 1927.

37 Hughes's life is shrouded in carefully cultivated mystery, which several biographers have set out to penetrate, sometimes with a liberal use of gossip and imagination, but thus far without conspicuous success. The most recent biography of which I am aware, Richard Hack's *Hughes: The Private Diaries, Memos and Letters* (Beverly Hills: New Millennium Press, 2001), provides countless trivial details about Hughes's life, but neglects to document any of the author's statements and conjectures about the issues that matter. Martin Scorsese's emphasis on Hughes's psychological disabilities in his ambitious epic film released in 2004, *The Aviator*, is difficult to reconcile with Hughes's undeniable achievements in the late 1920s and '30s. Though cleverly linked to the plot or Orson Welles's *Citizen Kane*, Scorsese's picture fails to explain the Hughes enigma. But perhaps this is too much to ask of a motion picture whose primary objective is to entertain, which it unquestionably does.

38 Hughes had been introduced to Neilan, by his uncle Rupert, a well-connected writer and director who lived in Los Angeles.

39 The first Academy Awards were given to films released between 1 August 1927 and 1 August 1928, the last year of the silent cinema. *Wings* won the award for "the most unique, artistic, worthy and original production without reference to cost or magnitude." Koszarski, *An Evening's Entertainment*, p. 316.

40 According to Farmer, *Celluloid Wings*, p. 49, Hughes received his license in December 1927 and learned to fly "under the careful tutelage of Charlie LaJotta at Santa Monica's Old Clover Field." Richard Hack writes that Hughes had begun his flying lessons in mid-1927 and was taught by J. B. Alexander for $100 a day. He dates his pilot's license to 7 January 1928. *Hughes*, pp. 64, 68. Moye Stephens claims that Hughes soloed in the summer of 1927. Quoted in H. Hugh Wynne, *The Motion Picture Stunt Pilots and Hollywood's Classic Aviation Pilots* (Missoula, Mo.: Pictorial Histories Publishing Company, 1987), p. 72. But in the same book Frank Tomick is quoted as saying that Hughes had just soloed when the shooting of the aerial scenes in *Hell's Angels* began, which would place the date around December 1927 or January 1928. Such varying accounts of events in Howard Hughes's life are common in the literature about him.

41 Quoted by Peter Harry Brown and Pat H. Broeske in *Howard Hughes: The Untold Story* (New York: Dutton, 1996), pp. 40–41. According to Richard Hack, Hughes had written the first three of these goals on the back of a receipt from a men's store already in January 1925. *Hughes*, p. 55.

42 Hughes's biographer Charles Higham claims that Neilan was responsible for both the title and plot of *Hell's Angels*. According to Higham, Neilan told Hughes that while in Havana in 1916 he had heard a story about two brothers in the air force fighting over a woman. Hughes then asked him to produce a draft of the story for a film. *Howard Hughes: The Secret Life* (New York: Berkley, 1994), p. 28.

43 For a probing analysis of these differences, see Robert Baird, "*Hell's Angels* above *The Western Front*," in Peter C. Rollins and John E. O'Connor, *Hollywood's World War I: Motion Picture Images* (Bowling Green, Ohio: Bowling Green State University Popular Press, 1997), pp. 79–100.

44 Commenting on the eccentric behavior of Hughes during the making of *Hell's Angels*, the cinematographer Elmer Dyer recalled: "He always ran the daily rushes at five o'clock in the morning. He used to sit there with his shoes off, wrapped in a dirty old overcoat, holes in his socks, unshaven." Quoted by Don Dwiggins in *Hollywood Pilot: The Biography of Paul Mantz* (Garden City, N.Y.: Doubleday, 1967), p. 39.

45 Hughes did so, however, only after Tomick convinced him that less well paid pilots would not be up to the task. Frank Tomick, quoted by Wynne in *Motion Picture Stunt Pilots*, pp. 75–6. Hughes could be extravagant, but he was not always generous with those who worked with him.

46 Carroll V. Glines, *Roscoe Turner: Aviation's Master Showman* (Washington and London: Smithsonian Press, 1995), pp. 88–9.

47 Tony Thomas, *Howard Hughes in Hollywood* (Secaucus, N.J.: Citadel Press, 1985), p. 45.

48 Ibid., p. 50.

49 Quoted by James Curtis in *James Whale: A New World of Gods and Monsters* (London: Faber & Faber, 1998), p. 86. For Whale's dislike of flying and Jean Harlow, see ibid. pp. 87–9.

50 Glines, *Roscoe Turner*, pp. 94–5. Glines quotes a revealing letter from Turner to an Army pilot who had been approached about doing the stunt, warning him that the Sikorsky was "in terrible shape" and that owing to its size Turner doubted that "it would be possible to clear it with a parachute in a spin." He went on to say that ". . . if you want to spin this baby, I would suggest that you watch everything very closely both as to the airplane and as to dealing with these people because, frankly, they think that whoever spins it will get killed and they won't have to pay" (p. 96). Turner complained bitterly to Hughes about the way he had been treated and the destruction of the Sikorsky, but Hughes responded with equal indignation. "I have tried to be fair in my dealings with you throughout the picture and the only thing I know that you can criticize is the deal for the purchase of the bomber and as you know I didn't make that deal with you and any misunderstanding is not my fault" (p. 99).

51 Dick Grace, *I Am Still Alive* (New York: Rand McNally, 1931), p. 162.

52 To Harlow's credit, it should be said that she hated the role she was asked to play and knew that her acting in the picture was dreadful. Certainly, Whale did nothing to help her. He was obviously appalled by her lack of acting experience and did nothing to hide his disdain for her. Yet whatever Harlow's failings, they did not prevent her from becoming a star and overshadowing Hughes and his girlfriend Billie Dove when they took to the road to promote the film throughout the United States. See David Stenn, *Bombshell: The Life and Death of Jean Harlow* (Raleigh, N.C.: Lightning Bug Press, 2000), pp. 39–46.

53 Brown and Broeske, *Howard Hughes*, pp. 69–70. They also claim that Hughes was personally responsible for Harlow's cleavage in the famous scene during which she seduces Monte before the two brothers go off to the front. According to David Stenn in *Bombshell*, pp. 33–5, Harlow scarcely needed Howard Hughes in order to learn how to dress provocatively.

54 All those attending the premiere were given a leather-bound souvenir program that provided a detailed breakdown of the cost of the film. Hack, *Hughes*, p. 81.

55 This quotation and other details are taken from Brown and Broeske, who date the premiere, incorrectly, to 30 June. *Howard Hughes*, pp. 70–71.

56 Thomas, *Howard Hughes in Hollywood*, p. 52.

57 Hack, *Hughes*, p. 82.

58 *New York Times*, 16 August 1930.

59 Glines, *Roscoe Turner*, p. 88.

60 Sherwood's review is quoted extensively by John Keats in *Howard Hughes* (New York: Random House, 1966), pp. 43–4.

61 "Emperor Hughes," *New Republic*, 1 October 1930, p. 180.

62 From a deposition given by John Monk Saunders in August 1930 and quoted in Rudy Behlmer, ed., *Inside Warner Brothers (1935–1951)* (New York: Viking, 1985), p. 338.

63 The cooperation the navy provided to Warner Brothers in making *Devil Dogs of the War* (1935), Navy Secretary Claude Swanson argued had been "more than compensated by the favorable publicity value of the product." Quoted by Lawrence Suid in *Sailing on the Silver Screen: Hollywood and the U.S. Navy* (Annapolis, Md.: Naval Institute Press, 1996), p. 39.

64 For the experiences of early air travelers, see Robert Wohl, "Des héros méconnus de l'aviation commerciale pionnière: les

passagers," in *Actes du Colloque "Pierre-Georges Latécoère"* (Paris: Service historique de l'armée de l'Air, 1994), pp. 305–17.

65 Donald Dale Jackson, *Flying the Mail* (Alexandria, Va.: Time-Life, 1982), p. 38.

66 Between October 1919 and July 1921, twenty-six Air Mail Service employees died in crashes, an average of more than one a month. Jackson, *Flying the Mail*, p. 54.

67 Gloria Stuart, who played the female lead in *Air Mail*, thought that it was "really a *potchkeh* [time-wasting] picture, low-budget and everything." At the time, she adds, Ford was not considered "a great big famous director." Quoted by Joseph McBride in *Searching for John Ford. A Life* (New York: St. Martin's Press, 2001), p. 178.

68 Ford himself received only $36,000 for directing it. McBride, *Searching for John Ford*, p. 179.

69 In creating this setting, Ford was assisted by Karl Freund, cinematographer of Fritz Lang's *Metropolis* and F. W. Murnau's *Der Letzte Mann.* Tad Gallagher, one of Ford's most astute critics, believes that no movie illustrates Murnau's influence on Ford better than *Air Mail.* Tad Gallagher, *John Ford: The Man and His Films* (Berkeley and Los Angeles: University of California Press, 1986), p. 79.

70 This scene marked Paul Mantz's debut as a Hollywood stunt flyer and was shot by Elmer Dyer at Bishop, California, a small town at the foot of the Eastern Sierras. The hangar Mantz was expected to fly through was only five feet wider than the wingspan of the Stearman with which he did the stunt. As Mantz approached the hangar, he was hit by a burst of heavy turbulence that unbalanced his wings. He succeeded in righting himself, shot through the hangar, and ended with an exuberant victory roll, which is shown in the picture. For Mantz's problems in breaking into the world of Hollywood stunt flyers, see Dwiggins, *Hollywood Pilot*, pp. 35–45.

71 In *Dirigible*, made the previous year, Wead had also shown indulgence for the daredevil pilot. Despite his neglect of his marriage and irresponsible flying that results in the death of two men, Frisky Pierce is redeemed and allowed at the end of the picture to reconcile with his wife. The dependable dirigible commander, Jack Bradon, who subordinates individual exploits to disciplined group action, gives up his hopes of marrying Frisky's wife, Helen, in a noble act of self-sacrifice.

72 "For ten minutes at the end of the second act the play holds all the screeching terror and mute impalpable doom that hang with invisible weight and mortal danger in the dead mist of a fog bank. It is Guinol [sic] stuff, if you please, but effective, racking, terrifying with all the subtlety of a torture chamber." *The New York Journal*, quoted in Frank Wead, *Ceiling Zero. A Play in Three Acts* (Richmond Hill, N.Y.: The Richmond Hill Record, 1935), p. 152.

73 Wead, *Ceiling Zero*, p. 134.

74 One of the two readers was Dalton Trumbo, who himself would later write an aviation movie, *Thirty Seconds Over Tokyo.*

75 Todd McCarthy, *Howard Hawks: The Grey Fox of Hollywood* (New York: Grove Press, 1997), pp. 111, 215.

76 For a sustained and stimulating comparison of Hawks and Ford, see Gallagher, *John Ford: The Man and his Movies*, pp. 81–3. Ford is a constant point of reference for Hawks in his long interview with Peter Bogdanovich in *Who The Devil Made It: Conversations with Legendary Film Directors* (New York: Ballentine, 1997), pp. 244–378.

77 For Hawks's account of his later relationship with Hughes, see Joseph McBride, *Hawks on Hawks* (Berkeley and Los Angeles: University of California Press, 1982), p. 51. "We played golf and lied to each other about our handicaps. He flew my airplane and I flew his . . . He could fly, and he had a lot of guts."

78 In an interview with Peter Bogdanovich, Hawks claimed authorship of the original story on which *Dawn Patrol* was based. Bogdanovich, *Who The Devil Made It*, p. 271. Saunders's wife at the time *Dawn Patrol* was made, Fay Wray, remembers Hawks coming to their house with a story idea that he wanted Saunders to sell. She also reproduces documents, signed by Saunders and Hawks', ascribing to Saunders any interest that

Hawks might have in the story. Wray, *On the Other Hand*, pp. 121–3. Wray concludes that "the mystery of that Sunday morning when Howard first went to John with the idea, the *why* of it, would remain!" (p. 122). Yet in a deposition, given in August 1930, Saunders describes a meeting he had in July or August 1929 during which Hawks "told me that he would like to obtain an air story with a war atmosphere as a starring vehicle for the well-known actor Ronald Colman . . . I then told Hawks the idea Mr. [Irwin S.] Cobb had given me at a dinner party at his apartment in New York and which I had further investigated at Oxford and during my travels in France and Germany. I told Mr. Hawks that I had in mind a story involving that tragic atmosphere of which Mr. Cobb had spoken, that to my knowledge the subject of a British aerodrome at the front and the comradeship and attitude of mind of the British pilots had never been shown on the screen and that we had therefore a story which was in background and atmosphere altogether original. Mr. Hawks stated that he believed that the part would be suitable for Mr. Colman and that Mr. Colman's producer would be interested in the purchase of such a story. I then gave Mr. Hawks a synopsis of the story which I had in mind [*The Flight Commander*] and which was later produced on the screen under the title of *The Dawn Patrol* . . ." Quoted in Behlmer, ed., *Inside Warner Bros.*, p. 339. Hawks's biographer Todd McCarthy sums up the evidence, commenting that in Saunders's original eighteen-page treatment there was a subplot involving women (but not included in the film) that may have represented a Hawks contribution. *Hawks*, pp. 102–5. I myself see no reason to doubt Saunders's account.

79 McCarthy, *Hawks*, pp. 114–5. In addition to *Dawn Patrol*, Hawks had directed the 1928 silent picture, *Air Circus*, and *Today We Live*, a 1933 MGM film, written by William Faulkner, that featured Gary Cooper as a First World War aviator. *Dawn Patrol* was so sound in its dramatic conception and structure and its aerial combat scenes so beautifully photographed that Warners would remake it in 1938 to great acclaim with another director, a totally different cast, minimal changes in its scenario and settings, and the same flying scenes. The reviews were even more enthusiastic than they had been in 1930.

80 McCarthy, *Hawks*, pp. 219–20.

81 Ibid., p. 214.

82 In the hospital, when it was clear that Tex was likely to die, Tex's wife Lou had told Dizzy that "You're no good . . . Everybody you touch you hurt, your friends most of all." Dizzy makes no effort to defend himself. But a Hawks hero will be more sensitive to the opinion of males he respects than to a woman, in this case one whom Dizzy has treated condescendingly during the early scenes of the picture.

83 When Wead wrote a similar scene for *Dive Bomber* five years later, he was careful to make Fred McMurray's act of self-sacrifice, testing a new device to prevent dive bomber pilots from passing out under heavy G-loads, more unambiguously altruistic.

84 During the previous year, Pat O'Brien had appeared in two Cagney pictures, *The Irish in Us* and *Devil Dogs of the Air*, a service film based on a story by John Monk Saunders.

85 In the play, Dizzy delivers these lines to Tommy, as he does other comments about aviation.

86 For the efforts of the commercial aircraft industry to alter Wead's play before its filming by Warner Brothers, see Dominick A. Pisano, "The Greatest Show Not on Earth": The Confrontation between Utility and Entertainment in Aviation, in *The Airplane in American Culture* (Ann Arbor: The University of Michigan Press, 2003), pp. 60–63. Those familiar with commercial aviation would not have been taken in, since both the play and the film make much of the existence of a new two-engine airliner capable of flying 220 miles per hour and taking off on one engine. This was a reference to the DC-2, which entered commercial air service in the United States in May 1934. No such airliner existed in the 1920s.

87 As a further concession to the airlines, Warners shortened Dizzy's flying career from twenty-four to sixteen years, thus

shifting the setting of the action from 1935 to 1927. The play specifies that Dizzy had begun flying in 1911.

88 *Time* began its review of *Ceiling Zero* by observing that it was unlikely "to whet the average citizen's appetite for flying, despite the moral that pilots are brave men willing to die for Science." 27 January 1936, p. 46. Writing in the *New York Times* on 20 January 1936, Frank Nugent pronounced *Ceiling Zero* "tersely written, handsomely produced, and played to perfection . . ." In a second review that appeared in the *Times*,' Sunday edition on 26 January, he added that he found Hawks's film "infinitely superior to the play in every respect."

89 "Other air pictures have been made," *Harrison's Reports* commented, "but for sheer thrills, this one leads them all because of the realistic way it has been done." 30 April 1938.

90 In an interview with Peter Bogdanovich, Hawks insisted that he had written the screenplay on which *Test Pilot* had been based. He even claimed to have joined Fleming in coaching Clark Gable and Spencer Tracy in their delivery of the dialogue. "I wrote the dialog for *Test Pilot* and Fleming came over and said, 'Tracy and Gable won't read that dialog.' So I said to Vic: 'Do you know the dialog?' 'Yes.' 'Well, let's you and I play it for 'em.' So I told him how to play it and we went down and said, 'Well, it's awful when two guys who can't act have to show two actors who are drawing a lot of money how to do a scene. Vic, let's how 'em how to do it.' And they didn't think we could bring it off. We read it just the way it was written and they said 'Oh, that's different.' We did it with an entirely different viewpoint than what they thought." Responding to Bogdanovich's observation that *Test Pilot* wasn't really a very good picture, Hawks commented: "No. The story was pretty good, but it's awfully hard to take someone else's stuff, as Fleming took mine, and make it work." *Who The Devil Made It*, pp. 296–7, 303–4.

91 In a brilliant essay about the movie that abounds in insights, Gerald Mast confesses his puzzlement about the title. *Howard Hawks, Storyteller* (New York and Oxford: Oxford University Press, 1982), pp. 130–1. But most aviators, I think, will understand its meaning immediately. Men were not meant to fly and their insistence on doing so implies the possibility of their death.

92 In conversation with Bogdanovich in *Who The Devil Made It*, pp. 308–9. The origin of the script for *Only Angels Have Wings* was a good deal more complicated than Hawks suggested. See Todd McCarthy's excellent reconstruction of the film's development from an early seven-page synopsis by Anne Wigton and a five-page sketch by Hawks himself to the finished script on which five writers and Hawks worked. *Hawks*, pp. 266–9.

93 "I got the idea for the story at a party one night. I was with a Mexican bush pilot. We were flying around Mexico landing in washes and having a lot of fun. He told me a marvelous thing I couldn't put in the picture. He went to a dinner where there was a very attractive girl who had been married for a year to a fellow with a burnt face and great eyes. A fellow got up at the dinner and made a speech. He said, 'A year ago tonight we were celebrating the marriage. About one o'clock you shoved us all out. You went to bed about two minutes past. Then you got up at ten minutes past one, and then you had at it again a bit later.' He told the story of the whole wedding night, and the girl said, 'You son of a bitch, you were peeping!' He said no, and brought out a graph that was made from a German machine that you attach to your airplane. It shows where you started the motor, when you bounced while taking off, when you got up. And he's hung it under the bed. The girl hung up the graph, she was so proud of it. That's where I got the story of *Only Angels Have Wings*." As good a yarn as this is, its relationship to the plot of *Only Angels* was obvious only to Hawks. He is more convincing when he says in the same interview that "I knew the fellow that jumped out of an airplane [during the making of *Hell's Angels*] and left somebody behind to get killed. He spent the rest of his life trying to make up for that, and he got killed, finally, trying to make up for it." McBride, *Hawks on Hawks*, p. 74. The pilot Hawks is referring to, Al Wilson, died in 1932 in a col-

lision with an autogyro at the National Air Races in Cleveland. According to H. Hugh Wynne, Wilson "was probably involved in more precarious aviation stunts than any other pilot in the world. His courage was matched by his piloting skill, and he was thoroughly professional in his work." *Motion Picture Stunt Pilots*, p. 128.

94 See Robin Wood, *Howard Hawks* (Garden City, N.Y.: Doubleday, 1968), pp. 22–3.

95 *New York Times*, 21 May 1939.

96 McCarthy, *Hawks*, p. 275.

97 According to Gerald Mast, Hawks claimed to have been inspired in his lighting of *Only Angels Have Wings* by the American painter Frederick Remington. Mast goes on to say that "If there is a single formal feature that distinguishes a Hawks film visually from that of any other Hollywood director, it is its sensitivity to the particular sources (and consequent qualities) of light." *Howard Hawks, Storyteller*, pp. 106–7.

98 Hawks had included a similar scene in *Dawn Patrol*, but there it was Richard Barthelmess's young comrade, played by Douglas Fairbanks, Jr., who was disgusted by the scene of British airmen drinking happily with a captured German pilot who was responsible for the death of a member of their squadron.

99 One of the best examples of the orientation of *Only Angels* toward what is happening on the ground rather than the air comes in the way that Hawks chooses to narrate Joe's death at the beginning of the film. We see the scene almost exclusively through the eyes and ears of people on the ground. See Mast, *Howard Hawks, Storyteller*, pp. 117–18. Todd McCarthy even argues that "the second-unit sequences of actual planes flying, the only recognizable exterior shots in the entire film, actually yank one out of the action, so disconnected are they from the artificial world of Barranca." *Hawks*, p. 277.

100 "I've known a lot of fliers and I've seen a lot of forced landings, and they don't moan about what's going to happen when they hit the ground. One of them's liable to say, 'Did you ever do this before?' 'Not me.' 'Well, this is going to be fun to watch.' They take *that* attitude about it. It doesn't do them any good to dramatize it." *Who The Devil Made It*, pp. 314–15.

101 In his study of Hawks, Leland A. Poague argues that it is not the woman but the male protagonist who is put to the test in *Only Angels* and other Hawks pictures; but I remain unconvinced by this and other points Poague makes. *Howard Hawks* (Boston: Twayne, 1982), p. 39. For the best assessment of the film, within the relevant contexts in which it needs to be placed and free of distracting jargon, see McCarthy, *Hawks*, pp. 276–7.

102 "Well, when you're all through, that's what it was [sic]. I'm a firm believer in that. Nobody causes anything exactly – things are destined to happen. So you have to turn around and say that." *Who The Devil Made It*, p. 312.

103 I take the term "useless service" from Henry de Montherlant, Hawks's coeval, who defined it in 1929 in the following way: "To search for a solution, knowing that the problem is insoluble; to serve, while smiling at what one serves; to subject oneself to an iron discipline, without end and without profit . . ." In *Un Voyageur solitaire est un diable*, reproduced in Henry de Montherlant, *Essais* (Paris: Gallimard, 1963), pp. 432–3.

104 When asked by Bogdanovich why he had chosen to set *Only Angels Have Wings* in such a remote and backward place, Hawks replied: "It was the one place in the world where that condition still existed and was made for drama. It had all the qualities of *Ceiling Zero*. These guys were a hard-boiled bunch. They weren't at that particular airfield at the time, but I met them and they *told* me about that airfield. So I just combined their stories." *Who The Devil Made It*, p. 310. The original treatment Hawks wrote for the film, called "Plane Four from Baranca [sic]," made it clear that the picture was to be about "a group of flyers who had migrated to South America because they could not fly elsewhere – outcasts because of troubles with the law, with drinking and smuggling, with accidents." Mast, *Howard Hawks, Storyteller*, p. 105. In McCarthy, this text runs somewhat differently; but the point remains the same. The pilots he

intended to portray in his new film, he wrote, were "collectively and individually the finest . . . I've ever seen but they had been grounded because of accidents, drinking, stunting, smuggling – each man's existence almost a story in itself." McCarthy, *Hawks*, p. 267.

105 For the perspectivism of *Only Angels Have Wings*, see Poague, *Howard Hawks*, pp. 35–8. My own approach to Hawks's perspectivism varies somewhat from Poague's.

106 For Hawks as the "Le Corbusier of the sound film," see Henri Langlois, "The Modernity of Howard Hawks," in Jim Hillier and Peter Wollen, *Howard Hawks, American Artist* (London: British Film Institute, 1996), p. 73.

107 Thus it comes as no surprise to discover that in the early 1950s Hawks announced that his next project would be a film version of *The Sun Also Rises*. McCarthy, *Hawks*, p. 512. One can only regret that the picture was never made. Having been so successful with one of Hemingway's worst novels, *To Have and Have Not*, one can only wonder what he would have done with one of his best. Hawks intended to cast Montgomery Clift as Jake Barnes and Gene Tierney as Lady Brett Ashley, a promising combination.

108 The term "regulation muddle" is Graham Greene's in his 1939 review reprinted in Hillier and Wollen, *Howard Hawks, American Artist*, p. 19. Even the generally uncritical *Harrison's Reports*, while praising the aerial photography as "exceptional," found the picture's story "routine." 27 May, 1939. The most incisive contemporary review of *Only Angels* I have found is by Richard Sheridan Ames in *Rob Wagner's Script*, 21, no. 509 (20 May 1939), 16, reproduced in Anthony Slide, ed., *Selected Film Criticism, 1931–1940* (Metuchen, N.J. and London: The Scarecrow Press, 1982), pp. 187–9. Ames declared himself "prepared to risk the ire of perspicacious and cultivated readers" by confessing his admiration for Hawks's film. He praised its "natural acting," its choice photography, and "incisive direction" and found that some of its "telling dialogue" had "Hemingway's bite." But even he concluded that it was "in no way important." What a shame that he didn't have the courage of his convictions!

109 Robin Wood in *Howard Hawks*, p. 17.

110 *New York Times*, 12 May 1939.

111 The message that we all have to die some time and that hence what matters is how we live is first conveyed through Geoff's attitude toward Joe's death, then reiterated in a different form by the doctor who insists on flying with MacPherson to attend the injured son of the mine owner, despite the risk. The doctor recites in Spanish a speech from Shakespeare's *Henry IV, Part One* that contains the lines: "A man can only die once. We owe God a debt. If we pay it today, we don't owe it tomorrow." To which MacPherson replies: "He's no fool." Mast, *Howard Hawks, Storyteller*, p. 123.

1112 *New York Times*, 16 April 1938.

113 Ibid., 12 May 1939.

114 For surveys of aviation pictures, see Pendo, *Aviation and the Cinema* and Farmer, *Celluloid Wings*. I am indebted to both these authors for their painstaking research.

115 *Variety*, quoted by Leslie Halliwell in *Halliwell's Film Guide*, 7th ed. (New York: Harper & Row, 1989), p. 303.

116 Wellman quoted in Harold Turney, *Film Guide to Paramount's Men With Wings* (1938), n. p. See also Ray Milland's enthusiastic report of his involvement in the picture in ibid.

117 For an informative summary of Mantz's career in Hollywood, see Pendo, *Aviation in the Cinema*, pp. 46–9.

118 Ibid., p. 47.

119 "Working in [*Dawn Patrol*] . . . was one of several things that made me want to join the RAF when the war broke out. But they wouldn't take me. In 1939 I met 'Pappy' Pope in France. He was the almost legendary RAF flier on whom my role was based. Pappy said, 'I saw you in *Dawn Patrol*, and it was all right.' That quiet praise was as good as a decoration." Quoted by Farmer in *Celluloid Wings*, p. 126.

120 Just before beginning work on *Only Angels*, Hawks took the woman he was courting, who would become his second wife, to Burbank Airport at 4:00 a.m. to witness the beginning of the Bendix Air Race. It was that morning, while sitting on the top of his station wagon watching the departing planes, that Hawks told her that he intended to marry her. McCarthy, *Hawks*, p. 264.

121 For a peculiarly unpleasant development of this theme, see Warner Brothers 1936 production *China Clipper*. Like so many other misogynist aviation movies, this was written by Frank Wead.

4. Knights of the Air

1 In his preface to Jean-Gérard Fleury, *Les Chemins du ciel* (Paris: Nouvelles Éditions Latines, 1933), p. 13.

2 Amelia Earhart, *The Fun Of It* (New York: Harcourt Brace Jovanovich, 1932).

3 *Les Nouvelles Littéraires*, 23 November 1929.

4 A "closed circuit" is a set course that takes the approximate form of a circle in contrast to a route from one point in the world to another.

5 Pierre Weiss, *L'Espace* (Paris: Louis Querelle, 1929), p. 217.

6 The comparison of flying to poetry was a leitmotif in Weiss's work. "One is born an aviator as one is born a poet." Quoted from Weiss's *Le Bouclier de Clésiphon* by Émile Krantz in his preface to Weiss, *Les Charmeurs de nuages* (Paris: Louis Querelle, 1928), p. 18.

7 *Les Nouvelles Littéraires*, 23 November 1929.

8 Edmond Rostand, *Le Cantique de l'aile* (Paris: Eugène Faquelle, 1922), originally published in *L'Illustration*, July 1911.

9 For a discussion of Driant's aviation novels, see Robert Wohl, *A Passion for Wings: Aviation and the Western Imagination 1908–1918* (New Haven and London: Yale University Press, 1994), pp. 81–9.

10 Marcel Proust, *A la recherche du temps perdu* (Paris: Gallimard, 1954), Vol. III, p. 106.

11 "And like an aviator who, up to that point, has laboriously been rolling along the ground, then suddenly 'taking off,' I ascended slowly toward the silent heights of memory." Ibid. p. 858.

12 Henry Bordeaux, *Vie héroïque de Guynemer: Le Chevalier de l'air* (Paris: Plon-Nourrit, 1918), p. 12.

13 *Dans le ciel de la patrie* (Paris: Draeger, 1918), n.p.

13 Jean Cocteau, *Œuvres poétiques complètes*, ed. by Michel Décaudin (Paris: Gallimard, 1999), p. 11.

14 *L'Archange*, a "heroic drama in three acts in verse," was first performed on 19 March 1925 in the Sarah-Bernhardt Theater in Paris. The text was published in *La Petite Illustration*, 9 May 1925. The critics, whose reviews are summarized by Robert de Beauplan in his introduction to the play, responded to Rostand's patriotism, but were clearly unenthusiastic about what the author himself confessed was the translation of Bordeaux's biography to the stage. See "*L'Archange* au theater Sarah-Bernhardt," published as a preface to the text of the play in *La Petite Illustration*, preceding p. 1 and following p. 28. Note also the two-volume biography of Roland Garros by Jean Ajalbert of the Goncourt Academy, *La Passion de Roland Garros* (Paris: Les Éditions de France, 1926). The hagiographic tone of the work is announced in its first lines. "Roland Garros who, by superhuman wings, rose to the conquest of infinite spaces . . . Roland Garros whose virtues equaled, both in the apotheosis of glory and in the abysses of sadness, the greatest examples of history and legend" (pp. 1–2). For a comprehensive and well-informed overview of French aviation literature in the 1920s and 1930s, see Bùi Xuân Bào, *Aviation et literature. Naissance d'un héroïsme nouveau dans les lettres françaises de l'Entre-Deux Guerres* (Paris: A. Dubin, 1961).

15 In skipping over the decade of the 1920s so cavalierly, I should recall that Louise Faure-Favier had been an indefatigable proponent of an aviation literature that would look beyond the exploits of wartime aces. Writing in *Les Nouvelles Littéraires* on 16 August 1924, she had pleaded for French writers to free themselves from their obsession with the past and take to the air. In these times, when the five continents had been explored and everything there was to say had been said about the sea,

Faure-Favier insisted, the adventure novel had no choice but to turn toward the sky. Alas, Faure-Favier's own major effort at aviation fiction, *Les Chevaliers de l'air* (Paris: Le Renaissance du Livre, 1923), though well informed about the life of French airline pilots in the early 1920s, was vitiated by the unqualified admiration she felt for her aviation friends and a style that makes Danielle Steele appear, in comparison, a master of prose. Greeted with applause in the aviation community for her contribution to "aeronautical propaganda," Faure-Favier's novel failed to find favor with the literary critics who were capable of making reputations. In surveying what he perceived to be the most important contributions to aviation literature in the introduction to his article on Weiss and *L'Espace*, Martin du Gard pointedly omitted Faure-Favier, a slight that must have been painful to someone who had devoted herself as totally as she had to the cause of aviation culture. Ungifted for fiction if persistent in its practice, Faure-Favier was at her best when writing "aerial guide books" aimed at attracting passengers to the fledgling airlines the French government was at that time subsidizing. See her *Guide des voyages aériens Paris–Londres* (Paris: Charles Bernard, 1921).

16 In *L'Espace*, Weiss left no doubt about his admiration for Lindbergh. "The exploit was prodigious. People experienced in all its totality in their imagination. An archangel had accomplished it . . . This event cured us [the French] of many of our debilities and tendencies toward decline. It had a touch of the divine that one finds spread throughout the world and it reopened the chivalric era. It had about it a color of dawn and hope" (pp. 170–71).

17 How many aviators would describe their experience of having lost their way in minimal conditions of visibility, as Weiss does here? "While the crew harvests the thoughts that rise in the horizon and picks a thousand flowers of dreams, on the ground the light evening fog has thickened and in the infinite distance an embroidery of cirrus clouds is being woven. Then other clouds appeared and, above as below, everything disappeared. Our airplane falls into the trap, strangled by uncertainty, indecision, and the impalpable." Pierre Weiss, *Escales et paysages* (Paris: Grasset, 1939), pp. 40–41.

18 See, for example, Weiss's hymn to Dieudonné Costes' glory in *Le Portrail bleu du Sagittaire* (Paris: Louis Querelle, 1931), pp. 92–103. Since the Armistice, Weiss claimed, France had known no greater day than that of Costes and Bellonte's 1931 nonstop flight from Paris to New York (p. 102).

19 Ibid., p. 185.

20 Pierre Weiss, *CIDNA ou l'Express d'Istambul* (Paris: Louis Querelle, 1932), pp. 11–12.

21 In 1928 (the year after Lindbergh's flight) Weiss described Lieutenant-Colonel Vuillemin as "this leader that all other aviation communities agree in recognizing as the world's leading pilot." Weiss, *Charmeurs de nuages*, p. 85.

22 Weiss to A. Pecker in an interview published in *Les Nouvelles Littéraires* on 27 May 1939 on the occasion of the publication of his book, *Escales et paysages*.

23 André Billy was perceptive when, reviewing *L'Équipage*, he observed that Kessel was "a storyteller who moves us by instinct, but he has none of the qualities of an intellectual, a thinker or a moralist." Quoted by Yves Courrière in *Joseph Kessel ou sous la piste du lion* (Paris: Plon, 1985), p. 224. See also Billy's sketch of Kessel in *Intimités littéraires* (Paris: Flammarion, 1932), pp. 131–6. ". . . an aura of uncertainty that is not without its charm, I would even say that is not without poetry, surrounds him and isolates him a bit. He doesn't say very much. It seems that he is caught up in some faraway dream. I would be tempted to write: 'Byronic (*beau ténébreux*),' if these two words didn't run the risk of making you smile by representing Kessel in some kind of banal Romantic pose. For there is nothing at all affected about him or less contrived than his way of being" (p. 133). For Kessel's own literary preferences and his view of himself as someone who wrote for "everyone" rather than for an elite, see his conversation with Frédéric Lefevre, "Une heure avec M. J. Kessel, journaliste et romancier," *Les Nouvelles Littéraires*, 13 June 1925. A writer's style, he told Lefevre, is like a "zipper." "Each

sentence must have a kind of hook that connects it to what comes next. Isn't that the great secret to being read?" Kessel was convinced that novels do not survive because of the distinctive style of their author. "It's the warmth that they contain, it's the élan vital of the writer that makes for the savor and value of the work." No one can dispute that Kessel's books contain an extraordinary degree of warmth, nor that they display an intense élan vital.

24 Léon Daudet, "Nouveaux Livres de Guerre: 'L'Équipage'," *L'Action Française*, 24 November 1923.

25 Returning to the front after a leave in Paris, the protagonist Jean Herbillon recalls a conversation he had with a veteran observer and agrees that what really counted in the squadron was not "the flights, the acts of bravery, the fear, not even death, but comfort and the art of organizing it." Joseph Kessel, *L'Équipage* (Paris: Librarie de la Revue Française, n.d.; originally published 1923), p. 133. Paul Souday commented favorably on this aspect of Kessel's novel in his review in *Le Temps*, 29 November 1923.

26 Kessel, *L'Équipage*, pp. 37, 77, 153.

27 Ibid., p. 33.

28 The admiration Kessel felt for his squadron leader is clear in this passage he wrote describing the circumstances of Thélis's death in October 1918: "He flew constantly on all kinds of missions, changing airplanes, taking on new observers who replaced the dead ones, making up for their lack of experience with an unequaled ability and an unfailing courage. No plea nor warning could stop him. He had reached a limit of exhaustion that can only be overcome by a frantic effort. One would have said that he wanted to intoxicate himself with fatigue and peril in order to forget the holocaust and attract the attention of death. He succeeded in doing so" (p. 193).

29 *La Nouvelle Revue Française*, 22 (January–June 1924), p. 118.

30 The phrase "rapid and flaming prose" is Léon Daudet's. He added that Kessel's dialogue sounded like "the clash of swords." *L'Action Française*, 24 November 1923. The description of "the intoxication of the air" is from Kessel, *L'Équipage*, p. 97.

31 Kessel, *L'Équipage*, p. 108. Compare Kessel's portrayal of the fraternity of aviators with the way Gabriele D'Annunzio had earlier described the relationship between his two aviator-protagonists in *Forse che sì forse che no* (Milan: Treves, 1910), p. 85: ". . . their friendship was composed of two equal statures, of two equal strengths, of two equal liberties, and of two indomitable fidelities. Each measured his value by the value of the other; each recognized his temper by the temper of the other; each knew that the most difficult assignment could be carried out by either and that the crudest adversary would not benefit from the substitution of one by the other."

32 The final sentence of Kessel's novel read: "Hélène [Jean's mistress, Claude's wife] would forget the young officer Jean Herbillon before he would" (p. 215). In *Le Repos de l'équipage* (Paris: Gallimard, 1935), Kessel expressed the misogyny that runs through the novel even more openly. When Maury's wife tries to persuade Jean Herbillon to escape service at the front by applying for a position as an instructor at Fontainbleau, he replies bitterly: "You have to be a woman to think of something so disgusting" (p. 136).

33 Quoted by Courrière, *Kessel*, p. 226.

34 Writing in *Le Temps*, Paul Souday complained that Kessel's plot was too contrived. "I mean that, even if it's not impossible, even if by chance the story he tells is true, it seems nonetheless to be concocted too deliberately and too skillfully by the author. In the process of writing, he has been unable to avoid the appearance of an excessive cleverness." 29 November 1923.

35 For the details of this extraordinary story, see Courrière, *Kessel*, pp. 106–29.

36 Leaving for the front, Herbillon remembers that he had volunteered for the air force because of the prestige that "men with wings" enjoyed with women. "A feeling of hate roused him against these feeble and perverse creatures for whom he was going to give his life. Denise [his mistress] seemed particularly detestable for not having dissuaded him from going." Kessel, *L'Équipage*, pp. 13–14.

37 In a letter to Kessel's publisher, Gaston Gallimard, quoted from at length in Courrière, *Kessel*, pp. 319–20. Gide said: "I would be curious to know whether Kessel hasn't sometimes inverted some personal experiences and reignited [for the purposes of his story] some embers of a hell that is specifically masculine" (p. 320).

38 From Kessel's preface to Marcel Reine and Edouard Serre, *Chez les fils du desert. Récits d'aventures au pays maures* (Paris: Éditions de France, 1929), p. 15.

39 For portraits of Reine and Serre, see Joseph Kessel, *Tous n'était pas des anges* (Paris: Plon, 1963), pp. 161–85 and *Des hommes* (Paris: Gallimard, 1972), pp. 233–7.

40 According to Kessel in his preface to *Chez les fils du desert*, p. 10.

41 The account Reine and Serre published in 1929 of their captivity, *Chez les fils du desert. Récits d'aventures au pays maures*, was published by Éditions de France and preceded by a preface by Kessel.

42 Joseph Kessel, *Vent de sable* (Paris: Éditions de France, 1929), p. 6.

43 *Vent de sable* was published simultaneously in the fall of 1929 by two houses, Horace de Carbuccia's Éditions de France, and Gallimard.

44 For the relationship between *Vent de sable* and the genre of *reportage* to which it belongs, see Michel Collomb, "Joseph Kessel et le roman de reportage," in *Presence de Kessel* (Nice: Publications of the Faculty of Letters, Arts, and Human Sciences of the University of Nice-Sophia Antipolis, 1998), pp. 130–32.

45 Kessel, *Vent de sable*, pp. 9–10.

46 Ibid., p. 14.

47 Ibid., p. 14.

48 Ibid., p. 92.

49 Ibid., p. 95.

50 Kessel, *Des hommes*, p. 251.

51 Kessel, *Vent de sable*, p. 181.

52 Ibid., pp. 182–3.

53 Kessel, *Des hommes*, p. 250.

54 Kessel recalled how Lécrivain assured him in a night club in Casablanca that he should not judge him in terms of his behavior there. "At work no one is more serious [than I am]. You'll see. Not so much during the way down [to Dakar], because when convoying people it's a tourist trip, but on the return. I'll have the mail." *Vent de sable*, p. 96.

55 Kessel, *Des hommes*, pp. 250–51.

56 Kessel, *Vent de sable*, pp. 230–31.

57 Kessel, *Des hommes*, p. 239. Lécrivain exaggerated slightly. Saint-Exupéry had spent only thirteen months at Cap Juby.

58 Ibid., p. 239.

59 Kessel, *Vent de sable*, pp. 80–81.

60 An excerpt from *Vent de sable*, describing Saint-Exupéry's rescue of a downed Aéropostale airplane, had been published in *Le Figaro Littéraire* on 30 November 1929. Kessel described this story as being told to him in Casablanca "by a sort of feverish choir." He added, however, that Serre was quick to interject that Saint-Exupéry was not the only one to have risked his life in the search to find himself and Reine. *Vent de sable*, pp. 84–5. It was typical of the camaraderie of *La Ligne* to emphasize the common qualities of the group rather than the virtues of heroic individuals.

61 In a letter of 1927 to Yvonne de Lestrange, Saint-Exupéry asked disdainfully how the "men of letters" were doing. They never changed professions because they didn't have one. They spent their time asking one another questions. "It's a joke." Antoine de Saint-Exupéry, *Œuvres complètes* (Paris: Gallimard, 1999), Vol. II, p. 864.

62 Quoted by Stacy Schiff in *Saint-Exupéry* (New York: Knopf, 1994), p. 162.

63 In a 1926 letter to Renée de Sassine in Antoine de Saint-Exupéry, *Œuvres complètes* (Paris: Gallimard, 1994), Vol. 1, p. 793.

64 Ibid., p. 799.

65 After a long conversation with Saint-Exupéry in August 1939, Charles Lindbergh's wife Anne confided to her diary "what a joy it was to talk [to him], to throw things out, to be understood like that without an effort. Summer lightning." Speaking of her book, *Listen! The Wind* (London: Chatto & Windus, 1938), for which he had written an introduction to the French translation, Saint-Exupéry commented on its classical qualities. There was something fundamental about it, "like a Greek play," which he was astonished to find in America. Two days later after further talk about literature, politics, and the impact of the machine on human life, Anne Lindbergh confessed that "My mind has been quickened, and my sight and feelings. For a week now [sic] the world has been almost unbearably beautiful. It cries out everywhere I turn." Anne Morrow Lindbergh, *War Within and Without: Diaries and Letters, 1939–1944* (New York: Harcourt Brace Jovanovich, 1980), pp. 23, 35.

66 Léon-Paul Fargue, quoted by Schiff in *Saint-Exupéry* in her caption to a photograph following p. 180.

67 See the 1925 letter to his mother in which he defends himself against the imagined familial accusation that he is "a superficial creature, talkative and sybaritic . . ." Saint-Exupéry, *Œuvres complètes*, Vol. I, p. 747–9.

68 In his notebooks, Saint-Exupéry reflected on the submission of men to objects and related it to the effects of advertising. "In this sense, we are barbarians . . . in this sense the retreat of religion is a disaster that has impoverished our spiritual world . . ." Ibid., p. 508.

69 See the 1927 letter to his mother in ibid., p. 714.

70 For the depth of the affection Saint-Exupéry felt for Guillaumet, see the dedication he wrote for him to *Courrier-Sud* in *Œuvres complètes*, Vol. II, p. 1054.

71 Saint-Exupéry to Yvonne de Lestrange, 23 October 1926, in ibid., p. 851.

72 "People blame Latécoère for pushing his pilots too hard, but I like the fact that they don't ask us if we want or don't want to take off, nor inquire about our impressions afterwards. They couldn't care less." Saint-Exupéry to Yvonne de Lestrange, November? 1926, in ibid., p. 854.

73 Saint-Exupéry, *Œuvres complètes*, Vol. I, p. 1171, n. 1.

74 For Saint-Exupéry's idea that men learn to communicate through gratuitous action, see ibid., p. 506. For all the literary inspiration that life at Cap Juby may have given him, Saint-Exupéry was not inclined in his letters to romanticize it. "This corner of the Sahara . . . bores me like a dirty suburb." From a 1928 letter to his mother in ibid., p. 769.

75 From a 1927 letter to Yvonne de Lestrange in Saint-Exupéry, *Œuvres complètes*, Vol. II, pp. 867–8. Saint-Exupéry's italics.

76 For Saint-Exupéry's dislike of Dakar, see ibid., pp. 867–9.

77 In a 1928 letter to Yvonne de Lestrange in ibid., p. 880.

78 See his 1927 letter to Yvonne de Lestrange in ibid., p. 860.

79 "L'Aviateur," fragments of a lost text entitled *L'Évasion de Jacques Bernis*, first published in *Le Navire d'argent* on 1 April 1926; now available in Saint-Exupéry, *Œuvres complètes*, Vol. I, pp. 27–35. Saint-Exupéry would nonetheless have been pleased to make his literary debut in a magazine that included a translation of one of his favorite poets, Rainer Maria Rilke.

80 The young Saint-Exupéry, then studying in Paris, was so carried away by the qualities of Yvonne de Lestrange that he wrote his mother that she was "the most charming person I know, original, refined, intelligent, a superior being in every sense and along with that as nice as she can be." Saint-Exupéry in a 1919 letter to his mother in ibid., p. 685. Eight years later he wrote her that she was the only person in the world in whom he could confide. Saint-Exupéry to Yvonne de Lestrange in *Œuvres complètes*, Vol. II, p. 866.

81 For Saint-Exupéry's description of a flight through a sandstorm in 1928, see his letter to Yvonne de Lestrange in *Œuvres complètes*, Vol. II, p. 874.

82 Remembering Saint-Exupéry, Kessel wrote: "I've met many men who are at the same time poets and men of action. But always one of these persons was undermined, bothered by the other . . . Only the author of *Vol de nuit* and the bearer of airmail above the desert, the jungle, and the pampas, is at the same time entirely a writer and entirely a pilot." Kessel, *Des hommes*, p. 240.

83 Saint-Exupéry, *Œuvres complètes*, Vol. I, pp. lxix, 199. In 1939 Saint-Exupéry told Anne Lindbergh that rhythm in writing was "almost the most important thing in a book." He went on to add: "That only the *conscious* gets across in words, the unconscious in the rhythm." Lindbergh, *War Within and Without*, p. 22.

84 Henri Peyre in *The Contemporary French Novel* (New York: Oxford University Press, 1955), p. 171. Peyre detected in Saint-Exupéry's style and his themes traces of his Jesuit education with its emphasis on the classics and French writers like Montaigne, Pascal, and La Rochefoucault. For Saint-Exupéry's cult of Pascal, see Léon Werth's testimony in René Delange, *La Vie de Saint-Exupéry* (Paris: Éditions du Seuil, 1948), pp. 180–81. "We [Werth and Saint-Exupéry] thought that among French writers no one had used words so powerfully. Each word is a drop of blood."

85 Maurice Martin du Gard, an admirer of Saint-Exupéry, later wrote that "what was fascinating and new in this novel was not the novel; it was *Courrier Sud*, the Aéropostale mail route Toulouse–Dakar, and the ordeal, of which the public was still unaware, of commercial pilots." *Les Nouvelles Littéraires*, 19 December 1931.

86 *Les Nouvelles Littéraires*, 6 July 1929. Nonetheless, Saint-Exupéry was pleased with this review by "the most famous of critics," perhaps because Jaloux had added that "everything that touches aviation [in *Courrier-Sud*] is remarkably well treated." See his 1929 letter to his mother in Saint-Exupéry, *Œuvres complètes*, Vol. I, p. 775.

87 *La Nouvelle Revue Française*, 1 September 1929, 417.

88 For a fascinating reading of *Courrier-Sud* that argues for its unity, see Michel Quesnel's essay in Saint-Exupéry, *Œuvres complètes*, Vol. I, pp. 888–905. But most of the evidence he produces from Saint-Exupéry's letters and later works to shed light on the novel would not have been available to those who read the work when it first appeared in 1929.

89 *Courrier-Sud* in ibid., pp. 108–9.

90 *Courrier-Sud* in ibid., pp. 39–40.

91 Saint-Exupéry's friend Ramón Fernandez had written the first draft of the preface, which Saint-Exupéry dismissed privately as the hasty work of a "a superficial mind." See his 1929 letter to Yvonne de Lestrange in which he express his irritation at the "protective irony" he found in Fernandez's pages, written in "a half hour at the most." *Œuvres complètes*, Vol. II, pp. 892–3. Saint-Exupéry's own letter to Fernandez (pp. 893–4) was more restrained.

92 For the text of Beucler's introduction, see Saint-Exupéry, *Œuvres complètes*, Vol. I, pp. 905–6.

93 On 20 November 1929 he wrote to his mother: "I can't tell you what pleasure my job gives me for your sake . . . It's not bad to be the head of such a big enterprise at twenty-nine. Don't you think?" In ibid., p. 778. For Saint-Exupéry's financial aid to his mother, see Emmanuel Chadeau, *Saint-Exupéry* (Paris: Plon, 1994), pp. 160–61.

94 Benjamin Crémieux in *La Nouvelle Revue Française*, October 1931, 610.

95 Saint-Exupéry, *Œuvres complètes*, Vol. I, p. 159.

96 Ibid., pp. 151–2.

97 Ibid., p. 123.

98 Ibid., pp. 160–61.

99 Reproduced in ibid., pp. 962–4.

100 See, in particular, Joseph Kessel's article "Le Dépanneur du Rio de Oro" in *La Matin*, 13 December 1931; and "Saint-Exupéry" by Maurice Martin du Gard in *Les Nouvelles Littéraires*, 19 December 1931.

101 Robert de Saint Jean in *La Revue Hebdomadaire*, 12 December 1931, 226.

102 Saint-Exupéry, *Œuvres complètes*, Vol. I, pp. 155–6.

103 For Saint-Exupéry's sober lyricism, see Crémieux's review in *Nouvelle Revue Française*, October 1931, 39; and John Charpentier's review in *Mercure de France*, 15 December 1931, 617.

104 *Les Nouvelles Littéraires*, 7 November 1931.

105 *La Revue Hebdomadaire*, 12 December 1931, 225–6.

106 From a press notice, dated 19 December 1931, in Alain Vercondelet, *Antoine de Saint-Exupéry, Vérité et légendes* (Paris: Éditions du Chêne, 2000), p. 94.

107 In addition to Jaloux's November review and Martin du Gard's December article, Georges Charensol reviewed Saint-Exupéry's novel in *Les Nouvelles Littéraires* on 24 October 1931. He proclaimed it "exceptional by its tone and composition." "But *Vol de nuit* isn't a novel, it's better than that: a great work – and all the greater because the author has to make a greater effort in order to win us over."

108 *Les Nouvelles Littéraires*, 19 December 1931.

109 Saint-Exupéry, *Œuvres complètes*, Vol. I, p. 167.

110 For a judicious account of the Aéropostale scandal that places it in the context of the *affaires* of the 1930s and the crisis of the Third Republic, see Nicolas Neiertz, "Argent, polititique et aviation. L'Affaire de l'Aéropostale (1930–1932)," in *Vingtième Siècle*, no. 24 (October–December 1989), 29–40.

111 According to Emmanuel Chadeau, the enthusiasm of center-right and right-wing journalists for Aéropostale was maintained with a public relations budget of over 400,000 francs a year; but he concedes that the enthusiasm of some journalists was genuine and sustained by the potent mixture of patriotism, exoticism, danger, technology, and sport that *La Ligne* represented. *Mermoz* (Paris: Perrin, 2000), p. 127.

112 Henri de Régnier of the French Academy, writing in *Le Figaro*, 14 January 1930; quoted in Chadeau, *Mermoz*, p. 128.

113 Chadeau, *Mermoz*, p. 186.

114 Kessel, *Des hommes*, p. 273.

115 See Jean-Gérard Fleury, *La Ligne* (Paris: Gallimard, 1939), which is dedicated to Kessel.

116 Kessel, *Vent de sable*, p. 11.

117 Fleury, *Chemins du ciel*, p. 20.

118 See ibid., p. 29, where Dautry and Verdurand are given credit for having reorganized this immense organization and continued "the glorious work that has prodigiously magnified French prestige in Latin America."

119 Ibid., pp. 31–2.

120 Ibid., p. 153.

121 Ibid., p. 35.

122 Ibid., p. 65–6.

123 Ibid., p. 73.

124 Ibid., p. 76.

125 On the basis of the information he had gathered from the technical staff of Aéropostale, Fleury argued that the period of great investment in Latin America was now over. The infrastructure was in place. Expenses had been reduced by fifty percent, and it would now be possible to maintain the service more inexpensively. Ibid., pp. 138–9.

126 Ibid., p. 157.

127 Ibid., p. 160. "In France we are unaware of their courageous exploits and their heroism. Little does it matter. The world knows about them. Some admire. Others envy. And thanks to them, the prestige of France increases in Latin America" (p. 158).

128 Ibid., p. 197.

129 Ibid., pp. 172–3.

130 Paul Morand, *Air Indien* (Paris: Grasset, 1932), pp. 80–81, 75. Nonetheless, if Fleury was upset with Morand he gave no hint of this in *Les Chemins du ciel*. Referring to lunches he shared with the "famous writer" in Buenos Aires, he went out of his way to praise Morand as "a knight of the leather helmet." "He [Morand] also regrets that our brave pilots in Latin America are not better known in France" (p. 143).

131 Fleury, *Les Chemins du ciel*, p. 170.

132 Ibid., pp. 194–5.

133 Quoted by Courrière in *Kessel*, p. 412.

134 Chadeau, *Mermoz*, p. 249.

135 See Mermoz's letter of 11 November 1935 to René Couzinet in which he explained that he was "up to his neck" in the Croix de Feu. "You know that my ambitions do not belong to this world, but I have such a desire to serve during my time on this

earth that I had no choice but to devote what remains of me to something that may affect the society in which we live." Bernard Marck, ed., *Jean Mermoz. Défricheur du ciel. Correspondance 1921–1936* (Paris: L'Archipel, 2001), p. 359. For Mermoz's fears of a Communist seizure of power, see his letter to Couzinet of late 1936 in ibid., pp. 371–3.

136 Chadeau, *Mermoz*, p. 245.

137 Jean Mermoz, *Mes vols* (Paris: Flammarion, 1937), pp. 150–53. See also his earlier notice in the newspaper of the Croix de Feu, *La Flambeau*, 28 March 1936. La Rocque added two lines in which he said: "Mermoz is with me. I am proud, moved, and happy."

138 Mermoz, *Mes vols*, pp. 136–7.

139 The phrase "more tomb-like than death itself" is Kessel's. From Joseph Kessel, *Mermoz* (Paris: Gallimard, 1938), p. 1. Shortly after Mermoz's death, a biography by Jacques Mortane appeared in which the author pronounced the dead pilot to be an "apostle" of aviation whose biography should be read "while kneeling." *Jean Mermoz* (Paris: Plon, 1937). The following year Mortane elevated Mermoz from "apostle" to "archangel," putting him on the same exalted level with Georges Guynemer, whose name had been inscribed on the walls of the Panthéon. Kessel may also have been aware of the article that Raoul Dautry had devoted to Mermoz in *La Revue des Jeunes*, in which he had written that "You could not see him, not even for an instant, without feeling in the depth of your being that he was a leader . . . This workers' son had the look of a prince. He made you think of those young captains, such as Roland or Bayard, Hoche or Guynemer, who over a period of so many centuries stand as monuments to the glory of our country." "La leçon de Mermoz," *La Revue des Jeunes*, 15 March 1937, 317.

140 See, for example, Kessel's article in *Le Matin*, 6 August 1934, entitled "Le Commandeur." ". . . I know no greater moral consolation nor more virile joy than an encounter with Mermoz. His presence tears you away from the pettiness, intrigue, and shabbiness in which we flounder every day. It makes you more demanding toward others and yourself." Reprinted in Mermoz, *Mes vols*, p. 186.

141 Kessel, *Mermoz*, pp. 1–2.

142 These terms are used in the national commendation issued by the Minister of Air Pierre Cot after Mermoz's death. In Catherine Herszberg and Anne Proenza, *Mermoz* (Paris: Le Cherche Midi, 2001), p. 139.

143 Kessel, *Mermoz*, p. 20.

144 Ibid., pp. 29–30.

145 Ibid., pp. 72–3.

146 Ibid., p. 115. Kessel understandably emphasizes Mermoz's dedication to *La Ligne* during the time he spent in Africa. But Mermoz's letters to his mother leave no doubt that he was seriously considering abandoning Latécoère for a more highly paying job with another airline. See in particular his letters of 1 April 1926, 13 April 1926, July 1926 (undated), 31 December 1926, and 11 February 1927. In Marck, ed., *Jean Mermoz*, pp. 160–62, 165–7, 182–3, 195–7, 202–3.

147 In a letter of 29 November 1927 to his mother, written after arriving in Rio de Janeiro, Mermoz explains his reaction to the administrative tasks being thrust upon him. Julien Pranville, Aéropostale's chief of operations in Latin America, had told Mermoz that because of his experience and demonstrated qualities of leadership, it was his duty to "make an effort for our aeronautical prestige here." He was among those destined to command rather than to obey. "Beautiful words that didn't exactly excite me, but which I've had to give into, on the condition that I will fly as much as any pilot, which has been promised to me." Marck, ed., *Jean Mermoz*, pp. 240–41.

148 Kessel, *Mermoz*, p. 207.

149 Ibid., pp. 261–2.

150 Ibid., p. 266. Mermoz had alluded clearly to his sense of frustration in his speech to the constituent assembly of the PSF in July 1936. "Certainly, when I return to my earthbound life, I'm used to every type of treachery, every type of cowardice. It's the worst aspect of my life, but when one has a goal and an ideal,

one disdains the obstacles that lie along the road. In spite of every obstacle, the work must go on. Your duty as a crew member is to close ranks as we do when we encounter a storm." Mermoz, *Mes vols*, p. 151. Yet if Mermoz had any doubts about the PSF, he did not reveal them to La Rocque. Eduard Carvallo later testified that he "never heard in [Mermoz's] mouth the slightest expression of a reservation or disillusionment. When he was in town, he came every day to his [La Rocque's] office. He was the only one allowed in to see the boss without being announced. The day when Air France informed me that they had no news of him, I opened his door. The Colonel said immediately: 'Mermoz.' Then he moved towards me. 'You see, my boy, it's all over.' For La Rocque, Mermoz represented the future; he was the one who would lead the next generation. He seemed overwhelmed. He considered Mermoz as his successor. And Mermoz was aware that he did." Quoted by Jacques Nobécourt, *Le Colonel de la Rocque (1885–1946) ou les pièges du nationalisme chrétien* (Paris: Fayard, 1996), p. 630. See also the testimony of the Air France pilot Joseph Portal, who dined with Mermoz in Marseille shortly before his death. According to Portal, Mermoz "venerated" La Rocque. Ibid., p. 1049, n. 12.

151 See the extracts from the letter Jean-Gérard Fleury wrote to Yves Courrière, Kessel's biographer. "With his Russian temperament, Jef [Kessel] could not resist the temptation to cast large shadows around the luminous face that was Mermoz. Whereas drugs in Syria were an insignificant thing in the life of the pilot, our friend [Kessel] gave the impression that he [Mermoz] was a drug addict who, by force of will, escaped from its hold. Mermoz was no more a slave of cocaine and opium than Kessel, who often wrote about [these drugs]. As far as the rest [of Kessel's biography] goes, Jef had admirably grasped Mermoz's personality." Courrière, *Kessel*, p. 497.

152 Kessel, *Mermoz*, p. 228.

153 Ibid., p. 226.

154 See for example the passage on p. 20 of *Mermoz*, where Kessel distinguishes between two "races of men." "The first – so numerous as to be suffocating – contents itself with satisfying the elementary needs of existence. Material preoccupations and family concerns limit his field of action. Love sometimes projects its shadow, but in a strictly egotistical way and proportioned to the rest. The other race, though submitted to the yoke of hunger, the pleasures of the flesh, and tenderness, extends further and higher its ambition. In order to grow and simply to breathe, it needs a climate that is more beautiful, purer and more spiritual . . . Mermoz belonged to this chosen blood, to its elite, to its flower . . . In order to live, he had to escape from life."

155 Ibid., p. 236. In his correspondence, Mermoz was more understanding of his wife's dilemma. Writing to René Couzinet, he confessed that he had separated from his wife (whom Couzinet would later marry) because he was unwilling to give up his "dangerous life." "I am ready to sacrifice my life and everything in order to accomplish what I consider to be an ideal and sacred task." But he added that he did not hold his wife responsible for what had happened. "I've reached a point where I can't give any more, even to a young kid – at twenty-three a young kid can remake her life. In my case, I won't remake mine. Besides, my life belongs to me so little, and all that matters to me is that it should be worthwhile from the point of view of sacrifices and results." Marck, ed., *Jean Mermoz*, p. 359.

156 Kessel, *Mermoz*, p. 274.

157 See Thierry Maulnier's review in *L'Action Française*, 6 October 1938, in which he lists the obstacles that condemned Kessel's biography to failure.

158 Which is not to suggest that biographies of Mermoz are not needed in order to complement and correct Kessel's. The best and most thorough to date is Chadeau's *Mermoz*.

159 Mermoz, *Mes vols*, p. 200.

160 Kessel, *Mermoz*, p. 120.

161 Saint-Exupéry's article "Pilot de Ligne" was a defense of Aéropostale against its enemies. He compared the men of *La Ligne* with members of a religious community who never

questioned the importance of the mail, nor the need to sacrifice in order to deliver it on time. But it was preceded on the first page by a spirited denunciation of Marcel and André Bouilloux-Laffont's financial maneuvers and a call for the resignation of Emmanuel Chaumié, the government's director of civil aviation. This earned Saint-Exupéry a stern reprimand by Raoul Dautry, the acting head of the company. Engaging in a game of biting irony that made the blow of Saint-Exupéry's severance from the company even more painful, Dautry went so far in a private letter as to remind Saint-Exupéry that, given the hymn to discipline in his literary work, he should be the first to give his unqualified approval to the policies of the new management. This was the equivalent of asking Saint-Exupéry to applaud his own dismissal. Saint-Exupéry's article is in *Marianne*, 26 October 1932 and reprinted in Saint-Exupéry, *Œuvres complètes*, Vol. I, pp. 301–5. Dautry's letter is reproduced in excerpted form in *Antoine de Saint-Exupéry, 1900–1944* (Paris: Archives Nationales, 1984), pp. 60–61.

162 When Kessel proposed to Mermoz that he do a newspaper article on his escape after crashing in the Andes, he demurred, saying "Oh no . . . this isn't for the newspapers . . . It's for us." Kessel, *Mermoz*, p. 227.

163 See the letter to Guillaumet in Yvette Guy, *Saint-Exupéry* (Monaco: Éditions Les Florts Bleus, 1958), p. 99, reproduced in part in English translation in Schiff, *Saint-Exupéry*, pp. 214–15. According to Stacey Schiff, Saint-Exupéry's gross income in 1934 was slightly over 48,000 francs, one-sixth of what he had been earning in Argentina. Schiff, *Saint-Exupéry*, p. 233.

164 Letter to Guillaumet, dated approximately December 1933, in Saint-Exupéry, *Œuvres complètes*, Vol. I, p. 862.

165 See his letter of 2 February 1934 to the Director of Operations at Air France, Monsieur Foa, in which he lists his grievances and his contributions to Aéropostale, while at the same time proudly insisting that he was not prepared to accept a secondary post. Reproduced in full in Didier Daurat, *Dans le vent des hélices* (Paris: Éditions du Seuil, 1956), pp. 241–4.

166 Schiff, *Saint-Exupéry*, pp. 294–5.

167 Modeled after the Bible and Nietzsche's *Also Sprach Zarathustra*, *Citadelle* has been treated harshly by its critics. For a more favorable view along with a discussion of the book's reception, see Michel Quesnel's essay in Saint-Exupéry, *Œuvres complètes*, Vol. II, pp. 1396–430.

168 Saint-Exupéry, *Œuvres complètes*, Vol. I, p. 1006.

169 Nonetheless, if Saint-Exupéry did heed Gide's advice and read *Mirror of the Sea* – and there is no evidence that he did – its ironic tone left no trace on the manuscript that would become *Terre des hommes*. We know that Saint-Exupéry had read Conrad and, in particular, *Typhoon*, which had been translated by Gide. In a letter to Yvonne de Lestrange, which unfortunately exists only in a fragmentary form, he explains that he finds in each of Conrad's books "two parallel novels – that of the characters and that of events – often badly connected." In Saint-Exupéry, *Œuvres complètes*, Vol. II, p. 860.

170 This may not seem impressive today, but according to Emmanuel Chadeau it constituted 200,000 French francs, enough to pay ten years of rent on Saint-Exupéry's large apartment on the Place Vauban. *Saint-Exupéry*, p. 273.

171 Schiff, *Saint-Exupéry*, pp. 300–05.

172 Saint-Exupéry, *Œuvres complètes*, Vol. I, p. 171.

173 One of its first reviewers claimed that not since Chateaubriand had anyone so skillfully coaxed poetry out of prose. André Thérive in *Le Temps*, 27 April 1939, quoted in Schiff, *Saint-Exupéry*, p. 309.

174 "The airplane is not an end; it's a means. It's not for the airplane that one risks one's life. Similarly, it's not for his plough that a peasant works." Saint-Exupéry, *Œuvres complètes*, Vol. I, p. 263.

175 Ibid., p. 282.

176 Ibid., p. 171.

177 Ibid., p. 197.

178 Ibid., p. 270.

179 Ibid., p. 188.

180 Nonetheless, Saint-Exupéry sent Daurat a copy of *Terrre des*

hommes with a long dedication that expressed his "profound affection" and "profound admiration" for Daurat's work. It was Daurat's "authority, his sense of man's grandeur, his faith in discipline and in enthusiasm for a common enterprise that had made it possible for him to make of the old Aéropostale a sort of special civilization in which men felt more noble than elsewhere." Saint-Exupéry, *Œuvres complètes*, Vol. II, pp. 1058–9.

181 Saint-Exupéry, *Œuvres complètes*, Vol. I, p. 188.

182 Ibid., pp. 186–9.

183 Notice that Saint-Exupéry pointedly omits from this passage on p. 197 in ibid. a reference to Guillaumet's sense of responsibility to his wife. This is a book about men.

184 Ibid., p. 197.

185 Ibid., p. 192.

186 Ibid., p. 296.

187 For Saint-Exupéry's passion for Nietzsche, see his letter of November 1926 to Renée de Saussine in ibid., p. 808. In late 1928 he wrote Yvonne de Lestrange that he was rereading *Zarathustra*. *Œuvres complètes*, Vol. II, p. 888.

188 Saint-Exupéry, *Œuvres complètes*, Vol. I, p. 180.

189 Ibid., p. 269.

190 Ibid., pp. 284–5. These are the closing lines of *Terre des hommes*, hence the final message its author wished to leave his readers.

191 Ibid., p. 263.

192 Like many intellectuals of his generation, Saint-Exupéry felt ambivalent about communism and fascism. In August 1939, he told Anne Morrow Lindbergh that the trend toward a spiritual revival was visible. "Witness even these movements like Communism and Fascism (which he dislikes but which he regards as a symptom). And what man seeks and wants he will find – he always *has*." Lindbergh, *War Within and Without*, p. 27. Though never tempted by fascism and disapproving of Mermoz's involvement in the Croix de Feux, Saint-Exupéry believed that socialism, by preaching individual enrichment, exalted men less than fascism, which preached sacrifice to something outside of the individual. What that "something" was mattered less than the sacrifice itself. Saint-Exupéry, *Œuvres complètes*, Vol. I, p. 506.

193 "Today's world is beginning to collapse around us. Everyone is moved by religions that promise this sense of plenitude. Under contradictory slogans, we all express the same yearnings. We are divided on the methods that are the result of our reasoning, not on the ends: these are the same." Ibid., pp. 277–8.

194 Ibid., pp. 277–8.

195 Ibid., p. 280.

196 Ibid., p. 178.

197 Ibid., p. 179. It was in the omnibus to Montaudran that Saint-Exupéry first heard of the death of Kessel's pilot, Émile Lécrivain. "It was three o'clock in the morning; the same silence reigned when we heard the director [Daurat], invisible in the darkness, raise his voice toward the inspector. 'Lécrivain didn't land last night at Casablanca.' 'Ah!' the inspector responded. 'Ah?' And torn from his dreams, he made an effort to awake; in order to show his concern he added: 'Ah! Yes? He didn't get through. He turned around?' To which in the back of the omnibus was simply added: 'No.' We waited for what would come next but no word came. And as the seconds passed, it became more obvious that this 'no' would not be followed by any other word; that this 'no' was without appeal; that Lécrivain had not only not landed at Casablanca, but that he would never again land anywhere" (pp. 178–9).

198 Ibid., p. 177.

199 See ibid., pp. 180–81, for a discussion of the changes that had taken place in aviation between 1926, when he went to work for Latécoère, and 1939. "The pilot, the mechanic, and the radio operator no longer undertake an adventure, but shut themselves up in a laboratory" (p. 180).

200 In his notebooks, written during the late 1930s, Saint-Exupéry subscribed to the idea of "useless service," a concept often associated with the writings of Henry de Montherlant and André Malraux in the same period. "It is by means of a gratuitous sac-

rifice that men communicate with one another. And by gratu-itous, I mean that the 'useful part' is 'useless'." Ibid., p. 506.

201 Ibid., p. 276.

202 For this phrase, see ibid., p. 264. Nizan's review, published in *Ce Soir* on 30 March 1989, is reproduced in *Saint-Exupéry* (Paris: Archives Nationales, 1984), p. 105.

203 François Le Grix in the *Revue Hebdomadaire*, 3 June 1939, p. 122. For the Catholic Le Grix, Saint-Exupéry was "a kind of Chateaubriand without window dressing" (*sans nulle draperie*).

204 Henry Bordeaux, "Antoine de Saint-Exupéry," *Écrits de Paris*, no. 47 (September 1948), pp. 91–2, 95. Bordeaux would no doubt have been astonished to learn that only eight years before the publication of the book he so much admired Saint-Exupéry had declared in a letter to Yvonne de Lestrange that to read something by Bordeaux one was to be "certain, absolutely cer-tain, desperately certain . . . of reading something idiotic." *Œuvres complètes*, Vol. II, p. 902.

205 Quoted by Chadeau, *Saint-Exupéry*, p. 281. Saint-Exupéry, by contrast, had a low opinion of Gide's writing. See his harsh cri-tique of Gide's *Voyage au Congo*. "This guy gives me the impres-sion of being a skeleton. I find nothing in him to get my teeth into . . . what impotence, it seems to me." In a 1926 letter to Yvonne de Lestrange, in Saint-Exupéry, *Œuvres complètes*, Vol. II, p. 858. Much later in his notebooks, Saint-Exupéry complained that "Gide judges without having 'experienced.' But a concep-tual system is only justified by the type of man it creates . . ." Saint-Exupéry, *Œuvres complètes*, Vol. I, p. 482.

206 Quoted by Curtis Cate, *Antoine de Saint-Exupéry* (New York: Putnam, 1970), p. 350.

207 In a series of interviews that appeared in *Les Nouvelles Littéraires* in response to the question of whether the airplane had changed our vision of the world, all the writers queried expressed their admiration for the author of *Vol de nuit*.

208 Jacques Baratier in *Les Nouvelles Littéraires*, 11 March 1939.

209 Ibid., 18 March 1939.

210 Ibid., 8 April 1939.

211 Ibid., 27 May 1939.

212 *Nouvelle Revue Française*, 1 June 1939, p. 1046.

213 Crémieux was especially troubled by a passage that appears at the beginning of the last chapter of *Terre des hommes*. "Truth is not something that can be proved. If orange trees develop solid roots and bear fruit in this piece of land and not in another, the first piece of land is the truth of the orange trees. If this religion, if this culture, if this system of values, if this form of activity and not another favors the fulfillment of man and delivers in him the great man of which he was earlier unaware, then it's this sys-tem of values, this culture, this form of activity that is the truth of man." Saint-Exupéry, *Œuvres complètes*, Vol. I, pp. 269–70.

214 When Crémieux referred to Saint-Exupéry's willingness to give priority to action over thought, he may have had in mind the first sentence of *Terre des hommes*. "The earth teaches us much more about ourselves than all the books ever written. Because it resists us. Man discovers himself when he comes to grips with an obstacle." Ibid., p. 171. Or possibly he was thinking of Saint-Exupéry's claim in his articles for *Paris-Soir* in October 1938 that "It's not in reasoning that we will find our salvation . . . A truth is not something that can be proved: it's something that simpli-fies the world." Saint-Exupéry, "La Paix ou la Guerre?" in ibid., p. 346.

215 *Nouvelle Revue Française*, 1 June 1939, p. 1049.

216 Saint-Exupéry, *Œuvres complètes*, Vol. I, p. 362.

217 "There's no more human life in cities . . . By means of the air-plane, one leaves the cities behind with their accountants, and one discovers the truth of peasants." Ibid., p. 263. One of *Terre des hommes*'s first reviewers, the future collaborator and Fascist Robert de Brasillach, also objected to the author's Romantic and Nietzschean cult of individual heroism, which he related to works by Henry de Montherlant and André Malraux. In Saint-Exupéry's book, he complained, heroism had been reduced to instinct. "How far we are from rationality." But even he con-ceded that *Terre des hommes* – which he would have preferred to call *Terre de la Solitude* – had a certain barbaric grandeur that a

sound philosophy would attempt to incorporate in "a vaster and more solid rationality." *L'Action Française*, 16 March 1939.

218 Reproduced in Kessel, *Des hommes*, pp. 217–20.

219 For Kessel's praise of Saint-Exupéry's literary innovations, see his contribution to *Les Nouvelles Littéraires*'s inquiry among writers as to how the airplane had changed their vision of the world, 7 November 1936. Kessel himself had responded that the airplane had given rise to a "new race of men: the race of cen-taurs of the sky." Maurice Bourdet's *Grandeur et servitude de l'avi-ation* (Paris: Éditions R.-A. Corrêa, 1933) bore a preface by Saint-Exupéry; his chapter on Aéropostale was entitled "Pages of Glory." For René Chambe in *Enlevez les cales!* (Paris: Baudinière, 1936), Mermoz was an "apostle of aviation." "What drives him is an internal flame, a conviction, a highly placed sense of honor vis-à-vis aviation; it's an ideal" (p. 143). Jacques Mortane's short and quickly produced hagiography of Mermoz, *Jean Mermoz*, may have helped to convince Kessel that his friend had to be reconstituted as a person of flesh and blood rather than left to serve as a heroic icon.

220 André Lichtenberger in his novel *Le Sang nouveau* (Paris: Plon, 1914), p. 90.

221 Alfred Leblanc in his preface to Roland Garros, *Guide de l'avia-teur* (Paris: Lafitte, 1913), pp. 6, 10.

222 This brochure is to be found in the papers of Pierre-Etienne Flandin, Bibliothèque Nationale (Paris), Carton 23.

223 For a useful, if not exhaustive list of the books, articles, films, and television documentaries devoted to Mermoz and Aéropostale, see Mermoz, *Mes vols* (Paris: Flammarion, 2001 ed.), pp. 227–34.

224 See, for example, Benoît Heimermann and Olivier Margot, *L'Aéropostale* (Paris: Arthaud, 1994); Jacques Legrand. ed., *Jean Mermoz* (Paris: Éditions Chronique, 1997); Herszberg and Proenza, *Mermoz*; and the children's book by Fabien Grégoire, *Les Disparus de l'Aéropostale* (Paris: Archimède, 1999). For a recent comic book devoted to Mermoz, see Jean-Michel Charlier, *Mermoz, chevalier du ciel* (Paris: Dupuis), with illustra-tions by Victory Hubinon.

225 Patrick Baudry and Cyril Le Tourneur d'Ison, *Un vol de légende sur les traces de l'Aéropostale: Mermoz toujours vivant* (Paris: Tallander, 1998).

226 Paul Morand, *Flèche d'orient* (Paris: Gallimard, 1932) and *Air Indien*; Jérôme and Jean Tharaud, *Paris Saigon dans l'azur* (Paris: Plon, 1932); Anne de Noailles, "Souvenirs de voyages en Afrique," *Les Grandes Conférences de l'aviation au Théâtre des Ambassadeurs* (Paris: Éditions du Comité des Oeuvres Sociales du Ministère de l'Air, 1933); André Malraux, *La Reine de Saba: une aventure géographique*, ed. Philippe Delpeuch (Paris: Gallimard, 1993), *Le Temps du mépris* in *Œuvres complètes* (Paris: Gallimard, 1989), Vol. I, pp. 818–25, and *L'Espoir* in *Œuvres com-plètes* (Paris: Gallimard, 1996), Vol. II, pp. 3–433.

227 Jean-Paul Sartre, *Lettres au Castor et à quelques autres* (Paris: Gallimard, 1983), pp. 441–2.

228 Jean-Paul Sartre, *Qu'est-ce que c'est que la littérature?* (Paris: Gallimard, 1948), p. 237.

229 Sixty years after he disappeared, the remains of Saint-Exupéry's P-38 and some of his personal effects were finally recovered off the island of Riou, not far from Marseilles. See Hervé Vardoit, Philippe Castellano, and Alexis Rosenfeld, *Saint-Ex. La Fin du mystère* (Éditions Filipacchi: La Provence, 2004).

230 Bordeaux, "Antoine de Saint-Exupéry," 89, 91.

231 François Mauriac, "Mermoz," *Le Flambeau*, 16 January 1937, in Mermoz, *Mes vols*, p. 190.

232 Jean-Gérard Fleury, *La Ligne de Mermoz, Guillaumet, Saint-Exupéry* (Rio de Janeiro: Atlantica Editora, 1942), pp. 5–6.

5. Bombs Away

1 Quoted by Samuel Hynes in *The Auden Generation* (London: The Bodley Head, 1976), p. 232.

2 Paul Claudel, *Journal*, Vol. I (Paris: Gallimard, 1968), p. 772.

3 Paul Claudel, "L'Étoile collective," in *Contacts et circonstances* (Paris: Gallimard, 1947), pp. 221–7.

4 Claudel, *Journal*, p. 801.

5 Claudel, "L'Avion et la diplomatie," in *Contacts et circonstances*, p. 210.

6 Claudel, *Contacts et circonstances*, p. 211.

7 Ibid., pp. 211–12.

8 For the context of Claudel's concerns about bombing, see Robert J. Young's article, "The Use and Abuse of Fear: France and the Air Menace in the 1930s," in *Intelligence and National Security*, 2 (1987), pp. 88–109.

9 Claudel, *Contacts et circonstances*, p. 214.

10 The French version of Douhet's book, translated by Jean Romeyer, introduced by Étienne Riche and prefaced by General Tulasne, was entitled more ominously *La Guerre de l'air* (Paris: Éditions des Ailes, 1932). For its impact in France, see Ladislas Mysyrowicz, *Autopsie d'une défaite. Origines de l'effrondrement militaire français de 1940* (Lausanne: L'Âge d'Homme, 1977), pp. 169–73.

11 Prefacing the French translation of Douhet's book, General Tulasne emphasized that if the Italian military theorist had exaggerated the possibilities of aircraft in 1921, when his work had first appeared, his conceptions were today "almost totally in the domain of reality or, at least, of the possible." Douhet, *La Guerre de l'air*, p. 20.

12 Giulio Douhet, *The Command of the Air*, trans. Dino Ferrari (New York: Coward-McCann, 1942), p. 58.

13 Ibid., p. 58.

14 Ibid., p. 181.

15 In his introduction to the French translation of *Il dominio dell'aria*, Charles Betrande explained that Douhet's espousal of airpower was a direct result of his attempt to escape from the dilemmas of trench warfare in the First World War. If national resistance was the sovereign force that it was necessary to overcome in order to defeat the enemy, what was the arm that would make it possible to achieve most rapidly the desired end? Douhet's answer was the bomber. This, said Betrande, led Douhet to his essential principle: offense in the air, defense on land and sea. Douhet, *La Guerre de l'air*, p. 36.

16 Douhet, *The Command of the Air*, p. 61.

17 Quoted by Eugen Weber in *The Hollow Years* (New York: Norton, 1995), p. 239.

18 Quoted by André Demaison in *Menaces dans le ciel* (Paris: Éditions Baudinière, 1933), p. 34. Ladislas Mysyrowicz argues in *Autoposie d'une défaite*, p. 173, that fear of an air attack by German commercial planes was widespread in France as early as 1921. Anxiety about the destructive possibilities of an air war was especially strong among French Socialists during the 1930s. Evoking the specter of such a war at the French Socialist Party's congress of Tours in May 1931, Georges Richard asked whether ". . . it would be a victory if our unhappy country of forty million inhabitants won a war after having destroyed thousands and thousands of enemies, and, drawing up the balance sheet of the battle, discovered, ten million or fifteen million cadavers spread throughout the towns and countryside of our country?" Quoted by Mysyrowicz, p. 175.

19 Quoted by Uri Bialer in *The Shadow of the Bomber. The Fear of Air Attack and British Politics 1932–1939* (London: Royal Historical Society, 1980), p. 128. Ladbroke Black's 1933 novel, *The Poison War*, had two years earlier provided a terrifying description of an air attack against London. "Oxford Street, Piccadilly, the Mall, Trafalgar Square, the Strand, Fleet Street, Ludgate Hill, were carpeted with the dead. The entrance to every tube station was piled high with the bodies of those who had made one last mad effort to escape from the poison gas. In the City itself the Bank of England had been blown to pieces and in the narrow streets in the neighborhood the stench was appalling . . . A wave of panic-stricken humanity, fleeing from the first bombs dropped by the raiding aeroplanes had stampeded inland; and this human wave had met another wave which had come running from London. At those points where the collision had taken place, fighting between the two panic-stricken mobs must have occurred . . . And then had come the rush of poison gas and the fighting and confusion had become suddenly stilled." Quoted by Martin Ceadel in "Popular Fiction

and the Next War, 1918–39," in Frank Gloversmith, ed., *Class, Culture and Social Change. A New View of the 1930s* (Atlantic Highlands, N.J.: Humanities Press, 1980), p. 161.

20 For *Things To Come* and the people who made it, see Christopher Frayling, *Things To Come* (London: British Film Institute, 1995).

21 Jesús Salas Larrazabal, *Air War Over Spain*, transl. Margaret A. Kelley (London: Ian Allan, 1974), p. 105.

22 For German and Italian intervention in the air war over Spain, see Gerald Howson, *Arms for Spain* (New York: St. Martin's Press, 1998), pp. 17–20. According to Salas Larrazabal in *Air War Over Spain*, only about a hundred aircraft remained in the Nationalist zone at the beginning of the war, whereas the government forces retained control of nearly two hundred (p. 49). By the end of 1936 the American Congress had passed the Neutrality Act, which made it unlawful to sell or ship arms to either the Republicans or the Nationalists, but it was easy to circumvent this statute by transporting planes by way of Mexico.

23 Raymond L. Proctor, *Hitler's Luftwaffe in the Spanish Civil War* (Westport, Colo.: Greenwood Press, 1983), pp. 56–7.

24 Williamson Murray argues that when Richthofen came to Spain, air support for the army ranked at the bottom of his priorities. "However, once in his position as chief of staff, Richthofen recognized that the theories of air power and Spanish political realities did not have much in common. The stalemate on the ground, the lack of suitable strategic targets, and the great Nationalist weakness in artillery led Richthofen to consider using the Condor Legion to support directly Franco's offensive against Bilbao." "The Luftwaffe Before The Second World War: A Mission, A Strategy?," *Journal of Strategic Studies*, 4, no. 3 (September 1981), p. 262. Murray bases this contention on conversations and correspondence with General Hans Asmus in 1980–81. See also Proctor, *Hitler's Luftwaffe in the Spanish Civil War*, pp. 257–8.

25 Wolfram von Richthofen, Spanish diary for 2 April 1937, reproduced in Klaus A. Maier, *Guernica, 26.4.1937. Die deutsche Intervention in Spanien und der "Fall Guernica"* (Frieburg: Verlag Rombach, 1975), pp. 86–8.

26 Gordon Thomas and Max Morgan Witts, *Guernica. How Hitler's Air Force Destroyed a Spanish City for Franco in Practice for World War II* (Chelsea, Mass.: Scarborough House, 1991; first published 1975), p. 63. Thomas and Witts's book, which reconstructs through interviews with participants of the period the events leading to the bombing of Guernica, needs to be used with caution but nonetheless contains valuable testimony from surviving members of the Condor Legion, especially Hans Asmus, assistant operations officer, who was in daily contact with Richthofen in this period and later rose to become commander-in-chief, NATO Air Force, Baltic. According to Hugh Thomas, 127 civilians, including 2 priests and 13 nuns, were killed in the country town of Durango on 31 March and 121 more later died in hospitals. Hugh Thomas, *The Spanish Civil War* (New York: Touchstone, 1986), p. 616.

27 For two opposing views, see Jesús Salas Larrazabal, *Guernica: el bombardeo* (Madrid: 1981), who doubts that there were more than 250 people killed (p. 23); and Paul Preston, *Franco. A Biography* (New York: Basic Books, 1994), who is inclined to believe that the figures given by the Basque government (1,645 dead and 889 injured) come closer to the truth (p. 244). Preston acknowledges that the exact figure of victims will never be able to be determined. For a recent account, based on interviews with survivors of the raid, see Maria Jesús Cava Mesa, *Memoria colectiva del bombardeo de Gernika* (Bilbao: Bakez, 1996). The persons interviewed by Cava Mesa and his collaborators estimated the number of dead at 200 and under no circumstances exceeding 1,000 (p. 145).

28 According to Thomas and Witts, *Guernica*, p. 63. Surveying the evidence, Klaus Maier concludes that Richthofen's objective of cutting off the withdrawal of retreating Basque troops could be achieved only through the destruction of the city. The type of bombs chosen by Richthofen, with a heavy emphasis on incen-

diaries, further indicates that his intention was to set fire to the town. Maier, *Guernica*, p. 109. Horst Boog, while denying that the Luftwaffe systematically pursued a policy of terror bombing between 1936 and 1942, agrees that the attack on Guernica and the German bombing of other cities during the Spanish Civil War ". . . can also be interpreted as a veiled attempt under the pretext of being a military necessity, to study the effects of those officially banned attacks on the civilian population, although accomplishment of the combat mission in the case of Guernica included blocking the approaches to the bridge, which was only possible from the air with the rubble of the houses." "The Luftwaffe and Indiscriminate Bombing up to 1942," in Horst Boog, ed., *The Conduct of the Air War in the Second World War* (New York and Oxford: Berg, 1992), pp. 336–7.

29 Richthofen, Spanish diary, in Maier, *Guernica*, p. 109.

30 In the book Steer wrote about the Abyssinian war, *Caesar in Abyssinia* (Boston: Little, Brown, 1937), he quotes from a report written by Colonel Konovaloff, who was present at Emperor Haile Selassi's last battle against the Italian invaders: "The moral effect of aviation in this war was enormous. If the land space was unconquered yet, the aerial already belonged to the Italians. From their heights they penetrated our life, turned it upside down. They could intervene on all our movements. They prevented us from eating and warming ourselves after a heavy march round our camp-fires, which we were afraid to light. They turned us into moles who dashed into their burrows at the slightest alarm" (p. 309). For Steer's life and his experiences during the Abyssinian War, see Nicholas Rankin, *Telegram from Guernica: The Extraordinary Life of George Steer, War Correspondent* (London: Faber & Faber, 2003), especially pp. 7–77.

31 "Gernika" is the Basque spelling of Guernica.

32 George Steer, *The Tree of Gernika: A Field Study of Modern War* (London: Hodder & Stoughton, 1938), pp. 244–5.

33 Steer made the point explicitly in a book he wrote about his experiences during the Basque campaign. "Assuming a German mastery of the air, the destruction of Gernika, with 10,000 souls, by a series of about forty planes in relay, would correspond to the destruction of a borough with 200,000 inhabitants by the size of fleet that Germany might send against Great Britain: in the same time, three and a half hours. The blotting out of Hull, for instance, with a fair number of bombs left over to polish off her shipping. Or the end of Portsmouth." Steer, *The Tree of Gernika*, p. 258. For the impact of the bombardment of Guernica on British public opinion, see Steer, *The Tree of Gernika*, p. 259.

34 For a refutation of most of Steer's claims, see Salas Larrazabal, *Guernica: el bombardeo*, pp. 7–23.

35 Herbert Routledge Southworth, *Guernica! Guernica! A Study of Journalism, Diplomacy, Propaganda, and History* (Berkeley: University of California Press, 1977), pp. 22–3. Nationalist planes had been grounded on 27 April, but the bombing had taken place on the 26th. Later, on 2 May, the Nationalists admitted that Guernica may have been bombed, but they insisted that it was a legitimate military target (pp. 37–8).

36 Southworth speculates that the Havas news agency and the French Foreign Ministry first held back news of the destruction of Guernica and then, when news reports were published in London, repressed various aspects of the story in order to prevent popular feeling in France from reacting violently and demanding aid for the Spanish Republic. *Guernica! Guernica!*, p. 352. For the slowness and incompleteness of the French press's reaction to Guernica, see pp. 20–30.

37 In January 1937 Picasso had composed an illustrated prose poem, entitled *Sueño y mentira de Franco* (Dream and Lie of Franco), which portrayed the Nationalist general as a ridiculous and disgusting knight with a sword and religious banner, who disemboweled horses and demolished classical statues of women. Herschell B. Chipp, *Picasso's Guernica. History, Transformations, Meanings* (Berkeley: University of California Press, 1988), pp. 11–15.

38 For these transformations and the history of the painting in general, see Chipp, *Picasso's Guernica*. Though in no way a work

of original research, Russell Martin's *Picasso's War* (New York: Dutton, 2002) sets the well-known story of Picasso's painting and its reception in the context of twentieth-century Spanish history and does so in a highly engaging way.

39 In May 1937, while working on *Guernica*, Picasso made public his feelings about the Spanish Civil War. "The war in Spain is a war of reaction – against the people, against liberty. My whole life as an artist has been a continual struggle against reaction, and the death of art. In the picture I'm now painting – which I shall call *Guernica* – and in all my recent work, I am expressing my horror of the military caste which is now plunging Spain into an ocean of misery and death." Quoted by Pierre Daix in *Picasso. Life and Art*, trans. Olivia Emmet (New York: IconEditions, 1993), p. 251.

40 Douglas Cooper, *Picasso Theater* (New York: 1968), p. 80.

41 Writing in 1938 when *Guernica* was exhibited in London, Stephen Spender was struck by this aspect of the painting. "The flickering black, white and grey lights of Picasso's picture suggest a moving picture stretched across an elongated screen; the flatness of the shapes again suggests the photographic image, even the reported paper words. The centre of this picture is like a painting of a collage in which strips of newspaper have been pasted across the canvas." *New Statesman and Nation*, 15 October 1938, pp. 567–8.

42 For a brief but well-illustrated description of the Spanish pavilion, see Mark Daniel, "Spain: Culture at War," in *Art and Power. Europe under the Dictators 1930–1945* (London: Hayward Gallery, 1995), pp. 64–7.

43 Catherine Blanton Freedberg, *The Spanish Pavilion at the Paris World's Fair* (New York and London: Garland, 1986), Vol. I, p. 633.

44 For a sensitive discussion of these issues and an exploration of their complexity, see Ellen C. Oppler, ed., *Picasso's Guernica* (New York: Norton, 1988), pp. 94–103.

45 Daix, *Picasso*, p. 251.

46 See Picasso's interview with Jerome Seckler (published in *New Masses* on 13 March 1945), where he first rejects the idea that the bull should be interpreted as fascism, saying instead that it represents "brutality and darkness"; then goes on to deny knowing why he used any of the objects that appeared in the painting. "They don't represent anything in particular. The bull is a bull, the palette a palette and the lamp is a lamp. That's all. But there is definitely no political connection for me." Reproduced in Oppler, *Picasso's Guernica*, pp. 148–50. See also Oppler's own interpretation of the bull, which differs from Picasso's (pp. 94–7).

47 *Cahiers d'Art*, nos. 4–5 (1937), p. 128. Quoted by Chipp in *Picasso's Guernica*, p. 153.

48 Major Helders (Robert Knauss), *Luftkrieg 1936. Die Zertrümmerung von Paris* (Berlin: Verlag Tradition Wilhelm Kolk, 1932). Knauss's novel was immediately translated into English by Claud W. Sykes and published by John Hamilton in 1932.

49 Quoted by Leonard Mosley in *The Reich Marshall. A Biography of Hermann Goering* (Garden City, N.Y.: Doubleday, 1974), p. 45.

50 Quoted by David Irving in *The Rise and Fall of the Luftwaffe. The Life of Field Marshal Erhard Milch* (Boston: Little, Brown, 1973), p. 30.

51 David Irving, *Goering. A Biography* (London: Macmillan, 1988), p. 131 and Irving, *The Rise and Fall of the Luftwaffe*, p. 33.

52 See Richard J. Overy, "Hitler and Air Strategy," *Journal of Contemporary History*, 15, no. 3 (July 1980), pp. 410–11. When Milch first met Hitler in Göring's Berlin apartment on 28 April 1932, the Nazi leader spoke to him at length about the ideas of Douhet. "As early as this he was principally interested in bombing warfare as the best means of deterring an aggressor. He talked of the importance of powerful armed forces, in which he saw the air force as occupying a position equal to the army's (at that time a totally novel concept); this was the only way for Germany to rid herself of the shackles of Versailles short of war itself." Quoted by Irving in *The Rise and Fall of the Luftwaffe*, p. 27. Overy claims that Hitler's attachment to bombing as a terror weapon led him to the astonishing conclusion that Allied

bombing attacks against German cities would work to the advantage of the Nazi regime ". . . because it is creating a body of people with nothing to lose – people who will therefore fight on with utter fanaticism." "Hitler and Air Strategy," p. 411.

53 Irving, *Goering*, p. 224; Irving, *The Rise and Fall of the Luftwaffe*, p. 63; Mosley, *The Reich Marshal*, p. 227; Paul Stehlin, *Témoignage pour l'histoire* (Paris: Robert Laffont, 1964), pp. 86–93.

54 Entry for 9 September 1938. *The Wartime Journals of Charles A. Lindbergh* (New York: Harcourt Brace Jovanovich, 1970), p. 70. At the suggestion of Major Truman Smith, American air attaché in Berlin, Lindbergh visited Germany as a guest of the Nazi government in 1936 and 1937 and provided reports on German air strength to the American government. These reports were shared with the French and British governments in the fall of 1938.

55 Quoted by Irving in *Goering*, pp. 225–6.

56 Quoted by Irving in *The Rise and Fall of the Luftwaffe*, p. 64. Williamson Murray concurs with Felmy's assessment in *German Military Effectiveness* (Baltimore: The Nautical and Aviation Publishing Company of America, 1992), pp. 53–67.

57 For Daladier's belief that the Luftwaffe had a "crushing superiority" over the French Air Force and its impact on his attitude toward the Munich settlement, see Young, "The Use and Abuse of Fear: France and the Air Menace in the 1930s," p. 89. Arthur Scheslinger, Jr. arrived in London on 29 September 1938, as Chamberlain was leaving for Munich. "Men were digging trenches in Bloomsbury Square and piling sandbags against basement windows. A notice posted at Carlton Mansions told us where to get gas masks, adding helpfully that there was an air raid shelter at 10 Bedford Place . . . I went that evening to see Robert E. Sherwood's antiwar play *Idiot's Delight* . . . Sherwood's lines about the impossibility of war, then its insanity, then its imminence had fruitful relevance, and the air raid that ended the play left the audience, including me, somewhat shattered." *A Life in the 20th Century. Innocent Beginnings, 1917–1950* (Boston and New York: Houghton Mifflin, 2000), p. 190.

58 Quoted by Irving in *The Rise and Fall of the Luftwaffe*, p. 77.

59 Olaf Groehler, "The Strategic Air War and its Impact on the German Civilian Population," in Boog, ed., *The Conduct of the Air War in the Second World War*, p. 282. Even Horst Boog, who denies that the Luftwaffe pursued a policy of terror bombing between 1936 and 1942, agrees that the air raids on Warsaw during the last week of September gave the appearance of terror raids because they were, in part, carried out by Ju-52 transport planes that were incapable of aimed bomb-dropping. See ibid., p. 386.

60 Lee Kennett, *A History of Strategic Bombing* (New York: Charles Scribner's Sons, 1982), p. 108.

61 In late 1939 Tobis was, for all practical purposes, controlled by the state. For the reorganization of the German film industry under the National Socialist regime, see David Welch, *Propaganda and the German Cinema 1933–1945* (Oxford: Clarendon Press, 1983), pp. 6–38.

62 Quoted by Hilmar Hoffmann in *"Und die Fahne führt uns in die Ewigkeit". Propaganda im NS-Film* (Frankfurt: Fischer Taschenbuch Verlag, 1988), Vol. 1, p. 207.

63 Discussing the realism of German wartime newsreels, Oskar Wessel wrote on 8 August 1941 that one has the impression that the same hand that wields a camera also, at another moment, is grasping a weapon. Hoffmann in *"Und die Fahne führt uns in die Ewigkeit"*, p. 207.

64 Quoted by Welch, *Propaganda and the German Cinema*, p. 208.

65 "Wir flogen zur Weichsel und Warthe, /Wir flogen ins polnische Land. /Wir trafen es schwer/Das feindliche Heer/Mit Blitzen und Bomben und Brand." Quoted by Hoffmann in *"Und die Fahne führt uns in die Ewigkeit"*, p. 207.

66 Quoted by Welch, *Propaganda and the German Cinema*, p. 214.

67 Norbert Schultze, the composer of the music for *Feuertaufe*, later claimed that he had taken the assignment in order to obtain a draft deferment. According to Michael Meyer, "the resulting music for the film . . . and its famous song for the air force,

Bomben über England, insured Schultze's fame as a composer of catchy marching songs, as well as future contracts. His music became a prototype for this kind of film-music throughout the Third Reich. As the air force song became an identification mark for the air force, similar songs were written by Schultze and others for other branches of the military, to identify military campaigns, and to create a pop-Wagnerian world of musical motifs which, even out of context, would later recall the service or battle." *The Politics of Music in the Third Reich* (New York: Peter Lang, 1991), p. 208.

68 Albert Speer, *Inside the Third Reich*, trans. Richard and Clara Winston (New York: Collier Books, 1970), p. 227.

69 "A Movie Warning to Neutrals," *Living Age*, June 1940, p. 360.

70 Quoted by Welch, *Propaganda and the German Cinema*, p. 214. William Shirer, stationed in Berlin as a foreign correspondent at the time *Feuertaufe* was released, saw the film on 8 May 1941 in a suburban movie theater. He recorded in his diary that the audience watched "the wanton destruction of Polish towns and villages, but especially of Warsaw . . . in dead silence." William L. Shirer, *Berlin Diary* (New York: Alfred A. Knopf, 1942), p. 265.

71 Quoted by John Keegan in *The Second World War* (New York: Viking, 1989), p. 55.

72 The term Stuka was an abbreviation for *Sturzkampfflugzeug*, dive-attack plane.

73 Quoted by Alistair Horne in *To Lose A Battle* (London: Macmillan, 1969), p. 248.

74 According to General Edouard Ruby, quoted by Horne in *To Lose A Battle*, p. 249. Even the historian Marc Bloch, a seasoned veteran of artillery fire during the First World War, confessed that he was unable to retain his composure under air attack in 1940. The dropping of bombs from the sky, he wrote in *The Strange Defeat* (New York: Norton, 1968 ed.), had a unique power of spreading terror. "They are dropped from a great height, and seem, though quite erroneously, to be falling straight on top of one's head. The combination of weight and altitude gives them an appearance of almost visible violence which no shelter, however thick, seems capable of resisting. There is something inhuman about the nature of the trajectory and the sense of power. Exposed to this unleashing of destruction, the soldier cowers as under some cataclysm of nature, and is tempted to feel that he is utterly defenceless – though, in reality, if one dives into a ditch or even throws oneself flat on the ground, one is pretty safe from the bursts, which are generally a good deal less effective than those of shells, always ruling out, of course, the effects of a direct hit . . . The noise is hateful, savage, and excessively nerve-racking, both that of the descending 'whistle' (deliberately accentuated) . . . and that of the actual burst, which shakes every bone in one's body. It seems to crush the very air with unparalleled violence, and conjures up pictures of torn flesh which are only too horribly borne out in fact by the sights one sees. It is not only that the bodies are terribly mangled. The effect of escaping gases adds to the appalling nature of the spectacle. A man is always scared of dying, but particularly so when to death is added the threat of complete physical disintegration. No doubt this is a peculiarly illogical manifestation of the instinct of self-preservation." But Bloch also thought that if the campaign in the West had lasted longer, the French would have grown accustomed to aerial bombardment. "Reason would have convinced them that, no matter how terrible it might be, its material effects were no worse than those of other forms of attack" (p. 57).

75 Kennett, *A History of Strategic Bombing*, p. 112; and Horne, *To Lose A Battle*, p. 296. Historians differ on whether the bombing of Rotterdam should be understood as a case of deliberate terror bombing. For contrasting views, see Charles A. Swint, "The German Air Attack on Rotterdam," *Aerospace Historian*, 21, no. 1 (March 1974), pp. 15–22 and Horst Boog, "The Luftwaffe and Indiscriminate Bombing up to 1942," in *The Conduct of Air War in the Second World War*, pp. 386–7. In *The March of Conquest*, (New York: Simon & Schuster, 1958), Telford Taylor concluded that the bombing of Rotterdam "was part of the German pat-

tern of conquest – a pattern woven by Hitler and the Wehrmacht. A Luftwaffe whose pilots would strafe the streets of The Hague in the first hour of the assault was a Luftwaffe whose leaders would not boggle at the destruction of Rotterdam as the capstone of aggression. Even as the bombs fell, the German radio was loudly predicting that Utrecht would soon receive the same treatment" (p. 203).

76 Quoted by Taylor in *The March of Conquest*, p. 203.

77 Kennett, *A History of Strategic Bombing*, pp. 113–14. In his essay on "German Air Superiority in the *Westfeldzug*, 1940," in F. X. J. Homer and Larry D. Wildox, eds., *Germany and Europe in the Era of the Two World Wars* (Charlottesville: University Press of Virginia, 1986), Kennett concludes that the function of the German air attack on Parisian aviation facilities and factories was "probably to deliver a psychological blow at the enemy's capital just as the second phase of the campaign was opening" (p. 149). Horst Boog insists that the demoralization of the Parisian population was secondary to the destruction of the French engine and aircraft industry as a motivation for the raid. *The Conduct of the Air War in the Second World War*, p. 387. Yet he himself reproduces a diary entry by the Chief of the Operations Department of the Luftwaffe General Staff, saying that the attack on Paris had been a "strike prepared with loving care" with the intention of achieving a "desirable influence on the morale of the [French] capital."

78 Walther Hubatsch, *Hitlers Weisungen für die Kriegführung 1939–1945* (Frankfurt: Bernard & Graefe, 1983), p. 54.

79 Quoted by Keegan in *The Second World War*, p. 91. No source given.

80 Quoted by Max Hastings in *Bomber Command* (New York: Dial Press, 1979), p. 237.

81 Gerhard Weinberg argues that the Germans had originally intended to delay the terror bombing of London until the launching of the invasion of Britain. "What slight evidence we have suggests that Hitler originally thought of a 'Rotterdam'-type operation which would cause the people of London to flee the city and block the roads just as German troops were about to land." *A World At Arms. A Global History of World War II* (Cambridge: Cambridge University Press, 1994), p. 149. The implication here is that British bombing of Berlin merely inspired Hitler to hasten the application of a tactic that he had already used against Warsaw and Rotterdam and always planned to employ against London and other British cities. In support of this interpretation, Weinberg notes that the Germans bombed Belgrade in 1941 when they initiated their invasion of Yugoslavia (p. 974, n. 109).

82 Horst Boog, *Die Deutsche Luftwaffenführung 1935–1945* (Stuttgart: Deutsche Verlags-Anstalt, 1982), p. 104. Yet writing a decade later Boog was inclined to emphasize Hitler's restraint in bombing civilians. On 14 September, he says, Hitler rejected Jeschonnek's request to bomb English residential areas. "He ordered that 'although the target area has been extended, air raids on London will continue to be directed primarily against installations of military importance and vital facilities in the city, including train stations. Terror raids on purely residential areas should only be a last resort to exert pressure and, therefore, should not be used at this time.'" Boog, "The Luftwaffe and Indiscriminate Bombing up to 1942," pp. 389, 390. From the evidence that Boog himself reproduces, Hitler reached this decision not on humanitarian grounds but because he felt that military targets would be decisive in determining the outcome of the battle. "As long as there is one remaining target of military importance," he told Jeschonnek, "it must not be let go" (p. 390).

83 Quoted by Kennett, *A History of Strategic Bombing*, p. 19.

84 See Richard Overy, *The Battle* (London: Penguin, 2000) for an account that de-emphasizes the aspect of reprisal in Hitler's decision to shift the brunt of the attack to England's cities. "Hitler insisted that only war-essential targets should be attacked, and rejected the idea of inducing 'mass panic' through deliberate attacks on civilian areas. The [British] raids on Berlin may have affected the timing of the decision, but even this is doubtful. At most they allowed German leaders what Goebbels described as an 'alibi' . . ." (p. 88).

85 Many civilians were killed by shrapnel and unexploded shells from antiaircraft fire plunging back to earth. According to Philip Ziegler, British antiaircraft guns killed more Londoners than they did German pilots. *London At War* (New York: Knopf, 1995), p. 118.

86 *Front Line* (New York: Macmillan, 1943), pp. 10–22.

87 Whatever the reason, the battle fought by the British to win American sympathy in the war against Nazi Germany was won during the second half of 1940. On 25 June 1940, a Gallup poll found that 64 percent of Americans believed that it was more important for the United States to stay out of the war than to come to Britain's defense. By late November, the numbers had reversed: 60 percent of Americans now believed that it was more important to aid Britain than to stay out of the war. James Chace, "The Winning Hand," in the *New York Review of Books*, 11 March 2004, p. 18.

88 Ian McLaine, *Ministry of Morale. Home Front Morale and the Ministry of Information in World War II* (London: George Allen & Unwin, 1979), p. 3.

89 In 1935 L. E. O. Charlton, former British air attaché to the United States, had painted a fearful picture of what would happen in the case of an air attack against London. "There will be undisciplined flight from London, disintegrating to the public transport facilities, and dislocating to the food supply . . . Large sections of this self-evacuated population will be soon existing in a state of semi-starvation, and lawlessness will add its quota to the upheaval." Of those who stayed in London, either by choice or through constraint, some would have their sanity strained to the limit and others would "cower" in their assigned shelters. Charlton was especially concerned about the reaction of the "labouring masses," and "factory employees in particular," who were the "most difficult people to control" and who would be "more susceptible than most to dismay and stampede when the air-raid warning goes." *War from the Air. Past, Present, Future* (London: Thomas Nelson & Sons, 1935), pp. 171–3.

90 Peter Stansky and William Abrahams, *London's Burning. Life, Death and Art in the Second World War* (London: Constable, 1994), p. 87.

91 Harry Watt, *Don't Look at the Camera* (New York: St. Martin's Press, 1974), pp. 137–41.

92 Quentin Reynolds, *A London Diary* (New York: Random House, 1941), p. 65. "I never knew that people were so wonderful. Taxicab drivers, waiters, charwomen, waitresses, actresses – even wealthy West Enders who I thought would crack first – all take their beating each night, shake the noise of the night from their heads, and face the new day and its dangers with calmness" (p. 66).

93 Ibid., p. 41.

94 Watt, *Don't Look at the Camera*, p. 141.

95 Reynolds, *London Diary*, p. 129. Watt later provided a colorful account of the means by which they had achieved the famous Reynolds growl. "We took Quentin down to Denham to record the commentary. He had never broadcast on radio, so we stood him in front of the mike and told him to have a go. The first words were 'I am speaking from London.' Quent bellowed them out like a barker in a fair-ground! I said 'That's great, Quent, great, but just take it down a bit, will you?' He did it again, and still sounded like a master of ceremonies at a banquet, so we gave him a drink, and got into a huddle in the sound booth. 'What in Christ's name are we going to do with this bloody awful bellowing bull?' Then Ken Cameron, the sound-man, had the flash of intuition that was to make Quentin Reynolds famous. He said 'Look, he's a big bugger with an enormous belly. Let's sit him down in an armchair, stick the microphone nearly down his throat, and let him whisper.' We did this, and rumbling out of that belly came the famous deep Quentin growl, that was destined to be listened to throughout the Allied world." Watt, *Don't Look at the Camera*, p. 141.

96 Actually, according to Angus Calder, the film itself was shot during the period between 26 September–11 October 1940. See *The Myth of the Blitz* (London: Jonathan Cape, 1991), p. 232. Reynolds was apparently not contacted by Bernstein until 6 October. See *London Diary*, p. 40. His narration situates the film five weeks after the beginning of the Blitz. This is important because he claims in *London Diary*, pp. 65–6, that reactions to the Blitz had changed by 10 October. "During the first two weeks of the Blitz, men and women lived like hunted animals. They ran toward shelters when the bombs began. They crept out when the immediate danger had past [sic]. Now they have fashioned a way of life and a method for living that if not entirely comfortable is at least reasonably safe. They line up calmly for the public shelters and the subways late each afternoon. Whole families go in carrying blankets, thermos bottles of tea, sandwiches, bottles of milk for the children. They usually stay in the shelters until about eight in the morning. It isn't too comfortable, but these civilians are good soldiers. It is their part of the war effort and they accept it."

97 In his diary, Reynolds put the same point rather differently. On 9 October 1940, he noted: "London tries to keep up the fiction that things are fairly normal. I will say they live the part too. I've never seen the faintest sign of fear on the face of any Londoner yet – even on the noisiest of nights."

98 Watt, *Don't Look at the Camera*, p. 142.

99 Ibid., pp. 146–7.

100 Ibid., p. 150.

101 *Time*, 3 November 1941, p. 86.

102 Watt, *Don't Look at the Camera*, p. 152.

103 "Report by Mr. Butt to Bomber Command on His Examination of Night Photographs, 18th August 1941," in Sir Charles Webster and Noble Frankland, *The Strategic Air Offensive Against Germany, 1939–1945* (London: HMSO, 1961), Vol. 4, p. 205. Robin Neillands, in a recent history of the Allied air offensive against Nazi Germany, comments that the Butt Report merely offered "objective, irrefutable proof of what most people in Bomber Command had known for two years: that the strategic bombing offensive was a failure . . ." *The Bomber War* (Woodstock and New York: The Overlook Press, 2001), p. 57. Neillands quotes testimony from Lord Sandhurst, who served as a navigator/bomb-aimer during the early phase of the bombing campaign. "I have read most of what has been written since the war about Bomber Command and have often been puzzled by the surprise at the errors made in 1941. My logbook only records six occasions when I positively claimed to have identified the aiming point" (p. 56).

104 Hastings, *Bomber Command*, p. 126.

105 On 24 January 1942, Captain Harold Balfour, prepared a confidential memorandum for the Air Minister, Sir Archibald Sinclair, in which he estimated that only ten percent of the bombs being dropped were falling in the target area. "The public are more and more questioning the effectiveness of bombing policy and beginning to wonder whether bombs can bring Germany's effort to a standstill and thus be a deciding factor in winning the war." Quoted by Hastings in *Bomber Command*, p. 113. A month later the Lord Privy Seal, Sir Stafford Cripps, made a speech in the House of Commons in which he pointed out that "a number of Honourable Members have questioned whether in the existing circumstances, the continued devotion of a considerable part of our efforts to building up this Bombing Force is the best use we can make of our resources." Quoted by Neillands, *The Bomber War*, p. 108.

106 Hastings, *Bomber Command*, p. 116. For a judicious discussion of Churchill's attitude toward bombing during the Second World War, see Geoffrey Best, *Churchill. A Study in Greatness* (London and New York: Hambledon, 2001), pp. 234–42.

107 Webster and Franklin, *The Strategic Air Offensive Against Germany*, Vol. 4, pp. 143–8.

108 Ibid., Vol. 1, p. 324.

109 For a sympathetic but not uncritical account of Arthur Harris's life, see Henry Probert, *Bomber Harris. His Life and Times* (London: Greenhill Books, 2001). Probert concludes that, with all his faults, Harris "deserves to rank among the great commanders of modern times" (p. 414).

110 Sir Arthur Harris, *Bomber Offensive* (New York: Macmillan, 1947), pp. 52–3. In June 1943, Harris submitted a paper to Churchill and his immediate commanding officer Peter Portal, Chief of Air Staff, arguing that a concentration of Allied air force bombers could raze to the ground thirty to forty of the major German cities and bring the war to an end within a year. Churchill replied, pointing out that the war was not going to be won by bombing alone and that there was no possibility of it being brought to an end in 1943. Probert, *Bomber Harris*, pp. 142–3.

111 John Terraine, *A Time for Courage. The Royal Air Force in the European War, 1939–1945* (New York: Macmillan, 1985), p. 488.

112 Harris, quoted by Hastings, *Bomber Command*, p. 154.

113 Alexander P. de Seversky, *Victory Through Air Power* (New York: Simon & Schuster, 1942). Much of the material in this book had earlier appeared in magazines, including the article "Why Lindbergh Is Wrong," *American Mercury*, 52 (May 1941), pp. 519–32.

114 Warren M. Bodie, *Republic's P-47 Thunderbolt. From Seversky to Victory* (Hiawassee, G.: Widewing Publications, 1994), pp. 69–70.

115 Alexander P. de Seversky, "Why Lindbergh Is Wrong," pp. 519–32.

116 Russell E. Lee, "Impact of *Victory Through Air Power*. Part I: The Army Air Forces' Reaction," *Air Power History*, Summer 1993, p. 3.

117 For Disney's enthusiasm for the project and the reaction of the critics, see Steven Watts, *The Magic Kingdom. Walt Disney and the American Way of Life* (Boston and New York: Houghton Mifflin, 1997), pp. 234–7. According to Watts, the film attracted "only meager audiences and ended up losing money for the studio" (p. 236).

118 Seversky, *Victory Through Air Power*, p. 7.

119 Ibid., p. 11.

120 Ibid., p. 12.

121 Ibid., p. 103.

122 Ibid., p. 27.

123 Ibid., p. 146.

124 Lee, "Impact of *Victory Through Air Power*," Part I, pp. 4–12.

125 Richard Overy, *Why the Allies Won* (New York: Norton, 1996), p. 109.

126 Walter J. Boyne, *Clash of Wings* (New York: Simon & Schuster, 1994), p. 303.

127 Clayton R. Koppes and Gregory D. Black, *Hollywood Goes to War: How Politics, Profits and Propaganda Shaped World War II Movies* (New York: The Free Press, 1987), pp. 225–30. According to George Froeschel, one of the writers of *Mrs. Miniver*, Goebbels is said to have screened *Mrs. Miniver* for his staff on several occasions, explaining to them that this was the way a propaganda picture should look. See Michael B. Druxman, *One Good Film Deserves Another* (South Brunswick and New York: A. S. Barnes, 1977), p. 45.

128 Axel Madsen, *William Wyler* (New York: Thomas Y. Crowell, 1973), p. 217.

129 Quoted by Jan Herman in *A Talent for Trouble. The Life of Hollywood's Most Acclaimed Director, William Wyler* (New York: G. P. Putnam's Sons, 1995), p. 249.

130 For Morgan's career in the Eighth Air Force, see Robert Morgan with Ron Powers, *The Man Who Flew the Memphis Bell* (New York: Dutton, 2001).

131 Quoted by Herman, *A Talent for Trouble*, p. 252.

132 Quoted by Herman, *A Talent for Trouble*, p. 251. Morgan remembers this incident occurring on the *Memphis Belle's* last flight. See *The Man Who Flew the Memphis Belle*, p. 208.

133 Quoted by Herman, *A Talent for Trouble*, p. 252.

134 Morgan with Powers, *The Man Who Flew the Memphis Belle*, p. 210.

135 Herman, *A Talent for Trouble*, p. 247.

136 Ibid., p. 261.

137 Koenig had replaced Jerry Chodorow at Wyler's request.

138 Quoted by Madsen, *Wyler*, p. 240.

139   See Bosley Crowther in the *New York Times*, 16 April 1944.

140   *The Nation*, 15 April 1944, p. 456.

141   Jules Roy, *Retour de l'enfer* (Paris: Gallimard, 1951), p. 185.

142   Robert Morgan shared the general anger against Japan. Though having flown twenty-five missions in Europe, he volunteered to fly bombing missions against the Japanese in 1943–4. "I had some payback I needed to deliver to the Japanese for what they did to us at Pearl Harbor." *The Man Who Flew the Memphis Belle*, p. 253.

143   For Hollywood's problems in making the transition from movies featuring aces to bombing crews, see Thomas Doherty, *Projections of War. Hollywood, American Culture, and World War II* (New York: Columbia University Press, 1993), pp. 103–11.

144   James Doolittle and Caroll V. Glines, *I Could Never Be So Lucky Again* (New York: Bantam Books, 1991), p. 213.

145   For the conception of the attack, see Carroll V. Glines, *Doolittle's Tokyo Raiders* (Princeton: D. Van Nostrand Company, 1964), pp. 13–19.

146   H. H. Arnold, *Global Mission* (New York: Harper & Brothers, 1949), p. 299. Some idea of Doolittle's attitude toward danger can be gathered from the following anecdote, which he recounts in his autobiography. Based on his record, there is no reason to doubt his sincerity. "One of the pilots [among those chosen to make the raid on Tokyo] asked me what I would do if my plane was badly damaged and would have to be abandoned. I replied, 'Each pilot must decide for himself what he will do and he'll tell his crew to do if that happens. I know what I'm going to do . . . I don't intend to be taken prisoner . . . I'm 45 years old and have lived a full life. If my plane is crippled beyond any possibility of fighting or escape, I'm going to have my crew bail out and then I'm going to dive my B-25 into the best military target I can find. You fellows are all younger and have a long life ahead of you. I don't expect any of the rest of you to do what I intend to do." Doolittle and Glines, *I Could Never Be So Lucky Again*, p. 250. The irony is that Doolittle had most of his life ahead of him. He died at the age of 96.

147   Doolittle and Glines, *I Could Never Be So Lucky Again*, pp. 228–9.

148   Ibid., p. 246.

149   The American garrison on Bataan in the Philippines had surrendered on 9 April 1942; what came to be known as the "Bataan Death March" had begun on 10 April. Hong Kong, Singapore, Rangoon in Burma, and the Dutch East Indies had been overrun by Japanese troops during the preceding months following Pearl Harbor.

150   Glines, *Doolittle's Tokyo Raiders*, p. 379–80. Hilton had been one of the Academy Award-winning scriptwriters of *Mrs. Miniver*.

151   Ibid., p. 138.

152   Ted W. Lawson with Robert Considine, *Thirty Seconds Over Tokyo* (New York: Random House, 1943).

153   Ibid., p. 179.

154   Ibid., p. 5.

155   Ibid., p. 7.

156   Ibid., p. 74.

157   Ibid., p. 40.

158   Ibid., p. 68.

159   Ibid., p. 212.

160   Ibid., p. 209. Curiously, Lawson does reproduce this comment in his narrative of the mission but instead inserts it in an epilogue entitled "After One Year." Trumbo, however, alluded to Jurika's remark in his script when he has Jurika warn Doolittle's men about being taken prisoner by the Japanese.

161   " 'You are to bomb military targets only,' I told them. 'There is nothing that would unite the Japanese nation more than to bomb the emperor's home. It is not a military target! And you are to avoid hospitals, schools, and other nonmilitary targets.' " Doolittle and Glines, *I Could Never Be So Lucky Again*, p. 246.

162   According to *Time*, 4 December 1944, 93, the twenty-eight-year-old Johnson was receiving eight thousand fan letters a week, the most of any star in Hollywood. Because of his appeal to young girls he was sometimes called "the voiceless Sinatra." Intensely ambitious, Johnson was said to live more simply than other stars. "His agent allows him $25 of his comparatively modest $750 a week for spending money; the rest goes into War bonds and toward buying a house. He gets to bed by nine each working night, studies his script for an hour and smokes his one cigaret of the day."

163   Lawson claims that he was taken by surprise by Pearl Harbor. He and Ellen had just had breakfast at the Pig 'n' Whistle on Hollywood Boulevard in Los Angeles when they heard the news on a radio at a news stand. "The Japs! I couldn't figure it out at first. What about that Peace Envoy – what's his name? How the devil did they get bombers as far east as Hawaii? I looked at Ellen and we walked away from there. I told her how strange it seemed to me, after thinking only about the Germans for so long. I told her that every bomb we had dropped, real or flour-sack, every real or blank machine-gun bullet we had fired, every scouting trip, every maneuver for weeks and weeks had been directed at the vision of one opponent – Germany. Every plane I dreamed of fighting was a Messerschmitt. Now Japan!" Lawson with Considine, *Thirty Seconds Over Tokyo*, pp. 12–13.

164   Ibid., p. 170.

165   Ibid., p. 211.

166   *New York Times*, 16 November 1944.

167   Bosley Crowther, "Happy Medium," *New York Times*, 26 November 1944.

168   For its lack of pretentiousness and "dogged sincerity," see James Agee in *The Nation*, 2 December 1944, p. 699; for its "documentary realism," Philip T. Hartung in *Commonweal*, 22 December 1944, p. 255.

169   Philip T. Hartung in *Commonweal*, 22 December 1944, p. 255.

170   John Lardner in *The New Yorker*, 2 December 1944, p. 85.

171   John Gassner and Dudley Nichols, eds., *Best Film Plays of 1943–1944* (New York: Crown, 1945), p. 90.

172   Gassner and Nichols, *Best Film Plays of 1943–1944*, p. 147.

173   Conrad C. Crane, *Bombs, Cities, and Civilians: American Air power Strategy in World War II* (Lawrence, Kans.: University Press of Kansas, 1993), p. 132.

174   Wesley Frank Craven and James Lea Cate, *The Army Air Forces in World War II* (Washington, D.C.: Office of Air Force History, 1983), Vol. V, p. 617; Kennett, *A History of Strategic Bombing*, p. 171; Boyne, *Clash of Wings*, p. 372.

175   Morgan with Powers, *The Man Who Flew the Memphis Belle*, p. 311.

176   Adolf Galland, *Die Ersten und Die Letzten: Die Jagdflieger im zweiten Weltkrieg* (Darmstadt: Franz Schneekluth, 1953), p. 205.

177   Ursula von Kardorff, *Berliner Aufzeichnungen 1942–1945* (Munich: C. H. Beck, 1992). On 2 May 1944, Ursula von Kardorff recorded in her diary the experience of a pregnant friend who was caught in a bombing attack while taking a train to Berlin. "It's inconceivable what people can bear, and how quickly they forget their anguish. And what if this situation becomes a habit? They'll never get us to give up with these methods. We'd rather crawl half dying from hunger out of our holes and bomb shelters and go back to work" (p. 184).

178   Quoted by Hastings in *Bomber Command*, p. 89.

179   For Air Vice-Marshal Donald Bennet's criticism of the low-level marking methods introduced by Cheshire, see Richard Morris, *Cheshire: The Biography of Leon and Cheshire, VC, OM* (London (Viking, 2000), pp. 166–7.

180   From C. Day Lewis's poem, "Bombers," in *Short Is The Time: Poems 1936–1943* (New York: Oxford University of Press, 1945), p. 5.

181   In late May 1944 Ursula von Kardorff got away from Berlin to spend a few days of vacation with friends at a thirteenth-century castle at Harbke. But not even the countryside was safe from aerial attack. "Just as we were sitting in deck chairs and roasting ourselves in the sun . . . the sirens began to shriek. Shortly thereafter squadrons of enemy planes began to fly overhead. In mathematical order, one after the other. We watched them with binoculars, happy for once not to be crouching in some dismal cellar and observed these modern instruments of death from which we for the moment had nothing to fear. Suddenly three planes dived toward us and fired, as if they were aiming at us.

The men in front, we ran like hares across the drawbridge behind the castle's walls. For a few seconds I thought that we were never going to get out of this alive. Why do I cling to this existence, which consists in great part of fear, tension, and sadness?" *Berliner Aufzeichnungen 1942–1945*, pp. 195–6. For a British account of the bombing of a German village, see Guy Gibson, *Enemy Coast Ahead* (London: Michael Joseph, 1946), p. 297.

182 See Elmer Bendiner, *The Fall of Fortresses* (New York: G. P. Putnam's Sons, 1980), p. 207, who tells the story of a pilot who baled out safely from his B-17 but had the misfortune to land "among people who did not recognize the war as a game. Rendered mindless by the rain of bombs or perhaps by earlier horrors, they spoke of lynching the bomb crews who came to earth. Johnny was rescued by German airmen who, in 1943, saw him as a member of their fraternity. They understood the bombing and the killing of total strangers in ways that a civilian could never appreciate."

183 "As much as [our commanding officers] Belcher, Deveraux, and Billings would have liked us to be flaming heroes, we could [not] manage to play the role. We were drab workingmen who did what we were told to do as best we could. Our best was our commitment to the hard task of war, which we met as common men enduring the trouble of each day as it came. We were rarely brave, and some of us were cowards. We trembled, cursed, and grumbled. When it was beyond bearing, we were silent. There were a few like Paul, who were indifferent to death, who praised God and flew their missions sure of glory, one way or the other. But they were, we thought, a little mad." John Muirhead, *Those Who Fall* (New York: Random House, 1986), p. 62.

184 See Wohl, *A Passion for Wings*, pp. 138–43.

185 John Muirhead, a bomber pilot, admits that "There were no words for the horror of our bombs, or for the thousands who perished in their flames, beyond the comfortable abstractions one used after a mission, 'Yes, we covered the target well today.' And by such fragile devices, we did our obscene work and endured, becoming strangers to our past, becoming uncaring men without pity." *Those Who Fall*, p. 93. Assessing the morality of the bombing over three decades after the end of the war in *The Fall of Fortresses*, Elmer Bendiner, who served as a navigator in B-17s in raids over Germany, writes: ". . . a question nags me: suppose our leaders were pure in heart and dedicated solely to the destruction of fascism, undistracted by lesser ambitions, not caring whether the Air Forces or the Navy won the war so long as it was won; and suppose that their minds as brilliant as their hearts were pure and that the blasting of cities was in fact the only key to victory; then would not the sacrifice of thousands of lives have been worth it? If one can practice a terrible and Godlike arithmetic, can we say that we were right to kill thousands because they number less than the millions who would have died or lived appallingly if Hitler had won? Could we have dared to refrain from such a sacrifice merely to keep our hands clean? Admittedly, this is a dangerous kind of bookkeeping, for if we allow it who can say that any terror is not justified in a cause we believe to be good? And if after the killing discerning critics point out that the strategists were not pure in heart or particularly wise and that therefore some of our victims died needlessly, where can we find absolution? Only in this: that our cause was just. This sets us apart from our enemies." But Bendiner goes on to say that he would "draw lines and maintain that some sacrifices are not acceptable even in a just cause. I would not have dropped the atom bomb even to wipe out Hitler, because the bomb makes possible the end of all life. We carried no such heavy freight in our B-17s. We carried death for ourselves or for others, but humanity was not doomed in the fall of Fortresses." Bendiner, *The Fall of Fortresses*, pp. 238–9.

186 Commenting over a half century later on the reluctance of the Germans to come to terms with the scope and horror of the bombing of German cities during the last three years of the war, W. G. Sebald also wondered whether it could not be ascribed to a feeling of just punishment for the atrocities of the Nazis. "With silent fascination . . . the Germans confronted the catastrophe [of the bombing of their cities] that was taking

place." *Luftkrieg und Literatur* (Frankfurt: Fischer Taschenbuch Verlag, 2002), pp. 21–2.

187 Im Gnadenlosen suchten wir die Leuchte,/die uns den Weiterweg erhellen soll./Und wundern uns, dass es noch tiefer finstert./Selbst riefen wir die grauen Furienchöre,/die nun durch unsern Heimathimmel jagen,/Ensetzen streuend: Stadt um Stadt erliegt." Quoted by Hans Rumpf, *The Bombing of Germany* (London: Frederick Muller, 1963), trans. Edward Fitzgerald, p. 223.

188 For a critique of the Nazi leadership of the Luftwaffe, see Werner Baumbach, *Zu Spät? Aufsting und Untergang der deutschen Luftwaffe* (Stultgart: Motorbuch, 1977, 3rd ed.) (1946). For the argument that Germany did not initiate the terror bombing of civilians, see Rumpf, *The Bombing of Germany* and Boog, "The Luftwaffe and Indiscriminate Bombing up to 1942," pp. 373–404. For a recent restatement of Boog's position that it was the British who began terror bombing against civilians, see his essay "Harris – A German View," in Sir Arthur T. Harris, *Despatch on War Operations* (London: Frank Cass, 1995), pp. xxxviii–xliii. "Only after the incendiary raids on the cities of Lübeck and Rostock in the spring of 1942 did Hitler order the terror bombing of smaller English towns. the so called 'Baedeker-raids.' This does not mean that German air attacks on Britain in the previous years did not also have a terroristic effect, but this was not the primary purpose" (p. xliii).

189 Jörg Friedrich, *Der Brand. Deutschland im Bombenkrieg 1940–1945* (Munich: Propyläen Verlag, 2002). Friedrich's book had been preceded by Hans Brunswig's comprehensive study of the bombing of Hamburg, *Feuersturm über Hamburg* (Stuttgart: Motorbuch Verlag, 1978) and was followed by others, including Volker Hage, ed., *Hamburg 1943. Literarische Zeugnisse sum Feuersturm* (Frankfurt am Main: Fischer Taschenbuch Verlag, 2003); Christoph Kucklick, *Feuersturm. Der Bombenkrieg gegen Deutschland* (Hamburg: Ellert & Richter Verlag, 2003); Stephan Burgdorff and Christian Habbe, eds., *Alrs feuer vom Himmel fiel. Der Bombenkrieg in Deutschland* (Munich: Deutsche-Verlags-Anstalt, 2003); and Friedrich's own illustrated history of the bombing war against Germany, *Brandstätten. Der Anblick des Bombenkrieges* (Munich: Propyläen Verlag, 2003). The appearance of Frederick Taylor's book, *Dresden. Tuesday 13 February 1945* (London: Bloomsbury, 2004), suggests that the Allied bombing campaign remains highly controversial and inspires strong emotions, both in defense of its necessity and against what some perceive as its unnecessary excesses. For a thoughtful discussion of the reasons for the failure of the bombing war to find a place in the German postwar historical consciousness, see W. G. Sebald's 1997 Zurich lectures in *Luftkrieg und Literatur*, pp. 11–74.

190 Paul Brickhill, *The Dam Busters* (Hambledon and London: Evans Brothers Limited, 1951). The film, *The Dam Busters*, written by R. C. Sheriff and starring Richard Todd, was released in 1955.

191 Richard Morris with Colin Dobinston, *Guy Gibson* (London: Viking, 1994), p. 184. For an assessment of the significance of the dams raid, see Webster and Frankland, *The Strategic Air Offensive Against Germany*, Vol. 2, pp. 168–89.

192 For Harris's bitterness about the lack of recognition accorded to Bomber Command by the British government following the defeat of Germany, see Probert, *Bomber Harris*, pp. 343–51. Probert concludes that it was not the Labour Government that denied Harris a peerage, but that he himself refused to accept it out of loyalty to the men and women of Bomber Command, who had been denied the campaign medal they deserved (p. 351).

193 Hastings, *Bomber Command*. In 1980, Geoffrey Best reached a similar conclusion in *Humanity in Warfare* (New York: Columbia University Press, 1980), pp. 280–85. "Denied opportunities for a proper scrutiny of what was going on, the British public was willy-nilly made participant in what seems in retrospect to have been the only big blot on Britain's war record, and to have sullied the cause for which some fifty thousand gallant airmen died and some untold much larger number of German civilians were

immolated" (p. 284). Horst Boog also concludes, with clear reference to Harris, that ". . . indiscriminate bombing was one of the most serious sins of highly industrialized nations this century" in his "Harris – a German View," p. xlv.

194 For more positive views of Harris, see Charles Messinger, *'Bomber' Harris and the Strategic Bombing Offensive, 1939–1945* (New York: St. Martin's Press, 1984), pp. 191–214; Denis Richards, *The Hardest Victory. RAF Bomber Command in the Second World War* (New York and London: Norton, 1995), pp. 289–305; Overy, *Why the Allies Won*, pp. 112–14; and Neillands, *The Bomber War*, esp. pp. 393–406.

195 The Mayor of Cologne pointed out the lack of sensitivity shown by the organizers of the ceremony to unveil the statue. The date they chose for this event, 31 May 1992, was the fiftieth anniversary of the thousand-bomber raid against Cologne. See Probert, *Bomber Harris*, pp. 416–18, for the public response to the inauguration of Harris's statue.

196 The phrases quoted are from John Terraine in his review of Richard Morris's biography of Guy Gibson in the *Times Literary Supplement*, 6 January 1995.

197 Noble Frankland, *History at War. The Campaigns of an Historian* (London: Giles de la Mare, 1998), pp. 80–113.

198 Even Harris's biographer, Henry Probert, who finds reasons to justify most of Harris's actions, concludes that, regrettably, he "does not emerge well from this affair." "There was an inevitability about Harris's hostility to the way the official history was compiled that reflected the set of his mind and the unshakeable conviction that he was right." *Bomber Harris*, p. 384.

199 Quoted by Ronald Shaffer in *Wings of Judgment. American Bombing in World War II* (New York: Oxford University Press, 1985), pp. 65–6.

200 I have in mind especially the films dealing with the dropping of the atomic bomb on Hiroshima: MGM's *Above and Beyond* (1953) and Viacom's *Enola Gay* (1980).

201 Webster and Frankland, *The Strategic Air Offensive Against Germany*, Vol. 4, p. 287. The ambiguity of Webster and Frankland's history is suggested by the fact that it was at first interpreted as arguing that the bombing campaign had been a "costly failure." See Frankland, *History at War*, pp. 114–17.

202 Trying to explain the reasons for the extraordinary success of *Target for Tonight* in Britain, Harry Watt wrote: "To give the real reason for its success one must realize the emotions of the people of this country at the moment it came out. All propaganda had been geared to encourage us to bear up, to stay cheerful and optimistic under bombs, mines, torpedoes, rationing and cold, while a constant stream of success stories came from the other side. There was no sign of cracking, but I believe, away back in many people's minds, there had arisen the doubt that we could ever win, although I am sure we would have fought to the end. Then came this film, actually showing how we were taking the war into the heart of the enemy, and doing it in a very British, casual, brave way. It was a glimmer of hope, and the public rose to it." *Don't Look at the Camera*, p. 152.

203 Overy, *Why the Allies Won*, p. 128; Shaffer, *Wings of Judgment*, p. 61.

204 John Boyer, *By the Bomb's Early Light* (New York: Pantheon, 1985), pp. 213, 183. As late as March 1995, 44 percent of Americans polled said they "would have dropped the atomic bomb" on Hiroshima. Robert Jay Lifton and Greg Mitchell, *Hiroshima in America. Fifty Years of Denial* (New York: G. P. Putnam's Sons, 1995), p. xvi.

205 In a memorandum to his combat commanders in 1943, Hap Arnold wrote that "used with the proper degree of understanding," the bomber was "the most humane of all weapons." Quoted by Shaffer in *Wings of Judgment*, p. 61. For a series of reflections on the cultural dimension and morality of bombing, see Sven Lindquist, *A History of Bombing* (New York: The New Press, 2001), an English translation by Linda Haverty Rugg of the original version in Swedish, *Nu dog du* (Now You Die).

6. A New Civilization

1 Le Corbusier (Charles Jeanneret-Gris), *Aircraft* (New York: Universe, 1985; orig. ed. 1935), p. 6.

2 Elias Canetti, *Die Provinz des Menschen: Aufzeichnungen 1942–1972* (Munich: Carl Hanser, 1973), p. 10.

3 Ernst Jünger, ed., *Luftfahrt ist not!* (Leipzig: Vaterländischer Buchvertrieb Thankmar Rudolf, 2nd rev. ed., n.d.), pp. 7–8.

4 Ernst Jünger, *Feuer und Blut: Ein kleiner Auschnitt aus einer grossen Schlacht* (Berlin: Frundsberg, 1929, 4th ed.), p. 84.

5 Jünger, *Feuer und Blut*, p. 82.

6 Jünger, ed., *Luftfahrt ist not!* pp. 6–7, 8–9.

7 See, for example, the chapter in Norman Bel Geddes, *Horizons* (Boston: Little, Brown, 1932), entitled "Speed – To-morrow," pp. 24–43.

8 For example, Jean Batten's purchase of an expensive Percival Gull 6 in 1935, with almost twice the speed of her Gipsy Moth and a range of two thousand miles, was vital to making her record-breaking flights to South America and New Zealand. See Ian Mackersey, *Jean Batten: The Garbo of the Skies* (London: Macdonald, 1991), p. 206.

9 Alan Cobham, *A Time to Fly* (London: Shepheard-Walwyn, 1978), p. 107.

10 Flying the British director of civil aviation, Sir Sefton Branker, to India in 1924, Cobham suffered the humiliation of having to send him from Lemberg to Bucharest by train when bad weather grounded his plane. ". . . our swift aircraft sat on the ground and did nothing." *A Time To Fly*, p. 86.

11 Pierre Weiss, *L'Espace* (Paris: Louis Querelle, 1929), pp. 31–2.

12 Weiss introduced this metaphor three years later in *CIDNA ou l'Express d'Istambul* (Paris: Louis Querelle, 1932), pp. 11–12.

13 Louise Thaden, *High, Wide, and Frightened* (Fayetteville: The University of Arkansas Press, 2004), pp. xi–xii. Thaden's memoir was first published in 1938, then reprinted in 1973 with a newly added prologue and epilogue.

14 Marcel Proust, *A la recherche du temps perdu* (Paris: Gallimard, 1954), Vol. II, p. 1029.

15 Charles A. Lindbergh, *Autobiography of Values* (New York and London: Harcourt Brace Jovanovich, 1977), pp. 63–4.

16 Anne Morrow Lindbergh, *The Steep Ascent* (London: Chatto & Windus, 1945), p. 69.

17 Jules Roy, *Comme un mauvais ange* (Paris: Gallimard, 1947), pp. 25–6, 41.

18 Ibid., p. 35.

19 Thaden, *High, Wide, and Frightened*, p. xi.

20 Reproduced in John Thorn, *The Armchair Aviator* (New York: Charles Scribner's Sons, 1983), p. 182.

21 Beryl Markham, *West With the Night* (San Francisco: North Point Press, 1983), p. 284.

22 René Chambe, *Sous le casque de cuir* (Paris: Baudinière, 1928), pp. 174–5.

23 Thaden, *High, Wide, and Frigthened*, p. xi. Unlike her friend Amelia Earhart, Thaden willingly gave up competitive flying to raise a family.

24 Louise Faure-Favier, *Les Chevaliers de l'air* (Paris: Renaissance du Livre, 1923), p. 25.

25 "Aviatrix" was the term that Elinor Smith chose as the title for her autobiography (New York and London: Harcourt Brace Jovanovich, 1981).

26 Amelia Earhart to Louise Thaden, quoted by Susan Ware in *Still Missing: Amelia Earhart and the Search for Modern Feminism* (New York: Norton, 1993), p. 89.

27 Thaden, *High, Wide, and Frightened*, p. xii.

28 A good example is Jean Batten. See Mackersey's biography, *Jean Batten*. Evaluating Batten's achievements, Sir Peter Masefield concluded: "Given that obviously there can be no comparison with a modern professional pilot, I think history will rank her as a competent, determined – and, eventually, experienced and skilful – amateur." Masefield added that "Indeed, she learnt the hard way – through two disastrous Australia attempts – to become reasonably adept at long-distance light aeroplane flying and, eventually, to modify her earlier obsessive 'press on regardless' approach. I would rate her also as one of the great

women navigators of the world." Quoted by Mackersey, pp. 279–80.

29 Gilbert Frankau, *Christopher Strong* (New York: Dutton, 1932). For the description of *Christopher Strong* as "silly," see David Thomson, *The New Biographical Dictionary of Film* (New York: Knopf, 2002), p. 393. For Dorothy Arzner's lesbianism and her career in Hollywood, see Judith Mayne, *Directed by Dorothy Arzner* (Bloomington and Indianapolis: Indiana University Press, 1994); for a brief sketch of Zoë Atkins's career in the Broadway theater, see Jennifer Bradley, "Zoë Atkins and the Age of Excess," in June Schlueter, *Modern American Drama: The Female Canon* (London and Toronto: Associated University Presses, 1990), pp. 86–96.

30 Actually, the only American woman aviators mentioned by Gilbert Frankau in his novel are Elinor Smith and Ruth Nichols. It is their altitude records that the heroine sets out to break in the flight that takes her life.

31 Dorothy Arzner herself insisted that the figure of Lady Cynthia was not inspired by Amelia Earhart. She goes on to say, however, that her story came from an "English novel based upon the life of Amy Lowell, who did make the around-the-world flight and also broke the altitude record in her time." Claire Johnston, *The Work of Dorothy Arzner: Towards a Feminist Cinema* (London: British Film Institute, 1975), p. 26. Here, I think, Arzner's memory failed her. Amy Lowell was an early twentieth-century American poet. She must have meant Amy Johnson.

32 Constance Babington Smith's biography, *Amy Johnson* (London: Collins, 1967), stresses the role that supportive men played in promoting her aviation career. For a skeptical assessment that places her in the context of the 1930s, see Ronald Blythe, "Miss Amy Johnson," in *The Age of Illusion. Glimpses of Britain Between the War, 1919–1940* (Oxford and New York: Oxford University Press, 1983), pp. 83–102. Blythe emphasizes Johnson's marginality. Running away, he says, was the recurring motif of her life. "She has almost no need for courage in the sense in which it was popularly attributed to her. It was always easier for her to go off into the unknown, be it jobs, digs or deserts, than to face the uncongenial certainties of life. Her intense conviction that these were not for her, that she was an exception to the rule and in a sense 'privileged' began to make itself felt in earliest childhood" (p. 85). Not everyone would agree with Blythe that Johnson had "no need for courage."

33 Antoine de Saint-Exupéry, *Œuvres Complètes* (Paris: Gallimard, 1994), Vol. I, p. 209.

34 Smith, *Aviatrix*, p. 33.

35 Ruth Nichols, *Wings for Life* (Philadelphia and New York: Lippincott, 1957), p. 68.

36 Nichols, *Wings for Life*, p. 26.

37 See, for example, the contribution of Ermanno Contini, who accompanied Balbo on his 1928 Mediterranean cruise, in *Passeggiate aeree sul Mediterraneo* (Milan: Treves, 1929). Contini asked what he and his fellow journalists had seen of Sardinia, Majorca, Spain, Marseilles. His answer was: almost nothing. "But the world appeared to us more desolately and monotonously the same" (p. 60).

38 Lowell Thomas, *European Skyways: The Story of a Tour of Europe by Airplane* (Boston and New York: Houghton Mifflin, 1927), p. 235.

39 Paul Morand, *Flèche d'orient* (Paris: Gallimard, 1932).

40 Quoted by Paul K. Saint-Amour in "Modernist Reconnaissance," in *Modernism/Modernity*, 10, No. 2, p. 350.

41 Quoted by Paul K. Saint-Amour in ibid. p. 349.

42 Anne Morrow Lindbergh, *North to the Orient* (London: Chatto & Windus, 1936), p. 3.

43 Ibid., p. 12.

44 Ibid., pp. 243–4.

45 Jérôme and Jean Tharaud, *Paris Saïgon dans l'azur* (Paris: Plon, 1932), pp. 196–8.

46 Ernst Jünger, *Das abenteulicher Herz, Erste Fassung* in *Werke*, Vol. 7 (Stuttgart: Ernst Klett, 1961), p. 154.

47 Jean Batten, *My Life* (London: George G. Harrap, 1938), pp. 257–8. Her biographer Ian Mackersey claims that her un-

published memoirs tell a different story: that all she wanted was marriage to the Australian airline pilot who had recently died in a plane crash. *Jean Batten*, pp. 258–9. But one thing does not exclude the other. Having lost the man she loved, she had no intention of giving up her career as a flyer. And there is little reason to believe that she would have given up flying, even if she had married. As Mackersey himself points out, she coveted fame and public adulation too much to abandon her career.

48 René Chambe, *Altitudes* (Paris: Baudinière, 1932), p. 171.

49 Lindbergh, *The Steep Ascent*, p. 67.

50 "The Airman," in Stephen Spender, *Poems 1928–1985* (New York: Random House, 1986), p. 17.

51 Note also the title Louise Thaden gave to her memoirs: *High, Wide, and Frightened*. In the introduction to the original 1938 edition, she wrote: "A pilot who says he has never been frightened in an airplane is, I'm afraid, lying . . . Actually we are human beings with the usual inhibitions, phobias, and frailties common among men. We are unusual only because of our constant devotion to and fierce defense of aviation. If you have flown, perhaps you can understand the love a pilot develops for flight. It is much the same emotion a man feels for a woman, or a wife for her husband" (p. xv). What Thaden omits here is that many pilots of the 1920s and 1930s craved and sought situations that produced fear.

52 Cobham, *A Time To Fly*, pp. 87–8.

53 Weiss, *L'Espace*, p. 217.

54 "Courage," reproduced in *The Armchair Aviator* (New York: Charles Scribner's Sons, 1983), p. 110.

55 Jean Mermoz, "Aux Obsèques de Bajac," in *Mes vols* (Paris: Flammarion, 1937), p. 144.

56 Charles A. Lindbergh, *The Spirit of St. Louis* (New York: Charles Scribner's Sons, 1953), pp. 261–2.

57 Virginia Woolf, *Mrs. Dalloway* (New York: Harcourt Brace, 1925), pp. 28–9.

58 Batten, *My Life*, pp. 102–3.

59 Charles A. Lindbergh, *Of Flight and Life* (New York: Charles Scribner's Sons, 1948), pp. 49–50. Lindbergh returned to this theme in *The Spirit of St. Louis*: "There was science in each curve of an airfoil, in each angle between strut and wire, in the gap of a spark plug or the color of the exhaust flame" (p. 261).

60 Anne Morrow Lindbergh, *Listen! The Wind* (London: Chatto & Windus, 1938), pp. viii–ix.

61 Lindbergh, *The Spirit of St. Louis*, pp. 288–9.

62 Joseph Kessel, *Vent de sable* (Paris: Éditions de France, 1929), p. 6.

63 Robert de Marolles, *Aviation, école de l'homme* (Paris: Plon, 1938), p. 25.

64 Ibid., p. 25.

65 Le Corbusier, *Aircraft* (Milan: Abitare Segesta, 1996; orig. ed., 1935), p. 13.

66 Ibid., captions to Plates 8, 78, 92.

67 Ibid., p. 5.

68 Ibid., p. 12.

69 Quoted by Jennifer Davis Roberts from the *Futurama* narration script in her very useful catalogue, *Norman Bel Geddes. An Exhibition of Theatrical and Industrial Designs* (Austin: The University of Texas at Austin, 1979), p. 43.

70 Roberts, *Norman Bel Geddes*, p. 44.

71 For the origins of *The Airborne Symphony*, which was first performed in New York on 1 April 1946 under the direction of Leonard Bernstein, see Eric A. Gordon, *Mark the Music. The Life and Work of Marc Blitzstein* (New York: St. Martin's Press, 1989), pp. 230–34; for a well-informed analysis by Gordon that relates *The Airborne Symphony* to other works of the period and a summary of its reception, see ibid., pp. 276–87.

72 F. Scott Fitzgerald, *The Love of the Last Tycoon* (New York: Scribner, 1993), pp. 7–8.

73 Ibid., p. 14.

74 Ibid., p. 20.

75 Ibid., pp. 20–21.

76 According to Fitzgerald's notes in ibid., pp. 151–4.

77 For Fitzgerald's final outline for the novel, see ibid., p. xviii.

78 Ibid., p. 138.

79 Marolles, *Aviation, école de l'homme*, pp. vii–viii.

80 Ibid., pp. 278–9.

81 Mermoz, *Mes vols*, pp. 135–6.

82 Jünger, ed., *Luftfahrt ist not!*, p. 10.

83 Jünger, *Das abenteuliche Herz*, p. 154.

84 *Daily Mail*, 27 July 1909.

85 Gabriele D'Annunzio, *Forse che sì forse che no* (Milan: Treves, 1910), pp. 78–9.

86 A. Scott Berg, *Lindbergh* (New York: G. P. Putnam's Sons, 1998), pp. 381–2.

87 Anne Morrow Lindbergh, *The Wave of the Future: A Confession of Faith* (New York: Harcourt Brace, 1940).

88 For the vogue of aviation among British writers during the 1930s, see Valentine Cunningham, *British Writers of the Thirties* (Oxford and New York: Oxford University Press, 1988), pp. 156–210.

89 Rex Warner, *The Aerodrome* (London: The Bodley Head, 1982; originally published in 1941), p. 223.

90 Ibid., p. 224.

91 Ibid., pp. 224–5.

92 Ibid., p. 226.

93 Ibid., pp. 261–2.

94 Ibid., pp. 279–80.

95 Guido Mattioli, *Mussolini aviatore* (Rome: Aviazione, 1938, 3rd ed.), p. 15.

96 In a speech to the men of his organization, the Air Vice-Marshal denounces the bourgeois civilization he is bent on transforming. "And in the cities you will see even worse things. There you will find people whose preoccupation is not even with an out-of-date machine, but whose lives are devoted to the lowest and meanest of all aims, the acquisition by cunning and hypocrisy of large or small sums of money. This is the type of man which our historical tradition has produced in our age, a monster whether he be sensualist or ascetic, a man whose power, if he is successful, is accidental and not deliberate, a slave in himself to the most commonplace modes of thought and action, a creature whom you will agree with me, I hope, to treat with undeviating contempt." Warner, *The Aerodrome*, p. 179. Later on in the same speech, he sets forth the aim of the Air Force. "Your purpose – to escape the bondage of time, to obtain mastery over yourselves and thus over your environment – must never waver. You will discover, if you do not know already, from the courses which have been arranged for you, the necessity for what we in this Force are in process of becoming, a new and more adequate race of men" (p. 187).

97 "Is it so hard for the earthling mind to glimpse the air-lovers' attitude to life and death? For true air-lovers, death in flight is what they would choose, and though it come sooner than is welcome, who shall say that death is the end?" Stella Wolfe Murray in Lady Mary Heath and Stella Wolfe Murray, *Woman and Flying* (London: John Long, 1929), p. 220. For the role of death in Nazism and fascism, see Saul Friedländer, *Reflections of Nazism. An Essay on Kitsch and Death* (New York: Harper & Row, 1984). "For the Nazis, this motif of death [stemming from Romanticism and reinforced by Wagner] takes on a special dimension – urgent, essential, in some ways religious, mythical. This is an attraction for death in itself as something elemental, opaque, intractable to analysis" (p. 42).

98 In *For Whom The Bell Tolls* (New York: Collier Books, 1987; orig. ed. 1940), p. 87.

99 Quoted by Stephen Tabachnick in *Fiercer Than Tigers: The Life and Works of Rex Warner* (East Lansing: Michigan State University Press), p. 159.

100 Saint-Exupéry, *Œuvres complètes*, Vol. I, p. 670. Though this letter is undated, it was probably written in June 1918 when Saint-Exupéry was studying at the Lycée Saint-Louis in preparation for the examination to the Naval Academy in Brest.

101 Ibid., p. 671.

102 Saint-Exupéry to his mother in June 1918, ibid., p. 674.

103 Ibid., p. 280.

104 Saint-Exupéry's 1942 bitter account of his experiences as a reconnaissance pilot during the German invasion of France in May–June 1940 already marked a distinct change in tone from *Terre des hommes*. Though able to salvage memories of camaraderie from what he (like others) perceived as a "disaster," he deplored the absurd sacrifice of aircrews. "One sacrifices the crews as one would throw glasses of water on a forest fire." *Pilote de guerre* in *Œuvres complètes* (Paris: Gallimard, 1999), Vol. II, p. 114.

105 Saint-Exupéry, *Œuvres complètes*, Vol. II, p. 333.

106 Ibid., p. 328. Some have suggested that this letter, which was written in June 1943 shortly after Saint-Exupéry arrived in Algeria from New York, may have been written to General Béthouart, whom Saint-Exupéry had met in the United States where Béthouart served as the emissary of General Henri Giraud. Given Saint-Exupéry's confession that he has lost his earlier enthusiasm for aviation and his reference to Mermoz's politics, however, Chambe seems the more likely addressee. See ibid., pp. 1373, 1380–81.

107 Saint-Exupéry to Pierre Chevrier, December 1944, in ibid., p. 963.

108 Describing himself as a young aviator in the mid-1930s, Roy wrote: "The airplane fascinated me at the same time that it frightened me. I suffered from airsickness, but I wanted to follow the example of my intellectual guides and imitate them. First, Kessel, and then Saint-Exupéry, so great both of them, so faraway and inaccessible." Roy, *Mémoires barbares* (Paris: Albin Michel, 1989), p. 160. Roy was among those who believed that Saint-Exupéry had taken the literature of aviation to a new level. "No one before him had known how to impress on our soul the vibration that accelerates the coursing of our blood from the very first pages of *Vol de nuit*, as if we were the first along with him to penetrate the realm that had been coveted since the beginning, as if the age-old desire, finally achieved, rose to our head and knotted our throat, and there were not enough images to cause our eyes to explode." Jules Roy, *La Passion de Saint-Exupéry* (Paris: Gallimard, 1951), pp. 30–31. "One had tried before *Vol de nuit* to show us people working, fighting, and dying in flying machines, or because of them, and we didn't feel anything. We hadn't shared their anguish and their joy, we hadn't scaled the sky seated behind them. Saint-Exupéry performed the miracle. A pilot makes us share his state of mind, just like the captains of Conrad" (p. 35).

109 See Roy's journal entry for 31 December 1939 in Jules Roy, *Les Années Déchirement. Journal 1925–1965* (Paris: Albin Michel, 1998), p. 158. For Roy's belief in the mystique of aviation, see his entry of 23 February 1938 in ibid., p. 130, where he compares passing his military aviator's course to his first communion; for Roy's belief in the knighthood of the air, see Jules Roy, *Passion de Saint-Exupéry* (Paris: Gallimard, 1951), pp. 86–7.

110 Jules Roy, *Trois prières pour des pilotes* (Algiers: Charlot, 1942). Roy later wrote that Saint-Exupéry had told him that *Trois prières pour des pilotes* had come close to reducing him to tears and weighed more heavily on him than "a kilogram of paper." *Mémoires barbares*, p. 221.

111 Roy, *Passion de Saint-Exupéry*, p. 70.

112 From a letter of July 1943 from Saint-Exupéry to Roy, which was never sent. *Œuvres complètes*, Vol. II, p. 335. In this heart-wrenching and highly emotional letter, Saint-Exupéry accused Roy of having insulted him in a conversation with other Gaullists.

113 Roy, however, was shocked by Saint-Exupéry's physical deterioration. "He seems old, worn out, wear. He's huge." Four days later, on 17 May 1943, Roy recorded in his diary that "Little by little, just as his Little Prince tames the fox, I tame him." Roy, *Les Années Déchirement. Journal 1925–1965*, p. 215.

114 Roy, *Passion de Saint-Exupéry*, p. 72. Though Saint-Exupéry was piloting a Bloch 175 when Roy described him, he had already begun his training on the much faster and more complex P-38, the so-called Lightning.

115 Roy, *Mémoires barbares*, pp. 222–4.

116 Ibid., p. 225.

117 Ibid., p. 227.

118 Cited in part in Saint-Exupéry, *Œuvres complètes*, Vol. II, p. 1385. The reference to winter, the sense of despair, and the lack of any reference to flying suggests that this letter was written not long after Roy arrived in England, perhaps in November 1943 when he was interned in a camp at West Kirby. This period, he later wrote, was "unbearable." *Mémoires barbares*, p. 230.

119 In the RAF, the commander of a bomber was always a pilot, but the British made an exception for the French crews. Roy, *Mémoires barbares*, p. 240.

120 Roy, *Comme un mauvais ange*, pp. 78–9.

121 Ibid., p. 64.

122 Jules Roy, *La Vallée heureuse* (Paris: Charlot, 1946), p. 162.

123 Roy, *Mémoires barbares*, p. 262.

124 Ibid., pp. 265–6.

125 Roy, *Comme un mauvais ange*, p. 25.

126 Ibid., pp. 25–6.

127 Ibid., pp. 31–2.

128 A half century earlier, after having completed his training as a military aviator, Roy had written: "It's said that men leave their father and mother in order to attach themselves to a woman. Their wife, that is their love. But our love is aviation . . . For us the airplane will replace all other loves. Woe to the person who hasn't understood this." Roy, *Les Années Déchirement. Journal 1925–1965*, entry of 8 December 1938, p. 141.

129 Ibid., p. 33; Roy, *Mémoires barbares*, p. 281.

130 Roy, *Mémoires barbares*, pp. 218–19.

131 Roy, *Comme un mauvais ange*, pp. 19–20.

132 Camus had written in *Combat* on 8 August 1945 that "Mechanized civilization has just achieved its highest degree of savagery. In a future more or less near, it is going to be necessary to choose between collective suicide and the intelligent use of scientific conquests." Roy was so struck by this statement that he quoted in his memoirs over forty years later. *Mémoires barbares*, p. 298. For Roy's trip to Germany where he and an aviator friend "meditated on the ruins," see ibid., p. 299.

133 Roy, *Comme un mauvais ange*, p. 55.

134 Ibid., p. 56.

135 Ibid., p. 66.

136 Ibid., p. 93.

137 Quoted by Antonio Foschini in *Baracca* (Rome: Editoriale Aeronautica, 1939 ed.), p. 105.

138 For a probing and far-ranging inquiry into the way the airplane transformed conceptions of space and influenced the visual arts, architecture, and design, see Christoph Asendorf, *Super Constellation: Flugzeug und Raumrevolution, Die Wirkung der Luftfahrt auf Kunst und Kultur der Moderne* (Vienna and New York: Springer, 1997).

139 Doris L. Rich, *Amelia Earhart* (Washington, D.C. and London: Smithsonian Institute Press, 1989), p. 236; Mary S. Lovell, *The Sound of Wings* (New York: St. Martin's Press, 1989), p. 227. Already in late 1934, Amy Johnson was worried about dropping out of the public eye. She realized that the press was losing interest in long-distance flights and she was looking about for ways to reinvent herself. Babington Smith, *Amy Johnson*, pp. 307, 309, 311, 320.

140 Italo Balbo, *Stormi in volo sull'oceano* (Milan: Mondadori, 1931), pp. 49–50).

141 Quoted by Gordon in *Mark the Music*, p. 278.

142 Thomas, *European Skyways*, p. 235.

143 Saint-Exupéry, *Œuvres complètes*, Vol. I, p. 200–01.

144 Ibid., p. 201.

145 Le Corbusier, *Aircraft*, plates 122 and 123.

146 Lindbergh, *North to the Orient* (New York: Harcourt, Brace, 1935), pp. 48–9. For a contrary view, however, see Jérôme Tharaud who, recounting his trip by air to Saigon in December 1931 to an audience at the Petit Palais in Paris, concluded: "Thank God, the unity of this flight and its rapidity do not abolish the diversity of things but, on the contrary, make it possible to grasp the harmonious and subtle transitions between one place and another. Marseille prepares you for Athens; Athens no longer seems so strange when you reach Damascus; Damascus is the sister of Baghdad, and Baghdad is already India. By diminishing, at least in terms of time, the distance that separates them, [the airplane has the effect of making] civilizations show their connections more readily than it appears when one approaches them in sequence after days of train or boat." "Dans le ciel des dieux," in *Les Grandes Conférences de l'aviation au Petit Palais, contées le 21 décembre 1933* (Paris: Éditions du Comité des Oeuvres Sociales du Ministère de l'Air, n. d.), p. 17.

147 Saint-Exupéry, *Wind, Sand and Stars* (New York: Harcourt Brace Jovanovich, 1968; orig. ed. 1939), p. 68. This passage does not appear in *Terre des hommes*.

148 See, for example, Reginald M. Cleveland and Leslie E. Neville, *The Coming Air Age* (New York and London: McGraw-Hill, 1944). "The so-called 'barrier of distance' is rapidly becoming meaningless – and with it goes, forever, our so-called 'security' . . . When the whole world is included within the possible range of a single overnight trip, any conception of 'far away' disappears completely . . ." (p. 42).

149 Quoted by Gordon in *Mark the Music*, p. 282.

150 Entry of 16 November 1939 in Charles A. Lindbergh, *The War Time Journals of Charles A. Lindbergh* (New York: Harcourt Brace Jovanovich, 1970), p. 286.

151 Entry of 5 September 1942 in Lindbergh, *War Time Journals*, pp. 706–8.

152 Lindbergh, *Autobiography of Values*, p. 147.

153 Entry of 29 May 1944 in Lindbergh, *War Time Journals*, pp. 834–5.

154 Entry of 6 June 1945 in ibid., pp. 978–9.

155 Quoted by Berg in *Lindbergh*, p. 478. Judging from Berg's notes, these comments come from letters written by Lindbergh to his wife between August 1947 and August 1948; but there is no way of telling which passages come from which letters and when they were written.

156 Lindbergh, *Of Flight and Life*, pp. vi–vii.

157 Ibid., pp. 51–2. For the development of Lindbergh's attitude toward science and technology, see Susan M. Gray, *Charles A. Lindbergh and the American Dilemma: The Conflict of Technology and Human Values* (Bowling Green, Ohio: Bowling Green State University Popular Press, 1988).

158 Wendell L. Wilkie, *One World* (New York: Simon & Schuster, 1943), p. 2.

159 Saint-Exupéry, *Œuvres complètes*, Vol. I, p. 186.

Photographic Acknowledgements

AEG Firmenarchiv: 350. Frédéric d'Agay: 197. *L'Aérophile*: 183. Air Force Museum, Dayton, Ohio: 294. Air Photo Archives, Department of Geography, UCLA: 361. John Alcock and Arthur Brown, *Our Transatlantic Flight*: 14. Dino Alfieri and Luigi Freddi, eds., *Mostra della rivoluzione fascista*: 118. Marc Alyn, *François Mauriac*: 188. American Airlines: 341. American Heritage Center, University of Wyoming: 148. Archives Charmet (Photo: Bridgeman Art Library): 181. Archives Nationales, Paris, France: 196, 204. © Association française pour la diffusion du Patrimoine photographique, Ministère de la Culture, Paris, France (Photo: F. Kollar): 256. Author's collection: 122, 132, 154, 176, 177, 192, 229, 240, 255, 261, 266, 287, 311, 321, 345, 346, 364. Italo Balbo, *Da Roma a Odessa*: 77, 78. Basque Government: 251. Bayerische Staatsbibliothek, Munich: 268. BBC: 271. Richard J. Beamish, *The Boy's Story of Lindbergh The Lone Eagle*: 17. Beaverbrook Collection of War Art, © Canadian War Museum (Photo: Bridgeman Art Library): 5. Norman Bel Geddes, *Horizons*: 333. Norman Bel Geddes Papers, Harry Ransom Humanities Research Center, University of Texas, Austin: 332, 334, 335, 336, 337, 338. Werner Beumelberg, *Kampf um Spanien*: 247. Bildarchiv Preussischer Kulturbesitz: 297, 298. *Britain Can Take It*: 272, 273, 275, 276. British Airways: 355. British Empire and Commonwealth Museum, UK (Photo: Bridgeman Art Library): frontispiece. British Film Institute: 245. Maria Fede Caproni and Baldassare Catalanotto, *Tutti a volare*: 68, 82, 102, 107, 126. Caproni Museum Archive: 71. Baldassare Catalanotto and Hugo Pratt (Photos: Italian Air Force): *Once upon a sky*: 103, 104, 243. Louis Castex, *Mon tour du monde en avion*: 327. H. Chrétien, *L'Aviation et la guerre future*: 259. Collection of the Presidency of the Italian Republic: 59. Yves Courrière Collection: 186. *Daily Mail*: 269. *Daily Mirror*: 318. Raymond Danel, *L'Aéropostale, 1927-1933*: 202. M. J. Bernard Davy, *Air Power and Civilization*: 270. D'Annunzio Foundation, 55, 56, 61, 62. *Dans le ciel de la patrie*: 184. Christian Delporte, Patrick Facon, and Jeannine Lepesant-Hayet, *Jules Roy*: 354. © Éditions Gallimard (poster Roger Parry): 232. EDO Corporation: 326. Elmer Dyer Collection: 162, 175. *L'Esposizione dell'aeronautica italiana*, 119, 120, 121. James H. Farman Collection: 135, 138, 152, 153. Cesare Falessi Collection: 74, 75, 81, 106, 108. *Front Line*: 274. Adolf Galland, *Luftwaffe*: 264. Orveille Goldner and George E. Turner, *The Making of King Kong*: 347. Giordano Bruno Guerri, *Italo Balbo*: 86. Howard Hawks Collection, Brigham Young University: 170. Hearst Collection, USC Department of Special Collections: 146. *Icare*: 206, 216, 222, 227, 230, 236. *L'Illustration*: 9, 207, 208, 209, 210, 211, 212, 213, 214, 216, 241, 263, 356. Imperial War Museum: 277, 278, 279, 296, 299, 300, 304 © ARS, 305, 306, 307, 308. Italian Air Force (Stato Maggiore Aeronautica, Rome, Italy): 79, 80, 83, 84, 88, 97, 99, 103, 104, 105, 109, 110, 111, 112, 114, 115, 116, 117. Ernst Jünger, *Luftfahrt ist not!*: 316, 349. Joseph Kessel, *Chez les fils du desert*: 189, 190. Latécoère Company: 195. Ted Lawson, *Thirty Seconds Over Tokyo*, 290, 292. Marie-Vincente Latécoère Collection, 191, 194. Le Corbusier, *Aircraft*: 3, 331. Lestrange Collection: 199. Library of Congress, Prints and Photographs Division: 16, 20, 21, 35, 242, 313, 340, 342. Lindbergh Picture Collection, Manuscripts, Yale University Library: 7, 8, 25, 38. *The London Illustrated News*: 4, 29. Attilio Longoni, *Fascismo ed aviazione*: 64, 67, 73. Domenico Ludovico, *Italian Aviators from Rome to Tokyo in 1920*: 72. The MacGilchrist Collection: 2. The Marconi Collection: 13, 49. McGuire Air Force Base: 362. MIT Archives and Special Collections. Jerome Clarke Hunsaker Collection: 12. Francis Trevelyan Miller, *The World in the Air*, Vol. 2: 69, 244, 330. Missouri Historical Society: 23, 33. Moderna Museet, Stockholm, 252. Musée Air France, Paris: 225. Musée de l'Air et de l'Espace, Le Bourget: 193, 201, 223. Musée de la Poste, Paris: 237, 239. Musée des Arts décoratifs, Paris (Photo: Bridgeman Art Library): 1, 358. Musée des Deux Guerres Mondiales – B. D. I. C., Paris: 303. Musée National d'Art Moderne, Centre Pompidou, Paris: 254. Musée Nungesser et Coli, Étretat, France: 19. Museo Caproni: 71. Museo di Arte Moderna e Contemporanea di Trento e Rovereto: 339. Museo Reina Sofia, Madrid: 258. Museo storico dell'Aeronautica, Bracciano, Italy: 51 © ARS. Museum of Modern Art: 280. National Air and Space Museum, Washington, D.C.: 11, 18, 24, 26, 27, 28, 30, 32, 34, 35, 36, 37, 41, 50, 325. *National Geographic*: 43. National Portrait Gallery, London: 6 © ARS, 278. Evelina Nazzari Collection: 124, 179. Heinz J. Nowarra, *Udet*: 352. Nürnberg Stadtarchiv: 363. *Il Palazzo dell'Aeronautica*: 87, 89, 90, 91, 92, 93, 94. 95, 96, 98, 100, 101. *Paris 1937*: 253. *Passeggiate aeree nel Mediterraneo*: 76. *La Petite Illustration*: 185. Pablo Picasso (Photo: F. Kollar): 257 © ARS. Port Authority of New York and New Jersey: 359. Private Collection, Milan: 329. Cesare Redaelli, *Iniziando Mussolini alle vie del cielo*: 52, 65, 66. Karl Ries and Hans Ring, *Legion Condor*: 246, 249. Giorgio Rochat, *Balbo*: 70. Art Ronnie Collection: 127, 128, 129. San Diego Air and Space Museum: 22, 44, 46. Margherita Sarfatti, *Dux*: 63. Heimo Schwilk, *Ernst Jünger*: 231, 314. Alexander de Seversky, *Victory Through Air Power*: 281. Michael S. Sherry, *The Rise of American Air Power*: 312 Constance B. Smith, *Amy Johnson*: 324. Städtische Galerie im Lenbachhaus, Munich, Germany (Photo: Bridgeman Art Library): 54. Clyde Sunderland Photograph Collection, courtesy of the Bancroft Library, University of California, Berkeley): 328. *Streamlined: A Metaphor for Progress*: 357. Madonna M. Turner Collection: 157. UCLA Special Collections: 322. US National Archives: 31, 260. US Navy: 291. *Il volo per Vienna*: 57, 60. Frank Wead, *Ceiling Zero*: 163. William A. Wellman, *A Short Time for Insanity*: 131. John Walter Wood, *Airports*: 344. Fay Wray, *On the Other Hand*: 130. H. Hugh Wynne Collection: 134, 136, 137, 143, 144, 156.

Index